D0214767

The General's General

HISTORY AND WARFARE
Arther Ferrill, *Series Editor*

THE GENERAL'S GENERAL: The Life and Times of
Arthur MacArthur   Kenneth Ray Young

TO DIE GALLANTLY: The Battle of the Atlantic
Timothy J. Runyan and Jan M. Copes, *editors*

THE HALT IN THE MUD: French Strategic Planning
from Waterloo to Sedan   Gary P. Cox

THE HUNDRED YEARS WAR FOR MOROCCO:
Gunpowder and the Military Revolution in the
Early Modern Muslim World   Weston F. Cook, Jr.

CRETE: The Battle and the Resistance   Antony Beevor

GOOD NIGHT OFFICIALLY: The Pacific War Letters
of a Destroyer Sailor   William M. McBride

SUN-TZU: ART OF WAR   Ralph D. Sawyer, *translator*

HIPPEIS: The Cavalry of Ancient Greece
Leslie J. Worley

FEEDING MARS: Logistics in Western Warfare from the
Middle Ages to the Present   John Lynn, *editor*

THE SEVEN MILITARY CLASSICS OF ANCIENT CHINA
Ralph D. Sawyer, *translator*

FORTHCOMING

THE ANATOMY OF A LITTLE WAR: A Diplomatic and
Military History of the Gundovald Affair (568–586)
Bernard S. Bachrach

ON WATERLOO
The Campaign of 1815 in France by Carl von Clausewitz
Memorandum of the Battle of Waterloo by the Duke of Wellington
Christopher Bassford, *translator*

A HISTORY OF WARFARE IN CHINA: The Period of the Classics
Ralph D. Sawyer

ORDERING SOCIETY: A World History of Military Institutions
Barton C. Hacker

WARFARE AND CIVILIZATION IN THE
ISLAMIC MIDDLE EAST, 600–1600   William J. Hamblin

THE GENERAL'S GENERAL

The Life and Times of Arthur MacArthur

KENNETH RAY YOUNG

WESTVIEW PRESS
Boulder • San Francisco • Oxford

History and Warfare

Copyright © 1994 by Westview Press, Inc.

Published in 1994 in the United States of America by Westview Press, Inc., 5500 Central Avenue, Boulder, Colorado 80301-2877, and in the United Kingdom by Westview Press, 36 Lonsdale Road, Summertown, Oxford OX2 7EW

Library of Congress Cataloging-in-Publication Data
Young, Kenneth Ray.
   The general's general : the life and times of Arthur MacArthur /
Kenneth Ray Young.
      p.   cm. — (History and warfare)
   Includes bibliographical references and index.
   ISBN 0-8133-2195-6
   1. MacArthur, Arthur, 1845–1912.   2. Generals—United States—
Biography.   3. United States. Army—Biography.   4. United States—
History, Military—To 1900.   I. Title.   II. Series.
E181.M115Y68   1994
355'.0092—dc20   94-12218
                                                                                      CIP

Printed and bound in the United States of America

 The paper used in this publication meets the requirements of the American National Standard for Permanence of Paper for Printed Library Materials Z39.48-1984.

10   9   8   7   6   5   4   3   2   1

In Memory of
Arnold Brackman
and
Major James Bradley, USAF Ret.

Contents

Part Four
Final Days

Illustrations

PHOTOGRAPHS

MAPS

Preface

IF DOUGLAS MACARTHUR'S FATHER, Lieutenant General Arthur MacArthur, had pursued the press as actively as did his son, he would likely be remembered today as an important man in American history. Arthur joined the 24th Wisconsin Volunteers in August 1862 when he was seventeen years old, and during the Civil War he fought in eighteen major battles in Tennessee and Georgia. Cited for bravery over a dozen times, he won the congressional Medal of Honor for his valor at Missionary Ridge in November 1863. The following spring, he assumed command of the regiment during the Atlanta campaign and soon after became the youngest lieutenant colonel in the Union army.

After the war, Arthur joined the Regular Army as an infantry captain when he was twenty-two years old, remaining at that rank for twenty years, which was not unusual in the postwar army that shrank from 1 million men in April 1865 to a mere 2,000 officers and 25,000 enlisted men in April 1870. As a company commander on the western frontier from 1867 to 1887, he never fired his gun against a "hostile" Indian force. Yet during his years on the frontier, MacArthur acquired skills that, combined with his knowledge of combat learned during the Civil War, made him an efficient trainer of men. He grew to know the problems of the enlisted men because he worked, ate, and lived with them. MacArthur's concern for his men led him to initiate reforms when he became the post commander at Fort Selden, New Mexico, in 1886. Because the post was too small for a sutler (a licensed merchant), MacArthur established an enlisted men's canteen, whose profits were returned to the men in the form of better recreational facilities and lower prices. Other post commanders copied MacArthur's idea, and the canteen developed, years later, into the modern army post exchange, or PX.

During his twenty years as an infantry captain, MacArthur was an insatiable reader, and he demanded that his sons also become knowledgeable in literature, economics, philosophy, and politics as well as military affairs. MacArthur became an expert on Asia and petitioned the War Department in 1882 to assign him to China as a military attaché. His request was ignored, but his interest in Asia did not decline. In 1889, he was finally promoted to the rank of major and transferred to the Adjutant General's Office in Washington, D.C., where he contributed to the movement for army reforms that led to a new promotion system based on ability. He was also instrumental in altering old injustices. During the Civil War, officers were not given medals for bravery in combat but rather were awarded brevets, or honorary promotions, that were often withdrawn after the war. MacArthur convinced the War Department to change its policy and to award medals to officers as well as enlisted men. In the 1890s, sixty-eight officers, including MacArthur, were awarded the congressional Medal of Honor for their acts of bravery during the Civil War.

When the Spanish-American War began in April 1898, MacArthur was a lieutenant colonel. The war meant instantaneous promotion as the U.S. Army quickly expanded to 100,000 men. Promoted to brigadier general, MacArthur was assigned to the Philippines. As a brigade commander, he was instrumental in capturing Manila from the Spanish in August 1898; subsequently, he was promoted to major general and assigned a division of 10,000 men. When the Filipinos rebelled against U.S. rule, MacArthur's division did most of the fighting. His military techniques achieved a quick victory for the United States, and military leaders carefully studied his campaigns. Those campaigns were particularly impressive to Japanese military leaders, who utilized his tactics in Korea and Manchuria during the Russo-Japanese War, 1904–1905.

In May 1900, President William McKinley appointed MacArthur the military governor of the Philippines. Under his command were 70,000 U.S. soldiers, the largest military force the United States had placed in the field since the Civil War. As military governor from May 1900 to July 1901, MacArthur carefully studied Filipino culture and insisted that the primary purpose of U.S. rule was to train the Filipinos in the principles of self-government. Many of his programs were so far-sighted that they were emulated forty-five years later by his son, Douglas, when he was the Supreme Commander of Allied Powers in occupied Japan.

During the Russo-Japanese War, MacArthur served as a military observer in Korea and Manchuria. After the war, he toured Asia with his wife, Pinky, and Douglas. During the year-long, 18,000-mile journey from Japan to China through Southeast Asia to India, emperors, kings, governors, and generals entertained the MacArthurs. Douglas's later claim that he knew the Asian mind was, in large part, a reflection of what he learned on this trip.

When MacArthur returned to the United States in 1906, he was promoted to lieutenant general—the highest rank in the U.S. Army, a rank that had been held by only twelve other men in U.S. history, including George Washington, Ulysses S. Grant, and William Tecumseh Sherman. Three years later, at the age of sixty-four, MacArthur retired from the army and settled in Milwaukee, Wisconsin. In September 1912, he died while giving a speech to the surviving members of his old Civil War regiment.

There are hundreds of biographies on far less significant U.S. generals than Arthur MacArthur. Why has he been ignored? One reason lies in his character. He was a reserved man who was comfortable only with other military men. While military governor of the Philippines, for example, he refused to give press interviews. Newspapermen did not dislike the general, but no reporter was ever permitted to truly know him. Pinky MacArthur knew the value of a good press and often chided her husband for his attitude toward publicity. She advised her son not to make the same mistake.

Possibly the foremost reason biographers have ignored Arthur MacArthur is the dearth of information about his personal life. When Douglas went to the Philippines in 1935, he took his father's papers with him; those papers were destroyed in Manila during World War II. Since Arthur MacArthur usually refused to give interviews and did not write an autobiography, most of his surviving writings are limited to official reports. In most instances, it is impossible to know how he felt about his father, mother, wife, children, and friends, as well as other such personal matters as whether he had a dog, what childhood diseases he contracted, the name of his favorite horse, or whether he liked cornbread. Given the lack of personal letters, any account of his life must deal primarily with his public life.

Fortunately, the material on MacArthur's public life is extensive. The military archives provide details on every major battle of the Civil War and the Philippine revolution. Although MacArthur's personal letters have not survived, many participants in the same events wrote diaries, letters, and autobiographies, and it is likely their experiences were comparable to MacArthur's.

I wish to thank my friends, colleagues, and students for their understanding during the long process of writing this book. Particular thanks are extended to David Detzer, John M. Gates, Stuart Creighton Miller, Carol M. Petillo, Joan W. Sherman, and Joan Gereg, who read portions of the manuscript and made invaluable suggestions. Any mistakes are mine. My gratitude is deepest for my wife, Midge.

Kenneth Ray Young

PART ONE

The Civil War

*Colonel MacArthur and the
24th Wisconsin Volunteers*

1

The Judge

As many observers have noted, Douglas MacArthur had a monumental ego, yet there was one bit of flattery he always rejected. When anyone implied that his achievements outshone the accomplishments of his father, Douglas became angry. His father was his hero. In Douglas's mind, no military man could ever equal the valor and brilliance of Lieutenant General Arthur MacArthur. Douglas struggled all his life to emulate his father's standards and to equal his attainments. Over thirty years after his father's death, Douglas would say, "Whenever I perform a mission and think I have done it well, I feel that I can stand up squarely to my dad and say, 'Governor, how about it?'"[1]

If Douglas often wondered if he was as good a man as his father, Lieutenant General Arthur MacArthur probably doubted that his successes in life ever equaled the record of his own father, Judge Arthur MacArthur, the founder of the family in the United States.

Judge MacArthur was born in Glasgow, Scotland, on January 26, 1817, and named Arthur after his father. The maiden name of his mother, Sarah, had also been MacArthur, making him, in his own words, a "double-distilled" MacArthur; in fact, both his grandfathers were named John MacArthur.[2] His paternal grandfather was a "genuine highlander" from north Scotland who lived "among the braes and hills" near Loch Kathrine, "a Loch consecrated ... by [Sir Walter] Scott in the *Lady of the Lake*." His maternal grandfather lived in Dumbarton and probably worked in a textile mill. In the family, there was a legend, repeated for generations, that the MacArthurs dated back to the sixth century and were descendants of King Aedan MacGrabhran of Argyll and the Scottish clan of MacArtair.[3]

After their marriage, Arthur and Sarah MacArthur settled in Glasgow among relatives and in 1815 had their first child, a daughter. Within months, Sarah was pregnant again, but before the birth of the second child, disaster struck. A few days before Arthur Jr. was born on January 26, 1817, his father and sister died, leaving the widow and young child to be cared for by the MacArthur clan. Although there are no records on this period in Arthur's life, in later years he exhibited a bravado often associated with younger children in a large family, and he further developed the independent nature frequently displayed by half orphans. His motto was to succeed, and success meant becoming an educated professional—a lawyer, a priest, a doctor, or a teacher.[4]

When Arthur was seven, his mother married Alexander Meggett, a man whom Arthur later described as "very worthy." Four years later, in 1828, the family migrated to the United States and joined one of Sarah's sisters living in Uxbridge, Massachusetts, a small town about 60 miles south of Boston and 30 miles east of Providence, Rhode Island. Uxbridge, established as a town in 1727 and located between Worcester, Massachusetts, and Providence, was growing rapidly; in 1828, it had a population of about 2,000. Its chief industry was textiles.[5]

The family prospered in Uxbridge, and in the next few years, a number of relatives, including Sarah's mother and one of her brothers, migrated from Scotland and settled in the area. Young Arthur had a good relationship with his stepfather, and in later years, he always referred to him as his father. Arthur had at least two half brothers, born after the family's arrival in the United States. Alexander Meggett's occupation is unknown, but he certainly was not a common laborer. The family could afford, for example, to send young Arthur to Uxbridge Academy rather than have him work in the mills.[6]

Uxbridge Academy was a one-room school that enrolled both young men and women. Years later, when he reminisced about his youth, Arthur remembered how thrilled the young girls were with his Scottish accent. He further gained their attention by recounting Scottish legends and describing his visits to Scottish castles. The reading rage that year was Jane Porter's *Scottish Chiefs*, and young Arthur was the expert in this field. Meanwhile, the school's teachers opened his mind to a new world of literature and history. His first teacher was Abiel Jaques, a Harvard College graduate; the next year, his instructor was William H. Williams, an alumnus of Brown University.[7]

Life in mill towns like Uxbridge was not pleasant for the workers, and young Arthur developed strong sympathies for the working man's demands for more political and economic equality. He would become a Jacksonian democrat. When an economic recession hit Uxbridge in 1831, closing the local academy, Arthur was sent to a boarding school in Amherst, Massachusetts, while the family moved down the Blackstone River into Rhode Island, probably settling in Woonsocket, where there were more textile mills. In September 1836, Arthur enrolled at Wesleyan College in Middletown, Connecticut.[8]

Arthur's stay at Wesleyan was brief. In the spring of 1837, the nation plunged into a depression, causing his family to suffer financial reverses. At twenty, he was on his own. He dropped out of school and moved to Boston, where he found a job as a clerk in a law office; in 1838, he moved to a comparable position in New York City.

While working as a law clerk in New York City, Arthur met Aurelia Belcher, the twenty-one-year-old daughter of Benjamin Barney Belcher, a wealthy industrialist in Chicopee, Massachusetts, a suburb north of Springfield. The Belchers of Chicopee were descendants of Jonathan Belcher, the colonial governor of Massachusetts and New Hampshire from 1730 to 1741 and of New Jersey from 1747 to 1757. The family owned the Belcher Iron Works in Chicopee, which produced castings and agricultural equipment, including plows, cultivators, harrows, corn shellers, hay cutters, and other farm tools that were sold nationwide.[9]

Over the Belcher family's objection, MacArthur married Aurelia in 1840. A year later, he was admitted to the New York bar. Before he opened a law office, his wife's father suggested that the young couple come to Chicopee for a family reunion. Realizing his wife missed her family, Arthur accepted the invitation. While there, Aurelia's father offered to help him establish a law practice in Springfield. Aurelia, delighted, pressed her husband to accept.[10]

Arthur realized that his wife's wealthy, aristocratic family could truly assist him in establishing a law practice, and he accepted Benjamin Belcher's offer. After Arthur was admitted to the Massachusetts bar in February 1842, he moved with his young bride to Springfield, where they lived in the Belcher family homestead off Broadway and Belcher Streets with Aurelia's aunt, Margaret Belcher.[11]

Arthur opened a law office on Elm Street in Springfield, and with his wife's family contacts, his practice prospered. The area was booming as textile mills were built to take advantage of the power generated by the Connecticut and Chicopee Rivers. The population of Chicopee increased dramatically as the factories expanded to employ 2,000 workers, primarily young women. Meanwhile, tenements to house them sprang up in town.[12]

In 1843, Arthur wrote a friend that he was happy in Springfield with his "aristocratic, black-eyed Yankee wife" and was successful in his profession as a lawyer. Active in local Democratic politics, he was appointed judge advocate for the militia in the Western Military District and a public administrator for Hampden County. The only thing lacking in his life, he said, was children. But even that deficiency was cured when Aurelia gave birth to their first son, Arthur Jr., on June 2, 1845.[13]

Although MacArthur might write to friends that he was contented in Springfield, he was not, in reality, happy living so close to the Belchers, who were displeased with his Democratic party loyalties. The Belchers were part of the Springfield aristocracy, and as Whigs, they supported the protective tariff, sound monetary policy, and Daniel Webster. As an outspoken Democrat, MacArthur favored James K. Polk over Henry Clay for president in 1844, applauded Polk's decision to annex Texas, and supported the government during the Mexican-American War. Moreover, aristocratic privileges irritated Arthur. With educational opportunities, the common man, he believed, could rise to aristocratic levels.[14]

The Belchers' pompous pride in their heritage also annoyed Arthur. He later observed: "In this country the aristocracy of birth is about as old as a modern photograph. ... When families grow grand and supercilious upon shoddy contacts [with the past], it is to be feared that they will have to look further back than the Garden of Eden for a first father and mother who will acknowledge them. ...

It is for some men an unfortunate provision of nature that they cannot deny having fathers at all."[15]

Hoping to get away from the Belcher family, Arthur opened a law office in New York City. Aurelia, however, was unhappy there, and he began to search for an alternative city with opportunities for an aspiring, young Democratic lawyer.

Arthur decided to move to Milwaukee, Wisconsin, a decision likely influenced by Rufus King or Alexander Mitchell. Part of the powerful King family of New York and Massachusetts, Rufus (named for his grandfather, who had been a delegate to the Constitutional Convention) had graduated from West Point in 1833. His father, Charles King, was president of Columbia College in New York City. In 1836, Rufus resigned his commission and became the editor of the *Albany Daily Advertiser* and later the *Albany Evening Journal.* In 1845, he moved to Milwaukee, where he established his own newspaper, the *Sentinel.* Alexander Mitchell, a wealthy Scot who owned a prosperous insurance company in Milwaukee, most likely seconded King's report that there were excellent opportunities for a young Scottish lawyer in Milwaukee.[16]

Cheap but fertile farmland attracted a swarm of immigrants to Wisconsin between 1842 and 1848, and the population grew from 45,000 to nearly 250,000 in just one decade. Admitted to the Union in June 1848, Wisconsin already had more people than six of the other twenty-nine states.[17]

Some time in 1849, MacArthur moved to Milwaukee, Wisconsin, with his wife and four-year-old son. Located on Lake Michigan 90 miles north of Chicago, Milwaukee was already superior to many an eastern city, including Springfield, in size and culture. Aurelia, probably frightened and depressed at having left her family in Chicopee, may have been relieved on arriving in Milwaukee. She found well-stocked stores and beautiful houses, many of them built of cream-colored brick, as well as newly graded and graveled streets, limestone-slab sidewalks, a spacious theater, and many of the other amenities of urban life. The population, over 40 percent German, numbered about 14,000, including 400 Scotsmen, and was growing rapidly.[18]

Initially, MacArthur and his family boarded on West Osborn Street, but they soon purchased a home at 448 Van Buren Street (now 762 N. Van Buren), in an exclusive section of town and next door to the King family. Attorney MacArthur established a network of powerful friends and quickly earned a reputation as an informative and entertaining speaker. Alexander Mitchell, the wealthiest Scot in the city, introduced him to the social elite and sponsored his membership in the Odd Fellows Club, the Milwaukee Literary Club, and the Milwaukee Boat Club. Mitchell, the same age as MacArthur (thirty-two in 1849), had migrated from Scotland to Milwaukee in 1839. There, he founded the Wisconsin Marine and Fire Insurance Company, whose assets totaled $60,000 in 1849 and grew rapidly to ten times that amount in the next decade. Mitchell was a powerful friend. Shortly after MacArthur arrived in Milwaukee, he and Mitchell organized the Robert Burns Society, a club for the Scotsmen living in the city; with Mitchell's support,

Judge Arthur MacArthur, daguerreotype print, c. 1850. (MacArthur Memorial Library, Ph-101)

MacArthur was elected the club's first president. Meanwhile, Mitchell's sons, William and John, became boyhood acquaintances of young Arthur. Like the Mitchells, the MacArthurs were Episcopalians, and they attended services at St. James Church.[19]

MacArthur became a rising star in Milwaukee politics. Representing the reform wing of the Democratic party, he was a favorite speaker at July 4th celebrations. Although he was friendly with a number of Whigs, such as Rufus King, he refused to join the Whig party because he believed it was too closely associated with the nativist movement epitomized by the Know Nothing party. Know Nothing membership was open only to U.S.-born Protestants; the party was hostile to Catholicism and to foreign immigrants. The Know Nothings wanted to extend the residency requirement for citizenship to twenty-one years and to prohibit any foreign-born resident, naturalized citizen or not, from holding public office. Yet Know Nothing membership was increasing in Wisconsin in 1850. Because the Germans were the prime producers of beer, the Know Nothings (along with many Whigs) supported the temperance movement and wanted to prohibit all alcoholic beverages.

The Know Nothings appalled MacArthur. He took their attacks on foreign immigrants personally. He certainly did not believe his love of Scotland, the land of his birth, indicated any lack of patriotism for the United States. At every opportunity, MacArthur attacked the nativists' bigotry and berated the Whigs for their support of the temperance movement. He had a personal interest in the issue as well, for he loved his Scotch whiskey; to his dying day, he would have at least one toddy before bedtime.

The Democratic party was not much better than the Whig party in MacArthur's mind, and petty squabbles and corruption racked the Democratic machine in Milwaukee. MacArthur joined the reform wing of the Democratic party, and in March 1852, he ran for city attorney on the People's party ticket. The Whig party, weak in the city, endorsed the reform slate, helping the People's party sweep into office with a new mayor and MacArthur as city attorney. For the next two years, MacArthur had a guaranteed income of $600 a year plus 10 percent of all sums collected in city suits. The security was fortuitous, for on September 20, 1853, Aurelia had a second son, whom they named Frank.[20]

In 1854, the Kansas-Nebraska Act tore the established political parties asunder as the slavery issue again became a topic of national debate. Supported by Illinois Senator Stephen A. Douglas, President Franklin Pierce, and the entire Southern bloc, the Kansas-Nebraska Act repealed the Missouri Compromise that had prohibited slavery in all of the Louisiana Purchase area north of the latitude 36° 30' except for Missouri. Under the act, settlers in the Kansas and Nebraska territories would decide whether they wished to allow slavery when they petitioned for statehood.[21]

In the South, there were cheers of victory. Proslavery forces developed plans to stimulate settlement in Kansas to ensure it would enter the Union as a slave state. The uproar in the Northern states was instantaneous, and the Kansas-Nebraska Act soon split the Wisconsin Democratic party into two hostile wings. Following the lead of President Pierce and Senator Douglas, the party organization, headed by Edward G. Ryan, a prominent Milwaukee attorney, supported the Kansas-Nebraska Act. But MacArthur and a sizable section of the party, including William A. Barstow, the Democratic governor, refused. Ultimately, the act destroyed the Whig party in Wisconsin. From its ashes, a new party—the Republican party—arose, drawing membership from disgruntled Democrats and Free Soilers as well as Whigs.

In November 1854, the new Republican party swept the elections in Wisconsin, gained control of the state legislature, and won two of the state's three seats in Congress. The governor and most state officers were scheduled to stand for election in November 1855, and the Republicans' chances seemed excellent. It appeared they would get the antislavery vote, and Governor Barstow's Democratic administration was notoriously corrupt. Elected to the post in 1853, Barstow was a magnetic but unscrupulous politician, and scandals rocked his administration. The new Republican assembly uncovered massive fraud, inspiring newspapers to refer to the administration as "Barstow and the Forty Thieves." Legislative investigative committees discovered corruption in the building of a state insane asylum, in the selling of school land that had been purchased by insiders of the Barstow administration for less than true value, and in the maintenance of state land records kept in such hopeless confusion that corruption was the inevitable conclusion.[22]

Attorney MacArthur, a lifelong Democrat, must have been chagrined, and it is possible that he considered leaving the Democratic party to join the Republicans. But then, the Republican legislature revived the temperance issue and passed a law prohibiting the sale of alcohol in the state of Wisconsin. Governor Barstow vetoed the bill, restored his following in Milwaukee, and convinced MacArthur to continue to support the Democratic party. For his loyalty in such chaotic times, MacArthur was selected as one of Milwaukee's delegates to the Democratic Convention to nominate the state ticket.[23]

The convention opened in Madison, the state capital, on August 29, 1855. Despite his liabilities, Governor Barstow was renominated (although one delegate insisted on casting his vote for Arthur MacArthur). Barstow's renomination was actually a foregone conclusion. The real debates centered around the platform and candidates for the other state offices—particularly state treasurer and lieutenant governor, listed separately on the ballot. Over the opposition of the Democrats aligned with Edward Ryan, who supported the Kansas-Nebraska Act, the convention adopted a platform opposing any law that allowed slavery to expand, passed resolutions condemning prohibition, and attacked the bigotry of the nativist elements in the Republican party.[24]

When the convention took up the question of the lieutenant governor, the delegates realized they needed an honest man to balance the ticket led by Barstow. The Milwaukee delegation nominated Arthur MacArthur. His popularity in the Democratic stronghold of Milwaukee, his excellent speaking ability, his friendly and gregarious nature, plus his proclaimed Scottish heritage all worked in his favor; consequently, he was nominated for lieutenant governor on the third ballot. *Argus,* a Democratic paper, applauded the selection and proclaimed that MacArthur added materially to the ticket. His nomination, the paper noted, served as clear proof of the antinativist position of the Democratic party.[25]

A week later, on September 5, the new Republican party held its convention, also in Madison, to nominate its first slate of candidates for state offices. Proclaiming slavery and its expansion to be the prime issue of the election, the convention nominated State Senator Coles Bashford for governor and C. C. Sholes for lieutenant governor. Bashford was a lawyer from Winnebago who had exposed the misdeeds of the Barstow regime. Unfortunately for the ticket, he was also a prohibitionist and was linked closely with the Know Nothing party, which immediately endorsed him. The convention tried to disassociate itself from the nativists by adopting resolutions proclaiming the "equal rights of men" and condemning all secret political organizations that advocated bigotry based on "birthplace, religion, or color."[26]

In the campaign, the Republicans concentrated on the slavery issue and the corruption charges leveled against Barstow. Barstow and MacArthur ignored both issues and instead appealed to the German voters in Milwaukee by taking an antitemperance and antinativist position, while branding the Republicans as Know Nothings in disguise.[27]

The election results were a clear-cut victory for MacArthur but very close in the governor's race. MacArthur received 38,040 votes to Sholes's 35,160, a majority of almost 3,000 votes, but in the governor's race, Barstow received just 36,169 votes to Bashford's 36,012—a mere 157-vote difference. When Democratic-controlled canvassers declared Barstow the winner, the Republicans protested and demanded a recount under court supervision. Bashford's lawyers claimed they had overwhelming evidence that fraud had been committed. Edward Ryan, the powerful Democrat supported by President Pierce, decided the controversy was an opportunity to destroy the reform wing of the Democratic party. He offered legal advice to the Republicans, and despite his support of the Kansas-Nebraska Act, the Republicans accepted his offer. Ryan proclaimed he had irrefutable evidence that proved Coles Bashford had won the election. The Wisconsin Supreme Court agreed to hear the case.[28]

Excitement on both sides grew as inauguration day—January 7, 1856—approached. Rumors circulated that the Republicans planned to occupy the state capitol to prevent Barstow's inauguration. For his part, Barstow mobilized the state militia and collected 250 armed supporters to guarantee there would be no interference by the Republicans. Violent confrontation seemed possible as large numbers of men on both sides equipped themselves for battle.[29]

In the end, the Republicans attempted no coup d'état as calmer heads prevailed. On January 7—a bitterly cold day in Madison—Barstow, MacArthur, and the other newly elected state officers were sworn in without disturbance.

Over the next two months, Bashford's attorneys presented evidence to the state's supreme court that revealed a devastating case of fraudulent election manipulation by Barstow's supporters. A Democratic-controlled election board had accepted forged supplementary returns and counted voters who did not exist in a number of precincts. One set of ballots, for example, was from Spring Creek, a nonexistent precinct purported to be somewhere in Polk County. Moreover, all the supplementary returns, regardless of where the votes were supposedly cast, were written on the same unusual kind of watermarked paper, with the same peculiar phrasing, and in the same handwriting. In one case, the supplementary returns from Waupaca added up to more voters than there were in the entire district, raising Barstow's count in that area from 288 to 547—enough votes to change the election results. Even Democratic-controlled newspapers, such as the *Evening Argus & Democrat,* admitted the evidence of election fraud was overwhelming and expected the supreme court to overturn the election and proclaim Coles Bashford the winner.[30]

But before the court ruled, in a move widely interpreted as an attempt to derail the case, Barstow resigned on March 21, 1856, after serving only six weeks of his second term. There had been no hint of scandal surrounding MacArthur's election as lieutenant governor, and after Barstow's resignation, MacArthur immediately assumed the governorship. The new governor relieved tensions in the state capital by ordering the militia home and disarming all Barstow supporters. MacArthur announced that he had no intention of holding the governor's seat by force and that he hoped the opposition would not resort to force to obtain the office. Civil disruption would not be condoned.

Nonetheless, MacArthur's tenure as governor lasted only three days. On the afternoon of Monday, March 24, the Wisconsin Supreme Court issued a unanimous decision: Fraud had been committed, and Coles Bashford had actually been elected governor on November 6, 1855. Consequently, around eleven o'clock on March 25, Bashford, accompanied by his lawyers, the sheriff, and about twenty supporters, appeared at MacArthur's office with the court decision. MacArthur teased Bashford about bringing so many men to oust him from office, and the group laughed, realizing that MacArthur intended to honor the court decision. Two days later, he returned to his duties as lieutenant governor.[31]

Public attention in the next few months focused on events in Kansas. When the Kansas-Nebraska Act opened Kansas for settlement, proslavery forces rushed to the area. At the same time, abolitionists in the North, determined to prevent the spread of slavery, sponsored settlement through the New England Emigrant Aid Society. Conflict erupted in early 1856 as fanatical elements from the North and the South flocked to the new territory, both sides determined to have Kansas. Congress did nothing as violence flared in mid-May. Proslavery forces burned sections of the town of Lawrence in northern Kansas; antislavery forces under John Brown responded by raiding areas in southern Kansas and murdering a number of farmers who had supported the proslavery government.

With "Bleeding Kansas" on the nation's mind, the Democrats held their national convention in early June in Cincinnati, Ohio. The two leading Democratic presidential contenders, Senator Douglas and President Pierce, were passed over. Instead, the delegates nominated James Buchanan from Pennsylvania for president and a Southerner, John C. Breckinridge from Kentucky, for vice president. The convention also adopted a platform in support of the Kansas-Nebraska Act. Two weeks later, on June 17, 1856, the Republican party held its first national convention and nominated soldier-explorer John C. Frémont for president on a plat-form opposed to the expansion of slavery into Kansas.

In Wisconsin, Lieutenant Governor MacArthur faced a dilemma, for he could not support the Kansas-Nebraska Act. Perhaps he thought of deserting the Democratic party for the Republican party, as many of his friends had done. James R. Doolittle, for example, refused to remain in a party committed to slavery in the Kansas territory. Yet MacArthur could not accept the close connection in Wisconsin of the Republican party with the Know Nothings, now calling them-selves the American party. He continued as a Democrat technically. He conceiv-ably refrained from voting for the national ticket and voted only for Democrats for state offices.

Buchanan won the presidential race, carrying fourteen slave states but only five free states. In Wisconsin, the coalition Republican party used the slavery issue and "Bleeding Kansas" with devastating results for the Democrats. Buchanan won Milwaukee County, with its high German population, but lost the state to Fré-mont, who polled 66,090 votes to Buchanan's 52,843. Wisconsin's three congres-sional districts went to the Republicans as well. In the state elections, the Republi-cans won the majority of seats in both the senate and the assembly.

In the spring of 1857, MacArthur began to think about running for governor on the Democratic ticket in the fall. Although the Republicans appeared to have overwhelming power in Wisconsin, the party membership was united only over the question of slavery. Moreover, the Bashford administration had proven to be as corrupt as Barstow's had been. MacArthur's chances of obtaining the Demo-cratic nomination for governor appeared excellent.

However, in April 1857, MacArthur decided not to run for governor, opting in-stead to run for a judgeship on the Second Circuit Court of Milwaukee. His deci-sion may have been based on family concerns, for his wife had returned to her parents' home in Chicopee, leaving behind two young sons who now needed more of their father's attention.

MacArthur's older son, eleven-year-old Arthur, is depicted in a few accounts as a spirited boy nicknamed *Mac* by his friends. As a typical youngster of the times, he spent his afterschool hours and summer days playing with the other boys in the neighborhood. During the summer, about a dozen boys met every morning at Charlie King's house on the corner of Mason and Van Buren Streets. "We raced and scuffled and wrestled" the day away, King later said. The boys sometimes per-suaded their fathers to take them hunting and fishing. Their favorite spots were on the Menomonee River, but they also enjoyed camping on the shores of many of the small lakes in the interior, away from Lake Michigan. The boys' favorite game on the camping trips was "war," in which they pretended they were soldiers on a scouting mission for Zachary Taylor or Winfield Scott in the Mexican-American War. On Sundays, the boys often went sailing with their fathers on Lake Michi-gan.[32]

In contrast to her son, who appeared well suited to life in Milwaukee, Aurelia MacArthur apparently never reconciled herself to the move and longed to return to her relatives in Springfield. There are no records that any contact was maintained with the Belcher family in Chicopee. It was almost as if Aurelia and her sons had been disowned. Thus, the only family Arthur had consisted of his mother, father, and younger brother, Frank. Arthur's father was a busy man, and his mother, like many other wives of the era, probably felt ignored. With only limited records to go on, it seems that Aurelia was a shy woman who brooded away her days in lonely contemplation of home while her husband went to dinner parties and was active in a number of social clubs.

Sometime after the birth of her second son in September 1853, Aurelia left her husband and children to visit Chicopee. She never returned. While there, she suffered a "mental breakdown" and was committed to a sanatorium in Northampton, Massachusetts. Thereafter, friends of the family never mentioned Aurelia in front of the boys.[33]

The effect that the loss of his mother had on Arthur as he entered puberty was probably dramatic. In effect, deserted by his mother, who had already been dividing her affection with a new sibling, Arthur appears to have withdrawn. Perhaps he decided that no love could be trusted if he could not trust his mother's love. Conceivably, he worried that his father would also abandon him. He may even have considered her "mental" condition a sign of weakness and vowed not to show such weakness himself. All his life, he would be reserved, polite, and formal, although not shy. Perhaps, in the end, he blamed his father. There always seemed to be a certain formality, a polite coolness, in their relationship.[34]

In April 1857, MacArthur was elected to the first of his two six-year terms as judge of the Second Circuit Court of Milwaukee. He remained as lieutenant governor through the fall elections, then resigned and began hearing cases in early October.[35]

Being a judge suited MacArthur and allowed him an opportunity to indulge in his other intellectual interests. Among other things, he gave a number of lectures on Scottish history and began to write. Except for the absence of Aurelia, life in Milwaukee was pleasant for the judge and his two sons. He was a gregarious man, and his home had a constant stream of visitors. As president of the Robert Burns Society (later known as the St. Andrews Society), the judge organized picnics, dances, boating trips, and curling tournaments for the Scots living in Milwaukee. At parties, he encouraged everyone to sing, recite poetry, or tell stories.[36]

Arthur, twelve years old in the summer of 1857, was almost the opposite of his father in terms of social graces. He was a quiet boy who preferred to be alone, and he dreaded his father's parties. The judge, with his playful Scottish humor, probably teased the boy about his shyness, about his studious ways, and about his interest in girls. It can also be assumed the judge forced his son to socialize when company arrived at the MacArthur home.

Arthur likely tried to avoid the judge's parties; it is even possible he resented his father's constant socializing and his activities with the Robert Burns Society, the Odd Fellows, and the Democratic party in Milwaukee that took him away from home night after night. Arthur may have considered the constant social gatherings to be a foolish waste of time and extremely boring; he certainly decided he did not want to be a lawyer or a "good time Charlie" like his father. It is possible that the judge's socializing extended beyond exclusively male companionship. And, as social psychologist Gail Sheehy notes, a "sudden puritanical intolerance [comes] over the young when Mom and Dad expose themselves as human." Thus, when his father had visitors, Arthur usually retreated to his room or to MacArthur's extensive library.[37]

The judge most likely felt his son's resentment. Arthur was not a rowdy adolescent—the judge might have liked that—but rather a serious young man who considered himself an adult. Charlie King and the other boys in his group were going through the same stages of development, and most were struggling with their fathers to obtain independence. All in all, they were good boys, each certain that his destiny was grand and glorious. The frontier mentality encouraged the boys to be self-sufficient, with a yearning for adventure. As psychologist Erik H. Erikson writes, "In a world which developed the slogan, 'If you can see your neighbor's chimney, it is time to move on' [mothers and fathers] had to raise sons and daughters who would be determined to ignore the call of the frontier—but who would go with equal determination once they were forced or chose to go."[38]

During the summer of 1858, young Arthur decided he wanted to be a soldier. Like many young men of the previous two generations, he had devoured Sir Walter Scott's *Waverly* tales, stories that glorified war and featured knights fighting for honor and displaying the most manly of virtues, courage in battle. In *Embattled Courage,* historian Gerald F. Linderman observed, "To those imbued with knightliness, warfare seemed a joust and the soldier a knightly warrior or holy crusader, an exemplar of brave and noble manhood."[39]

In all probability, Arthur visualized himself as a returning hero, wounded in battle but triumphant over fear, a man among men. "In the adolescent image," Sheehy writes, "the hero always walks out of the debris, blood-crusted but grinning, and oh what a story to tell some beautiful girl." Years later, writing about another MacArthur (Douglas), historian Carol Petillo observed, "These fantasies allowed him to see himself as hero—unafraid as he could not be in his real life."[40]

Arthur hoped to go to a military academy, pointing out to his father that many of his friends were leaving home to go to school. Charlie King was going to New York to live with his grandfather, the president of Columbia College; William Mitchell was off to the U.S. Military Academy at West Point, New York; and Charlie Cotton was going to the U.S. Naval Academy at Annapolis, Maryland.[41]

Arthur, like other young boys, wanted to "stand on his own two feet and make good." Throughout time, the motto of most adolescent boys in the United States, Sheehy notes, has been, loud and clear: "I have to get away from my parents," accompanied by another refrain, "I know exactly what I want!" "The conviction is that *real* life is somewhere out there away from family and school 'waiting to happen.'"[42]

The judge, however, rejected his son's pleas to attend a military school and instead enrolled Arthur in a two-year program at Milwaukee University High, locally referred to as Mercantile High because the curriculum emphasized business, law, and accounting. The judge wanted his son to become a lawyer rather than a soldier; perhaps, too, he simply did not want Arthur to leave home.

While Arthur was in his second year at Milwaukee University High, sectional animosity reached a fever pitch. On October 16, 1859, abolitionist John Brown seized the U.S. armory and arsenal at Harpers Ferry, Virginia. His plan was to distribute arms to the slaves in the area and to incite slave insurrections throughout the region. Captured by federal troops, Brown was convicted of treason and hanged on December 2, 1859. Six other captured raiders later suffered the same fate. Enraged Southerners blamed the Republicans for Brown's raid and threatened to secede from the Union if a Republican were elected president in 1860.[43]

Arthur spent many evenings with his father discussing Brown's raid as the slavery issue plagued the country. Although Southern fire-eaters threatened secession, Judge MacArthur did not believe the slavery issue would lead to civil war: Compromises had always been reached in the past. It is possible his son disagreed and continued to push for military school.

Arthur graduated from Milwaukee University High in June 1860, when he was fifteen years old. That summer, he again pressured his father to send him to a military academy to prepare for West Point or Annapolis. Charlie King, home on vacation, regaled Arthur with stories of evenings he spent with General Winfield Scott, who lived just down the street from the King home in New York City. After a summer of arguments, the judge finally agreed to send Arthur to a military academy in Illinois.[44]

While his son was away at school learning to be a soldier, Judge MacArthur watched the political situation slowly deteriorate. Meeting in Chicago, the Republican Convention nominated Abraham Lincoln of Illinois on a platform opposed to any further expansion of slavery into the territories. Meanwhile, the Democratic party split over the issue of slavery. Northern Democrats nominated Stephen Douglas, who ran on a platform of allowing the people in the territories to decide whether slavery should be accepted; Southern Democrats nominated Buchanan's vice president, John Breckinridge of Kentucky, who ran on a states'-rights and proslavery platform. Out of the ruins of the Democratic party and the old Whig party, the Constitutional Union party was formed, nominating Senator John Bell of Tennessee on a platform of compromise to save the Union.

Lincoln won the election as voting split clearly along sectional lines. He received 1,866,452 votes (approximately 40 percent) but did not get a single vote in ten Southern states. He carried seventeen of the eighteen free states, losing to Douglas only in New Jersey, and won 180 electoral votes, a clear majority.

Breckinridge won in eleven slave states with 79 electoral votes; Bell won three border states (Virginia, Kentucky, and Tennessee) with 39 electoral votes; and Douglas took New Jersey and Missouri with 12 electoral votes.

South Carolina greeted Lincoln's victory with a call for a state convention to consider secession from the Union. The convention met in Charleston on December 17, 1860, and voted to secede on the basis that a Republican president, committed to "unconstitutional goals," was unacceptable. South Carolina had freely entered the Union in 1788, and it considered that it had the right to withdraw as an independent sovereign state. Within sixty days, Alabama, Georgia, Florida, Mississippi, Texas, and Louisiana also withdrew from the Union. Delegates from the seven states met in Montgomery, Alabama, on February 4, 1861, and formed the Confederate States of America. In six days, the delegates drafted a constitution and elected a provisional president, Jefferson F. Davis, a former soldier, U.S. congressman and senator from Mississippi, and Franklin Pierce's secretary of war. Davis appealed to the remaining eight slave states to join the Confederacy. Flag-waving crowds in Montgomery did not expect a war; on the contrary, as James M. McPherson notes in *Battle Cry of Freedom*, "they believed that 'the Yankees were cowards and would not fight.'" "Just throw three or four shells among those blue-bellied Yankees," said a North Carolinian, "and they'll scatter like sheep." In Southern eyes, the North was a nation of shopkeepers. It mattered not that the Union's industrial capacity was many times greater than the Confederacy's. "It was not the improved arm, but the improved man, which would win the day," said Henry Wise of Virginia. "Let brave men advance with flint locks and old-fashioned bayonets on the popinjays of Northern cities ... and he would answer for it with his life, that the Yankees would break and run."[45]

The crisis deepened as Lincoln took office in early March. As the Southern states seceded, they attempted to take over federal forts and arsenals in their states. In four cases, they were unsuccessful. The most significant exception was Fort Sumter, located on an island in the middle of Charleston harbor. South Carolina demanded the fort's surrender. Lincoln ordered the Union forces under Major Robert Anderson to resist. As the leading state of the secession movement, South Carolina refused to accept the situation, and Confederate batteries opened fire on the fort on April 12, 1861. Forty hours later, Anderson surrendered.

Huge crowds poured into the streets of Southern cities, waving Confederate flags and cheering the glorious victory for the Southern cause. Within weeks, Virginia, Arkansas, North Carolina, and Tennessee withdrew from the Union and joined the Confederacy, bringing the number of Confederate states to eleven.[46]

Lincoln called on the free states to enlist 75,000 volunteers to supplement the small Union army, which numbered less than 17,000 men. "The response from free states was overwhelming," according to McPherson.

> War meetings in every city and village cheered the flag and vowed vengeance on traitors. "The heather is on fire," wrote a Harvard professor. ... "I never knew what a

popular excitement can be. ... The whole population, men, women, and children seem to be in the streets with Union ... flags." From Ohio and the West came "one great Eagle-scream" for the flag. "The people have gone stark mad!" In New York City ... a quarter of a million people turned out for a Union rally.

The time before Sumter was like another century, wrote a New York woman. "It seems as if we never were alive till now; never had a country till now." Stephen Douglas, in Chicago, told a huge crowd, "There are only two sides to the question. Every man must be for the United States or against it. There can be no neutrals in this war, *only patriots—or traitors*."[47]

Judge MacArthur organized a Union rally in Milwaukee. Although a Democrat, he was appalled by South Carolina's attack on Fort Sumter. Before a packed crowd at Albany Hall on April 19, the judge declared that the Union was above any sectional or party loyalties and pledged to never submit to the dissolution of the United States. Joined by Matthew H. Carpenter, Charles D. Robinson, and many other Wisconsin Democrats, MacArthur formed the Union Democratic party. The Union Democrats supported Lincoln, with MacArthur leading the way. Before packed crowds throughout the state, the judge repeated his belief that the Union came before party politics.[48]

Young men flocked to enlist in state volunteer regiments. When Arthur Jr. returned home in June, he learned that seventeen-year-old Charlie King had joined the 6th Wisconsin as an orderly. Using his friend as an example, Arthur tried to persuade his father to let him join one of the volunteer regiments forming in Milwaukee.

The judge rejected the idea, and his son's arguments did not sway him. Arthur was barely sixteen years old, not seventeen like Charlie, and besides, the judge knew the King family had allowed Charlie to join the 6th Wisconsin only because his father, General Rufus King, was the commander of the regiment. Small for his age, Arthur was only about five feet tall and weighed around ninety pounds. In his father's eyes, he was still a young boy.[49]

When Arthur threatened to enlist without his father's permission, the judge hired a detective to follow him around the city and contacted a number of officers to request they not enlist his son. As a powerful Union Democrat, the judge and his desires could not be ignored. Arthur went from recruiting office to recruiting office, trying to enlist, but since no regimental commander wanted to irritate the judge, no officer listened to the pleas of the sixteen-year-old boy.

Arthur did not give up. He went to Camp Sigel just outside Milwaukee to watch the new regiments drill. When a regiment left Milwaukee, he was usually at the railroad station, trying one last time to enlist. Sergeant Jerome Anthony Watrous saw Arthur at the station when the 6th Wisconsin left Milwaukee for the eastern front in July 1861. He later recalled that one of the men yelled out, "Enlist the boy! The lad's General material for sure." Several soldiers laughed. Looking at the slim, pale-faced lad, one of the men sarcastically remarked that the boy would not last a month in the army. Dismayed yet undeterred, Arthur kept trying, but all the regiments that passed through the city that summer refused to enlist him.[50]

As the North and South built up their armies, June passed into early July. The raw recruits took up defensive positions around the two opposing capitals, Washington and Richmond. On July 21, small contingents, about 25,000 on each side, clashed at Bull Run, a sluggish, meandering river a few miles north of Manassas, Virginia. The inexperienced Union troops panicked and fled in disarray back to Washington. Although technically victorious, the Confederate forces were badly disorganized and did not follow the routed Union army.[51]

The day after Bull Run, Lincoln signed a bill to enlist 500,000 three-year men. Three days later, he signed a bill authorizing another 500,000.

The atmosphere at the MacArthur home in the summer of 1861 was tense. Arthur was afraid the war would end before he could enlist and prove his bravery. Meanwhile, the judge negotiated a compromise with his young son. If Arthur would return to his military academy in Illinois for one more year, the judge would try to obtain an appointment for him to West Point. When Arthur learned Charlie King, his best friend, was also pursuing a West Point appointment, he agreed. His desire to enlist remained strong, but he went back to the military school that fall. "One more year, and that's it," he probably proclaimed to his father. Only a West Point appointment, he asserted, would prevent him from enlisting when he returned home.

Through the fall of 1861 and the spring of 1862, Arthur could not keep his mind on his studies as the war dominated the news. Lincoln eased seventy-four-year-old General in Chief Winfield Scott, hero of both the War of 1812 and the Mexican-American War, into retirement on November 1, 1861, and replaced him with thirty-four-year-old Major General George B. McClellan. McClellan spent the fall and winter stockpiling equipment and training his troops.[52]

In the west along the Mississippi Valley, Union forces under General Ulysses S. Grant initiated a number of actions during the late winter. In February 1862, Grant captured Fort Henry and Fort Donelson, two strategic Confederate positions along the Tennessee-Kentucky border. Union forces under General Don Carlos Buell occupied Nashville, Tennessee, on February 23, bringing most of central Tennessee and all of Kentucky under Union military control, although guerrilla activity and periodic Confederate cavalry raids continued.

In early April, Confederate forces under General Albert Sidney Johnston attacked Grant's army at Shiloh, Tennessee. Considered a Union victory, Shiloh was the first bloody battle of the Civil War; the casualty totals staggered both sides. Union losses were 1,754 killed and 8,408 wounded; Confederate losses were 1,723 killed and 8,012 wounded.

Arthur wired his father that he could no longer wait and intended to join an Illinois state Volunteer regiment. In the preceding months, Judge MacArthur had tried to honor his promise to obtain a West Point appointment for his son, but despite his political connections, no Wisconsin congressman had an appointment still open. The judge knew he could not block Arthur's enlistment much longer—thousands of sixteen- and seventeen-year-olds were enlisting in state Volunteer regiments.

The judge decided to appeal to President Lincoln. In mid-May 1862, he collected his son from his military school, and together they traveled to Washington, D.C., to see the president of the United States. Indeed, politicians, businessmen, and jobseekers of every description had flocked to the capital to see Lincoln. When Judge MacArthur arrived with his son on May 22, 1862, the city was crowded with soldiers; at long last, McClellan was beginning his military offensive.[53]

Judge MacArthur contacted Wisconsin Senator Doolittle, who arranged an interview with Lincoln. The president needed the support of the Union Democrats not only in Wisconsin but throughout the North. Without a decisive victory on the battlefield, Northern enthusiasm for the war had waned perceptibly, and the faultfinders multiplied. Higher taxes, inflation, profiteering, arbitrary arrests, suppression of the press, and military conscription aggravated the discontent, as did Lincoln's call for 300,000 more troops. At the same time, the Democratic party attacked Lincoln for incompetency, corruption, and stupidity, and his military blunders and acts of dubious constitutionality were grist for the political mills. As discontent and criticism of Lincoln's war policies escalated with each passing month, the Republicans desperately needed the continued support of the Union Democrats, and Lincoln obviously did not wish to alienate the most important Union Democrat in Wisconsin.[54]

On the morning of June 3, the day after Arthur's seventeenth birthday, he and his father visited the White House. Unfortunately, however, Lincoln could not appoint young Arthur to the West Point class of 1862. The president was allowed to appoint ten cadets each year, and he had already filled his quota. To Arthur's chagrin, Charlie King, his boyhood chum, was one of the ten presidential appointees.[55]

Lincoln instead offered young Arthur an appointment to the West Point class of 1863. Judge MacArthur thought that was an ideal solution—another year for his boy to grow strong, to study, and to avoid the war. As father and son left Washington the next day, the enlistment argument continued. By the time they were back in Milwaukee on June 7, the judge had admitted defeat. He could no longer prevent his son from enlisting in the army—the war beckoned too strongly.

The judge had one option left, and he used it.

2

Into the War

SHORTLY AFTER Judge MacArthur and his young son returned home from Washington, D.C., the judge learned that the Milwaukee Chamber of Commerce was forming and outfitting a new regiment, the 24th Wisconsin Volunteers. Alexander Mitchell, a friend of the judge's and the leading Scottish businessman in the city, had obtained appointments in the new regiment for his son John and for Robert J. Chivas, who lived with the Mitchell family. Nineteen-year-old John L. Mitchell was to be a second lieutenant in Company I, and Bob Chivas, the twenty-year-old secretary of the St. Andrews Society, was to be appointed first lieutenant in the same company.

With Alexander Mitchell's backing, the judge took a train to Madison to see Governor Edward Salomon, who had been in office only four months and who owed his lofty position to MacArthur. In November 1861, the Republicans ran Louis P. Harvey as their candidate for governor and, with MacArthur's support, selected Salomon, a young Milwaukee lawyer and a Union Democrat, as their candidate for lieutenant governor. The Harvey-Salomon ticket had won the elections, but after just over a hundred days in office, Harvey drowned in a boating accident on April 19, 1862, and the thirty-three-year-old Salomon became governor.[1]

Salomon, who respected Judge MacArthur and needed the continued support of the Union Democrats to run the state effectively, had already written a letter to Lincoln recommending the appointment of young Arthur to West Point. Now, the judge wanted more. He wanted his son appointed to the 24th Wisconsin as regimental adjutant with the rank of first lieutenant.[2]

Salomon wished to approve the judge's request, but Arthur was only seventeen years old, which was simply too young for such a responsible position. An adjutant handled all regimental paperwork and delivered orders from the commanding officer to his line, or company, officers. Many military men considered the adjutant as second in importance only to the colonel commanding a regiment. A mistake by an adjutant could be as devastating to a regiment as a mistake by the commanding officer.

Lieutenant Arthur MacArthur, c. 1862, probably taken at the time Arthur joined the 24th Wisconsin in August 1862, at age seventeen. (MacArthur Memorial Library, Ph-2035)

Judge MacArthur solved Salomon's dilemma by lying. He informed the governor that young Arthur was really nineteen years old and fully qualified to hold the position. Furthermore, Arthur was a high school graduate at a time when many officers in Union Volunteer regiments were practically illiterate. He also had two years of training at a military academy. Although agreeing that nineteen was still young for such a responsible position, the judge pointed out that the 24th Wisconsin had a number of young officers, including Lieutenants Mitchell and Chivas, and that most of the enlisted men were under twenty-two. The judge won his case, and Salomon made the appointment. MacArthur returned to Milwaukee later that evening with the papers in hand. His son was to report to Camp Sigel, just outside Milwaukee, on August 21 to be mustered into the 24th Wisconsin.[3]

The first order of business was to outfit the new first lieutenant. Officers in Volunteer regiments provided their own uniforms and equipment, and the judge paid more to equip his young son than the $1,000 annual salary of a first lieutenant. Photographed in his new uniform, Arthur was a slim young man with a full head of light brown hair and a face not yet touched by a razor. Weighing a little over a hundred pounds and standing five-feet-seven-inches tall, he looked about fifteen years old; in his lieutenant's uniform, he resembled a military cadet playing soldier.[4]

On August 21, Arthur reported to Camp Sigel. Lieutenant Colonel Charles H. Larrabee, the commander of the 24th Wisconsin, was shocked when he saw the young boy who claimed to be his new adjutant.[5] Larrabee sent a frantic wire to Governor Salomon. Having an inexperienced boy as an adjutant would make the 24th Wisconsin the laughingstock of Camp Sigel. Larrabee requested that MacArthur's appointment be rescinded.

Salomon wired back: "Try him."[6]

Larrabee did not like it, but, as a politician, he recognized a political appointment. The forty-two-year-old Larrabee had been a judge and congressman before the war. Commissioned as a second lieutenant in Company C of the 1st Wisconsin shortly after Fort Sumter, he had utilized his political connections to quickly obtain a promotion to major and was assigned to the 5th Wisconsin. In June 1862, Governor Salomon selected Larrabee to command the 24th Wisconsin with the rank of lieutenant colonel.

Larrabee decided to "try" his new adjutant. When 1,020 men reported to Camp Sigel the next day, Arthur was in charge of all the paperwork. Most of the men were from Milwaukee and represented the spectrum of society—there were merchant clerks, railroad men, carpenters, mechanics, bakers, and tinsmiths as well as farm boys from the surrounding areas. They were predominantly of German descent, and many were Catholics. The 24th would be the first Wisconsin regiment to have a Catholic priest, Father Francis Fusseder.[7]

The men were mustered into the regiment by declaring their allegiance to the Constitution and to the government of the United States. The Volunteers assumed the Union side was the side of justice, and as abstract as the concepts might have been, they were willing to fight to maintain the Union, the Constitution, and democracy.

After the men received cursory physical examinations by the regimental surgeon, the quartermaster issued them their uniforms. Although officers purchased their uniforms and equipment, enlisted men were provided with the bare necessities, including a double-breasted dark blue jacket and light blue trousers. After dressing in their uniforms, they received their assignments from the adjutant. The regiment was divided into 10 companies, A to J, of approximately 100 men in each company. A captain, assisted by 2 lieutenants, commanded each company.[8]

That night, amidst much comaraderie, the men slept for the first time in large Sibley tents. Named after Major Henry Hopkins Sibley, who had invented the design, each tent could house twenty to twenty-two men. With two door flaps on its sides, the Sibley was raised on an iron tripod and supported by a center pole; it looked like a large tepee. The men slept with their feet toward the center and their heads near the outer walls. That first night was probably a restless one; when they moved or shifted positions, the men disturbed their neighbors. When a cannon boomed at five o'clock to announce the beginning of their first day of training, most of the men ached from sore hipbones.[9]

The new recruits quickly discovered that life in the army, even the volunteer army, was not a pleasant experience. Marching around the camp in company formations, they drilled through the morning and afternoon. No rifles or muskets were available, so the men never fired a gun during their two weeks of training. Nor did they engage in any field maneuvers or hear a lecture on any topic of war. They spent their days marching and learning some of the rules of military discipline.

Colonel Larrabee gave his young adjutant a special assignment by ordering MacArthur to prepare the regiment for a dress parade. Having spent two years in military school where dress parades were the rage, Arthur felt up to the task. Larrabee had invited Milwaukee's city fathers, embodied by the Milwaukee Chamber of Commerce, and its citizens at large to attend the parade on Saturday, August 28. The regiment had less than seven days to prepare.

For the next week, company commanders drilled the men in company formations every morning; in the afternoons, MacArthur led the regiment in rehearsal dress parades. His prime problem was convincing the officers and men to take him seriously. When he shouted out his orders, the men laughed at his high, squeaky voice: The farm boys proclaimed that he sounded like a young rooster trying to crow for the first time. As he strolled around the camp at night, Arthur heard the officers and men laughing at him. He returned to his tent and worked hard studying military manuals.

The week passed quickly. On Saturday morning, August 28, about 10,000 people turned out to see the regiment's first dress parade. The day would be a disaster for Arthur. He dressed carefully for the parade in a new uniform, complete with sword and sash. As the large crowd settled down, the regiment formed by companies to march onto the parade grounds. Arthur was at the head of the formation with Larrabee and the other staff officers. Behind them, ten companies marched in step, with company commanders and their lieutenants a few feet in front of their companies. As the regiment proceeded onto the parade ground, the crowd cheered the impressive formation of 1,000 soldiers marching in step. Arthur shouted out the order to halt when the regiment reached the reviewing stands. The regiment stopped and then turned to face the crowd. The ten companies stretched for 100 yards, with 100 men to a company.[10]

"Lieutenant MacArthur!" Larrabee shouted.

"Yessir!" Arthur barked back.

"Pass the regiment in review."

"Yessir!"

Arthur stepped forward in the best military tradition. Facing the regiment, he shouted, "Attention!"

To his horror, the command came out as a high-pitched squeak that was heard no more than twenty or thirty yards down the line, and only the men of the first three or four companies heard the order. The regiment came raggedly to attention. Larrabee stewed in irritation.

"Shoulder arms!" Arthur shouted. Again his voice did not carry, and companies down the line followed the example of their comrades rather than acting in unison with them. The scene looked even more ludicrous because the men were carrying sticks rather than guns.

"Open ranks to the rear!" Arthur yelled. Fortunately, the regiment had been through the drill a number of times, and the men turned sharply in ranks and marched across the parade ground. As the troops circled the field, Arthur marched in step until the regiment reached the original position in front of the reviewing stands. The men halted on command and then faced front toward the regimental staff officers and the 10,000 onlookers.

As the regiment stood at attention, Arthur faced the men. He was required to make a half-turn, march back to Colonel Larrabee to take his position with the other staff officers, and then turn back to face the regiment. With stiff military bearing, he marched toward the staff officers as the whole regiment and audience watched. Unfortunately, the scabbard for his sword was too long, and it kept hitting the ground. He was forced to hitch his sword higher and shove the scabbard up so that it rested more on his shoulder than on his side. When it was time for him to stop and about-face, disaster struck: As he turned, he tripped. His legs tangled in his scabbard, and he almost fell on his face.

The audience erupted in laughter, and some of the men of the regiment joined them.

For Arthur, the ordeal was not over. The ritual called for him to order the first sergeants to the front and center, and he shouted out the command.

The sergeants knew the drill. They stepped forward and shouted out, "All present and accounted for, Sir!"

Arthur turned smartly, saluted the colonel, and shouted, "Parade formed, Sir!"

Larrabee barked, "Very well, Lieutenant."

Arthur saluted again before moving to take his place on the colonel's left while Major Elisha C. Hibbard, the second in command, stood to the right. As Arthur took up his position, Larrabee glared at him with contempt.

When the dress parade ended, Larrabee told his officers he was going to request that the governor give him a man for an adjutant instead of a white-faced, chicken-voiced boy.

No one needed to tell Arthur that the dress parade had been a disaster—he knew it. The image of tripping on his sword's scabbard haunted him all his life, and he looked back on the incident with horror as perhaps the lowest point in his military career.

That warm August evening, Arthur left the officers' quarters because the other men insisted on talking about his hilarious performance. As he strolled in the dark through the rows of tents, the night was filled with the voices of soldiers yelling out in high-pitched tones: "First Sergeants to the front and center! March!"

"Present arms!" One soldier shouted, "Who's got a baby adjutant?" and was answered, "The Twenty-fourth Milwaukee." Someone else proclaimed "Colonel Larrabee has bought a new milch cow." "What for?" "For the nurse who will have charge of our adjutant."[11]

In the next few weeks, Arthur was subdued but determined to prove the colonel and the men wrong. He avoided shouting out orders and remained in the background. Larrabee ignored him, and the other officers treated him as the colonel's orderly rather than as the regimental adjutant. Arthur accepted his fate, convinced that once the regiment was in battle, the colonel, the other officers, and the men would change their minds. He still dreamed of performing heroic actions. As one of his heroes, Davy Crockett, had once said of battlefield courage, "Pluck doesn't depend on the length of one's beard, otherwise a goat would be a better fighter than any man." Arthur would not give up. Indeed, throughout his life, perseverance in the face of adversity was one of his prime personality traits.[12]

The 24th Wisconsin held no more dress parades for the citizens of Milwaukee. A desperate need existed for Union troops on both the eastern and western fronts. McClellan's campaign to capture Richmond had bogged down, and the Union Army of the Potomac suffered reverses in a series of battles fought from June 25 to July 1 on the peninsula east of Richmond. Seeing an opportunity to counterattack, Robert E. Lee sent Major General Thomas J. "Stonewall" Jackson north and west into central Virginia. McClellan withdrew his army from the peninsula to support other forces defending the Union capital. On August 29, units of the two armies clashed in the second battle of Bull Run near Manassas, Virginia. Union forces commanded by Major General John Pope were decisively defeated in three days of heavy fighting and suffered 16,000 casualties to Confederate losses of 9,200. The news was particularly grim for the people of Milwaukee. The "Iron Brigade," composed of three Wisconsin regiments (the 2nd, 6th, and 7th) and the 19th Indiana, had been hit hard at Bull Run, suffering 33 percent casualties (751 men).[13]

On the western front, the Union line stretched southwest from Louisville, Kentucky, through Nashville, Tennessee, to Corinth, Mississippi. The Confederate Army of Tennessee, commanded by General Braxton Bragg, controlled southeastern Kentucky and eastern Tennessee from Knoxville south to Chattanooga. Confederate president Jefferson Davis ordered Bragg to launch an attack into northern Kentucky toward Indiana and Ohio. Lincoln ordered Major General Don Carlos Buell, the Union commander in western Kentucky and northern Tennessee, to stop Bragg and then attack Knoxville, the major Confederate supply base in eastern Tennessee. Thus, both armies in the west were gearing up for an offensive. The 24th Wisconsin received orders to join Buell's army, mobilizing near Louisville, Kentucky.

On September 3, 1862, the 24th marched from Camp Sigel to the railroad station in downtown Milwaukee. The citizens of the city packed the streets, and cheer after cheer went up as the regiment marched down Main Street. At the depot, an estimated 7,000 friends and relatives crowded around the railroad cars to shake hands and say goodbyes. Judge MacArthur and his younger son, Frank, were there to send Arthur off to war.

The regiment was in high spirits; the men bragged to their friends that they would whip all the Johnny Rebs in Kentucky and Tennessee. The men of the 24th bubbled with enthusiasm as many of them visualized their future valor in battle. Their biggest worry was that the war might end before their regiment reached Kentucky.[14]

A train took the regiment from Milwaukee to Chicago, where the men changed to a train bound for Louisville. They traveled through the night and the next day. Aboard the crowded train, the men amused themselves with cards and jokes as they munched peaches and watermelons. As Colonel Larrabee's "orderly," Arthur ran errands from car to car, with the men teasing him as he hustled past. The officers smiled at the enlisted men's humor and noted that Arthur took the hazing with good grace. Bob Chivas and John Mitchell, two of Arthur's friends in the regiment, were always ready with words of encouragement.[15]

The train traveled south through Michigan City, Indiana, to Lafayette, then southward through Indianapolis to Louisville, arriving on September 5. The regiment disembarked for a two-day rest before proceeding to Cincinnati, Ohio, 40 miles north, to report to Brigadier General Philip H. Sheridan (see Map 2.1).

Sheridan, a bowlegged former cavalryman called "Little Phil" because he was only five-feet-five-inches tall and weighed about 115 pounds, commanded the 11th Division, composed of 10,000 men organized into three brigades, the 35th to 37th. The 24th Wisconsin was assigned to the 36th Brigade, commanded by Colonel Nicholas Greusel. Besides the 24th Wisconsin, the brigade included the 36th Illinois, the 88th Illinois, and the 21st Michigan.

The 24th Wisconsin was outfitted with supplies from the Union depot in Cincinnati. Adjutant MacArthur worked with the regimental quartermaster to complete the paperwork to obtain rifles, ammunition, knapsacks, canteens, mess equipment, and tents from the depot. There were forms for everything and an army way of completing each form. Since many of the enlisted men were illiterate, MacArthur had to complete their forms and make sure each man had the proper equipment.

Austrian rifled muskets were finally issued to the men. A single-shot, muzzle-loading rifle, the guns were cumbersome weapons but sturdy and dependable, with an effective range (the distance a good marksman could consistently hit a target) of about 300 yards. The rifle fired a conical bullet, called a minié ball after its inventor, French Captain Claude E. Minié. It took an infantryman approximately twenty-five seconds to load and fire the rifled musket.

After receiving their supplies, the regiment marched 2 miles south, crossed the Ohio River, and camped near Covington, Kentucky. From their campgrounds, they saw steamboats moving lazily down the river conveying supplies to Louisville 40 miles south.

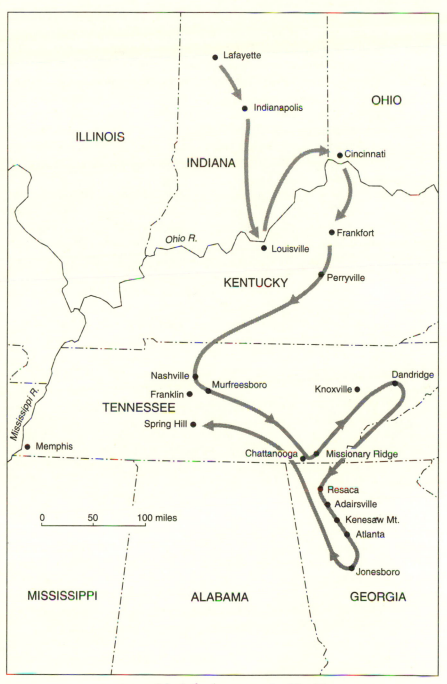

MAP 2.1 MacArthur's movements, 1862–1865

Few of Arthur's letters to his father have survived, but Bob Chivas and John Mitchell wrote home at least once a week. Lieutenant Howard Greene, Company B, and Sergeant Henry T. Drake, Company A, were also prolific letter writers. They reported that the mood in the regiment was one of anticipation.[16]

Drills were the order of the day. The buglers woke the division at 4:30, brigade by brigade and company by company. The clear-toned bugle sounds of reveille ("The Devil is loose, the Devil is loose") echoed about the camp and jarred the men awake. Soon the camp was alive with activity. Campfires sent sparks high in the faint dawn light and cast flickering shadows as the men hurried to roll call. After lining up by company and responding as their names were called, the men dispersed for breakfast.[17]

Within days, they were complaining about the monotonous army food. They ate hardtack, beans, flapjacks, and rice for breakfast, lunch, and supper. Called teeth-pullers or sheet-iron crackers by many of the men, hardtack was a form of dried crackers. It came in barrels or boxes marked "B.C." Although this was an abbreviation for "Brigade Commissary," the troops claimed with mock seriousness that the initials represented the hardtack's date of manufacture. The crackers were often wormy. One soldier complained in a letter home, "All the fresh meat we had came in hard bread, and preferring my game cooked, I used to toast my biscuits." Flapjacks were made from fresh flour mixed with water, grease, and salt. The batter was thrown into a mess pan, and the resulting flapjacks were as heavy as lead and almost indigestible.[18]

After eating, the men busied themselves with policing their camp. Around 7:30, a roll of drums signaled the end of the breakfast period.

The adjutant brought each company the orders of the day and picked up the morning reports. Knowing Lieutenant MacArthur was still in disfavor with the colonel, the men teased him when he delivered messages to the company commanders. He bore it well. Men assigned to brigade and campguard duty marched off with the first sergeant to the accompaniment of music provided by the regimental band. The guards formed into lines for inspection before going to their respective posts.

Company marching drills began at nine o'clock and continued until eleven. After a two-hour lunch break, the companies reformed for more drills. The afternoons were hot, with the temperature climbing as high as 110 degrees. Southern Ohio and northern Kentucky had suffered through a long, hot summer, and the heat wave continued. The boys from Milwaukee had seldom experienced such weather, but even on the hottest days, when the sun's scorching rays came down in full force and perspiration rolled off them in torrents, the men were still drilled. In the afternoons, the wind blew great dust clouds over the marching men and made the air suffocating.[19]

Around four o'clock, the troops were dismissed. The regiment was lucky to be camped near the Ohio River, with its gentle, sloping banks and picturesque scenery. Many went swimming to escape the heat. Returning to camp, they brushed their uniforms, polished their brass buttons, and cleaned their weapons for an evening dress parade around six o'clock. The officers and the men took great pride in the evening parades, which were always accompanied with music from the regimental band.

Shortly after retreat, a bugle called the men to supper. Blazing campfires lit up the lowering clouds with a lurid glow. After eating, the men had a brief period of free time to write letters, play cards or dominoes, or socialize. Around 8:30, the bugles and drums signaled evening roll call, bringing the companies back into formation. On dismissal, the men returned to their tents. Shortly afterward, a bugle call announced the end of a long day. Lights were extinguished, and silence descended over the campgrounds.

The young adjutant's busiest day was Sunday, when he accompanied Larrabee on an inspection of personnel, equipment, quarters, grounds, and other facilities. The colonel was a strict disciplinarian and blamed MacArthur if anything was amiss. After Larrabee's inspection, Colonel Greusel, the brigade commander, held his own inspection. He marched up and down the regimental ranks, scrutinized the men's uniforms and arms, and looked into knapsacks that the men kept opened on the ground for his examination.[20]

The 24th Wisconsin remained in camp near Covington for two weeks. The men became sunburned, and many sported ragged beards or mustaches. They were a jolly lot, pleased with their training. Many in the regiment prayed for action, believing the Johnny Rebs did not stand a chance against the 24th. Sergeant Drake wrote, "We can clean out anything that comes our way. If we don't, then my name is not Henry Drake."[21]

The 24th was soon to get its opportunity. Sheridan's division was ordered to Louisville to reinforce the 20,000 Union troops already there. Braxton Bragg's Confederate Army of Tennessee was 20 miles to the south, and Confederate cavalry raids were occurring in the area near Louisville.

On September 18, the 10,000 men of Sheridan's division broke camp and marched 4 miles to Covington on the Ohio River, directly opposite Cincinnati. At Covington, ten steamboats waited to transport the division down the river to Louisville. As each regiment reached the Covington levee, they boarded one of the steamers. The 24th embarked on the *Pocahontas*. As the sun sank low in the west, the signal to start was given, and one after another, the ten steamers moved out into the middle of the river. The *Pocahontas* took the advanced position of the fleet.

Crowds lined the banks of the river, waving handkerchiefs and cheering as the boats steamed away. The troops returned the cheers. Larrabee ordered the regimental banners unfurled and the brass band to play. The other regimental bands took up the songs, and a number of steamers tooted a few notes as the drummers joined the bands. Late that night, fog enveloped the river, and the steamers pulled to shore to moor until daylight. With the rising sun and the dissipating fog, the steamers moved off again. Around nine o'clock, they encountered sandbars, and the men were off-loaded to lighten the boats. They marched along the shore about 2 miles; then, beyond the sandbars, they were reloaded onto the boats.

It was a lovely autumn day, and the trip seemed more like a pleasure cruise than a wartime movement of troops. When the steamers passed towns, Union sympathizers lined the riverbanks in a show of support. Regimental flags flew over the boats, and periodically, the bands struck up a rousing tune. Here and there along the broad river, a boat passed by from the opposite direction, then disappeared slowly, its black smoke curling into the sky. Around nine o'clock that evening, the fleet reached Louisville and moored at the levee. Because of the hour, the troops remained aboard overnight.[22]

The next morning, they marched through Louisville. Union supporters lined the sidewalks, waving miniature U.S. flags. The balcony of the Louisville Hotel was packed with women who threw kisses to the troops as they marched past. The division camped on the Salt River Turnpike, 3 miles south of the city.

Rumors were rampant that a major battle was imminent. Confederate cavalry under General Edmund Kirby Smith were harassing rail lines in the area, and Union sympathizers in Louisville were in an uproar, frightened that the Confederate army might capture the city. Braxton Bragg's Army of Tennessee, 40,000 strong, was entrenched 40 miles to the south, near Bardstown. Although there were 30,000 Union troops in and around Louisville under the command of Major General William "Bull" Nelson, they were raw troops, much like the 24th Wisconsin. Nelson proclaimed he could hold the city, but he later issued orders that all noncombatants should evacuate north into Ohio and Indiana.

News from the eastern front was dismal. On September 17, McClellan's Army of the Potomac clashed with Lee's Army of Northern Virginia at Antietam Creek near Sharpsburg, Maryland. McClellan won a strategic victory, forcing Lee to withdraw back into Virginia, but the cost was horrifying. At Antietam, 6,000 men lay dead or dying and another 17,000 were wounded before the day ended. The numbers were staggering.[23]

Union forces continued to gather around Louisville, and through mid-September, the 24th Wisconsin returned to drills and marches as the officers tried to train their men. The regiment still had no rifle practice because ammunition was being conserved for an impending offensive. Rumors abounded, but camp gossip centered around the murder of General "Bull" Nelson by another Union general, ironically named Jefferson C. Davis.

Davis, a thirty-four-year-old brigadier general who had served with distinction under General Grant in Corinth, Mississippi, came to Cincinnati on sick leave in July 1862. When Bragg threatened Louisville in late August, Davis offered his services to General Nelson, who accepted. After Davis arrived in Louisville in early September, he learned that Nelson had no intention of giving him a brigade but instead ordered him to train the civilian population in the use of arms. Soon, Buell's army would leave, and Louisville would have to defend itself for a while. Insulted, Davis returned to his hotel room, sulked for two days, and made no attempt to fulfill his assignment. Nelson demanded a report. When Davis showed up at 3rd Corps headquarters at the Galt House, a local hotel, he admitted he had done nothing, declared he deserved a brigade, and demanded an assignment equal to his military talents. Nelson, a former naval officer with a notorious temper, gave Davis a verbal lashing, relieved him of duty, and ordered him to report to General Horatio G. Wright in Cincinnati for reassignment. When Davis objected, proclaiming Nelson was being unfair, Nelson called in his adjutant and said, "Captain, if General Davis does not leave the city by 9 o'clock tonight, give instructions to the provost marshal to arrest him." Highly indignant, Davis withdrew and reported to Wright in Cincinnati.[24]

On September 25, General Buell arrived in Louisville with another 31,000 men and united his army, dubbed the Army of the Ohio. Buell had 61,000 men divided into three corps. The 24th Wisconsin was in Sheridan's division, which was part of the 3rd Corps commanded by Major General Nelson. The other two corps were commanded by Major General Alexander McD. McCook and Major General Thomas L. Crittenden, younger brother of Confederate General George B. Crittenden.[25]

With Buell's army gathered at Louisville, General Wright in Cincinnati suggested that Davis report to Buell for reassignment. Davis arrived at the Galt House in Louisville on the morning of September 29. There, relaxing after breakfast, Nelson was standing outside the hotel office, leaning against the counter. Having been informed that Davis was reporting to Buell, Nelson said nothing but gave him a look of contempt. Davis, still incensed over Nelson's earlier tongue-lashing, refused to ignore the look and marched over to Nelson. He challenged him to a duel, demanding satisfaction. Nelson snorted contemptuously and said, "Go away little puppy. I don't want anything to do with you." Fidgeting with a blank registration card he had absentmindedly picked up off the desk, Davis squeezed the card into a small ball and flipped it into Nelson's face. Nelson stared at Davis, stepped forward, and slapped him, then turned his back in disdain and headed for his office.

Unarmed, Davis glanced around and saw an officer with a sidearm. Davis walked over to him and asked for his pistol. The officer handed him the gun without comment. Nelson meanwhile walked back through the lobby, heading for Buell's apartment on the second floor of the hotel. Davis charged toward him, met him at the foot of the stairs, and fired his pistol from less than three feet. The bullet struck Nelson in the chest. He stared down in disbelief then stumbled in a daze up a flight of stairs before collapsing outside Buell's door.

Crittenden, commander of the 2nd Corps, was at breakfast when he heard the shot. He hurried into the lobby to see Davis with the gun and Nelson dragging himself up the stairs. Crittenden found Nelson collapsed outside Buell's door. He bent over and clutched Nelson's hand. "Nelson, are you seriously hurt?" Looking very white, the general said, "Tom, I think that bastard just murdered me." He died in less than an hour.[26]

Davis was arrested but never tried for murder because he had influential friends. In a few months, he reappeared in command of a division at the battle of Murfreesboro in Tennessee.

Brigadier General Charles C. Gilbert replaced Nelson as temporary commander of the 3rd Corps. Two days later, on October 1, Buell's army left Louisville to search for the elusive Confederate army, which had been harassing Union supply lines between Louisville and Cincinnati. Leaving their tents behind, the troops carried knapsacks that contained a change of clothing, an army blanket, toilet articles, and other personal items. Each man carried three days of rations in a leather haversack that hung from a strap across the left shoulder and looked like an old-fashioned school satchel. He also carried a canvas-covered metal canteen, a small cartridge box loaded with forty rounds, a leather box with forty explosive caps used to fire his weapon, a bayonet, and a sewing kit. When mess equipment was added, an infantryman's load weighed about forty pounds.[27]

As a staff officer, Adjutant MacArthur rode horseback while all line company officers marched with the men. MacArthur was constantly on the move, riding up and down the regiment's line to deliver orders and returning with reports from the company commanders. Dust clouds rose high in the air, indicating for miles the direction taken by the lead troops. Artillery carriages rattled past the men, and baggage trains spread out behind them. Uniforms turned the color of dried earth, and the men's faces grimed over with dirt that discolored their eyelashes and eyebrows. When the 24th Wisconsin set up camp that night, the men wanted to bathe, but water was too scarce. After cooking and eating their evening meals, they fell exhausted into their blankets and slept soundly. It turned bitterly cold during the night, and toward morning, the first frost fell. With no shelter other than their blankets and rubber ponchos, the men woke shivering.

When the bugles sounded reveille at four in the morning, the camp was still encased in darkness. Around six o'clock, the men formed in line for the day's march. They traveled twenty miles the second day. By the time they had set up camp and eaten their evening meals, the men were so exhausted they immediately rolled up in their blankets and fell asleep, too tired even for conversation. Lieutenant Greene wrote home,

> We get up anywhere from 4 to 5 A.M., march until sundown, and sometimes until late at night, and by the time we have got into camp and cooked our supper we are always ready to go to sleep. I have at times been so tired when I got into camp that after getting my men into line I would drop right where I was, roll my blanket around me, and go to sleep, too tired to wait for supper. It is a rough life, and none but an iron constitution can stand it.[28]

During the night, rifle fire woke the regiment when Union pickets fired on a Confederate cavalry patrol. MacArthur was kept busy running from company to company to investigate. Few of the men could sleep, and rumors were rampant that a major battle was on the horizon. At 6:00 A.M., they were back on the road, moving toward Perryville, Kentucky, 80 miles southeast of Louisville.[29]

As the Army of the Ohio approached Perryville, McCook's 1st Corps was on the left flank, Crittenden's 2nd Corps was on the right flank, and Gilbert's 3rd Corps occupied the center. In Gilbert's 3rd Corps, Brigadier General Robert B. Mitchell's division had the lead, followed by Brigadier General Albin Schoepf's division. Sheridan's division, including the 24th Wisconsin, was in the rear.[30]

Around two o'clock in the afternoon of October 7, Mitchell's division occupied the high ground on an almost dry tributary of the Chaplin River. Bragg's Confederate Army of Tennessee was entrenched on the south bank of the river. The need for drinking water had brought both armies to Perryville. After a few shots were exchanged, musket fire erupted along the line. The 24th Wisconsin arrived late in the evening, and around the campfires that night, many speculated that a major battle would occur the next day. The men of the 24th were confident and felt that, at last, they were in the war.

Around 3:30 in the morning, Confederate artillery opened fire.

The 24th Wisconsin formed into line as Union artillery responded. The cannon fire blasted for a few minutes and then died out.

Few of the men went back to sleep. While preparing breakfast, they heard musket fire south toward the Chaplin River and Perryville. The Union army was drawn up in a semicircular line with a front of about 5 miles lying east to west. The main action was on the east end, where McCook's corps fought off a number of Confederate attacks. All morning, cannon boomed as the Union and Confederate artillery exchanged fire. Sheridan's division occupied the right center of the line, and he kept the raw 24th Wisconsin as his division's reserve 3 miles behind the line.

The men played cards, slept, wrote letters, or socialized to hide their apprehensions. The battle sounds made most of them nervous as they realized men were actually dying nearby. Some reported feeling a dull pain in their chests that made breathing difficult.[31]

MacArthur was anxious and a little scared, but he was probably as concerned with being a coward as with dying or being maimed. In battle, no one knew whether honor or fear would triumph. He longed for action, but the regiment remained in place through the morning hours.

Around 1:00 P.M., Larrabee received orders to move his regiment forward to a small hollow a quarter of a mile from the front lines. After reaching the position, they halted to await new orders.

A rebel cannon shell exploded nearby. No one was hurt, but the tension increased. The regiment was close enough to the front for unspent musket balls to whiz overhead. The distant rifle fire sounded like the noise boys made when rattling a stick along a picket fence. As the bullets flew past, the men ducked, then laughed nervously, knowing full well that one heard the whistle only after the ball had passed. A Union artillery unit immediately in front opened fire, and a Confederate battery responded. Exploding shells fell all around the 24th.[32]

Larrabee became impatient and ordered Adjutant MacArthur to reconnoiter. MacArthur galloped to the top of a small hill where he could see the battle. Bullets were flying and cannons were blasting as, fully exposed to fire, he sat on his horse and calmly observed the situation. From below, many of the men in the regiment gawked in amazement at Little Mac's courage.

It was a scene from one of the novels by Sir Walter Scott that had captivated young Arthur: the brave young warrior defying danger to do his duty, watching the enemy mobilizing in the distant mist. Death does not frighten him, for the hero always returns if not unscathed then at least with his honor and courage a legend among the other warriors. Gail Sheehy suggests that young warriors, like Arthur, are "insulated by some soft-walled childhood sack" that they think provides for their own indestructibility.[33]

MacArthur's reckless exposure to enemy fire epitomized bravery to many Civil War officers, who often inspired their troops to display courage by being the most courageous themselves. Stories of officers standing calmly atop barricades as enemy artillery fire exploded nearby, of cavalry officers recklessly charging a blazing infantry line, of the coolness of Stonewall Jackson or Little Phil Sheridan when bullets buzzed about their ears were told around campfires at night and eulogized in Northern and Southern accounts of the war. That night, Little Mac's courage would be a topic of conversation, and most of the men agreed the young adjutant had grit. But his bravery would only be a small part of the talk that night for the men of the 24th Wisconsin were about to have their first taste of battle and their first taste of triumph in war.[34]

From the hilltop, MacArthur had seen a Union battery on a ridge protected by a Union regiment that was firing at Confederate forces across a large cornfield littered with dead bodies. The Confederates appeared to be preparing for another attack.

Wheeling his horse about, MacArthur dashed back to the regiment huddled low in the hollow. A few of the men cheered him as he rode to report to Larrabee.[35]

MacArthur recommended that the regiment move up to support the battery and the other Union regiment before the Confederates attacked. As Larrabee contemplated the advice, a division staff officer galloped up.

"Colonel," he shouted, "the general wants you to march your regiment to the left of that battery and hold it at all hazards. The rebels are about to charge it."

Larrabee was hard of hearing. He placed his hand to his ear and said, "What's that, sir?"

The order was repeated.

Larrabee's chest swelled, and he shouted out in answer, "I will, by God, sir."

The regiment formed up and quickly marched to a position at the crest of a ridge overlooking the cornfield next to the Union battery just as the Confederates attacked.[36]

"Open fire!" Larrabee shouted, and the regiment responded like seasoned troops. The barrage caught the Confederates halfway across the field, and their attack sputtered. The Confederate troops withdrew to their original position.

The 24th moved down the ridge and formed a line on a road immediately in front of the Union battery. They were going to attack across the cornfield.

"By the left flank," Larrabee shouted. MacArthur galloped down the line, conveying the order.

The regiment charged across the cornfield.

The Confederates soon abandoned their position and ran south toward the Chaplin River. The 24th took eight prisoners before receiving orders to fall back to their position next to the Union battery.[37]

The regiment's part in the battle lasted less than ten minutes, and they lost only one man. Officers and men grinned broadly, relieved at surviving their first firefight. They had known they could whip the Johnny Rebs.

Other parts of Buell's army, including some of the other regiments of Sheridan's division, were not as lucky. Union losses were 845 killed, 2,851 wounded, and 515 captured or missing, a total of 4,211 casualties. Sheridan's division alone reported 44 dead and 293 wounded. Confederate losses were almost the same, but for Bragg, the losses were more devastating because his army was much smaller. At the start of the battle, it numbered only 16,000 to Buell's army of 61,000.[38]

That night, the men of the 24th Wisconsin relived their bravery around glowing campfires. The talk of war was easier now. The men felt they could whip any Confederate force, and they were looking forward to the next day's fight. Rain fell during the night, and with no tents, the men were cold.[39]

In the chilly, early morning hours, they were rousted from their blankets and called to arms. For two hours, they stood in line shivering and waiting to march into battle.

The sun rose, but nothing happened. During the night, the Confederate army had withdrawn.

Despite his force's overwhelming numerical superiority, Buell decided to regroup his army before pursuing. The 24th Wisconsin broke ranks to reestablish camp, and during the next two days, the men of the 24th wandered the battlefield and saw the horrors of war for the first time. In the heat of battle, war had seemed heroic; now, reality sank in as they walked through the cornfields. "The sights and smells that assailed us were simply indescribable," one soldier wrote home. "Corpses swollen to twice their original size, some of them actually burst asunder with the pressure of foul gases. ... The odors were nauseating and so deadly that in a short time we all sickened and were lying with our mouths close to the ground, most of us vomiting profusely." Another soldier remembered that the corpses were "swollen to twice their natural size, black as Negroes in most cases. [Here lay] one without a head, there one without legs, yonder a head and legs without a trunk ... with fragments of shell sticking in oozing brain, with bullet holes all over the puffed limbs."

Lieutenant Mitchell wrote home that Confederate dead lay over the fields in numbers too large to be counted. They had been killed by cannon balls, shells, grapeshots, and rifle balls. Mitchell saw one dead Confederate soldier who "had half a thigh shot away and his bowels completely torn out by a shell; another had his head taken from his shoulders as clean as if done by a knife." Lieutenant Greene also wrote home of the horrid sights he saw in the field, where killed and wounded men lay in all sorts of shapes and positions. Union surgeons probed the wounds of some, extracted balls from others, and amputated the legs and arms of still others. Greene saw one rebel in a curious position: "He had evidently taken off his Butternut Pants, thrown them to one side, and taken a pair from a Union soldier. He was just in the act of putting them on, and had got them drawn on his right leg, when a ball struck him and laid him over, still in the position of drawing on his pants."[40]

On October 11, Buell learned that Bragg's army was retreating southward toward strongly held Confederate territory. Buell realized that he had made a mistake by delaying for two days and frantically ordered his army to pursue.

Three weeks of hell began for the 24th Wisconsin and Buell's entire army. At four o'clock in the morning of October 11, the 24th was on the road; they marched 24 miles that day before camping well after sunset. Larrabee, who had not been feeling well, turned over command to Major Elisha "Lish" Hibbard and went to Louisville for medical treatment. Although Larrabee would later return to the regiment, he would be on sick leave so often that he never again effectively commanded his troops.[41]

The trials of the 24th Wisconsin had just begun. The regiment was on the move for the next two days, covering 12 to 18 miles each day. The country they marched through was ravaged by war—the fields destroyed for miles, the houses plundered by the retreating Confederate troops. The regiment marched south through central Kentucky—through Mount Washington, Bardstown, Shepardsville, Springfield, and Harrodsburg. In most of the towns they passed through in southern Kentucky, civilians stared at them sullenly. Kentucky was a divided state, with three slave states and three free states touching its borders. The people were evenly split in their loyalties, and Kentucky men fought on both sides. Ironically, the state was also the birthplace of both Abraham Lincoln and Jefferson F. Davis.

Nearly every day, artillery boomed in their front as the forward elements briefly caught up with the retreating Confederates. The sounds became so commonplace that the men no longer even took notice. By the end of the third day, the troops were exhausted, and many had raw, blistered feet. That night it rained. At first, the rain was a relief from the earlier heat, but when the march began the next day, it was a nuisance, for large puddles formed in the muddy roads. The line became ragged as the men scrambled around the bogs and then double-timed to catch up with the forward regiments.[42]

On October 15, Buell finally gave up the pursuit and halted his army for a much needed rest. The 24th encamped just south of Harrodsburg at a place called Crab Orchard. Bragg's army was long gone.

Five days later, when Buell received a report of a major Confederate cavalry raid along the Nashville-Louisville-Cincinnati railroad line, he thought that a large force had gotten to his rear. He turned his army around and made a mad dash to save the Union base at Nashville, over 160 miles away.

A few days' rest had not relieved the footsore and weary men of Buell's army. But the general refused to listen to complaints and marched his army hard for ten straight days. He even issued strict orders to force stragglers forward at the point of a bayonet. The 24th Wisconsin's rearguard refused to comply with the order, but others in Buell's army did. Several soldiers died from bayonet wounds.

The men grumbled and questioned Buell's ability to command. Lieutenant Greene wrote his family that he was disgusted.

> We make forced marches until we catch Bragg, fight him, whip him, and then instead of following up our victory, we are ordered to lay on our "ars" for two or three days. After that we make forced marches ... then rest for two days, and then retrace our steps as through the Devil himself was after us. Anyone to see us ... would have thought we were making a forced retreat and that Bragg was right on our heels. ... Give us more fighting and less marching, say we all, and we will so much the sooner end the war.[43]

Sergeant Drake wrote to his brother, advising him, "Don't volunteer—wait till you're drafted."[44]

After ten days of hard marching, the 24th Wisconsin reached Nashville without sighting a single Confederate soldier. The mad dash had taken its toll—the regiment had shrunk down to less than 600 men.[45]

Buell's failure at Perryville angered Lincoln. His army had been four times larger than Bragg's, yet Buell had failed to achieve a dramatic victory. Lincoln decided to replace Buell and on October 30, named Major General William S. Rosecrans as the new commander of the Army of the Ohio. A new era was about to begin for the 24th Wisconsin.[46]

3

The Battle of Murfreesboro

THE 24TH WISCONSIN settled into camp south of Nashville in early November 1862. The regiment had shrunk to less than 500 men, about 40 to 50 for each company. Many were home on sick leave, and others had returned home to settle family problems. The regiment's supply train arrived from Louisville; after sleeping in the open for a month, the regiment finally had its tents again.

Colonel Larrabee spent most of his time in Nashville rather than with the regiment. Adjutant MacArthur enjoyed the colonel's absence because he had a better relationship with his replacement, Major Hibbard. Most of the officers in the regiment now accepted MacArthur, and many relied on him for his knowledge of army regulations.

Camp routine, complete with drills and parades, returned. The men grumbled that being in the army meant march and countermarch, drill after drill, little fun, and almost no fighting. The monotony of the camp routine was broken up by picket duty on alternate weeks, which involved just enough danger and excitement to make the men feel like soldiers. On picket duty, they crouched close to the Confederate lines, observed the movements of the enemy, and occasionally fired their muskets at Confederate cavalry patrols.

The 24th greeted Major General William S. Rosecrans's arrival at Nashville in early November 1862 with enthusiasm. They had disliked Buell, and "Old Rosey," as the men called him, delighted them because he was a fighter, not a marcher. A hero in battles on the eastern and western fronts, Rosey was articulate and colorful. At forty-three, he was in his prime, a solid six feet of nervous energy. A West Point graduate, he was a heavy drinker, with a drinker's red nose and a boisterous personality. He was a curser and a shouter, but he was also a deeply religious man. A devout Roman Catholic, he refused to fight or march on Sundays, and he wore a crucifix on his watch chain. Drinking, chewing on a cigar, and expounding on his favorite topics of religion and war, he often kept his staff up half the night. He also enjoyed comparing the battles of the Civil War with great battles in history. An energetic, restless man, he needed little sleep and tended to bounce around, agitated. He shouted out commands so rapidly his staff often had to ask him to repeat his orders.[1]

Rosecrans maintained his headquarters in Nashville, with his army in a defensive line south of the city. Nashville was the Union's largest supply base in the West, and soldiers outnumbered civilians there by as much as two to one. Railroad lines radiated out from Nashville north to Louisville, south to Decatur, Alabama, southeast to Chattanooga, and west to Johnsonville. To feed and equip tens of thousands of men and thousands of horses required millions of tons of supplies. Away from the railroads, Rosecrans could not have kept his army in food, arms, and ammunition.

Bragg's army was at Murfreesboro, Tennessee, about 30 miles south of Nashville. A railroad brought supplies for the Confederate forces from Atlanta via Chattanooga. With an established supply line, Bragg's troops were reinforced, and the strength of the Confederate army rose from a mere 15,000 men to over 51,000. Bragg established a defensive line 2 miles north of Murfreesboro at Stones River.[2]

Confederate cavalry patrols ranged north, harassing Union positions and raiding the countryside. With a cavalry brigade of 2,100 troopers, Brigadier General Nathan B. Forrest launched raids into western Tennessee, while Colonel John H. Morgan and his 3,100-man cavalry division raided north and threatened Rosecrans's supply line from Louisville. Most of the civilian population south of Nashville was hostile to the Union forces, but as with Kentuckians, Tennesseans fought on both sides. North and east Tennessee was laced with Union sympathizers; most southern Tennesseans supported the Confederacy. Raiding parties from both sides depleted the normally rich Tennessee Valley of food and livestock, and farmhouses between Stones River and Nashville were burned—only chimneys marked the spots where they had once stood.

Throughout November and most of December, Rosecrans reorganized and resupplied his army of 56,671 officers and enlisted men—51,822 infantry and artillery and 4,849 cavalry. Rosecrans shuffled divisions and commands and renamed his force the Army of the Cumberland. He retained two of the three corps commanders, but in the reorganization, General Gilbert was relieved. Major General George Henry Thomas was placed in command of the 2nd Corps and General Crittenden moved from the 2nd Corps to command of the 3rd Corps. General McCook retained command of the 1st Corps. Every corps was composed of three divisions, each of which was divided into three brigades with four regiments. Thus, there were a total of thirty-six regiments per corps.

The 24th Wisconsin remained part of the 1st Brigade of Sheridan's division, which became the 3rd Division in McCook's 1st Corps. The brigade included the 36th Illinois, the 88th Illinois, and the 21st Michigan, plus the 4th Indiana Battery commanded by Captain Asahel K. Bush. The brigade received a new commander, Brigadier General Joshua W. Sill. Colonel Nicholas Greusel, who had commanded the brigade at Perryville, returned to regimental command of the 36th Illinois and ranked as the brigade's second in command. The 24th Wisconsin had liked Greusel, but Sill was an equally respected commander. He had graduated from West Point in 1853, ranking third in a class of fifty-three that included such fa-

Major General William S. Rosecrans, commander of the Army of the Cumberland, November 1862. (National Archives, 111-B-2505)

Major General George Henry Thomas, commander of the 2nd Corps,
Army of the Cumberland, November 1862. (National Archives,
111-B-5583)

mous generals as Sheridan, James B. McPherson, John M. Schofield, and John B. Hood. Sill was a fearless and able soldier. The 24th was proud to be part of his brigade, just as they were proud to be part of Sheridan's division.

Lieutenant John Mitchell left the 24th Wisconsin to join Sill's staff; consequently, Arthur had a contact at brigade headquarters. John was two years older than Arthur, and though the two had not been close boyhood companions, they were friends who shared a common Scottish heritage. The MacArthur and Mitchell families had socialized with each other, and Judge MacArthur and Alexander Mitchell, John's father, were close personal friends.

Rosecrans delayed launching an offensive against Bragg until after Christmas. On December 26, 1862, the Army of the Cumberland was mobilized. Three corps moved simultaneously down different turnpikes, heading south toward Murfreesboro. With 56,000 men, thousands of horses and mules, and hundreds of wagons and artillery caissons, Rosecrans's army packed the roads.

Larrabee rejoined the regiment just as the 24th broke camp, leaving their tents behind and carrying their rations and ammunition. The 24th marched south along the Nolinsville Turnpike and formed the west end of the line. Thomas's 2nd Corps was in the center and moved along the Wilkinson Turnpike. Crittenden's 3rd Corps comprised the east wing of the army and followed the railroad line and the Nashville Turnpike.

The 24th Wisconsin was on the march less than an hour when a cold, drenching rain began, which soaked through the men's clothes down to the skin. The unsurfaced roads were never meant for the heavy traffic of a moving army, and when it began to rain, the turnpikes became quagmires. Wagons bogged down and blocked the roads. The 24th took to the muddy corn- and cottonfields that stretched along the sides of the turnpikes. MacArthur and the other staff officers dismounted, and both the officers and men slogged through mud up to their ankles. Every step was an effort, and the pace was laborious and slow. They marched less than 5 miles that first day before stopping to camp around 5:00 P.M.

Under a heavy, overcast sky, MacArthur checked with each company commander before eating a half-warmed supper of hardtack and beans. He rolled up in his blanket just as the rain started again. During the night, his uniform and blanket became completely soaked, leaving him cold and miserable.

Around four o'clock, he woke to sporadic musket fire as Union picket lines engaged Confederate skirmishers. Although the rain had stopped, the sky was overcast. Patches of snow covered the ground, and ice had formed on the camp's water. The sounds of the brigade and Sheridan's division were all around: Drums rolled and bugles blared as campfires were started, pickets were relieved, and horses were taken to water.[3]

After one day and night in the field, Larrabee returned to Nashville, for he had the flu. The inclement weather worsened his condition, and he could barely talk because of an ulcerated throat. Another commander might have remained with his regiment, but Larrabee turned the 24th over to Major Hibbard. MacArthur breathed a sigh of relief—Larrabee had never accepted him and still referred to him as a baby.

Larrabee's departure left the regiment severely understaffed at a critical time. Hibbard promoted Captain Carl von Baumbach, commander of Company C, to the rank of acting major, but Baumbach had no experience as a staff officer and was not even sure of his duties. During a battle, staff officers communicated orders to the ten company commanders, usually captains, who were assisted in comparable fashion by a staff of lieutenants conveying orders to the platoons. The officers grumbled at this late change in command. The only element of continuity was the adolescent adjutant, who was still not shaving on a daily basis. In the officers' view, MacArthur was a good kid but still only seventeen years old.[4]

Around ten o'clock, the regiment received orders to march. As they moved out, it started to rain again. Bragg's remaining cavalry, under the command of twenty-six-year-old Brigadier General Joseph Wheeler, raided along the road, attacking supply wagons and throwing the march into havoc as troops stopped to seek cover. Each order to halt echoed back down the line, and there were long delays. The regiment was forced off the turnpike to go around the wagons. As on the previous day, they marched through muddy corn- and cottonfields, only occasionally traveling along the Nolinsville Pike when it was clear of wagons. After traveling only 10 miles, they camped in a wooded area near a cotton plantation. It rained most of the night.[5]

The next morning, the sun shone for the first time in three days, but it was Sunday, and Rosecrans did not march on Sundays. Instead, the 24th explored the plantation, where they discovered cellars packed with food. Short of rations, the men needed no invitation to plunder, and that night, the whole regiment had a good meal.[6]

The regiment was on the march again the next day, moving south toward Murfreesboro. They made good time as the road continued to dry. Along the route, large wooded areas separated the corn- and cottonfields. Although beautiful, the rough terrain was not suited for cavalry or artillery. Composed mostly of Tennessee red cedar, the woods grew in dense brakes and glades where the cedar limbs hung down and created impassable barriers that had to be skirted. The trees also often covered limestone ledges broken up by deep crevices.

That night, the regiment camped in a cornfield less than 5 miles from the Confederate line near Stones River. During the night, the rain began again, and no one got much sleep. The officers met to discuss the coming battle as picket fire echoed periodically in the distance. Hibbard was nervous because he had never led a regiment in battle.

When the buglers of Sheridan's division sounded reveille around 4:00 A.M., the 24th Wisconsin rose in the chilly, wet morning to the sounds of horses stamping, canteens and skillets rattling, and men talking quietly while starting morning fires. Up and down the line, a musket occasionally fired as the pickets of the two armies exchanged shots. By five o'clock, the 24th was standing at arms and awaiting orders. Hibbard and MacArthur, both mounted, moved among the troops shouting encouragement.[7]

At eight o'clock, the regiment received orders to advance down the Wilkinson Pike toward the Confederate line. The rain continued, and it drizzled off and on all day. Along the turnpike, the terrain became more wooded, with fewer and fewer corn- and cottonfields (see Map 3.1).

A quarter of a mile from the Confederate line, the regiment left the turnpike and took up defensive positions in the woods with the rest of Sheridan's division. Two divisions, one commanded by General Richard W. Johnson and the other led by General Jefferson C. Davis of "Bull" Nelson fame, occupied the right flank. To the left, east of Sheridan's division, Thomas's corps guarded the center of the line,

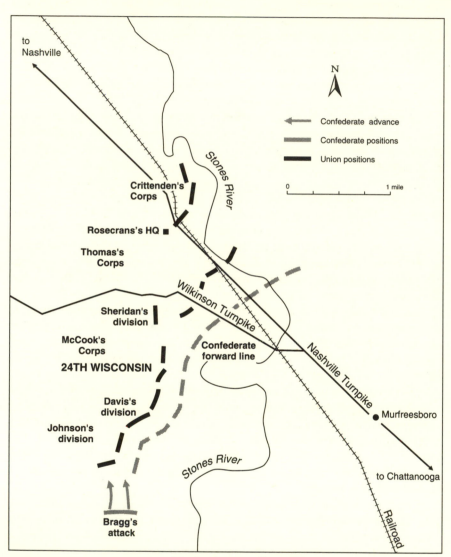

MAP 3.1 Murfreesboro, or Stones River

and Crittenden's corps took up the extreme left near the railroad along the north bank of Stones River.[8]

With his army in position, Rosecrans ordered an advance at one o'clock. The Confederate forward line was about 2 miles north of Murfreesboro and stretched 2 miles west from the railroad to a point just beyond the Wilkinson Pike. In Sheridan's sector near the pike, Sill's brigade moved forward about 1,500 yards through some woods and into a cornfield.

A Confederate artillery unit opened fire.

Cannon balls crashed around the 24th Wisconsin, which was in an exposed position beyond the tree line. The men immediately dropped to the ground. Staff officers dismounted and sent their horses to the rear just as Captain Asahel Bush's Union artillery battery arrived in the woods behind them. The Union artillery opened fire on the Confederate battery.

In an accident of war, the 24th suffered its first Murfreesboro casualty. When a Union cannon ball splintered above, pieces of shrapnel dropped down into the 24th's ranks. A shell fragment struck First Lieutenant George Bleysen, commander of Company F, in the knee. He died in the hospital.

When the Confederate battery ceased firing and withdrew, the 24th Wisconsin moved forward through the cornfield to the next set of woods, where they again halted and awaited orders.[9]

Around three o'clock, Bush moved his guns through the cornfield and took a new position next to the 24th Wisconsin. The 36th Illinois and five companies of the 24th Wisconsin under the command of Captain Baumbach took up supporting positions around Bush's guns, while the rest of the regiment and Sill's brigade advanced into a cottonfield beyond the woods.

A camouflaged Confederate battery fired on the 24th from less than 500 yards. Shells exploded all around the 24th Wisconsin. Several men were wounded, and two died gruesome deaths. A man in Company K had his head sliced off by a shell fragment; another man in Company D was struck in the stomach, his guts spilling out as he died.

Stunned, the 24th retreated out of the cottonfield back into the woods as Bush's battery opened fire on the Confederate battery. This was not like Perryville: MacArthur and his comrades had not even seen the enemy as death arbitrarily struck down their friends.

In the rain and chill of the winter afternoon, a fierce artillery duel occurred. When dusk approached, the Confederate artillery withdrew, and silence settled over the battlefield.

Bush's battery also withdrew as the 24th settled in for the night. Hibbard sent Company G, under Lieutenant William Kennedy, to establish a forward picket line. In the early evening, Kennedy reported that there was considerable activity on their front, a warning he repeated every couple of hours. Hibbard sent MacArthur to report to General Sill, who was receiving similar reports from his other regimental commanders. While at brigade headquarters, MacArthur talked with Johnny Mitchell, and they agreed that a Confederate attack appeared imminent.

Sill reported the enemy movement on his front to Sheridan, who immediately inspected his division line. The other two brigade commanders, Colonel Frederick Schaefer and Colonel George W. Roberts, also noted unusual Confederate activity all along the right wing of the Union army. Sheridan ordered his division to remain alert.

The men of the 24th had not eaten since breakfast, and they went without supper that evening as they remained in formation. Each company detailed a few men to prepare coffee, but no food was cooked. In the chilly early evening, the men of the 24th Wisconsin stared across the cottonfield toward the next span of woods about 1,000 yards away. On their right flank, campfires lit up the night sky as the men of Johnson's and Davis's divisions cooked their evening meals.[10]

On the Union left and center, in the stillness of the winter night, the military bands began to play. A Union band played "Yankee Doodle" and was answered by a Confederate band that played "Dixie"; "The Bonnie Blue Flag" brought out a resounding version of "Hail Columbia." When a federal band struck up the familiar "Home Sweet Home," almost immediately a Confederate band caught up the strain, then one after another the bands of both armies played "Home Sweet Home" in unison. The music was a sad reminder of the nature of this war where brother was fighting brother.[11]

Confederate movement in front of Sheridan's division continued. Three times during the night, Sill sent warning messages, and he eventually rode to division headquarters. Sheridan was awake, and he, too, was concerned. It seemed possible that the Confederate army was massing on the Union right for an attack.

After a conference with his brigade commanders, Sheridan rode to corps headquarters to report his concerns to General McCook. After consulting with his other division commanders, Davis and Johnson, McCook was not impressed with Sheridan's report of unusual Confederate activity on the right flank. After all, the Union army was on the offensive, not the Confederate forces who were now in defensive positions. The idea that Bragg would attack the Union right seemed absurd to McCook. Sheridan disagreed and insisted that McCook ride with him to Rosecrans's headquarters near the railroad on the Union left flank.

After testing the Confederate defensive positions all day, Rosecrans was busy working on his attack plans for the morning. He hoped to fake an attack on the right while Crittenden's corps crossed Stones River on the railroad bridge and hit Bragg's army on the Union left. Rosecrans expected Bragg to evacuate Murfreesboro when his supply line was threatened.

Sheridan's report of Confederate activity on the right flank did not impress Rosecrans any more than it had McCook. He rejected Sheridan's suggestion that McCook's entire corps remain on alert for an early morning attack: Rosecrans wanted his troops to be fresh. Once Bragg's army was routed from its positions,

Rosecrans intended to use Thomas's and McCook's corps to pursue Bragg's retreating army.

When Sheridan returned to his division, he decided to take no chances. He ordered his regiments to remain at arms. No campfires were to be lit, and the division was to be prepared for a possible attack at dawn.

The men of the 24th Wisconsin lay on the ground with their guns at their sides. The night was intensely cold, not the cold of a Wisconsin winter but a damp, heavy cold that pervaded the atmosphere and drilled right into the marrow of the bone. Adding to the misery of the men, an icy wind swept down from the north and brought occasional rain. The men stamped about to keep warm. Sergeant Thomas J. Ford of Company H remembered that he was so cold he could not move his fingers. When he tried to grip his rifle, it kept dropping from his benumbed hands.[12]

In the gray, frosty light, the regiment formed in line. A shot rang out and startled everyone. The cold had caused an accident that seemed amusing in the tense situation—Private Charles Ellmaker of Company B had dropped his rifle. When it discharged, its ball had passed through his hand, between the thumb and the forefinger, and continued upward to graze his head. Miraculously, he was not badly hurt, and he, too, was soon laughing about the incident.[13]

As dawn broke, the men of the 24th saw on their right flank McCook's two other divisions, commanded by General Davis and General Johnson, rising from their blankets and preparing campfires. Whispering to each other, the men of the 24th pointed to the blazing campfires: Was a Confederate attack not expected?

The men did not know that only Sheridan's division—twelve regiments in three brigades, numbering about 5,000 men—had remained on alert through the night. The rest of McCook's corps, two divisions of some 12,000 men, were not prepared for an attack despite Sheridan's warnings.

Around six o'clock, bugles sounded from Johnson's area, signaling the artillery to take their horses and mules to water at a small stream 100 yards behind the forward line. Sergeant Drake of Company A shook his head in disgust. Artillery batteries without horses would be practically useless if an attack occurred.[14]

Around 6:10 A.M., from the far right, the 24th heard popping noises. Softly at first, then louder came the sounds of rifle fire, cannons thundering, and Rebel yells. A major Confederate attack had begun.

Bragg struck the Union right flank with two divisions composed of 12,000 men. His plan was to roll up the Union line, smashing one Union division after another. If Bragg could shove the Union troops back and capture the railroad line, Rosecrans would be forced to retreat. The two Confederate divisions poured out of the woods and struck Johnson's division, located a half mile to the 24th Wisconsin's right.

Johnson's division was totally unprepared for the attack. Most of his men were still in their blankets or just beginning to move around their cooking fires. They scrambled to get their weapons, but most were too late as the Confederate tidal wave hit their lines. Almost half of the division's 6,000 men were killed, wounded, or captured in the first few minutes of the battle. The rest broke and ran, with 12,000 charging Confederates chasing them.

Johnson's men ran east straight into Davis's division, stationed to the immediate right of the 24th Wisconsin. Given a few minutes' warning, Davis was better prepared but still could not withstand the onslaught. Within minutes, the Union troops broke and ran east toward Sheridan's division, straight at the 24th. Routing one Union division at a time, the Confederates were indeed rolling up the line.[15]

Sheridan galloped down the line and ordered General Sill to prepare his brigade for an attack. Major Hibbard sent MacArthur to bring in the 24th's pickets. As MacArthur and the pickets rejoined the regiment, the remnants of Johnson's and Davis's divisions—a shouting, cursing, crying, hysterical mob—tumbled through the 24th's line. Most of the fleeing mob of soldiers had dropped their weapons in their desperate scramble to escape the attacking Confederates. Limping along behind the first charge came the wounded, their blood-stained uniforms a testament to their bravery or misfortune. Occasionally, a riderless horse crashed into the line and galloped after the retreating horde.[16]

The 24th Wisconsin had never seen Union soldiers in frantic retreat, and the spectacle frightened them all. Some of their officers and men broke and ran, joining the fleeing mob.[17]

Over the cacophony of the retreating masses, faintly at first, and gradually increasing in volume, the men of the 24th heard the din of thousands of weapons at work. Approaching nearer and nearer, it sounded as if some mighty power was breaking every tree in the forest.

The attacking Confederate divisions came within 1,000 yards of the 24th Wisconsin. Only Sheridan's division, less than 5,000 men, stood between the Confederate army and victory.

Across the cottonfield from the 24th Wisconsin, a Confederate brigade emerged from a clump of black cedars. Silence descended over the battlefield as the brigade formed into two lines for an attack.

"Stand fast, 24th Wisconsin," Hibbard yelled. MacArthur galloped up and down the line shouting out the order to the company commanders. The trees around him were alive with the buzz and *zap-zap* sound of musket balls. Captain Baumbach, the other staff officer, had disappeared—he had forgotten his duties and taken cover behind a tree. Throughout the battle, Hibbard relied on MacArthur to convey his orders to the ten company commanders.

A Confederate artillery battery opened fire. Around the 24th Wisconsin, the trees exploded, and the debris buried a few of the men.

With a war whoop, the Confederate brigade charged. A volley of musket fire ripped into the ranks of the 24th Wisconsin, and there were screams as dozens of the men were hit. George Cole, Lieutenant Greene's orderly, was killed instantly when struck in the right eye by a musket ball.

The 24th returned the fire, reloaded as quickly as possible, and fired again. Although they shot from prone positions, they had built no defensive barricades, nor had they stacked logs or provided themselves with any protection from the onslaught. Officers were trained not to entrench their troops, and even such illustrious generals as Sherman and Grant initially believed that "digging-in" was bad psychologically. At Shiloh, neither had entrenched their men because they believed it would rob them of their aggressive spirit. "Fight man-fashion" was the prevailing slogan. "I cannot tell how often I heard that agreeable aphorism set forth in war days," Charles Frances Adams said later. "The old fogy, West Point, regular army theory [was] that fieldworks made the men cowardly." The ideal unit remained compact and cohesive during a battle as the men moved and fired with machine-like efficiency. But the rifled-musket, with a longer range than the old smoothbore musket of the Napoleonic era, made such tactics an anachronism, as the 24th Wisconsin was now learning.[18]

Shouting out orders, the officers could barely be heard. The noise was deafening: the shrieking of artillery shells followed by explosions, the buzzing of bullets slicing through the air, and the chugging noise when the bullets hit human forms, causing cries of pain. The fearful groans of the wounded men intermingled with the agonizing screams of injured horses. When a man fell, his friends often dropped their guns, forgetting the battle, and stared at him in horror and curiosity. There were no medics, no stretchers, no hospital attendants, and no first-aid kits.[19]

The Confederates rolled forward in deep columns like an irresistible wave. Union artillery and musket fire cut gaps in the charging line but did not deter the attack. "Never before did I see such incessant and determined fighting, and never was I among such a perfect storm of bullets and shells," Lieutenant Greene later wrote. "The bullets came zip, zip, around me on all sides and over my head, and it seems to me a perfect miracle that I escaped without a scratch."[20]

The charge came within 50 yards of the 24th Wisconsin's line before a Confederate bugler sounded recall. The remnants of the Confederate brigade retreated back across the cottonfield into the woods 1,000 yards away.

The field was littered with Confederate dead. One participant later said, "I cannot remember ever seeing more dead men and horses, all jumbled together, than that scene of blood and carnage. The ground was literally covered with the dead."[21]

The breathing spell for the 24th Wisconsin was brief, no more than ten minutes. All around them were their comrades, many dead, others frightfully wounded. Hibbard and MacArthur tried to reestablish the 24th's line.

In the woods, the Confederates regrouped. The initial brigade was joined by two others. Again, they attacked across the field, seemingly as strong and as fierce as in the first charge. They came with their colors flying, shouting and hollering as if certain of victory.[22]

Behind the 24th Wisconsin, the Union artillery battery withdrew. This act badly frightened the men because they realized the meaning—General Sill did not want the battery to be captured. Hibbard had no orders.

Faced with three charging brigades, it was obvious the 24th could not withstand the attack. Some of the men leaped up and ran. "The truth is," admitted one soldier, "when the bullets are whacking against tree-trunks and solid shot are cracking skulls like egg-shells, the consuming passion in the breast of the average man is to get out of the way." "For thousands of them," historian James McPherson observed, "the shock of 'seeing the elephant' (the contemporary expression for experiencing combat) was too much."[23]

With no other choice, Hibbard shouted, "Break to the rear by companies!" Sergeant Drake observed that for the 24th to have remained would have been "perfect folly."[24]

MacArthur repeated the order to several company commanders on the left and then charged across the field to contact the units on the right. On horseback, he was an exposed target, but his luck held. The four companies on the right were almost surrounded when he galloped up with the order to retreat. The rest of the regiment was already frantically running into the cornfield behind them, desperate to get into the next batch of woods, over 1,000 yards away, where Colonel Schaefer, commander of Sheridan's 2nd Brigade, had established a defensive line.

The retreat, at first ragged, turned into a rout. It became every man for himself as the ten companies ran through the muddy field. The regiment was in plain view of a Confederate battery, which opened fire, and cannon balls and canister shells exploded all around the running men. Before the 24th could make it across the 1,000 yards of open ground to the next strip of wooded area, Confederate rebels opened fire from the woods behind them and then charged into the cornfield, right on the 24th's heels.

Slipping and sliding, the men tore frantically through the muddy terrain. MacArthur hung back, firing his revolver at the charging rebels; even though bullets buzzed around him, neither he nor his horse was hit.

The 24th suffered horrendously as dozens of men were killed or wounded. Stumbling across the final few yards, the survivors reached the woods where Schaefer's 2nd Brigade was in position. Schaefer's brigade opened fire as the 24th cleared the line, and the Confederates reeled back.[25]

The 24th Wisconsin regrouped. They were a blood-stained, powder-blackened, muddy group whose numbers had shrunk from over 500 to less than 200 men. The officers reformed the remnants of the regiment and moved up to support Schaefer, who ordered a retreat before the Confederates attacked again. Retreating but no longer running, the 24th Wisconsin would be fighting for its life for the rest of the day.[26]

General Sill had been wounded in the first attack while directing his brigade. Lieutenant John Mitchell, on Sill's staff, discovered the general lying on the ground on his side with his face and beard covered with blood. When Mitchell found him, Sill was "still breathing, and as the air bubbled through the stream of blood, he seemed like a drowning man." Shot in the middle of the head near his left eye, he died. In this war, officers on both sides led by example, and the casualty figures testify to their bravery. In both armies, officers suffered 15 percent higher deathrates than enlisted men, and generals led the grim list. In fact, a general's chance of dying in battle was 50 percent greater than that of a private.[27]

Mitchell ordered several men to carry Sill's body to the rear. Meanwhile, Colonel Greusel assumed command of the 1st Brigade around eight o'clock, two hours after the battle had begun.

Three miles east, near the Nashville Turnpike and the Nashville Railroad, Rosecrans at first refused to believe that Bragg was attacking the Union's right flank. At approximately 8:00 A.M., Rosecrans finally realized his entire army was in danger. Two-thirds of the Union right wing had been wrecked by the Confederate onslaught. If the rebel troops continued to roll up the Union line, half Rosecrans's army would be annihilated. He needed time to form a defensive line along the railroad and to bring the 30,000 men of Thomas's and Crittenden's corps into the battle. Therefore, Rosecrans ordered Sheridan's decimated division to delay the Confederate forces as long as possible.

Seven times that day, Sheridan's division made a stand. It was fight and retreat, then rally and make a stand until flanked, retreat again, then rally and fight once more. The 24th overcame the ghastly horrors of war and continued to fight, blood-stained and covered with soot from the black powder they used in their muskets. Hazy smoke surrounded them, and the thunder of muskets and artillery was deafening. Amid it all, everywhere one turned, were the dead, often gruesomely mangled, and the wounded, writhing in agony. Dead soldiers, dead horses, and thousands of pieces of lost, broken, or abandoned equipment littered the battlefield.[28]

MacArthur galloped up and down the line carrying messages from Colonel Greusel to Major Hibbard to the company commanders. Low on ammunition, the 24th Wisconsin fell back over 1 mile. Around ten o'clock, they formed a defensive line in a cypress swamp, known locally as Round Forest, just north and east of the Wilkinson Turnpike. The regiment took cover behind trees, limestone rocks, portions of fences, depressions in the ground, or whatever else offered any protection. The woods were alive with birds, rabbits, and other small animals frightened by the sounds of war.

Bragg ordered two Confederate divisions to attack Sheridan's position. Major Hibbard and Colonel Greusel counted five different regimental battle flags as the rebel forces approached. Sheridan's division repulsed the attack, but the 24th Wisconsin was subjected to a terrific artillery barrage. Exploding shells tore up the trees around them. "So thick and fast did the rebels send their shot and shell, it seemed impossible for even a bird to escape," declared Sergeant Ford of Company H. Many of the men stuffed their ears with cotton to deaden the noise.[29]

Cannon and musket fire on the right warned Sheridan that his division was again flanked. Soon, firing was also erupting on the left and then in the rear. They were completely surrounded, being attacked from all directions.

In front of the 24th, Confederate officers galloped up and down the line to urge their men forward as they tasted victory. Lieutenant Greene of Company B later wrote, "I, for one, thought the Rebels had us" and would "capture our whole Brigade. Visions of Vicksburg, Mobile & other southern cities floated before my eyes rather too vividly to be pleasant." The rest of the war might have been spent in a Confederate prison camp, assuming one was lucky enough to survive the battle.[30]

At this most desperate time, fresh Union troops came on line as Thomas's corps finally entered the battle. The Confederate charge stalled, and the lines stabilized. Union batteries belched forth shell after shell, and Thomas's corps shoved the attackers back, punching a hole in the Confederate encirclement of Sheridan's division.

For six hours, the division had fought and retreated and fought again. All three of Sheridan's brigade commanders were killed. His division lost 1,663 men, killed, wounded, and missing—one-third of its fighting force. Eight artillery batteries had abandoned their guns and run for their lives. But the division had slowed down the Confederate attack and bought Rosecrans the time he needed to reorganize the Union army. In the words of one authority, their fighting retreat was "possibly never surpassed during the Civil War." Because of Sheridan's division, Bragg's attack lost momentum.[31]

Sheridan's battered veterans, a procession of exhausted, bloodied men, stumbled to the shelter of the railroad line, where Rosecrans had thrown up entrenchments. They staggered another few hundred feet to the Nashville Turnpike to replenish their ammunition. Supply wagons, ambulances, stragglers, and the walking wounded clogged the road. After obtaining ammunition, the division marched back to the railroad line to regroup and to act as headquarters guards. Tattered, cold, tired, and hungry, only willpower kept them moving.[32]

With the rest of Sheridan's division, the 24th Wisconsin was spread along the railroad line to protect it from bands of Confederate cavalry that harassed the flanks of Rosecrans's army. Afternoon faded into twilight as fighting continued all over the 3-mile battlefield. At dusk, quiet finally settled over the battlefield.

Major Hibbard ordered roll call. It was a sad affair. Sheridan's 1st Brigade, now commanded by Colonel Greusel, had lost more men than any other brigade in the entire Union army. Greusel's four regiments reported 104 killed, 365 wounded, and 200 missing, for a total of 669, over half the brigade's effective strength at the beginning of the battle. Of that number, the 24th Wisconsin suffered 19 killed, 58 wounded, and 98 missing, about a third of its original strength. Some of the regiment's companies suffered disproportionately. Company B went into battle with 47 men and 2 officers; at roll call, only 16 men and 1 officer were present. Company I had had 45 men and lost 20—1 killed, 8 wounded, and 11 missing.[33]

The 24th Wisconsin threw up barricades and sent three companies out on picket duty. The day's battle had taught them a lesson. The regiment never camped again, even for one night, without fortifying their position with temporary barricades.

Despite orders, the men built campfires. They were exhausted, hungry, and frozen. Although they had not eaten in thirty-six hours, the rations that evening were only one ear of corn per man. A few of the men still had some coffee and biscuits in their haversacks; they boiled the coffee over the campfires and shared the few biscuits with their comrades. On this cold and rainy winter night, only a few men had managed to save their blankets, and those without blankets were soon chilled to the bone. The ground was frozen, the wind was strong, and sleet pounded them. The men sat on rocks or the ground and shivered around small campfires.[34]

It was December 31, but there was no New Year's Eve celebration that night. Most of the men felt fortunate to have survived. Understandably, those survivors formed a bond with each other that they would remember their entire lives.

From the front came the moans of the wounded still lying among the limestone boulders, the cedar thickets, and the fields. All night long, wounded soldiers called out for a fire, for a stretcher, for water, or for death. Many of the wounded froze to the ground in their own blood.[35]

Interestingly, both Rosecrans and Bragg believed they had won the battle—Bragg because he had pushed the Union army back over 3 miles, Rosecrans because his final defensive line had saved his link with Nashville via the turnpike and railroad. Both commanders expected the other to withdraw at first light.

The weather cleared during the night. Up at four o'clock, the 24th Wisconsin took a position near the Nashville Turnpike next to Rosecrans's headquarters, about a mile north of Stones River. Emotionally drained and exhausted, the regiment was assigned guard duty. They finally obtained supplies. After throwing up breastworks, they stacked their arms, ate, and lay down to rest. Their rest was not peaceful. Every hour or so, an outbreak of firing occurred in their front. Sharpshooters harassed the Union pickets, and there were sporadic exchanges of artillery. Officers on horseback soon discovered it was dangerous to group together; enemy spotters would aim artillery in their direction. When one group of mounted officers, including Hibbard, MacArthur, and Baumbach, stopped to talk, it was less than ten minutes before "they were discovered by some battery." Lieutenant Greene reported that "the shell and round shot fell around so thick and fast that all sociability immediately terminated." The officers dismounted, and most stayed off horseback as much as possible since enemy sharpshooters were all over the area.[36]

On Friday, January 2, Bragg tried again to oust Rosecrans from his position. Around three o'clock in the afternoon, he attacked the Union left defended by Crittenden's corps. Still in reserve, the 24th heard the battle rage and expected to be called into action. Near sundown, a terrific artillery duel occurred. Captain

Alva Philbrook, commander of Company D, timed the reports: "There were sixty-five per minute and a continual roar of musketry." Later, the 24th learned that the "rebels charged on Crittenden's corps across open fields and were defeated." The fighting was severe, but the Union forces were behind strong breastworks and effectively used their artillery, forcing the rebels to retreat back to their original positions.[37]

That night, the rain began again. The next day, Saturday, neither Bragg nor Rosecrans initiated any action. There was skirmishing up and down the line but not much fighting. When the sun set, the rain turned to sleet. Under the cover of the rain, Bragg withdrew around midnight, retreating south toward his major base camp in Chattanooga.

On a clear, bright Sunday morning, Rosecrans's army occupied Murfreesboro. Deciding he needed time to regroup his troops, he chose not to pursue Bragg.

Over 3,000 men, Union and Confederate, were killed in the battle of Murfreesboro, and almost 16,000 men were wounded. Many of the wounded still lay in agony on the battlefield waiting for the attention of the doctors. Young, middle-aged, and old soldiers from both sides were scattered all over the woods and fields for miles. John Beatty, an officer in another regiment, reported that he saw men with their legs "shot off; one with brains scooped out with a cannon ball; another with half a face gone; another with entrails protruding; [another] with one foot off, and both legs pierced by grape at the thighs; another boy lay with his hands clasped above his head, indicating that his last words were a prayer." He also saw "a young boy, dressed in the Confederate uniform, [who] lay with his face turned to the sky and looked as if he might be sleeping." Burial parties were engaged in their somber task in the fields where thousands of dead and wounded horses and mules were intermixed with the fallen soldiers.[38]

The death and maiming of thousands was a spectacle that no man could ignore. "We realized," remembered one veteran of Murfreesboro, "what war really was. Most of us, I suppose, were at one time in our experience as soldiers rather anxious to participate in a battle. Perhaps we were not quite willing that the war should end without our having had that experience. If," he concluded, "the writer had cherished any such feeling, it disappeared after Stones River." Sergeant Drake put it succinctly when he wrote home, "I assure you, such fearful carnage, I never wish to witness again."[39]

The battle of Murfreesboro was the first true test for Lieutenant MacArthur and the 24th Wisconsin. Though many of the officers in the regiment proved themselves unfit for command, MacArthur had been cool and courageous in battle. His comrades recognized his bravery, and one veteran later recalled that the 24th was "glad indeed" that Colonel Larrabee "hadn't ... traded off" MacArthur, who "was a hero in the eyes of the whole Brigade."[40]

As in the British system, medals were not awarded to individuals for bravery but to regiments for campaigns. Commanding officers recognized individual courage in their official reports submitted within weeks of the battle. These reports were generally published in hometown newspapers. Any officer receiving a mention was considered a hero, and the report became part of the officer's official military service record. Colonel Greusel and Major Hibbard lavishly praised MacArthur in their reports. Greusel wrote, "Adjutant MacArthur of the 24th Wisconsin behaved with great coolness and presence of mind ever ready to obey my commands." Hibbard was even more generous in his praise. He wrote, "I am more than indebted to Arthur MacArthur, Jr., for his aid and efficient service rendered during the engagements. Young and gallant, I bespeak for him an honorable career." Hibbard proved to be an excellent prophet.[41]

Years later, during long evenings on the western frontier, Arthur's children insisted that he recount his Civil War deeds time and again. In his memoirs, Douglas, one of his sons, remembered his father's bravery at Murfreesboro in the glowing tones that only a MacArthur could use. He adored and admired his father, and his account reflects that adulation, but perhaps it also holds as much truth as the dull official records. Douglas recalled his father describing the battle at Murfreesboro as

> one of the fiercest of the war. ... Fourteen times that day the Wisconsin regiment changed front[s]. ... The carnage was merciless. The regiment lost nearly 40 percent of its strength. ... Every mounted officer of the 24th was down except the adjutant. In effect, he became its commander. He was everywhere, rallying the ranks, reorganizing the companies, holding on with tooth and nail. The indomitable Sheridan was roaring in his ears, "Pivot, Arthur, pivot! Roll with the punch! He must not turn you!" And when Sheridan rode up that night, he patted the lad and with a grin [said,] "Arthur, my boy, congratulations."[42]

The battle of Murfreesboro, or Stones River, was declared a victory in the North but only because Rosecrans's army had not been crushed. The Army of the Cumberland had been bruised, and Rosecrans would take several months to regroup his forces for another battle.

4

Interlude

THE 24TH WISCONSIN settled into winter camp about 3 miles south of Murfrees-boro on January 4, 1863, with Bragg's Confederate Army of Tennessee less than 20 miles south at Tullahoma. The regiment's supply wagons arrived two days later with tents and clean clothing. For the first time in two weeks, the men could relax. From December 26 to January 6, they had lived and slept in the same clothes. At last, they took baths and changed into clean, dry clothing.[1]

While the regiment recuperated, the major topic around the campfires was the battle of Murfreesboro. Although Rosecrans's army had come close to annihilation, the men did not blame "Old Rosey," whom they still adored. Rather, they criticized General Richard Johnson, whose division had been so poorly prepared. Moreover, MacArthur and the other survivors of Murfreesboro were ashamed that so many in the 24th had run at the first shot. A good number of the regiment's officers had also disgraced themselves. Eventually, a half dozen officers submitted their resignations.[2]

Colonel Larrabee remained in Nashville, and many in the regiment hoped his absence was permanent. Colonel Greusel wrote to Alexander Mitchell in Milwaukee that the 24th Wisconsin needed new leadership. With the support of Lieutenant MacArthur, Major Hibbard's men had fought well, but Hibbard was inexperienced as a regimental commander.[3]

General Sheridan was the true hero of the battle for Murfreesboro, and the 24th Wisconsin was proud to be part of his division. Sheridan received a promotion to major general in early January, and the division honored him with a party and gave him a beautiful silver service. That evening, the men even serenaded their general. The regimental bands played as Sheridan entertained his officers, including Lieutenant MacArthur, the youngest officer in Sheridan's division and possibly in the entire Army of the Cumberland.[4]

Winter camp took on a life of its own. The cold, wet weather made life miserable, but the troops from Wisconsin soon transformed their campsite. From the plentiful timber in the area, they constructed log cabins that began to feel like home, complete with the crude furniture they had built. The officers shared reinforced, rectangular wall tents that they made quite comfortable. Lieutenant

Chivas, for example, reported that his quarters were fitted "with two bedsteads, with straw mattresses, a table with oil cloth cover, a large brick fireplace, and the floor covered with clean oak flooring." MacArthur shared his tent with Captain Carl Baumbach, the other staff officer.[5]

The winter camp of the 24th Wisconsin was a mere suburb of a tent city that stretched for miles east, west, and north. There were over 50,000 soldiers in the Army of the Cumberland, and thousands of civilians flocked to Murfreesboro to sell their wares—merchants, prostitutes, photographers, gamblers, candlemakers, lithographers, and even traveling theatrical and minstrel troupes.

Unfortunately, the new city bred diseases, for sanitation and water supplies simply were inadequate to deal with the influx of 60,000 to 70,000 people. In fact, twice as many soldiers died of disease in the Civil War as died in battle. The principal killers were typhoid and intestinal infections caused by contaminated water. Bacteriology was an unknown science at the time, and no one knew the water was unsafe. Typhoid probably was responsible for one-fourth of all deaths from disease, followed closely by dysentery, influenza, bronchial ailments, scurvy, measles, and malaria. Poor sanitation was a principal cause. Latrines were simply open pits, and filth was everywhere. Thousands of horses and mules contributed to the problem, and refuse and offal accumulated in and around the camps, attracting hordes of flies that crawled over the food and spread the germs. Body lice and fleas were rampant; if the victims did not take care of themselves, many developed complications.[6]

The 24th Wisconsin suffered heavily. Nearly everyone had the "Tennessee quickstep," or a looseness of the bowels, and MacArthur, though fastidious in his personal habits, was not immune. The food itself was contaminated because it was prepared in infected water. Although over 350 men were listed on the official rolls, the regiment had only 140 able-bodied men by the end of January. Company A reported 20 men; Company B had 9; Company D, only 8; the rest of the companies had about 15 men each.[7]

Most of the men attributed their stomach ailments to army rations of wormy hardtack, beans, and rice. They hungered for fresh fruit, but they had no money to purchase any additional food. Five months after being mustered into the army in August 1862, they still had not been paid a dime. MacArthur accepted responsibility for the delay, for the War Department claimed he had incorrectly completed the enlistment forms—his first lesson in the importance that petty bureaucrats placed on proper paperwork. In letters home, the men of the 24th Wisconsin let it be known that MacArthur was not to blame. No one in the Army of the Cumberland had been paid in months, a source of demoralization throughout the army.[8]

Officers also felt the pinch because they did not draw food rations. When they were not paid for six or eight or even twelve months, as frequently happened, they had to beg food from the quartermasters or hope for packages from home. For weeks at a time, they received no mail because the U.S. postal service was not trustworthy; pilferage and poor management were rampant.

The enlisted men also suffered from lack of pay. Few wanted to exist on army food rations alone, and most liked to supplement their diets with items purchased from authorized merchants, called sutlers, who demanded payment in cash. Assigned to a regiment, a sutler arrived in camp with a wagon loaded with supplies, which he transferred to a strong, rectangular tent that opened only in the front. His stock usually included tobacco, cigars, lemons, oranges, apples, candy, raisins, soda crackers, cakes, canned fruits, sugar, salted fish, bacon, ginger ale and other soft drinks, and even liquor for the officers. The sutler also stocked other items not provided by the army commissary, such as rubber ponchos and stoves for Sibley tents and log cabins. Realizing his customers might be dead after the next battle or die of illness in the diseased camps, the sutler wanted cash payment up front. Yet his outrageous prices made it difficult even when the men were paid. A private received only $11 a month, later raised to $16, plus an annual clothing allowance of $52. Thus, the men were hard-pressed to keep themselves in tobacco when they were not paid for months. For his part, the sutler guarded his goods with a passion, and the soldiers took delight in stealing from him. Like most of the officers who served in the Civil War, MacArthur developed a bitter hatred toward these merchants.[9]

Colonel Larrabee returned to the regiment on March 3. Although absent during the battle of Murfreesboro, Larrabee had been promoted to full colonel. Hibbard was made a lieutenant colonel, and Carl Baumbach rose from captain to major.[10]

Some of the officers were glad to see Larrabee because discipline had been lax under Hibbard. Lieutenant Mitchell, on Colonel Greusel's staff at brigade, wrote his father that Larrabee's prolonged absence from the regiment was unfortunate. Larrabee, he noted, was "sometimes eccentric and always obstinate, but his discipline was firm. Since he relaxed his hold, the regiment has gradually been losing its position." According to Mitchell, Larrabee had been an unfortunate victim of circumstance. Lieutenant Chivas, one of Arthur's close friends in the 24th, wrote home that although Larrabee was not perfect, he was better than Hibbard. Chivas was not, however, entirely pleased with Larrabee, who perhaps was a "good disciplinarian and trainer" but had "no tactical sense."[11]

Many of the officers, including MacArthur, were unhappy to see Larrabee return. Hibbard resigned in protest. Captains Richard H. Austin, Alva Philbrook, and Howard Greene notified Colonel Greusel that they did not wish to serve under Larrabee. Greene wrote to his brother that he not only disliked Larrabee but felt he was totally unfit for command. "As the boys say," Greene wrote, "I wouldn't go a cent for him. … Larrabee knows nothing of military matters, … is rash, … childish, … and a man of very poor judgment. He is tricky [and] unprincipled."[12]

The complaints were effective. On March 31, Governor Salomon appointed Theodore S. West as lieutenant colonel of the 24th Wisconsin. West had seen action on the eastern front in 1862 as adjutant of the 5th Wisconsin. He arrived at the 24th's winter camp on April 13 and took command as Larrabee again retired to

Nashville. West was exactly what the regiment needed. At approximately the same time, the 1st Brigade received a new commander, Brigadier General William H. Lytle.[13]

With West now in command, drills returned as an integral part of camp life for the 24th Wisconsin. Each morning, buglers woke the regiment around 4:30. The sergeants called roll as the aroma of boiling coffee drifted about the camp. The men consumed vast quantities of coffee. As the soldiers crushed the coffee beans on flat stones with their rifle butts or fed them into primitive grinders, the camps were musical with this clangor. The tin canteen was also useful equipment: It came unsoldered when thrown into a fire, resulting in two dishes that furnished the soldier with both a washbasin and a skillet. If one half of the canteen was stabbed full of holes, it made a perfect grater for corn fritters.[14]

After breakfast, MacArthur carried duty rosters to the company commanders and picked up the day's muster rolls. Around nine o'clock, drills began, and having learned the value of discipline in battle, the men no longer grumbled about them. In the mornings, they drilled by company and then by squads. In the afternoons, MacArthur led the regiment in drills until about 4:30, when he returned to his quarters, brushed his uniform, polished his brass buttons, and cleaned his weapons for the evening dress parade. Shortly after dress parade, the bugler sounded supper call. After eating, the men had a period of free time, an interval devoted to socializing around the campfires. At ten o'clock, bugles sounded and officially ended the day. All lights were extinguished, and silence descended over the campgrounds.[15]

Many of the volunteers complained of the "monotony and most tedious irksomeness" of camp life. Rufus R. Dawes of the 6th Wisconsin moaned that "military life in camp is the most monotonous in the world. It is the same routine over and over every day." "Bugles, drums, drills, parades—the old story over and over again." "I am ... worn out with idleness," John Beatty of the 3rd Ohio wailed, complaining that he had "hardly enough to do to keep me awake."[16]

Perhaps Arthur was a rarity in actually enjoying camp life, but he probably found it uplifting. As adjutant of the 24th Wisconsin, he had staff duties that kept him busy. During breaks, on his days off, and in the evenings, MacArthur read books, magazines, and newspapers, which were passed around camp until they literally fell apart. Around campfires, he talked tactics with the other officers and listened to advice from the enlisted men. Most soldiers believed they knew more than the generals and were willing to advise officers on any topic. The men talked politics, analyzed war strategy, and reviewed battles late into the evenings. While they talked, they enjoyed playing checkers, dominoes, and chess. Gambling was pervasive, the men staking their meager wages on poker, twenty-one, and keno. Dice was also a popular game among the gamblers. Sporting gentlemen chalked squares on their rubber ponchos to play chuck-a-luck and honest John, and they often bet on horse races, wrestling matches, boxing contests, and cockfights.[17]

In the evenings, the regimental bands played, or the men broke up into little groups that surrounded musicians who had brought their own fiddles, banjos, and harmonicas. Civil War soldiers enjoyed singing, and the songs they sang inspired MacArthur for the rest of his life. Nearly every Union regiment had a singing group that entertained comrades. The most popular song among the soldiers was "Home Sweet Home," and the men enjoyed other songs such as "When This Cruel War Is Over," "The Girl I Left Behind Me," and "Tenting on the Old Camp Ground." They sang comic songs like "The Blue Tail Fly," "Shoo Fly," and "Pop Goes the Weasel." Patriotic and marching songs included "Battle Hymn of the Republic," "John Brown's Body," "Tramp, Tramp, Tramp," "Battle Cry of Freedom," and "Yankee Doodle." On Sundays, they sang grand old hymns like "Rock of Ages," "Nearer My God to Thee," and "On Jordan's Stormy Banks I Stand."[18]

While in winter camp, the 24th Wisconsin was slowly resupplied. In early March, the regiment was issued new Enfield rifles to replace the old Austrian ones. In late April, they were issued new tents. Holding up to 24 men, the Sibley tents were ideal for camp conditions but a liability on the march. They were so large they had to be hauled by supply wagons. On the march, the tents were left behind and often did not catch up with the regiment for weeks while the men slept in the open and braved the elements. Recognizing the problem, the War Department began issuing shelter tents in early 1863.

The shelter tent was constructed by joining two four-by-six-feet pieces of canvas. On the march, each man carried one canvas piece rolled up and slung over his shoulder. At night, each soldier found a buddy with whom he would build a tent by buttoning or tying together their two canvases. The tent was then mounted on a horizontal ridgepole that was supported at each end by a stick or a musket stuck in the ground. The shelter tent looked like a doghouse, and hence, it acquired its nickname, pup tent. Inside, the pup tent measured six feet by seven feet. Three or four soldiers could combine their halfshelters to make a larger tent, or a man could simply tie the corners of his canvas to the top of four upright sticks to create a single tent.[19]

The soldiers recognized that pup tents were better on the march than the old Sibley tents, but they thought it was hysterically funny that the government expected them to sleep in doghouses. When Rosecrans ordered the tents pitched for inspection, every regiment competed to come up with the funniest slogans to adorn their new tents. Many of the men scribbled charcoal letters on the outside of their tents. When Rosecrans rode out on inspection, he whooped gleefully as he read the charcoaled signs. "Dog Hole No. 1," one declared, and others proclaimed "Pups for Sale," "Rat Terriers," "Bull Pups Here," or "Sons of Bitches Within." As the general rode down the line, a red-faced soldier on his hands and knees suddenly peered out from one of the tents and barked, "Bow-wow!" Soon, at the inverted V of every tent, faces appeared, yowling, barking, and baying. Rosecrans roared with laughter as he passed down the line.[20]

The 24th Wisconsin entered into the competition with humorous signs that represented nearly every occupation. Lieutenant Drake wrote to his brother that "one fellow had a sign on his tent—'Dogs for Sale, Inquire Next Door'; another said, 'Hotel Murphy, barn in rear.'" Another soldier illustrated his black humor by drawing a skull and crossbones on his tent.[21]

The pup tents were soon put to use. About once a month, Sheridan volunteered his division to pursue Confederate cavalry raiding outlying Union posts and harassing Rosecrans's supply line from Nashville to Murfreesboro. There was little chance of catching the Confederate raiders, but the marches kept Sheridan's division away from the diseased camps and put the men in fighting trim. Leaving his supply wagons behind, Sheridan required each man to carry forty rounds of ammunition, a canteen with three pints of water, a knapsack with a change of clothes, a blanket rolled up in his half of the pup tent, a rubber poncho, and a haversack with three days' rations. Sheridan chased Confederate raiders as far south as the Duck River and as far north as Nashville. He pushed his men hard, and soon the division was being referred to as "Sheridan's Cavalry." When on the march with Sheridan, the men rose at sunrise and marched until sundown.[22]

When not marching or drilling, the men of the 24th Wisconsin were often on picket duty. As the days turned warmer in early April, this duty was preferred over the infected camp near Murfreesboro. After posting guards, checking their barricades, and pitching their pup tents, the men would go off into the woods to search for berries and small game to supplement their camp rations. At night, they took torches into the woods, Lieutenant Drake reported to his brother, and knocked blinded doves and wild turkeys from the trees and roasted them over their evening campfires. They also went frog hunting and speared frogs "so big they bleated like lambs." The major irritant were the flies, wood ticks, and mosquitoes that were more prevalent than in Milwaukee.[23]

There was little exchange of fire with Confederate pickets. Men on both sides, as Private Thomas F. Galwey of the 8th Ohio noted, were "accustomed to see one another on picket and ... unwilling to harass or to be harassed unless an advance, retreat, or some decided movement is attempted by the opposite side." Most of the officers agreed with the men and, like Michigan's General Alpheus S. Williams, were "always unhappy when picket fire broke out and always glad when it ceased, for it could have no effect on the war's outcome and was 'a miserable and useless kind of murder.'" "Wanton cruelty," Sergeant Wilbur F. Hinman of the 65th Ohio called it.[24]

On June 24, three weeks after MacArthur celebrated his eighteenth birthday, Rosecrans began a spring offensive. Twenty miles south of Murfreesboro at Tullahoma, Braxton Bragg and the Confederate Army of Tennessee waited. Bragg's defensive line stretched along the foothills east from Shelbyville on the Duck River to McMinnville in the mountains to the northeast. With six months to prepare, Bragg's elaborate defensive positions verged on being impregnable. All along his line, which stretched 20 miles east to west, Bragg built forts and barricades. In front of the forts, he cleared the trees for a half mile. Cut trees were stacked to prevent a charge and to force any attacking force to crawl and stumble over these barriers.[25]

Rosecrans's intelligence on Bragg's defensive position was excellent. The Union cavalry had carefully observed the building of the Confederate fortifications. Although a frontal assault on the enemy line would have been suicidal, that line was thin. Therefore, Rosecrans flanked the Confederate positions by sending Thomas's corps east toward McMinnville and Crittenden's corps west toward Shelbyville. Bragg soon withdrew from his defensive line to protect his supply route to Chattanooga, the major Confederate base. Without firing a shot, Sheridan's division occupied Tullahoma on July 3.

While Rosecrans paused at Tullahoma, news from the eastern front reached the Army of the Cumberland. Robert E. Lee's offensive into Pennsylvania had been stopped at Gettysburg on July 3, 1863. Both sides suffered horrendous casualties in what would be the most analyzed battle of the Civil War. Repulsed at Gettysburg, Lee's Army of Northern Virginia withdrew into Virginia, and the city of Washington celebrated. "I never knew such excitement in Washington," wrote one observer.[26]

Three days later, Washington learned of another dramatic Union victory. On July 4, General Ulysses S. Grant had finally captured Vicksburg, the last major Confederate stronghold on the Mississippi River. Grant later considered this victory, which placed the entire Mississippi River in Union hands, as the most strategic of the Civil War. "Within two weeks, unarmed merchant ships from St. Louis, Missouri arrived in New Orleans without incident. 'The Father of Waters again goes unvexed to the sea,' announced Lincoln." The Confederacy was thus cut in two.[27]

Rosecrans remained at Tullahoma, as the Army of the Cumberland was being ravaged by typhoid. The symptoms were high fever, diarrhea, enlargement of the spleen, and a rash covering most of the body. Patients wasted away, and the mortality rate was as high as 30 percent. The only real cure was rest and a well-balanced diet, something simply not available in the army.

Lieutenant MacArthur fell desperately ill with typhoid in early July. When Judge MacArthur learned that his son was ill, he obtained a military pass to travel over 600 miles to visit him. He found Arthur in the Tullahoma hospital on the verge of death.

With Colonel West's approval, the judge bundled Arthur up in blankets, and they left Tullahoma on July 15. Traveling by train, they arrived in Milwaukee on July 17.[28]

There is no way of knowing whether his father's appearance and rescue upset Lieutenant MacArthur. Considering his struggle for independence, he must have felt ambiguous. He might have died in the Tullahoma hospital, but as he returned to his father's house, he also returned to being a boy again—back in a dependent state, living at home.

Under the care of the best doctors in Milwaukee and with the help of hired nurses, Arthur slowly recovered. Although not ready for the rigors of military life, he was out of danger by early August.

Greatly relieved, the judge returned to his own war with the "Peace Democrats" or "Copperheads" (so named because many of them wore copper penny badges to advertise their position on the war). The power and influence of the Copperheads varied according to the fortunes of Union armies on the battlefield. After two years of war and the death of thousands in battle after battle on the eastern and western fronts, Union victory had still not been achieved. Many blamed Lincoln and the Republicans. A number of Copperheads wanted peace at any price and were even willing to let the Southern states become a separate, independent nation.

In August, when casualty lists from Gettysburg were published, the fruits of victory tasted less sweet. In the three days of fighting around Gettysburg, the Union forces had suffered 3,155 men killed and 14,529 wounded. Confederate forces had 3,903 killed and 18,735 wounded. The nation gasped in horror at the death and maiming.[29]

In Washington, generals were fired, new commanders appointed, and time passed. Lincoln demanded action, but the generals procrastinated, proclaiming they needed more recruits, more training time, and more supplies.

In Wisconsin, where the governor's election occurred in odd-numbered years, some of the old-guard Democrats saw an opportunity to regain the office in November 1863. The party held its convention in Madison on August 5, and Judge MacArthur led the Milwaukee delegation. It was quickly apparent that the Peace Democrats under Edward Ryan controlled the majority of the delegates. The convention adopted a platform that attacked the Lincoln administration and advocated an immediate peace conference to end the war. They nominated Henry L. Palmer, a lawyer from Milwaukee, as their candidate for governor.[30]

Judge MacArthur and thirty other delegates who represented the Union wing of the party withdrew from the convention. The Republican leaders, seeing an opportunity, opened negotiations with the Union Democrats, soliciting the opinion of Judge MacArthur and others on whom they should nominate for governor. The judge preferred Salomon, but compromised on James T. Lewis, a former lieutenant governor and Salomon's secretary of state. Lewis, who for years had been a leading Democrat, was an acceptable candidate for the judge and his colleagues. Judge MacArthur campaigned through the fall for Republican Lewis, who would defeat his Democratic opponent in a landslide victory.[31]

As Arthur convalesced, his father's friends probably paraded through his sickroom to wish him well, but they adjourned to the parlor to discuss politics with the judge. Little Mac was recognized as a brave young soldier, and they applauded his devotion to his duty and his courage in battle. Like many other combat veterans, he took their praise in silence, realizing they had never walked a battlefield strewn with the dead nor felt the overwhelming fear of bloodshed. Civilian talk of patriotism and war no longer seemed appropriate, and their talk of politics probably bored or infuriated him. Gerald F. Linderman, in *Embattled Courage*, observed that most soldiers were convinced, "quite accurately, that those at home did not understand the experiences through which they were passing, and they resented … that civilian incomprehension." Veterans on home furloughs were often irritated at the reactions of neighbors when they told their stories of war. While the returning soldier usually thought of the horrors of war and remembered the maimed and the dead, the civilians talked of patriotism and duty. When home on a brief leave, Corydon E. Foote of the 10th Michigan sought out the only person with whom he felt at home, an invalided veteran. "Gosh, Pop, the rest of 'em can't imagine what it's like down there. No use tryin' to tell 'em, either." "Not much, Cordie. Not much, because most of 'em think they know such a goldern lot more about it than we do!"[32]

Arthur, anxious to return to his regiment, read the newspapers and letters from his comrades avidly.

5

Hero of Missionary Ridge

WHILE ARTHUR WAS HOME on sick leave, Rosecrans stumbled into a major disaster. When Bragg withdrew from Tullahoma on July 2, he retreated 30 miles south to new fortifications at Chattanooga, Tennessee, a natural fortress nestled in a river valley on the east bank of the Tennessee River.

Rather than attacking Bragg in Chattanooga, Rosecrans sent McCook's and Thomas's corps swinging west and attacked Confederate forces at Caperton's Ferry, Alabama, 35 miles southwest of Chattanooga. With his smaller army on the verge of being surrounded, Bragg withdrew from Chattanooga and moved his troops about 12 miles south to Chickamauga Creek. On September 9, Rosecrans occupied Chattanooga without firing a shot. Meanwhile, Union General Ambrose E. Burnside, commanding a force of 15,000 men, had captured Knoxville, Tennessee, 100 miles northeast of Chattanooga, on September 2.

Union telegraph wires sang in triumph, and celebrations occurred throughout the North. In Milwaukee, Arthur probably beamed with pride. Coupled with Grant's conquest of Vicksburg, the victories crippled the South. The railroad that ran north from Atlanta through Chattanooga and Knoxville had been an essential supply link for Lee's Army of Northern Virginia, which depended on Tennessee and Georgia for food, horses, coal, and gunpowder. Equally important, with Chattanooga in Union hands, Rosecrans could potentially attack Atlanta.

Believing he had Bragg on the run, Rosecrans did not wait to consolidate his gains but lunged south from Chattanooga into the mountains of north Georgia. This proved to be a major strategic blunder.

In mid-September, Bragg received reinforcements that dramatically altered the power balance. Two veteran divisions led by Confederate Generals William H.T. Walker and John Breckinridge arrived from armies fighting along the Mississippi. Shortly thereafter, Lee sent a crack corps from Virginia, under the command of General James Longstreet, that raised Bragg's total forces to over 66,000 men. Rosecrans's army numbered less than 58,000.

Unaware of Bragg's new strength, Rosecrans stumbled against the Confederate army at Chickamauga Creek, 12 miles south of Chattanooga, on September 20. Bragg attacked and caught Rosecrans unprepared.

The 24th Wisconsin was in the heart of the battle. Stationed on the right wing at Chickamauga Creek, McCook's entire corps, including Sheridan's division, was routed. Now a veteran outfit, the 24th Wisconsin did not run but rather retreated in good order. Again, they lost their brigade commander: General Lytle was killed early in the morning. Later in the day, Colonel West was wounded in the foot and was left behind. He was captured, leaving Major Baumbach in charge. Of the approximately 350 men in the regiment, over 100 were missing by the end of the conflict. In a single day, Rosecrans's Army of the Cumberland had over 16,000 men killed, wounded, or captured.[1]

Rosecrans ordered a retreat back to Chattanooga. On the morning of September 21, Sheridan's division, including the 24th Wisconsin, joined Thomas's corps of 15,000 men to participate in a rear-guard action to give Rosecrans time to stabilize the Union army in Chattanooga. Known for his defensive skills, Thomas placed his corps between Bragg and Chattanooga. Bragg attacked and was repulsed three times. Thomas stood immovable, the "Rock of Chickamauga."[2]

On September 22, Thomas withdrew to Chattanooga with Bragg on his heels. Bragg's army captured the heights south of the city, and his cavalry swept north to cut Rosecrans's supply line to Nashville.

As the news of Rosecrans's defeat was reported in Northern newspapers, hysteria swept the North: What had been annnounced as a great victory turned into a bitter defeat. Disaster appeared imminent. Rosecrans had lost most of his artillery in the battle at Chickamauga, and he had only enough ammunition for one day's fight. Bragg placed the Union army under siege and dispatched Longstreet's corps to recapture Knoxville.

Although not fully recovered from his illness, Arthur insisted on rejoining his regiment. Judge MacArthur tried to persuade his young son to wait and regain his health, but Arthur was obstinate, as always.[3]

His desperate need to rejoin his regiment was not unique. In *Embattled Courage*, Linderman observes that experienced combat units often developed a cohesiveness:

> Men began to speak of the mess as home, of their group as a family, and of their comrades as brothers. The strength of such ties found its most dramatic demonstration in the determination of some soldiers to return to the war when nothing save comradeship impelled them to do so. Those were cases … of furloughs cut short, of extensions unapplied for, of subterfuges employed to thwart doctors' refusals to release the sick or wounded.[4]

On September 28, Arthur boarded a train in Milwaukee to return to the front. The trip took him from Milwaukee to Louisville to Nashville to Bridgeport, Alabama, 28 miles west of Chattanooga. When he arrived on October 1, he discovered that the railroad to Chattanooga was closed. Although the Tennessee River flowed from Bridgeport to Chattanooga, it could not be used either, for from mountain peaks along the river, Confederate artillery bombarded any Union steamships or barges trying to make that journey.

Lieutenant MacArthur joined a wagon train carrying supplies along an old mountain road that twisted and climbed 60 treacherous miles through the mountains along the northern bank of the meandering Tennessee River. As the wagon train left Bridgeport, it began to rain. The road turned into a quagmire, and the heavy wagons bogged down in knee-deep mud. Even lightly loaded wagons sank up to their axles in the soft, sticky goo. Mountain passes were washed out, and broken-down wagons and abandoned supplies littered the road. The area had been devastated by war. The carcasses of thousands of dead horses and mules lay along the entire course of the supply road as it traveled up one steep mountain and down another. Confederate sharpshooters harassed the column. The 60-mile trip took four days.[5]

As his wagon train neared Chattanooga, MacArthur understood the dire straits of Rosecrans's army. Surrounded by mountains and ridges, Chattanooga was located on the east bank of the Tennessee River where it made a lopsided S-shaped loop, called Moccasin Bend. The city was in the center top of the S loop and in the C bend, protected on the north and west by the river but vulnerable because of the heights on the south and east. At the bottom of the C bend was Lookout Mountain, rising 2,200 feet and towering over the entire Chattanooga valley. From the top of the mountain, Confederate artillery lobbed shells down on Union positions in the city. To the east of the C bend, blocking the opening and stretching north to south for 10 miles, was Missionary Ridge. Confederate artillery dotted the top of the 500- to 800-foot-high ridge, and Confederate rifle pits studded the top, side, and base of it. Deep ravines cut the crest of the ridge, which in places was as narrow as 75 feet but in other spots was over 600 feet wide (see Map 5.1).

The Confederate positions on Lookout Mountain and Missionary Ridge seemed impregnable. About 30,000 Union soldiers were trapped in Chattanooga, with little hope of breaking out of the Confederate encirclement. Rosecrans's besieged army had fortified the town and built breastworks that stretched 2 miles from the river north of the city to the river on its south side. Homes became blockhouses, and the men dug pits to escape the daily Confederate artillery bombardment that tore gaping holes in various structures. Soot covered the city as smoke from the heavy black gunpowder lingered in the air.[6]

When MacArthur's wagon train crossed the Tennessee River and entered Chattanooga, the plight of the men shocked him. The proud Army of the Cumberland was starving to death. The men were emaciated, walking skeletons with pale, gaunt faces. Some were so weak they staggered as they followed the wagons, pleading for food. Others waited around animal feed troughs to steal grains of corn.[7]

The 24th Wisconsin was camped on the southern end of the Union line, near the base of Lookout Mountain. The regiment had shrunk to less than 150 men, who gathered around MacArthur to hear news from home. One veteran observed,

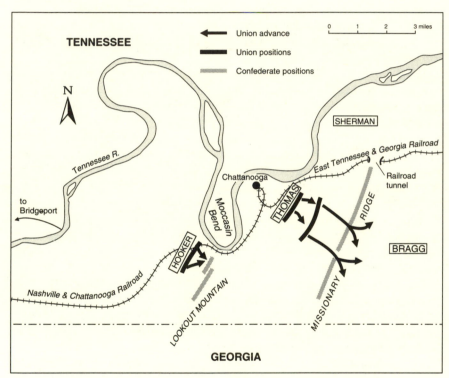

MAP 5.1 Missionary Ridge, Chattanooga, October–November 1863

"No greater pleasure is known to the soldier than the warm welcome extended him after a long absence, by his comrades." Major Baumbach, temporarily in command of the regiment, was particularly pleased to see MacArthur.[8]

The men had done a good job in building defenses for their camp. They had cut, hewed, dug, and built barricades to protect themselves against long-range enemy artillery fire from the top of Lookout Mountain. Inside their defensive citadel, the men ripped down fences, barns, sheds, and houses and erected huts along orderly company streets, using their pup tents for roofs. Sibley tents were unloaded from regimental wagons, and tepee tent villages sprang up throughout the city. Within the Union lines, all the trees were cut down for barricades and firewood, leaving the city bare.

The weather had turned wet and chilly. Scarce firewood supplies were soon exhausted. In the evening, homemade candles made from grease and old rags provided the only light. Wagon trains from Bridgeport brought only food and ammunition, and many of the men had neither shoes nor clothing suitable for the advancing cold season.

Food rations were issued every fourth day. The normal ration was some hardtack, dubbed "Lincoln platforms," and a small piece of fatty bacon. The few beef cattle transported over the road from Bridgeport were so lean the men jokingly called their meat "beef dried on the hoof." The troops ate the meager four days' ration as soon as it was issued and hoped somehow to scavenge more. Roasted acorns became a delicacy, and armed guards kept desperate soldiers from stealing the three ears of corn fed to the horses and mules each day. Thousands of horses and mules died of starvation; the men ate the carcasses but obtained little sustenance from the lean meat. The few horses that survived grew too weak to pull even the lightest wagons, and they often gnawed their hitching posts, wagon spokes, and even the tails of other horses. Artillery horses, the least needed, were fed less and died first. The batteries sank in the mud and became stationary.[9]

As the siege dragged on into its fourth week, the Union position in Tennessee was on the verge of disaster. Another Confederate army placed Burnside's Army of the Ohio in Knoxville under siege. The loss of both the Army of the Cumberland at Chattanooga and the Army of the Ohio at Knoxville could have dealt a shattering blow to the Union.

President Lincoln and Secretary of War Edwin M. Stanton became increasingly nervous. They decided something had to be done. On October 17, they created a new Military Division of the Mississippi and appointed Major General Grant to command it. With the exception of General Nathaniel P. Banks's army far south at New Orleans, Grant was to command all Union forces in the West, including William T. Sherman's Army of the Tennessee, Burnside's Army of the Ohio, and Rosecrans's Army of the Cumberland. Lincoln dispatched to Grant another 15,000 men from the Army of the Potomac under the command of General Joseph Hooker. Excluding garrison troops, Grant's combined armies included over 90,000 men. His prime directive was to relieve the siege at Chattanooga.

As Grant reviewed the situation, he believed he had two immediate problems. One was Rosecrans, who seemed to have lost his will to fight after his defeat at Chickamauga. With the approval of Lincoln and Stanton, Grant relieved Rosecrans and replaced him with General Thomas, the "Rock of Chickamauga." McCook and Crittenden were also relieved, and the Army of the Cumberland was reorganized into one corps under General Gordon Granger.

Grant's second problem was to open a more effective supply line to Chattanooga. He ordered Sherman to march with his 30,000 men from the Mississippi River to Bridgeport. While Grant waited for Sherman's arrival, he devoted all his efforts from mid-October to mid-November to breaking the Confederate encirclement of Chattanooga. In a series of small battles, he gained control of a better road, which alleviated some of the Army of the Cumberland's suffering. The men remained on half rations as Grant concentrated on stockpiling desperately needed supplies for an offensive to break the siege.

At the same time, Grant developed a battle plan. Before assuming command of the new Division of the Mississippi, he had commanded the Army of the Tennessee with Sherman as his second in command. They had been together since 1862 and had fought many battles from Shiloh to Vicksburg. A trust developed between them, a respect that would continue for the rest of their lives.

Sherman's Army of the Tennessee reached Bridgeport in mid-November and arrived on the outskirts of Chattanooga on November 21. Grant placed Sherman's 30,000-man army on the north flank and positioned General Hooker, who had arrived from the east with 15,000 men, on the south flank. Thomas's Army of the Cumberland occupied the center of the 2-mile line with 25,000 men. Grant's plan called for the Army of the Cumberland to defend the main Union line south of Chattanooga while Sherman and Hooker attacked the Confederate flanks. Grant did not seriously consider attacking the center of the line; he assumed that Bragg had made the naturally strong Confederate position atop Missionary Ridge impregnable to a direct attack.

The Army of the Cumberland was chagrined at Grant's lack of confidence in them. Sherman's western Army of the Tennessee bragged that they were the best in the Union, and they were proud of both their fighting abilities and their disheveled military appearance. Hooker's men from the eastern Army of the Potomac, where discipline and military posture were emphasized, were teased for their soldierly appearance and natty uniforms. Sherman's boys were quick to point out that only the Army of the Tennessee had been victorious in battle after battle, while the Army of the Potomac had suffered defeat after defeat under innumerable military commanders—including Hooker himself, who had failed as dismally as the rest. Sherman's men held a certain grudging respect for the Army of the Cumberland, for General Thomas, and particularly for General Sheridan and his fighting division. "Better fighters than those Easterners," most in the Army of the Tennessee admitted, but in their minds, Sherman was the best general in the Union army, and the Army of the Tennessee was the "best damn army." The 24th

Wisconsin disagreed. To a man, they believed that they were the best regiment, that Sheridan was the best general, and that the Army of the Cumberland was the best Union army.[10]

Sherman and Grant admired Thomas for his defensive abilities, but neither particularly liked him. They considered him to be ineffective when attacking Confederate strongholds; they also believed he was a military martinet who over-emphasized West Point codes and military discipline. From his days at the academy, where he graduated in 1840 (the same year as Sherman and three years before Grant), Thomas had been known as a stickler for military discipline and appearance. Despite being under siege for two months with his men on meager rations, he insisted the troops dress appropriately and drilled them continuously. Every Sunday and sometimes twice or three times a week, he ordered full regimental dress parades. He was convinced that infantry drills prepared the troops to follow orders on the battlefield. Sherman and especially Grant, who hated West Point and its formal military traditions, believed parade ground drills were ridiculous and taught the men nothing of value.

Lieutenant MacArthur agreed with General Thomas, and as adjutant of the 24th Wisconsin, he conscientiously led the regiment in drills and dress parades. The regiment took great pride in their marching skills.

Thomas got a chance to illustrate the courage of his men when Grant ordered him to capture Orchard Knob, a small hill that rose 100 feet from the valley floor about 1 mile from the base of Missionary Ridge in the exact center of the line. Less than a half mile from the Union line, the Confederates had built barricades on the knob, and the entrenched Confederate line extended north to south for 1 mile. Confederate pickets occupied rifle pits in a heavy stretch of timber that ended abruptly a quarter of a mile from the Union line. Between the belt of timber and the Union line, there was an open field, 300 yards wide, without a tree, a fence, or any other obstruction. Pickets from both armies dug so many pits in the field that the little mounds of dirt marking the spots looked like prairie dog villages. Only 100 yards separated the forward pickets of the two armies. In such an exposed position, the pickets agreed to an informal truce—"I won't shoot at you if you won't shoot at me" was the rule. Grant was about to change that rule.[11]

Thomas selected two divisions, one commanded by Thomas J. Wood and the second commanded by Sheridan, to attack Orchard Knob. The 24th Wisconsin was still part of Sheridan's division.

About half past one on November 23, a sunny Monday afternoon, Sheridan's and Wood's divisions marched through the Union barricades into the open field. "It was an inspiring sight," proclaimed Colonel Joseph S. Fullerton. "Flags were flying; the quick, earnest steps of thousands beat equal time." Drums rolled and bugles sounded up and down the line of the two divisions as regiments and then companies wheeled into line for an assault. Shouted commands were picked up by company officers, who echoed them across the field.[12]

For almost the only time in the Civil War, nearly every man in both armies was about to see a battle. Surrounded by mountains, Chattanooga was a gigantic amphitheater. The low-lying areas had been denuded of trees, giving everyone an excellent view. No battle of the Civil War provided so many observers with such good seats. Thomas used the stage to illustrate the superiority of his military training tactics.

The 24th Wisconsin was in the thick of it again. With Major Baumbach, Lieutenant MacArthur, and the regimental color sergeant in the lead, the 24th formed in ranks. The bright sun reflected off the officers' highly polished swords and "flashed like flying showers of electric sparks." The troop movement looked more like a dress parade than a true preparation for an attack on a heavily fortified position. Less than 100 yards away, Confederate pickets in front of Orchard Knob came out of their rifle pits and stood to admire the regiments marching in review.[13]

Around two o'clock, the drums and bugles blared out the signal to advance. The two divisions moved forward in formation, with the drummers rolling out the beat to double-time. There was not a single straggler as they moved across the field.

There were shouts from the Confederate pickets who suddenly realized this was an attack, not a review. They fell back to their entrenched lines at the foot of Orchard Knob. As Confederate artillery opened fire from the top of Missionary Ridge, cannon balls came tumbling down from the six-hundred-foot-high ridge that towered over the battlefield. Because of atmospheric conditions, the men of the 24th Wisconsin saw the balls rise high and float down toward the field, where they smashed huge holes in the charging Union line. Rolling musket fire mixed with the artillery bombardment as puffs of smoke rose from the battlefield. Bodies soon covered the ground, dotting the field as the Union line double-timed across the field directly into the woods before Orchard Knob.

As the Union forces struck the Confederate forward line, it was obvious that Bragg had no intention of making his stand here. The position could not be as easily defended as Missionary Ridge, which towered over Orchard Knob. The Confederate defenders therefore retreated back to prepared barricades and rifle pits at the base of the ridge.

As grand and glorious as it appeared, the battle for Orchard Knob lasted less than a half hour. A cheer swept through the two attacking divisions as they ascended the knob. They had proven their bravery and shown Grant that they were as good as Sherman's boys in the Army of the Tennessee.[14]

In a festive mood, the 24th Wisconsin camped near Orchard Knob that night. In a letter to his father, Arthur described the brief battle. He did not mention his friends nor his inner turmoils but rather formally reported on the status of the 24th. Although the records over the years illustrate that Arthur loved his father, there always appeared to be a gulf between them. There was little gossip in his letter and no indication that he felt homesick. Instead, he reported that by sundown, firing ceased almost entirely. We were ordered to remain in the same place during the night, that is, in line of battle. This was a rather unpleasant order to comply with, seeing that we had marched out without anything but guns and ammunition. To alleviate this difficulty, details were made from the several companies in the regiment to return to camp and bring out rations and blankets to their comrades. At length the hungry were fed, the bivouac was made complete by blankets, and everything passed off quietly.[15]

The 24th's new position encompassed a wooded area; the men built bonfires and clustered around the flames to warm themselves.[16]

The next day, Tuesday, November 24, was wet and chilly. The assault on Orchard Knob had merely been a diversion to force Bragg to concentrate more of his troops in the center of the line and thereby weaken his flanks. Grant's plan was simple: He would simultaneously assault Bragg on both flanks. Sherman would attack on the Union left at the north end of Missionary Ridge. On the right, Hooker and his 15,000 men would attack Lookout Mountain. Thomas's Army of the Cumberland remained in the center as a threat to prevent Bragg from reinforcing his flanks. Grant assumed that Sherman would capture the north end of the ridge and threaten the Confederate supply line. No one really believed that Hooker's men could capture Lookout Mountain—the attack was intended to divert Bragg while Sherman's army hit the right flank.

But the battle did not proceed according to plan. Although Sherman's army captured the north end of Missionary Ridge, rolling up the Confederate line proved impossible, for the top of the ridge was broken by ravines that made rapid movement impossible. The Confederate defenders beat a slow retreat.

Meanwhile, to everyone's surprise, Hooker was more successful. Ordered to attack the Confederate rifle pits halfway up Lookout Mountain, he discovered that Bragg had, indeed, weakened his defenses on Lookout to strengthen his center and right flank.

Down in the valley, the 24th Wisconsin heard the battle on Lookout Mountain but could not see it because a thick mist of cloud reached almost halfway down the mountain. Around noon, a tremendous artillery barrage erupted; it was followed by rifle fire that lasted for hours. All day long, the men stared up at Lookout Mountain anxiously, wondering and worrying about Hooker and his men. Finally, in the late afternoon, the cloud covering dissipated, and the men in the valley saw Union soldiers climbing onto the peak, 2,200 feet high, as the Confederate defenders fled.

The Army of the Cumberland gave a spontaneous cheer that echoed through the valley. As the sun went down, the clouds rolled away. The night came on clear and cool.[17]

Around camp that night, the men of the 24th were a cheerful lot. On their right flank, Lookout Mountain was ablaze with the campfires of Hooker's men. On their left flank, reaching far above the valley, the north end of Missionary Ridge was aflame with the lights of Sherman's army. The only thought that dampened the 24th's enthusiasm was that the enemy was being destroyed on the flanks while the regiment was tied down in the center.[18]

The next day was a beautiful and crisp fall day in Tennessee. The sun quickly burned off the morning mist that hung over the summits surrounding the valley. Grant and Thomas moved their forward headquarters to the top of Orchard Knob, a point from which they had an excellent view of the action along the entire line. Grant ordered Sherman to renew the attack on the left end of the ridge. From early morning, the 24th Wisconsin heard the sounds of battle.

Around ten o'clock, the 24th received orders to move forward a quarter mile to the edge of the woods bordering the no-man's-land between the two armies. The Army of the Cumberland's 4th Corps, under the command of General Granger, eased into a line that stretched for more than 2.5 miles. Composed of 23,000 men, the 4th Corps was divided into four divisions. Brigadier General Absalom Baird's division was on the far left, then came Brigadier General Thomas Wood's division, followed by Sheridan's division. Finally, on the far right, was Brigadier General Richard Johnson's division. Each division had three brigades, and most of the brigades had nine regiments. All the regiments were undermanned—MacArthur's reports indicate that only 150 men in the 24th Wisconsin were ready for action. The 24th Wisconsin was part of Sheridan's 1st Brigade, commanded by Colonel Francis T. Sherman.

By eleven o'clock, the 24th Wisconsin was in place. Hidden by a thin belt of woods, they waited for the command to attack. After forming into lines, they were ordered to lie down. Their field pieces were masked with brush, and for a time, all seemed as still as death. The distance from where they lay to the base of Missionary Ridge was about three-fourths of a mile.

As they lay waiting, Major Baumbach received new orders. Grant wanted to divert Bragg and decided to attack the center of the Confederate line. At the signal of six guns fired in succession from the Union forts surrounding Chattanooga, Sheridan's division was to charge across the open field and attack the first line of Confederate rifle pits at the base of the ridge. The men were not to attempt a major frontal assault up the ridge.

The 24th Wisconsin was located almost exactly in the center of the 2-mile Union line that stretched north to south from river bank to river bank. Above them, the ridge rose abruptly to almost 600 feet, its northern side scored with ravines, gulleys, and Confederate rifle pits. The Confederate position looked impregnable. The trees on the side of the ridge had been cut to give the defenders a better field of fire. There were also barricaded rifle pits at the base of the ridge and a second major line of barricades about halfway up the side of the ridge; finally, at the very top, Bragg had stationed 10,000 men and fifty heavy siege guns. A small house on the ridge top that served as Bragg's headquarters was directly in front of the 24th's position. From the valley's floor, the 24th saw Confederate officers moving between barricades lined with heavy artillery pieces.[19]

Noon passed, then one o'clock and two o'clock. On the Union left, musket fire erupted, then abated as Sherman's attack faltered. There were too many intervening ravines on top of the north end of the ridge for him to roll up the Confederate line.

Around three o'clock, the big siege guns behind the Union lines finally signaled Granger's corps to attack. The Army of the Cumberland did not rush out of the woods. As in their previous attack on Orchard Knob, the four divisions marched into the open field and formed into battle lines by brigades under eighty regimental battle flags. Bugles sounded, drums rolled, and the bands played as the four divisions formed their ranks as carefully as if they were on dress parade. General Thomas's training clearly showed.

A line of skirmishers went forward and was followed by a double line of infantry. The Union line stretched for 2 miles in a vast panorama.

The 24th moved forward in common time, with the officers and color sergeant in the lead. Then, to the beat of drums and the sound of bugles, they charged at a dead run toward the rifle pits three-quarters of a mile away. Shouting and cheering, the 24th wanted to be the first to hit the Confederate rifle pits at the base of the ridge.

The ridge came alive with flame as fifty Confederate cannon blazed and roared. Solid cannon balls arched high in the air, and again, the men saw each round fired from the moment it left the cannon's muzzle. The cannon balls plowed into the attacking Union troops; canister shells screamed overhead, bursting to spray hot pieces of iron down into the ranks.

The big Union siege guns in the Chattanooga forts thundered. Patches of acrid, dirty-white smoke from the black powder used in the guns filled the valley.

The enemy's rifle pits were ablaze. Little puffs of smoke drifted upward as the unmistakable sound of musket reports echoed through the valley.

A storm of bullets tore into the Union ranks, mortally wounding hundreds of men, but the Confederate volleys did not stop the charge. Amid the overwhelming noise of men yelling, horses screaming, muskets firing, and cannon shells bursting, the attack continued.

The Confederate defenders in the first line of rifle pits wavered. An unstoppable force of 23,000 blue-clad troops raced forward. Opposing that wave in the rifle pits at the base of the ridge were just 3,200 Confederate soldiers.

The Union line hit the rifle pits and broke through the barricades in several places. Some of the Confederates threw down their weapons and surrendered, while others scrambled up the side of the ridge, under heavy Union artillery fire, toward a second line of pits. On top of the ridge, Confederate soldiers watched helplessly as the rout developed; they could not fire to assist their comrades for fear of hitting them. The Union charge paused with the capture of the Confederate rifle pits at the base of the ridge. The bluecoats had captured their objective, and the mile-long dash had exhausted them.

Their respite was brief, however, for they soon discovered they were in an exposed position. From midway up the slope and crouched near the crest, the Confederates were shooting as fast as they could load and fire. The barrage was lethal.

The 24th Wisconsin scrambled for cover. Confederate artillery zeroed in on the Union position, and the shelling was brutal. The just-won trenches turned into death traps as Confederate infantry and artillery blazed away with devastating results.

Given the pride of the 24th Wisconsin, the men could not retreat. Although it appeared suicidal, the only answer was to attack the seemingly impregnable, 600-foot-high ridge. Several officers up and down the line leaped from the rifle pits and shouted, "Up the ridge!" Captain Edwin B. Parsons, Company K, jumped out of the pits with MacArthur right on his heel.[20]

Within seconds, the men of the 24th followed their leaders and leaped from the rifle pits to seek cover among the boulders and fallen trees. The 24th Wisconsin took the initiative for the entire Union line. "Our only hope was to charge the hill," Major Samuel F. Gray of the 49th Ohio observed later, "[and we] raced to the protection of the mountain side."[21]

Back on Orchard Knob, Grant was furious. He turned to Thomas and angrily demanded, "Who ordered those men up the ridge?"

Slowly shaking his head, Thomas replied, "I don't know. I did not." Turning to Granger, also on Orchard Knob with his staff, Thomas asked, "Did you order them up?"

"No," Granger replied. "They started up without orders. When those fellows get started, all hell can't stop them."[22]

Grant turned back to look at the ridge and stoically watched the battle. By this time, smoke (the infantry soldier's godsend before the era of smokeless gunpowder) had wrapped the mountainside and obstructed Grant's view. General Granger dispatched his chief of staff, Colonel Joseph Fullerton, to see what was happening. Leaping on a horse, Fullerton hurried to the front, where he discovered that neither General Wood nor General Sheridan had ordered the charge up the ridge. The men had done it on their own initiative, and it was too late to turn back. "I didn't order them up," said Sheridan, "but we are going to take the ridge." He then galloped off to personally lead his division.[23]

The Union attack was no longer a desperate charge. Several times, the men stopped to rest, taking cover behind tree stumps, rocks, or in the numerous ravines. The Union troops dashed from one natural obstruction to the next. Lieutenant MacArthur later wrote his father that "the men took advantage of all obstacles" as they advanced "steadily and surely toward the top." As they moved slowly up the side of the ridge, deadly volleys of musket fire were hurled at them every step of the way.[24]

A crude, unfinished second line of Confederate rifle pits halfway up the steep slope proved worthless for the defenders. The troops in the rifle pits retreated back up the slope.

The side of the ridge became half gray with the uniforms of the retreaters, then half blue with the pursuers. Now and then, the Confederates stopped to let loose a blast of musketry. For a few precious minutes, the defenders on top of the ridge could not fire at the attacking Union men without hitting their own comrades scrambling in front toward the peak. Confederate and Union artillery fire subsided as friend became intermingled with foe.[25]

The 24th Wisconsin broke up into little groups, small platoons of men all trying to keep their regimental color sergeant in sight. The formation was like a triangle, or wedge, with officers and color sergeants leading the way, followed by the rest of the men. Waving their regimental flags to rally the men, the color-bearers were easily identifiable and favorite Confederate targets. They dropped all over the field, with many regiments losing a half dozen. As one fell, a comrade would grab the flag to lead the charge.

The going was inconceivably rough. To climb the ridge on a calm, clear day would have been an accomplishment. In the face of the devastating Confederate fire, the ascent seemed impossible.

Halfway up the ridge, John Booth, the 24th Wisconsin's color sergeant, stumbled and dropped to his knees in exhaustion. MacArthur was next to Booth when he fell. He grabbed the flag, waved it high, and shouted, "24th Wisconsin!" as he charged. Fast on his feet, Little Mac was soon ahead of the entire Union line, the 24th's colors first in the race to the top.[26]

The Confederate defenders saw him and directed a withering fire of bullets toward the flag. As the regiment got closer to the top, they discovered that the defenders could not depress their artillery guns enough to fire on them. Bragg had placed his artillery on the geographical top of the ridge rather than the military crest—the topmost line from which the enemy could be seen and fired on. From the geographical peak, intervening ravines and gulleys hid the charging Union soldiers in many spots. The Confederates solved the problem by lighting the fuses on hundreds of canister shells and bowling them down the ridge.

Canisters exploded around MacArthur as he charged up the slope. A shell burst near him, knocked him to the ground, and blew his hat 20 feet away. The shrapnel tore through the regimental battle flag. Miraculously, he escaped with only a minor scratch. The flag was tattered, but still intact.

Without hesitation, MacArthur leaped back to his feet, waved the flag high, and again charged with the men of the 24th right behind him.[27]

It is possible that young Arthur MacArthur felt much like Teddy Roosevelt did later when he charged up San Juan Hill in the Spanish-American War. Roosevelt admitted that some "primeval force" drove him. In the heat of battle, he was aware of very little that was going on outside the orbit of his ears and sweat-fogged spectacles. "All men who feel any power of joy in battle," he wrote, "know what it is like when the wolf rises in the heart."[28]

When MacArthur reached the crest of the ridge, he leaped over the Confederate barricades, with a pistol in one hand and the 24th's battle flag in the other.

As the Union troops scrambled to the top of the ridge, the Confederate defenders broke and ran. There was no place on the narrow ridge where they could reform; therefore, they retreated down the eastern slope, which was almost as steep as the western.

MacArthur dashed forward and planted the 24th's battle flag directly in front of Bragg's old headquarters. Standing next to MacArthur, Sergeant Thomas Ford, Company H, pointed at the retreating Confederates and said, "That's a splendid sight." He shouted, "Chickamauga! Chickamauga!" at the retreating Confederates.[29]

The charge had lasted one hour and twenty-six minutes, and when it was over, the afternoon sun hung low on the horizon. "Union soldiers could hardly believe their stunning success," historian James McPherson observed. "When a student of the battle later commented to Grant that southern generals had considered the position impregnable, Grant replied with a wry smile: 'Well, it was impregnable.' Bragg himself wrote that 'no satisfactory excuse can possibly be given for the shameful conduct of our troops. ... The position was one which ought to have been held by a line of skirmishers.' "[30]

Although most men who participated in the attack later claimed they charged the ridge because they had no choice, Sergeant Ford admitted he had another motivation—he was hungry. At the time of the battle, the men were still on half rations. Ford hoped that if they captured the ridge, they would also capture some Confederate supplies. "The first thing I did after the rebels skedaddled," Ford declared, "was to grab a full haversack and jerk it off a wounded rebel captain's neck. I opened it and divided its contents with my comrades. It was saturated with the rebel captain's blood, but we ate it all the same."[31]

When Sheridan came galloping up on horseback, he shouted out, "Where's the 24th's color-bearer?" MacArthur stepped forward and proudly showed the general the tattered flag. Sheridan complimented him and the entire regiment for their bravery. The men clustered around cheering, then they good-naturedly called for a reward.

"How about some food, General?" Ford yelled. Some shouted for hardtack, some for sowbelly and some for beef, while others shouted for whiskey.

Sheridan raised his hat until silence prevailed. "Boys," he answered, "in less than two hours' time you will have all the hardtack, all the sowbelly and all the beef you want."

Sheridan kept his word. In less than two hours, Ford reported, "there were sixteen hundred head of cattle driven up on that ridge, and in an hour's time they were in the frying pan. You could see men as far as the eye could reach, several lines of them, with boxes of crackers on their shoulders." The moon was full and shining brightly that victorious evening, and "the boys all felt happy."[32]

It had been a glorious victory. Sheridan's and Wood's divisions captured 31 pieces of artillery, several thousand small arms, and 3,800 prisoners. However, their losses had also been sizable. In the hour-and-a-half assault, the two divisions lost 2,337 men killed and wounded, over 20 percent of their whole force. In comparison, Sherman's losses in two days of fighting were 1,697 killed and wounded. The 24th Wisconsin suffered 4 dead and 31 wounded out of their complement of about 150. Two of MacArthur's closest friends, the prolific letter writers of the regiment, died that day: Lieutenant Robert Chivas and Captain Howard Greene.[33]

Veterans and Civil War historians argued for decades over which Union flag first reached the crest of the ridge. Many proclaimed that several banners reached the top of the ridge simultaneously. The men of the 24th Wisconsin knew better— the flag carried by their Little Mac was the first on the crest. Viewing the battle from Grant's headquarters on Orchard Knob, Colonel Fullerton supported the 24th's contention. He wrote that although Union troops broke over the crest of the ridge at six different points almost simultaneously, the first banner sighted was the battle flag of the 24th Wisconsin near Bragg's headquarters.[34]

In the eyes of his comrades, MacArthur was the hero of the battle. Captain Parsons, commander of Company K, wrote Judge MacArthur, "Arthur was magnificent. He seems to be afraid of nothing. He'd fight a pack of tigers in a jungle." The judge glowed with pride.[35]

Major Baumbach, the regiment's commander, praised his young adjutant in his official report and later wrote:

> Among the many acts of personal intrepidity on that memorable occasion, none are worthy of higher commendation than that of young MacArthur, ... who seizing the Colors of his regiment at a critical moment, contributed materially to the general result. He was the most distinguished in action on a field where many in the regiment displayed conspicuous gallantry, worthy of highest praise.[36]

The MacArthur family legend later proclaimed that Sheridan said he was going to recommend Arthur for a congressional Medal of Honor, but the story is unlikely. In truth, the officers and men had never heard of the Medal of Honor, which had only recently been established.[37]

6

The Atlanta Campaign

THE 24TH WISCONSIN's victory celebration lasted only a few brief hours. After being issued one day's rations and more ammunition, they moved out to pursue Bragg's army around eleven that evening. It was a cold, moon-lit night. The regiment marched for 3 miles, picking up Confederate stragglers along the way. Around 3:00 A.M., Sheridan ordered a halt. The men rested, but most could not sleep because of the cold; they shivered in the predawn hours. When the sun rose, the 24th was on the march again. In the next two days, the Union army captured 6,100 Confederates, 40 artillery pieces, and over 7,000 rifles.

With Grant's army in hot pursuit, Bragg retreated south 12 miles to his supply depot at Chickamauga Station. He burned his supplies and continued his retreat. Grant halted the pursuit on Saturday, November 28, and dispatched Gordon Granger's corps of 23,000 men to relieve the siege at Knoxville, 85 miles northeast of Chattanooga. The 24th Wisconsin was part of Granger's corps.[1]

Marching hard through freezing rain, the corps made 10 miles the first day. They followed the course of the Tennessee River, which was swollen with rain. The following day, the weather improved, and the men foraged through the rolling farmlands of central Tennessee. As they recovered from their two months of starvation in Chattanooga, their appetites were huge, and they took what they wanted from a recent bountiful harvest. They liberated hams, corn, molasses, eggs, pork, liver, sweet potatoes, and even tenderloins from the farmers' houses and barns.[2]

When Granger's corps was still about 20 miles from Knoxville, word reached them that Confederate General Longstreet had withdrawn his corps from Knoxville and retreated northeast into the Cumberland Gap. He could not go south to rejoin Bragg because Grant's army blocked the way. The 24th Wisconsin reached the outskirts of Knoxville on December 7, and Sheridan's division paused a few weeks to rest and recuperate.

Shortly after reaching Knoxville, Carl Baumbach, the acting commander of the 24th Wisconsin, resigned his commission and returned to Milwaukee. For the next two months, either Captain Alva Philbrook or Captain Edwin Parsons would serve as the acting commander while the regiment waited for the return of Lieutenant Colonel Theodore West. Captured at Chickamauga in September, West had engineered a dramatic escape from a Confederate prisoner of war camp. In the interim, Parsons and Philbrook depended on Adjutant MacArthur to keep the regimental paperwork in order—they were company commanders, not staff officers.

In early January 1864, the 24th Wisconsin moved out with Sheridan's division to pursue and harass Longstreet, who had halted his retreat near Danridge, Tennessee, 75 miles northeast of Knoxville. The 24th Wisconsin left Knoxville and marched through the cold and wet winter days into the mountains of northeastern Tennessee. On January 14, they came into contact with Longstreet's rear guard at Blain's Cross Roads near Danridge. After a brief skirmish, Longstreet withdrew his army further into the mountains. For two weeks, the 24th Wisconsin remained near Danridge. Then they marched south to Loudon, Tennessee, 15 miles west of Knoxville, and went into winter camp.[3]

In early February, word reached the regiment that Lieutenant MacArthur had been promoted to major to fill the post vacated by Baumbach. Most of the officers felt the promotion was justified: MacArthur had performed the adjutant's job well, proven his courage in battle, and knew the regiment better than any other officer. But some of the senior captains, such as Parsons and Philbrook, grumbled about political influence. The judge denied the implication and proclaimed his son had fairly won the promotion. Colonel West, recuperating in Milwaukee after months in a prison camp, approved of MacArthur's promotion. Although only eighteen years old, Arthur was the logical choice. An experienced staff officer, he had won the respect of his comrades at Murfreesboro and Missionary Ridge. An informal vote revealed that the men of the 24th approved the promotion.[4]

As the regiment's commanding officer until West returned, MacArthur continued the 24th Wisconsin's training program as new recruits were sent to fill its ranks. Unlike most states, Wisconsin sent recruits to established regiments instead of forming new units. Although never at full strength, the 24th averaged about 300 men before a campaign. MacArthur drilled the recruits until they became an integral part of the regiment.

General Thomas, the commander of the Army of the Cumberland, remained a stickler for military detail. Stern and austere, he demanded absolute conformity to military rules and regulations. He ordered constant drills and repeatedly warned his officers that sloppy dress led to sloppy battlefield performance.

MacArthur agreed; throughout his career, he would regard Thomas as the model of the proper commander. While in command of the 24th, MacArthur drilled the regiment to perfection. Sheridan was impressed and assigned the regiment to be the division's provost guards. Stationed at Sheridan's headquarters, the 24th entertained visitors to the 2nd Division with well-performed dress parades. Following these parades, MacArthur met most of the generals in the Army of the Cumberland, a heady experience for an eighteen-year-old soldier. As reflected in

Major Arthur MacArthur, c. September 1864. (MacArthur Memorial Library, Ph-1552)

later letters of recommendation, the senior officers were duly impressed with the young man.[5]

In early March, Lincoln made a dramatic change in the command of the Union armies. Disappointed with the failure of commander after commander on the eastern front, Lincoln promoted Grant to lieutenant general, a revived three-star rank last held by George Washington, and placed him in command of all the armies of the Union.

On March 18, Grant left Nashville to take up his new position in Washington, D.C. The redheaded, grizzled, forty-four-year-old William Tecumseh Sherman,

"Uncle Billy" to his men, became the new commander of the Military Division of the Mississippi. Sherman's department had over 100,000 men, divided into three armies spread throughout Tennessee. The Army of the Ohio, with 14,000 men, was in Knoxville under a new commander, General Schofield; the Army of the Cumberland, with 60,000 men commanded by Thomas, was spread in garrison duty from Loudon down to Chattanooga; and the Army of the Tennessee—Sherman's favorite unit, under the command of his protégé General McPherson—had 25,000 men near Nashville.

When Grant reached Washington, he summoned Sheridan. Sheridan subsequently became a legend in the Union army as Grant's cavalry commander. The news that their Little Phil was departing for the eastern front saddened the 2nd Division, which gave him a grand party on March 22, the day before he left. The regimental bands played, and the officers danced with the local ladies.[6]

Brigadier General John Newton became the new commander of the 2nd Division. The 24th Wisconsin remained part of the 1st Brigade of the 2nd Division of the 4th Army Corps, now commanded by General Oliver O. Howard. The 1st Brigade also received a new commander, Brigadier General Nathan Kimball. The brigade had 2,500 officers and men divided into seven regiments, including the 24th Wisconsin. Newton, the 2nd Division's new commander, was apparently as impressed with the 24th Wisconsin as Sheridan had been. He retained the regiment as his headquarters guards.

Sherman spent March and April preparing his theater of operations for a major offensive, collecting a force of 100,000 men, 23,000 support animals, and 254 heavy artillery guns, which required tons of military equipment. Sherman's supply line ran from Cincinnati through Louisville to Nashville. Nashville itself became a vast Union storehouse. Warehouses and repair shops covered city blocks, and acres of land were used to stable the mules and horses. Sherman built blockhouses along the railroad from Nashville to Chattanooga and posted guards at every bridge and tunnel to protect his forward supply line.

In early April, Sherman began to concentrate his army near Chattanooga. Thomas's Army of the Cumberland was ordered to form near Ringgold, Georgia, 20 miles south of Chattanooga. At Loudon, 70 miles northeast of Chattanooga, the 24th Wisconsin broke winter camp on April 10 and began a leisurely march southwest through eastern Tennessee. The regiment stopped at Cleveland, Tennessee, 15 miles from Ringgold, on April 19 and made camp.

On April 21, Colonel West and many of the officers who had been home on leave rejoined the regiment. MacArthur arranged a rousing party to celebrate the colonel's return. West was a popular commander, and the men considered him "a gentleman and a gallant leader." West would continue the regiment's training exercises and hold dress parades almost every day. In the evenings, the officers often went to Catoosa Springs, a few miles away. A Georgia resort for the wealthy, the town had a hotel and several boarding-houses surrounded by magnificent mountain scenery.[7]

While Sherman mobilized his army near Chattanooga, Confederate forces concentrated 40 miles south at Dalton, Georgia. Bragg's retreat had halted there more by accident than by design, but it was an excellent area to defend. Dalton was 3 miles south of Rocky Face Ridge, the last gap in the mountains before the land leveled out into the gentle rolling hills of the north Georgia plains that led directly down to Atlanta, 100 miles farther south. Atlanta was Bragg's major supply base, and there was a railroad running from Dalton to Atlanta.

Bragg was never given the opportunity to defend Dalton. After years of controversy, Confederate president Jefferson Davis had lost confidence in Bragg following his disastrous defeat at Missionary Ridge. On December 27, 1863, Davis relieved him and appointed General Joseph E. Johnston to command the Confederate Army of Tennessee. Irascible, taciturn, and brilliant, Johnston was a superb military man. Older than most of the commanders in both armies, he had graduated from West Point in 1829. During the Mexican-American War, he led a regiment and was wounded five times. In the 1850s, he rose to the rank of brigadier general. When the Civil War began, Johnston opted for the Confederacy. After winning fame in battles around Richmond, he was appointed, in late 1862, to command all the Confederate armies operating in Tennessee and Mississippi.

Technically, Bragg had been one of Johnston's field commanders. The Confederate command structure was unclear, and Johnston's position was primarily that of an administrator rather than a grand strategist. He had little control over the department's field commanders, but when he returned to direct field command, he revitalized the Confederate Army of Tennessee.

Sherman was sorry to hear of the Confederate change in command, preferring to meet Bragg in battle rather than Johnston, who was a true artist of defensive strategy with few peers in either army. Sherman had tremendous respect for "Old Joe's" defensive skills.[8]

Johnston reorganized the Confederate army at Dalton, obtained new recruits, and collected supplies. By early May, his force numbered 37,652 infantrymen, 2,812 artillerymen with 112 guns, and 2,392 cavalrymen. He fortified the mountain passes north of Dalton and waited for the inevitable Union attack. Being outnumbered two to one by Sherman's army, his strategy was to prepare for an orderly retreat. Consequently, he had his people construct fortified positions along the rail line south toward Atlanta. He expected Sherman to attack his flanks, and he hoped that at some point as the Confederate troops retreated down the railroad to previously prepared positions, Sherman would blunder.

The Union strategy was broader. Grant, now in command of all the Union armies, consulted with his major field commanders, including General Benjamin F. Butler, commander of the Army of the James; General George G. Meade, commander of the Army of the Potomac; and General Sherman, commander of the Division of the Mississippi. They decided on a concerted military operation to destroy the Confederacy. As soon as weather permitted, all Union armies would take the offensive. Butler's army at Fort Monroe on Old Point Comfort, at the tip of the Virginia peninsula, was the extreme east, or left, edge; Meade's army near Washington, the center; and Sherman's army at Chattanooga, the right wing. The main objectives were to destroy Lee's Army of Northern Virginia, concentrated near Richmond, and Johnston's Army of Tennessee, concentrated near Dalton. Butler was to cross the James River and move against Richmond from the southeast. Meanwhile, Meade would cross the Rapidan River and attack Lee's army entrenched north of Richmond, and Sherman would attack Johnston and push him to and beyond Atlanta.

The 24th Wisconsin marched out of Cleveland on May 3. They were a small but disciplined veteran regiment. They reached Ringgold the next day and camped near the rest of the 1st Brigade.[9]

Two days later, Grant's plan was implemented. In the East, Grant's armies crossed the Rapidan and James Rivers to begin the Wilderness Campaign, the bloodiest offensive of the Civil War. Grant pounded Lee's army in battle after battle in a densely wooded marshland south of the Rapidan River. Both armies suffered heavy casualties.

In the West, Sherman marched his armies south from Ringgold to confront Johnston's troops. Three days later, Sherman's forces were before the heights of Rocky Face Ridge, where the Confederate army was entrenched. The ridge rose about 500 feet and extended south for 10 miles. Its perpendicular face presented a formidable wall.

Sherman halted before the fortification on May 9 and pondered his options. All day long, there was a constant exchange of artillery fire, and the sound of musketry rang up and down the line. Johnston, a defensive artist, had had six months to construct barricades and install gun placements that made his position almost unassailable (see Map 6.1).

Sherman had little stomach for direct frontal assaults, and more than most generals, he recognized that new weapons had changed the nature of war. Artillery could lob shells farther, and rifled-muskets made the classic military assault obsolete.[10] Sherman therefore opted for a flanking movement to threaten Johnston's supply line that ran south from Dalton to Atlanta. Using Thomas's Army of the Cumberland to keep Johnston on the defensive, he sent McPherson's Army of the Tennessee around the line to swoop down on Resaca, 18 miles south of Dalton. Johnston evacuated Rocky Face Ridge and fell back to Resaca on the night of May 12. The Army of the Cumberland pursued and skirmished with the rear guard of the Confederate army.[11]

Sherman's forces were near Resaca on May 14. Around two that afternoon, Newton's 2nd Division reconnoitered the Confederate line. As the advanced skirmishers of the division, the 24th Wisconsin met stiff resistance. MacArthur reported that the regiment was subjected to a "galling fire" of both artillery and small arms. The air was full of screeching shells and whizzing bullets. The ill-fated Colonel West, commander of the 24th, was wounded in the foot and evacuated from the field.[12]

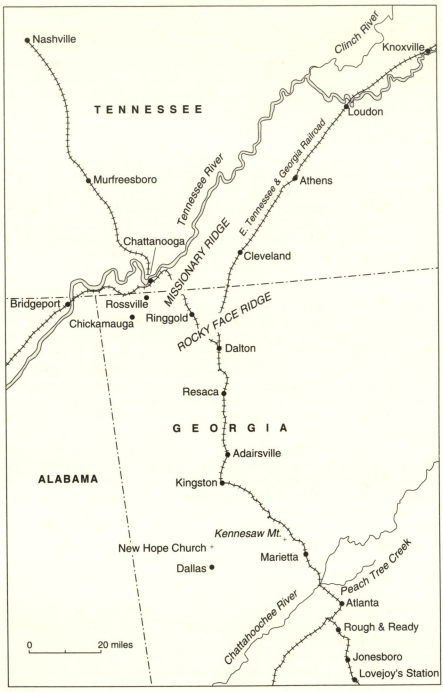

MAP 6.1 The Atlanta campaign

MacArthur was in command. Despite the new commander's youth, General Newton remarked that the 24th Wisconsin was in good hands and could take care of itself. Although still only eighteen, MacArthur was a veteran, and his company commanders were also experienced.

MacArthur withdrew the regiment from the forward position only after his men had expended all their ammunition. Before allowing the men to bed down for the night, he ordered the regiment to construct defensive barricades. The rolling hills north of Resaca offered little natural protection, and MacArthur expected a Confederate attack. He remembered Murfreesboro, where, with almost disastrous results, the 24th had not entrenched. This time, the barricades the 24th Wisconsin built were the envy of engineers. The men dug a trench and tossed the dirt to the front to built a parapet 4 to 6 feet high. Cutting trees, they placed a top log across the parapet to offer protection when they fired at any attacking enemy force. They dug a ditch in front of the earthworks and planted sharp wooden stakes to slow down a charge. They also cut the trees and brush for 100 yards in front of the breastworks to obtain a clear field of fire. In battle, one veteran observed, "experienced men ... always availed themselves of any shelter within reach. ... Only recruits and fools neglected the smallest shelter."[13]

Despite the hard work involved, the men of the regiment understood the need for defensive fortifications. While MacArthur was in command, the regiment never stopped, even for a few hours, without building barricades. Their leader had been in too many battles to be caught by a surprise attack. The well-constructed barricades saved the regiment from crippling casualties time and again in the next few months.

Early in the evening of May 14, MacArthur and Captain Parsons, commander of Company K, were up near the barricades talking quietly when a staff officer (named Lieutenant Sutherland, Parsons later remembered) appeared to check on the 24th's new commander. The three officers talked softly as they stared over the barricades at the Confederate campfires clearly visible less than 1 mile south. When Sutherland asked MacArthur about his hopes, dreams, and ambitions if he survived the war, MacArthur remarked that he intended to stay in the army and make the military his career. Sutherland nodded, teased the young major on his ambitions, then asked the burning question. "Major," he inquired, "suppose the Rebs down there should make a charge and attempt to capture this position? What would you do?"

"Fight like hell!" was MacArthur's quick reply. Sutherland left shortly afterward and reported MacArthur's answer to General Newton, who grinned, nodded, and left MacArthur in command of the 24th Wisconsin.[14]

MacArthur's chance to fight like hell occurred early the next morning. Johnston had decided to test Sherman's position, and around eight o'clock, the Confederates attacked. From behind their barricades, the 24th easily fended off the first attack. The Confederates attacked again. Private George A. Cooley, Company A, recorded in his diary that "the sounds of musketry and cannon rose all day."

The Confederate forces came within yards of the 24th Wisconsin's entrenchments but were finally repelled. Only with darkness did the battle end and silence descend over the field.[15]

Sherman began another flanking movement the next day to threaten the railroad behind the Confederate lines. He had no intention of wasting his army by attacking Johnston in fortified positions. Using the Army of the Cumberland as his battering ram in the center, Sherman sent the Army of the Ohio and the Army of the Tennessee sweeping east and west around the Confederate fortifications to attack Johnston's railroad. During the night of May 16, Johnston conducted another orderly retreat from Resaca and fell back 5 miles to new fortified positions at Adairsville.

With the 24th Wisconsin as the advance skirmish line, the Union army pursued. Two days later, the 24th caught up with Johnston at Adairsville and engaged in a firefight with the Confederates that lasted until long after sundown. In the forward position, the 24th was exposed to constant artillery and musket fire and suffered crippling casualties. By torchlight, they moved their wounded to a nearby field hospital. The 24th Wisconsin had over a 30 percent casualty rate that day, losing 58 men, killed or wounded.[16]

During the night, the Confederate army withdrew, and the next morning, the Union army passed through Adairsville and pursued the Confederates toward Kingston. General Thomas used Newton's 2nd Division as his forward line. Newton, in turn, used Kimball's 1st Brigade as his advance force, and Kimball used the 24th Wisconsin as his point regiment. Major MacArthur excelled at reconnaissance, and the 24th seldom lost as many men as other regiments when in the exposed position at the front of the entire army.[17]

The 24th marched, skirmished with Johnston's rear guards, then camped behind barricades. The next day, they moved forward 2 or 3 miles, engaged in sporadic fire with rebel troops, and then constructed breastworks for the night. They repeated the process for three more days, and each day, the regiment lost more men.[18]

The weather turned nasty: It began to rain, and the rain continued for seventeen straight days. Supply wagons bogged down on the roads, which were ankle deep in mud.

Life for the men of the 24th was miserable. It was impossible to keep dry: The rain soaked their clothing, and their boots constantly filled with water. They were plastered with sticky, red mud at the end of each day. To add to their discomfort, it was hot and muggy. Even when not drenched by rain, they were soaked by their own perspiration. At night, it was hard to start campfires, and sleeping was difficult with only their shelter tents to ward off the rain.[19]

Johnston moved back through Kingston to New Hope Church, 4 miles north of Dallas, Georgia, where he fortified his position and waited. The 24th reached the outskirts of town on May 25, constructed their barricades, and began once more to feel out the Confederate position.

For eleven days, Sherman and Johnston sparred near New Hope Church. The muddy roads made quick flanking movements impossible, and as Sherman waited for the weather to improve, constant skirmishes occurred up and down the line. The 24th Wisconsin was slowly being depleted, losing more men in combat each day. Sickness also continued to take its toll. The number of officers with the regiment shrank from a high of 34 down to 5, and the roster of enlisted men shrank from over 300 to less than 100.[20]

Johnston withdrew from New Hope during the night of Saturday, June 4. The next morning, the 24th woke to silence for the first time in ten days. The eleven-day battle had devastated the area around New Hope. Private Cooley wrote in his diary that "large trees, ten, twelve, and fourteen feet high, some two feet through, were broken and shot off as though made of glass."[21]

Sherman rested his army for five days. News from the eastern front described a new type of warfare, one of attrition, initiated against Lee's Army of Northern Virginia. From May through June, Grant used the Union's superior numbers to hammer Lee's forces. Over these two months, Union casualties totaled 65,000 killed, wounded, or missing to Confederate losses of 35,000, but Grant had the manpower to smother Lee's smaller army with sheer numbers. Clearly, the war of attrition favored Grant.[22]

Sherman's army also had superior numbers, and he resumed his pursuit of Johnston's Army of Tennessee on June 10. Johnston retreated slowly south to a formidable defensive position on top of Kennesaw Mountain. Between Dalton, where the campaign began, and Kennesaw, the terrain consisted of rolling hills and farmland interspersed with cedar woods. Just north of Marietta, Georgia, Kennesaw Mountain rose about 1,000 feet above the surrounding countryside and offered Johnston an ideal defensive position. From Kennesaw's peak, the city of Atlanta, 20 miles south, was clearly visible. Johnston fortified the top and sides of the mountain and placed his reserve forces in Marietta, 5 miles to the south.[23]

Sherman's forces reached the base of Kennesaw Mountain on June 19. For the next seven days, there was not an hour or even a minute when the two armies were not engaged somewhere along the 10-mile front. Union artillery batteries exchanged fire with the enemy atop Kennesaw Mountain, and skirmishers were constantly in contact. Continuous rain and muddy roads made any flanking movement difficult.

On Wednesday morning, June 24, General Kimball ordered the 24th Wisconsin to reconnoiter the Confederate positions on the south face of Kennesaw Mountain. Going up the side of the mountain, Major MacArthur was struck in the wrist by a musket ball, but the wound was a minor one, and he continued to lead the regiment in its forward reconnaissance. The regiment forced the Confederate pickets back up the hill, but as the 24th pursued, they found themselves encircled and attacked from all sides. The enemy troops were dug in, and their rifle pits covered the side of the mountain. Moreover, fallen timbers and traps created impassable barriers. When the Confederate artillery zeroed in on the regiment, MacArthur ordered a retreat.[24]

From hidden rifle pits, rebel sharpshooters harassed the regiment as it withdrew. A musket ball struck MacArthur in the chest and bowled him over. He lay stunned on the ground while the men stared in shock. MacArthur had led a charmed life; now the regiment thought their young commander was dead.

They were wrong. In minutes, MacArthur was back on his feet, wounded but still able to conduct an orderly retreat. Leaving behind 25 dead and wounded comrades, the 24th finally reached the base of the mountain and reentered Union lines.[25]

MacArthur hurried to Kimball's 1st Brigade headquarters to submit a report. After describing the strength of Confederate fortifications and reporting the loss of his men, MacArthur strongly recommended that Kennesaw Mountain be flanked. Kimball praised him for his fine leadership on the dangerous reconnaissance mission, but the decision to attack or flank was General Sherman's.

When he returned to the regiment, MacArthur's wounds were examined by the surgeon. The wrist wound was minor, but the chest wound was more serious; there was a musket ball embedded just under the skin, right over his heart. He had not been killed because he was carrying some letters from his father in his jacket pocket, and the letters acted as a cushion against a musket ball that had almost been spent. Although the wound was painful, MacArthur refused to relinquish his command.[26]

Around midnight, the regiment was relieved and sent to the rear to recoup. A number of officers and men who had been slightly wounded in earlier engagements returned to the 24th the next day. Even with reinforcements, however, the regiment numbered less than 125 men.

They rested behind the line most of the day, but around three in the afternoon, MacArthur received orders to return his regiment to the front line. Kimball wanted the 24th and his other experienced regiments on the front for an impending attack.

For two months, Sherman had flanked again and again to avoid costly frontal attacks. To keep Johnston off balance, Sherman decided that a frontal assault, even one doomed to fail, was necessary. Over General Thomas's objection, an attack was ordered for the morning of June 27. As usual, Sherman used the Army of the Cumberland as his battering ram and spared his beloved Army of the Tennessee, or so it seemed to some of the men in the 24th. Recognizing the impending danger, none of the men had any desire to charge a fortified position. They had, after all, been at Murfreesboro and Chattanooga.

At 8:30 that Monday morning, the Army of the Cumberland charged up the heavily timbered slope of Kennesaw Mountain, with the 24th Wisconsin in the lead. For two and a half hours, they struggled up the side of the mountain. Hitting one Confederate defensive position after another, the 24th was subjected to heavy artillery and musket fire. They lost 1 officer and 8 enlisted men before capturing the first line of Confederate rifle pits.

The other Union regiments behind the 24th wavered, then withdrew down the side of the mountain. The 24th then slowly retreated to the protection of the Union barricades.

The men grumbled: To attack fortified positions was a stupid waste of manpower. In the two-and-a-half-hour battle, the Army of the Cumberland lost over 3,000 men; Confederate losses were 600 to 700.

The 24th was placed on the forward picket line, and during the night, they lost 3 more men in firefights with Confederate skirmishers. Fortunately, they also received some reinforcements as more of the men wounded in May returned to the regiment.[27]

The next day, the battlefront quieted down for the first time in a month. Sherman was unwilling to renew the attack; instead, he waited patiently for the rains to end and for the roads to dry.

For the next few days, the men of both armies relaxed, and the 24th Wisconsin's pickets worked out an agreement with the Confederate pickets in their immediate front—"Don't shoot!"

When the weather improved, the men sunned themselves on their breastworks and socialized with the "rebs." Combat veterans from both sides felt a paradoxical friendship for men of the opposing forces, with whom they had more in common than with the civilians at home. When General Thomas learned of the informal truce, a staff officer was sent out to investigate. He then ordered the regiment to open fire on the Confederate pickets. MacArthur sent out an officer to tell the rebs that the truce was over, and shortly afterward, the 24th fired a few shots to obey their orders, but no one really tried to hit the enemy pickets.[28]

When the rain ended on July 2, Sherman returned to his flanking movements. He sent the Army of the Tennessee wide around the Confederate defenses to threaten Johnston's supply base at Marietta. Realizing once more that he could not protect his railroad line with his smaller army, Johnston withdrew south from Kennesaw Mountain to Marietta.

Sherman's boys were in hot pursuit. Johnston retreated through Marietta south to the Chattahoochee River, only 5 miles north of Atlanta, where he had prepared additional fortifications. He crossed the river and burned all the bridges.

When Sherman and his army reached the Chattahoochee on July 5, he ordered his engineers to construct pontoon bridges while his forces rested.

The 24th rushed madly for the river for their first bath in two months. The day was hot and humid, and the river water was delightfully clean and cool. While the engineers laid pontoon bridges, thousands of naked men bathed and enjoyed the sun on the banks of the river.

For eight days, there was a lull in the fighting. The men washed their clothes, played cards, and cooked hot meals. While on the march, they had eaten hardtack and strips of raw pork sprinkled with brown sugar. Now, around campfires, they pounded the hardtack into flour to make griddle cakes. The crumbs were fried in pork fat, seasoned, and added to their "hell fire stew." Beans were thrown into an iron pot, covered with pork fat, and sunk in a pit of coals to bake all night; at dawn, the men lifted the kettle out of the fire with their bayonets. They ate the pork and beans for breakfast, lunch, and dinner.[29]

On July 12, Sherman sent McPherson's Army of the Tennessee east, up the north bank of the Chattahoochee River, and Schofield's Army of the Ohio west, down the river to swing wide of Johnston's position. Sherman kept Thomas's 60,000-man army before the Confederate forces to prevent Johnston from reinforcing his flanks. Once again, Johnston withdrew; he retreated south 2 miles to a new line at Peach Tree Creek, only 3 miles north of Atlanta.

The citizens of Atlanta demanded that Johnston stand and fight to stop Sherman's invasion. Johnston's reply was that his intent was to save an army, not a city. This answer was unacceptable. Atlanta was a symbol of the Confederacy in the West, much like Richmond was in the East. Its foundries, ammunition plants, warehouses, and railroad links were glorified in the Southern press. The loss of the city to Sherman would be a devastating blow to the Confederacy.[30]

On July 17, Confederate president Davis relieved Johnston of command and named General John Bell Hood as his replacement. Sherman was overjoyed. Johnston had conducted a brilliant retreat from Dalton to Peach Tree Creek, and Sherman knew that a lesser general would have had his smaller army trapped a half dozen times. In Sherman's opinion, Hood was a lesser general.[31]

Only thirty-three years old, Hood had achieved a reputation as a fighter in Lee's Army of Northern Virginia as he rose from company to brigade to division commander. At Gettysburg, he was wounded in the left arm, paralyzing it for the rest of his life. After sick leave, he was sent to Bragg in Tennessee; as a corps commander, his boldness there had contributed to the Confederate victory at Chickamauga, where he was wounded once again. A bullet struck him in the right thigh, and his leg was amputated. But as soon as the stump healed, Hood returned to active duty on crutches. To ride a horse, he had to be strapped to the saddle.

Sherman's three army commanders knew Hood intimately. McPherson and Schofield had been at West Point with him in the class of 1853. While McPherson had been first in the class and Schofield seventh, Hood had graduated forty-fourth in a class of fifty-two. Furthermore, Thomas had served with Hood in Texas before the war. McPherson, Schofield, and Thomas agreed that Hood was rash, erratic, and headstrong. In their opinion, he would attack. Sherman hoped so, for he was positive that Hood would suffer serious losses in the process.[32]

Sherman ordered that Union skirmishers be sent beyond the barricades to warn of any Confederate troop movement. General Kimball selected MacArthur's 24th Wisconsin as his forward reconnaissance team. On the morning of July 20, the 24th was several hundred yards beyond the Union barricades when their forward skirmishers reported that Hood's forces were advancing. Sending a runner back to Kimball, MacArthur remained with a dozen men as the rest of the regiment fell back about 200 yards. They established a defensive position to cover the forward line as it fell back; then the process was repeated. In good formation and without the loss of a single man, the 24th reentered the Union lines.[33]

Hood's first attack was repelled, but he was obstinate and charged six more times that day. Each time, his attack was repulsed. The Confederates lost a staggering 4,796 men to the Union's 1,710.

The next day, Hood retreated south to his main defensive line, which surrounded the city of Atlanta. Sherman's army rapidly followed. Believing he saw an opportunity, Hood attacked again on Saturday, July 22, but again he was repulsed with severe losses—8,499 to the Union's 3,641. The Union's prime loss was the death of the brilliant McPherson, Sherman and Grant's protégé.

Sherman's forces formed a half circle to the north of Atlanta, constructed breastworks, and placed the city under siege. The weather was hot and humid.

For the next few days, the two armies skirmished. The thunder of Sherman's 223 artillery guns sounded almost constantly as he bombarded the city that he considered a military installation rather than a civilian center. The "entire South, man, woman and child is against us, armed and determined," he observed. As long as the citizens of Atlanta remained in rebellion, they were enemies of the Union, and as enemies, they risked annihilation. "A people who will persevere in war beyond a certain limit ought to know the consequences. Many, many people with less pertinacity have been wiped out of national existence." "The cost of the war," Sherman concluded, was "not chargeable to us, but to those who made the war." The rebels "had forced us into war, and … deserved all they got and more."[34]

Sherman's engineers repaired the railroad all the way back to Nashville, and supplies and reinforcements soon rolled into the Union camps surrounding Atlanta. Each day, Sherman's army became stronger while the Confederate forces in Atlanta slowly weakened.

Hood tried to break the siege on July 28 when he again ordered his battered army to attack. It was a dismal defeat for the Confederates, as Hood lost 4,632 men to Sherman's 700. His attacks against Sherman's fortified positions failed time after time, but Hood refused to learn the lesson. In a mere ten days after assuming command, he had lost 18,000 men killed and wounded, more than Johnston had lost in three months. With desertions, Hood's army shrank to less than 30,000 men while Sherman's army, through constant reinforcements, still numbered almost 100,000. Hood could not sustain any more losses and still defend the city.

During the siege, Sherman promoted General Oliver Howard, commander of Thomas's 4th Corps, to command the Army of the Tennessee. General David S. Stanley became the new commander of the 4th Corps. General Kimball was promoted to command a division, and Colonel Emerson Opdycke became the new commander of the 1st Brigade. Only thirty-four, Opdycke was a veteran officer who had participated in the bloody battle of Shiloh; he had led a brigade for almost a year. The 1st Brigade had 1,143 men divided into seven regiments: the 24th Wisconsin, the 15th Missouri, and five Illinois regiments (the 36th, 44th, 73rd, 74th, and 88th). Like Kimball, Opdycke used the 24th Wisconsin as his reconnaissance unit; the men were sent out daily to test Confederate defensive positions.[35]

Gradually, Sherman tightened his siege. On August 25, he sent elements of the 1st, 2nd, and 3rd Divisions of the 4th Corps, including Opdycke's 1st Brigade and the 24th Wisconsin, west into the interior. They marched beyond Hood's defenses and then turned south. After seven days' march, they struck the Macon railroad line 20 miles southwest of Atlanta at a train station called Rough and Ready. It was Thursday morning, September 1. Hood's only remaining supply line was a railroad that ran southeast from Atlanta to Savannah, and that line was also threatened.

With the 24th Wisconsin in the lead, the Union forces moved southeast down the line and ripped up the rails. In the late afternoon, they struck a Confederate force entrenched at Jonesboro.

Opdycke's brigade was ordered to oust the Confederate forces. He divided his force into three lines for an attack. The first line was composed of the 24th Wisconsin on the left and the 44th Illinois on the right. With the other five regiments formed 300 yards behind the first line, the 24th Wisconsin and the 44th Illinois attacked across an open field and struck the Confederate forward pickets entrenched in a stretch of cedars. The pickets retreated.

MacArthur moved the 24th Wisconsin through the woods without breaking formation and entered the next field, beyond which was the Confederate main line, protected by more trees. It was almost dark, but Opdycke ordered the 24th to press on. Charging across the field, they struck the Confederate barricades, with the entire brigade quickly coming up to support them. After a brief but stiff defense, the smaller Confederate force withdrew under the cover of darkness. The 24th Wisconsin repaired the enemy barricades before they settled down for the night.

The Union flanking force had accomplished its task. With his supply line cut, Hood abandoned Atlanta during the night. He set fire to all military supplies his army could not carry. Twenty-six miles away, outside Jonesboro, the 24th Wisconsin heard the resulting massive explosion. Fires engulfed Atlanta and lit up the night sky. Hood's depleted army retreated south, then west, with Sherman in hot pursuit. The Confederate force established a new line at Lovejoy's Station near Macon, a few miles south of Jonesboro.

The next morning, the 24th Wisconsin was up at four o'clock and on the march by daylight. In the early light, they marched through Jonesboro as Confederate citizens stared in frozen silence. Opdycke ordered the regimental bands to play and the color sergeants to unfurl their flags. In parade step, the brigade passed through the town and continued for about 4 miles until they reached Hood's new forward defensive line. After a brief testing attack, the brigade constructed barricades and waited for Sherman's orders.

Sherman's goal had been achieved: Atlanta was in Union hands. Hood had fled with his army in tatters, his men starving and undersupplied. In two months, the Confederate Army of Tennessee had shrunk from over 60,000 men to less than 23,000. Sherman decided not to expend his energies chasing Hood. He had other plans now that Atlanta was in his hands, but first, his army needed to be rested and reinforced.

For four days, the 24th Wisconsin remained behind the barricades near Lovejoy's Station. Late in the afternoon of September 5, MacArthur received orders to march the regiment to Atlanta. Traveling slowly, the fatigued troops took three days to march the 30 miles to the city.

Around noon on Thursday, September 8, MacArthur led the 24th into Atlanta. As they marched through the principal streets in parade formation, they saw the damage inflicted on the city during the six weeks of Union bombardment.

The 24th camped near the railroad station. Debris littered the area. When Hood had set fire to his military supplies, the explosion had blown railroad cars all over the area near the depot. According to Private Cooley, "the ground was covered with shells, musket balls and old iron."[36]

The men of the 24th Wisconsin were bone-weary and tried to relax. To celebrate the capture of Atlanta, Sherman approved a ration of whiskey for the men. In the 112-day campaign ending in the capture of Atlanta, the 24th had marched over 200 miles, fought thirteen major battles, and engaged in dozens of skirmishes. A total of 3 officers and 21 enlisted men had been killed, 5 officers and 71 enlisted men had been wounded, and 3 men were missing in action. Illness had also taken its toll. Even with replacements and the return of some of the wounded, the regiment had only 125 men on the active roster.[37]

Sherman rested his army as he prepared for a new, dramatic campaign. The timing was fortunate for MacArthur. The mail had brought the sad news that his mother, ill for years, had become sicker, and his father felt her older son should visit her.

7

The Battle for Franklin

AURELIA BELCHER MACARTHUR was only forty-five years old in 1864. The illness she suffered after the birth of her second son, Frank, in 1853 might today be diagnosed as postnatal syndrome, caused by a hormonal imbalance. But in the 1850s, the diagnosis was a mental breakdown, and the doctors recommended that she be sent back to her family in Chicopee, where she might recuperate. Judge MacArthur accepted the diagnosis and the recommended treatment.

In Chicopee, Aurelia's condition apparently did not improve, and she was eventually placed in a sanatorium in Northampton, a town a few miles north of Chicopee. The Belchers perhaps blamed the judge for Aurelia's breakdown. In any case, there are no records of any contact between the Belchers and the judge's children: Arthur and Frank never knew the Belcher side of the family.[1]

The judge remained in Milwaukee, where he prospered and became a respected man in the community. Arthur and Frank's mother was seldom mentioned around the dinner table, and though Milwaukee newspapers gave prominent coverage to all the judge's political and social activities, they never mentioned his wife.[2]

In September 1864, Aurelia MacArthur's condition worsened, and Dr. Henry Fuller, the sanatorium director, recommended that Major MacArthur visit his mother. She had fixated on her soldier-son and had anxiety attacks about his death or maiming in the war. Fuller suggested that a visit by the major might ease his mother's mind.[3]

On September 13, MacArthur was granted a month's leave to visit his mother. He probably left the regiment reluctantly—the "boys" of the 24th Wisconsin were his family now. Besides, the war had changed him from an adolescent boy to a man who, in later wars, would be described as having the thousand-yard stare. He had seen more death in two years than most souls would have seen in a thousand lifetimes. The cumulative effect of these encounters with injury and death made the horrid sights of the dead on the battlefield "horrid no longer," as historian Gerald Linderman observed in *Embattled Courage*.[4]

Major MacArthur reached Northampton in mid-September, where he joined his father and brother in visiting his mother at the sanatorium. Although he remained in Northampton for two weeks, his mother's condition did not improve. With his month's leave almost expired, he left Northampton for a brief visit to Milwaukee before returning to his regiment in early October.[5]

While Arthur was on leave, the 24th Wisconsin was transferred from Atlanta to Chattanooga. Veterans returning from sick leave and new recruits restored the strength of the regiment to 250 enlisted men and 16 officers. Every few days, the regiment went on patrol into the countryside to discourage marauding Confederate cavalry units. As the weather turned colder each day, the 24th made preparations to winter in Chattanooga.[6]

Major MacArthur and the other veterans hoped the war was over for the 24th Wisconsin. They had no more romantic illusions about combat. Sherman accurately expressed their feelings when he wrote a St. Louis friend, "I confess without shame [that] I am tired ... of war. Its glory is all moonshine. Even success, the most brilliant is over dead and mangled bodies. ... Only those who have not heard a shot, nor heard the shrills & groans of the wounded & lacerated (friend or foe) ... cry aloud for more blood & more vengeance [and] more desolation."[7]

The soldiers talked often about the upcoming presidential elections. Only nineteen years old, MacArthur could not vote, but he probably enjoyed debating the issues with the other officers. Normally shy around civilians, MacArthur was at ease with the 24th Wisconsin. The soldier, as one Civil War veteran observed, "has to look for happiness in the kindness and good will of his comrades. Their joys and sorrows are his; he learns to look upon them as brothers; there is no sacrifice that he will not make for them; no trouble that he will not cheerfully take. Fellowship becomes almost a religion." "In all wars," a military historian noted, "there is in units subjected to rigorous campaigning and suffering high casualties a propensity for shrinking circles of survivors to strengthen their ties—'the camaraderie of misery,' Ernie Pyle called it."[8]

In the camp debates, most of the men favored President Lincoln, who was running on a platform to continue the war until the Union was reunited. The Democrats nominated General McClellan, a war hero and former commander of the Army of the Potomac, who, like MacArthur, was affectionately referred to as "Little Mac" by his men. The Democrats were confident that anti-Lincoln sentiment was strong throughout the North and adopted an antiwar plank calling for a cease-fire and negotiations to end the war. The Republicans branded the Democrats "copperheads." McClellan personally rejected his party's antiwar plank, and many Democrats hoped they would win voters on both sides of the issue.

The election results in early November showed that Lincoln received over 55 percent of the popular vote, which translated into 212 electoral votes to McClellan's 21. The men of the 24th believed it was Sherman's capture of Atlanta in September that had swung the election to Lincoln.[9]

The war in the West was not yet over. Sherman had triumphed in invading Georgia and capturing Atlanta, but his army was now deep in Confederate territory and surrounded by hostile citizens.

After losing Atlanta, Hood reformed his broken army 100 miles southwest of Nashville at Decatur, Alabama. A visit by President Jefferson Davis revitalized Hood, who laid plans for a new offensive. Because of the overwhelming strength of Sherman's forces, Hood could not recapture Atlanta or Chattanooga, but he could harass the Union supply line that stretched from Atlanta north to Chattanooga and then to Nashville. By threatening and, with luck, even breaking the supply route, Hood hoped to force Sherman to withdraw. Hood's cavalry raided north into Tennessee, attacked small garrisons, tore up railroad track, and burned minor supply depots.

The Confederate cavalry raids irritated but did not frighten Sherman, who had no intention of playing cat and mouse with Hood. Indeed, he regarded his opponent as a nuisance, not a threat. Sherman had other plans. He was convinced the way to end the war was to send a Union force marching through Georgia to cut a path from Atlanta to Savannah on the Atlantic Ocean. Sherman expected to lead the Union forces. Once he reached Savannah, he could turn his army north toward Richmond. With Grant attacking Richmond from the north and Sherman from the south, Lee's army would be trapped and annihilated. Sherman submitted his plan to Lincoln and Grant who, albeit reluctantly, approved the plan. Sherman was to take his beloved Army of the Tennessee, with some 60,000 men, and march through Georgia from Atlanta to Savannah. General Thomas would remain behind with the Army of the Cumberland to protect southern Tennessee from an invasion by Hood.

Thomas protested. Hood's Confederate Army of Tennessee still numbered 40,000 to 45,000 men, yet Sherman proposed to leave Thomas with General Stanley's 4th Corps of 12,000 men, of which the 24th Wisconsin was part, and General Schofield's 23rd Corps of 10,000. Although Thomas would have another 70,000 men under his command, the troops were spread over 200 miles in small garrisons to protect the towns, railroads, and supply depots from Atlanta north to Nashville. The Union supply line was vulnerable to Confederate cavalry raids, and the area was too vast for a Union mobile force of 22,000 men to patrol and defend (see Map 7.1).

Sherman acknowledged the problem. He wrote Grant that it would be impossible for Thomas to protect the railroad from Atlanta to Nashville "now that Hood, Forrest, and Wheeler, and the whole batch of devils, are turned loose without home or habitation."[10] Sherman estimated that Thomas would lose 1,000 men a month protecting the railroad lines. He suggested that Grant allow Thomas to abandon Atlanta and concentrate his forces around Nashville. Sherman had never intended to occupy Atlanta permanently. The goal of the summer campaign had been to destroy the Confederate supply base, and Sherman now had no interest in holding onto the city. In the West, battles were fought for strategic reasons, not for a particular city such as Richmond. Moreover, cities like Nashville and Knoxville were strategically significant, but Atlanta was not. If Thomas concentrated his 90,000 men at Nashville, his army would vastly outnumber Hood's. Thomas,

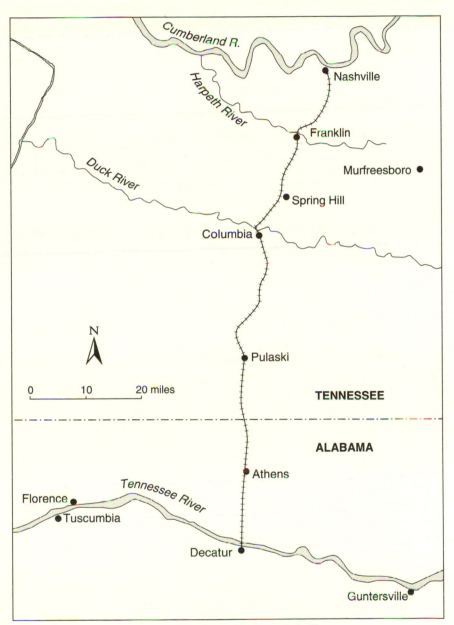

MAP 7.1 Hood's approach to Nashville

the "Rock of Chickamauga," was a master of defensive tactics. If Hood attacked Nashville, it was inconceivable that he could capture any position defended by Thomas. All the Union general needed was time to bring his forces together. Grant agreed, and Thomas returned to Nashville to begin preparations for its defense.

Cavalry reports indicated that Hood was mobilizing his army 100 miles southwest of Nashville at Decatur, Alabama. In late October, Thomas sent his mobile forces to Pulaski, Tennessee, a few miles north of Decatur, to slow Hood's advance. Stanley's 4th Corps left Chattanooga and arrived in Pulaski on October 26. The 24th Wisconsin was part of Stanley's 2nd Division, now commanded by General George D. Wagner. The thirty-five-year-old Wagner had commanded a division since early 1863 and was a veteran of Murfreesboro, Chattanooga, and the Atlanta campaign. His division had around 3,000 men, divided into nineteen regiments organized in three brigades. The 24th Wisconsin was in the 1st Brigade, still commanded by the fiery Colonel Opdycke.[11]

While in Pulaski, Arthur received news that his mother had died on November 10, at the age of forty-six, in the sanatorium in Northampton. The death certificate proclaimed the cause of death was insanity. She was buried in the Belcher family plot in East Street Cemetery in Chicopee. Although his mother's death probably saddened Arthur, there is no way to document his reaction.[12]

Schofield's 23rd Corps, composed of 10,000 men, arrived in Pulaski on November 14. As the ranking officer, Schofield assumed command of the combined Union forces. On the same day, Sherman burned the rest of Atlanta, abandoned the city, and began his march through Georgia to the sea.

As Sherman's army disappeared into the depths of the Confederacy, Hood's response was predictable. He had a plan even more grandiose than Sherman's. He would attack Schofield in Pulaski, destroy or capture his army, then march on Nashville and capture that city and all its supplies. If Hood captured Nashville, Sherman would be forced to return to defend northern Tennessee and southern Kentucky. When Sherman came charging back, Hood intended to march east to Knoxville, capture that city with its stockpile of Union equipment, and then march through the Cumberland Gap to join Lee's army near Richmond.

On November 15, Union cavalry reported that Hood's army was on the move and headed for Pulaski. The advancing army numbered 45,000 men to Schofield's force of 22,000, but Schofield did not panic even though he was outnumbered two to one. He was a calm, methodical man, representative of his middle-class New York background. A solid administrator, he looked like a businessman in uniform. Schofield's orders were to slow Hood's advance and give Thomas time to concentrate Union forces around Nashville. Schofield planned to skirmish with the Confederate army while he slowly retreated up the turnpike that ran from Pulaski to Nashville, a distance of about 60 miles.

Hood's advance columns reached Lawrenceburg, a small town 16 miles west of Pulaski, on November 22. Meanwhile, Schofield slowly began the Union withdrawal from Pulaski. He refused to leave anything behind, and his supply train of 800 wagons stretched for miles. It was extremely cold for southern Tennessee, and ice covered the turnpike and made rapid military movements impossible.

The Union rear guard fought several skirmishes with advancing Confederate units, but the cold weather also prevented Hood from moving rapidly. The countryside was rolling hills, not severe mountains, and most of it was cleared farmland much like that encountered around Murfreesboro. Any movement off the roads bogged down in muddy and frozen fields.

There were two critical points on the turnpike along the withdrawal route— Columbia and Franklin. At both points, there were major rivers with bridges that were essential to secure if Schofield was to keep his artillery and wagon train intact. Columbia was a small town on the Duck River about 22 miles north of Pulaski. Both the Columbia Pike and the Decatur-Nashville railroad crossed the Duck River at Columbia. Some 20 miles farther north on the turnpike and railroad was the small town of Franklin, located on the Harpeth River. Franklin was less than 20 miles south of Nashville and only a few miles west of Murfreesboro.

Schofield ordered Wagner's 2nd Division to move as rapidly as possible to Columbia to secure the bridges over the Duck River. Wagner then sent Colonel Opdycke's brigade forward as his advance line. The brigade, including the 24th Wisconsin, was a veteran outfit not likely to panic in an emergency, and its seven regiments had been together since May 1863. Led by the best brigade commander in Stanley's corps, the troops worked well as a team. Further, the brigade had marched and fought over the entire area in the previous two years.[13]

Opdycke's brigade arrived at Columbia early on the morning of November 24, just in time to prevent a Confederate cavalry unit from capturing the town. The brigade threw up breastworks and exchanged musket fire with the Confederate cavalry until the rest of Stanley's corps arrived.

Schofield's corps brought up the rear and arrived in Columbia the next morning. The combined Union forces crossed the Duck River and burned the bridges behind them. On the north bank of the river, Schofield constructed barricades and waited for Hood. His orders were to slow Hood's advance without getting into a major battle. In Nashville, General Thomas was still collecting his forces and needed at least two more weeks before he would be ready to take the offensive.

Schofield waited almost too long in Columbia. A dramatic change in the weather occurred on November 29, as the cold, freezing rain and hail stopped and sunny weather returned. Indian summer had begun in Tennessee. The good weather allowed Hood's cavalry greater mobility, and they discovered a number of alternate fords across the Duck River. Confederate advance units raced toward Spring Hill, the next small town on the turnpike about 12 miles north of Columbia.

Early that morning, Stanley's corps left Columbia and marched north toward Spring Hill to secure the town for the Union retreat. Around 11:30, while still 2 miles from Spring Hill, Stanley learned that a Confederate force was in his front. He ordered Wagner's division, with Opdycke's brigade in the lead, to proceed double-quick toward Spring Hill. Once again, Opdycke's unit arrived just in time to prevent the Confederate cavalry from capturing the town. The brigade engaged in a fierce firefight with the advance Confederate units as Wagner brought up his entire division.

Hood had almost succeeded. Crossing the Duck River, his troops had marched through the open fields and had flanked Schofield's army. Hood had pushed his men to the limit to capture Spring Hill, but when his advance forces reached Spring Hill and encountered stiff resistance, he believed he had failed. In reality, only Wagner's division held the town. If Hood had attacked, he might have delivered a crushing defeat, and perhaps his grandiose scheme to capture Nashville might have been realized. Instead, he waited until his whole army arrived. By that time it was dark, and Stanley's entire corps now occupied Spring Hill.

Schofield's 23rd Corps was still on the turnpike in Hood's rear. Under the cover of darkness, Schofield slipped by the rebel forces and reached Spring Hill. He now recognized the danger and continued the retreat toward Franklin, 8 miles up the turnpike. The Harpeth River was at Franklin, and the Union army needed to cross the river before Hood attacked. Schofield left Wagner's division in Spring Hill to act as the rear guard.

Wagner assigned Opdycke's brigade to be the last Union unit to leave Spring Hill. He also ordered Opdycke to delay Hood's advance elements as long as possible.

The 24th Wisconsin spent a nervous night astride the railroad and turnpike in Spring Hill. Around 4:30 A.M., the last Union stragglers finally moved through the town. Advance elements of the Union army were already in Franklin. As dawn approached, Opdycke withdrew his brigade. Divided into two battle lines, the brigade leapfrogged north up the turnpike. Every few hundred yards, the advance regiments established a defensive position while their companion regiments retreated north to repeat the operation.

The debris of a retreating army littered the turnpike. The ground was strewn with pup tents, blankets, rifles, and knapsacks dropped by raw recruits marching as they had never marched before. Stragglers were everywhere.

Opdycke was disgusted. Proclaiming that no one was to be left behind, he ordered all stragglers rounded up, at bayonet point when necessary. Over 500 men were collected, loaded on a number of abandoned wagons, and sent toward Franklin. Considering the stragglers to be worthless raw recruits, Opdycke refused to allow them to join his veteran brigade.[14]

Throughout the morning, the brigade engaged in brief firefights with Confederate cavalry units that made dashes at the road. The brigade took up defensive positions, fought little pitched skirmishes, and then withdrew by regiments to a new line.

Eight hours after leaving Spring Hill, they were 2 miles from Franklin, with the bulk of Hood's army visible on the rolling farmlands to their rear. It was a sunny, summerlike day that felt even warmer after the recent cold weather. When the brigade halted in a new defensive line on Stevens Hill, they had a perfect view of the advancing Confederate army. Hood skirmishers approached, and behind them was his main force of 45,000 men advancing with their flags flying and officers on horseback dashing about the field.

After exchanging a few long-range artillery shots, Opdycke ordered his men to withdraw around one o'clock in the afternoon. By that time, the other two brigades of Wagner's division were within sight of Franklin. General Schofield ordered Wagner to occupy Winstead Hill a half mile in front of the Union barricades.

Schofield did not wish to fight a major battle with Hood, but he was prepared. While Opdycke's brigade was still 8 miles south in Spring Hill, Schofield's advance columns had entered Franklin in the early morning hours of Wednesday, November 30. The Union troops discovered that an advance Confederate cavalry unit had destroyed the bridges across the Harpeth River. The river was at flood level, and Schofield had no pontoon bridges. He therefore ordered his engineers to immediately begin repairing the bridges. They replanked the railroad bridge and made it strong enough to allow marching men and small wagons to cross the river; however, it would not support Schofield's heavy artillery caissons. There was another bridge that could be repaired, but the engineers predicted it would take most of the day to complete the job, and by that time, Hood's army would be near Franklin. Reports from Wagner's division informed Schofield that the rebel army was in hot pursuit and could be expected in Franklin by late afternoon. The Union force could be trapped, with the river at its back and no means of retreat. At this point, it seemed that Hood was going to get that battle he so desperately desired.

But Schofield's situation was not as critical as it first appeared. Franklin was a good defensive position, for the town had been occupied and fortified by various Union forces since 1862. Located in a bend in the Harpeth River, much like Chattanooga on a smaller scale, Franklin enjoyed a naturally strong position. Moreover, it had been encircled with breastworks on the south side. With the south bank of the river on each flank, the barricades stretched for almost 2 miles. The works needed repairing, but that would not take too long.

Schofield assigned General Jacob D. Cox to repair the fortifications. Along the line of old Union barricades that enclosed the entire town of Franklin, Cox placed thirty-four guns to blast any assaulting enemy troops. Head logs were repaired and placed properly, and the men cut a ditch in front of the breastworks.

A mile south of town where the Union line crossed the turnpike, there was a weak spot. To allow wagons and heavy artillery caissons to enter through the Union line, Cox left a gap in the fortifications at the turnpike, and 70 yards behind the main Union breastworks, he constructed a retrenched line. Wagons could then come up the turnpike, pass the main fortifications, roll off the road and around the retrenched line, and move on toward the river, where they waited in a crowd to cross the river once the bridges were repaired (see Map 7.2).

Recognizing the weak spot, Cox established his headquarters in the Carter family farmhouse near the turnpike. The main building stood on the crest of a small hill about 15 yards west of the pike. The red brick structure was simple but impressive–50 feet long with steep parapet walls topped with chimneys at each end. Next to the main house was a small frame building for the household slaves; a little further south, there was a brick smokehouse, a barn, and some small structures used by the field workers. About 80 yards to the east of the pike was a cotton mill. From the Harpeth River southward, the land rose gently, and the Carter house, a mile from the river, was on slightly higher ground. Open fields lay south of the house, the land almost flat. Only a few farm buildings and orchards here and there blocked the view in any direction. Clearly visible a half mile south was Winstead Hill, where Wagner had positioned his two advance brigades.

By noon, General Cox was satisfied that the fortifications could withstand any frontal assault, even by a force that outnumbered the defenders two to one. Work on the bridges proceeded rapidly. To reinforce the railroad bridge, which had remained intact, the engineers ransacked nearby houses for planking boards. Work was also begun on an old wagon bridge whose main posts had not burned and were still firmly grounded. The posts were sawed off at the water's edge, and new crossbeams and stringers were attached and planked over. The engineers expected to be finished with the repairs by sundown.

Colonel Opdycke and the 24th Wisconsin reached Winstead Hill around 2:30 P.M. with Hood's army right on their heels. As the brigade approached the hill, they formed into columns, and General Wagner rode out to greet them. As Wagner drew near, Opdycke's aides saw their leader's blue eyes flash with anger. Hot-tempered and headstrong, Opdycke began a shouting match with his division commander: His men had been worked to a frazzle and left as the rear guard for the entire army for over twenty-four hours. He believed the duty should have been shifted between Wagner's three brigades. When Wagner ordered Opdycke to halt and place his regiments in line with the rest of the division on Winstead Hill, Wiley Sword reports,

> Opdycke fairly exploded. His men had been on arduous rearguard duty since before daylight, most of them hadn't slept in forty-eight hours, and they hadn't been given the opportunity to eat or make coffee that day. Furthermore, the position he was told to occupy was untenable, being exposed and without natural cover. Angrily, Opdycke rode on without bothering to halt, even while Wagner trotted beside him, demanding his compliance. Opdycke, his blue eyes flashing and his lusty voice booming, would have no part of it. He kept telling Wagner that his men needed a respite; they were exhausted beyond the point of further service, and they deserved to eat. All the while, his men kept marching for the line of breastworks. ... It was insubordination, pure and simple.[15]

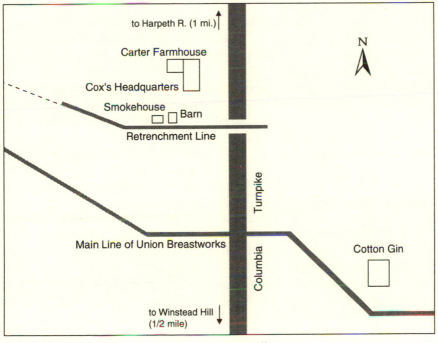

to Harpeth R. (1 mi.)

Carter Farmhouse

Cox's Headquarters

Smokehouse ☐ ☐ Barn

Retrenchment Line

N

Turnpike

Columbia

Main Line of Union Breastworks

Cotton Gin

to Winstead Hill
(1/2 mile)

MAP 7.2 Carter Hill

Shouting out orders to stand and fight if the rebs attacked, Wagner followed Opdycke's brigade as it marched the half mile to the Union breastworks and passed through the Union line near the Carter house around three o'clock. The barricades were fully manned, in some places three men deep, and fully repaired. Opdycke marched his brigade to a cleared field about 300 yards behind the barricades.

The brigade broke ranks, and after stacking their arms, the men sank wearily to the ground under some shade trees. A few fell asleep, but most were too hungry. They had not eaten for almost twenty-four hours. After a brief rest, some of them built campfires to heat up their coffee and beans. The firing from the front was steady but normal. They heard the pop-pop sound of musket fire, but they had heard such sounds for days, and it did not worry them. They felt absolutely safe behind the well-constructed and strongly defended Union breastworks.

Not really believing that even the impetuous Hood would dare attack, the Union generals also relaxed. At places like Kennesaw Mountain during the Atlanta campaign, they had all learned that it was suicide to attack a well-entrenched force. Meanwhile, with the bridges across the Harpeth River repaired by three o'clock, Schofield made plans to retreat under the cover of darkness. Artillery was brought across the river and strategically placed to cover the retreat. Schofield established his headquarters in an old fort on the north bank of the river.

Around 4:30, the sounds of heavy firing erupted near the Carter house. Some 300 yards behind the Union lines, the 24th Wisconsin rested as best they could and ignored the increased noise of battle in their immediate front. The men munched on hardtack as they waited for their campfires to slowly heat up their coffee and beans. It was a sleepy summerlike afternoon, and some of the men dozed under the shade trees, assuming they would not be called back to the front until after sundown. They had done their share of fighting for the day; if needed, they would receive orders to move up. Until that time, they intended to enjoy their few minutes of rest.[16]

But near the Carter house, the inconceivable was happening. Despite the well-fortified Union position, Hood had attacked, and the attack was an unbelievable success. The Union generals had made a fundamental defensive blunder. The true weak point in their defenses was not the retrenched line near the Carter house but Wagner's division on Winstead Hill, a half mile south of the Union fortifications. When Wagner rode to the Carter house to report Opdycke's insubordination and left his division with orders to stand and fight if attacked, he violated a military axiom: Never place a force that might block fields of fire in front of a major defensive line. Although too small to stop Hood's army, Wagner's two brigades (some 2,000 men) could nonetheless easily interfere with Union artillery and musket fire from the main line around Franklin. The Confederate defenders had erred in the same way at Missionary Ridge and had lost the battle.

Around 4:30, Hood's Army of Tennessee, 45,000 strong, gathered near the Columbia pike just south of Winstead Hill. With bands playing and flags flying, the Confederates formed into regiments and brigades, their line stretching east to west for over a mile and a half. On horseback, staff officers dashed up and down the line shouting out commands. Directly in front of the Confederate army, Wagner's 2,000 men watched, still not convinced that Hood was about to attack.

Orders were relayed, and the Confederate line moved forward in double-quick time, with its center aimed at Winstead Hill. Horrified, Wagner's men suddenly realized that the enemy was charging. When the Confederate force was less than 100 yards away, Wagner's two brigades fired one volley, then broke for the rear. Every man in the division instantaneously concluded that he was doomed if he remained on the hill.

With thousands of Confederates hot on their heels, Wagner's troops started to run across the half mile of open country toward the Union barricades. Trying to obey their orders to stand and fight, the brigade officers had waited too long. Confederate marksmen picked off the fleeing Union troops, and by the hundreds, Wagner's men dropped their weapons, threw up their hands, and surrendered. The rest ran frantically toward the Union lines. Fleeing in utter confusion and disorder, the retreating mob actually formed a shield for the Confederate soldiers fast behind them. Union defenders did not open fire for fear of hitting their comrades.

Confusion and chaos reigned as the remnants of Wagner's brigades hit the barricades at the pike near the Carter house. Confederate officers shouted, "Into the works with them!" Striking the weak point where the line was retrenched to allow wagons to move down the turnpike, the Confederates charged and breached the Union line.

In some of the Union regiments, panic erupted among the raw recruits. Horrified at the death all around them, they dropped their guns and joined in the mad dash for safety in the rear. The contagion spread, panic feeding panic. A disorderly mass of men poured down the pike. Posted near the pike, eight Union artillery guns were captured.

The Confederate success was amazing. In the first few minutes of the battle, they had taken over 800 men and broken through the Union fortifications. They soon controlled about 300 yards of the Union line near the Carter house. The breakthrough occurred at a critical point from which the Confederate troops and artillery could wreak havoc. They could roll up the Union line in either direction while their artillery bombarded the bridges crossing the Harpeth River 1 mile away.

Three hundred yards behind the lines, the 24th Wisconsin heard the increased musket fire but ignored it. Even if Hood attacked, it was inconceivable that he could break through the heavily fortified positions. The 24th's coffee was beginning to boil, their beans were finally hot, and their sowbelly and crackers were frying.

The men of the 24th had their first inkling that something was wrong when the fleeing mob of Union troops came stampeding through the campgrounds, destroying their fires and upsetting their pots and pans. Several artillery caissons, with horses running wild, galloped through to add to the bedlam. Sergeant Thomas Ford, Company H, reported that at first, he was mad as hell: He had not eaten in twenty-four hours, and the damn recruits were destroying his dinner. He knocked one man down and screamed at him, then saw the terror in the young face and realized that Hood was attacking. In their front, the 24th heard the almost demonic yells of victorious Confederates. Musket balls crashed into the trees around the 24th, and they again heard the familiar buzz of passing minié balls.[17]

In seconds, MacArthur was on his feet and in the saddle. Rising high in the stirrups, he shouted, "Stand fast, 24th."

His men responded instantly. Grabbing their rifles, they formed in line. "Fix bayonets," MacArthur yelled as he drew his saber.[18]

Without orders, Colonel Opdycke's entire brigade of seven regiments, about 1,200 men, formed into a battle line. These were not raw recruits but veterans of dozens of battles, from Murfreesboro to Atlanta. If the Confederates had penetrated the breastworks, the brigade knew that it could be a disaster for the entire army. General Stanley later reported that the moment was more critical than any he had known in previous battles. The Confederates had captured the breastworks around the Carter house and taken eight guns that they were in the process of turning on the Union line. If they held the position, they could destroy the bridges across the Harpeth River and capture most of Schofield's forces.[19]

At this point, Opdycke's brigade saved the entire Union army from possible annihilation. Without waiting for orders, his veteran regimental commanders leaped into action. Their regiments advanced through the frightened raw recruits still fleeing to the rear. Major Thomas Motherspaw, commander of the 73rd Illinois, took the lead as he galloped in front of his regiment calling, "Go for them, boys."[20]

MacArthur galloped forward with a pistol in one hand and a saber in the other. Guiding his horse with his knees, he shouted, "Give them hell, 24th!"[21]

The roar of musket fire on their right, left, and front was deafening. With strained muscles and set teeth, Opdycke's brigade shoved the Confederates back, officers and enlisted men alike fighting like demons.

The sudden appearance of Opdycke's veteran brigade startled the Confederates, who were chasing the fleeing Union troops. After an initial volley, Opdycke's troops did not stop to reload but used their rifles as clubs. In fierce hand-to-hand combat, the bayonet was the best weapon. Dismounting, MacArthur and the other officers were in the thick of it. Opdycke later remembered being "in the midst of the fighting, firing his revolver until it was empty. Quickly reversing the pistol, he grabbed it by the barrel and violently swung with the butt at the heads of the enemy. When the cylinder wedge came out and the barrel fell off [he] grasped an abandoned rifle musket and began bludgeoning the enemy with it."[22]

Opdycke's brigade drove the Confederates back, recaptured the retrenched line, and reloaded. From behind this barricade, the men opened a deadly fire on the rebel forces near the forward breastworks. The distance between the retrenched barricade and the breastworks was less than 70 yards, and the brigade's fire was deadly accurate. Confederates trapped on the north side of the works leaped over them to join their comrades.

The battle raged with indescribable fury for the next two hours. General Cox and General Stanley quickly rushed in reserve forces. With the Confederate forces holding the outer breastworks near the pike, neither side could withdraw. To retreat from the protection of the breastworks meant almost certain death. The two forces were so close that men could stand up and reach over the barricades to bayonet their enemy. Raising their rifles perpendicularly over their heads, they fired over the barricades into the massed enemy troops. It was dangerous to lean too far forward; several men were grabbed by the hair and dragged over the breastworks. With not a breath of wind, dense, black gunpowder smoke settled over the battlefield, and it was impossible to see more than a few feet ahead.

Hood threw in his reserve forces and ordered his men to attack, but they were beaten back. In a frenzy, Hood ordered thirteen separate charges over the next two hours, all doomed to failure. Each man of the 24th Wisconsin shot off hundreds of rounds of ammunition as the minutes lengthened into hours. The roar of musket fire would subside for a few minutes only to be renewed as fresh troops poured in or more ammunition was brought up.

In one of the attacks, MacArthur's incredible luck finally ran out. A musket ball hit him in the left leg, just below the knee. As he fell to the ground, another hit him in the shoulder near the clavicle. He lay dangerously wounded on the battlefield, like thousands of others.[23]

Hours passed as Hood attacked again and again. The wounded lay everywhere, but they could not be removed from the field. Twilight came, then darkness. Sporadic fire continued until around nine o'clock, when the last Confederate attack ended.

When the fighting finally ceased, the men of the 24th went to look for their Little Mac. Captain Parsons found him still alive but badly wounded. The men carried MacArthur to a field hospital, where bandages were applied to his wounds. Nearby, several burning houses lit up the night sky.[24]

Around 11:30, Mac was loaded into an ambulance. Shortly thereafter, General Schofield ordered the last of his men across the Harpeth River, burned the bridges, and retreated toward Nashville, 20 miles away.

The twelve-hour ambulance ride from Franklin to Nashville was long and painful. The ambulance train had over sixty wagons to carry the 2,000 men wounded in the battle of Franklin. Each drawn by two horses, the spring wagons had canvas tops with benches to seat eight patients on either side. On the floor or in swing stretchers lay the seriously wounded, including Major MacArthur. The ambulances rattled and bounced down the turnpike, the wounded moaning and suffering. During the slow, jolting trip, flies swarmed over open wounds and around bandages. Finally, the ambulances reached Nashville around noon on Thursday, December 1.

The Nashville hospitals were efficiently run. In the first years of the Civil War, the wounded suffered horrendously in unsanitary hospitals, operated on by poorly trained surgeons. But by late 1864, the doctors were experienced in treating gunshot wounds.

Although in critical condition, MacArthur had been lucky. The wound in his left chest was serious, but fortunately, the musket ball had passed right through his body. The wound in the leg required an operation to remove the ball lodged there. After surgery, MacArthur was placed in comfortable quarters where convalescent soldiers nursed the wounded. Young and strong, his body quickly began to mend.

In the next few days, nearly every member of the 24th Wisconsin came to visit MacArthur. They talked about the battle of Franklin, and the men of the 24th were justifiably proud of themselves. Veterans of Murfreesboro, Chickamauga, Missionary Ridge, and the entire Atlanta campaign, they believed that the battle at Franklin was the severest test they had ever endured. Schofield's army had suffered 2,326 casualties, about 10 percent of his command. Opdycke's brigade had lost 216 men. Of that number, the 24th Wisconsin had 2 dead, 16 wounded, and 3 missing. Among the dead was Captain Alva Philbrook, acting field officer. Captain Parsons was temporarily in command of the regiment. Confederate losses had been even more horrific. Hood had lost over 6,000 men—1,750 killed and 4,500 wounded. The dead included 6 Confederate generals; another 7 generals had been wounded and 1 captured.[25]

General Thomas recognized the significance of Franklin and praised the men of Opdycke's brigade for their bravery. They had recaptured 8 Union guns and had captured 400 Confederate soldiers, including 19 officers and 10 battle flags. Ultimately, the brigade had saved Schofield's entire army. Colonel Opdycke was promoted to brigadier general.

The men of the 24th Wisconsin and their young commander also received praise for their courage. Opdycke declared that Major MacArthur "bore himself heroically" and "with a most fearless spirit" in the battle of Franklin. General Stanley also lauded the young major's bravery and manliness and proclaimed that MacArthur could serve as a model for the entire Union army.[26]

8

A Hero's Return

AFTER TWO WEEKS in the hospital in Nashville, MacArthur was able to travel. His chest and leg wounds were healing, and the doctors recommended that he return to Milwaukee to recuperate. On December 12, he was issued a six-week medical leave. Captain Edwin Parsons, the temporary commander of the 24th Wisconsin, accompanied him on his return home.

The war news was good on all fronts. On December 13, Sherman emerged from the heart of Georgia and captured Savannah. His march through Georgia shattered the Confederacy, and most people hoped the war would soon be over. Sherman and Grant immediately began to plan a joint spring offensive to trap General Lee and capture Richmond.

Meanwhile, General Thomas marched out of Nashville on December 13 to confront the remnants of Hood's army. Thomas was a slow, meticulous planner who had delayed the offensive for two weeks to guarantee an absolute victory, which he achieved on December 15. In the battle, Hood lost 15,000 men (to Thomas's losses of 3,057), and the Confederate Army of Tennessee was destroyed as a fighting force.

The MacArthur home on Van Buren Street in Milwaukee was a sad one. When Arthur was wounded at Franklin on November 30, his father was still back East, where his wife had recently died. The judge hurried home, ill himself, to greet his son. The MacArthurs had a somber and lonely Christmas that year. The judge even refused to attend the annual meeting of the St. Andrews Society.[1]

Arthur could have easily ended his military service at this point because his wounds were serious, but he desperately wanted to return to his regiment. He took an additional fifteen days' leave in late January 1865 to complete the healing process, but in mid-February, he returned to Nashville. The 24th Wisconsin was occasionally sent out on patrol to round up marauding Confederate bands, but there was no longer a real rebel force west of the Alleghenies.

Arthur began to think about his future. When the war was over, the 24th Wisconsin, as a state Volunteer regiment, would be demobilized, and he would no longer have a job. Yet he wanted to remain in the army and decided to petition the War Department for a commission in the U.S. Regular Army. He asked several of his superior officers to write letters of recommendation, and they happily complied. His brigade commander, General Opdycke, praised MacArthur as a "true soldier ... thoroughly informed in military art and tactics," who had displayed exceptional leadership and bravery in battle after battle while under his command. General Kimball, MacArthur's brigade commander before Opdycke, was equally generous and wrote that "Major MacArthur has no superior as an officer in the army." General Stanley, MacArthur's corps commander, noted in his letter to the secretary of war that, though MacArthur was a very young man, he deserved a commission in the Regular Army at the highest possible rank. While under Stanley's command, MacArthur had illustrated his ability in numerous battles while commanding the 24th Wisconsin. Stanley wrote:

> This officer's name will be found favorably mentioned in reports of all the battles this gallant regiment has fought in this department, which are all the great battles of this army. At the battle of Franklin, where ... MacArthur received two service wounds, his services were most important, and were gallantly performed. In command of his regiment, he retook our batteries at the very moment the enemy was about to turn them on us. Of good moral habits, possessing a good education, well informed and experienced in arms [Major MacArthur] will fill any position in the regular Army, up to the command of a regiment, usually a Colonel, with credit. If this rank cannot be given, I recommend him for the next highest.[2]

Generals Thomas and Sheridan also wrote the secretary of war, recommending that MacArthur be awarded a commission.

When Wisconsin's senators and congressmen learned that Major MacArthur wanted to join the Regular Army, they sent a joint letter to the secretary of war, urging his appointment. MacArthur possessed, the congressmen wrote, "a remarkable love and genius for the profession of arms. He has acquired a reputation for skill and bravery surpassed by no soldier in the Union Army from our State."[3]

Months passed before the War Department responded, but the state of Wisconsin was more appreciative of MacArthur's heroic actions. Other than the congressional Medal of Honor, which had not yet received wide acclaim, there were no medals for Civil War soldiers. Rather, bravery was noted by awarding brevet ranks. A brevet had no monetary or command value but was an honor noted on the uniform; on social occasions and in official correspondence, an officer was addressed by his brevet rank. On March 13, in recognition of his services from Perryville to Atlanta, Wisconsin awarded MacArthur the brevet rank of lieutenant colonel. For his valor at Franklin, he was also awarded the brevet rank of colonel. Often, a brevet award was the first step to permanent promotion.

Meanwhile, Grant and Sherman began their spring campaign against General Lee in Richmond. With Grant hammering from the north and Sherman marching up through the Carolinas, Lee was forced to abandon Richmond on April 2. His army had shrunk to less than 30,000 men; Grant had 115,000, and Sherman had over 60,000. Lee was doomed. On April 9, he surrendered at Appomattox Court House, a small village about 95 miles west of Richmond. The war was over.

The Union's initial jubilation, however, was soon subdued. Five days after Lee's surrender, the nation suffered a devastating blow when John Wilkes Booth assassinated President Lincoln while he sat in his box at Ford's Theater, watching a performance of *Our American Cousin*. It was the first of three presidential assassinations that would occur in MacArthur's lifetime, and for young Arthur, it was the most crushing. Death transformed Lincoln into a martyr of the Union, and over the years, his legendary intellect and wisdom would grow to gigantic proportions. The soldiers of the 24th, like the rest of the nation, were shocked, and they mourned the death of a great man. In later years, Major MacArthur would relate to younger officers how he had actually met Lincoln in the summer of 1862. Few other officers of his generation could make the same claim.

Despite Lincoln's death, the end of the war was cause for relief throughout the North. A grateful Wisconsin rushed to honor its heroes. On May 18, the state legislature promoted MacArthur to lieutenant colonel of the 24th Wisconsin Volunteers. The state wanted to make him a colonel, but the 24th, with only 250 enlisted men and 16 officers, was simply too small. Thus, at the age of nineteen, MacArthur became the youngest lieutenant colonel in the Union army. A few other boy soldiers were close to his age, the most notable being Lieutenant Colonel Henry W. Lawton, who, at the age of twenty-one, commanded the 30th Indiana.[4]

With the war over, state Volunteer regiments were quickly returned home to be mustered out of the service. In Nashville, General Thomas demobilized his beloved Army of the Cumberland. In the first week of June, just after MacArthur turned twenty, the 24th Wisconsin left Nashville by train and headed back to Milwaukee.

The 24th was Milwaukee's "Chamber of Commerce regiment," and the city planned a grand reception to honor their famous regiment and its boy colonel. The 24th had been depleted by war. Of the 1,150 men who served in the regiment, 750 had died in battle, of diseases, or in prison camp. Another 100 were so badly wounded that they never returned to the regiment. A few had resigned or had transferred to other regiments. The remaining 266 enlisted men and officers were MacArthur's comrades in arms, the men he would honor above all others for the rest of his life.[5]

The regiment arrived in Milwaukee on June 5. As their train neared the city, a field gun posted at the edge of town boomed out its welcome. Thousands waited for them at the railroad station, including Judge MacArthur, the mayor, former governor Salomon, and members of the regiment on leave recuperating from wounds. As the 24th emerged from the train, soldiers were clasped in loving arms and greeted by cries of joy from mothers and fathers and friends. For a few minutes, it was absolute bedlam.

Colonel Arthur MacArthur, c. June 1865. (MacArthur Memorial Library, Ph-37)

Colonel MacArthur finally restored order by shouting for his men to form in line. They were about to engage in their last dress parade. With their regimental flag flying and their band playing, they marched through the city streets to the cheers of thousands who lined the way. At the Fair Building, the ladies of the city had prepared a grand repast, and a carnival atmosphere prevailed. There were speeches by the mayor, the judge, and Salomon. Nervous in front of the crowd, Colonel MacArthur said a few words, to the delight of his men.[6]

Five days later, on June 10, 1865, the 24th Wisconsin was mustered out of the army after two years and ten months of service. One day later, the state legislature promoted MacArthur to full colonel. If the 24th Wisconsin was ever needed again, young Mac would be in charge. The final appearance of the regiment was on July

4, when the city again honored them. Along with General Frederick C. Winkler, Colonel MacArthur led the Independence Day parade that year.

It was a bittersweet time for Arthur. At the age of twenty, he was already famous and had achieved high rank—he was a man among men. Now that the regiment no longer existed and the war was over, he was a young man without a job. He probably suffered a period of disorientation as the rules that governed his daily life changed dramatically. And he no doubt had to deal with the disturbing memories of war that most veterans keep to themselves. Yet if his future was uncertain, his past clearly illustrated his potential to achieve almost unlimited success.[7]

PART TWO

Frontier Days

9

Into the Wilderness

THE HEROIC TIMES WERE OVER. Although young Colonel Arthur MacArthur continued to be honored by his former comrades, the question of career was a haunting one. His father wanted him to become a lawyer, but the war remained the foremost influence on Arthur's life, and to ignore that grand experience seemed impossible for the young man. He waited impatiently for word from the War Department on his application for a commission in the U.S. Army.[1]

Months passed before his application was processed. The size of the army shrank rapidly as Congress slashed the Union army from a million men to a mere 54,000, organized into forty regiments (twenty-five infantry, ten cavalry, and five artillery). The new army needed only 3,400 officers. Thousands of Civil War Volunteer officers had applied for a mere 1,530 open positions, and the authorities moved slowly in reviewing the many applications.[2]

Arthur studied law while he waited. In late April 1866, the War Department finally offered him a commission as a second lieutenant in the 17th Infantry Regiment, being reorganized in New York City. He had hoped for more (at least the grade of major), but given the extreme competition for the few openings, he was fortunate to be offered any commission. Even Regular Army officers who had served bravely during the war were forced to accept positions at lower grades: Generals became lieutenant colonels, colonels became majors, and majors were lucky to remain in the army at all. Moreover, some of Judge MacArthur's friends in Washington assured young Arthur that he would be quickly promoted to captain if he accepted the commission.

He decided to accept the appointment. Historian Carol Petillo, in analyzing his decision, speculated:

> At an age when self-definition often required rejection of roles which seemed safe, the young man was drawn inexorably to a career of risk and romance. He had always loved tales of military adventure, and his recent martial experience only served to reinforce his predilection. If the Civil War had not occurred when it did, he might have been content to contain his military enthusiasm in fantasy. If he had not succeeded so completely and performed so brilliantly in the war, the attraction might have waned. But social reality, coupled with personal needs and adequate reinforcment, provided

many reasons for his decision. Others might seek advancement in the opportunity offered by what has come to be known as the "age of big business," but for Arthur MacArthur, Jr., the parapet called. The borders of his identity were defined by what he would *not* do. His self-image needed a broader canvas than that provided by an urban legal career. He would wait nearly twenty years before this inner choice was validated by external events.[3]

As he completed the final application forms, there was one minor problem: According to regulations, officers had to be at least twenty-one years old, but he was only twenty. He solved the problem by again lying about his age. On the application, he wrote he was twenty-two, soon to be twenty-three, a lie that would later come back to haunt him.[4]

Arthur left Milwaukee on June 3, 1866, one day after his twenty-first birthday, to join the 17th Infantry Regiment. Traveling at his own expense, he arrived in New York on June 11. The 17th was stationed on David's Island, a recruiting depot in New York harbor. MacArthur's first job was to instill respect for military discipline in the new recruits. He drilled the men and taught them to obey orders—absolute obedience to commissioned and noncommissioned officers was emphasized. Life at the recruiting station soon revealed one difference between Civil War Volunteer regiments and the Regular Army. In the Regular Army, officers did not socialize with enlisted men, even sergeants, because fraternization might interfere with discipline.

Shortly after his arrival at David's Island, MacArthur was promoted to first lieutenant, and he continued to hope for promotion to captain or major. His father wrote to Postmaster General Alexander W. Randall, a former governor of Wisconsin and an old friend, for assistance and indicated his son would accept an appointment to one of the new regiments being formed from black veterans of the Civil War. Randall contacted President Andrew Johnson, praised MacArthur's military record, and reminded the president of Judge MacArthur's popularity and political influence in Wisconsin. Senator Matthew Carpenter, Representative Halbert Paine, and Governor Lucius Fairchild of Wisconsin wrote both the president and the secretary of war to request a promotion for young MacArthur.[5]

The political pressure worked. On Saturday, October 13, three days before the 17th Regiment was due to leave David's Island for Texas, MacArthur was promoted to captain, retroactive to July 28. The official July date was significant because it determined seniority in grade or rank. Grade and rank had strict military definitions, and the terms were not synonymous. Grade indicated position: MacArthur was a captain, and all captains held the same grade. Rank referred to position in relation to all officers in the same grade. Thus, no two men could be of the same rank. In each grade, rank was determined by the official date of appointment, and promotions were based on both performance and seniority. Because there was no captain's vacancy in the 17th, MacArthur was reassigned to the 36th Infantry stationed in Nebraska Territory.

However, there was a catch. Before taking up his new assignment with the 36th, he needed the approval of an examining board. To cut back the size of the officers corps to 3,400 men, Congress authorized the establishment of examining boards, sarcastically nicknamed "benzine boards" after a powerful cleaning solvent, to weed out unqualified officers. Each officer was scrutinized and forced to testify before a board, and if he failed to receive the board's approval, he was forced to resign his commission.

The Adjutant General's Office ordered MacArthur to appear before a board meeting in Chicago. He left New York on October 14 and traveled by train to Chicago, where he spent a few days with his father and brother. On October 22, at 10 A.M., MacArthur appeared before the board at the Sherman House in downtown Chicago. He presented a list of impressive documents that supported his appointment to captain, including excerpts from the official records of battles of the Civil War, letters of recommendation from Generals Thomas, Kimball, Opdycke, Stanley, and Sheridan, and letters from both senators and every congressman from Wisconsin. General Sidney Burbank, the president of the board, was impressed with the young man. In his official report, he recommended that MacArthur be retained and described him as an educated, experienced officer who was respected by all who had served with him in the Volunteer forces. The captain breathed a sigh of relief. The board could have ended his military career.[6]

Traveling from Chicago, MacArthur stopped for a few days in Milwaukee, then collected his law books and proceeded to Fort Kearny in Nebraska Territory, headquarters of the 36th Infantry Regiment. The regiment was protecting Union Pacific railroad crews constructing sections of the first transcontinental railroad. The Union Pacific was laying track westward from Omaha, Nebraska, while the Central Pacific was building eastward from Sacramento, California. For each mile of track, the companies received huge land grants and loans, amounting to $16,000 per mile on level ground, $48,000 in the mountains, and $32,000 in intermediate country.

As Union Pacific crews moved west through Nebraska, they were protected by troops from the 36th Infantry to which Captain MacArthur had been assigned. The ten companies of the regiment were spread thin along the railroad line. At the end of the tracks, troops lived in tents and moved almost monthly to new encampments or small towns along the route. Under the direction of its chief engineer, General Grenville M. Dodge, Union Pacific construction crews, composed largely of Civil War veterans and Irish immigrants, laid 568 miles of track that year. The 36th Infantry followed the crews as the tracks moved past Fort Kearny to Platte City and Beauvais Rancho, then to Coal Creek, Colorado. Finally, in July 1867, the 36th Regiment took up station at Fort Sanders, about 3 miles south of the town of Laramie in Wyoming Territory. Regimental headquarters would remain at Sanders for almost a year (see Map 9.1).[7]

Sanders was a typical frontier fort that looked more like a small town or village than a military outpost. Constructed by the troops, the fort was a collection of

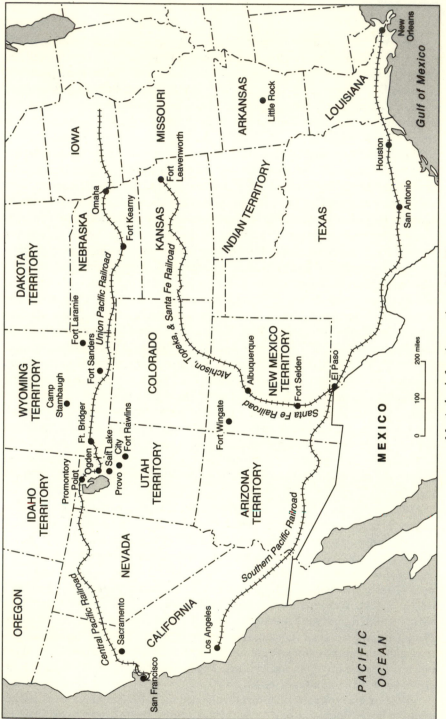

MAP 9.1 MacArthur's frontier postings, 1867–1889

wooden buildings of almost identical design. The buildings surrounded a parade ground with a high flagpole to raise the colors above the fort. On one side of the parade ground was the enlisted men's barracks, and directly across were small houses for officers. At either end of the parade ground stood administrative offices, warehouses, workshops, corrals, and the post trader's store. The married enlisted men built shanties beyond the perimeter area.

Contrary to the image depicted in popular magazines, no stockade surrounded the fort. In fact, the chances of an Indian attack were minute. Grouped together, there were less than 270,000 Indians divided into 125 distinctive tribes. Some of the tribes, such as the Pueblos in the Southwest and the Crows, were peaceful. Only a few powerful tribes, such as the Sioux, Cheyenne, Kiowa, Comanche, and Apache (about 100,000 Indians in all), were hostile.

The infantry was used more as a labor brigade and a police force than as a fighting force. Eventually, hundreds of thousands of people followed the railroad lines west and built mining camps, cowtowns, and farming communities. Policing the myriad of new settlers, some of whom were ruffians and outlaws, was the prime job of the 36th Infantry, and companies were detached to the diverse communities that sprouted up near the railroad tracks. The infantry's first task was to curtail the murder, mayhem, and violence that abounded on the frontier. As a labor brigade, it also built bridges, roads, and telegraph lines. The troops cut lumber, quarried stone, made adobe bricks, plastered, built, painted, repaired wagons and harnesses, and even planted hay. All this was in addition to constant military drills and guard duty.

The 36th Regiment moved west from Sanders to Fort Bridger in May 1868, where they remained for an entire year. The first transcontinental railroad was finally completed when the Union Pacific and the Central Pacific tracks met on May 10, 1869, at Promontory Point near Ogden, Utah. The Union Pacific had laid 1,086 miles of track; the Central Pacific, building through the Rocky Mountains with construction crews composed mainly of Chinese coolies, had laid 689 miles. The national press heralded the meeting of the two lines as a grand event in U.S. history, and Captain MacArthur was there to see the driving of the final, golden spike.

Shortly thereafter, the 36th Infantry Regiment received a shock. Congress instituted additional military cuts and reduced the army from 54,000 to 30,000 enlisted men; the officers corps was to be cut from 3,400 to 2,100. Cutting back on enlisted personnel simply meant curtailing enlistments, but shrinking the size of the officers corps meant eliminating over 1,000 officers. New benzine boards were formed and given the unpleasant task of weeding out undesirable officers.

Officers in the 36th Regiment were in a delicate position. When Congress reduced the army from forty to twenty-five regiments, the 36th Infantry was one of those demobilized. The officers were thus placed on detached duty while boards examined their records in hopes of eliminating some. MacArthur returned to the family home in Milwaukee to await orders. He would be without a job for almost four months.

While MacArthur was on the northwest frontier with the 36th Infantry, a dramatic change had occurred in his father's life. In the summer of 1867, Judge MacArthur had met a young woman in Chicago named Zelia Hodges. From North Adams, Massachusetts, less than 30 miles from Chicopee, Hodges had many endearing qualities that enticed the judge to propose marriage. She accepted, and on January 29, 1868, three days after the judge's fifty-first birthday, they were married.[8]

When Captain MacArthur returned to Milwaukee in May 1869, he met his new stepmother and discovered that his father was again unfortunate in love. The new Mrs. MacArthur had developed consumption and was dying. During his stay, Arthur gave his father some emotional support but spent most of his time with his younger brother, Frank.

Arthur was not idle during his months in Milwaukee. The disbanding of the 36th Infantry had shocked him, and he realized that he had little security in the military since the officers corps was constantly shrinking. While on the frontier, he had studied his law books, and he therefore decided to take the Wisconsin bar examinations in August 1869. To the judge's delight, Arthur passed the exams. If his military career ever faltered, he could now practice law in the state of Wisconsin.[9]

Shortly after being admitted to the Wisconsin bar, Arthur received orders to report to New York City. The family decided to travel east with him, for Zelia wanted to visit her relatives in North Adams while she could still travel. On a stopover in Boston, the judge was hit by a runaway horse and suffered several injuries but soon recovered. When his father and stepmother went on to North Adams to visit her family, Captain MacArthur proceeded to New York City. Zelia and the judge remained in North Adams until mid-September. Unfortunately, the trip did not improve Zelia's health, and less than a month after they had returned to Milwaukee, she died, on October 11, 1869, at the family home on Van Buren Street. She had been seriously ill for over eight months.[10]

The death of his second wife was hard on Judge MacArthur. Despite the pleas of many friends, he refused to run for reelection for circuit judge. Because of painful memories, he wanted to leave Milwaukee and open a law office in Chicago. The Milwaukee Bar Association was extremely disappointed, and on several occasions it petitioned him to reconsider, but he always refused. After twelve years as a circuit judge, he resigned in November 1869, with less than two months left in his second term of office. When the Milwaukee Bar Association honored him with a retirement dinner on December 16, 1869, nearly every lawyer in the city attended. Shortly thereafter, the judge put his house up for sale and announced he was moving to Chicago.[11]

The judge's friends recognized his depression and went to work on his behalf. Supported by all the Wisconsin congressmen, Senator Carpenter petitioned Presi-

dent Grant to appoint Judge MacArthur to the federal court. To the delight of his
friends, MacArthur was made an associate judge of the Supreme Court of the District
of Columbia on July 15, 1870, a position he would hold for seventeen years.[12]

When the judge moved east in the summer of 1870, he visited his son in New
York City. Captain MacArthur had been assigned to the Cavalry Recruiting Office
in the Bowery. Desertions among the enlisted men were so high that the army was
in constant need of new recruits and maintained recruiting offices in most of the
major cities. In 1871, for example, over 8,000 enlisted men (approximately one-
third of the army) deserted. Throughout the 1870s, the annual desertion rate averaged about 3,000 men, approximately 10 percent of the army each year.

The Cavalry Recruiting Office in New York City was a busy place. The cavalry
was the glamour service, and newspapers and dime novels recounted heroic tales
of mounted campaigns on the western frontier. MacArthur interviewed many
young men who dreamed of going west to fight the Indians. The law allowed recruits to be between the ages of sixteen and thirty-five, although those under
twenty-one needed the permission of their parents. The average age was twenty-
three. The recruits signed on for five years, and no married men could enlist. The
pay for a recruit was only $13 per month. The backgrounds of the recruits were as
varied as the nation itself, and every occupation was represented—hatters, watch-
makers, shoemakers, tailors, preachers, lawyers, mechanics, students, and businessmen. Many were new immigrants and unskilled laborers. There were also
Bowery boys, toughs, gamblers, and petty criminals.

To improve his efficiency as a recruiting officer, MacArthur studied cavalry tactics, and he slowly became convinced that he should transfer from the infantry to
the cavalry. On the western frontier, the infantry acted as a police force and garrisoned supply depots for the cavalry, which campaigned against the Indians. The
infantry's role was one of drudgery; the cavalry's role one of action. Equally significant for an ambitious young officer, promotion in the infantry was going to be
glacially slow for years. As the officers corps shrank in 1870 to 2,100 men, the surviving captains, majors, lieutenant colonels, and colonels were almost all in their
midthirties or early forties. Since the retirement age was sixty-five, few openings
would occur for twenty or thirty years. In 1870, MacArthur ranked three-hundredth on the captains' seniority list and could not expect a promotion to major
for at least fifteen years. Opportunities for promotion were far greater in the cavalry because there were more field-grade positions available. An infantry regiment consisted of ten companies. The commanding officer was a colonel, assisted
by a lieutenant colonel and a major. Each cavalry regiment, by contrast, was made
up of three squadrons of four troops each, or twelve troops to the regiment, and
was commanded by a colonel, assisted by a lieutenant colonel and three majors.

When General Sheridan, commander of the Division of the Missouri, visited
New York in July 1870, MacArthur went to see him. By looking at MacArthur's
service record, Sheridan knew the young man had been one of his officers during
the Civil War. It is not likely the general remembered the adjutant who had

charged up Missionary Ridge, but comrades in arms formed a club. Sheridan listened to MacArthur and endorsed his request for a transfer to the cavalry. For some reason, however, the War Department ignored the application.[13]

MacArthur's dream of joining the cavalry ended in August 1870, when the War Department assigned him to the 13th Infantry Regiment. MacArthur was appalled. The 13th Infantry was on duty in Utah and Wyoming, guarding the construction of new railroad lines, and he felt he had already served his time in isolated frontier garrisons. His wishes, however, were not important to the War Department.

MacArthur left New York in early September 1870 and arrived at Fort Rawlins, the headquarters of the 13th Infantry, on September 27. Rawlins was located on the Timpanogos River near the base of the Wasatch Mountains in Utah Territory, about 50 miles southeast of Salt Lake City. Colonel Philippe Regis de Trobriand, the commander of the 13th, assigned MacArthur to command K Company, a position he would retain for the next twenty years.[14]

As the army shrank in size and was spread thin in garrison duty, the company became the prime military unit. Seldom were all ten companies of the 13th stationed at one fort. Rather, they were dispersed throughout Utah and Wyoming in small temporary posts, guarding mining camps, small towns, and railroad construction crews. During the winter of 1870–1871, two companies, including MacArthur's K Company, remained at Rawlins. Permanent buildings were not erected, and the men were quartered in tents and in the town of Provo, Utah. The next year, K Company moved to another primitive post called Camp Stambaugh near the Sweetwater River on the Oregon Trail. Living in tents in the frigid northwest, known for its blizzards and deep snow, Company K suffered through the winter of 1871–1872 there.

The greatest burden for the men stationed in the sparsely settled western districts was the loneliness and unbearable tedium of garrison life. Assigned to areas with no civilized amenities, regiments often remained at the same stations for years. The daily drills and guard duty were monotonous, with each day's activities determined by a rigid routine beginning at reveille and followed until lights were doused at 11:00 P.M. To alleviate the tedium, company commanders organized baseball teams, track meets, and horseshoe tournaments. The officers acted as umpires or judges rather than active participants. Singing was one of the popular pastimes with the men, and Civil War songs (such as "Marching Through Georgia" and "The Girl I Left Behind Me") remained the favorite selections. Regimental headquarters maintained a band, but nearly every company also had its own musicians who played for the men in the evenings on banjos, guitars, violins, harmonicas, and, occasionally, accordions. After payday, gambling was popular, and the men spent long hours playing three-card monte, seven-up, high-low, blackjack, and, of course, stud poker. Although all forms of gambling violated army regulations, the officers usually ignored small-limit poker games.

Under a rigid caste system, Colonel de Trobriand forbade fraternization between the ranks because he believed it interfered with proper maintenance of authority. Even when there were only two or three officers at one camp, as at Stambaugh, they maintained separate quarters, separate latrines, and even separate messes. MacArthur began to assume the distant, almost austere manner that would characterize him for the rest of his life. He was friendly but formal with the troops under his command.[15]

Although he enjoyed playing an occasional game of whist with his brother officers, MacArthur spent most of his evenings reading to alleviate the boredom of garrison duty. He had a voracious appetite for books on almost any topic, from Greek and Roman history to the culture of China. His intellectual interests were encouraged by Colonel de Trobriand. Although de Trobriand was not popular with his subordinate officers, they respected him, and MacArthur was proud to have him as a commander. De Trobriand was an educated man and used regimental funds to purchase the popular journals and magazines of the day. The *Army and Navy Journal* led a list that included *Harper's Weekly, Puck, Appelton's Weekly, North American Review, Colburn's United States Magazine, Blackwood's Magazine,* the *New York Herald,* and the *San Francisco Examiner.*

From his father, MacArthur received a constant stream of books. Economics fascinated him, and he read, among many other authors, Adam Smith, Thomas Malthus, David Ricardo, John Stuart Mill, Matthew Carey, Walter Bagehot, and Thomas Leslie. He also read Francis Parkman's seven-volume history of France and England in North America, and Parkman ensnared him on history. MacArthur became fascinated with the colonial and revolutionary periods of U.S. history, the formation and adoption of the Constitution, and the subsequent constitutional development of the republic. He also did extensive reading into the civilizations and institutions of China and Japan.[16]

Captain MacArthur requested a short leave in January 1871 to attend his father's third wedding. The move from Milwaukee to Washington in 1870 had revitalized Judge MacArthur. Fourteen months after the death of his second wife, he married Mary Hopkins, the widow of Congressman Benjamin F. Hopkins. He had known Mary for almost twenty years. As old friends mourning the deaths of their previous mates, they soon realized they had much in common and were perfectly suited for each other. Their wedding was held at her home in Madison on January 11, 1871, a few days before the judge's fifty-fourth birthday. His new bride was forty-seven and had one son by her former marriage.[17]

Captain MacArthur's request for leave was delayed, and he did not reach Madison to meet his new stepmother until the last week in January. He was glad to see his father so happy, and the new Mrs. MacArthur was an easy person to like. After only a few days, he left to return to his regiment at Fort Rawlins.

Two years passed before MacArthur visited the family in Washington, D.C. In April 1872, he was a guest in his father's home at 1201 N Street. At that time, the captain's nineteen-year-old brother, Frank, was in Boston attending Harvard University. The judge's third marriage was a happy one. The MacArthurs were active in the social life of the capital, often dining at the best restaurants in the city and entertaining friends at home. Their parties were informal, usually with about forty guests. Most people who knew the MacArthurs liked them, and their guests particularly enjoyed the dinner table conversations; after dinner, there was usually music and dancing. The judge liked to have people around him, and he enjoyed dancing.[18]

Arthur had a delightful time. His father introduced him to his friends and political acquaintances, including judges, senators, congressmen, cabinet members, and even Ulysses S. Grant, the president of the United States. Judge MacArthur was one of Grant's favorite people, and they enjoyed each other's company on many occasions. The president was always impressed with the judge's wit and great eloquence as a speaker. Only two months before, in February 1872, the judge had been the keynote speaker at a Wisconsin congressional reception for the president and vice president.[19]

The home at 1201 N Street was crammed full of books, and Captain MacArthur spent a number of evenings simply reading. The judge was a bibliophile, and his library included not only law books but hundreds of volumes on literature, philosophy, history, and politics. Judge MacArthur, of course, was particularly fond of Scottish history, Robert Burns, and Shakespeare, but he lectured on a myriad of topics to many clubs and societies in Washington, D.C., and wrote a number of books on subjects ranging from education to Scottish humor.

In discussions with Senator Carpenter, Captain MacArthur learned that the University of Wisconsin was in dire need of a military instructor. Specializing in agriculture, civil engineering, mining, and law, the university was one of the most prosperous educational institutions in the country. Because the school had over 500 students, the state ordered it to establish a military department. But though the state was willing to provide the equipment and even a building, the university did not have a qualified military instructor. Senator Carpenter wondered if MacArthur would be interested in the job.

The offer was, indeed, enticing to him. Garrison life on the frontier was not only boring, it also offered little chance to display his battlefield experience and his knowledge of military tactics. In MacArthur's opinion, such duty was a waste of time and manpower. He also believed that the infantry could be more effective in campaigns against the Indians than the cavalry had been. Year after year, the cavalry chased and captured a few Indian raiding parties, yet the Indian attacks continued. If properly used in the field, MacArthur felt, the infantry could actually end the Indian wars. The Indians were mobile only in the summer; in winter, they returned to their base camps, and the braves spent the winter with their women and children. MacArthur believed the infantry could capture the winter base camps, as well as any braves who escaped, because the Indian ponies would be weak at that time of year. An infantry company could walk down a horse in four days: MacArthur had seen it happen in long campaigns during the Civil War.[20]

MacArthur did not want to return to Fort Rawlins, and the teaching position at the University of Wisconsin sounded like a wonderful opportunity. Senator Carpenter contacted J. H. Twambly, the president of the university, who immediately offered MacArthur the job.[21]

First, however, MacArthur needed the permission of the Adjutant General's Office to accept Twambly's offer. Twambly wrote to President Grant, and Senator Carpenter met with the president to request that MacArthur be detailed to the University of Wisconsin. Despite the president's support, the adjutant general, Edward D. Townshend, rejected the application for detached duty. He piously observed that too many officers had been assigned to detached duty and that MacArthur was desperately needed by his company and regiment.[22]

Thus, MacArthur's dream was shattered. He was ordered to return to Fort Rawlins without delay, and he arrived back on the frontier on August 31.

Two years passed before the 13th Regiment was relieved from frontier duty and returned to civilization. The unit was transferred to Jackson Barracks just outside the city of New Orleans in October 1874. It was a momentous assignment for young Captain MacArthur.

Until his assignment to Jackson Barracks, MacArthur viewed congressional reconstruction policies as no more than general abstractions. He now found himself and his regiment surrounded by a hostile Southern populace that resented Northern carpetbag control. Although the Southern states had been readmitted to the Union by October 1874 under the Reconstruction Acts, Northern carpetbag politicians, not native-born Southerners, continued to dominate. Some of the carpetbaggers were true reformers, but many others were extremely corrupt. For example, Henry C. Warmouth, the governor of Louisiana from 1868 to 1872, did not even pretend to be honest. On a salary of $8,000 annually, he managed to retire with a personal fortune of $500,000. "Corruption is the fashion," he said with a smile.[23]

The 13th Regiment was at Jackson Barracks for less than three months when it was called on to defend another corrupt carpetbag administration, headed by Governor William P. Kellogg. Like most of the South, New Orleans was in an economic depression, stimulated by wartime destruction and financial losses. Neither Congress nor the state government did much to alleviate the economic problems, and poverty was rampant in the city. Carpetbag corruption made the depression even harder to bear, and reformers tried to take over the state. In response, the army was ordered to maintain law and order and to defend the Kellogg administration. In January 1875, Colonel de Trobriand marched contingents of the 13th Regiment into the state capitol in New Orleans to oust political opponents of the Kellogg regime.

The New Orleans aristocracy condemned the use of federal troops but did not blame de Trobriand for obeying orders. Most Southerners realized that their foe was not the army but rather the Republican Congress. In fact, there was less animosity toward Union officers in New Orleans than in most other Southern cities. Union Civil War heroes, such as Captain MacArthur, were actually honored by the Southern veterans who had fought against them. MacArthur was invited to dinner parties, dances, and picnics, and, over tea and cakes, he refought the battles of Murfreesboro, Missionary Ridge, Kennesaw Mountain, and Franklin with his former enemies. For both the victorious and the defeated, the glory was greater in retrospect.

Almost thirty years old, MacArthur had reached the age when he wished to have a family. With all the balls and dances in New Orleans, it was almost inevitable that he would meet a young woman and fall passionately in love. The Southern belle who won his heart was named Mary Pinkney Hardy, whom he met during the Mardi Gras. Their son Douglas would later recall in his memoirs that Pinky, as the captain called her, "came from an old Virginia family dating back to Jamestown days. Her ancestors had fought under George Washington and Andrew Jackson, and her brothers, products of the Virginia Military Institute, had followed Robert E. Lee's flag on Virginia's bloody fields. A Hardy was at Stonewall Jackson's elbow that dark night when he fell on the sodden Plank Road near Chancellorsville. Her father, Thomas Hardy, was a wealthy ... merchant" in Norfolk, Virginia.[24]

The eleventh of fourteen children, ten of whom lived to maturity, Pinky was born on May 22, 1852, at Riveredge, the Hardy family plantation, near Norfolk and was nine years old when the Civil War began. Her four brothers joined the Confederate army. In May 1862, the Union army occupied Norfolk, and General Benjamin F. Butler established his headquarters on the Hardy estate. The family fled to their summer home near Henderson, North Carolina. Until the closing stages of the war, Henderson was far from the scene of the fighting, but in November 1864, Union troops occupied the town, "much to the disgust and dismay of the Hardys."[25]

As a merchant family dealing in fertilizer rather than cotton, the Hardys emerged from the war with their fortune somewhat intact. While the old plantation in Norfolk was being restored, the family lived in Baltimore, where Pinky attended an exclusive girls' school (Mount de Sales Academy) and became a true Southern belle, proficient in dancing, embroidery, watercolor painting, and the decoration of chinaware.

Perhaps Pinky appealed to Captain MacArthur because she was Scottish and proud of it. From his father, Arthur had inherited an intense pride in his heritage. He often recounted how his father had taught him to love Scottish poets, philosophers, whiskey, and, of course, Scottish women.[26]

Impulsively, Arthur proposed to Pinky, and she accepted, assuming the marriage would meet the approval of her family since three of her older sisters had already married Northerners they had met at the family's new summer home in Massachusetts. She left New Orleans to return to Norfolk, Virginia, to prepare for

Mary Pinckney (Pinky) Hardy MacArthur, c. 1870. (MacArthur Memorial Library, Ph-3086)

a May wedding. Her decision to marry a Union officer initially displeased the Hardy family, but apparently Judge MacArthur visited Riveredge and charmed them with his Scottish humor. Some members of the family changed their minds, although two of her brothers who had fought for the Confederacy refused to attend the wedding.[27]

The wedding took place on May 19, 1875, at St. Mary's Catholic Church in Norfolk. Pinky asked Father Matthew O'Keefe, a family friend, to perform the ceremony, and O'Keefe agreed even though the bride was a Methodist and the groom an Episcopalian. The reception was at Riveredge.[28]

The adjutant general could be kind on occasion. Recognizing MacArthur's long years of service on the frontier, and perhaps given a gentle push by friends of the judge's and of the Hardy family, he assigned Captain MacArthur to detached duty in Washington, D.C. For sixteen glorious months, he would serve on various army review boards while living in the nation's capital.

The judge was delighted with his new daughter-in-law, particularly when Pinky informed the family she was pregnant and due to give birth in June 1876.

Meanwhile, the young couple became part of the Washington social scene. The judge kept them entertained, and they were invited to numerous parties by congressmen, senators, and business leaders.

The social scene delighted Pinky, but Captain MacArthur was not as impressed as his wife was by the parade of politicians at his father's house. Corruption was rampant in Washington in 1875, and although the judge was an honest man, many of his friends were not. Senators and congressmen were often unprincipled spokesmen for steel corporations, oil and sugar refining companies, and railroads. The heroes of the day were sly businessmen like John D. Rockefeller, Commodore Cornelius Vanderbilt, Henry and Jay Cooke, J. P. Morgan, and Jim Fisk. These powerful men manipulated the government with well-placed gifts to politicians. As William Allen White observed,

> A United States senator ... represented something more than a state, more even than a region. He represented principalities and powers in business. One senator, for instance, represented the Union Pacific Railroad system, another the New York Central, still another the insurance interest of New York and New Jersey. ... Coal and iron owned a coterie from the Middle and Eastern seaport states. Cotton had a half a dozen senators. And so it went.[29]

For Pinky, the year in Washington was possibly the happiest of her marriage. Her first son, named Arthur III after his father and grandfather, was born at Norfolk on June 1, 1876, one day before his father's thirty-first birthday. Arthur III would be the apple of his father's eye, the truly beloved son. In mid-June, Captain MacArthur's younger brother, Frank, graduated from Harvard. Frank would follow in the judge's footsteps; after studying law in New York City, he was admitted to the New York bar in 1880. He specialized in patent law and even wrote a book on the subject. The only sad event in Pinky's life that year was the death of her father in late 1876.[30]

The nation was not having such an idyllic year as the MacArthurs. A depression that began in September 1873 with the collapse of the New York Warehouse and Securities Company lingered on as thousands of businesses went bankrupt. In 1876, another 18,000 firms failed, railroads halted construction and defaulted on their bonds, factories closed down, and unemployment reached levels never before approached in U.S. history. Millions of skilled and unskilled laborers, small businessmen, and white-collar workers were forced to seek public charity in order to survive.

In December 1876, MacArthur received orders to report back to the 13th Regiment, still stationed at Jackson Barracks, and resume command of Company K. The year in Washington had not prepared Pinky for the realities of army life. Located on the west bank of the Mississippi River about 50 miles north of New Orleans, Jackson Barracks was an old army post, established in 1831. Because of congressional budget cuts, many of its buildings were in a state of permanent decay. Moreover, Jackson Barracks was a typical inbred army post, where relations were based on the position of each officer in his regiment. A stylized code of conduct was maintained in a rigidly graded, caste stratification. At social functions, subordinate officers and their wives deferred at all times to those of higher rank.

MacArthur was a relatively junior captain in the regiment, his commission dating back ten years. Promotion in the infantry was notoriously slow, and captains often remained in grade for twenty years. Now, his advancement depended as much on his wife's social skills as on his own ability as a company commander. Fortunately, Pinky's Southern charm complemented the captain's more distant manner. He seldom attended social functions at the post, leaving this aspect of army life to his wife. Pinky soon learned to bow to all her husband's superiors, to listen patiently to their wives, and to display a proper respect for the system at all times.[31]

Houses on the post were assigned according to rank. The best house belonged to the colonel, the second best to the lieutenant colonel, and so on straight down the line to the lowly second lieutenants. As on nearly all army posts, the buildings were constructed around a parade ground. On one side was an imposing structure where the colonel lived. Nearby were the officers' quarters. Bachelor officers shared quarters, and married officers lived in small two- or four-room cottages that were boiling hot in the summer.

Across the parade ground was the enlisted men's barracks, a long, one-story building with porches in front. Privates and corporals of each company bunked in a large, common room. Sergeants bunked in small cubicles, separated from the other enlisted men. Each company had an ordnance sergeant, a quartermaster sergeant, and a first sergeant. The latter was the most important man in the company next to the captain, who relied on the first sergeant to enforce discipline in the enlisted ranks.

Behind the barracks was the mess hall. On the other sides of the parade ground were administrative buildings, a guardhouse, a hospital, and a post trader's store.

Beyond the post's perimeter, small cabins, usually with tent additions, served as homes for the families of the enlisted men. This area was referred to as soapsuds row because the enlisted men's wives worked as laundresses and servants for the officers' families. A vast gap separated an officer's family from the families of enlisted personnel, and only on holidays did the two groups socialize.[32]

Pinky soon learned that life at Jackson Barracks followed an absolute routine. First bugle call was 5:45 A.M., reveille was at 6:00, and the garrison flag was raised at exactly 6:10. Breakfast was at 6:30, stable call at 7:10, sick call and fatigue duty at 7:30, assembly at 8:00 with duty assignment by platoons, and so on through the day. Every afternoon at 5:40, the captains marched their companies to the parade ground, where each unit formed up in line. The troops went through portions of the manual of arms, roll call was taken, and orders and assignments were read aloud before the parade was dismissed. The men were in their quarters by 9:00, and lights were out by 11:00. On Sundays, dress uniforms were worn for inspections.

The enlisted men ate their meals in the mess hall, sitting on long benches at bare wooden tables. Army rations remained basically the same for thirty years. Breakfast was salt bacon, hardtack, brown sugar or molasses, vinegar, and stew left simmering from dinner the night before. Because everything was thrown into the stew, it was called slumgullion. Lunch was more stew, perhaps some baked beans, some coarse bread, and coffee. Dinner was the same as lunch. Vegetables were not included in the rations, but each company maintained a vegetable garden to supplement the spare provisions.

Provided they had the money or credit, the men could augment their diet by purchasing food from the sutler, or post trader. But with congressional budget cuts, pay was low and sporadic: Regiments often did not see the paymaster for months. Like the food rations, the army pay scale had remained the same for thirty years. A private received $13 a month, $16 after six years, plus an annual clothing allowance of about $38. A sergeant major received $23 a month plus allowances. A second lieutenant was paid $113 a month, a captain $150, and a brigadier general $460. The annual salary of the ranking lieutenant general was $13,500. Officers also received an annual allowance to purchase all their equipment, including uniforms, weapons, and horses.

Most equipment was purchased at the post store, which operated under a franchise from the War Department. Other merchants were not permitted to compete with the post store, which had everything from canned peaches to shoelaces. The store also had a bar for enlisted men and a separate one for officers. Beer was the favored beverage. Packed in quart bottles in straw-filled barrels, it generally sold for $.50 a quart; in town, a quart of beer was only $.18. The sutler normally overcharged for everything since he had a monopoly, and on payday, he sat at the pay tables. The first priority of all army personnel was to take care of the debt they owed to the sutler. Officers and enlisted men considered the post trader a parasite, a vulture from which there was no protection.

Although the young bachelor officers at Jackson Barracks found New Orleans to be a mecca, married officers like Captain MacArthur did not have the time or the funds to socialize. Congress did not help matters. A House of Representatives controlled by the Democrats made conditions in the army almost unbearable following the disputed presidential election in 1876. The Democratic candidate, Samuel J. Tilden, a rich corporation lawyer and former governor of New York State, received a plurality of 250,000 votes over Republican candidate Rutherford B. Hayes in the November balloting; but after the Republicans manipulated the electoral college system, Hayes was declared the winner in late February 1877 by one electoral vote. Voters in New Orleans reacted violently to the decision, and the 13th Regiment was sent to the city to control the riots. Grant's decision to use federal troops to control the demonstrations irritated members of the Democratic-controlled House of Representatives, and they soon took it out on the army. For six months, Congress refused to appropriate funds for the army, and the troops went unpaid. Pinky, upset at having to borrow money simply to survive, began to pressure her husband to resign his commission and accept an offer to join the Hardy family business.

In the summer of 1877, the public's antimilitary attitude deepened when federal troops were used to control labor strikes in the industrialized cities of the Northeast and Midwest. A national railroad strike turned violent and was supported by sympathetic coal miners, stevedores, farmers, small businessmen, and tens of thousands of unemployed workers. MacArthur found himself in Scranton, Pennsylvania, assisting in the suppression of labor riots that seemed on the verge of destroying the social and political structure of the United States.

The antimilitary attitude was reflected in newspaper editorials that attacked the use of the army to support the corrupt political system and protect the interests of giant corporations. Fighting the Indians had also provoked major opposition from religious and pacifist groups, who depicted the Indians as noble savages and the soldiers as cruel and inhumane.

The attitude of the civilian public toward the military as a whole carried over in its opinion of the individual soldier. "A respectable American citizen," declared one newspaper, "would no more think of joining the Regular Army than he would volunteer for the penitentiary." Indeed, the rank and file were considered to be bums, loafers, and foreigners. General Sherman once said to a lady critical of the regular soldier, "Well, madame, you surely can't expect the possession of all the cardinal virtues for thirteen dollars a month," the base pay of a private.[33]

The disrespect civilians displayed for the enlisted men was not directed toward the officers, although their abilities were questioned. With all the economic opportunities available to a literate man, why would anyone be content to remain an officer in the army, where his job was in constant jeopardy and where the possibility of promotion was practically nil? Most businessmen, politicians, and even some scholars felt that a man of ability would never remain in the army when there were such lucrative and fruitful outlets in industry and finance.[34]

The *Army and Navy Journal* complained that "the name soldier, as [people at large] use it, seems to be a synonym for all that is degrading and low, and whenever they meet a person bearing it they cannot forbear showing their contempt." For example, when Charlie King, suffering from wounds sustained in the Indian campaigns, returned to Milwaukee on sick leave in 1878, people on the streets reacted to his uniform with "impudent jeering comment." Businessmen were no less mean-spirited: "Well, old fellow, how do you manage to kill time out in the Army—nothing but play poker and drink whiskey?" Historian Gerald Linderman observed, "When Andrew Carnegie exclaimed in 1881 that to him 'the real glory of America lay in the fact that she had no army worth the name,' he deftly caught the mood of his society in the fifteen years following the war."[35]

Pinky was not thrilled with army life, but Captain MacArthur, like most of his fellow officers, enjoyed the peaceful routine at Jackson Barracks. After seven years on the frontier, he knew this was a good duty post. Meanwhile, Pinky sought relief from the routine and the hot Louisiana weather by fleeing back to Riveredge each summer to be with her mother. In the spring of 1878, she became pregnant again and that year remained with her mother through the fall, even traveling north to New Britain, Connecticut, with the Hardy family. In fact, it was there that her second son, Malcolm, was born on October 17, 1878. Reluctantly, she rejoined her husband in early 1879.

Because of an outbreak of yellow fever in New Orleans, the 13th Regiment moved north to Baton Rouge, then was on the move again, first to Chattanooga, then to Atlanta, and finally to Little Rock, Arkansas. Pinky was back with her husband for only a couple of months when she became pregnant again. She seemed destined, like her mother who had borne eleven children, to be perpetually with child. On January 26, 1880, Douglas, her third son, was born. Judge MacArthur was delighted, for his third grandson had been born on his own sixty-third birthday. As the captain and his first son Arthur shared birthdays, one born on June 1 and the other on June 2, now Douglas shared his day with his grandfather.

Although Pinky was often moody (and having three young children to care for certainly justified her moodiness), married life agreed with Captain MacArthur. A relatively contented man, he became stocky as the years passed, and as his hair thinned on top, he grew a mustache. He now needed glasses to read, but he still spent most of his evenings devouring books. His dream was to command a regiment again before he retired, and he wanted to be well prepared. Therefore, he read all the books he could find on military strategy and tactics and read and re-read the many articles and memoirs appearing on the battles of the Civil War. He practiced his knowledge on a small scale with Company K as he drilled his men, engaged in field maneuvers, and demanded that every man in the company be an expert marksman. Target practice was obligatory, and sharpshooters were honored; in fact, no single aspect of training received more emphasis than small arms target practice. Most soldiers enjoyed target shooting as a sport and took great pride in their skill and marksmanship. The best shots in the company were awarded marksmen's badges and prizes, including furloughs. "The United States regular," one historian later concluded, "was probably the world's best military marksman, compared man for man with the soldiers of any of the world's standing armies."[36]

The primary change in terms of infantry equipment was the adoption of the Springfield '73 rifle (a breech-loading, single-shot, .45-caliber carbine) and the six-shot Colt .45 revolver. Metallic cartridges replaced the conical minié ball. Although a single-shot rifle, the Springfield's range, accuracy, and loading speed were excellent. Repeating arms, such as the Winchester '73, might have given the soldier the psychological feeling of greater potency, but the Springfield was superior in power and accuracy. With a maximum range of 1,000 yards, more than a half mile, the Springfield was an accurate, brutal weapon up to 500 yards. Its kick was severe, but its killing power was ferocious. The Springfield '73 remained the issued weapon until the Krag-Jorgensen rifle was adopted in 1892.

In June 1879, the 13th Infantry received a new commander, Colonel Luther P. Bradley. During the Civil War, Bradley had been with the Army of the Cumberland and participated in many of the same battles as Captain MacArthur. At the battle of Murfreesboro, he had commanded the 51st Illinois in Sheridan's 3rd Division. Bradley was promoted to brigadier general in July 1864 during the Atlanta campaign. Like many Volunteer officers, he joined the Regular Army after the war but had to accept the grade of lieutenant colonel. Finally, in June 1879, he was promoted to full colonel and assigned to command the 13th Infantry. Bradley liked and respected MacArthur and considered Company K one of the best infantry companies in the Regular Army.

The 13th Infantry's tour of duty in Little Rock, Arkansas, came to an end in the summer of 1880. To Pinky's horror, the regiment was assigned to Fort Wingate, New Mexico, an isolated post 100 miles northwest of Albuquerque. The regiment embarked by train on a trip that would take at least a week. Traveling through the deep South into Texas in the hot summer months could be enervating even for healthy young men; for Pinky, the trip was probably a nightmare. With three small children in tow—the oldest, Arthur III, was only four years old, Malcolm was nineteen months, and the baby, Douglas just six months old—the long train ride through Texas and into New Mexico drained Pinky.[37]

Arrival at Fort Wingate did not improve her mood. Wingate was not very attractive under the best of circumstances. "I never heard of a place," one officer later recalled, "which, for pure monotony, dreariness, and general worthlessness, could approach Fort Wingate." Established in 1860, periodically abandoned then reoccupied, the fort had decayed from neglect. Located high in the Zuni Mountains near the continental divide, Wingate was brutally hot in summer and brutally cold in winter. The area around the fort was laced with mesas, basins, and sandstone outcroppings, and the surrounding mountains rose as high as 11,000 feet.[38]

The 13th Regiment rebuilt and garrisoned the fort to guard the crews building the Atchison, Topeka and Santa Fe Railroad. Two cavalry companies also used the fort for operations against the Apache Indians. Five of the ten companies of the 13th Infantry, including Company K, were permanently stationed at the fort. The other five manned outposts south to the Rio Grande River. While the cavalry fought the Indians, the infantry policed the towns to curtail the activities of numerous outlaws in the area. In his *Reminiscences*, Douglas MacArthur romanticized this period in his father's career.

> In the eyes of the MacArthurs' three young sons, life at Fort Wingate was packed with adventure. Stories and rumors of notorious outlaws circulated often in the little world within the walls of the fort. Indians, whether sullen Chiricahua prisoners or peaceful Navaho sheepherders, were a daily sight. ... The mornings were filled with the cadenced sounds of barking sergeants and marching soldiers in close order drill. The crackling of [Springfield] rifles and the booming of field guns on practice ranges were everyday noises. ... All of life seemed regulated by the crisp, sometimes harsh

notes of bugles. A troop of cavalrymen would infrequently stop at the fort. ... For young and old at Wingate, the highlight of the year was the Fourth of July when parades, shooting contests, sack races, and other competitions marked the joyous celebration from early morning until late in the evening.[39]

For the boys' mother, life at Wingate was considerably less ideal. If Pinky had thought army life was hard at Jackson Barracks and Little Rock, it was almost unbearable at Wingate for a Southern belle with three small children. There were few luxuries and even fewer women with whom Pinky could socialize. Officers' families lived in cramped quarters. In fact, the facilities for families were mere hovels rather than homes. The buildings were one-story, adobe structures that were scattered in an irregular square around the omnipresent parade ground. They had flat dirt roofs that leaked rivulets of mud when it rained. To protect the occupants from the mud and the tarantulas and centipedes that nested in the dirt roofs, the ceilings inside were covered with canvas. The buildings had tiny windows that swung outward on hinges like doors because the ceilings were too low to allow them to slide up. The rooms were dark and uncomfortable. Most of the houses at least had rough floor boards. The officers' quarters barely conformed to army regulations that prescribed the minimum number of rooms for each grade: A lieutenant with a family was allotted a small cabin with one room and a kitchen; Captain MacArthur's family of five had two rooms and a kitchen. A tent lean-to in the rear expanded the space, but the tent area was unbearably hot in summer and freezing in winter. There was no school for the children.

Army life in an isolated post was monotonous and limited. According to one military historian, the shared hardships of a bleak climate and daily perils often made the army pioneers "closer to each other in some instances than many brothers and sisters." Supposedly, the garrison became one big, happy family. In reality, the residents engaged in constant bickering and gossip. Living so close together in an isolated community, it was impossible to hide anything, and personality conflicts were almost inevitable. Thus, "the dreary monotony of frontier garrison duty took its toll in alcoholism, excessive gambling, and cruelty to enlisted men on the part of weaker officers." Not surprisingly, the troops' morale was low: In 1881–1882, 248 of the 440 enlisted men in the 13th Infantry deserted.[40]

Life at Fort Wingate was more than Pinky had bargained for and beyond anything she could have imagined for herself and especially for her children. William Manchester, after extensive research, concluded that Pinky was "a complex woman, being both meek and tough, petulant and sentimental, charming and emotional. Under her mannered, pretty exterior she was cool, practical, and absolutely determined" that her children would be given every educational and social opportunity. She wanted her husband to resign his commission and take a job in business or practice law and perhaps, as he grew older, go into politics. In the meantime, she constantly harped on the dirty, primitive, and isolated conditions in which she was raising her three boys. They needed proper schooling, they needed playmates, and they needed the graces only obtainable in the polite society of the East. With Judge MacArthur's influence in Washington, D.C., and Milwaukee, plus the business connections of the Hardy family, Pinky thought the captain could easily get a good job in the civilian world. Given his talent, he would rise to the top of the corporate ladder, where he might amass millions.[41]

The captain, much like another famous army officer, William T. Sherman, wanted to please his wife "yet could not accept her uncompromising demands." MacArthur "felt financially and psychologically secure in the army despite its many shortcomings." Although he acknowledged that he dreamed of being more than a mere captain at an isolated frontier post, he, like most other army officers, wanted to remain in the service. He was convinced he was "perfect[ly] dependent" on the army "for a living." He probably assured his wife that, as he gained in rank, life in the army would be better. But she was not dissuaded from her desire to return to the more civilized eastern society. The captain might dream of better times, but Pinky knew it would be years before her husband would be promoted. The army was top-heavy with majors, colonels, and generals who still had years to go before retirement.[42]

The arguments Pinky and her husband had were reminiscent of the arguments Arthur had had with his father when he joined the 24th Wisconsin in 1862. Arthur did not want to be a lawyer, had no desire for the dull life of the business world, and was appalled at the suggestion that he might join the corrupt world of politics. He loved the democratic principles of the republic, but politicians and business leaders did not have his respect. As a rule, he felt superior to businessmen and politicians and thought being a military officer was a far more honorable profession. Most Civil War veterans, historian Gerald Linderman noted, "did not much like" the new industrial magnates. While MacArthur had fought at Missionary Ridge and Franklin,

> J. Pierpont Morgan, John D. Rockefeller, and Andrew Carnegie had hired substitutes [and] had built the foundations of great wealth. Phillip Armour's first great strike had come when he sold pork short in 1864. Jay Gould, Jay Cooke, Jim Fisk, and Collis Huntington had established or multiplied their fortunes while soldiers fought. So it was with a combination of anger and envy that veterans regarded the financial and social success of such people.[43]

MacArthur considered most businessmen to be money-hungry, power-hungry, selfish men. Like many other professionals—such as teachers, doctors, and ministers—he rejected the idea that the purpose of life was the pursuit of the almighty dollar.

Besides, he felt he should remain in the army for practical reasons as well. His job was secure, and his pay, through seniority raises and deflation, was actually increasing. The cost of living dropped almost 50 percent in the 1870s, while MacArthur's pay increased over 50 percent through annual seniority raises. He was not likely to become a millionaire, but he had a secure job in a profession that he loved.[44]

It was easy, he felt, for Pinky to advocate that he resign his commission—she did not have to deal with the economic realities. Though a few men were making fortunes, millions of others were unemployed. In the rapid economic transformation of the United States from 1865 to 1880, most men worked long hours in insecure jobs for dismal wages. The average U.S. urban worker earned $6 to $9 for a sixty-hour week, or from $300 to $500 a year. In the depression that lasted from 1873 to 1879, thousands of small businessmen went bankrupt and soon found themselves working in the offices of giant corporations, lost in a world of conferences, consultations, and compromises.[45]

The captain was convinced that the quiet army life was best for him. If he joined a business, he would have to start at the bottom and lose almost twenty years of seniority. At Wingate, he was isolated from the raging economic and political storms, and even the assassination of President James A. Garfield in July 1881 created only a minor ripple on the far-flung frontier post. Despite the isolation (or perhaps because of it), the captain returned to reading with a passion as he continued to receive a stream of books from his father. Though he enjoyed playing cards in the evenings with his brother officers, he did not enjoy social functions where the ladies were also invited. He preferred the company of men who had comparable interests and whose opinion of him determined his position within the closed ranks of the officers corps. In turn, his brother officers respected him for his stable personality, his well-researched beliefs, and his long military experience, but they noted that he was not an overly friendly man. He seldom went to the officers' club or took part in social affairs. Edward Brown, at Fort Wingate in 1882, noted that MacArthur was respected but that he was not as popular as "rough and profane" officers like Adna R. Chaffee, a cavalry captain at Wingate.[46]

MacArthur did take an interest in his children but apparently spent most of his time with his eldest son. By the age of five, Arthur III could be taken on rides and often accompanied his father's troops on short supply trips. Arthur became much like his father, serious and responsible. Douglas, only a year old at the time, and Malcolm, almost three, remained with their mother. Because there were few children at the post, Douglas and Malcolm were each other's playmates. Biographer Carol Petillo later speculated that "Malcolm was probably Douglas's first friend, the bigger brother who could walk and talk, and who had developed capacities for achievement for which the baby Douglas could only aspire."[47]

When her mother died in the fall of 1881, Pinky wanted to return to Virginia to be with her family and to settle the estate, which had been left to the nine surviving children. Captain MacArthur was granted a leave in April 1882, and the family arrived in Norfolk in early May. In delicate negotiations at Riveredge, the Hardy family estate was divided up, with Pinky inheriting $40,000, a fortune at the time. The captain invested the money, and the family would remain on sound financial footing for the rest of his life; there was enough money to eventually send the boys to private academies and to provide Pinky with the luxuries of life.[48]

While Pinky and the children spent most of their time at Riveredge, the captain visited his father in Washington, D.C. The judge was at the height of his political influence. In talks with his son, he realized that life on the frontier was difficult for a married man, so he contacted a number of his friends to see if his son could be assigned a better duty.

The idea that most appealed to the captain developed in a meeting with former president Grant. When in Washington, Grant nearly always visited the judge. He loved to listen to the judge's stories, particularly ones that involved Grant's own administration. Perhaps his favorite was the judge's story on the appointment to the Supreme Court of Chief Justice Morrison R. Waite in 1874. When Chief Justice Salmon P. Chase died in 1873, Grant was besieged by people wanting the appointment. His first two nominees had been rejected by the Senate, and Grant agonized over whose name he should submit next. A number of people wanted Judge MacArthur to suggest a particular candidate to Grant, and the judge reluctantly agreed to intervene. The president apparently expected MacArthur to solicit the appointment for himself, so when the judge asked, "Mr. President, may I speak about the matter of the Supreme Court appointment?" Grant had replied rather curtly, "Certainly, on one condition."

"And that condition?"

"That you are not a candidate and are not going to urge your own appointment."

"On, no!" said Judge MacArthur with a smile, "I would never suspect this administration of making so sagacious a selection."[49]

When Grant was invited to the MacArthur house in May 1882 to meet the judge's older son, he accepted. He was impressed with the young captain, who did not fit the stereotyped image of a frontier officer. Scholars, politicians, and businessmen assumed that most frontier officers were uneducated, semi-illiterates. The image presented in books and newspapers suggested that army officers were lazy and narrow-minded and commanded troops who were dirty, stupid, and illiterate; as the years progressed, the officers' only claims to fame were Civil War deeds that were exaggerated in the retelling. In the minds of many, the officers were not true professional soldiers who studied warfare, economics, and philosophy.

That stereotype certainly did not fit Captain MacArthur, and perhaps it fit only a few of the officers of the period. At Wingate, he was physically isolated from the mainstream of American life, but he was not isolated intellectually, for even there, books, newspapers, and magazines were available. Equally significant, he had served on many posts throughout his military career. Most civilians lived their lives out in one place, but Captain MacArthur had lived in nearly every area of the United States except the extreme West Coast.

He was intensely proud of his intellectual heritage, and all his life, be it in the comfort of his father's home or in a desolate frontier garrison, he would pursue knowledge. Military history interested him, of course, and he studied the great battles of Western history, from the Peloponnesian Wars to the Franco-Prussian War of 1870. Certainly, when General Grant and Captain MacArthur met, they reviewed the crop of Civil War memoirs appearing each year and compared these accounts to what they remembered from the common battles they had seen. The two men talked of other subjects as well.

Grant was particularly delighted with the captain's interest in Far Eastern culture and history. The general had just returned from a trip to the Far East, and the Orient fascinated him. He discussed his China tour with MacArthur, and the two analyzed the situation there. Grant enjoyed the conversation so much that he invited MacArthur to continue the discussion later, and the two met several times in May 1882. Learning that the captain's wife was dissatisfied with life on the frontier, Grant suggested that MacArthur apply to the War Department to be sent to China as a military attaché. The idea thrilled MacArthur. Grant then offered to use his influence with the War Department and President Chester A. Arthur to obtain the appointment. Honoring his promise, Grant wrote a number of letters recommending MacArthur for an assignment to China because of his impressive knowledge of Chinese affairs.[50]

The bureaucratic machinery in Washington was notoriously slow, but the secretary of war eventually requested an updated service record from the Adjutant General's Office. MacArthur filled out a formal application for the assignment and updated his service record. On May 15, hoping desperately to be assigned to China, MacArthur requested a six months' leave extension. Since he had had no leave for seven years, army regulations permitted him to request up to four months on full pay plus two months on half pay.

Two things happened. First, he got in trouble. In filling out the request for transfer, MacArthur correctly stated his birth date as June 2, 1845, his age as thirty-six. The adjutant general, in reviewing the captain's records, noted a discrepancy: When he had joined the Regular Army in April 1866, he had declared he was twenty-two, which would have made him thirty-eight in 1882. MacArthur tried to explain, but it was obvious to the adjutant general that he had lied. The War Department asked for clarification, and it took a number of letters before the corrected birth date was accepted.[51]

MacArthur's request for extended leave time also irritated his division commander, General Sheridan. Nearly every officer stationed on the frontier was attempting to pull strings to be reassigned to other duties. So, despite presidential interest in the case, Sheridan denied MacArthur's request and ordered him to report back to the 13th Regiment at Fort Wingate by May 24. By the time MacArthur received his orders, he had only six days to make the trip back to Wingate, over 2,000 miles away. Pinky refused to contemplate such a journey and argued that her husband should resign his commission rather than submit to the orders. He rejected the idea. Leaving Pinky and his children at Norfolk, he made a frantic journey and arrived at Wingate within the allotted time. Railroads now criss-crossed the nation, and the trip reinforced in the captain's mind the idea that the days of the outlaw and the Indian raider were numbered.[52]

Back with the 13th Regiment, MacArthur still hoped that his request to be assigned as a military attaché to China would be approved. In early September, he again requested a leave of absence to return to Norfolk to be with his family. Surprisingly, what had been so arbitrarily rejected in May received approval only four months later. Colonel Bradley, commander of the 13th Infantry, liked MacArthur and was sympathetic. Bradley approved the leave and noted, "Captain MacArthur's long & faithful services entitles him to favorable consideration at all times." The request received endorsement through the chain of command and finally was approved on October 2, 1882.[53]

While in Norfolk sorting out Thomas Hardy's will, MacArthur also worked on preparing a strong case to support his appointment to China. He carefully wrote and typed a forty-four-page manuscript that he titled "Chinese Memorandum" and sent the manuscript to General Grant, who forwarded it to the president.[54]

MacArthur's first scholarly paper represented the best and the worst of the new bureaucratic, academic literary style that had become popular in the 1870s. It illustrated that MacArthur had done extensive reading in Chinese, Russian, European, and U.S. history, and the opinions he expressed echoed the advanced ideas of his time. For example, ten years before Frederick Jackson Turner published his famous essay on the disappearing American frontier, MacArthur noted its passage. He observed that, because of the expanding railroad network, problems with hostile Indians and frontier outlaws would diminish. He foresaw that the major security problem facing the nation was the labor upheaval in the industrialized Northeast. Labor strikes were already ravaging the nation, and on several occasions, the army had been used in riot suppression. To avoid depressions and labor uprisings, MacArthur believed the United States needed to expand its markets to absorb the overproduction made possible by industrialization. "No matter how rich we may be in accumulated capital," he wrote, "restriction of production, by reason of restriction of markets, means stagnation of business and social disturbances." The solution, he said, was to increase U.S. exports to China. "The American Republic," MacArthur wrote, "can never acquire its full complement of riches and power if it permits itself to be excluded from the field of Asiatic commerce."[55]

It would be absurd to believe that either the president or the secretary of war bothered to read the ambitious paper written by a mere infantry captain. If they had, they would have needed a dictionary and a sheet of paper to outline the ideas and discover the enlightened meaning hidden by MacArthur's esoteric vocabulary and convoluted sentences. His model (and probably his adviser) was his father, who eventually wrote seven books and dozens of articles on topics as varied as Mary, Queen of Scots, to the need to establish vocational educational institutions in the United States. The judge was a magnificent public speaker but merely an adequate writer, primarily because of his desire to be taken seriously. When he took up his pen on scholarly topics, he wrote meticulous prose that was heavy with words of Greek and Latin origin. As a self-educated man, the judge tried to impress his readers with his extensive vocabulary. Unfortunately, he had a tremendous influence on his son's writing style. Indeed, the style became a trademark in the MacArthur family. Just as the judge had taught his sons, the captain taught his own boys. Captain MacArthur, however, was even less adept at the style than either his father or his son Douglas. Arthur had worked on expanding his vocabulary and enjoyed using grandiose words, but if he seldom misused them in the sense of distorting their meanings, he did abuse them by stringing together too many inflated and obscure terms. Yet his paper on China could have easily been delivered to a graduate seminar, and it did reflect the captain's vast reading.

Nonetheless, Captain MacArthur's dream of being appointed as a military attaché to China had no chance of being realized, for in 1883, the United States maintained no military attachés in any foreign country. Six years later, they were sent for the first time to sixteen countries, mostly European.

While the family was still at Norfolk, tragedy struck. In early April 1883, all of the MacArthur children fell ill with the measles. The captain helped Pinky nurse their children through the attack, but on April 12, four-year-old Malcolm died. His death was a shattering blow, particularly for Pinky and three-year-old Douglas. Malcolm had been Douglas's best friend, and with the loss, the young child turned to his mother for more affection. Carol Petillo observed,

> Coming as it did on the heels of her mother's death, the tragedy may even have had a more vital effect on Pinkie's immediate response. If, as so frequently happens, she dealt with the first loss by incorporating some of the dimensions of her mother's personality into her own outlook, Malcolm's death might have resulted in an even more intense guilt than usual. In her last years, Pinkie's mother had retreated into a maternal pessimism unrelieved by the comfort of her religion or the attention of her children. Malcolm's death, therefore, occurring as it did in Pinkie's childhood home, may have stirred and intensified the feelings of remorse which always accompany the death of a close family member.[56]

Malcolm's death caused Pinky to hug her youngest child even closer in her grief. She wanted him to remain her baby; despite the captain's objections, Pinky dressed Douglas in a skirt and a long, full blouse for the funeral, attire that perhaps fit the eastern social dress code for three-year-old boys but would have been inappropriate for the rough-and-tumble life of a frontier army post like Wingate.[57]

With his bid to become a military attaché rejected, the captain decided, in May 1883, to rejoin his regiment at Fort Wingate, where he could hide his sorrow in work. "As we reach midlife in the middle thirties or early forties," social psychologist Gail Sheehy noted, "we become susceptible to the idea of our own perishability." "The first time that message comes through is probably the worst." Some of us

Fort Selden, New Mexico, c. 1885. (Photo by J. R. Riddle, courtesy Museum of New Mexico, neg. 14523)

respond, as Captain MacArthur, by "keeping busy, pretending to carry on as if nothing has changed." "We elude it by pretending to function as before. Some people press down harder on the career accelerator."[58]

In June, Pinky and the children joined MacArthur at Wingate. For the family, the winter of 1883–1884 was a sad time. The captain channeled his emotional energies into the fort's routine and grieved over the loss of his son only in the privacy of his home. He became even more withdrawn, avoided all informal social affairs, and stopped playing cards. Pinky pleaded with her husband to resign his commission and return to civilization. He ignored his wife's pleas. Military life at Wingate was familiar and reassuring. If he persevered, the captain believed he would be promoted; then, things would become easier for the family. The army was his life, and perhaps the battles of the Civil War still echoed in his ears.[59]

In February 1884, Company K, under the command of Captain MacArthur, was detached to Fort Selden, a post 300 miles south of Wingate near the Rio Grande, about 60 miles north of El Paso. Although Selden had been established in 1865, the fort had been abandoned between 1877 and 1882. In 1882, Company D of the 13th Infantry took up garrison duty at Selden to protect crews building the Santa Fe Railroad from Albuquerque to El Paso.

MacArthur welcomed the new assignment because it meant an independent command. On February 25, 1884, Company K—three officers on horseback (the captain, First Lieutenant William W. Tyler, and Second Lieutenant William Hughes), an assistant surgeon, five sergeants (including First Sergeant Peter Riply), four corporals, a musician, and forty privates, plus the wives and children—marched out of Wingate. They had a supply wagon as well as an ambulance, each pulled by four mules. The first 100 miles down the banks of the Rio Puerco to Albuquerque took almost a week.[60]

At Albuquerque, the company turned southwest and followed the Rio Grande about 100 miles to Fort Craig, a one-company garrison post about 10 miles north of Fray Cristobal, near the beginning of the dangerous dry route west known as the Jornada del Muerto. "In crossing the Rio Grande [by ferry] on March 8th near Fort Craig," MacArthur reported, "the cable parted. The river was high and four mules and a loaded wagon were on the boat. Sergt. Henry R. Jameson saved three mules. Sergt. George Chapman and men were able to save the wagon."[61]

The final and most grueling stretch of the journey was the last 100 miles from Fort Craig to Fort Selden. It was a dry desert area, a monotonous, level plain only sparsely covered with dingy grass and low bush greasewood that stretched until it met the horizon in all directions. The trail diverted away from the banks of the Rio Grande, and for about five days, it was necessary to ration water. Company K finally reached Selden on March 14, taking about three weeks to make the journey from Wingate. MacArthur relieved Company D of the 13th Infantry, which departed on March 17 for Wingate.[62]

Selden was a miserable little fort in a godforsaken land, and Pinky was no doubt appalled. The fort would be her home for the next two and one-half years. Located at the southern end of the Jornada del Muerto in the Mesilla Valley about 1.5 miles north of the Rio Grande, Selden was one of the most isolated garrisons in the entire nation. El Paso was a long 60 miles south. A mile and a half south of Selden, there was the tiny village of Leesburg, which had a general store, a grog shop, and a few miserable huts for the Mexican workers of the area. Eighteen miles south of Selden was the small town of Las Cruces, where there was a hotel called L'Amador. The English translation was "Lover," and apparently, the twenty-three rooms were used by prostitutes.[63]

The site for Selden had been chosen to guard a major ford across the Rio Grande and to provide a base for cavalry operations in the area. A ferry operated across the river to the base of the only high ground in the area, Mount Robledo. There were no trees and little grass near Selden, and the countryside was flat, sandy desert laced with gulleys. A mule-drawn wagon hauled water daily from the Rio Grande to the fort. From November through April, the weather was relatively cool, but by July, the heat was dreadful, and there was not a green thing anywhere—only tarantulas, scorpions, centipedes, rattlesnakes, lizards, and rabbits survived in the sun-scorched land.

The buildings at Selden were in a sad state when Company K arrived. There were about a dozen crude, single-story, adobe buildings with flat, dirt roofs and earthen floors. The largest was the enlisted men's barracks, which was about 90 feet long and 24 feet wide. There were four small cottages for the officers. All the buildings had front porches to provide shade during the long, hot summers.[64]

MacArthur's first job was to repair and whitewash the buildings, inside and out. The company did most of the work, but some civilian craftsmen were also used. MacArthur hired blacksmiths, carpenters, bricklayers, saddlers, wheelmakers, and teamsters who received between $40 and $60 a month for their labors. With the buildings neatly repaired, MacArthur felt the pride of his first independent command.[65]

Bleak as Selden was, the move was the exact prescription needed for the MacArthurs to heal from the wounds caused by Malcolm's death. At Selden, the small company was isolated; no social duties were required of Pinky, and as commander, the captain decided what was needed and what was not needed. In May 1884, Pinky wrote to one of her sisters in Massachusetts that she liked Selden very much. Although the garrison was a "lonely place," she wrote, at least "Arthur is in command and I can do just as I want. I have only three rooms and small kitchen, but it is enough for my family." She informed her sister that she and the captain had decided to have no more children. Pinky was fitted with a pessary, a birth control device. This, as Carol Petillo observed,

> was less than usual for women of that time period. She probably would have had to make the arrangements for obtaining the device while on one of her trips East, and might have had to visit several doctors before finding one who would supply her with the pessary. That she had gone to these lengths confirms the strength of her decision to escape the fate her mother suffered, and the forthrightness with which she approached her goals.[66]

Far from any interference by superiors, MacArthur implemented some of his theories for the proper training of men, albeit on a small scale. He insisted on absolute conformity to military rules and regulations. His Civil War experiences and his later readings in military theory and tactics convinced him that future wars would be won not by individual acts of bravery but through team performance and through the troops' total obedience to their commanding officers. Modern weapons had altered the qualifications of the ideal soldier: Rather than being a strong physical specimen who could win in hand-to-hand combat, he would be a trooper who could obey orders under heavy rifle and artillery fire. Victory depended on the skill of the men in using modern weapons, so MacArthur insisted on constant target practice. To achieve discipline and ready obedience to orders, there were morning and afternoon drills, daily inspections, and weekly rifle practice.[67]

With only one infantry company, Selden was too small for a post trader. This pleased the captain because he was able to open a company canteen where the enlisted men could socialize outside the barracks: They could buy beer, snacks, and smoking tobacco and play a game of pool or cards without worrying about the officers. The canteen's profits went into buying special foods for the enlisted men's mess, a pool table, books and magazines, and seeds for a company vegetable garden. Selden's canteen was the first established on an army base, and its success stimulated the formation of a canteen system that eventually replaced the franchised sutlers.[68]

The training exercises worked. The men of Company K began to believe they were the best company in the U.S. Army, and they performed accordingly. Significantly, in the two years at Selden, one of the worst garrison duties in the nation, Company K had the lowest desertion rate in the army. The unity and spirit of the company was noted by officers passing through. The men of Company K had become one big family: They lived together, worked together, and shared hardships and joys together. But they always remained Regular Army. No one forgot proper military protocol, and no one viewed the captain as a chum.[69]

Although the captain was a reserved, almost austere man, in the eyes of his two little boys he was the most romantic figure that ever lived. Douglas and Arthur would look back on their days at Selden, where their father was constantly with them, as the happiest time of their lives. Both the boys and their father assumed that they would enter one of the military academies and become officers someday. In the interim, the captain quietly took over their education. Along with the three Rs, he instilled in them a stern sense of discipline and pride in the family heritage. They were expected to obey his orders and conform to the same strict discipline as his men. Doug, as the captain called him, was only four when they arrived at Selden and seven when they left, but in those three years, his father's teachings, in the words of one biographer, were "tamped down into his subconscious being." Douglas and his brother learned that a MacArthur was a man of superior talents, who was obligated to conduct himself with honor and gallantry. The boys would never lose their love of country, flag, and honor that their father implanted in them during these early formative years. And there was another word that the captain used constantly—duty. Douglas remembered that his father insisted that a MacArthur must "do what was right no matter what the personal sacrifice might be."[70]

The captain taught his sons that an officer, besides being brave in battle, must also be a scholar and a gentleman. As William A. Ganoe would later observe, he taught his sons that "the word 'gentleman' ... was sacredly higher than any title, station, or act of Congress. It was an attitude of life to be cherished in every gesture and spoken word. It comprehended and excused no letdown in its execution." If the boys displayed any temper tantrums, the captain disciplined them. "Flying off the handle, berating or bawling out were cardinal sins." If the boys irritated him, the captain's "voice grew low, falling to a deep bass and intoning, with a control so strong, it held motionless everyone within its sound. ... With all his high-strung impulses, he held himself in check. ... And in about ten words he summoned up a deserved and consummate loathing. Even in reproof and rebuff, he kept the lofty manners of a gentleman."[71]

Although the captain insisted that the boys study their books, life was not all dull schoolwork. He allowed his two boys to spend much of their time in the barracks and stables with the soldiers, to the mutual enjoyment of both men and

Captain Arthur MacArthur and family, c. 1886. From left: Douglas, Captain MacArthur, Arthur III, Pinky. (MacArthur Memorial Library, Ph-69)

boys. As army brats, riding and shooting became an integral part of their lives, and the captain bought them two spotted Navajo ponies. It is easy to visualize, as William Manchester did, the boys "shoeless and shirtless, wearing only head-bands and fringed leggings of tanned hide [riding] off into open country taking potshots at rabbits." Sometimes, the boys hitched rides on the mule-drawn water wagon "that made its regular trip to the Rio Grande, a mile and a half from the post. And there were visiting officers and mounted details from the cavalry post at Fort Stanton to the east that guarded the nearby Mescalero Apache reservation. Toward twilight each evening the company would go through the ceremony of re-treat and the lowering of the flag, and while the bugle sounded, the two little boys would stand at stiff attention."[72]

Douglas would remember the Fort Selden days with romantic fondness. All his life, he would consider himself a frontiersman, and in later years, he loved to watch western movies. In *Reminiscences,* he recalled cowboys, Indians, cavalrymen, and gunfighters visiting the fort. Douglas saw Selden as a place where the plains broke off and the land gets rough and unruly—a lonely land of sun and silence. Not yet had the plough turned over the grass, nor the land been spanned by ribbons of steel; not yet tamed by the snorting iron horses, frightening off the buffalo herds; not yet the barbed wire to choke off the endless acres. ... A bright land of promise scarred only by wind and weather—a land with unknown mountains to be climbed, alluring trails to be ridden, streams to be navigated by the strong and vigorous—a land of water holes, dusty sagebrush, of sturdy pines. ... It was the Old West of frontier days, with its thrilling adventures into which Captain MacArthur plunged. ... He knew the badmen of those days—the James boys, the Youngers—and the picturesque scouts and lawmen such as "Wild Bill" Hickok and "Buffalo Bill." He was at the center of disorder and violence, the fighting involved in this drama of undisciplined and untamed men.[73]

The reality, however, was vastly different. Selden was a hard post in a hard land. Ironically, for all that hardship, Company K never had even one contact with hostile Indians during the years of MacArthur's command. When Geronimo and a small band of Chiricahua Apaches broke out of the Arizona reservation in May 1885, the last Apache war began, striking terror in settlers and travelers across the Southwest. Traveling light, Geronimo headed for Mexico and raided isolated ranches and small communities along his path. Experts at ambush, the Apaches struck savagely and fled before the cavalry appeared.

Army tactics were based on pursuit, and the role of the infantry was to maintain strategic garrisons to resupply the cavalry. Although Company K often found evidence of prior Apache attacks, the men never saw an Apache and never fired a shot at one. Ultimately, General Nelson A. Miles pursued Geronimo until he was captured; Captain Henry Lawton accepted the chieftain's surrender in northern Mexico in September 1886.[74]

The Apache uprising affected Company K and Captain MacArthur in a subtle but permanent way. In September 1885, Major G. H. Burton, assistant adjutant general of the Department of the Missouri from Fort Leavenworth, visited Selden. Burton was impressed with the fort's combat readiness and wrote a glowing report back to his superior:

> Captain MacArthur's company was inspected and drilled in full dress, and, subsequently, ordered into camp. The military bearing and appearance of the troops were very fine. Captain MacArthur impresses me as an officer of more than ordinary ability, and very zealous in the performance of duty. The company and post show evidence of intelligent, judicious, and masterly supervision. This company has more comforts in the barrack and amusement room than any other organization I have visited, and, in fact, there are no criticisms of an unfavorable nature that could be made on this organization.[75]

Major Burton's report came to the attention of brevet Major General Alexander McCook, commandant of the newly established Infantry and Cavalry School at Fort Leavenworth, Kansas. During the Civil War, McCook had commanded Rosecrans's 1st Corps in the battle of Murfreesboro. Sheridan's 3rd Division, in-

cluding the 24th Wisconsin, had been part of McCook's corps. Although it is unlikely that he remembered MacArthur from Civil War days, McCook did recognize the name because he knew Judge MacArthur: They had met in Washington
in November 1879 at the eleventh reunion of the Society of the Army of the Cumberland. Thousands attended the event, including the president, the secretary of
war, and Generals Sherman, McDowell, Hancock, Hunter, Garfield, Davis, and
Buell. MacArthur introduced McCook as the keynote speaker, and the judge's humor and entrancing speaking style impressed everyone, including McCook.[76]

MacArthur's Company K received a plum assignment in September 1886, when
the 13th Infantry was reorganized. With Geronimo's capture, the army high command concluded the Indian wars were over; thus, there was no need to garrison
isolated forts like Selden. The number of western posts occupied by the army consequently dropped from a high of 111 in 1880 to less than 62 by 1891. The 13th Infantry was withdrawn from isolated posts along the Rio Grande and dispersed
over a wide territory, from Fort Crawford in Colorado to Little Rock, Arkansas.
Regimental headquarters was established at Fort Supply in Indian Territory. General McCook requested that MacArthur's Company K be detached as an "instructor" company for Fort Leavenworth's Infantry and Cavalry School. It was a dream
assignment for Captain MacArthur.

Company K packed up and left Selden for Leavenworth on September 6, 1886.
MacArthur's frontier days had finally come to an end, and his career would soon
undergo a dramatic change.

10

On Staff

LEAVENWORTH WAS A welcome change for Captain MacArthur's family. Located on the Missouri River near Lawrence, Kansas, it served as a supply depot for forts west of the Mississippi, as the headquarters post for the Department of the Missouri, as the site of the army's major military prison, and as the location of the army's new Infantry and Cavalry Training School. Thousands of officers and men were permanently stationed at Leavenworth.[1]

In late September 1886, the MacArthurs moved into an apartment in a large, two-story frame house on officers' row. After years of living in adobe huts at Selden and Wingate, the apartment seemed luxurious, and Pinky was delighted. There were excellent schools for Douglas and Arthur III, libraries with thousands of books to satisfy the voracious appetite of the captain, and, for Pinky, stores, theaters, and restaurants for socializing with the wives of other officers. Pinky enrolled the boys in the post school, and due to the captain's excellent tutoring, the teachers placed Douglas, only six years old, in the second grade and his ten-year-old brother Arthur in the sixth grade. The boys now had playmates, but they still never tired of watching their father's company march in the afternoon parades.[2]

MacArthur enjoyed his new assignment. Lieutenants from every regiment came to Leavenworth for a two-year course of instruction at the Infantry and Cavalry Training School. The school designed its curriculum and routine to teach the young lieutenants their duties at the company level. The school provided more than the basics. Courses in mathematics, world history, military theory, and military law supplemented constant drills and field maneuvers. During his long years on the frontier, MacArthur had been preparing to train men for battle. His knowledge of all aspects of military affairs was impressive, and his students were in awe of his Civil War record. He emphasized that an officer's prime responsibility was to train enlisted men to obey orders instantaneously. Training and discipline counted in war as nowhere else, and the officer who knew his trade was more effective than the novice. Civil War battles were analyzed, each movement of troops examined in depth, and personal accounts by participants were required reading. Drawing on his war experiences, MacArthur lectured to the young officers on the battles of Murfreesboro, Missionary Ridge, and the Atlanta campaign.

He advised them never to attack a fortified position if the position could be flanked and warned them that a company of troops should never form into columns for an attack. He also carefully explained the purpose of reconnaissance. Modern weapons dictated that officers examine the terrain, select a spot that provided some protection, then charge to that position, halt, reform, and push forward by a series of rushes that slowly closed in on the enemy. "Seek protection behind any tree or rock or in gulleys," he advised.[3]

MacArthur's knowledge of infantry tactics impressed his fellow instructors. When he described to a class the 24th Wisconsin's reconnaissance up Kennesaw Mountain on June 22, 1864, fellow instructor Captain Arthur L. Wagner took careful notes; when Wagner later wrote a textbook, required at the school, he cited the action as a classic example of proper infantry tactics.[4]

Although MacArthur was happy at Leavenworth, he was disappointed that his career was not proceeding more rapidly. In 1887, 110 of the 2,100 officers in the army had not received a promotion for twenty years. Fifty-nine of these were infantry captains, and MacArthur was on the list. Infantry captains were passed over time and time again as cavalry, artillery, and staff captains obtained promotions to major. Gail Sheehy observed that most men in an age group and a position comparable to MacArthur's at that point have felt "a sense of stagnation, disequilibrium, and depression." Some "intruder" usually shakes them as they "enter the passage of midlife" and shouts: "Take stock! Half your life has been spent. What about the side of you that wants to contribute to the world? You've done some good work, but what does it really add up to?"[5]

In the summer of 1888, MacArthur learned there was a staff opening, grade of major, in the Inspector General's Office, and he applied for the position. Perhaps he felt this was his last chance to pull away from the pack. It was no longer enough to be the loyal junior officer, the promising but no longer young infantry captain. It was time to command his own destiny.

At that time, the army was divided into two basic components: line and staff. Line officers were members of infantry, cavalry, and artillery units. Staff officers belonged to departments charged with the purchase and distribution of supplies, the payment of troops, and the performance of other administrative duties. There were ten such departments, each with a bureau chief and a large staff. The most powerful of the staff departments was the Adjutant General's Office, in charge of personnel, followed by the Inspector General's Office and the Quartermaster General's Office. Line officers eagerly sought staff positions, making the competition fierce. Staff officers had much greater opportunities for promotion and enjoyed privileges and working conditions that line officers envied. Over one-fourth of the 2,100 army officers served in staff departments, and staff was swollen with high rank: Staff had 7 of the 13 brigadier generals, 31 of the 75 colonels, 37 of the 80 lieutenant colonels, and 172 of the 242 majors. When a staff position opened, line officers strenuously competed and pulled every possible string to secure the appointment. Once appointed, a staff officer had lifetime tenure.[6]

MacArthur supported his application to the Inspector General's Office with an impressive array of documents that dated back to August 1862. His service record included recommendations from Civil War generals, Wisconsin politicians, and every commanding officer he had served under since 1866. He supplemented the official record with new letters of recommendation from his fellow officers at Leavenworth, who rushed to support his application. The highest praise came from his commanding officer, Colonel McCook, brevet major general, who wrote the secretary of war that MacArthur "was beyond question the most distinguished captain in the army of the United States."[7]

MacArthur's prime competitor for the position was Henry Lawton, a dashing cavalry captain whose career ran a parallel course with MacArthur's. At the age of twenty-two, Lawton commanded a regiment during the Civil War, with the rank of lieutenant colonel. After the war, he joined the Regular Army as a first lieutenant and remained in grade from 1867 to 1879, when he was promoted to captain of the 4th Cavalry. Lawton achieved national fame when he accepted the surrender of the Apache chief, Geronimo, in September 1886. The public fell in love with him. Over six feet tall, slim and physically attractive, intelligent and humorous, Lawton looked and acted like a future general. While many officers considered the rather staid MacArthur to be the army's foremost infantry captain, many also considered Lawton its foremost cavalry captain. MacArthur was a rock of stability, Lawton a fountain of animation. In grade less than ten years, Lawton was junior in rank to MacArthur. Of the 662 captains in the U.S. Army, MacArthur ranked number 34 in seniority, and Lawton ranked 234.

On September 18, 1888, MacArthur received bad news: The appointment to the Inspector General's Office had gone to Lawton. MacArthur was crushed. With twenty-two years in grade, he had been jumped over by junior captains fifty-two times, primarily because of favoritism shown to the cavalry. If seniority alone had been the criteria, he would have achieved the rank of major in 1881. To make matters worse, just five months later, on February 12, 1889, Lawton received another promotion to lieutenant colonel, while MacArthur remained a captain.[8]

In Washington, Judge MacArthur was extremely upset. He had often tried to obtain appointments for Arthur, but in the 1870s and 1880s, the judge was more concerned with his younger son. After graduating from Harvard, studying law, and being admitted to the New York bar in 1885, Frank joined a law firm in New York City. In 1886, he published a book on patent law, his speciality. In May of that year, he married Rose Winston, a girl from Alabama, and two years later had a son, whom they named Malcolm. The judge visited them often and enjoyed his new grandson.

With Frank settled into a career and family life, the judge turned his attention to his other son once again. He had retired from the federal bench at the age of seventy in January 1887 to devote his time to writing and his family. When Arthur applied to the Inspector General's Office, the judge was delighted. The appointment to staff would mean that Arthur and his family would probably move to

Washington, and the judge looked forward to having his grandchildren near him. Understandably, Lawton's appointment to the staff post upset the judge, who was convinced that his son should have received it.

Shortly thereafter, when a new staff vacancy occurred in the Adjutant General's Office, Judge MacArthur used his political influence to obtain the position for his son. At the judge's request, friendly congressmen, senators, and business leaders wrote to the president and the secretary of war recommending Captain MacArthur. Postmaster General William F. Vilas, a close friend of the judge's, even talked to President Cleveland on MacArthur's behalf.

While his friends worked to obtain Arthur's promotion, the judge was not idle. He composed a twenty-two-page legal brief to support his son's application and presented it to the secretary of war on June 26, 1889. In that brief, the judge attacked the army promotion system that had treated his son unfairly for twenty-two years.[9]

The judge's legal brief was forwarded to Adjutant General John C. Kelton. After reading the arguments, Kelton examined Captain MacArthur's service record and was particularly impressed with his legal talents, which were well illustrated in a twenty-year feud he had had with the War Department over the issue of brevet ranks.[10]

The brevet issue was close to the hearts of many U.S. Army officers who had served in combat units during the Civil War. Because officers had received no medals for bravery under fire, these combat veterans took great pride in the only outward recognition they were awarded for their heroic deeds—the brevet rank.[11]

At the end of the Civil War, a problem developed when state legislatures showered hundreds of brevet commissions on staff officers and politicians for meritorious service rather than battlefield bravery. Many a politician and staff officer who had never even been in combat now strutted about at parties in a general's uniform, and most acted as if they had been awarded the grand rank for heroic acts during the war.

Combat officers resented these armchair generals, but few advocated ending the brevet system. Although the phony generals might fool the public, military veterans knew instantly if a brevet commission was for battlefield bravery or political influence. Every officer wore campaign badges, or ribbons, on his dress uniform, so with a single glance, an officer knew a fellow officer's entire combat record. The left breast of MacArthur's dress uniform, for example, was heavy with campaign badges that showed he had fought at Perryville, Murfreesboro, Missionary Ridge, Kennesaw Mountain, Atlanta, and Franklin as well as in the Indian wars. Thus, although the honor of holding a brevet commission declined because of the indiscriminate bestowal of hundreds to staff and rear echelon personnel, brevets remained important as the way the army acknowledged an officer's bravery during the Civil War.[12]

When MacArthur joined the U.S. Army in 1866, he had petitioned the War Department for recognition of his brevet ranks of lieutenant colonel and colonel, awarded by the state of Wisconsin in June 1865. The Adjutant General's Office notified him in October 1868 that the War Department recognized those commissions. Six months later, in March 1869, Congress changed the regulations on brevet grades, and the War Department informed MacArthur that his brevet commissions had expired due to constitutional limitations. Henceforth, he was not to wear the uniform or be addressed as colonel. MacArthur immediately requested an explanation.

What had happened was the result of simple bureaucratic obstinacy, based on a legal technicality. Although the War Department had approved MacArthur's brevets in October 1868, the commissions needed official confirmation by the U.S. Senate. The confirmation process bogged down in the congressional machinery. Finally, on March 3, 1869, the Senate confirmed MacArthur's brevet rank of lieutenant colonel, although no action was taken on his nomination as colonel. At the same time, the Senate confirmed brevet ranks for over 100 other officers.

When the commissions were sent to John A. Rawlins, the secretary of war, he noted a legal problem. On March 1, 1869, Congress had passed a law that forbade the awarding of any brevet commissions except "in time of war for distinguished conduct in the presence of the enemy." Did the law of March 1 invalidate the brevets the Senate confirmed two days later? Rawlins asked Attorney General Ebenezer R. Hoar for an opinion, and after examining the law, Hoar wrote Rawlins that the officers confirmed by the Senate on March 3 could not be commissioned because the authority, in these cases, was "swept away by the statute even before such confirmation was made." Consequently, as members of the Regular Army, these officers now held no brevet ranks and were to refrain from referring to their former brevet ranks in all official correspondence or at any social function.

The decision angered MacArthur. Why should his commissions be withdrawn when hundreds of others remained officially recognized? Any officer whose brevet rank had been confirmed prior to March 1, 1869, continued to hold that rank. MacArthur believed he deserved the commissions and decided to fight.

Over the next twenty years, in dozens of letters to the Adjutant General, MacArthur debated the legal aspects of the case. He went to his law books. He analyzed the law passed by the Senate on March 1, 1869, read the *Congressional Record* on the confirmation hearings, requested and received a copy of Hoar's opinion, and concluded that it was inconceivable that the attorney general's interpretation of the law was correct. For one thing, Hoar's opinion implied that the Senate was incompetent: It passed a law prohibiting brevets except for bravery in the face of the enemy; and then, a mere two days later, confirmed brevets for over 100 officers. MacArthur argued:

> Considering the body in which this action was taken, the character, and vast experience of the then chairman of the Committee on Military Affairs on legislation of this kind, the act of the Senate in confirming the appointments when presented for its ac-

tion, must be accepted as tantamount to a resolution, to the effect, that the law of March 1 did not embrace the cases there before it. It is hardly possible that body, together with a committee having full knowledge of the entire subject, would proceed in violation of a law, which from the nature of things must have been fresh in the minds of Senators.

MacArthur believed Congress had passed the law of March 1 to end "the practice of conferring brevet rank upon non-combatants and not to sweep away existing rights of meritorious officers who had acquired a status in actual conflict with an armed enemy." Furthermore, MacArthur wrote, the new law did not strike down appointments that were in the hands of the Senate at the time of its passage. The attorney general and secretary of war had misinterpreted the law. "The seminal principle of the law is embraced in the line making brevets depend upon service in the presence of the enemy." In MacArthur's case, as well as dozens of others, this principle was maintained. His commissions may not have been confirmed until after March 1, 1869, but that did not alter the fact that the awards were for valorous service in the face of the enemy. MacArthur believed that he had a legal and moral right to the brevets and that the adjutant general should immediately issue the commissions. The withdrawal of the honors, he contended, was illegal and even cruel. "To bestow honor for martial deeds then to forbid the use of the title and insignia is mortifying and discouraging," he observed.[13]

Even those officers who retained their brevets were upset because of additional congressional action. On July 15, 1870, Congress passed a law that restricted brevet commissions to strictly social functions. In all official correspondence, an officer was to be addressed by his actual rank rather than his brevet rank as demanded by military courtesy. In essence, brevets were to exist in name, but they lost any privileges worth claiming. Most officers wanted the honorary features of the brevets restored, and a petition was circulated and sent to Congress. MacArthur signed the petition and so did Adjutant General Kelton.

Year after year for twenty years, MacArthur had written letters to the War Department, the attorney general, and the adjutant general demanding a redress of his grievance. When Adjutant General Kelton reviewed MacArthur's service record in 1889, the captain's letters on the issue impressed him. They illustrated a fine legal mind at work, and the topic was one that interested Kelton.

On July 1, 1889, Kelton telegraphed MacArthur: "You are appointed Major and Assistant Adjutant General." MacArthur immediately wired back his acceptance. There was a party at Fort Leavenworth that night as his fellow officers congratulated the major on his new assignment.[14]

On July 16, after a frantic two weeks of packing, the MacArthurs left for Washington, arriving around July 20. They lived with the judge for a few weeks before finding a house on Rhode Island Avenue. While Major MacArthur settled into his new job at the Adjutant General's Office, Pinky visited the Hardy family in Norfolk. In the fall, she enrolled her two sons in the Force Public School on Massachusetts Avenue. Nine-year-old Douglas was placed in the fourth grade, and Ar-

Judge Arthur MacArthur, c. 1890. (MacArthur Memorial Library, Ph-2903)

thur, now thirteen, entered the ninth. With Pinky's inheritance from her family's estate, money was no problem. Douglas's major annoyance in life in those days was that his father insisted that he wear the glasses that a physician had prescribed to strengthen his eyes: As Theodore Roosevelt learned in his adventures out west, cowboys and cavalry officers (real men) did not wear glasses. MacArthur laughed and pointed out that he himself wore glasses. In fact, the major now looked much like a fifty-year-old Teddy Roosevelt—chunky but strong and still dynamic in body and mind.[15]

After thirteen years in the wilderness, Pinky was again partaking in the glitter and pomp surrounding national politics. It was like her honeymoon days again. Judge MacArthur was at the height of his political and social influence, and the first year of Benjamin Harrison's administration was a good one for the Mac-Arthur family. "Our country's cornucopious bounty seemed to overflow," sighed one Washington matron forty years later. "Never again shall any of us see such abundance and cheapness, such luxurious well-being, as prosperous Americans then enjoyed."[16]

Politicians, intellectuals, and business leaders flocked to the judge's dinner parties, and although Major MacArthur disliked social gatherings, Pinky insisted that they attend. She probably wished her husband was more like his father, who loved socializing while his son enjoyed solitude. As D. Clayton James noted, the major was "always dignified, usually formal, and never guilty of the common officer's vices of excessive cursing, drinking, gambling, and promiscuity." He also lacked a sense of humor while the judge enjoyed teasing people, who generally loved the attention. Pinky knew the judge's political connections had gotten her husband the job in the Adjutant General's Office. That impressed her, and she never forgot the lesson. Pinky carefully cultivated a network of powerful acquaintances that she would later use to help promote the men in her family. She remembered the names of all the officers who served with her husband, and if any later rose to influence and power, she was not averse to calling in old debts and friendship obligations.[17]

Being in Washington delighted the major as much as it delighted his wife. With a job that allowed him to illustrate his legal and administrative talents, he took a refresher course in law at the National University, where the judge served on the board of trustees.

On December 1, 1889, however, the general happiness of the MacArthur family was shattered when Frank, the major's thirty-four-year-old brother, died suddenly in New York City. The judge was devastated.

As was the major's tendency when confronted with emotional problems, he threw himself into his work. The adjutant general was the recordkeeper for the U.S. Army and was in charge of issuing orders, instructions, and regulations. His office received reports from distant posts, compiled army registers and directories of personnel, published and distributed manuals and miscellaneous documents, and was in charge of preserving all records of the military establishment.

General Kelton assigned MacArthur to work with Lieutenant Colonel Henry C. Corbin in redrafting army regulations on promotions. For years, infantry officers had suffered under a system that ignored seniority. They were promoted by regiment up to the grade of major. The only way a lieutenant was promoted was if a captain's vacancy occurred in his regiment, and some unlucky lieutenants remained in grade for twenty years. Promotion from captain to major was also slow in the infantry, as illustrated by MacArthur's own career. General Kelton wanted these inequities eliminated.

Corbin and MacArthur were careful and methodical staff officers. After thoroughly reviewing the literature, they recommended many of the reforms that William B. Hazen had suggested as far back as 1872 and that had been supported by the *Army and Navy Journal* for over a decade. Corbin and MacArthur recommended that infantry and cavalry officers be promoted on the basis of seniority rather than by regimental affiliations. They also recommended that all officers be required to pass written and oral examinations prior to promotion. Sensitive to civilian criticism that military officers were uncultured and ignorant on the intellectual topics of the day, they suggested that all officers be required to study not only military science and tactics but also history, politics, economics, sociology, and even psychology. Years later, when Douglas was superintendent of West Point, he implemented his father's ideas and broadened the academy's curriculum.[18]

Kelton accepted the Corbin-MacArthur report and forwarded it to the House and Senate Committees on Military Affairs. In October 1890, Congress passed an army reform bill that incorporated the suggestions, inaugurating lineal promotion by branch of service through the grade of colonel and requiring both "physical and professional examinations for all lieutenants and captains who came up for promotion. Since promotions were still granted on the basis of seniority, these examinations were not competitive," but officers were required to meet physical requirements and demonstrate professional competence.[19]

Kelton next assigned MacArthur the task of improving the life of the army's enlisted men—a project dear to MacArthur's heart. Since Civil War days, he had believed that the franchised sutler, or post trader, should be replaced with stores operated by regiments and companies, and while in command at Fort Selden, he had established a company canteen whose profits went back to the men. He suggested that the example be applied throughout the army. Working with Major Theodore Schwan, MacArthur developed a plan to abolish the post trader system. Kelton accepted it, and over the next ten years, canteens replaced the sutlers on army posts across the nation.[20]

As one of the sixteen assistant adjutant generals, MacArthur was required to travel to military posts and recruiting stations to examine records and to sit on courts-martial. In May 1891, he went to Fort Bliss, Texas, near El Paso, then to Fort Grant and to San Carlos in New Mexico. On the way back to Washington, he stopped at Columbus Barracks in Ohio and later Fort Thomas in Virginia. MacArthur's work pleased General Kelton, who wrote in MacArthur's file, "I regard your assignment to duty in the Adjutant General's Office a most fortunate circumstance for the office and the Army. Every duty assigned to you, you have performed thoroughly and conscientiously. Every recommendation you have made has been consistent and without color of prejudice or favor, but solely for the good of the Army."[21]

MacArthur's position in the Adjutant General's Office gave him an opportunity to redress an old injustice. In 1890, while reviewing records of officers, MacArthur discovered a technicality that had been ignored by the officers corps, a technicality that would alleviate some of his bitterness over the army's failure to officially recognize his Civil War achievements. In April 1890, when he learned that a military board was meeting to consider an application by First Lieutenant Matthias W. Day for a congressional Medal of Honor for bravery against the

Apaches in 1879, a bell went off in MacArthur's head. Up to that time, he and nearly every other Regular Army officer believed the Medal of Honor was meant for enlisted men only. MacArthur went to the statutes and found that, as legislated by Congress in July 1862, the medal *was* meant only for enlisted men and noncommissioned officers. But in March 1863, Congress had amended the statute to allow officers to be awarded the medal. This revision had been ignored by the secretary of war: Not a single officer received the Medal of Honor during the Civil War.[22]

After the war, three officers did receive the medal, but the awards went unnoticed. The first officer to receive the Medal of Honor (on June 10, 1877) was Lieutenant Francis E. Brownell, cited for bravery in the Indian campaigns. On January 27, 1880, Second Lieutenant Hampton M. Roach was given the medal for valor in the Indian wars, but the award was for action that occurred when he had been a sergeant. The third medal awarded was the significant one for MacArthur. On November 16, 1887, twenty-five years after the event, a military review board had awarded retired Captain John G. Bourke the Medal of Honor for heroism under fire at the battle of Murfreesboro. MacArthur had been at Murfreesboro in December 1862 and had later been awarded the brevet rank of major for his bravery. That brevet had been withdrawn, but MacArthur suddenly realized his heroic actions could be acknowledged by a Medal of Honor. If the medal could be granted retroactively to one officer, why not to others? It was the fact of valor in the face of the enemy that was the significant point, as MacArthur had argued in his brevet case. It was an interesting legal question.

After Day received his award in April 1890, MacArthur submitted an application for the medal while the board was still meeting. He documented his case with official reports and letters from old commanders and comrades. He had been cited in the "Official Reports" of the Civil War for bravery in the battles of Stones River (Murfreesboro), Missionary Ridge, Kennesaw Mountain, and Franklin, and he supported the reports with letters from Generals Opdycke, Stanley, Kimball, and Thomas that had been part of his personnel file since 1866. MacArthur also asked some of his old comrades in arms to supply accounts of his bravery. E. K. Holton, a lieutenant with the 24th Wisconsin at Murfreesboro, wrote:

> I cannot refrain from recalling the heroic part which Adjutant MacArthur played in the tragedy of that eventful day, December 31, 1862. At the supreme moment, when the enemy was charging us in solid columns, overwhelming in numbers, and with almost irresistible impetuosity, the Major in command of our regiment was disabled. For an instant a panic seemed imminent; indeed, there was a break to the rear, and in a moment a wild stampede would have followed. The Adjutant at once grasped the situation, and being the only mounted officer in sight for the moment, assumed command, and by his ringing orders and perfect coolness checked the impending panic, restored confidence, rallied and held the regiment in line, until completely flanked we fell back slowly and in order, delivering our fire as we did so. It was a mere

boy of seventeen and one-half years, who saved our regiment from dishonor. A medal of honor was rightfully his for his conduct at Stone[s] River.[23]

Major Carl Baumbach, the commander of the 24th Wisconsin at Missionary Ridge, also wrote the board:

> The forcing of Missionary Ridge may be considered as one of the finest assaults in the annals of the war. Among the many acts of personal intrepidity on that memorable occasion, none are worthy of higher commendation than that of young MacArthur, then only eighteen years old, who seizing the colors of his regiment at the critical moment, contributed materially to the general result. I remain impressed now as I was then, by a sense of the vast importance of this officer's splendid efforts on that occasion. I think it no disparagement to others to declare that he was most distinguished in action on a field where many in the regiment displayed conspicuous gallantry, worthy of the highest praise.[24]

Testimonies from other veterans of the 24th Wisconsin, including Captain Edwin Parsons, Lieutenant George Allanson, and Lieutenant J. E. Armitage, supported Baumbach's report on Missionary Ridge.

On June 30, 1890, the military board awarded MacArthur the congressional Medal of Honor for conspicuous bravery during the battle of Missionary Ridge. He could have been awarded the medal for Murfreesboro or Franklin, but the board decided the most illustrious example of MacArthur's valor was his charge up the ridge.

MacArthur was delighted. He had redressed an old grievance and, after twenty-seven years, been rewarded for his Civil War actions. He had triumphed over the bureaucrats and was pleased not only for himself but for all the officers who had displayed conspicuous bravery during the war. Like most combat officers, he had always believed that medals commemorative of the event or actual promotions in rank were preferable to brevet commissions. The medal was now available, and MacArthur made sure other officers became aware of that fact. He persuaded the adjutant general to list Medal of Honor winners in the official *Army Register* in 1891. Six officers had received the medal by then, and MacArthur's name topped the list.

As MacArthur intended, publication of medal winners in the *Army Register* opened the floodgates. Hundreds of applications for the medal poured into the Adjutant General's Office. Nearly every Union officer who had been awarded a brevet commission for bravery during the Civil War applied. Military boards carefully reviewed each application, and in the next six years, 1891 to 1896, sixty-seven officers (forty-five still on active duty, twenty-two retired) received the medal for their heroic deeds in the Civil War.[25]

Douglas and Arthur glowed with pride when their father received the Medal of Honor. They loved to listen to his Civil War stories, but though the major enjoyed studying and analyzing the battles, he seldom spoke of his own accomplishments.

His father, the judge, was not so reticent. After Frank's death, Judge MacArthur had retreated into his study, but having his grandsons around helped him to recover. He was a good storyteller, and his two teenaged grandchildren listened in awe to his words of wisdom. Douglas later remembered his grandfather "as a large, handsome man of genial disposition and possessed of untiring energy. He was noted for his dry wit and I could listen to his anecdotes for hours."[26]

The judge was a witty man who knew that humor was the most effective when it was directed at one's own follies. He admitted that, as a member of the human race, he was a fool among fools. The judge warned his grandchildren, perhaps unsuccessfully, to watch out for vanity because a fool was within all of us. "If one is desirous of seeing the greatest of all fools," he would write, "let him look into a mirror and he will see the very person he is looking for. He will at least be sure to see something very like a fool of uncommon size, just about as big as they make them." When his grandsons asked about his writing, the judge sarcastically labeled it a hobby that was "a wonderful combination of goose quill and attenuated vapor." He asked their forgiveness but reminded them that "we should not murmur if our hobby is not a lion. The wildest beasts can be tamed and made useful by industry. In a word, our subject teaches the inestimable value of having a purpose and an aim through life, and to earnestly pursue it."[27]

The boys enjoyed the judge's repartee, but their favorite evenings were when they persuaded him to tell them stories about their father's heroic actions during the war. The boys listened wide-eyed as the judge recounted and embellished on MacArthur's courage in battle after battle. All their lives, they would dream of being a hero like their father, and the dream inspired Douglas until the day he died. According to Frazier Hunt, the "lore and romantic details ... seeped into [Douglas's] conscious and subconscious being. Fellow officers [would] say that when he went to France in 1917 as chief of staff of the 42nd Infantry Division, he had already fought ... the Civil War. ... Certainly he knew intimately every battle and every leader of the great civil conflict that ended almost fifteen years before he was born."[28]

In his memoirs, Douglas recounted his grandfather's Civil War stories, and although exaggerated, each held an element of the truth, perhaps more of the truth than the dull official records reflected. For example, in describing his father's charge up Missionary Ridge, Douglas wrote:

> No one seems to know just what orders may have been given, but suddenly the flag of the 24th Wisconsin started forward. With it was the color sergeant, the color guard of two corporals, and the adjutant. Up they went step by step. The enemy's fire was intense. Down went the color bearer. One of the corporals seized the colors as they fell, but was bayoneted before he could move. A shell took off the head of the other corporal, but the adjutant grasped the flag and kept on. He seemed to be surrounded by nothing but gray coats. A Confederate colonel thrust viciously at his throat, but even as he lunged a bullet struck and the deflected blade just ripped a shoulder strap. ... Above the roar of battle, sounded the adjutant's voice: "On, Wisconsin!"

They come then; they come with a rush and a roar, a blue tide of courage, a whole division of them. Shouting, cursing, struggling foot by foot, heads bent as in a gale! Gasping breath from tortured lungs! Those last few feet before the log breastworks seemed interminable! Men tumble over like tenpins! The charge is losing momentum! They falter! Officers are down! Sergeants now lead! And then, suddenly, on the crest—the flag! Once again that cry: "On, Wisconsin!" Silhouetted against the sky, the adjutant stands on the parapet waving the colors where the whole regiment can see him! Through the ragged blue line, from one end of the division to the other, comes an ugly roar, like the growl of a wounded bear! They race those last few steps, eyes blazing, lips snarling, bayonets plunging! And Missionary Ridge is won.

The adjutant suddenly falls to the ground exhausted, his body retching, racked with pain. He is a terrible sight—covered with blood and mud, hatless, his smoke-blackened face barely recognizable, his clothes torn to tatters. Sheridan, the division commander, utters not a word—he just stares at him—and then takes him in his arms. And his deep voice seems to break a little as he says: "Take care of him. He has just won the Medal of Honor."[29]

No man could hope to exceed the heroism he attributed to his father, but Douglas would alway try to equal the exploits.

The boys and their father read every book they could get on the Civil War, and the battles were analyzed and then reanalyzed. Each movement of troops was examined in depth as they compared the accounts of scholars and participants. They read Sherman's, Grant's, and Sheridan's memoirs and the accounts of dozens of lesser generals. Pinky insisted they also read the biographies of Confederate generals, for she retained pride in the Confederacy all her life.

As the older brother, Arthur got the first opportunity to follow in their father's footsteps. In early 1892, he was offered an appointment, obtained by the judge, to the U.S. Naval Academy. Only sixteen years old, almost the same age as his father when he joined the 24th Wisconsin back in 1862, Arthur went to his father for advice. Should he accept the appointment?

Over Pinky's objections, the major advised his son to go to the naval academy. The U.S. Navy was on an upsurge, and opportunities there appeared better than in the army. Between 1883 and 1890, Congress had authorized the building of nine new cruisers, and construction had begun on the first modern American battleship, the *Maine*. Naval construction was also stimulated when Captain Alfred T. Mahan published *The Influence of Sea Power upon History* in 1890. Major MacArthur and his sons read the book, which would influence a whole generation of U.S. intellectuals, policymakers, and military men. Mahan's thesis was that national security and international greatness could be obtained only if a country had a modern navy, with seaports around the world. The major no doubt pointed out to his older son that he had made the same observations himself back in 1882 in his "Chinese Memorandum." Mahan's ideas influenced Congress, which ultimately authorized a naval building program that would lead to the construction of many new battleships, cruisers, and gunboats as well as three naval maintenance yards in the 1890s. Within a decade, the United States would have the third largest navy in the world.

In early September 1892, Arthur entered the U.S. Naval Academy as the youngest member of the freshman class, composed of ninety-four cadets. Within a year, the class had shrunk down to fifty-four cadets, but Arthur survived the cut.[30]

After three wonderful years in Washington, Major MacArthur was assigned, in September 1893, as assistant adjutant general for the Department of Texas, headquartered at Fort Sam Houston in San Antonio, Texas. Pinky packed the bags, and they were off again.

Departure from the capital was almost a relief. Shortly after Grover Cleveland was inaugurated in March 1893, the nation fell into a severe depression; millions were thrown out of work, and the wages of millions of others were drastically reduced. MacArthur blamed the depression on corrupt politicians and greedy businessmen, a conclusion he had come to, like many other progressive thinkers, after a careful study of the major works on economics, political science, and sociology. He rejected out of hand the arguments of the social Darwinists, such as English philosopher Herbert Spencer and his American disciple, Yale sociologist William G. Sumner. Beginning in the 1860s, Spencer and Sumner wrote a series of books to illustrate how Darwin's theories on evolution could also be applied to the world's social and economic development. According to Spencer and Sumner, Darwin's theory of the "survival of the fittest" applied to the business world where, in a laissez faire environment, the better businesses survived and swallowed up their weaker competitors through a process of natural selection. Social and economic progress, according to the social Darwinists, demanded that these complex industrial organisms be left entirely to their natural bent. When Andrew Carnegie first read Spencer, he recalled in his *Autobiography,* "Light came as in a flood and all was clear."[31]

MacArthur did not think the leading businessmen represented the "fittest" within U.S. society. He agreed with Samuel L. Clemens (Mark Twain), who berated the greed of the Morgans, Carnegies, and Goulds and wrote that to these giants of the business world, the axiom was: "Get Money. Get it quickly. Get it in abundance. Get it dishonestly if you can, honestly if you must." Henry Demarest Lloyd expressed the same idea in a more academic style in *Wealth Against Commonwealth* (1894). After noting that an 1890 Census Bureau statistic indicated that 71 percent of the country's wealth was held by 9 percent of its families, Lloyd wrote, "Our barbarians come from above. Our great money-makers have sprung in one generation into seats of power kings. ... The forces and the wealth are new ... without restraints of culture, experience, pride, or even the inherited caution of class or rank; these men, intoxicated, think they are the wave instead of the float."[32]

MacArthur was in tune with the economists and philosophers classified as Progressives, men like William James, Henry George, Richard T. Ely, William Dean Howells, Lester Ward, John R. Commons, and Edward Bemis. The Progressives believed that the government had a moral obligation to improve society and that one of the greatest threats to democracy was corrupt politicians and greedy businessmen. They advocated government regulation of business to eliminate abusive labor practices and to control the trusts and railroads. Perhaps MacArthur hoped that the United States would achieve Edward Bellamy's vision of the future. Bellamy, a journalist and fiction writer from Chicopee, Massachusetts (MacArthur's birthplace), was troubled by the suffering and poverty in the textile mills and factories of the town. In *Looking Backward,* published in 1888, Bellamy "penned a vision of an ideal society flowering in the year 2000 whose beauty, tranquility, and efficiency contrasted vividly with the smoky and strike-ridden America of the '80's. The Golden Age had dawned after the nationalizing of the great trusts."[33]

MacArthur's transfer to Fort Sam Houston in San Antonio meant that he was relatively isolated from the violent labor disputes that racked the nation in the next few years. However, Sam Houston was not a small, isolated post on the deserted frontier. Located just north of the cultured city of San Antonio, the fort was the headquarters of the Department of Texas and the largest army post in the Southwest. Besides the headquarters staff, two cavalry regiments, two infantry regiments, an artillery regiment, and auxiliary units were stationed there. The fort's prime responsibility was to patrol the turbulent Mexican border. As the adjutant general in charge of all paperwork, Major MacArthur held a powerful position. "It can be assumed," Carol Petillo observed, "that Major MacArthur was delighted [to] be right in the middle of [the] military activity he loved so much."[34]

Pinky enjoyed life at Fort Sam. The family moved into pleasant quarters, and the major hired a maid for his wife. There was a constant exchange of calls, teas, and dinner parties with the other officers' wives, although the major continued to refuse to socialize and often retreated into his study. Pinky and the other wives also socialized with the local San Antonio aristocracy and had access to excellent shops and restaurants. As one army wife, Anna Maus, noted in her memoirs, "The garrison and town of San Antonio were filled with the most charming and lovely women including Mrs. John Weston, Mrs. Arthur MacArthur, Mrs. Herbert Slocum, and Mrs. Wade Smith."[35]

With one son safely away at school, Pinky focused her considerable energies on Douglas, who was thirteen years and nine months old when the MacArthurs arrived in San Antonio. His father enrolled him in the ninth grade at the West Texas Military Academy, which had just opened its doors. Run by Reverend J. S. Johnston, an Episcopal bishop, West Texas was located on Government Hill, overlooking the Alamo and the city of San Antonio. The academy offered courses for students from grades seven to twelve, with many classes taught by officers from Fort Sam. Tuition was $15 per twelve-week term, and the cadet's uniform cost $13.50.

The major kept close tabs on his son. He often visited the academy and reviewed the cadets' military training, attended baseball and football games, and watched Douglas play in tennis matches. At home, he discussed school subjects with his son, who now had a "desire to know," a thirst for knowledge that would soon equal that of his father. Douglas's studies enveloped him. "Abstruse mathematics began to appear as a challenge," he later wrote, and "dull Latin and Greek seemed a gateway to the moving words of the leaders of the past." Douglas did well at the academy, and he would remember his life in San Antonio with affection. In his memoirs, he proclaimed that his days at West Texas "were without doubt the happiest of my life. Texas will always be a second home to me." The MacArthurs were Episcopalians, and in Washington and San Antonio, they attended church regularly. Douglas was confirmed on April 1, 1894, at St. Paul's Memorial Church in San Antonio.[36]

The years at Fort Sam were also good years for Major MacArthur. He worked hard, was respected by his fellow officers, and received excellent efficiency reports from successive department commanders. MacArthur remained a spokesman for the reform wing of the army, and in 1895, his name again was in the forefront. Even though he had received the congressional Medal of Honor for his valor at Missionary Ridge, MacArthur was not satisfied. The issue of his brevet commissions still rankled him. When he petitioned Congress for redress and was ignored, he decided to pursue the legal route. In April 1895, he contacted a San Antonio attorney, John C. Dermody, who agreed to represent MacArthur in a legal suit against the War Department. This time, MacArthur won. In late April, the War Department notified him that his brevet commissions of major and lieutenant colonel for acts of bravery at Perrysville, Murfreesboro, Missionary Ridge, Kennesaw Mountain, and Franklin were again recognized by the department. In the *Army Register,* the commissions would be dated May 3, 1865. Once again, MacArthur opened the floodgates, and other Civil War officers who had been denied their brevet commissions suddenly found them officially honored.[37]

On June 8, 1896, six days after his fifty-first birthday, MacArthur was promoted to lieutenant colonel. The same month, his son Arthur MacArthur III graduated from Annapolis. He had done adequately but not brilliantly at the Naval Academy; his main accomplishment was that he survived the four years, and that was no mean feat. When he entered the academy at the age of sixteen, he was one of ninety-four cadets of the class of 1896. Four years later, only twenty-six cadets had survived, and Arthur ranked fifteenth among them. He had stood out in only one area—running—setting the Annapolis record in the half-mile run at two minutes, ten and four-fifths seconds. He was assigned to the *Philadelphia* in San Francisco, with the rank of naval cadet.[38]

In July, the family traveled back East to visit with Arthur before he took up his new post. They met in Washington at the judge's house. Seventy-nine years old, the judge was ill, but he recovered his good spirits for the visit. Suffering from the grippe, the judge rarely left his house, but he still insisted on his evening toddy as he proclaimed any good Scotsman would. His mind had not deteriorated, and he spent most of his time in his study writing his final book, a small volume of witty and insightful essays that he hoped to finish before he died. He did complete this work, the best of his six books.[39]

The judge was no longer part of the elite social scene in Washington. His older generation considered the rising politicians like Theodore Roosevelt, Henry Cabot Lodge, and William Howard Taft to be young upstarts. Nor did the judge have much use for the aristocratic Henry Adams, although he admired Adams's work as a historian. Adams and John Hay ruled the elite of Washington in 1896. They lived in matching red "Richardson" mansions on Lafayette Square in Washington, D.C., and represented the bluest of the blue bloods in the United States. Lodge, Roosevelt, and Taft were welcomed into Adams's circle of friends, and they all believed they were the best and the brightest of their day. The group's intellectual capacity was profound, but their aristocratic snobbery irritated the judge.[40]

The judge still had his Wisconsin contacts, and when he learned that Douglas wanted to go to the U.S. Military Academy at West Point, he began his networking. Unfortunately, he would never finish his efforts on behalf of this grandson.

Shortly after Lieutenant Colonel MacArthur returned to San Antonio in late July, his father went to a health clinic in Atlantic City, New Jersey. On Wednesday afternoon, August 26, 1896, the judge died. The *Atlantic City Daily Press,* the *Atlantic City Daily Union,* and the *Milwaukee Sentinel* carried stories on his death on their front pages the next day. After three weeks at a sanatorium on Pacific and Mt. Vernon Avenues, the judge had appeared to be recovering, and just three days before he died, he enjoyed a Sunday afternoon stroll along the Atlantic City boardwalk. But on Monday, he complained of not feeling well, and a doctor was summoned. The judge's condition worsened, and he died two days later. The next morning, his widow took the judge's body by train to Washington for interment in Rock Creek Cemetery, the burial ground of many wealthy and prominent people, including the Adams family.[41]

Although his father's death was not completely unexpected, Lieutenant Colonel MacArthur was deeply upset by the news. Coming face to face with man's mortality, he soon made out his own last will and testament and dropped the "Jr." from his name.[42]

Douglas's future was now uncertain, but his father began to write letters to all the judge's old friends, soliciting their help. Meanwhile, he encouraged his son to do well at West Texas Military Academy so that he would be fully prepared for an appointment to West Point. The academy had grown and now had 115 cadets in 4 forms, with 16 teachers and 5 buildings. A number of colleges accepted graduates of the academy without requiring entrance exams. Douglas excelled there, winning medals in Latin, mathematics, and competitive speaking. In his senior year, he was the quarterback of the football team, which had an undefeated season; in the spring, he played shortstop on the baseball team, which also went undefeated that year. In addition, he was on the elite, 10-cadet drill team, called the Crack Squad, that staged exhibitions at other schools. On June 8, 1897, as his proud parents watched, Douglas graduated as valedictorian, with a four-year grade point average of 97.33.[43]

One of Judge MacArthur's old friends, Wisconsin Congressman Theobald Otjen, informed Colonel MacArthur he would appoint Douglas to the U.S. Military Academy if the boy could fulfill two conditions: live in Otjen's district in Milwaukee and surpass all the other boys who wanted the appointment in a competitive examination. Initially, the residency stipulation seemed the more difficult, but fortuitous circumstances allowed the family to meet the requirement.[44]

In October 1897, Colonel MacArthur was assigned as the new adjutant general to the Department of Dakotas, with headquarters in St. Paul, Minnesota, 330 miles west of Milwaukee. To satisfy Otjen's first requirement, the colonel moved Pinky and Douglas to the Plankinton House in Milwaukee. Douglas was enrolled in West Side High, and private tutors were hired to help him prepare for the competitive examinations. The colonel then proceeded to his station in St. Paul. On nearly every weekend of the next six months, he made the long commute back to Milwaukee by train to be with his family.

Colonel MacArthur considered Milwaukee his hometown, and for the first time in his marriage, he enjoyed socializing more than Pinky did. His father's friends and many of his childhood friends still lived in the city, where the name MacArthur meant something. He therefore spent the weekends renewing old friendships. The veterans of the 24th Wisconsin Volunteers were delighted to have their old commander in the city, and many of its members dropped by to see the colonel and reminisce about the war.

John Mitchell and Charlie King still lived in Milwaukee, and the three old friends got together. John, who had served with MacArthur in the 24th Wisconsin, had prospered. The Mitchell family, still involved in banking and insurance, remained one of the wealthiest and most powerful families in the city. John had been elected to the House of Representatives in 1890, and three years later, in 1893, the state legislature selected him to be a U.S. senator. Douglas, almost eighteen, fell hopelessly in love with one of the senator's daughters, who "heartlessly" ignored him; he also became friends with Senator Mitchell's eighteen-year-old son, William, who would become famous as the army's air force advocate in the 1920s.[45]

Charlie King had followed in the footsteps of his father, Rufus King, and become a famous writer. A close boyhood friend of MacArthur's, Charlie had obtained an appointment to the U.S. Military Academy back in 1862, the appointment that had almost gone to Little Mac. While Arthur won fame in the Civil War, Charlie went to West Point and graduated in 1866. In October 1874, while serving as a lieutenant in the cavalry, he was wounded in action against the Apaches. The wound kept him off active service for a year, and he never completely recovered. Though he returned to active duty in 1876 and was promoted to captain on May 1, 1879, King would retire six weeks later, at the age of thirty-four, to take a position as military instructor at the University of Wisconsin. While teaching, he wrote ar-

ticles for the *Milwaukee Sentinel* on his army experiences—articles that were collected and published as his first book in 1880. By 1897, King had written over forty
books and hundreds of articles for newspapers and national magazines such as
Lippincott's, Century, and *Harper's Weekly.* Twenty-seven of his novels sold well
enough for more than one edition to be published. Considered serious literature,
not dime novels, King's books were filled with a profusion of material derived
from his army experiences on the frontier, and they were almost as popular as
Teddy Roosevelt's more famous books in the *Winning of the West* series.
MacArthur especially appreciated King's books because they depicted the frontier
army life he himself had lived.[46]

Pinky liked Milwaukee because the MacArthurs were among the social elite
there, and politicians and businessmen invited them to their parties. Though the
colonel disliked parties, he did enjoy private gatherings of the men while the
women socialized in another room. At these times, the men talked politics, analyzed the economic situation, and discussed the new books appearing on a variety
of topics. MacArthur was a hard-currency man and opposed the printing of
greenbacks or the unlimited coining of silver. For that reason, he had been delighted when William McKinley defeated William Jennings Bryan in 1896. The hot
topic that fall and winter was the possibility of war with Spain over Cuba. The
outcome of that debate would change MacArthur's life.

PART THREE

General MacArthur and the Philippines

11

The Spanish-American War and the Philippines

*T*HE FALL OF 1897 was a happy time for Colonel MacArthur as he continued to socialize in Milwaukee and commute to his job in St. Paul. Arthur Jr. was doing well in the navy, Douglas was studying hard for his competitive exams, and Pinky was part of the Milwaukee social circuit she loved. MacArthur's career was also on solid ground, and he could hope that, before he reached the mandatory retirement age of sixty-four in twelve years, he would be promoted to brigadier general and become the adjutant general of the army. His prospects improved when his old friend Henry Corbin became the new adjutant general that year. However, events intervened—events that would propel MacArthur to an even higher rank.

War was in the air that fall as the national press, led by Joseph Pulitzer of the *New York World* and William Randolph Hearst of the *New York Journal*, advocated U.S. intervention in Cuba. Cuba was only 90 miles from Florida, and U.S. investment in the sugar and mining industries totaled $50 million; U.S. trade with the island exceeded $100 million a year. When a major rebellion erupted in Cuba in 1895, Spanish authorities sent 200,000 men to suppress the upheaval. The insurgents fled into the hills and harassed the Spaniards with guerrilla tactics. The Spanish governor, General Valeriano Weyler, responded with a campaign of systematic torture and murder, winning him infamy in the United States in headlines that referred to him as "the butcher," a "human hyena," and a "mad dog." Weyler herded large segments of the island's population into concentration camps, where they died by the tens of thousands.[1]

Cuban refugees from the war settled in New York and Florida and lobbied Washington to intervene. At the same time, Pulitzer's *World* and Hearst's *Journal* were involved in a circulation war, each attempting to outdo the other in printing outrageous stories to capture the reader's attention. They increased their circulation by dramatizing labor upheavals, fires, murders, elections, and innumerable social movements. Dubbed the yellow press after the yellow ink used in their comic strips, the *World* and the *Journal* had no qualms about engaging in questionable journalistic practices. Their style was emulated by dozens of other newspapers around the country, for jingoism and disasters sold papers. Many printed the gory details of Spanish brutality in Cuba and moralistically demanded that the United States intervene to protect our "little brown brothers."[2]

A group of young politicians, led by Theodore Roosevelt and Henry Cabot Lodge, joined the press in clamoring for intervention in Cuba. Roosevelt, the young, aristocratic firebrand from New York, was assistant secretary of the navy under John D. Long; he was also the most outspoken of the new imperialists who visualized an age of U.S. expansion beyond American shores to create an empire larger and more profitable than the British Empire. The imperialists echoed the theories of Admiral Mahan on the necessity of having naval bases and seapower throughout the world to increase the nation's trade and influence. A war with Spain over Cuba would propel the United States into the international arena as a major player. As Roosevelt told a friend, "I should welcome any war, for I think this country needs one."[3]

Lieutenant Colonel MacArthur found that soldiers, particularly combat veterans from the Civil War, were once again admired and respected as the new surge of nationalism swept the country. In the first decade after the war, the public wanted to forget the bloody conflict. "The 1870s," Linderman noted, "saw the publication of fewer Civil War novels than any other decade. Popular magazines published little on the war. Between 1869 and 1873, *Harper's* printed two Civil War articles, and between 1869 and 1876, the *North American Review* carried one." But around 1880, public interest in the war slowly revived, and Civil War books became popular. Linderman estimated, "The circulation of the *Century* nearly doubled when, between 1884 and 1887, that magazine ran its series 'Battles and Leaders' of the Civil War.'" Membership in the Grand Army of the Republic (GAR) "jumped from 30,000 in 1878 to 146,000 in 1883, then to 233,000 in 1884 and to 320,000 in 1887. In 1890—at 428,000 members—it touched its crest."[4]

Patriotic societies sprang up across the nation. The press, the churches, politicians, and businessmen sang the praises of the country's greatness and its manifest destiny to lead the world. "The place of this nation is at the head of the column of civilization," stated one contemporary. "Not that we would put other nations down. Our idea has always been to point out to other nations the way up higher."[5]

President McKinley and the more conservative wing of the Republican party wanted to avoid a war, but events forced them to alter their position. On February 8, 1898, a private letter written by Depuy de Lôme, the Spanish minister in Washington, to a friend in Havana fell into the possession of Hearst's *New York Journal*. The letter was a time bomb. De Lôme loathed Americans and despised the newspapers' tirades against his country. In the letter, he characterized President McKinley as a "weak bidder for the admiration of the crowd." On February 9, Hearst published a translated version of the de Lôme letter on the *Journal's* front page under the headline: "WORST INSULT TO THE UNITED STATES IN HISTORY." Spain apologized, and de Lôme resigned.[6]

Feelings might have calmed down if the letter had not been followed by an even more dramatic event six days later. On the night of February 15, 1898, the USS *Maine,* a battleship sent to protect U.S. citizens in Cuba, blew up in Havana harbor, killing 262 U.S. sailors. No one knew the cause of the explosion, but the yellow press charged the Spanish with sabotage, and patriots screamed for revenge as the slogan "Cuba Libre!" was replaced with "Remember the *Maine!*" A bellicose fury seized the nation as almost every segment of U.S. society clamored for intervention.[7]

Although prodded by the press and the war enthusiasts, President McKinley procrastinated for two months before sending a war message to Congress on April 11. Congressmen hotly debated the issue but at last formally declared war on Spain on April 21 to save the 1.5 million Cubans from Spanish tyranny. To prove the United States had only altruistic motives, Congress attached a resolution to the war declaration that Senator Henry Moore Teller of Colorado had introduced. The Teller Amendment disavowed any U.S. intent to annex Cuba and proclaimed the war would be fought to assist the Cubans in obtaining their independence.[8]

MacArthur immediately sent a note to Adjutant General Corbin requesting a transfer back to the infantry. The colonel desperately wanted a field assignment. At fifty-two, he was still in good physical condition; although one authority later described him as looking like a grocery clerk, this description was unfair. He had put on some weight, but in comparison to the grossly overweight leaders of the era, his 180 pounds on a five-foot-ten-inch frame was merely stocky. With his mustache and glasses, MacArthur resembled Teddy Roosevelt, although the emotional make-up of the two men was markedly different: Roosevelt was spirited, while MacArthur was almost subdued, a man who fit in easily with the bureaucratic society that demanded obedience to rules and dress codes.[9]

While awaiting a reply to his request for a transfer to the infantry, MacArthur met with many of the survivors of his old Civil War regiment who flocked to his door and offered to join any regiment he commanded. He smiled his thanks, but his comrades knew they were too old to enlist. An exception was MacArthur's friend Charlie King, a West Point graduate and former Regular Army officer, whose petition to the War Department for an appointment was being seriously considered. In fact, Adjutant General Corbin's office was flooded with requests from staff officers for transfers to fighting units and with petitions from former officers for commissions as volunteer officers. The machinery moved rapidly in some cases, as it did for Colonel Henry Lawton, who was almost immediately promoted to brigadier general of the Volunteers and placed in command of a brigade mobilizing at Camp Thomas near Chattanooga, Tennessee.[10]

Unfortunately, General Corbin considered MacArthur too important to transfer immediately back to the line. Thirty years of congressional parsimony had to be overcome in weeks, and trained staff officers were desperately needed at the mobilizing camps. At the beginning of the war, the Regular Army, under the command of Major General Nelson A. Miles, consisted of 28,183 men and less than

2,200 officers. But in the first few weeks of the war, the army mobilized 125,000 Volunteers. Quick expansion meant innumerable problems, particularly for the Quartermaster Corps, responsible for feeding and equipping the army, and for the Adjutant General's Office, responsible for personnel assignments and paperwork.

MacArthur received orders in early May to proceed to Camp Thomas at Chickamauga, Georgia, where he was to assume the duties of chief of staff and adjutant general of the 3rd Army Corps. General Corbin promised MacArthur a field assignment as soon as things stabilized.

Camp Thomas, just south of Chattanooga, was in chaos when MacArthur arrived. The army had assigned 76,000 trainees to a camp where there were facilities for only 20,000 men. It was MacArthur's job to straighten out the chaos and to keep all the paperwork in order. He organized the Volunteers into regiments, brigades, and divisions and instructed the new officers on army regulations. MacArthur was a strict taskmaster, but he was also very precise in his instructions because he knew these troops were merely civilians playing at being soldiers. He recognized them as the same type of boys he had shared many a campsite with during and after the Civil War. Young men rushed to join the army because they wanted to take part in the grand adventure called war. One aspiring writer among the Volunteers described them as a motley band: "There was the clerk, the cook, the convict, the confidence man, the gambler, the saloon keeper, the professional man, the farmer, and all other trades, callings, and professions, all boiling over with patriotism." And all were soon complaining about the facilities, the food, the uniforms, the paperwork, and the drills. There were shortages of everything, from uniforms to ammunition, food, and bedding. Suffering from years of limited budgets, the army had no major stockpiles of weapons or foodstuffs. The War Department, led by Russell A. Alger, was bloated with incompetent bureaucrats who were engaged in constant squabbles with General Miles, the army chief.[11]

When typhoid fever raged through Camp Thomas, the 3rd Army Corps moved to Tampa, Florida, where conditions were almost as bad because the 5th Army Corps was also mobilizing nearby. A tent city arose that covered miles on the savanna grass outside of Tampa. Teddy Roosevelt, now second in command of the Rough Riders, was there, and he recorded in his diary that "no words can paint the confusion." Roosevelt considered Brigadier General William R. Shafter, the gouty old commander of the 5th Army Corps who weighed over 300 pounds and could barely sit on a horse, an incompetent. Yet Shafter had been assigned to lead the first Cuban expedition of 17,000 men. Since the navy had no transport vessels, a merchant fleet was slowly being converted to transport the troops, and there was nothing but delays.[12]

The focus of the war news swung from Cuba to the Philippines, a distant Spanish possession in the Pacific that few Americans had ever heard of before. While assistant secretary of navy, Roosevelt had prepared the service for war and sent Commodore George Dewey to Hong Kong with orders to attack the Spanish fleet in Manila if war erupted. Dewey steamed out of Hong Kong on April 27 with a small squadron of four armored cruisers, one unprotected cruiser, one gunboat, one coast guard cutter, and a few supply ships. Early in the morning of May 1, the squadron entered Manila Bay to confront the Spanish fleet and achieved one of the greatest naval victories in history. Dewey's ships destroyed the entire Spanish fleet, consisting of seven ships, while suffering only 8 men wounded to Spanish losses of 381 killed. The news of Dewey's victory reached Washington on May 7, and the nation went wild in celebration. Patriotic fervor swept the country, with Dewey as its symbol. Stores soon had Dewey hats, buttons, and soap; smokeshops sold Dewey cigars; and bars made Dewey cocktails. Mothers named their children Dewey, and crowds sang a popular song that proclaimed that "Dewey was the hero of the day," the man who had "remembered the *Maine* in the good old fashioned way." Meanwhile, Congress promoted Dewey to rear admiral and then to full admiral and ordered that a bronze medal be issued to all the men in his fleet to commemorate the victory. The Democratic party talked of nominating Dewey for president in 1900.[13]

Colonel MacArthur again petitioned Corbin in late May for reassignment to an infantry command. In peacetime, a staff assignment was fine, but in wartime, it was the battlefront for a man like MacArthur. He hoped to be commissioned as a brigadier general of the Volunteers and assigned a brigade in the 3rd Army Corps before the Cuban invasion. As Volunteer regiments were organized, Regular Army officers were promoted to lead them—overnight, captains became colonels, and colonels became generals. The promotions were only temporary commissions, however. At the end of the war, officers would revert back to their permanent grade and rank in the Regular Army.

On June 1, MacArthur received a telegram notifying him that he was commissioned brigadier general of the Volunteers. It was good news, but his new orders were a shock. He had assumed he would be assigned to the 3rd Army Corps, destined to invade Cuba, but instead, he was ordered to San Francisco to join Major General Wesley Merritt, who was assembling a force for the invasion of the Philippines. Carol Petillo speculated that MacArthur "was not adverse to nor totally unprepared for the new assignment. His still intense ambition was encouraged by the opportunities that he believed awaited him in the Philippines, and his earlier interest in Asia was reawakened."[14]

The public assumed that Dewey's victory placed the entire Philippine archipelago in the hands of the United States. Few Americans knew anything about the Philippines, and fewer still were aware of the history and culture of the islands. Spain had 35,000 men stationed in various towns in the 7,000 islands of the archipelago; its garrison in Manila alone was estimated at 13,000 to 15,000 men. Although Dewey could have bombarded Manila, he had no ground forces to capture the city. Therefore, the Navy Department ordered him to blockade the city and await the arrival of U.S. troops.

General Merritt was ordered to San Francisco to organize the 8th Army Corps, with an initial strength of about 10,000 men. Assigned as one of Merritt's brigade commanders, General MacArthur left Tampa on June 2 for Chicago to meet his wife at the Palmer House for a few days before proceeding to San Francisco. Pinky was not thrilled with her husband's resignation from the Adjutant General's Office. As the youngest lieutenant colonel in the department and a friend of General Corbin, it was likely that MacArthur would have become adjutant general before he retired in ten years. A Volunteer's commission was not permanent, and if the war ended quickly (as most observers were predicting), MacArthur would find himself a lieutenant colonel without a job because his staff position would no longer be available. Moreover, Pinky had vowed never to return to isolated garrison living. The fight between the couple on this issue must have been a dandy, but General MacArthur was an obstinate man. He believed that he was the best infantry officer in the U.S. Army, and he had trained all his life to lead men into battle. It was his duty to volunteer, and it was inconceivable that he would have been content with a staff position in wartime. Pinky knew this but declared she would not accompany him to San Francisco. She would remain with her son Douglas in Milwaukee.[15]

In early June, Douglas took the competitive West Point examination for Congressman Otjen's appointment to the U.S. Military Academy, and while the general was in Milwaukee, the results were made public. Douglas placed first among thirteen candidates, with a remarkable score of 93.3 percent against the closest competitor's score of 77.9 percent. He scored 700 points out of a possible 750. Although his father was proud of him, Douglas was almost saddened by the results.[16]

With the outbreak of war, Douglas wanted to forgo West Point, as his father had done back in 1862, and to enlist in a Volunteer unit. He dreamed of being as courageous and famous as his father, and he envied his older brother, who was now an ensign aboard the *Vixen*, a gunboat steaming toward Havana. General MacArthur, proud of his older son, had informed the press, "The military record of the MacArthur family is being maintained." Wanting to prove he was as brave as his brother, Douglas pleaded with his father—he wanted to go to war. General MacArthur rejected Douglas's request. Pinky would have exploded, and besides, the general definitely wanted him to go to West Point, an experience that he wished he had had himself. Douglas could not imagine disobeying his father, even though at eighteen he could have enlisted without his parent's permission. Because his West Point appointment was for the class of 1899, he and Pinky were to remain in Milwaukee for another year while he received medical attention to correct a curvature of the spine so that he could pass the academy's physical exams.[17]

After five days with Pinky and Douglas, General MacArthur left Milwaukee by train for San Francisco. He would not see either of them again for over three years. Pinky, still unhappy with her husband's assignment, wired Adjutant General Corbin on June 12 to ask that her husband's orders be changed to "anything else" but the Philippines.[18]

General MacArthur arrived in San Francisco the same day Pinky sent her telegram to Corbin. The city was in a festive mood, full of patriotic fever, and the citizens of the city cheered the soldiers who were collecting in camps just to the west of town. MacArthur was greeted by his old friend Charlie King, who had obtained an appointment as brigadier general and had also been assigned to the Philippine Expedition.

MacArthur met the other major officers at a staff meeting the next day at the Palace Hotel in downtown San Francisco. The 8th Army Corps commander was Major General Merritt, a sixty-two-year-old, overweight, gray-haired veteran of the Civil War. A West Point graduate, class of 1860, Merritt had won fame during that war and reached the rank of brevet major general of the Volunteers before he was thirty. He was not happy at being assigned to lead the Philippine Expedition; as the second-ranking general in the U.S. Army after General Miles, he believed he, rather than General Shafter, should have been placed in charge of the Cuban Expedition. Major General Elwell S. Otis (a sixty-one-year-old veteran of the Civil War and a former commander of the Infantry and Cavalry Training School at Fort Leavenworth) was second in command of the 8th Army Corps. A stickler for paperwork, Otis was a tall, balding, taciturn officer with white muttonchop sideburns. Besides Charlie King and MacArthur, Francis V. Greene was the other brigadier general. Like King, he was a graduate of West Point, class of 1870, who had resigned his commission but had returned to active duty as a Volunteer for the duration of the war.[19]

None of the generals at the staff meeting knew much about the Philippines, and Merritt admitted to the group of assembled officers that he had little information on the current situation in Manila. Before confronting the Spanish fleet on May 1, Admiral Dewey had cut the telegraph cable between Manila and Hong Kong as a precaution. The cable was still out, and it took almost two weeks for news of conditions in Manila to reach San Francisco. Since Dewey's great victory in Manila Bay, there had been hundreds of newspaper articles on the Philippines, but Merritt did not know how accurate these articles were. Further, there were no books on the Philippines in any San Francisco bookstore, and Merritt knew nothing of the history, culture, or geography of the archipelago except for the information available in any encyclopedia. He knew that the Philippines were a Spanish colony composed of a chain of islands off the southern coast of China. The islands were about 7,000 miles from San Francisco, about 150 miles southeast of Taiwan. They stretched south from the South China Sea for about 1,152 miles, down to the Dutch East Indies near the equator. The islands were tropical and produced bananas, tobacco, coconuts, sugar, and rice. Of the 7,000-plus islands in the archipelago, the 11 largest contained more than 95 percent of the population, estimated to be about 13 million.

The most important island was Luzon in the north, on which Manila, the capital, was located. Next in importance were the central islands of Cebu, Leyte, Panay, Samar, and the Negros. The southern islands, called the Mindanaos, were inhabited by Moslems, and the majority of the population on the other islands was Catholic. There were over 87 different tribal groups in the Philippines; the most important was the Tagalogs on Luzon. Manila was the largest city in the Philippines and had an estimated population of 300,000. Although Admiral Dewey retained control of Manila Bay, the Spanish still held the city.

The 8th Army Corps was assigned to get to Manila as rapidly as possible and capture the city. Since the navy had no transports available, Merritt had chartered seventeen merchant ships to transport the 15,000 men of the 8th Army Corps to the Philippines. The transports were being reoutfitted in San Francisco harbor; that is, the vessels were being ripped apart to install sleeping quarters and army messes. Each transport was expected to hold about 1,000 men. Traveling at an average speed of 9 knots, the transport ships would take almost forty days to travel the 7,000 miles from San Francisco to Manila. Three transports, the *City of Pekin,* the *Australia,* and the *City of Sidney,* had left San Francisco on May 25 with about 2,500 men under the command of Brigadier General Thomas M. Anderson.

At the conference, Merritt assigned each of his new staff to command functions. Greene was placed in charge of the 2nd Expeditionary Force, scheduled to depart on June 15 with 3,600 men. The 3rd Expedition, to leave around June 27 with 4,500 men, was placed under the command of King, although Merritt would also be aboard one of the ships. Otis and MacArthur would remain in San Francisco to organize the raw recruits flooding into the city into a 4th Expedition that would depart in early July.[20]

After the conference, MacArthur waited behind to see Merritt. He objected to Merritt's plan to send Greene and King to the Philippines and to leave him in San Francisco to organize the 4th Expedition. He had transferred from the Adjutant General's Office to see active duty, not to continue as a staff officer. MacArthur requested that he be assigned to command either the 2nd or 3rd Expeditionary Force. He supported his request by referring to army regulations. The Adjutant General's Office had intentionally placed him as fourth in command following Merritt, Otis, and Anderson. Since MacArthur outranked, by date of commission, both Greene and King, who was the most junior, Merritt's plan violated the principle of seniority. MacArthur realized that Merritt and King were old comrades in arms, having served together in the 5th Cavalry in the 1870s, and he also acknowledged King's military competence. Moreover, MacArthur liked Charlie. But that did not mean he could allow an injustice to be done. He had served in the Regular Army for thirty-two years, studying and training for the possibility of war. King had been retired for almost twenty years and was a Volunteer officer. Consequently, MacArthur knew he was more qualified to lead a brigade into battle than King. His arguments were persuasive, for Merritt reluctantly switched assignments and placed MacArthur in charge of a provisional brigade due to sail for the

Philippines as the 3rd Expedition. Hurt and bitterly disappointed, King accepted the decision.[21]

General MacArthur immediately went to work to get his brigade into shape. Camp Presidio, a permanent military base with well-planned grounds and administration buildings, was the 8th Corps headquarters, but most of the men were at Camp Merritt, a tent city in a vast picnic ground on the bay west of San Francisco. The mornings and evenings there were cold and foggy, and when the cold wind swept down through the bay, it whipped the sand into clouds of dust that pervaded everything. Bronchitis and pneumonia plagued the troops. Although conditions were better than at Tampa or Chickamauga, supplies were still limited. Volunteer units were outfitted in blue woolen uniforms and issued old Springfield '73 rifles rather than the newer repeating, bolt-action Krags that the Regular Army units had. The Volunteer officers knew nothing about training men, army regulations, or campsite sanitation. As a result, the garbage and latrine waste of 10,000 men soaked into the soft sand, and foul water accumulated as a breeding ground for disease.

With San Francisco so close, Camp Merritt was easily accessible to hordes of visitors. It proved impossible to isolate the men for drills and training exercises, as mothers, sisters, wives, and sweethearts roamed the unfenced areas and interfered with military discipline. The troops considered it all a magnificent lark: The Volunteers did not take the training seriously, complained about daily drills, and slipped out of camp at night to visit the beckoning fleshpots of the city. The saloons were a mere trolleycar ride away, and most of the men spent their evenings carousing through the city. Venereal diseases ran wild through the camps and became a pressing problem.[22]

In spite of the city's distractions, MacArthur insisted that the men engage in four hours of drills every day to learn basic army commands. He met with his officers and organized lectures for the noncommissioned officers. Due to sail on June 27, his command totaled 197 officers and 4,650 enlisted men. With only two weeks to prepare, MacArthur barely had time to process the brigade's paperwork and select his staff.[23]

On June 15, the 2nd Expedition of four ships with 3,600 men under General Greene sailed out of San Francisco, bound for Manila. Meanwhile, General Shafter and the Cuban Expeditionary Force of 17,000 had finally left Tampa for Cuba. The newspapers concentrated their coverage on the Cuban invasion, and even in San Francisco, there was much more popular interest in news on Cuba than events in the distant Philippines. Most of the officers, including MacArthur, wished they were with Shafter. Since it was only six days' steaming time between Cuba and Tampa, U.S. forces might be attacking Fort Santiago, the Spanish stronghold in Cuba, within days, and the war would probably be over before U.S. troops ever reached the Philippines.

Despite this fact, preparations for the Philippine Expedition proceeded rapidly. On Sunday, June 26, with MacArthur in the lead, his brigade marched from the camps west of town 5 miles through the cobblestone streets of San Francisco to the Pacific Mail Wharf, where six transports waited. Crowds lined the streets to watch the soldiers parade past. MacArthur ordered the bands to play, and John Philip Sousa's marching tunes lifted the spirits of the men as the crowds cheered them on to victory.[24]

At the wharf the crowds were even thicker as family and friends pushed to see the men off to war. The troops waited most of the morning, and ladies of the Red Cross served them sandwiches and coffee for lunch. It took most of the day to load the men aboard the six transports—the *Para,* the *Ohio,* the *Morgan City,* the *Valencia,* the *Newport,* and the *Indiana.* Each transport held about 1,000 men. Merritt would be aboard the *Newport,* the fastest of the transports, and would remain in San Francisco for two more days. MacArthur boarded the *Indiana* with his staff, Companies D and H, 18th Infantry, Companies C, G, and L, 23rd Infantry, Company H, 1st North Dakota, Company A Engineers, 47 men of the Signal Corps, 11 men of the Hospital Corps, and the band of the 23rd Infantry. The loading was not completed until late afternoon.

The transports steamed out into the middle of the bay to take on additional supplies and remained there for the night with the lights of San Francisco surrounding them. Officers were placed in staterooms on the stern and upper decks. The Hospital Corps and noncommissioned officers had the lower deck. For the rest, quarters were cramped. Almost 1,000 men were crammed into the reoutfitted cargo hold, or the "blackhole," as the men were soon calling it. Measuring only 60 feet by 100 feet, the hole was just large enough for each man to have a small bunk with a straw mattress. Despite the crowded conditions, the men sang that night. Everyone was in a good mood, but few had ever taken a forty-day sea voyage.[25]

The next day broke clear and cool with a strong breeze from the west. Throughout the morning, the vessels remained anchored in the bay taking on supplies. From shore came hundreds of boats of all descriptions, loaded with enthusiastic people, pretty girls, and brass bands. As the small boats passed from ship to ship, the men cheered and sang patriotic songs. As the bands played, the visitors threw fruit, flowers, and kisses to the men. Around 2:00 P.M., the transports weighed anchor and steamed down the bay, the *Indiana* in the lead. Ceremonial cannon boomed, while crowds jammed the shore and shouted themselves hoarse as they waved hats, handkerchiefs, and small American flags. Numerous boats ladened with enthusiastic people followed the troopships for several miles.[26]

As the shoreline disappeared from view around five o'clock, a mild catastrophe struck. Everyone had expected good weather, but as the transport ships reached the open sea, a violent gale struck. It was a wild night of terror for the 3rd Expedition. Bunks broke from lashings, and mess kits, clothes, cameras, and other equipment were strewn everywhere. For four days, the transports corkscrewed through the turbulent ocean. Nearly everyone, including General MacArthur, became seasick, and some became violently ill. Vomit and saltwater sloshed through the enlisted men's quarters.[27]

Even when the weather improved on July 1, the stench hovered over the vessels. With 1,000 men jammed in an unventilated cargo hold, the smell was unspeakable and could not be eliminated. The straw mattresses and clothes were soon infected with bugs. Freshwater was at a premium, and when the men washed their clothes in saltwater, the fabric came apart. There were no mess tables; therefore, the men squatted on the deck at mealtime. Private Frank Merrill of the 13th Minnesota Volunteers remembered that trying to eat on a rolling, slippery deck was "conducive to the spilling of soup or slum or coffee down the necks or over sprawled legs, and the spilling too of strong language." Soon the decks were greasy messes. The sick bay, as one soldier recalled, "was a small wooden structure built on the main deck, constantly in danger of being washed overboard." Food was difficult to prepare because the "cook's galley was poorly arranged; the stoves were not securely fastened to the ship." To make matters worse, on nearly all the transports, the generators had been smashed during the storm, and smoky kerosene lanterns provided the only light at night.[28]

The men grumbled. Most had never made an ocean voyage of any kind, and they were soon tired of the empty expanse of water and the narrow confines of the ships. They were seasick, homesick, and miserable. Clearly, the forty-day voyage to Manila was not going to be a pleasure cruise. Fortunately, the mood improved with the weather and with the knowledge that Honolulu, Hawaii, was only a few days away. The small fleet celebrated the Fourth of July with patriotic songs, speeches, and toasts to almost everyone. Aboard the *Indiana,* the band of the 23rd Infantry played "Red White and Blue," "Marching Through Georgia," and Sousa's marches.[29]

In the early morning hours of July 6, the ship steamed into beautiful Honolulu harbor. Aroused from his sleep by the bugle call, MacArthur stood on deck and watched the fairylike scene spread out before him. Hawaii was truly the "paradise of the Pacific." Mountains crowned with the halo of the rising sun surrounded the placid, blue waters of Honolulu Bay.[30]

The city was decked out to greet the soldiers. With the islands on the verge of annexation by the United States, patriotic enthusiasm was the order of the day. In fact, Congress adopted a joint resolution annexing Hawaii to the United States that very day, and the city of Honolulu was jubilant. Private Merrill recorded in his diary that "the city was agog with anticipation, hundreds of American flags flying." Businesses closed, and the people turned out in masses as the troops disembarked and paraded down the palm-lined streets to the park and government grounds. As a special treat, MacArthur ordered the troops to drill in the streets and the parks of the city. The citizens cheered their martial spirit. After the parade, the men marched to a bathing area, where clean clothes were provided. Dismissed from duty, many of the soldiers swam at Waikiki Beach, while others went sightseeing and souvenir hunting; many had the new, inexpensive Kodak camera, and they snapped hundreds of photographs. The city fathers gave a dinner that night for the officers.[31]

The news from Cuba was limited, and no one knew whether Shafter's forces had captured Fort Santiago. Meanwhile, there were rumors that a Spanish fleet had sailed from European waters to intercept the Philippine Expedition, which was defenseless against war vessels. The transports had no guns, and there were no U.S. naval vessels to protect the convoy. If the rumors were true and the transports were sighted by a Spanish fleet on the high seas, surrender would be the only option available.

The *Newport,* with Merritt aboard, arrived in Honolulu during the night. The next day, July 7, the citizens of the city provided a midday tropical lunch for all 4,800 men of the 3rd Expedition. Beneath coconut and palm trees, long tables groaned with native foods as the ladies of the city served a bountiful feast to the men while bands played in the background. Cigars were provided as an after-dinner treat. Private Jesse George of the 7th California Volunteers remembered the troops rising, regiment by regiment, to give "three cheers for the people of Honolulu." In the afternoon, the men organized athletic competitions on the baseball field and invited the citizens of the city. Track and field sports were very popular entertainment that day. In the early evening, the men returned, relaxed and cheerful, to their ships.[32]

Honolulu restored the spirits of the men. After two glorious days, on the morning of July 8, the six vessels of the 3rd Expedition steamed out of Honolulu. A war was waiting.

Five miles out of the harbor, the boilers of the *Indiana* broke down and brought the fleet to a halt. After consultation between MacArthur and Merritt, the expedition split. Five of the vessels returned to Honolulu while the *Newport,* the fastest vessel in the fleet and Merritt's command vessel, continued on alone. The *Ohio* towed the *Indiana* back to Waikiki harbor, with the other ships following. The *Indiana's* boilers were repaired overnight, and the next day, the five transports began their journey once more.[33]

The fleet took a southwesterly course from Honolulu, skirting the south coast of Oahu and passing Pearl Harbor. Splendid sugar plantations lined the coast. The Pacific Ocean was calm and peaceful, with only a few fleecy clouds in the sky. At an average speed of 245 miles a day, it would be twenty-two days before the transports reached Manila. As they steamed southwest, the days and nights became hotter, and heavy rains doused the transports daily. In the evenings, the officers sat on the upper deck in wicker chairs and watched the stars come out one by one. The transports were absolutely alone, cut off from the world, surrounded by ocean, and destitute of news.[34]

For the troops, life aboard the transport was more demanding than it was for the officers. A bugle call at 5:00 A.M. woke them, and they marched on deck for a saltwater bath to remove the stink of a night in the blackhole. At six, breakfast was served and was followed by cleaning of quarters. Every two or three days, the bedding was aired on deck. MacArthur ordered frequent inspections and demanded that the men keep their quarters as clean as possible. Beyond that, officers and sergeants gave daily lectures on army regulations, maintenance of equipment, and basic military tactics; the medical staff also lectured on tropical diseases. Two or three evenings a week, the band assembled on deck to play for the troops. The men enjoyed singing the favorite tunes of the day, such as "Good By My Love, Good By," "The Girl I Left Behind Me," "In the Greenfield of Virginia," "On the Banks of the Wabash," and "The Girl I Left in Sunny Tennessee." Many of the soldiers had brought mandolins, guitars, or other musical instruments, and in the evenings, they often played on deck. At other times, boxing bouts and wrestling matches were organized. On Sundays, religious services were held at 11:00 A.M. and 7:30 P.M. Other pastimes included cards, chess, and checkers. Many of the men had brought magazines or books, which circulated throughout the ship.[35]

In the vast expanse of the Pacific, water stretched for an eternity, the days became hot and humid, and boredom and monotony settled over the expedition. The men complained constantly about the food and water, which was brackish, almost nauseating, and served so warm it was practically undrinkable. Some of the men tied ropes to their canteens and lowered them into the ocean to cool the contents; others washed their clothes in a similar manner. The Volunteers groused about the food, but it was the same food the Regular Army had been eating for forty years. Day after day, the men were served the same diet. Breakfast was rice, some bean soup, hardtack, and dishwater coffee. Lunch was corned beef, called "red horse" or "canned jackass," and doughy biscuits that could be stretched out in the men's fingers like wads of warm putty. Dinner was slumgullion stew made with boiled salt pork, potatoes, and a trace of onions. The stew smelled and tasted awful, and many threw the disgusting slum overboard. They could buy pickles, crackers, and candies from the ship's store, but with the base pay of a private still at $.50 a day, or $15.60 a month, few of the men could afford any high-priced delicacies. The officers were better fed than the enlisted men, but the privileges of rank were paid for with hard cash. Officers paid $1.50 to $2.50 a day for meals and purchased additional foodstuffs from ship's stores at outrageous prices. Because there were no fresh or canned fruits on board, many of the men and a few of the officers became ill. Medical facilities, inadequate for dealing with sea sickness, were unable to deal with the more deadly outbreaks of measles and typhoid fever. The *Indiana* buried 1 lieutenant and 6 privates during the voyage.[36]

MacArthur took advantage of the privileges of rank. His quarters were spacious, and he ate a more varied diet in the ship's dining hall. The special privileges did not make MacArthur feel guilty, any more than Teddy Roosevelt did when he traveled by transport to Cuba; Roosevelt would describe that voyage as a "very pleasant" trip "through the tropic seas." In fact, MacArthur knew the lot of the enlisted men aboard the ships better than Teddy, for he had survived comparable conditions for twenty years on far-flung frontier posts. He, too, had eaten hardtack, bully beef, and slumgullion stew.[37]

After twenty days at sea, the fleet sighted the northeast coast of Luzon on the morning of July 29 (see Map 11.1). "As soon as the first dim outlines of the island could be traced upon the horizon," Forest A. Haight of the U.S. 6th Artillery remembered that "everybody crowded to the side of the ship and watched with keen interest. As the vessels approached, the island took the form of a mountain rising abruptly from the ocean, and towering skyward." Within sight of land, they steamed north, then west past the northern coast of the island into the South China Sea. The transports were still two days from Manila. That night and through the next day and night, the turbulent ocean tossed and turned the vessels. Heavy rains doused the ships several times.[38]

Around 7:30 on the morning of July 31, 1898, the five transports sailed past the rocky island of Corregidor that guarded the mouth of Manila Bay. A sea in itself, the bay was 35 miles wide at its mouth and stretched northeast for 30 miles before reaching Manila. Even at that hour of the day, the blinding sun reflected off the water, and saturated heat waves rose in the air and created a steambath effect that made everyone gasp for breath. Around ten o'clock, it rained so hard that the world disappeared into a sheet of water so thick that the front of the ships could not be seen even from the forward decks; water poured down from the heavens in buckets. Although it was easier to breathe, the heat remained stifling. When the rain stopped, the sun returned with a new intensity and sucked the moisture back into the air. Heavy black clouds soon formed overhead again.

It took five hours for the ships to steam from the mouth of the bay to Manila's inner harbor. Around eleven o'clock, the transports passed Cavite, a small peninsula jutting into the bay 10 miles south of Manila. On deck, the men rushed to the landward side of the transports to see the wrecks of the old Spanish fleet: Cavite had been the site of Dewey's great naval victory on May 1. Near the shoreline, the hulks of the destroyed Spanish ships rose high out of the shallow water; twisted rigging and battered funnels protruded above the waterline.[39]

The heart of Manila Bay was before them. Large warships and freighters of many nations loomed high on the flat plain of the sea. With over fifty ships of various nationalities present, there was a forest of masts in the deep harbor. The war had brought out the hawks: The Germans, British, French, and Russians each had a fleet in the bay. The U.S. contingent included Dewey's small squadron and most of the transports of the 1st and 2nd Expeditions.

Beyond the ships, the red-tile roofs of the old city of Manila gleamed in the sun. The city lay in an area almost as flat as a Kansas prairie. Built right on the ocean, Manila was invariably flooded in the rainy summer monsoon season. Beyond the inner city, an ocean of brown nipa huts stretched for miles north, south, and east into the interior of Luzon. With over 300,000 citizens, Manila encompassed a number of smaller suburbs stretching south 10 miles to Cavite and north 30 miles to Malolos. Beyond the flat lands, blue and purple mountain ranges rose high on the horizon. Here and there, a single, softly rounded mountain stood alone (see Map 11.2).

MAP 11.1 The Philippine archipelago

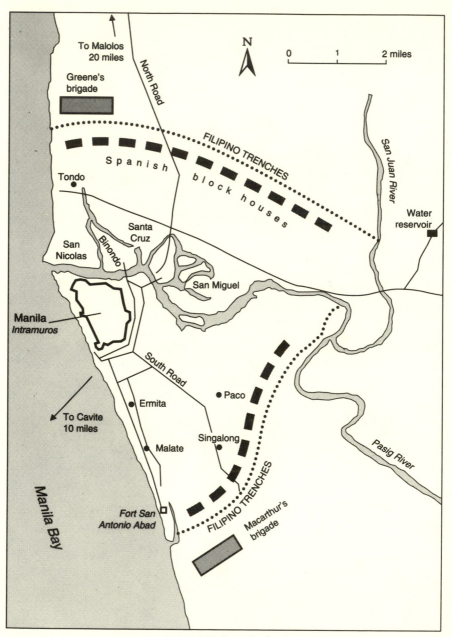

To Malolos
20 miles

Greene's
brigade

North Road

N

0   1   2 miles

S p a n i s h   FILIPINO TRENCHES

Tondo

b l o c k   h o u s e s

San Juan River

Santa
Cruz

San
Nicolas

Binondo

San Miguel

Water
reservoir

Manila
Intramuros

South Road

To Cavite
10 miles

Ermita

Paco

Malate

Singalong

FILIPINO TRENCHES

Pasig River

**Manila
Bay**

Fort San
Antonio Abad

Macarthur's
brigade

MAP 11.2 Manila and suburbs

The bay was alive with activity. Launches, cutters, and gunboats plied to and fro. Ships flew their foreign or U.S. colors and signaled constantly to one another with flags. Smaller Filipino *bancas* competed for room with majestic warships, ocean freighters, tugs, and hemp barges. On the small native boats, which resembled Indian canoes with outriggers, the boatmen paddled about from ship to ship selling fresh vegetables and souvenirs to the sailors and soldiers. Some of the Filipino craft resembled small Chinese junks. Painted in every conceivable color, the cumbersome-looking boats had rounded deckhouses roofed with bamboo and straw matting to protect the cargo as well as the Filipino families who lived on board.[40]

As he stood on the *Indiana*'s deck, MacArthur got his first look at the Filipinos. He had entered a new world teeming with a dense population and felt an instant affinity for the Filipinos, probably because they reminded him of his days in San Antonio, Texas. The Filipinos looked like Mexicans, not Orientals, and he knew many spoke Spanish. The men were small, about five-feet-four-inches tall on the average, with straight black hair cut very short. The petite, delicate, and shapely women had beautiful long hair. Though the men looked rather surly, the women smiled good-naturedly and waved at the men on the arriving transport.

Around 11:45 A.M., the five transports anchored near Dewey's flagship, the *Olympia*, one of the two cruisers in his small squadron of five ships supported by smaller gunboats and supply ships. Although not nearly as powerful as a battleship, a cruiser was still a formidable naval force, with 6-pound rapid-firing cannons and guns ranging in size from 5 to 8 inches set in steel-plated turrets. The transport captains were relieved to be under the protective guns, although no new Spanish fleet had materialized. It was raining again, but some of the sailors on the *Olympia* still came on deck to yell a greeting to the arriving transports and got a return cheer from the men on the *Indiana*.

"What's the news?" some of the men shouted. They had been isolated at sea for more than twenty days, and everyone hungered for information on the war. A launch soon arrived from the *Olympia* with English-language newspapers from Hong Kong and orders for MacArthur to attend a conference onboard Dewey's flagship.[41]

MacArthur quickly read the papers and learned for the first time of the U.S. victories in Cuba. U.S. forces had attacked San Juan Hill, the heights overlooking the city of Santiago, on July 1. Colonel Teddy Roosevelt, a true fighting gamecock and the commander of the 1st U.S. Volunteer Cavalry (more popularly known as the Rough Riders), had charged up San Juan's Kettle Hill in front of his regiment as dozens of newspaper correspondents watched. They wrote glowing accounts of the colonel's bravery, which he later embellished in minute detail in articles, books, and speeches.[42]

The U.S. forces captured the hill, gained control of the heights above Santiago, and placed the 13,000-man Spanish garrison under siege. A U.S. naval blockade kept the Spanish fleet bottled up in the harbor. On the morning of July 3, the fleet tried to run the blockade, and the ensuing naval battle up and down the Cuban coast lasted for four hours. The U.S. fleet, commanded by Admiral William T. Sampson, overwhelmed the Spaniards. Spanish losses were 474 killed and wounded and 1,750 taken prisoner; U.S. casualties were 1 killed, 1 wounded. In Manila, General MacArthur would celebrate the victory with a toast to his son Ensign MacArthur, who was aboard the gunboat USS *Vixen* and had participated in the naval battle.

The destruction of the Spanish fleet virtually ended the war in Cuba. On Sunday, July 17, the Spanish garrison in Santiago surrendered.

As a launch transported MacArthur to a meeting of the general officers onboard the *Olympia,* he must have wondered if the entire war would soon be over. Perhaps Pinky had been right and he had been foolish to resign his post in the Adjutant General's Office.

At the conference, MacArthur met Admiral Dewey and Brigadier General Anderson. Dewey, a slim, sixty-year-old naval veteran of the Civil War, had been in the right place at the right time to obtain one of the greatest naval victories in U.S. history. Wearing an immaculate, tailored dress-white uniform and polished high-instep boots, Dewey may well have been the smartest dresser in the navy. "It was said of him," wrote one reporter, "that the creases of his trousers were as well-defined as his views on naval warfare." And he was enjoying his new status as national hero. Anderson was a sharp-eyed, leathery Civil War veteran who had last served in Alaska.[43]

MacArthur was briefed on the military situation. Although Dewey's squadron controlled the bay, a Spanish garrison of 15,000 men still held part of Manila, called the *Intramuros,* and a string of fifteen blockhouses about 2 miles out that served as their forward outposts. The *Intramuros* was an old fortress that loomed over the harbor and the mouth of the Pasig River. Built in the sixteenth century, the old fortress was surrounded by a gray stone wall that was about 30 feet high and 10 to 20 feet thick. The wall was capped with parapets and bastions for cannons. Some of the Spanish cannons dated back to the seventeenth century, but the garrison did have a few modern 10-inch guns along the waterfront area. Entrance to the fortress was through one of eight gates. The arched gateways had drawbridges, worked by heavy chains, that stretched across a moat that ran around the walls of the fortress. The modern naval guns of Dewey's warships could have easily pounded the Spanish fortress into oblivion, but the United States wanted the *Intramuros* intact, not annihilated.[44]

The *Intramuros* represented only a small section of greater Manila, which stretched for miles into the interior. The outer regions of the city were controlled by a Philippine revolutionary army led by General Emilio Aguinaldo y Famy, a young Filipino firebrand who had visions of establishing an independent state. Admiral Dewey briefly recapped the growth of Aguinaldo's army for the officers at the conference.

Emilio Aguinaldo, c. April 1901. (National Archives,
111-SC-98358)

In 1896, Andres Bonifacio, founder of a revolutionary party called the *Katipunan*, led a rebellion against Spain's authority and attacked isolated Spanish garrisons on Luzon. The Spanish had retaliated with a policy of harsh repression, much like that of "Butcher" Weyler in Cuba. Filipinos were herded into concentration camps, where many were tortured and some were publicly decapitated. A power struggle erupted among the Filipino leaders that led to the death of Bonifacio and the succession of Aguinaldo, a serious, almost humorless, twenty-eight-year-old rebel. In 1897, Aguinaldo's small force achieved a few victories, but in the end, the rebellion failed because of a lack of weapons. Armed with bolos, spears, and a few decrepit rifles, Aguinaldo's peasant army could not win against modern Spanish weapons that included breech-loading Mausers and artillery. A compromise was negotiated. In August 1897, in return for Spain's promise to liberalize its rule in the Philippines, the thirty-four major leaders of the *Katipunan* ended the rebellion and accepted deportation to Hong Kong.

Aguinaldo soon realized that Spain had no intention of granting the promised concessions. The revolutionaries plotted and schemed to return to their homeland and renew the rebellion. When war appeared imminent between the United States and Spain in early 1898, Aguinaldo contacted the U.S. consulate in Hong Kong, hoping to form an alliance. After war erupted on April 21, Dewey left Hong

Kong for Manila, where on May 1, he destroyed the Spanish fleet. Dewey could not follow up his victory because he had no ground troops. He therefore decided an easy way to threaten the Spanish would be by supporting the Filipino revolutionaries. He sent a small revenue cutter, the *McCulloch,* to Hong Kong to retrieve Aguinaldo and the other exiled leaders. They arrived in Manila Bay on May 19 and, after a brief conference with Dewey, were put ashore with some guns. The Filipino leaders quickly reorganized the revolution, and in the next two months, they attacked and seized most of the isolated Spanish garrisons on Luzon. Aguinaldo's forces had captured about 3,000 Spanish soldiers and were holding them in a prisoner of war camp at Cavite.

The Filipino army surrounded Manila and placed the last major Spanish garrison on Luzon under siege. Aguinaldo's army around the city numbered about 15,000 men, about 75 percent of whom were armed with captured Spanish Mausers. The Filipinos constructed trenches just beyond the Spanish blockhouses that encircled the old city. The trenches began on the bay 2 miles south of the *Intramuros* near an area called Malate, curved inland about 4 miles, then curved back to the bay 2 miles north of the *Intramuros* near an area called Tondo. From bay to bay, the line covered about 8 miles. The two forces engaged in small firefights along this line.

Aguinaldo established a temporary capital 30 miles north of Manila at Malolos. On June 12, 1898, the rebel leaders declared their independence from Spain and proclaimed the formation of the Philippine Republic, with Aguinaldo as president. In correspondence with Dewey, Aguinaldo suggested that the Americans henceforth refer to the Filipino army as the Republican Army, not the Insurgent Army, and refer to him as President Aguinaldo rather than General Aguinaldo. The Filipinos were insurgents against Spain, but they were U.S. allies in the war.

Although Dewey had helped Aguinaldo return to the Philippines and had provided some arms to the Filipino rebels, he did not believe his actions committed the United States to support an independent Filipino government under Aguinaldo's leadership. Filipino nationalists, the U.S. military, and historians have argued for years over the U.S. commitment made to Aguinaldo during this stage; but despite Dewey's implied support for the Filipino revolution, he did not have the power to commit the U.S. Congress or the president to any political or diplomatic policy.[45]

Dewey refused to refer to Aguinaldo as president, and when General Anderson arrived in Manila on June 30 with the 1st Expeditionary Force of 2,386 men and 117 officers, Dewey suggested that Aguinaldo place the Republican Army under Anderson's command. The suggestion angered Aguinaldo, who refused. Forewarned, the Filipino rebels became suspicious and were reluctant to let Anderson land his troops. Aguinaldo wanted diplomatic recognition and guarantees that the United States would not attempt to remain in the Philippines, but the U.S. military commanders were under strict orders to make no commitments. The United States was at war with Spain, and what occurred in the Philippines after the war was a decision for the president and Congress. The military's task was to defeat Spain, and it would be difficult to accomplish that task without the assistance (or at least the acquiescence) of the Philippine Republican Army.

Under the pressure of Dewey's naval guns and still hoping for U.S. support, Aguinaldo allowed Anderson to land his troops at Cavite, the site of the old Spanish naval base, 10 miles south of Manila. Cavite was on a narrow peninsula separated from Manila by 10 miles of practically impassable roads and some 10,000 armed Filipinos. When General Greene arrived on July 17 with the 3,500 men of the 2nd Expedition, Aguinaldo allowed his forces to land 2 miles north of Manila at an old peanut farm, which the U.S. troops immediately dubbed, sarcastically, Camp Dewey. Camp Dewey was located on the bay and was practically underwater because of the continuous rain.

The first contingent of the 3rd Expeditionary Force under Merritt anchored in the bay on July 25, with about 1,000 men. The arrival of MacArthur's force of 4,650 men and 197 officers increased the U.S. ground forces to approximately 12,000 men. Merritt would remain aboard the *Newport* while placing Anderson in charge of the forces in the field. Greene's brigade at Camp Dewey was designated the 2nd Brigade; MacArthur was placed in charge of the 1st Brigade, which was to land as soon as possible in a designated area 2 miles south of Manila. Although there would be some minor personnel swapping, the 1st Brigade was composed primarily of the troops of the 3rd Expedition. The brigade included the Astor Battery, Battery B of the Utah Artillery, five companies of the 14th Infantry, the 23rd Infantry, the 1st Idaho Volunteers, the 13th Minnesota Volunteers, the 1st Wyoming Volunteers, plus headquarters staff, a Signal Corps detachment, and an engineering company, for a total of 3,691 men and 139 officers.

Merritt instructed his field commanders to cooperate with the Philippine Republican Army but to do nothing that might imply U.S. recognition of the Philippine Republic. In Merritt's opinion, the Filipino "insurgents" were an undisciplined, untrained, and poorly led rabble that could not be trusted. The crusty old U.S. general did not take Aguinaldo seriously. Merritt considered him to be a "bandit" leader, not the president of a republic, and refused to even meet with him. Merritt's opinion of Aguinaldo was derived from Dewey, who described him as a wild young man, tiny in stature and in mind, who had grandiose dreams comparable to those of a Latin American dictator. Dewey portrayed Aguinaldo's army as composed of "poor soldiers under poor leadership." In Dewey's opinion, the Philippine Republic was a "myth" and the U.S. Army should "take no notice of the insurgents."[46]

After the briefing, MacArthur returned to the *Indiana* for a conference with his brigade officers to plan their landing the next day. That night, the sounds of war echoed about the bay. All ship lights were extinguished at eight o'clock, and searchlights from Dewey's warships swept the bay, creating eerie shadows. Around midnight, there were flashes of gunfire from shore, and the reports rolled across the 3 miles or more of darkness. The troops on the transports stood on deck and watched the fireworks. They felt as if they were, at last, in the presence of war. Excitement was in the air, and the men could hardly wait to get ashore.[47]

The landing of MacArthur's brigade proved more difficult than expected as constant tropical storms swept Luzon. But despite the drenching rains, the 1st Brigade began landing on August 1 about 3 miles south of Manila, near the districts of Malate and Ermita. Spanish fortification began near Malate at Fort San Antonio Abad. With the transports 3 miles out in the bay, the men were loaded in small groups onto steam launches with light drafts and carried as near shore as possible. Then, they were transferred to small boats purchased from the Filipinos and manned by sailors from Dewey's fleet. Gale-force winds and heavy rains made disembarking difficult and dangerous. Large breakers crashed on the beaches, and the landings were treacherous: Boats were frequently swamped, drenching the troops, damaging supplies, and losing equipment.[48]

It took seven days for all 3,800 men of MacArthur's brigade to come ashore. The brigade occupied about three-fourths of a mile of trenches near Fort San Antonio Abad, right on the bay. North of the brigade, soldiers of the Philippine Republican Army manned barricades that stretched inland for 3 miles before circling west, back to the bay. Greene's brigade occupied three-fourths of a mile on the bay north of Manila. The total combined line was approximately 7 miles, with U.S. forces resting at both ends.

Fortunately, the Filipino reception was a friendly one. In a festive mood, the Filipino soldiers joked with the big U.S. soldiers. Private Ernest Hewson of the California Volunteers reported that the Filipinos greeted him with, "Americano, Filipino, amigos! Español Malo!" The U.S. troops smiled and shouted back, "Amigo!"[49]

The Republican Army was not the rabble described by Dewey, although the Filipinos were not as well equipped as the U.S. forces. The common Filipino soldier was usually a barefooted peasant, but most wore the Republican Army uniform of red-striped khaki trousers, loose fitting blue-and-white blouses, and large, broad-brimmed straw hats decorated with wide red bands. The lucky ones were armed with Mausers that shot a bullet weighing about 170 grains, a much lighter load than the U.S. Springfields and Krags. Except for the officers, who carried enormous swords, all the Filipinos carried bolos (the Filipino machete or long knife). Made of iron or steel, the bolos came in all sizes and shapes. Some were practical tools for cutting meat, rice, and bamboo. Others were more practical as weapons of war. For generations, Filipinos had used bolos to hack up their enemies.

As his men landed and took up their position in the trenches, MacArthur depended on the goodwill of the Filipino people to obtain much-needed supplies. Fresh food was most important because his men had been eating primarily canned meat for almost forty days. The Filipinos willingly sold him vegetables, bananas, pineapples, coconuts, rice, and sugarcane that was as sweet as maple sugar. Fresh firewood and bamboo were also desperately needed. Because of the torrential rains, the ground was a boggy morass, and tent areas were constantly flooded. Using bamboo frames, sleeping cots were raised two feet off the ground.

Along the front line, MacArthur ordered barricades built and trenches dug. Mud was everywhere, and the trenches quickly filled with water. Behind the trenches, a narrow gangway was constructed and protected by piles of sandbags. The rain poured down, and soldiers' feet dangled in water 3 or 4 feet deep. Their skin shrank with the constant soaking. Clothes stayed wet for days and literally rotted on the men's backs, equipment mildewed, and rifles rusted unless given constant attention. It was impossible to keep dry. The men ate, slept, and drilled in drizzle and downpour. They went to bed wet and woke up to put on wet clothes. Cooking was also a problem because of the scarcity of dry wood. In addition, drinking water had to be boiled for at least fifteen minutes or the men came down with intestinal problems.[50]

When it was not raining, the sun poured down in waves of intolerable heat. The temperature hovered around 90 degrees by 6:00 A.M., and humidity hung heavy in the air. By 10:00 A.M., the clouds overhead were black and heavy and the atmosphere as thick as soup. The air was so damp breathing became difficult.[51]

Around noon, there was often an absolute deluge as if a bucket in the sky had been turned upside down. For two or three hours, it poured, then drizzled, then stopped. The heat waves began again as the sun pulled the just-dropped moisture back into the air. The men sweated profusely and swore at the bloody heat. Many wandered around clad only in their underwear, and some swam for relief. Then, after the heat and dampness of the day, the evenings seemed cold. When the thermometer dropped below 78, everyone shivered miserably.

The tropical jungle vegetation surrounding them was alive with scary, crawly things. There were mosquitoes by the billions, rats by the millions, and ants, spiders, tarantulas, centipedes, monkeys, grasshoppers, brightly colored parrots, snakes, and multicolored lizards. As uniforms rotted or were torn by the vines and undergrowth, the skin was exposed to all types of pests. Worst of all were the slimy leeches. Most were less than 1 inch long, but some were almost 4 inches. They crawled along the leaves of the vegetation like inchworms. As the men passed, the leeches hooked onto them with suckers from both ends of the body. At night, half-naked men covered with welts danced around the evening campfires as they picked the leeches off each other and doctored the wounds with tobacco juice.

In the next few days, the troops of MacArthur's brigade explored the area. Nipa huts lined the roads. Constructed of bamboo and palm that grew in marshy areas around the rivers and near the sea, the nipa hut protected the people from both heavy rains and tropical sun. The huts were raised about 4 to 6 feet above the ground on stilts to avoid the myriad small animals and the constant floods. One climbed into the huts by means of a bamboo ladder. A single room served as sleeping quarters for an entire family. The bamboo floors were laced together with strips of rattan, and the thatched walls had easily removable shutters for air circu-

Nipa hut and U.S. soldiers in front, c. September 1898. (National Archives, 111-SC-98340)

lation in the hot, humid climate. The huts had no locks or bolts, no means of preventing outsiders from entering. In the evenings, the peasants lit their huts with candles or cotton wicks floating in cups of coconut oil. Pictures of saints or images of the Virgin Mary usually hung on the walls. Chickens and pigs lived beneath the sheltering huts, and the garbage and animal excrement generated a horrible smell that was nauseating to the Americans but did not seem to bother the Filipinos too much, although they often burned incense to disguise some of the odor.

There were immediate cultural clashes as the giant, brash U.S. boys flirted with the beautiful young Filipina girls. The peasant women wore loose blouses and slit skirts that were comfortable in the hot tropical climate. The blouses were cut low at the neckline and revealed smooth coppery skin. When the women squatted to perform a variety of tasks, from washing clothes to cooking, flashes of flesh enticed the U.S. soldiers to stare and flirt with the girls. Filipino males fingered their bolos and contemplated violence. As in most Spanish cultures, the sexes were segregated in the Philippines. Other than on festival days (of which there were many), the sexes did not intermingle socially. Seldom did they walk together, and even in church, the sexes occupied different aisles. To the Filipinos, the Americans were fierce-looking, unshaven giants. When war erupted in April, the Spanish authorities had described the Americans as barbaric butchers of little children and rapists. The peasants understandably feared the soldiers and disliked their brusque and direct behavior.

There was a cultural shock for most of the U.S. troopers as well, and many formed an instantaneous dislike for the "niggers," as they began to call the Filipinos. Some of the social habits of the Filipino peasants appalled the U.S. soldiers. For example, nipa huts had no inside plumbing, and bathrooms were nonexistent. Filipinos casually relieved themselves in the street, unconcerned about the presence of the opposite sex. The males went around half naked in cotton pants and seldom wore shirts. They squatted around their huts most of the day eating foods, such as fried grasshoppers, that many Americans found nauseating. In the evenings, they crouched around cooking pots and twisted little round balls of rice in the tips of their fingers. With a deft toss, the ball disappeared into their mouths: They had no need of knives and forks. Many of them chewed betel nuts that stained their teeth red and gave them strange, garish smiles. Nearly everyone smoked. The men smoked cigarettes, and the women (and even many young children) smoked fat cigars rolled in natural tobacco leaves and tied with bits of bamboo fiber. The resulting cigar appeared ridiculously gigantic in the mouths of old women and young boys.

MacArthur maintained good relations with the local Republican Army officers and concentrated on getting his men back into shape after forty days at sea. His principal creed remained the same: Drill the men and expect absolute obedience to orders. He knew that parade ground drills did not make a combat soldier, but he believed, as General George Thomas had taught, that parade drills instilled discipline and obedience.

Despite their physical discomforts, the men were in good spirits. On the whole, U.S. soldiers expressed a spirit that was almost embarrassingly gung-ho. The realities of this war were boredom, heat, rain, and more boredom. Still, the soldiers remained intensely patriotic.

Every night, the men listened to the sounds of war being fought without them. After dark, the Spanish and Filipinos were playing war games. Nearly every evening around ten o'clock, there was a furious exchange of small-arms fire between the lines that continued at intervals throughout the night. The nocturnal fusillades did little harm to either side, with only a few men killed or wounded, but both sides appeared to be pleased with their bravery. Neither side left the cover of their barricades.[52]

As the men of the 1st Brigade slowly became accustomed to life in the tropics, MacArthur attended daily meetings aboard the *Newport* with Merritt, Dewey, Greene, Anderson, and a large staff. The generals mapped out a strategy to capture the Spanish garrison in Manila. The plan was for MacArthur to attack the Spanish blockhouses south of Manila while Greene engaged in a simultaneous assault from the north. Merritt was very specific on one point—the Filipinos were not to participate. As Spanish positions were captured, MacArthur and Greene were to leave behind guards and establish roadblocks to prevent armed insurgents from pouring into the inner city. The brigade commanders were authorized to use force, if necessary, to prevent indiscriminate killing by armed Filipinos.

Merritt sent Aguinaldo an order to keep his men out of the confrontation. His reasons were simple: He had worked out a deal with the Spanish. Without the knowledge of his field commanders or the Filipino insurgents, Merritt had opened secret negotiations (through the Belgian consul in Manila, Edouard E. Andre) with the Spanish governor of Manila, Fermin Jaudenes. Cut off from reinforcements, starving, threatened by the guns of Dewey's fleet, and surrounded by hostile forces numbering almost 35,000 men, the Spanish had no chance of winning. Jaudenes knew his garrison was doomed. The question was not how the Spanish could win the war but rather how they could prevent Filipino atrocities while simultaneously appearing gallant in defeat. Jaudenes was terrified of a bloody massacre. Rumors were rampant that the Filipinos were torturing the Spanish prisoners at Cavite, rumors that Merritt believed. Jaudenes was convinced that if the Filipinos captured Manila, they would torture and then execute every Spaniard in the city. In the negotiations with Merritt, he indicated that Spanish resistance would be nominal if Merritt agreed that the battle for Manila was to be an affair only between Spain and the United States. Appreciating his concerns, Merritt willingly made the assurances.

Merritt did not tell his field commanders of his arrangement with the Spanish because he wanted MacArthur and Greene to act as if they were engaged in a real battle. "So far as I knew," MacArthur later said under oath, "there was no feint. All my orders were to the effect that we were to fight a battle, that we were making an assault on the city of Manila. Acting in accordance with those orders I got into a fight." In an article in the *North American Review,* General Anderson confirmed that the field commanders did not know of any arrangement with the Spanish. He reported: "I can say that, if there was any agreement that Manila was to surrender with only a semblance of a fight, it was not communicated to the Army. I was directed to draw up and submit what is known as the tactical plan of attack. And I did it on the theory that there would be resistance."[53]

Early in the morning of August 13, 1898, MacArthur ordered his brigade to attention. Bugles rasped out reveille at four o'clock as a fine drizzle descended. In the predawn haze, the troops checked their weapons as a deluge struck. Heavy rain fell for most of the day.[54]

Around 9:30, four warships of Dewey's squadron and portions of the Utah Artillery opened fire on Fort San Antonio Abad and the Spanish front lines. The men of MacArthur's 1st Brigade lay in the trenches in assaulting columns. Unable to see the shells explode, they heard the thunder of the heavy naval guns, the rattle of rapid-fire machine guns, and the scream of shells across their front. The shells crashed and exploded in the enemy's works with dull thuds. Jesse George of the 7th California Volunteers remembered the constant explosions as awesome, and he was convinced the bombardment unnerved the Spanish defenders. The shelling lasted for almost an hour, then silence descended on the battlefield.[55]

Around 10:30, MacArthur moved his brigade forward as the regimental bands played "There'll Be a Hot Time in the Old Town Tonight," perhaps the favorite American tune of the war. The road was a river of mud as the troops moved in columns toward the first Spanish blockhouse, which had a large number 14 emblazoned on its side. The Spanish forward blockhouses extended out from the *Intramuros* for about 2 miles and encircled the city from bay to bay. They were numbered from north to south 1 to 15, with Fort San Antonio Abad on the southernmost end.[56]

As MacArthur's brigade moved forward, his men were jostled by throngs of Filipinos who were in heavy force on their right flank. Seeing the Filipinos surge forward, the Spanish defenders in blockhouse 14 were horrified that they might be captured and tortured by them. The frightened Spaniards opened fire and offered stiff resistance. In a brief skirmish, two Americans were killed and several wounded.

MacArthur was on the front line, with Spanish Mauser bullets singing about his head. Private William Compton, Company C of the 13th Minnesota Volunteers, later wrote that "General MacArthur walked up and down the firing line as cool as if there wasn't a Mauser bullet within a thousand miles." Henry W. Lyon, also of the 13th Minnesota, recalled that MacArthur was "calm and collected, a splendid officer to follow. He was in plain sight of the enemy most of the time."[57]

The Spanish were across the road in a house fortified with sandbags. MacArthur ordered up the Astor Battery, commanded by Lieutenant Peyton C. March. The battery had been equipped by John Jacob Astor with six twelve-pound, rapid-fire, mobile Hotchkiss guns. Much like Roosevelt's Rough Riders, the men of the Astor Battery were handpicked, and a number were college graduates. "Only three of our guns could be brought into position," Private J. W. Watterson remembered, and "we immediately opened fire ... and planted shell after shell into the blockhouse. However, the Spaniards had our range calibrated to the yard. Their first salvo exploded a few feet from my head." A piece of the shell, he added, "tore away a spoke from one of the gun carriages, sliced off the barrel of Private Dunn's revolver, plowed through his canteen, and then ripped away eight inches of his right thigh muscle." Standing nearby, MacArthur encouraged the battery to continue firing. The battery got the range and lobbed shell after shell at the blockhouse, setting it on fire. When the enemy's ammunition started to explode, the Spaniards rushed from the blockhouse, firing as they ran.[58]

The Spanish fled north up the Paco Road to another stronghold near Singalong, perhaps a half mile away. MacArthur dropped off two battalions at the blockhouse to prevent the Filipinos from following, and with the rest of his brigade, he pursued the Spaniards. However, the Filipinos refused to desist, and many went around the roadblock to charge after the U.S. troops. MacArthur ordered them to withdraw, but most refused. Suddenly, the brigade was under attack from two sides—the Spanish were firing in their front, and angry Filipinos were sniping at their rear. MacArthur established additional roadblocks to his rear as his men returned fire.

The skirmish with the Filipinos ended quickly, although occasional shots were exchanged throughout the morning. Filipino soldiers buzzed around the edge of the front line, angry at the U.S. attempt to exclude them from the battle and deny them the prize they had worked so hard for—Manila.

MacArthur moved his brigade forward to the Singalong crossroads, where the Spanish had established another defensive position. In a brief firefight, his brigade suffered several more casualties before the Spanish retreated behind the walls of the old city and into the hands of General Greene. Attacking from the north of Manila, Greene's brigade had encountered no opposition; around 11:20 that morning, they had entered the old city unmolested to accept the Spanish surrender.

MacArthur left several small detachments at key bridges and street intersections to hold back the Filipinos. Then he and the remainder of his brigade entered old Manila through the Paco district.

As the troops tramped through the gates into the walled city, they felt as if they had returned to the seventeenth century. The narrow cobblestone streets literally formed a maze as they twisted and turned, and the alleys and walkways were so narrow that it was necessary to flatten oneself against a building to let another person pass. Except for a few massive, stone structures housing government offices and grandiose churches, the buildings were two stories or less because of the danger of earthquakes. The Spanish-styled houses had exterior walls of stone covered with moldy plaster painted a dirty cream or pink. The first-floor windows, with panes of seashell rather than glass, were heavily barred. Most of the houses had roofs of red tiles or corrugated tin and second stories with wooden balconies that hung over the street; little sunlight penetrated to street level because of those balconies. In many places, the walls of the buildings were completely hidden by tropical vegetation. Towering over the walled city were the steeples of a dozen Catholic cathedrals and the buildings of St. Thomas University.

MacArthur commandeered several empty houses to shelter his men from the constant rain. As night descended, angry Filipinos periodically fired shots into the U.S. lines and threatened to attack. The city they had been waiting two months to capture had been denied them by foreign manipulation. By seven

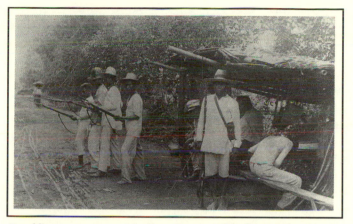

Republican outpost near Manila, c. January 1899. (National Archives, 111-SC-81696)

o'clock in the evening, some 4,000 Filipinos were massed south of the city just beyond the U.S. picket lines. Fires lit the night sky as angry mobs set ablaze sections of the outer city and a number of boats on the Pasig River. Because General Merritt feared looting, he ordered the Spanish civil guards, or police, to remain on duty as part of the outer defenses until U.S. troops could relieve them the following morning. The explosive situation was defused only by a tropical storm that raged most of the night and made movement along the roads almost impossible.[59]

During the night, soldiers of the Philippine Republican Army occupied the fifteen Spanish blockhouses that defined the city limits of Manila. Although Aguinaldo was forced to acknowledge the U.S. occupation of Manila, he issued a proclamation confining the foreigners to the city itself. Thus, the U.S. Army found itself surrounded by a hostile force, although both sides wanted to avoid an open confrontation. An uneasy truce developed.

Merritt placed the city under martial law and named MacArthur provost marshal, with three regiments under his command. His job was to maintain the peace, implement all army general orders, and assume control of all public buildings, including the customhouse, the post office, the arsenal, and particularly the *Ayuntamiento*, the main government building in the old walled city. General Anderson was in charge of the outer defenses of the city, and General Greene was appointed inspector general in charge of inventorying all Spanish assets and setting up a custom-collecting system. Merritt took up residence in the governor's house, called *Malacañan*, located just north of the walled city near the Pasig River.

The area of Manila under U.S. control included much more than the walled city, which encompassed only 1 square mile on the bay south of the Pasig. The army also controlled an area 2 miles out from the walled city that encompassed almost 15 square miles. U.S. forces occupied outposts 200 yards inside the old line of Spanish blockhouses now controlled by the Philippine Republican Army. The area between the U.S. outposts and the Filipino blockhouses became a no-man's-land where any American or Filipino wandering about could easily be shot. The terrain between the lines varied: There were both swamps and low-dyked ricelands. To the north, the country was perfectly flat, although the horizon was often obstructed by bamboo groves or wooded areas. No Filipino was allowed to carry arms within the area under U.S. jurisdiction.

The most pressing matter MacArthur faced was the sanitation problem, for during the two-month siege, refuse had been dumped in the streets. "The dirt and filth are unbearable," Lieutenant Colonel Enoch H. Crowder reported in a letter home. Rotting garbage was everywhere, and it acted as a breeding ground for diseases such as cholera, dysentery, typhoid, and malaria, which were already ravaging the U.S. Army. Sewage systems were open canals full of horrid beds of ooze and rank swamp vegetation; the canals often overflowed in the rainy season and mixed the sewage with the garbage lying in the streets. In the damp tropical heat, the musty smell was overpowering. Manila might have qualified for the name some journalistic boosters had given it, "Venice of the Pacific," had its water not been so vile and odoriferous. A crucial need was to obtain potable water for the troops. The city's drinking water was pumped from the Mariquina River some 8 miles east of the city to reservoirs about 4 miles out. However, Aguinaldo's army controlled the reservoirs and pumping stations, and it would be almost two weeks before the water supply was restored.[60]

MacArthur set to work policing the city. "Although this 'police action' was undoubtedly one of the more unpleasant assignments during this period of waiting," Carol Petillo observed,

> it provided Arthur MacArthur an excellent opportunity to confront at first hand several of the problems which would be his twenty months later when he was appointed military governor of the entire archipelago. He kept his eyes open, saw more of the Filipinos than his superiors, Merritt or Otis, and recognized their obvious desire for independence. He did not support the Philippine goals, but he never underestimated them. He, unlike most of the Americans already present or on their way to Manila, accepted the fact that most Filipinos preferred to undertake the responsibilities of self-government rather than follow the dictates of another white colonial master, no matter how benevolent.[61]

MacArthur hired hundreds of Filipino laborers to clean away the rubbish from streets and the garbage from the gutters, and property owners were required to clean up their premises and keep them clean. A few hundred Filipinos were arrested and fined for failure to conform to the new orders. All the while, MacArthur assured the Filipinos that U.S. intentions were benevolent. He promised the local Filipino and the Spanish aristocracy that personal property rights would be respected under American rule and that all peoples would be treated equally before the law.[62]

Within two weeks, Manila was almost back to normal. The water supply was restored, streetcars resumed operation, stores opened, and people returned to their homes. As the citizens reoccupied their homes, the population in the U.S. zone swelled to an estimated 300,000. There was generally a mass of humanity in the streets of the old walled city, except during the siesta hours (noon to four), when the heat drove most people inside. Brown-skinned Filipina women, barefoot and dressed in bright reds and yellows, squatted in the streets and hawked their wares. Decked out in gaudy jewelry and smoking giant cigars, street vendors quickly picked up pidgin English to peddle their goods to passing soldiers. Young Filipino boys and girls ran about the streets completely nude, with no concern for Western morality, as teenagers pitched pennies or chased the foreigners to beg for a dime. Poor, barefoot laborers wore baggy cotton pants, cotton skirts, and broad-brimmed straw hats; young Filipina girls wore loose-fitting cotton skirts and off-the-shoulder blouses with flowing sleeves; and Chinese coolies dashed about the waterfront dressed in nothing but loincloths. Pony carts sped down the streets dodging carabao carts, with their gigantic beasts of burden. A carabao was a thick-skinned, hairless, gray, black, or brown water buffalo that moved at a snail's pace. As one American maintained, "Nobody can possibly know just what the word slow signifies until he has seen a carabao move. He chews and walks at exactly the same pace." Horse and carabao droppings were everywhere, and the smell of the piles of manure assaulted the nostrils and attracted swarms of flies.[63]

The Pasig River, north and east of the walled city, divided the rest of Manila down the middle. The Pasig was a giant thoroughfare. Cargo boats of all sizes plied the river and brought sugar, coconuts, bananas, rice, and other products from the interior. Filipino boatmen, naked to the waist, pushed long bamboo poles firmly in the mud at the bottom of the river as they walked the length of their boats. Hundreds of *bancas*, narrow canoes hewed out of a single log and kept on even keel by graceful outriggers of bamboo, packed the river. The *bancas*, some large enough for twenty or thirty rowers, were loaded with tobacco, hemp, fruit, vegetables, and tons of raw sugar. Entire Filipino families lived on many of the boats.

Stone bridges spanned the 100-yard-wide river at various points. To the north lay the Binondo district and to the east the San Miguel district. Businesses in Binondo catered to the U.S. soldiers and the hundreds of foreigners who came to the Philippines in search of adventure and profit. Along with the new troops that continued to arrive came newspaper reporters, businessmen looking for grand opportunities, and the wives of many officers. The exclusive shops in Binondo were located on a narrow cobblestone thoroughfare called the Escolta. A horse-drawn streetcar ran from the old city right down the middle of Escolta road.

Scene along the Pasig River, Manila, 1900. (National Archives, 111-SC-80928)

Pulled by small, diseased ponies, the streetcars were usually full of Filipinos who jammed the doors and even stood on the steps. Americans seldom rode the street-cars; the soldiers soon discovered that the cars were so tiny they had to sit on the floor or their heads would bang against the ceiling. The major businesses in the city were located along the Escolta, where European and Chinese proprietors sold almost everything available in cities like New York, San Francisco, or even Lon-don. There were English clothing shops, foreign dealers of Filipino art (particu-larly woodcarvings), French-designed clothes, Stetson hats, Swiss watches, expen-sive jewelry, and handmade shoes. Cafés and fancy restaurants also lined the thoroughfare, and streets that angled off the main road were loaded with Chinese and native shops. On Rosario Street, there was the Great Common Market, where Filipino hawkers urged passersby to examine wares that varied from handmade baskets to bead shawls, tin items, fruits, and farming utensils. The Escolta was jam-packed with people in the evenings.[64]

North of the Binondo district came the Tondo area, a red-light district full of bars, opium dens, cockpits, and houses of prostitution. Thousands of poor Fili-pino laborers lived in nipa huts in the Tondo area. They worked in the many small shops that produced cigars, textiles, woodcarvings, candies, and a myriad of other products. Although Tondo had no streetcar, small native two-wheeled vehicles, called *carromatas* or *carretala,* serviced the area. Forerunners of the modern jeepneys, the *carromatas* were drawn by tiny native ponies. Passengers climbed or, more commonly, jumped on the *carromatas* from the rear. The ride was bumpy, and everyone held tightly onto a narrow seat. The driver, or *cochero,* ignored any pleas to slow down except to pick up one more passenger, and there always seemed to be room for one more. The people did not walk long distances because of the tropical heat. The fare on a *carromata* was only two cents.

North of Tondo, U.S. picket lines marked the end of the area under U.S. occupation. Beyond the Filipino line, nipa huts surrounded by sugarcane and ricefields stretched north 5 miles to the next town, Calacoon. The principal farming area in Luzon began at Calacoon and continued north for about 200 miles. A railroad, the only one in the Philippines, ran north through this farming country toward Malolos, 20 miles away. This area was denied to the Americans. Although unarmed Filipinos passed freely through the U.S. picket lines, Aguinaldo refused to allow Americans into the interior of the island.

Moving east from the bay inland along the north bank of the Pasig River, beyond Binondo, was the San Miguel district, a wealthy residential area with magnificent mansions including *Malacañan,* the former Spanish governor's residence that now served as Merritt's headquarters. Along the bay south of the old city was the Luneta, the most famous ocean drive in all the Philippines. The Luneta was a lovely public promenade that overlooked the bay for about 2 miles. Oval-shaped, like a racetrack, the Luneta was glaringly open with not a tree or even a sprig of grass. Along the promenade, there were a few dusty benches around bandstands but nothing else. Deserted during the heat of the day, the Luneta was packed in the cool of the evening as many in Manila turned out each dusk to watch the grand tropical sunsets and hear bands that featured guitars and trumpets. On holidays, children performed Filipino dances on raised, nipa-covered stages.

People began to congregate around five o'clock, and soon there were thousands strolling along the walkway. The wealthy came in private carriages drawn by little Filipino horses that were a joke to the Americans. The ponies stood less than 4 feet high, had shaggy manes and foretops, and were often covered with sores. Flies and other insects swarmed around the heads of the native horses. Most private carriages had both a coachman and a footman, usually dressed in white linen trousers and thin shirts that hung outside their trousers. They wore wide, floppy, shapeless straw hats. The carriage drivers were speed demons who traveled at a pace that was truly terrifying to the Americans. No *cochero* liked to have another *cochero* pass him, and the result was constant, indiscriminate racing on any kind of street, under any circumstances. Carriages had the right of way, and the drivers paid absolutely no attention to native pedestrians.[65]

The area south of the Pasig River included the suburbs Ermita, Paco, and Malate. The American southern picket lines began south of the Malate district on the bay and curved inland about 4 miles to the Pasig.

In the first few days of the occupation, U.S. troops had a holiday spirit, and the festive atmosphere spread when the Hong Kong cable was restored on August 20. News from the United States now reached Manila within fourteen hours. The men learned for the first time that the war was over and had been for a week. One of the ironies of the war was that the battle for Manila occurred one day after a cease-fire had been arranged at the Paris negotiating table. Most of the Volunteers began to think of home, and many went out and got drunk. Since they had enlisted for the duration of the war, most expected to be sent home within days.

But instead of sending the troops home, the U.S. Army was increasing its forces in Manila. Major General Otis arrived from San Francisco on August 29 with the 4th Expeditionary Force of 4,000 men. A 5th Expeditionary Force followed shortly and increased the U.S. strength in Manila to 20,000 men—15,000 Volunteers and 5,000 Regulars. General Merritt had requested that he be relieved of command, and Otis was named as his replacement. On August 30, Merritt, accompanied by General Greene, left Manila for Paris to update the U.S. peace negotiators on the situation in the Philippines.

Otis reorganized the 8th Army Corps into two divisions, naming Major General Anderson to head the 1st Division and recommending MacArthur as the commander of the 2nd Division. Washington agreed and, on September 3, promoted MacArthur to major general of the Volunteers. Otis assigned Anderson's division the area south of the Pasig River, up to and including Cavite, and MacArthur's division the area north of the river. Charlie King arrived with Otis and was assigned to Anderson's division. MacArthur smoothed over relations with his old friend, but Charlie would remember to the end of his days that Mac had usurped the role of brigade commander, a position that led to fame and rapid promotion for MacArthur.[66]

MacArthur's promotion and assignment as a division commander was the dream of a lifetime. He had under his command 9,000 men and 400 officers, organized into eleven regiments in three brigades. His division's left flank rested on Manila Bay north of the walled city and swung inland (east) about 6 miles in a rough semicircle to the San Juan River, close to its conjunction with the Pasig. South of the Pasig, the 1st Division's line stretched about 4 miles from the river to Malate on the bay, thereby completely encircling the greater Manila area. Along his 6-mile line, MacArthur placed seven regiments; four others were held in reserve.

MacArthur established his division headquarters in the prestigious San Miguel district. He commandeered a mansion about 2 miles from the front lines for his residence and headquarters. The mansion was the former home of Admiral Patricio Montojo, whose fleet had been sunk by Dewey on May 1. Dozens of staff officers quartered in the rooms of the large house, served by numerous Filipino maids and houseboys. Regimental commanders were often invited for conferences at the mansion. The Signal Corps strung telegraph lines from MacArthur's headquarters to the regimental command posts to maintain constant contact along the 6-mile line.

Otis's orders to his division commanders were to maintain law and order, to prevent armed Filipinos from entering Manila, and to prepare the troops for a possible attack. A well-armed, often menacing, Filipino army occupied the old Spanish blockhouses that encircled the city just beyond the U.S. lines. Aguinaldo assigned General San Miguel to a command in the south and General Antonio

Luna, his best (or at least his most aggressive) field commander, to the north, directly opposite MacArthur's division. Tensions escalated between the Filipino revolutionaries and the U.S. occupying forces as rumors spread that the United States might remain and supplant the Spanish as the new colonial masters of the islands. The Filipinos wanted independence.[67]

Surrounded by a potentially hostile army, MacArthur insisted that his brigade and regimental commanders keep their men ready for an attack at any time. Remembering Murfreesboro and other lessons learned during the Civil War, MacArthur placed pickets in outposts on every road or path that led from the north into Manila. While maintaining outposts 200 yards south of the Filipino blockhouses, he constructed barricades about a half mile behind the lines. Armed Filipinos were not allowed through these lines, although unarmed civilians could pass freely. The situation was especially sensitive because Aguinaldo knew the location of every artillery emplacement and the quarters of every regiment. MacArthur's orders to his brigade commanders were to do nothing to provoke an attack, but if they were attacked, he expected them to strike back with all their force and to capture or destroy the enemy.

Despite MacArthur's strict orders to treat all Filipinos with dignity, the U.S. guards often harassed Filipinos entering the city. Although many Filipinos spoke some Spanish, few spoke English, and barely any Americans spoke Tagalog, the local language. Interpreters were at a premium.

As was his habit, MacArthur read everything he could find on the Filipinos and the former Spanish administrations. He placed a standing order with Kelly's, a bookseller in Hong Kong, for every book published on Far Eastern matters, particularly those devoted to colonial administration. MacArthur was a scholar and a reader, like his father before him. His passion for research and the knowledge he accumulated were two of his strongest attributes as a general.[68]

MacArthur's prime task was to mold the 9,400 officers and men of the 2nd Division into a well-drilled and disciplined fighting force. He insisted on a ceaseless round of daily drills, carried on in the narrow streets, in small courtyards near the quarters, or in vacant lots. Indeed, Manila rumbled with the 2nd Division's constant activity, with the tramp of companies going to or from guard duty day and night, with the noise of mess lineups, and with the shouts of noncommissioned officers in charge of cleanup squads.

The Volunteers groused about the constant drills and all the military rules. MacArthur expected them to conform to regulations, but he applied the same rules to himself. "While in no sense a military Beau Brummel," Lieutenant Peyton March of the Astor Battery later told friends, MacArthur "believed that neatness in dress of a soldier, under all conditions, has much to do in estimating his worth." The general always appeared before his troops immaculately attired and cleanly shaven. In the field, he dressed in khaki uniforms, but at all social functions, he wore his dress whites. He preferred wearing a kepi, or infantry cap, at headquarters, but in the field, he wore a Stetson cavalry hat for protection from the sun. At headquarters, he went unarmed; in the field, he carried a revolver in a flap holster on the left side, with the butt handle pointing forward.[69]

Colonel Frederick Funston of the 20th Kansas, Lieutenant March, and many other officers respected MacArthur's knowledge of military tactics and training programs. Funston expressed the general consensus among the officers when he proclaimed that MacArthur epitomized the ideal commander—the elder, experienced soldier who was still made of iron. Funston, who later named his first son after the general, was particularly impressed with MacArthur's method of training regimental commanders. Each of these officers took a turn at being the division's commanding officer of the day, carefully inspecting the entire line of outposts and reporting back to MacArthur. These duties gave the regimental commanders an idea of the overall position of the 2nd Division.[70]

Life in Manila settled into a boring routine for the U.S. occupying forces. When not on duty, the men engaged in endless arguments and riotous poker games. It was unusually warm and sticky in Manila late that year, and the days passed slowly. The Volunteers, almost to a man, clamored to go home: After all, the war with Spain was over, and garrison duty was the rightful task of the Regular Army. As they marked time waiting for a speedy mustering out, the citizen soldiers complained about life in Manila. As one disgruntled Volunteer of the 3rd Artillery, Charles Soules, proclaimed in a letter home, "It is the same thing over and over again. There is constant guard duty. One day on guard, one day of work, and one day to burn. The burn means to go to sleep all day. It is the same thing over and over again. I tell you I get tired of it. I wish I was not in the Army." Louis Hubbard of the South Dakota Volunteers wrote to his parents, "You never saw such a homesick lot of fellows. They would give all they ever hope to be worth just to get orders to go back to the States."[71]

A few of Manila's 300,000 people were very wealthy, but the vast majority lived in semipoverty that often appalled the boys from Ohio and Kansas. William B. Landon, a band member in one of the Volunteer units, hated the Philippines and declared that he would "prefer to be in an American prison than to being in the Army in the Philippines." Nothing was there, he said, except bananas and rice. Many other Volunteers wrote that the Filipinos were nothing but dirty "gugus," an epithet derived from the tree bark used as shampoo by the local women. They were savages who would "be the best friend that you have to your face, but as soon as your back is turned, they are your foe."[72]

Jesse George of the 7th California expressed the typical soldier's attitude toward the Filipinos when he said, "Ninety percent of the native inhabitants of the Philippine Archipelago still squat to shit, live in primitive little huts, sleep on the floor, eat with their fingers, and have none of the comforts of civilization." George admitted that one could not technically call the Filipinos dirty savages, for they were clean "both in person and dress. They bathe everyday and their scanty clothing is generally spotless. They are active and energetic." Lieutenant March noticed that the public water hydrants were always surrounded by people washing themselves.[73]

The American soldiers developed many devices for passing the time and relieving some of the tedium of the daily routine. Too much time to think made them homesick, and letter writing became the major pastime. The mail that left Manila soon assumed enormous proportions and would be calculated by the ton. Next to letter writing came collecting relics and souvenirs to send home. The soldiers quickly picked up a smattering of "carabao" Spanish in order to negotiate with street vendors and merchants. The U.S. dollar was twice as valuable as the silver peso, and the troops had money burning holes in their pockets. They bought hand-rolled Filipino cigars, perfumes, woodcarvings, and war relics such as Spanish pistols, uniforms, and battle flags. Bolos were also prized as souvenirs. And many soldiers adopted monkeys or native dogs as pets.

To help the men pass the time, MacArthur encouraged sports, as he had while commanding a company on the western frontier. Regiments formed baseball and football teams and played hotly contested games. Some of the men swam at the beach each day, and others formed amateur theatrical troupes. Many officers volunteered to set up schools to teach the Filipinos English.[74]

Throughout the fall, the Volunteers remained disgruntled, but at least the weather improved; November to February is the most delightful time of year in the Philippines. It is still warm, but the evenings are often cool enough for light wraps. The constant tropical rain ceases, and the days are bright and sunny. The islands become a true tropical paradise.

The Volunteers' social life in Manila became more active. For many of the soldiers, their tour in the Philippines was an opportunity to violate the strict social codes of middle America. The provost marshal, Brigadier General Robert P. Hughes, was kept busy arresting drunks, curtailing brawls, and intervening between rowdy soldiers and the native population. One U.S. officer admitted that a Volunteer was a "mighty poor peace soldier." Bars all over the city catered to the American soldier. Beer was the preferred drink, with a variety of brands available, including Schlitz, Blatz Star, and San Miguel, a Filipino beer much esteemed by the soldiers.[75]

General Otis, called Grandpa by the men, concentrated on obtaining needed supplies for his army. A dapper sixty-one-year-old man, Otis compensated for his receding hairline by growing a mustache and long, thick sideburns, called muttonchops. From an aristocratic New England family, he had graduated from Harvard Law School in 1860 and joined a law firm in New York City. When the Civil War erupted in April 1861, Otis joined the 140th New York Volunteers. Two years later, he was severely wounded in the head; although suffering no permanent mental damage, he often had headaches and suffered from insomnia. Before the end of the war, he was a brevet brigadier general. In 1867, he joined the Regular Army and steadily climbed up the ranks. While a colonel, he was appointed, in 1881, to be the first commandant of the Infantry and Cavalry Training School at

Fort Leavenworth. In 1893, Otis was promoted to brigadier general and placed in command of the Department of Columbia, where he remained until he took over the Department of the Colorado in the spring of 1897. On May 4, 1898, he was promoted to major general of the Volunteers and assigned as second in command of the Philippine Expedition forming in San Francisco.

Otis's knowledge of military organization and army regulations was extensive, and he loved paperwork. He concentrated on organizational charts, obtaining equipment and food for his army, and other administrative chores and left the training of the troops to his division commanders. When the expeditionary force was in San Francisco, the troops had been issued uniforms with blue woolen shirts, which were hot in the tropics, and the cloth quickly rotted. Otis ordered new, dust-colored khaki uniforms from Hong Kong, which proved to be durable and washable. Each man was issued two khaki uniforms for outpost, drill, and fatigue duties. The army also provided each man with two dress white uniforms and one dress blue. The waterproof pith helmet, made of cork with a hood attached that covered the back of the neck and shoulders, was the authorized head covering, but few actually wore the British-designed headgear; the troops preferred the western-style campaign hats. Otis continued the practice of purchasing local fresh fruits and vegetables, but he also contracted to obtain frozen beef from Australia. Although army rations still included rice, the ever-present pork and beans, and canned salmon, called "goldfish" by the troops, the men now had fresh tomatoes, potatoes, onions, bananas, coconuts, and even dried prunes, apples, and peaches. Oats, sugar, coffee, mustard, salt, pepper, and vinegar rounded out the menu, except on special occasions, such as Thanksgiving when Otis somehow obtained turkeys for the men.[76]

A paramount problem faced by the general staff was the outbreak of venereal disease among the troops as prostitutes from all over Asia flocked to Manila. Venereal disease accounted for almost 25 percent of all sicknesses in the army. Otis's answer was practical rather than moral: He realized he could not prevent prostitution, so he licensed and ordered medical inspections of all prostitutes.

Otis was not so liberal on opium dens and gambling. He found the Filipino sport of cockfighting shocking, and it seemed as if no nipa hut was complete without a fighting cock tied to the leg of a table or some other prominent place. Outside, one of the rooster's legs was tied to a length of string 2 or 3 yards long, and the string was attached to a small stake driven into the ground. The rooster always got the best of everything, and its owner was continually petting it. Filipino males lovingly carried their fighting cocks with them everywhere. On Sunday afternoons in large bamboo cockpits throughout Manila, the roosters fought before large crowds. The cocks wore two-and-a-half-inch gaffs, or spurs, and all fights were to the finish. A good deal of money was won or lost each Sunday in betting on the cocks. General Otis outlawed the sport, but the Filipinos passionately ignored the law.[77]

Attracted by local pastimes but still longing for home, nearly all the troops avidly read every word of news on the Paris Peace Conference. The 13th Minnesota boys began publishing a weekly newsletter, *The American Soldier,* on September 10. Other papers quickly followed, such as *Freedom, Uncle Sam,* and *The Soldier's Letter,* all published by enlisted men. *The Manila Times* and the *American* became permanent Manila newspapers.[78]

The soldiers discussed U.S. policy, and many wondered whether the United States intended to keep the Philippines as a colony. At the beginning of the war with Spain, Washington clearly had no territorial ambitions, as illustrated by the Teller Amendment that pledged the United States would leave Cuba in control of the Cuban people. Aguinaldo hoped that the U.S. purpose in the Philippines was exactly the same as it was in Cuba. President McKinley could have easily cleared up the issue by announcing that the Teller Amendment also applied to the Philippines, but he made no such pledge.

A number of young Republican politicians, such as Henry Cabot Lodge, Theodore Roosevelt, and Albert Jeremiah Beveridge, believed the United States should retain the Philippine Islands. Dubbed the imperialists, they emphasized that Manila was essential for U.S. commercial expansion in Asia and as a military base for the U.S. Navy. The imperialists believed the periodic depression cycles that had hammered the United States since the Civil War could be eliminated by obtaining new markets for America's surplus manufactured and agricultural products. The supply of industrialized goods was too great for the internal market, they proclaimed, but the solution was simple—find new markets to allow the economic laws of supply, demand, and competition to function.

For the United States to compete in international markets, it needed to improve its strategic position. By 1898, all the major European countries had staked out colonial empires where U.S. goods were excluded. Britain, with its vast colonial empire that stretched east from Africa through India and Singapore to Hong Kong, was the prime example. To compete in the international market, the imperialists contended, the United States needed colonies and naval bases throughout the world. Lodge, Beveridge, Roosevelt, and others hoped the United States would begin an age of expansion and create an empire larger and more profitable than the British Empire. Roosevelt told a friend that the Philippines "must be ours. [If] we hold the other side of the Pacific, ... the value to this country is almost beyond imagination." With a base in the Philippines, the United States could easily penetrate the Chinese market.[79]

To gain the support of the public, the imperialists needed a cause beyond economic gain. That cause was obvious: The spread of the U.S. empire would mean the spread of American ideals of liberty, justice, and equality for all. Worldwide republicanism would be the goal as the United States assumed an obligation to protect, in the words of Rudyard Kipling, our "little brown brothers" in the Philippines. The imperialists asserted that the Filipinos simply did not have the education or ability to govern themselves; if independence were granted, it would lead to anarchy in the islands. In this period, racism and Anglo-Saxon superiority were themes that ran through the fabric of American society. And most people—whether labor leaders, politicians, academics, or generals—assumed that the Filipino race was inferior to the white race.

If the United States did not annex the Philippines, the imperialists argued, the islands would not necessarily become independent. Nations such as Germany and Japan stood on the sidelines like wolves awaiting the lambs. Shortly after the battle of Manila Bay, Kaiser Wilhelm had sent a large German naval squadron to Manila. In fact, in August 1898, German "neutral" warships in Manila harbor outnumbered U.S. warships. The kaiser suggested dividing the islands up. Meanwhile, Japan was entering its imperialistic period and might also try to claim sections of the Philippines. The U.S. imperialists assumed that the Filipino people would be delighted to be annexed, although Aguinaldo had actively attempted to present the position of his government. In September, he dispatched Felipe Agoncillo to Washington. On October 1, President McKinley saw Agoncillo, who presented Filipino demands for the withdrawal of U.S. troops and for U.S. recognition of the new Philippine Republic. The Filipino envoy informed McKinley that the Philippine government would probably accept a protectorate status as a compromise position, but McKinley refused to make a commitment. Agoncillo went on to Paris in mid-October, hoping for a better hearing, but the U.S. delegates refused to allow him to attend any meetings.[80]

Some Americans strongly opposed the annexation of the Philippines, including the leaders of the Democratic party. The Anti-Imperialist League was formed in Boston in June 1898 to campaign against the annexation of Cuba and the Philippines. The roster of the league, as historian Stuart Creighton Miller observed,

> read like a combination of the Social Register and Who's Who in America. There were politicians, such as former President Grover Cleveland, House Speaker Thomas B. Reed, former Treasury Secretary George S. Boutwell, Senators George F. Hoar, Benjamin Tillman, R. F. Pettigrew, and J. B. Weaver, and Democratic presidential hopeful William Jennings Bryan. ... There were educators, such as Yale's William Graham Sumner, Harvard's Charles W. Eliot, John Fiske, Charles Eliot Norton, and William James, and Columbia's Felix Adler, Frederick W. Starr, and John Burgess. And there were writers, such as Edgar Lee Masters, Mark Twain, Edwin Arlington Robinson, William Dean Howells, Ambrose Bierce, Lincoln Steffens, Finley Peter Dunne, and William Vaughn Moody. Even such diverse figures as the reformer Jane Addams, labor leader Samuel Gompers, and the industrialist Andrew Carnegie were united ... in their denunciation of imperialism.[81]

League members did not oppose U.S. involvement in foreign affairs and actually advocated an expansion of foreign trade. They were only opposed to colonization. The anti-imperialists argued that the Constitution of the United States forbade the acquisition of territory unless that territory was destined to become a state. They held as an axiom that all people living under U.S. control were equal citizens. No one (not even the most devoted imperialist) ever suggested that the Philippines would eventually become a state, nor that the Filipino people would be equal in citizenship to all other Americans. Moral axioms dictated that all people had the right of self-determination and that no government should be imposed by force alone. Thus, the Filipinos should be allowed to pursue their own destiny. Moreover, the league members felt, if the islands were colonized by Germany, Britain, France, or Japan, that would not threaten the security of the United States: The islands had no conceivable geographical link with the United States since they were over 7,000 miles from San Francisco.

The anti-imperialists did not represent the views of the majority of the American people, who favored retention of the Philippines. In September 1898, the *Literary Digest* polled 192 editors and reported that "a solid majority favored" annexation. Furthermore, Republicans scored dramatic victories in the November 1898 elections over the key issue of imperialism. Expansion was immensely popular. As McKinley confided to a friend, "You and I don't want the Philippines, but it is no use disguising the fact that an overwhelming majority of the people do."[82]

After fluctuating on his position for months, President McKinley finally decided in favor of annexation in late November. He explained his decision to a Christian delegation visiting the White House.

> The truth is I didn't want the Philippines, and when they came to us as a gift from the gods, I did not know what to do with them. I sought counsel from all sides—Democrats as well as Republicans. I thought first we would take only Manila; then Luzon; then the other islands. I walked the floor of the White House night after night, and I am not ashamed to tell you that I went down on my knees and prayed to the Almighty God for light and guidance. And one night it came to me. We could not give them back to Spain—that would be cowardly and dishonorable; we could not turn them over to France or Germany, that would be bad business; we could not leave them to themselves—they were unfit for self-government and they would have anarchy and misrule. There was nothing left for us to do but to take them all, and to educate the Filipinos, and uplift and civilize and Christianize them, and by God's grace do the very best we could by them, as our fellow men for whom Christ also died. And then, I went to bed, and went to sleep and slept soundly.[83]

President McKinley ordered the U.S. delegation at the Paris Peace Conference to acquire the entire Philippine archipelago. The Spanish delegates were surprised; they had hoped that the United States would be satisfied with Cuban independence and, at most, the city of Manila. According to international law, the Spanish delegation argued, the United States should not have demanded any area it had not actually conquered, and even Manila had been captured after the official cease-fire. The Spanish arguments did not impress President McKinley, who threatened to renew the war. A compromise was negotiated to save Spanish honor—the United States agreed to pay Spain $20 million for the Philippines. On December 10, 1898, the delegates in Paris initialed the settlement.

When Manila newspapers published the proposed treaty seventy-two hours later, there was an uproar. Aguinaldo and the Filipino revolutionaries felt betrayed. They began to prepare for war.

12

The Philippine Revolution

THE TREATY OF PARIS infuriated the Filipino Republican leaders, who cursed the day they had agreed to deal with the Americans instead of driving them out. A cabinet crisis ensued in the Republican capital of Malolos, 30 miles north of Manila. Aguinaldo's sharpest adviser, Apolinario Mabini, a thirty-four-year-old intellectual, suggested an immediate declaration of war. General Antonio Luna, the army's field commander, was in a blind rage and demanded history be made with the sword as he advocated independence or death.

The Republican military position was a strong one. Aguinaldo had 40,000 men in fortifications around Manila, with his army supported by hundreds of thousands of Filipinos throughout the island of Luzon. Although additional U.S. troops were pouring into Manila, the 8th Army Corps numbered only 20,000 men in December 1898.

Aguinaldo decided against immediate military action, but he issued orders that the U.S. troops were henceforth to be confined to Manila. He hoped that a solution could be negotiated, and he contacted General Elwell Otis, commander of the U.S. Army, suggesting that discussions be opened.

Otis refused to negotiate with the Republican government, a decision that a number of scholars have criticized. In *Benevolent Assimilation,* Stuart Creighton Miller berated the general and concluded that it was unfortunate that "American relations with the Filipino nationalists were, from the beginning, left to professional military men, who were ill-suited to play diplomatic roles due to their training and temperaments." In Miller's evaluation, officers like Otis had "spent their careers terrorizing Apaches, Commanches, Kiowas, and the Sioux"; moreover, Otis had "egregiously mishandled diplomatic functions and, more seriously, failed to keep Washington accurately informed of the nature and complexity of the insurrection against Spain and on the degree of organization of and popular support for General Emilio Aguinaldo's revolutionary government."[1]

Miller's criticisms are harsh. Otis, MacArthur, Anderson, and most of the other senior officers of the 8th Army Corps were actually well qualified for their jobs as military commanders. They were not diplomats, but they were under instructions not to commit the U.S. government to any course of action. Nor was Washington ignorant of the situation in the Philippines. Even if Otis failed to keep the War Department informed of the delicate situation, Washington had many other sources of information. As early as July 1898, General Anderson told Adjutant General Henry Corbin that any attempt by the United States to establish a government in the Philippines would "probably bring us into conflict with insurgents." Furthermore, a number of the Volunteer officers were important in civilian life, and they kept their friends in the government informed. The Republic of the Philippines' ambassador, Felipe Agoncillo, a wealthy Manila lawyer, was in Washington and in constant contact with Secretary of State John Hay and many U.S. senators. The War Department, Congress, and President McKinley knew a peaceful settlement was possible, and the failure to negotiate was Washington's failure, not the army's.[2]

Instead of opting for a peaceful settlement, President McKinley ordered Otis to extend U.S. military occupation of the Philippines "with all possible dispatch." The president's directive required that all Filipinos lay down their arms and accept U.S. sovereignty over the islands. The U.S. military in Manila knew Aguinaldo would not surrender without a struggle. Thus, the prime question was when, not if, hostilities would erupt.[3]

Throughout December 1898, MacArthur met with Otis, Anderson, and Dewey to plan a military offensive to break the Republican encirclement of Manila. The apparent strength of the Republican Army did not worry the U.S. generals. Units under MacArthur conducted detailed reconnaissance and learned that the Filipino army suffered from a number of liabilities, despite its numerical superiority.

The Filipinos occupied the old Spanish blockhouses that encircled Manila. The curved line, stretching around the city from bay to bay, was about 15 miles long. Just behind the blockhouses, Aguinaldo's army dug trenches and built barricades. About half of Aguinaldo's 40,000 men were armed with rifles, the rest carrying only bolos. The rifles were kept in the trenches, and relief units took over not only the ground area but also the weapons of those returning to the rear. With no modern artillery to protect his line, Aguinaldo was overextended. MacArthur reported the weaknesses in the Filipino line to Otis (see Map 11.2).

The U.S. line was much more compact. MacArthur's division protected the northern hamlets of Manila, while Anderson's division guarded the southern half of the city. The two divisions were separated by the Pasig River, which flowed through the center of the city. A hundred yards wide, the river was spanned by stone bridges at various points. The U.S. defensive line paralleled the old line of Spanish blockhouses now controlled by the Filipino army.

MacArthur placed his forward outposts about 200 yards inside the line along the various roads that entered Manila from the north and the northeast. He ordered barricades constructed about a half mile behind the forward outposts as his major line of defense. His line stretched for 6 miles from the bay north of the city east to the San Juan River near its conjunction with the Pasig River. To cover that distance, MacArthur had eleven infantry regiments plus a number of batteries of light artillery. From the bay eastward, he stationed first the 20th Kansas, then the 3rd Artillery (Infantry), followed by the 1st Montana, the 10th Pennsylvania, the 1st South Dakota, the 1st Colorado, and, on the extreme right, the 1st Nebraska. Each regiment was assigned a small area to defend and remained concentrated in one camp area with an outpost line usually manned by one of the ten companies in a revolving fashion. In battle, the U.S. regiments would be instant fighting units.[4]

Recognizing the need for constant surveillance of the enemy, MacArthur drew men from every regiment and formed special reconnaissance units that patrolled along the Filipino line and reported back the strength of the enemy army at every location. Telegraph lines connected the regiments to brigade and division headquarters, where MacArthur always kept four regiments in reserve for an emergency.[5]

Otis, MacArthur, Anderson, and Dewey worked on a plan to break the Republican siege and quickly quell any uprising. The generals were all experienced combat veterans of the Civil War. They knew war, and they knew it was won by well-trained, well-armed, and well-supplied armies. In their collective opinion, the U.S. Army was vastly superior in every respect to the Philippine Republican Army.

Supported by the U.S. fleet in Manila Bay, the 8th Army Corps had much greater firepower than Aguinaldo's army. Dewey's heavy naval guns controlled Manila Bay both north and south of the city and could easily annihilate the Filipino blockhouses near the water. While Aguinaldo had old, Spanish brass cannons, Otis's army had excellent ground artillery support. Both U.S. infantry divisions had mobile artillery composed of several batteries of Hotchkiss 3.2- and 1.65-inch guns. The Hotchkiss 12-pound mountain gun was an excellent mobile artillery weapon that shot a 1.65-inch shell that weighed 2 pounds. A breech-loading rifle, the rapid-fire Hotchkiss was accurate at ranges up to 4,000 yards. Attached to a wheeled gun carriage, the light, compact Hotchkiss was pulled by a team of six horses. The divisions also had less mobile but longer-ranged 3.2-inch guns.[6]

MacArthur's 2nd Division included the Astor Light Battery, the Utah Light Artillery, and Battery E of the 1st U.S. Artillery, Battery F of the 4th Artillery, Battery D of the 6th Artillery, and four batteries of the 3rd Artillery. Anderson's 1st Division had comparable artillery support. On the Pasig River, the gunboat USN *Laguna de Bay* was also under MacArthur's command.

The generals of the 8th Army Corps expected the greatest Republican resistance in the area north of the Pasig River protected by MacArthur's 2nd Division. The only railroad in the Philippines ran north up the island of Luzon through the Pampanga Plain. The plain encompassed only about one-tenth of the land area of Luzon, but it was the primary source of supply for the Republican Army; the breadbasket of Luzon, it was also the most strongly held Republican area. The farmland of the plain was bordered on the east, toward the interior, by the towering ranges of the Benguet Mountains and on the west, near the coast, by the Zambales Mountains.

By early January 1899, the Filipinos were in an ugly mood. Shooting incidents occurred nightly as tensions increased in Manila. Security was tightened. MacArthur and Anderson ordered their pickets to search all Filipinos entering the city, including women and children. No armed Filipinos were allowed through the lines, although unarmed civilians were allowed to enter Manila. Since few Americans spoke Spanish and even fewer spoke Tagalog, there were constant language problems.

The U.S. guards took particular delight in harassing Filipinos dressed in the blue-and-white uniforms of the Republican Army. Filipino soldiers entered Manila looking for trouble, and the U.S. soldiers cordially advised the "niggers" that in due time they would be shot down like rabbits. Hissing threats of their own, the Republican soldiers drew their fingers across their throats. Fights at checkpoints were inevitable as Filipinos pushed back when shoved, and tempers flared. On January 12, five natives were killed at one garrison outpost when they refused to halt. Along the outer perimeter, shots were exchanged nightly. In the city, troops of the provost marshal searched houses and shot any Filipino who argued with them. Off-duty U.S. soldiers did as they pleased; many got drunk, refused to pay for goods or services, started barroom brawls, and stole at will from the local merchants, confirming Republican propaganda that the Americans were turbulent, undisciplined, and licentious racists.[7]

By mid-January 1899, rumors were flying that war was imminent. Army intelligence estimated that there were over 8,000 armed Filipinos in the city—most male Filipinos carried a bolo or a small knife under their clothing. Nightly knifings occurred, encouraging U.S. soldiers to carry their weapons even while off duty. Business in Manila halted when Aguinaldo ordered all Filipinos to stop working for the Americans by January 23. Expecting a major battle, civilians fled Manila, and 40,000 refugees choked the roads leading out of the city. General Otis added to the flight on February 2 by firing all the remaining Filipinos employed by the U.S. Army. He ordered a full alert and warned Admiral Dewey that war was imminent. In the previous three months, both sides had ignored dozens of minor shooting incidents, but Otis apparently decided that the next incident would be his excuse to initiate an offensive that would force the Filipinos to lay down their arms and accept U.S. sovereignty. When an army looks for an excuse to attack, it is merely a matter of time before it finds one.[8]

MacArthur and Anderson issued new directives to their outposts to prevent any Filipino from loitering in no-man's-land, the 200 yards of unoccupied territory between the lines. Filipino soldiers often stood in the area and shouted insults at the U.S. pickets. MacArthur and Anderson ordered the pickets to investigate and search the miscreants, an order guaranteed to stimulate an incident. Any Filipino walking in the area between the lines was to be considered hostile, and all outposts were instructed to open fire if a Filipino refused to halt and be searched for arms. If the insurgents initiated any offensive movement, the pickets were to "strike with all force, and to capture or destroy the insurgents."[9]

The long-awaited incident occurred on Saturday evening, February 4. It had been one of those delightful, low-humidity, tropical winter days, with the temperature hovering in the midseventies under a clear and brilliant blue sky. Many of the U.S. soldiers had spent a relaxing day in Manila. On the Luneta, the crowds saw a spectacular sunset and enjoyed a cool evening while they strolled along the ocean front. Although there was no moon that night, the sky was clear, and the stars twinkled above. The city seemed covered in a blanket of peacefulness.

MacArthur invited a number of his officers and their wives to Montojo Mansion, his headquarters in the San Miguel district, for an early dinner party that night. Although he seldom socialized with civilians, he did enjoy evenings with his officers. He expected his officers to be punctilious and to dress for dinner. Conversation around the table ranged from the specifics to the broad theories of history, philosophy, politics, and military strategy.

Around 7:30 that Saturday evening, MacArthur's dinner party split up. The married officers left with their wives to return to the *Oriente,* the only place in the city that could truly be described as a hotel, while the remaining staff officers settled in for an evening of cards. The general enjoyed an after-dinner glass of Scotch, lit his cigar, and played whist with the bachelor officers. Occasionally, horses' hooves clattered on the cobblestone courtyard as couriers reported to division headquarters.[10]

About 1 mile northeast of headquarters, the 1st Nebraska Volunteers guarded an area near the confluence of the Pasig and San Juan Rivers, under the command of Colonel John M. Stotsenburg. Firing along the line, particularly in the Nebraska section, was a nightly occurrence. Directly across from the 1st Nebraska was blockhouse number 7, commanded by a Filipino officer who enjoyed harassing the Americans by sending his men into no-man's-land. On several occasions, he tried to establish his pickets within a few yards of the 1st Nebraska's forward outposts. MacArthur notified General Luna, the Filipino commander, that the 1st Nebraskans would not tolerate any activity in the area between the lines, and he authorized the pickets to open fire to protect their positions. The new orders delighted the Nebraskans, who wanted "to shoot a few niggers." They all expected hostilities to erupt within days.

Around 8:30 on that Saturday evening, several Filipinos ventured along a tiny dirt road into the area in front of the advanced Nebraskan picket line. Private William Walter Grayson, a lean youth of twenty-three from Beatrice, Nebraska, one of the two soldiers in the outpost, shouted out, "Halt! Who comes there?"

"!Alto!" one of the Filipinos shouted back mockingly as they kept right on advancing toward the outpost.

"Halt!" Grayson shouted again, and he was again ignored as the Filipinos continued to advance.[11]

At that point, Grayson and his companion, frightened and under orders to assume any advancing Filipinos were hostile, raised their Springfields and opened fire. Their first volley killed two men.

Yelling obscenities, the other Filipinos quickly retreated back to blockhouse number 7. Secure behind their trenches, they opened fire on the Nebraskan outpost. The U.S. sentries responded. Within minutes, the entire Nebraskan line was ablaze as both sides reacted to the incident.[12]

Colonel Stotsenburg wired a report back to division headquarters, and a staff officer interrupted MacArthur's whist game. Throwing the cards aside, MacArthur ordered all officers to their regiments and wired his brigade commanders to mobilize all their units and move forward to protect their picket lines.

Manila was soon alive with U.S. soldiers swinging down dark streets in columns of four, heading for the front line. Near the front, Mauser bullets whistled through the air and some struck nipa huts with a peculiar popping noise. Rockets flared overhead, and Filipino artillery (composed of old, bronze, muzzle-loading guns) opened fire. The cannons fired spherical, cast-iron shells of solid shot rather than canister shells. Although the cannon balls did no damage to the U.S. line, the booming of their artillery guns briefly bolstered Filipino morale.

MacArthur ordered the Utah Artillery and the Astor Battery to open fire with explosive shells. When the tops of the Filipino trenches blew up, the Republican soldiers ducked for cover, no longer enjoying the fireworks display. The noise was as intense as many a battle of the Civil War: Artillery guns boomed, heavy canister shells exploded, Mausers popped, and Springfields rattled in response. Despite the noise, little damage was suffered by either side.[13]

The outskirts of northern Manila resounded with the clatter of an army at war, and nipa huts and bamboo thickets burst into flame in the suburbs. "As the heated air inside the bamboo expanded," Captain George Deshon recalled, "it split open the wood with a sharp explosion resembling a rifle crack. The noise of one burning hut resembled the firing of a company of infantry." When patriotic Filipinos, hungering for independence rather than colonization, sniped at the provost marshal's fire brigades, MacArthur detached several of his companies to protect those brigades. During the night, six Filipinos were killed as they attempted to cut fire hoses.[14]

By midnight, the firing along the front line lessened, and the men of MacArthur's division settled down for the night. As they watched the fires burning in the surrounding suburbs, the men talked, laughed, smoked, and napped the night away. No one complained, except a few who had forgotten their pipes and tobacco. Before the battle, the Volunteers had growled for release from military service, but now they looked forward to a good scrap with the "niggers."[15]

With daylight, the front became quiet. Aguinaldo now expected to be invited to negotiate a cease-fire with General Otis. The Filipino experience in war had been against the Spaniards, and the tactics employed had followed a fairly set pattern: Nightly firefights ceased with daybreak, and both sides negotiated for several days before renewing the engagement. Otis, however, had no intention of negotiating; he had been waiting over a month for an excuse to attack the encircling Filipino army. During the previous three months, Otis, his division commanders, and Admiral Dewey had carefully worked on a battle plan. Now was the time to implement that plan.[16]

In conformity with the plan, Dewey's warships opened fire at 6:00 A.M. Shells from the heavy naval guns of the U.S. fleet tore gaping holes in the Filipino trenches both north and south of the city near the bay. The barrage along the shore signaled MacArthur's land-based artillery to open fire on the interior eastern end of the Filipino trenches. Anderson's artillery to the south also began to batter the enemy. MacArthur checked his regiments and placed himself near his artillery in the 1st Nebraska section, where the Utah and Astor batteries were using their guns to destroy the blockhouses and trenches along the northeast end of the line. The devastating artillery fire killed hundreds of Filipinos before they fled from their trenches.

At 8:00 A.M., MacArthur ordered Stotsenburg's Nebraska regiment to occupy the deserted Filipino trenches on the division's right flank. In MacArthur's area, Aguinaldo's army remained strong only in the center. South of the Pasig, Anderson attacked the Republican forces in his area, and the battle continued most of the day as his division moved south to Macati, extending his line by 2 miles.[17]

With his right flank secured, MacArthur moved his artillery to the center of the line where the Filipino defenses were strongest. With his artillery in place around noon, MacArthur renewed the offensive. Opening up with a half hour of artillery bombardment to cover his advance, his division moved forward about a quarter of a mile into no-man's-land to within 400 yards of the Filipino line. The U.S. troops boomed away with their heavy Springfields, and the enemy returned fire with their smaller-caliber Mausers. Soon, a pall of white smoke from the black-powdered cartridges of the Springfields hung over the battlefield.

In the first exchange of small-arms fire, the U.S. soldier proved to be a vastly superior marksman to the Filipino soldier. American accuracy with the rifle became legendary in the Philippines. For a Filipino to rise above the trenches meant almost certain death. Horrified, the Filipinos saw the heads of their comrades explode from the impact of the .45-caliber Springfield bullets. After the first few minutes of the battle, they were afraid to stand in the trenches to fire. Instead, they returned fire by sticking their rifles over the top and pulling the trigger without taking any aim. When forced out of their trenches, the Filipinos rested the butts of their rifles on their hips and pulled the trigger.[18]

The U.S. soldiers joked that the Filipinos were such poor marksmen that they would be better off using their rifles as clubs. In truth, they were such poor shots because they were sorely undertrained. Pulled directly from sugarcane fields and ricefields, the peasant soldiers had little idea how to fire their guns and no idea how to shoot them with accuracy. They did not know to squeeze the trigger gently, and they had no conception of bullet drift or the effect of the wind on bullets over distances much greater than 100 yards. Although the Mauser had a range of almost 1 mile, compared to the Springfield's effective range of only 1,000 yards, to hit a target at 1,000 yards or even at 100 yards required practice that the Filipino generals were never able to give their soldiers because of a shortage of ammunition. Each soldier with a rifle was issued six cartridges, and he had to account for each shot fired. If he accidentally discharged his gun or even lost a bullet, he was punished by being lashed twelve times (twenty-five times for repeat offenders). Furthermore, the Republican soldiers generally sighted along the barrel with the rear sight, which meant they invariably fired over the heads of the advancing U.S. units. Many years later, in an interview with historian Glenn Anthony May, one of the Filipino veterans admitted he had never killed any Americans, but, he added with a smile, "I killed many birds." Volley after volley missed the U.S. troops, and the failure scared the Filipino soldiers, who suffered a devastating return fire.[19]

Around 12:30, MacArthur passed the order down the line to fix bayonets, and the ominous clatter of metal striking metal sounded along the whole front. Using tactics he had advocated while an instructor at Leavenworth, MacArthur ordered his regiments forward by platoons. There would be no grand parade with regiments and brigades forming for an open attack as at Missionary Ridge. Modern weapons made such tactics ridiculous, and the 2nd Division's commander had learned that lesson at Kennesaw Mountain and at Franklin. MacArthur had trained his men to use all available cover when attacking, and they brilliantly executed his tactics. A platoon rushed forward about 50 yards, threw themselves prone, and provided covering fire as another platoon rose to rush past and repeat the maneuver. Although the ground was flat, bamboo growths, wooded spots, and fences sprinkled the 400 yards between the lines. The division advanced by leapfrogging companies, the rear line pelting the tops of the Filipino trenches with deadly accurate fire. Slowly but surely, the troopers moved forward.

When they were about 70 yards from the enemy's entrenchments, the buglers sounded the charge. The men yelled and dashed forward to leap atop the Filipino trenches. As the Filipino line crumbled, the Republican soldiers fled in panic. Charging over the trenches littered with dead Filipinos, the Americans raced after the enemy.

With the division flag flying proudly, MacArthur and his staff galloped forward. As the general passed, his men cheered and waved, and he raised his hand in a victory salute.[20]

Pressing the retreating Filipinos, MacArthur's division pushed on until they reached the outskirts of Calacoon, 4 miles north of the old line. Otis frantically telegraphed MacArthur to halt the advance. The U.S. line was stretched thin, and hundreds of Filipino were trapped behind it.[21]

MacArthur established his division headquarters at La Loma Church, 4 miles north of Manila near the Calacoon road. While some of his men searched the battlefield for wounded and enemy stragglers, the rest dug trenches and created a new defensive line.

MacArthur and his staff reconnoitered the battlefield. For those who had never been in war, the carnage was shocking. The old enemy trenches were in shambles, lined with 160 dead Filipinos. John F. Bass, a correspondent for *Harper's Weekly,* observed that bodies littered the landscape "like great disfigured dolls thrown away by some petulant child." On the field that night, U.S. soldiers buried 612 Filipinos. Casualties in MacArthur's and Anderson's divisions amounted to a total of 59 killed and 278 wounded.[22]

It was impossible to determine how many Filipino soldiers had been wounded that day, for any not killed outright were usually carried from the field by their comrades. If captured, Filipino soldiers expected to be executed or tortured, and they were very diligent in helping the wounded off the battlefield. Conservative estimates placed Filipino wounded at about 2,000.[23]

The Philippine Republican Army had been overmatched in both firepower and battlefield experience. Superior U.S. artillery, including Dewey's heavy naval guns, had played a role, as did the superior training of the U.S. soldier. But perhaps most significant was the superior leadership of the U.S. Army. No Filipino general had the battlefield experience of MacArthur, who represented the best in the U.S. military profession. He was a combat veteran, a company commander, a trainer of men, a teacher, a lawyer, an administrator, and a scholar. As commander of the 2nd Division, MacArthur applied all he had learned about soldiering in a career that extended over forty years. Inherently calm, he was never impulsive or rash in his methods. He prepared his division for action, and he displayed great personal courage in battle. In his official report, MacArthur described the second battle for Manila as a grand skirmish—nothing to compare to Murfreesboro, Missionary Ridge, or Franklin but more like the minor battles in the Atlanta campaign, such as Resaca or Adairsville.[24]

The U.S. attack had surprised the Filipino generals almost as much as Dewey's attack had surprised the Spanish fleet nine months earlier. One captured Filipino officer observed that he had been shocked when the Americans charged. When the Filipinos had fought the Spaniards, the officer observed, "we would fire and they would fire, and after a while we would stop and they would stop. [The] Americans jumped up and ran at us."[25]

After the battle, Aguinaldo thought the United States would discontinue its military offensive. To the Filipinos, the next logical step was a cease-fire and negotiations. After all, the Spaniards (who would never have attacked in the first place) would have negotiated until the Republican leaders made some concessions. The Americans were different: They were aggressive, they moved fast, and they were excellent shots.

Early on Monday morning, February 6, Aguinaldo sent an officer through the U.S. lines to suggest a cease-fire while working out a way to prevent a recurrence of "accidental" hostilities. He recommended that a neutral demilitarized zone be created as both armies withdrew a few hundred yards.

General Otis rejected Aguinaldo's offer and told the courier that the fighting would continue until the Filipinos laid down their arms and swore allegiance to the United States. There would be no negotiations or compromises. "The fighting has begun," Otis told the courier. "It must go on to the grim end."[26]

The Filipino leaders were stunned. Unlike the Spanish, the Americans did not understand the need for compromise, the need for face-saving negotiations. As Aguinaldo noted to his friends and fellow revolutionaries, "We have no honorable course but to resist" for death was better than dishonor. But they were no fools. They realized their only hope was to delay and gain time to win a propaganda victory in the United States and perhaps obtain foreign assistance from Japan or Germany.[27]

Halting to restore his line, MacArthur's men remained in place on February 6, except for one expedition. The reservoirs and pumping statons for Manila's drinking water, which lay beyond the confines of the city, were controlled by Aguinaldo's army. MacArthur therefore ordered Colonel Stotsenburg, commander of the 1st Nebraska, to take his regiment and two others to capture the waterworks. The Republicans quietly withdrew from the area, and the essential Manila water supply was in U.S. hands by nightfall.[28]

In the United States, events were moving rapidly against the Filipinos' desire for independence. The outbreak of hostilities came just as the Senate was finishing its debates on ratification of the Treaty of Paris. The debates had echoed the imperialist and anti-imperialist arguments that had been heard throughout the country for months. On February 6, Senator Henry Cabot Lodge, the leader of the fight for ratification, called for a vote. Lodge later observed that it was "the hardest, closest fight" he had ever known. With eighty-four senators voting, the final tally was twenty-seven no and fifty-seven yes—one more than the two-thirds required for ratification.[29]

Since the treaty was a popular, patriotic issue, most observers believed that Senate ratification was inevitable, but it is possible, even likely, that the outbreak of hostilities outside Manila on February 4 swung a vote or two. It is equally possible, since the treaty was a patriotic issue in itself, that a few senators might have switched their votes if it were necessary for ratification.[30]

Whatever the Senate's motivation, the U.S. government had now officially annexed the Philippines. Thomas Brackett Reed (the elephantine speaker of the House of Representatives known as "the Czar" because of his power in that chamber and a premier Washington wit) caustically commented on the $20 million indemnity owed Spain for the Philippines: "We have about ten million Malays at two dollars a head unpicked, and nobody knows what it will cost to pick them."[31]

Meanwhile, outside Manila, February 6 was a quiet day for MacArthur's division until nightfall, when firing erupted along the line. Nervous U.S. troops, with no real targets to shoot at, frantically returned Filipino sniper fire. The booming Springfields were deafening, and the muzzle flashes sparkled like a fireworks display.

Seeing the U.S. response as a senseless waste of thousands of rounds of ammunition, MacArthur ordered an immediate cease-fire, but a half hour passed before his orders were obeyed. In many places, the officers had to physically kick the men to make them stop. The incident embarrassed many regimental and company officers, but the panic firing by untested troops did not surprise or anger MacArthur. From Perryville to Franklin during the Civil War, he had observed hundreds of incidents where frightened raw recruits had fired wildly at unseen enemies. He teased his regimental commanders about discipline, then told them to learn from the experience; in the future, he expected better control.[32]

MacArthur kept his special intelligence teams busy collecting information. On February 7, he learned that the Republican Army was fortifying its position across the railroad line outside Calacoon, 1 mile north of the U.S. line. MacArthur telegraphed Otis for permission to attack. He especially wanted to capture the railroad maintenance plant at Calacoon, where there were a number of locomotives and considerable rolling stock. During the Civil War, he had learned the military value of the railroads and knew an army moved on its supplies. The best supply line in central Luzon was the railroad, and its capture, with bridges intact and with as much rolling stock as possible, had to be the major objective in future battles. Built and owned by an English firm, the railroad ran northward though the central Luzon plain through Malolos, Calumpit, San Fernando, Angeles, Tarlac, and Bayambang to Dagupan on the Lingayen Gulf, a distance of about 150 miles.[33]

MacArthur recommended an immediate attack on Calacoon to secure the railroad line while it was still intact. As MacArthur waited impatiently, Otis delayed taking action because he felt his army was already overextended—U.S. forces were thinly spread around a 15-mile perimeter circling greater Manila. MacArthur protested and noted that the delay would allow Aguinaldo to prepare a new fortified line only 7 miles north of the city. Otis ignored MacArthur's protest. Five days passed, and the front was quiet except for the nightly exchange of small-arms fire and a few skirmishes to straighten out the line.[34]

Finally, on February 10, Otis gave MacArthur permission to attack. The Filipino trenches south of Calacoon were within range of Dewey's guns, and MacArthur arranged for a naval bombardment that began at 3:00 P.M. At 3:30, he attacked the right flank, and despite stubborn Filipino resistance, he quickly captured the position. He then attacked in the center. The Filipinos abandoned their trenches, burned the town, and retreated just as the sun was setting.

Mounted on his favorite gray horse, MacArthur rode into Calacoon in the fading light of the day. As he passed, the men cheered. John Bass was with the general, and he reported that in the fading twilight "the dry nipa huts, set afire, shot great gothic spires of flame into the sky. The main street of the town was roasting hot, and we rode through on a gallop. ... Homeless dogs ran howling through the streets. Motherless broods of chickens peeped helplessly. ... Over the battlefield, doctors were still wandering about in the darkness, calling into the night to make sure that they had left no wounded."[35]

MacArthur's victory, as minor as it was, propelled him into national prominence as newspaper headlines in the United States proclaimed that in the Philippines, "'Tis Dewey on the Sea, and MacArthur on the Land." Since MacArthur refused to give interviews, few of the reporters knew anything about him, and he never became a darling of the press. However, a number of his officers, such as "Fighting Fred" Funston of the 20th Kansas, were not so reluctant. A five-foot-four-inch, thirty-six-year-old bantamweight, Funston was a news reporter turned soldier, and he always had a quotable line. His fame did not irritate MacArthur; in fact, Funston was one of the general's favorite officers, whom he often praised in his official reports.[36]

MacArthur wanted to continue the advance toward Malolos as quickly as possible, but Otis again ordered him to remain in place and to resupply his division. MacArthur established his headquarters in Calacoon near the railroad tracks, less than 100 yards behind the U.S. front line. The division had captured 5 railroad engines, 50 passenger coaches, and over 100 freight- and flatcars. The English-made trains were smaller than their U.S. counterparts, but possession of this rolling stock, repaired by MacArthur's troops, would enable the division to make use of the railroad on its future advances. The tramway from downtown Manila to Calacoon, a distance of 7 miles, brought out supplies to the 2nd Division. In a few days, the whole U.S. line along the Calacoon front was sufficiently entrenched to have resisted the assault of a modern army.[37]

Slipping through the overextended U.S. line, soldiers of the Republican Army harassed the supply line. On February 20, several fires erupted in the Paco area of Manila, and a number of Americans were killed. The provost guards rounded up hundreds of Filipinos, claiming they were insurgents in disguise. In the early evening of February 22, new fires erupted in the Santa Cruz suburbs only a few blocks from the Escolta. The flames lit up the sky, and the attention of Otis's army was drawn to the conflagration. When the fire brigade attempted to put out the flames, Filipino youths dashed in to cut fire hoses, and several were killed. Around midnight, new fires erupted in the Tondo district, the oldest and poorest section of Manila, near the *Intramuros*.

Simultaneously, Filipino guerrillas attacked a number of houses in the *Intramuros* where U.S. troops were quartered. When the provost guards responded, the guerrillas barricaded themselves in the old Spanish stone villas in the area and forced the guards to fight them from house to house. From narrow streets, roofs, buildings, and dark alleys, the guerrillas shot at the U.S. soldiers. Women, children, and noncombatants sought safety in the churches. Through the night, a red glare painted the sky over the burning city, and the sounds of firing Springfields, Krags, and Mausers were punctuated by the loud cracks of burning bamboo exploding in the air. At dawn, smoke lay in thick clouds over the city as the fires in Tondo continued to burn.[38]

At dawn, General Luna attacked MacArthur's fortified line at Calacoon. MacArthur's outposts were on the alert, and within minutes, his division was ready to respond. The Filipino army crossed the fields north of Calacoon in a line that stretched east to west for 2 miles. "A certain thrill of admiration ran along our ranks," observed one U.S. Volunteer, as the Republican soldiers marched toward the U.S. line as steady as veteran soldiers. Unfortunately for the Filipinos, an attack in formation was a foolish maneuver. MacArthur simply waited for the advancing enemies to come into artillery range and then ordered his batteries to open fire. The rapid fire of the breech-loading artillery guns, supported by Dewey's naval guns, collapsed the Filipino charge before the men even came within rifle range.[39]

MacArthur telegraphed Otis and requested permission to counterattack. To MacArthur's irritation, the cautious Otis refused permission and again failed to listen to his field commander; he decided instead to wait for U.S. reinforcements before extending his line beyond Calacoon.

The 2nd Division remained at Calacoon for the next four weeks. The days were comparatively quiet, although after dark the insurgents usually opened fire on the U.S. positions. Nearly every evening, a furious exchange of small-arms fire erupted between the lines and continued at intervals through the night. The nightly fusillades did little harm to either side, and few men were killed or wounded.

The troops of the 2nd Division were quartered in the deserted homes in the area as well as in tents near the railroad station. As during the Civil War, regimental line officers lived in walled, rectangular tents surrounded by sandbags to protect themselves from the nightly small-arms fire. As the temperature rose with each passing day, some of the officers and many of the enlisted men opted to sleep under the open sky, but a good night's sleep was fairly impossible because of the heat and the mosquitoes. The insects bit through shirts and trousers and brought blood that dried into small scabs. When scratched, these scabs became open sores, and skin diseases spread rapidly. In addition, drinking water had to be boiled for at least fifteen minutes, and sickness ravaged the division. Dysentery was as great a killer of men in this war as during the Civil War.[40]

MacArthur ordered daily drills to prevent the troops from becoming lax. His principal credo remained the same: Train the men to obey through drills and expect absolute obedience to orders, but in return, do everything possible to make the troops comfortable. The men accepted the drills with good humor. The constant nightly exchange of rifle fire with the Filipino army convinced them of the necessity of preparing for battle.[41]

As the days passed and became weeks, the common soldiers of both armies developed an informal agreement not to fire unless ordered or attacked. Regimental bands played at night, and Filipinos crowded atop their trenches to hear the music. Colonel Funston remembered the Filipinos "vigorously applauded pieces that struck their fancy. Every concert closed with the playing of 'The Star-Spangled Banner,' at which not only our men but all the Filipinos stood at attention."[42]

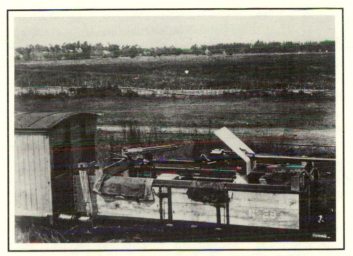

MacArthur's armored train. (National Archives, 111-SC-98052)

MacArthur was actively preparing for an offensive to be launched as soon as he could obtain permission from General Otis. A prime liability for the U.S. Army was the lack of detailed maps of Luzon. In fact, the only maps MacArthur had were those he obtained from foreign companies doing business in the Philippines, such as the New York and Java Trading Companies. He realized he needed more information and decided to form a special reconnaissance unit composed of 3 officers and 19 enlisted men, under the command of Major J. Franklin Bell. MacArthur ordered Bell to provide him with careful intelligence reports and reliable maps. Bell, who had been acting as MacArthur's special intelligence officer since early February, was an aggressive, enterprising officer who had graduated from West Point in 1878. Promotion was slow in the Regular Army, and after twenty years, he was still a first lieutenant in the cavalry. But, rapid promotion came with the war. He became a major of Volunteers in June 1898 and was sent to the Philippines with Merritt's expedition. MacArthur, who had known Bell previously, decided almost immediately to make him the division's intelligence officer. His boldness in reconnaissance paid great dividends for MacArthur, who was constantly informed on the line situation and the strength of his enemy.[43]

MacArthur also used the railroad cars he had captured to create an armored train of four cars, the first and last being flatcars and the other two boxcars. MacArthur mounted a rapid-fire, 6-pound naval gun and three machine guns on the first flatcar. The other three cars were to carry supplies. When the division took the offensive, the armored train became MacArthur's command headquarters and provided sleeping quarters for the general and his staff.[44]

As reinforcements arrived from the United States, new regiments were constantly added to the 2nd Division. Brigadier General Loyd Wheaton arrived in late

February with the 20th Infantry. A veteran of the Civil War with a reputation for being a fighter, Wheaton was a striking individual. Slender in build, he sported a long, bristling beard that covered his face. He was assigned to command the 3rd Brigade of the 1st Division that was temporarily detached to serve under MacArthur. Wheaton was a dependable officer. MacArthur liked him, and the two worked well together.

The most famous general in the U.S. Army, Major General Henry Lawton, arrived in Manila on March 17 with two battalions of the 17th Infantry and one battalion of the 4th Infantry. Many junior officers had eagerly awaited Lawton's arrival. It was rumored that he was to replace Otis as overall field commander. Otis's plodding, meticulous style had irritated many, including MacArthur, and it was assumed that the dashing Lawton would actively pursue the enemy. "In some ways," historian Stuart Miller observed, "Lawton was America's Lord Kitchener. He had had a string of successes from the Civil War, in which he won the Congressional Medal of Honor, to the Indian Wars, ... and finally in Cuba where he led the attack on El Caney on the outskirts of Santiago."[45]

MacArthur and Lawton were prime contenders for high rank in the U.S. Army. The two men were about the same age (midfifties), and both had careers dating back to the Civil War. MacArthur had been the youngest regimental commander in the Union army during the Civil War; Lawton had been the next youngest. In 1862, when eighteen, Lawton enlisted in the 9th Indiana Infantry as a sergeant. Before the end of the war, he had risen to the rank of colonel commanding the regiment, much as MacArthur had risen to command the 24th Wisconsin. Both had participated in over twenty-eight major engagements, including the Atlanta campaign, and both had received congressional Medals of Honor for their heroism in the war.

After the Civil War, Lawton's career continued to parallel MacArthur's. Both had entered the Regular Army in 1866 as second lieutenants, and shortly thereafter, both were promoted to captain. As a cavalry officer in the years from 1866 to 1888, Lawton won fame as one of the men who had captured Geronimo. When the two captains contended for an opening in the Inspector General's Office in 1888, Lawton got the position and the promotion to major. Soon, he was a lieutenant colonel. MacArthur meanwhile obtained an appointment to the Adjutant General's Office, but it was years before he became a lieutenant colonel. Before the outbreak of the Spanish-American War in April 1898, Lawton ranked third among all lieutenant colonels in the army; MacArthur was ranked fifty-sixth. Immediately promoted to major general of Volunteers, Lawton won additional fame in Cuba and promotion to brigadier general in the Regular Army; he also retained the rank of major general of Volunteers.

Lawton was very popular with his fellow officers, the politicians, and the press. Many observers thought he was the ideal commander. In military bearing, looks, dash, and ability, he was a model officer. Over six feet tall, he had a ruggedly

Major General Henry W. Lawton, 1899. (National Archives, 111-SC-90829)

handsome face beneath a crop of iron-gray hair. Vigorous and energetic, he had a reputation as a fighting cavalry man who disliked red tape.

Nearly everyone in Manila (except Otis) was thrilled with Lawton's arrival. Lawton, it was said, would have the Filipinos whipped in two weeks if he replaced Otis as commander.

The troops and Lawton were to be disappointed. It turned out that Lawton was on probation. The one black spot on his otherwise dynamic career was a drinking problem dating back to the 1880s. Normally an easygoing man, Lawton had violent fits of temper when drunk. Although he usually controlled his intake, he got into trouble during the Cuban campaign for drinking too much. Before leaving the United States in January 1899, he had met with McKinley and promised the president to give up alcohol. In return, McKinley indicated that he intended to place Lawton in command of the U.S. forces in the Philippines.

McKinley had second thoughts while Lawton sailed from New York on a forty-nine-day voyage via the Suez Canal to India, then to Singapore, and finally arriving in Manila on March 17. During his voyage, the second battle of Manila had occurred, and MacArthur and Anderson had successfully broken the Filipino encirclement of the city. The victories propelled Otis to the status of national hero as U.S. newspapers described him as a grand strategist. The official political line in Manila and Washington was that Otis expected to complete the pacification of the Philippines within a month.

McKinley decided to retain Otis in command while Lawton adjusted to the tropical climate and familiarized himself with the field position of the U.S. troops. Lawton felt betrayed and had difficulty controlling his temper when he learned he would replace General Anderson as commander of the 1st Division.[46]

Lawton's arrival created tensions in the command structure for both Otis and MacArthur. Lawton's popularity with President McKinley and with the other officers alarmed Otis, who subsequently favored MacArthur. The role of Lawton's 1st Division was to protect Manila while MacArthur's 2nd Division took the offensive. By mid-March, the U.S. strength had risen from 15,000 to 26,000 men. But eliminating administrative personnel, the sick, and others, the effective fighting strength was still only 16,500 men. Since MacArthur's division occupied the hot spot, he received most of the reinforcements, and his division swelled to over 10,000 men.

Because Lawton outranked MacArthur, there was a delicate command problem. Despite his successes on the battlefield from August 1898 to March 1899, MacArthur had received no promotions in the Regular Army. Officers in the Regular Army held two commissions—their Regular Army grade and rank, which they would revert to at the end of the war, and their temporary grade and rank in the Volunteer forces. MacArthur was a major general in the Volunteers but only a lieutenant colonel in the Regular Army, while Lawton was a brigadier general. Moreover, the number of general officers was severely limited in the Regular Army. Even though the army had increased from 25,000 to 65,000 enlisted men during the war, the officers corps had increased by only 332, from 2,168 to 2,500, and by law, the army was limited to 1 lieutenant general, 2 major generals, 6 brigadier generals of the line, and 10 brigadier generals of administration.[47]

General MacArthur desperately needed a promotion before he returned to the United States; otherwise, once he left the Philippines, he would automatically revert to the rank of lieutenant colonel. Considering his successes in the field, he deserved a promotion. Unfortunately, however, he would have to wait until a vacancy occurred in the generals' rank.

Back home, Pinky was upset that the War Department had not promoted her husband, and she took pen in hand and wrote to her contacts in Washington. She had learned from Judge MacArthur the importance of influence, and she often tried to persuade people to support her husband's career, just as she later did to help her son Douglas. The response was gratifying. Letters from powerful friends poured into the White House and the Adjutant General's Office recommending MacArthur's promotion.[48]

Lawton's arrival in Manila stimulated Otis into action. After a month's delay, he ordered MacArthur to attack along the railroad and capture Malolos 20 miles up the line. Otis was sure the Filipinos would surrender their arms and swear allegiance to the United States if MacArthur captured the Republican capital. He was convinced that most Filipinos welcomed the U.S. presence and only supported the revolution out of fear of Republican reprisals.

At sunrise on March 25, MacArthur's 2nd Division attacked the Filipino forces north of Calacoon. Using his artillery and his armored train, MacArthur bombarded the Filipino trenches for a half hour before he attacked. The armored train was a rolling powerhouse with its three machine guns and naval 6-pounder, a rapid-fire pom-pom gun. As the train neared the trenches, the pom-pom, supported by the machine guns, bombarded the enemy trenches while the infantry moved forward and added to the firepower with their Krags and Springfields.[49]

MacArthur advanced with one flank that broke through the line and then immediately shoved forward with the center and the other flank to exploit the breakthrough. After a brief but bloody firefight, the troops captured the fortifications as the Filipino army fled north toward the Tuliahan River. The deserted trenches lined with dead illustrated the Filipino will, but once again, the Filipino generals had been outmaneuvered by better-trained U.S. troops supported by superior artillery.[50]

After a short delay to reorganize, MacArthur moved his division up the railroad line, with his flanks extended out for about 8 miles on both sides of the tracks. The regiments moved forward by alternating companies, the rear company providing protective fire for the advancing one. Brief skirmishes occurred up and down the line as the retreating Filipino army destroyed bridges across several small streams and burned the nearby towns.

The U.S. regiments near the railroad bed had an easier time than those moving cross-country. Although the land was flat, it was broken up by wooded areas, bamboo groves, fields of cotton, sugarcane, and rice, and innumerable streams that made troop movements difficult. The going was particularly rough, historian William T. Sexton noted, when a regiment crossed a series of rice paddies that were "enclosed by earthen dikes at least a foot high. Crossing the dikes not only made the going hard for infantrymen but was tremendously exhausting to artillery horses or to gunners when the guns were pulled by hand."[51]

The U.S. troops became unbearably exhausted by late afternoon. The hot, dry season had descended on Luzon, and the tropical sun baked the central plains; by midday, the temperature hovered around 100 degrees. The heat disabled many of the men, despite the short marches between firefights. They staggered forward, and stretcher-bearers were kept on the run picking up men who collapsed from heat exhaustion. Part of the problem was that the men were packing a wide assortment of equipment that weighed them down. Each carried a bedroll, a rubber blanket, half a shelter tent, extra clothes, a second pair of shoes, toilet items such as soap, towel, and razor, a canteen filled with freshly boiled water, six days' food rations, a tin cup, and two plates that fastened together and hung from the belt. One of the plates had a small handle and was called a soup plate; it served as a coffeepot, a frying pan, and a tool for digging rifle pits. All this was in addition to a rifle and 150 rounds of ammunition fitted on a thick, canvas belt to which loops had been stitched to hold the cartridges. Uniforms varied, and many foreign observers thought the men looked more like *banditti* than regular soldiers. The men boasted of the way they adapted their equipment to fit their needs.[52]

The division camped that night on the south bank of the Tuliahan River, 5 miles north of Calacoon. The men dug trenches that encircled their encampments, posted guards, and placed their shelter tents in the center. MacArthur demanded that all camps be kept immaculately clean, and within the encircled line, deep ditches were dug for refuse.[53]

The men settled down to their evening meal of unpalatable hardtack, pork and beans, canned salmon, canned tomatoes, and rice. Some of them had foraged on the march; despite MacArthur's orders against looting, many a Filipino chicken and pig were added to the pot.[54]

During the early evening, MacArthur visited each regiment and consulted with their commanders. The major problem of the day's march had been the heat, and the general altered his plans to alleviate some of the worst aspects of the march. He ordered reveille for 3:00 A.M., with the next day's advance to begin at 5:00 while it was still cool. He also organized a brigade of Chinese coolies to carry the men's surplus equipment. The Chinese population in Manila numbered almost 90,000, and although some were prosperous merchants and shopkeepers, the majority were poor laborers; hundreds were hired to transport supplies.[55]

Early the next morning, the division crossed the Tuliahan River, dislodged the Filipinos from their trenches after a brief but sharp skirmish, and continued up the railroad to the next small town. The Filipinos had destroyed the railroad bridge across the Tuliahan, but that did not slow down the division. MacArthur ordered supplies ferried across the river, reconstructed his armored train from captured rolling stock on the far side, and continued up the line. Because of the lack of engines, the armored train was pushed along the track by Chinese coolies.

About every 5 miles along the railroad line, there was a small town composed of a stone government building, a large church, and a few hundred nipa huts. The retreating Republican Army burned the nipa huts in a scorched-earth policy. Frightened townspeople loaded their possessions onto carabao carts and fled before the invading army, for Republican propaganda proclaimed the U.S. soldiers would butcher their children and rape their women. Thousands of refugees poured into the mountains east and west of the central Luzon valley. The plain was a major food-producing area, and when the flow of farm produce slowed to a trickle, the poor of Manila felt the pinch.[56]

For the next five days, MacArthur moved his division forward as the Filipino army retreated, burning villages, destroying bridges, tearing up railroad tracks, and then establishing a new defensive position on the north side of the next major river. In the 20 miles between Calacoon and Malolos, there were dozens of small streams and six major rivers. During the dry season, troops could easily cross the streams at fords, but to keep his supply line open, MacArthur had to repair the railroad bridges. The repairs took time because of the lack of suitable building material—there were no large timbers in central Luzon. Therefore, rather than halt and wait for days for bridge repairs, MacArthur ferried his army and supplies across the rivers. He then took the armored train to the end of the tracks, where he left it and advanced with his forward artillery units.[57]

On the north side of the rivers, MacArthur repaired the track and reconstituted the armored train with captured rolling stock. The Filipinos were inept in their attempts to destroy the tracks. Usually, they simply unbolted the rails and shoved them off their ties. MacArthur smiled: General Sherman would have berated any regiment that engaged in such inadequate destruction. To prevent quick repair, as the 24th Wisconsin had learned, the rails had to be heated, then bent around a nearby tree. Even though parts of the track were partially destroyed, MacArthur's division captured large sections of the line intact, as well as a considerable amount of rolling stock and a number of locomotives.[58]

The division would then continue to the next major river, where once again the Filipinos were entrenched. MacArthur would pause for the night to repair the railroad in his rear and to build pontoon bridges over the smaller streams to ease the flow of supplies. Early the next morning, he would attack, always using the same tactics employed by General Sherman during the Atlanta campaign back in 1864: MacArthur's artillery would bombard the Filipino barricades as he swung two of his brigades wide to attack both flanks. Outmaneuvered, outnumbered, and outgunned, the Filipinos would flee north to new positions beyond the next major river. MacArthur then ferried his men across the river and pursued as his reserve forces repaired the railroad bridge. Reaching the next river, he would pause for the night and repeat the operation again the following day.

The success of MacArthur's invasion of central Luzon, in the words of one historian,

> appeared to be predetermined. This was not ... a contest between armies of comparable strength. There would be few of the dramatic scenes one might find in campaigns in which the result was in doubt—no matching of wits by rival commanders at the climax of a battle, no moments of crisis when the actions of a single company or battalion would determine the outcome of the fighting. This was rather to be a merciless thrashing. The Filipinos would fight bravely but they would lose every set-piece encounter.[59]

MacArthur's division shoved the Philippine Army back 18 miles and was within 2 miles of Malolos by the afternoon of March 30. MacArthur halted for the night to plan his attack and bring up supplies. Since Malolos was the Republican capital, he assumed the town would be well defended: Aguinaldo had had three months to prepare the defenses (see Map 12.1).

During the night, MacArthur visited each of his regiments and reconnoitered the forward positions of the enemy. As he and his staff "walked abreast of the Filipino" line, Captain Jacob F. Kreps of the 22nd Regiment reported, they "were fired upon by sharpshooters hidden in the trees. Although bullets kicked up dirt on all sides of the officers, MacArthur did not blink an eye" even when one of his aides was hit by a Mauser bullet.[60]

During the night, MacArthur formed his division for an attack. At 7:00 A.M., he opened with a twenty-five-minute artillery barrage. After the barrage, he moved his left flank and center forward. The advance was not resisted. During the night, Aguinaldo had pulled out, leaving only a rear guard in the trenches in front of Malolos. He had decided not to defend his capital. He tried to burn the city, but U.S. troops were in town so rapidly that little damage was actually done. In six days, MacArthur had achieved his objective.[61]

Aguinaldo's army retreated 3 miles to a new line on the north bank of the Quingua River. Evaluating reconnaissance reports, MacArthur estimated the Republican Army now numbered between 8,000 and 9,000 men. Aguinaldo's supply base was at Calumpit, 5 miles north of the Quingua River. The Republican Army's supply line stretched north along the railroad through San Fernando and Angeles City to Tarlac, the new Republican capital 50 miles north of Malolos.[62]

MacArthur wired Otis for permission to pursue the Philippine Army. His division had not suffered undue casualties in the campaign and was still capable of action. He had lost 33 killed and 501 wounded, and he estimated that Aguinaldo had suffered 801 killed and 3,000 wounded. The division had also captured 100 Filipino soldiers, who were being treated as prisoners of war. MacArthur was sure the Republican forces were demoralized and that if his division moved rapidly, he could capture Tarlac before the onset of the rainy season in late May.[63]

MacArthur wanted to continue the offensive at least to Calumpit, a small town on the Rio Grande River 8 miles north of Malolos. He considered Calumpit to be the most important strategic point in central Luzon. There, the Republicans had an almost ideal defensive position. The town was located on the southwest tip of a gigantic swamp called the Candaba. The triangular-shaped swamp extended northeast for twenty miles from Calumpit and prevented a flanking movement to the east. To the southwest of Calumpit, several major rivers splintered into a maze of small rivers and estuaries that ran all the way to Manila Bay and made a flanking movement in that direction difficult. If delayed until the rainy season, MacArthur's division would have to engage in a frontal assault to capture Calumpit, and the longer Aguinaldo was allowed to improve his fortifications, the greater difficulty MacArthur expected.

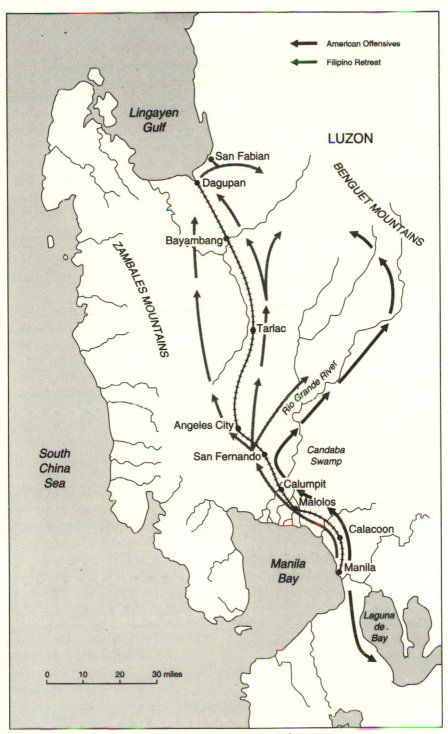

MAP 12.1 U.S. conquest of central Luzon

There were other considerations that made the general recommend an immediate offensive operation. The enlistment dates for his Volunteer regiments expired at the end of June, and their release from the service would deprive him of veteran units, units he had spent nine months training. New regiments arriving from the United States would need time to be trained and to become adjusted to the tropical climate. Equally important were the conditions associated with the coming rainy season. In the Philippines, weather controls military action, particularly for an army with heavy artillery. When the monsoons began in late May or early June, the area around Calumpit would become a lake, and any military operations would be impossible.[64]

Otis rejected MacArthur's pleas. Grandpa Otis constantly worried about supply problems and overextension of his forces. He believed that an army was like "a dog fastened to a chain—within the length of the chain, irresistible, beyond it, powerless." The chain was the army's supply train. He did not wish to spread his army too thin and jeopardize the tremendous victories achieved by MacArthur's division.[65]

With the fall of Malolos, Otis expected the Philippine Republic to collapse. He reported to Washington that the back of the insurgency was broken and that only a few Filipino bandits remained in the field. He was also convinced that the majority of the Filipino people were now ready to swear allegiance to the United States. But his positive reports were based on discussions with wealthy and well-educated Filipinos in Manila, rather than on true conditions among the population at large.

Otis's conclusions were also politically motivated. In the United States, a major debate raged between the imperialists and anti-imperialists. Otis wanted to support the McKinley administration, whose position was that most Filipinos were delighted with U.S. rule. Nearly every page of Otis's reports spoke of another disastrous blow to the enemy that presaged the imminent collapse of the rebellion. And official press releases presented a rosy picture of the situation as Otis inflated battlefield statistics and claimed fantastic victories. He suppressed or censored contradictory news reports through his control of the telegraph.

MacArthur disagreed with the official propaganda line in his reports to the War Department. In his opinion, the majority of the people of the Philippines supported Aguinaldo and the independence movement. Most news reporters agreed with MacArthur, but their reports seldom squeaked past the censors.[66]

For most of April, MacArthur waited for the ever-cautious Otis to allow the offensive to be renewed. After three weeks of idleness, Otis finally granted MacArthur permission to advance. On Sunday, April 23, MacArthur sent Major Bell's reconnaissance unit 3 miles north to the Quingua River, where the Filipino army was entrenched. During the night, MacArthur moved his division to the south bank of the river and at dawn, opened fire with his artillery. The Filipinos immediately abandoned their positions and retreated north 8 miles, where they had established a major defensive line on the north bank of the Rio Grande just south of Calumpit.

MacArthur crossed the Quingua and later the Bagbag River, reaching the south bank of the Rio Grande two days later, on April 26. The river was 400 feet wide, deep and swift, and the bridge crossing it had been destroyed. The Republican Army, estimated to be 4,000 strong under the command of General Luna, was entrenched on the north bank.

During the night, MacArthur's men constructed a pontoon bridge, and at dawn, he again ordered an attack, using his heavy artillery to batter the Filipino fortifications. After a fierce battle that lasted about an hour, Luna abandoned his position and retreated. The victory had been easier than MacArthur had expected, but his division still suffered 181 casualties—155 wounded and 26 killed. Among the dead was Colonel Stotsenburg of the 1st Nebraska, one of MacArthur's favorite regimental commanders. The strategic town of Calumpit was occupied that morning by the 2nd Division.[67]

MacArthur remained at Calumpit for a week, repairing bridges and railroad tracks until the supply trains caught up. On May 4, he moved again with the objective being the important city of San Fernando, located about 12 miles north. At several points, the Filipino army fought small skirmishes from entrenched positions, but the troops were overrun each time. Moving with a speed that surprised both Otis and Luna, MacArthur's division captured San Fernando the next day. The Republican Army did not even have time to destroy the attractive town, which was to serve as MacArthur's summer headquarters.

MacArthur wanted to continue the offensive before the Filipino army could destroy the railroad bridges and tracks. He believed his division could charge up the railroad all the way to the Lingayen Gulf, 100 miles north, before the rainy season began. He assumed that the sooner his division attacked, the sooner the war would be over.[68]

To MacArthur's irritation, Otis again refused permission and ordered him to remain in San Fernando until the railroad back to Manila was completely repaired. From the beginning of the campaign, Otis had constantly interfered with field operations, yet he knew very little about field conditions. He never visited the front lines, never inspected the troops, and, in fact, never left Manila. Nonetheless, he demanded that MacArthur constantly report to headquarters via telegraph and often ordered him to terminate operations prematurely.[69]

Otis was a good administrative general who kept his army well supplied and well fed, but many observers believed he should have let his division commanders take charge of field operations without interference from headquarters. Colonel Theodore S. Schwan, Otis's chief of staff and an old friend of MacArthur's from his days in the Adjutant General's Office, praised his boss as a man with "tremendous capacity for work." But he was critical of Otis's "fondness for details [that] make him loath to lodge discretion with anyone." Otis insisted on making all the decisions, even minor ones, that a commanding general ordinarily left to his staff.

Administrative work was his specialty, and he enjoyed arranging for supplies, developing organizational charts, and completing army regulation forms.[70]

Many of the officers in the 8th Army Corps considered Otis "fastidious, pompous and fussy." General Irving Hale, commander of the 1st Colorado, not only made his disrespect for Otis obvious but also engaged in shouting matches with him in front of the men. On one such occasion, Otis threatened Hale with "official action." MacArthur, in a rare unguarded moment, remarked to his staff that Otis was like "a locomotive bottom-side up, its wheels revolving at full speed but going nowhere." General Lawton, in command of the 1st Division, was equally critical of Otis's caution and remarked to news reporters that the commanding general was an interfering old busybody.[71]

Despite MacArthur's protests, Otis ordered him to remain at San Fernando. San Fernando was a pretty little town. Nipa huts surrounded the town center, where there was a massive Catholic church and several public buildings. Some of the division troops quartered in the public buildings; others occupied a number of abandoned Spanish villas. Several regiments guarded the front to the north, and a number guarded the railroad in garrison towns all the way back to Manila. Unarmed Filipinos were permitted to return to their homes and resume their lives. San Fernando was soon bustling with life.

The major problem faced by the division stemmed from the ravages of the tropical climate. Although battlefield casualties in April and May were relatively light (32 killed and 219 wounded), the men needed a rest from marching in the hot, humid climate. Many suffered from heat exhaustion, and others were debilitated by dysentery, cholera, typhoid, and malaria. In one regiment, 70 percent of the men were on sick leave. Of the 4,800 combat troops in the division on May 12, 45 percent, or 2,160, were on sick report. Few of the remaining men were healthy enough for a major campaign or even a day's march.[72]

To improve the men's health, MacArthur's quartermaster purchased fresh vegetables, bananas, pineapples, coconuts, rice, and sugarcane from native vendors. These diet improvements helped, but disease continued to ravage the division. The medical staff blamed filthy conditions, lack of proper sanitation, and poor water. Consequently, sanitation in every town and village controlled by the division became a priority item. The stink of rotten food, urine, and animal waste permeated the market centers of all the towns and villages. Carabao and small ponies defecated at will, and the smell was overpowering in the tropical heat. Further, because Filipinos disposed of their human waste near their nipa huts or in nearby streams that often served as the local water supply, polluted water contributed to the spread of dysentery, typhoid fever, and other diseases.[73]

MacArthur ordered all towns and villages to conform to stringent health standards. To guarantee his orders were obeyed, he appointed one of his best officers, Colonel William A. Kobbé, to act as liaison with the Filipino town councils. Kobbé hired a corps of native laborers to clean the rubbish from streets, and property owners were required to keep their premises clean. The town councils resented the sanitation rules but obeyed them.

Although MacArthur insisted that all sanitation rules be adhered to, he was not insensitive to the attitudes of the Filipino people. He abhorred the racial prejudice sometimes displayed by his officers and men; on several occasions, he reminded them that the purpose of the United States in the Philippines was to benefit the people, not to intimidate them. For U.S. soldiers to insult an individual Filipino or to burn or loot unprotected property was not only criminal, it also defeated the very purpose of the occupation. Every officer was ordered to punish any thoughtless or ignorant behavior that interfered with the establishment of friendly relations. MacArthur observed that the Republican leaders had persistently represented the U.S. soldiers as turbulent, undisciplined, and given to gross and licentious behavior. To eradicate the effects of such "mendacious misrepresentation," he felt it was essential that all his men "sedulously abstain from practices in any way calculated to annoy or engender the feelings of timidity or mistrust."[74]

MacArthur knew that most Filipinos resented the American presence and that many supported the Republican forces. The Filipinos in the area under his control acted as spies for the Republican Army, whose guerrilla forces harassed U.S. patrols along the rail line back to Manila.[75]

The Republicans' main army north of San Fernando was quiet for most of the month of May as the leaders engaged in another power struggle. Aguinaldo decided that the explosive and violent-tempered General Luna had to be replaced. Possessing a monumental ego, the aristocratic Luna knew he was always right and proclaimed that incompetent underlings had caused his earlier defeats. After losing a battle, he viciously turned on any subordinates who had erred, no matter how minor the mistake. He angrily stripped officers of their rank or threw them into jail. Peasants were shot if he suspected they had aided the U.S. troops in any way, and talking to a U.S. soldier was suspicion enough. Filipino leaders felt the only way to remove Luna from command was to kill him, and on June 8, 1899, he was assassinated while visiting Aguinaldo's headquarters. General Gregorio del Pilar replaced Luna as field commander. Only twenty-three years old, del Pilar was selected because of his loyalty to Aguinaldo rather than for his military brilliance.

Eight days after Luna's assassination, the Republican Army attacked MacArthur's stronghold at San Fernando. Early in the morning of June 18, 7,000 Filipinos massed north of town. If del Pilar expected to catch MacArthur by surprise, he was disappointed. Colonel Funston, commander of the 20th Kansas, recorded that his regiment and the entire division were fully prepared for the attack and were simply surprised at del Pilar's stupidity in hitting fortified positions protected by heavy artillery. As Funston later wrote: "We could not believe that they were actually going to charge us, but that is what they did, and did gamely too. It seemed a pity, as they certainly deserved a better fate."[76]

The U.S. artillery dispersed the attackers, and MacArthur ordered his regiments to counterattack as the Filipino army fled north from the battlefield. In the battle, del Pilar lost over 100 men while MacArthur lost only 12. In his official report, MacArthur observed that "the attack lacked nearly every element of professional sagacity." Although the attack illustrated that the Republican Army was poorly trained, it also showed that Filipino morale was high despite the army's setbacks. The attack, in MacArthur's words, displayed a "recuperative pertinacity" that proved the conflict was not yet over. He again recommended an immediate counteroffensive to crush the Republican Army before his Volunteer regiments were released to return to the United States.[77]

Otis rejected the proposal because Lawton's division was already engaged in military operations around Laguna de Bay, a large lake 18 miles southeast of Manila. Fishing and farming villages dotted the shoreline of the lake, which was 28 miles wide and 32 miles long. Most of the peasants around Laguna de Bay willingly supplied food to the Republican Army south of Manila. Lawton's orders were to clear the area of insurgents, a campaign he began on June 10.[78]

People in the United States found Lawton's military operations around the lake more fascinating than those of MacArthur to the north. MacArthur was cold and distant and discouraged news reporters in his area, but Lawton invited his favorite correspondents to accompany him on his operations. These reporters gave him excellent copy, noting that his troops adored him and were ready to follow him anywhere. The correspondents were convinced that Lawton could win the war in weeks if Otis would let him. After all, Lawton had captured Geronimo, and the "puffed-up crack brained egoists of Aguinaldo's had to realize they were no match for him," chided an editor of the *New York Times.* Lawton looked like a hero, talked like a hero, and acted like a hero. Correspondents noted that he walked erect and tall even when exposed to enemy fire. Wearing a glistening white British pith helmet and standing six-feet-four-inches tall, he was an inviting target as he rode astride his black horse or paced back and forth behind his forward firing line. Like MacArthur, he felt the proper role of the officer was to display valor in the face of enemy fire. Both men had exposed themselves to dangers during the Civil War, and neither appeared afraid to die. Also like MacArthur, Lawton was scrupulously accurate in describing a battle, never attempted to inflate it or himself, and he was always quick to praise the courage of others.[79]

The Laguna de Bay campaign ended quickly because of the onset of the rainy season. Lawton had not fully comprehended the effects of the weather on military operations. Torrential rains made most of Luzon a quagmire during the monsoon season, and it was impossible to travel overland as the island became a sea of mud full of swollen streams and swampland. The heat and humidity also decimated the ranks of the 1st Division. Lawton reported that "on foot, our men cannot stand the extra exertion in this awful heat; those who suffered sunstroke fell as though shot."[80]

Although his division captured most of the villages on the shores of Laguna de Bay, the campaign ended with a whimper in late June when the captured areas were abandoned. Despite the setback, Otis described the campaign as a complete success in his reports to Washington and asserted that the insurrection was over with only a few bandits and murderers remaining in the field. Correspondents traveling with Lawton disputed Otis's claim, and years later, politicians and historians blamed him for his failure to keep Washington properly informed on conditions in the Philippines. Historian Stuart Miller condemned Otis for always presenting an optimistic picture and constantly issuing "press releases full of exaggerated claims. ... Every military probe was launched with great fanfare and the claim that it was to be 'the last stroke of the war.' Otis invariably called each probe a 'complete success' in press releases."[81]

Correspondents who disagreed with Otis discovered their dispatches were censored, and they themselves were classified as troublemakers and denied access to future press briefings. The correspondents dutifully submitted to censorship until late June, when they became increasingly suspicious of Otis's rosy outlook. They banded together and wrote a protest that charged him with misrepresenting the real situation in the Philippines. To circumvent the censors, they smuggled a copy of their report to Hong Kong, where it was then transmitted to their newspapers in the United States.[82]

As news reports gradually became critical of Otis's optimistic briefings, Washington received information from many other sources that clearly contradicted the general's official propaganda line. Lawton and MacArthur, for example, disagreed with him in their official reports. General Nelson Miles, the lieutenant general commanding the army, read their reports and realized that Otis was glossing over the situation. Miles informed the president and Secretary of War Elihu Root that the conflict was not over; indeed, its end was not even within sight. But neither McKinley nor Root wanted to hear such an evaluation and instead supported Otis's position.[83]

As the Volunteers arrived back in the United States in August, reporters were surprised when the veterans described Otis as "a foolish old woman." The commander of the Colorado regiment, General Hale, denounced Otis as an incompetent, and Charlie King, in an article in *Call's Sunday Magazine*, criticized Otis's military and diplomatic skills. Other veterans "insisted that the war could never be won under Otis" and recommended that Lawton replace "the silly old Grandmother." Among the veterans, the overriding sentiment was "damn Otis and damn the Filipinos."[84]

The onset of the rainy season effectively ended all military operations, and the remaining Volunteer regiments in the Philippines clamored for release from the service. They had enlisted for the duration of the Spanish-American War and did not wish to serve on garrison duty through the long, hot rainy season that would last for five months, until October. They were state Volunteers, so the federal government had no choice but to release them. In late June, twenty-five new army regiments arrived in Manila to relieve the Volunteers. Recruited for service in the Philippines, the new units were numerically designated the 26th to 49th Infantry Regiments.

MacArthur looked forward to letters from home as much as any other soldier, and the news was good. Pinky and Douglas had left Milwaukee in early June for West Point, New York, where they arrived on June 3, the day after the general's fifty-fourth birthday. While Douglas enrolled in the U.S. Military Academy, his mother moved into Craney's Hotel, an antebellum structure of yellow brick with a broad wooden veranda located on the northern edge of the academy. Douglas visited his mother at every opportunity, and Pinky shared in his academy experiences. Mother and son had a photograph taken and probably sent a copy to Douglas's father. Nineteen years and four months old, Douglas was a handsome cadet, standing five-feet-ten-inches tall and weighing 133 pounds. In the photograph, as noted by William Manchester, Pinky is a formidable woman dressed "in black satin and white lace shirtwaist, her hair piled high in an intricate pompadour. She is staring evenly at the camera, her hands tense at her side."[85]

Douglas, like fellow cadet Ulysses S. Grant III, was marked for special attention because of his father's new status. "We always prepared a warm reception for the sons of well-known men," said Robert E. Wood, a firstclassman, and "the well-known man in this instance was General Arthur MacArthur." The senior cadets delighted in making Douglas recite his father's military record from Perryville to Manila, not once but hundreds of times. Pinky reported proudly that Douglas took the hazing with "fortitude and dignity."[86]

Cadet MacArthur's passion at West Point was to come in first in every subject and category so that his father would be proud of him. A fellow cadet, Marty Maher, reported later that Douglas "often wondered if he could ever become as great as his father, and he told me that if hard work had anything to do with it, he had a chance." Arthur P.S. Hyde, one of Douglas's roommates at the academy, recalled that Douglas often spoke of his father "with affection and pride" and felt a filial duty to become the general's "worthy successor."[87]

Meanwhile, as the Volunteers were relieved, the personnel of MacArthur's division drastically changed. Once again, the general had thousands of raw recruits. Fortunately, some of the veteran Volunteers elected to accept a generous government offer of three years of bonus pay ($450–$500) to stay in the Philippines for one more year. The bonus enticed over 10 percent of the Volunteers to remain, and they were formed into two core regiments, the 36th and 37th. The 36th was assigned to MacArthur's division, and he promoted one of his best officers, J. Franklin Bell, to colonel to command it. MacArthur also obtained promotions for other Regular Army officers in his division, including Colonel Kobbé. A Civil War veteran, he would be promoted to brigadier general of the Volunteers and placed in charge of MacArthur's 43rd and 47th Infantry Regiments.[88]

The U.S. forces swelled in size despite the withdrawal of the Volunteers. By early August, there were 30,000 U.S. troops in the Philippines, and the number increased to over 50,000 by November. MacArthur's division was composed of 11,000 enlisted men and 300 officers divided into sixteen regiments, plus artillery, cavalry, engineers, and other support units. MacArthur retained personal command of ten of the regiments, while forming the other six into two brigades, one commanded by Brigadier General Frederick D. Grant and the second by Brigadier General Joseph Wheeler.

MacArthur carefully studied the qualifications of his new brigade and regimental commanders. He talked to each of them separately and discussed topics much broader than the war itself. He also encouraged his officers to express their opinions and assured them that anything they said would remain confidential. In the interim, the new troops needed to be trained, and the order of the day was drills and rifle practice. Except for an occasional night firefight or an isolated attack on one of the division's outposts, July was an exceedingly languid period for military operations. The rains were torrential, as more than forty-two inches fell. The men sweltered in the heat, swore about the constant rain, and drilled.[89]

Despite the rains, MacArthur wanted to continue the offensive, for he felt he needed a training exercise for the new men. After obtaining permission from a reluctant Otis, he attacked north up the railroad line on August 9 and quickly shoved the Filipinos from their entrenched positions. In his report, he observed that the tactics of the Filipino army had changed. The enemy no longer attempted to hold positions but instead provided just enough opposition to make the U.S. forces deploy for battle. The Republican forces had shrunk to some 6,000 to 7,000 men, and MacArthur speculated that Aguinaldo was dispersing his army to harass the U.S. supply lines. Retreating north along the railroad, the Filipinos continued to burn bridges and to destroy tracks, but they no longer burned the towns and villages.[90]

MacArthur's major problem was Brigadier General Wheeler, commander of the 1st Brigade composed of the 12th, 16th, and 19th Regiments. "Fighting Joe" Wheeler had been a major general in the Confederate army and had fought at Stones River and Chattanooga. After the Civil War, he settled in Alabama and was elected to Congress in 1885. He served in the House of Representatives until 1898, when President McKinley appointed him a brigadier general of the Volunteers to show that "the boys in blue and gray" were now fighting together. During the Cuba campaign, Wheeler had commanded a cavalry division and had caused difficulties for his immediate superior, General Samuel B.M. Young. Only five-feet-two-inches tall, Wheeler was a regular "gamecock." Despite not having been in the army for thirty-five years, the sixty-three-year-old Wheeler believed he knew more about war than MacArthur. Rash and obstreperous, Wheeler often disregarded MacArthur's orders, but as an important political appointee, he could not be removed.[91]

MacArthur assigned Wheeler's brigade the easiest task—serving as the center of the line where the railroad bed made marching easier. He ordered Wheeler to move slowly up the line as a demonstration rather than as a full-scale attack. Using other regiments under his personal command, MacArthur began a flanking operation to encircle the Republican Army and to trap the rebels. Since Wheeler's regiments traveled up the railroad bed, they moved much faster than the division's flanks, who were tramping along muddy roads and through flooded ricefields. MacArthur ordered Wheeler to slow down: His role was to distract the Filipinos while the other regiments moved to entrap them.

"Fighting Joe" protested. He felt that his brigade should attack and was infuriated when MacArthur rejected his suggestion. So Wheeler ignored the orders. When his brigade encountered a Filipino force, he ordered his men to charge. The attack sent the Filipinos fleeing before MacArthur's flanking regiments could complete their encirclement.

MacArthur angrily sent Wheeler a message to report to division headquarters. When he arrived, MacArthur ordered him to recall his skirmishers and to send forward only a few scouts to demonstrate against the Filipino line. "Wheeler saluted, mounted his horse, and galloped back to the firing line. There, despite the definite instructions he had just received, he ordered his entire line forward."[92]

It is easy to imagine what occurred when Wheeler next reported to MacArthur. The general chastised him for disobeying direct orders and wired Otis requesting that Wheeler be relieved. But the former Confederate general retained his command because of his political influence and because of administration propaganda that in the Philippines, the "boys of the blue and gray are fighting under the same flag." Prevented from removing Wheeler for political reasons, MacArthur did the next best thing: He ordered Wheeler's brigade to the rear and used them to guard the railroad and supply trains back to San Fernando.[93]

Despite heavy rains, the offensive moved rapidly north along the railroad. MacArthur captured Angeles City, 10 miles north of San Fernando, on August 16. Larger than San Fernando, Angeles City was strategically located, with roads radiating out in every direction.

MacArthur settled his division into quarters at Angeles and waited for Otis to give him permission to advance. He spent the next three months at Angeles reorganizing his division, training his men, and collecting supplies. The division held 60 miles of railroad from Angeles south to Manila but did not control the surrounding countryside. Consequently, guerrillas harassed the railroad line and attacked isolated garrisons. A common guerrilla tactic was to excavate a hole under the railroad tracks so that when heavy locomotives passed over, the tracks collapsed and wrecked the train. To limit the damage, MacArthur placed his locomotives at the rear of the trains rather than the forward position; he lost a few flatcars but saved the more precious engines.[94]

With no direction from Manila, the general prepared for a dry-season offensive. He expected that when his division attacked, the Filipinos would withdraw, destroying the railroad tracks as they retreated north. To pursue the Republican Army, he would need pack animals to transport supplies while the railroad was being repaired in his rear. He therefore began to collect horses, mules, and carabao, plus innumerable vehicles.[95]

Off the railroad, the main means of transport was the carabao cart. Crudely constructed, the cart was pulled by a trained water buffalo weighing about 1,600 pounds. Throughout the wet lowlands in the rainy season, the carabao had no equal as a heavy draft animal. Looking like a cross between an ox and a rhino, it was the Filipino beast of burden, used both in the fields and to pull wagons and carts. Its meat was eaten, its skin was used to make leather goods, and its horns were generally used for bolo handles. A gentle creature, the carabao loved the mud, and at every opportunity, it would submerge its huge body in watery muck to prevent overheating. In the ricefields, which were plowed while under water, the carabao was invaluable. If tied to a cart and not released periodically, it would take the cart into the nearest water or mud hole whether it was a rice paddy, swamp, river, or the ocean. It was a common sight to see dozens wallowing in ponds, streams, and rivers during the heat of the day. The carabao was not a fast animal: When hooked to a cart, it plodded forward at less than 1 mile an hour. There were horses in the Philippines, but they were tiny ponies that made poor beasts of burden. The carabao, by contrast, could pull 600- to 800-pound loads through the mud, averaging about 5 miles per day.

MacArthur sent out reconnaissance patrols that discovered carabao in large numbers in the refugee camps of the nearby mountains and jungles. He purchased the animals for between 30 and 60 Mexican dollars each, and then he impressed the Filipino drivers and paid them 10 Mexican dollars a month. Each regiment was allowed to hire 100 as carriers.[96]

However, MacArthur's preparations for an early fall offensive were soon crippled by headquarters. After five months of silence, Otis finally revealed his grand strategy to his field commanders in early October. MacArthur's division was to attack up the railroad toward Dagupan, 80 miles north of Angeles, while Lawton's division swung inland, climbed the Benguet Mountains, and flanked Aguinaldo's army. Otis ordered MacArthur to turn over most of his vehicles and animals to General Lawton. General Wheaton's brigade would be transported by sea to land in the Lingayen Gulf at Dagupan, the terminus of the railroad. From Dagupan, Wheaton was to move inland to link up with MacArthur's forces pushing northward. Otis hoped to annihilate the Republican Army when it became trapped between the three forces.[97]

On November 8, MacArthur began the campaign. The plan called for his division to push rapidly up the railroad and flush the Republican Army north toward Wheaton and east toward Lawton. MacArthur used Colonel Bell's 36th Regiment to spearhead the attack. He trusted Bell, and the 36th was composed of battle-tested veterans recruited from the departed Volunteer regiments.[98]

MacArthur accompanied the 36th Regiment in his normal flanking movements. Off the railroad tracks, the march moved over open country and through ricefields whose crops had not yet been harvested. The farmers kept the fields irrigated and flooded to a depth of about 3 feet. Separating the fields, narrow dikes provided insecure footing for thousands of marching men. The ground was still a slippery morass from earlier rains, and the rain continued about every third day. Rapid advance in such conditions required pushing the men hard, and MacArthur's rigorous training again proved invaluable.

In six days, the division advanced 30 miles. On November 12, MacArthur's men captured Tarlac, the second Republican capital, but Aguinaldo and his government fled north to Bayambang, about 26 miles up the railroad line. At a conference at Bayambang, Aguinaldo decided further frontal resistance was impossible; it was time to disperse the remaining troops in the Republican Army into small bands for guerrilla operations.

Guerrilla war had always been the revolution's last resort. After the disastrous attack on San Fernando in early June, Aguinaldo had realized that a massed head-on confrontation with the U.S. Army would lead to disaster for the Republican forces. The U.S. troops had the firepower and the trained forces. The Filipino army could not match U.S. leadership, tactics, artillery, or marksmanship. Aguinaldo had delayed dispersing his army through the summer months because Otis had applied no pressure. Now, it was necessary to save the revolution. Future operations would harass the U.S. troops by attacking their supply lines and isolated outposts.[99]

Accompanying his forward reconnaissance units, MacArthur immediately recognized the change in strategy. On Monday, November 13, he wired Manila: "The enemy on this line is pretty near in a state of collapse, and I may get through to Dagupan without any further troops. I will crowd them with men, leave everything behind, including officers' horses, and go as far to the front as possible, with a very fair prospect of getting through to the end of the line, or getting far enough north to make a strong diversion in favor of Lawton and Wheaton."[100]

The Republican leaders almost left the decision to disperse until it was too late. They would have been captured if Lawton and Wheaton had fulfilled their assignments as well as MacArthur.

With one small band, Aguinaldo moved northeast in hopes of escaping into the Benguet Mountains and joining another Republican force commanded by General Manuel Tinio. Lawton's division was supposed to block that escape route. To do so, his division had to travel through the interior jungle, up high mountains, then back down to attack the retreating enemy. But if the terrain and weather proved difficult for MacArthur's division, they proved impossible for Lawton's men.

Moving along the edge of the Benguet Mountains to block the passes, Lawton became bogged down by the weather and the terrain. The rains returned, rendering the roads and fords impassable. For four days, November 13 to 16, it poured constantly, and the interior of Luzon seemed to be afloat. Bridges collapsed, and the incessant rain created hundreds of unfordable streams with currents so strong that both carts and animals were often carried away by floods. Bogs spread out from the streams and lagoons, and carts and horses sank deep into sticky mud. Lagoons and estuaries became impenetrable swamps of mangrove and bamboo thickets. Resembling islands in the ocean, only the high ground remained above water; low areas became broad, shallow lakes.[101]

The men ate, slept, and marched in the drizzle and downpour. Their perpetually wet clothes slowly rotted on their backs. Rifles rusted, and all the equipment was covered with a thin coat of mildew. When it was not raining, the sun baked the ground, and the air became heavy with humidity as the temperature hovered around ninety degrees by 6:00 A.M. The men gasped for breath like fish out of water.

Stalled by the rain, Lawton's encircling column could not block the passes into the Benguet Mountains. In desperation, he sent his cavalry brigade, commanded by General Young, ahead as a flying column toward Dagupan. Meanwhile, Wheaton landed at San Fabian and moved southeast to unite with Young. But Aguinaldo's party slipped through the trap by scaling the Benguet Mountains and hiding in the sleepy town of Palanan in Isabela Province. Young's cavalry did, however, capture a number of Aguinaldo's party, including his mother, Dona Trinidad, his son, Miguel, and his wife.

While Lawton's division was bogged down in the mountains, MacArthur continued the offensive on the plains. On November 17, he left Tarlac with 1,000 handpicked men, including the 36th Regiment, veterans from the 17th Regiment, and his own Headquarters Scouts, on a mad dash north up the railroad line. In the next three days, the forward column occupied the line all the way to Dagupan. From Dagupan, MacArthur wired Manila that "the country is entirely free from armed insurgents. The people generally are remaining in their towns, and the fields are swarming with laborers. There seems to be an absolute absence of fear [and] absolutely no danger. The attitude of the natives is a plain indication that there are no insurgents in this vicinity."[102]

U.S. troops took ten months to secure control of the 150 miles of railroad line stretching from Manila to Dagupan. If Otis had allowed MacArthur to move in April, he could have accomplished the task in less than four months.[103]

MacArthur praised his officers and enlisted men in his official reports. They had performed admirably under difficult conditions: To deploy and attack at the end of the rainy season on the island of Luzon was an arduous task. After two weeks of strenuous marches through rice- and canefields, the men were exhausted from exposure to rain, mud, heat, mosquitoes, leeches, and tropical diseases. However, their training had triumphed. Despite the heavy rains, MacArthur's division moved over 60 miles in twelve days. Their advance was so rapid, in fact, that the retreating Filipinos did not have an opportunity to remove a single rail or destroy a single bridge or culvert. MacArthur's men had displayed great fortitude and courage throughout the campaign, and in his official reports, MacArthur described their bravery in glowing terms.[104]

He was equally generous in his praise for his officers. Many an officer, young and old, would be promoted on his recommendation. Perhaps his favorite was Colonel Bell, who was made brigadier general of the Volunteers with MacArthur's strong support.[105]

Although Aguinaldo and most of the Republican Army had escaped, Otis claimed a complete victory and an end to the Filipino insurrection. All that remained, according to Otis, were a few bandit groups. MacArthur disagreed; he believed that Aguinaldo would continue to fight. His prediction proved true—the most brutal part of the war still lay ahead.

13

Military Governor

THE U.S. OFFENSIVE dispersed but did not destroy the Philippine Republican Army. Filipino troops returned to their various home provinces to rally support for the revolution. Luzon was divided into guerrilla districts, each under a general officer, and into subzones commanded by majors or colonels. Some of their men were full-time guerrillas, but most were part-time militia who operated in bands of five to ten men that harassed U.S. patrols. The militia operated near their own villages, dressed in peasant clothes, and blended into the village population. They watched the Americans and passed on information about their movements to regular guerrilla units in the vicinity. Aguinaldo's hideout remained secret even to his own provincial commanders. Everything now depended on whether the people at large would support and provision the resistance movement.[1]

From Dagupan, MacArthur telegraphed Otis with a proposed plan of operations to search out and destroy the remnants of Aguinaldo's army. He suggested that his division establish several strategic bases along the railroad line and begin a new offensive to quickly occupy the entire Pampanga Plain between the Zambales Mountains on the east and the Benguet Mountains on the west. Using his bases along the railroad line, MacArthur predicted that he could "insure permanent ... control of the great plain in less than sixty days."[2]

Otis rejected MacArthur's plan. Officially, the rebellion was over, with only a few "hot-headed" Filipino insurgents remaining in the field, and their surrender was inevitable. Otis directed MacArthur to disperse his division along the railroad line to protect the villagers against the many bandits that had appeared during the war.

MacArthur protested. He had trained his division to fight as a unit, not to waste its time occupying every tiny village in central Luzon. As an infantry captain from 1867 to 1887, he had commanded a company of troops at a number of isolated garrisons throughout the Southwest. The duty had been an idiotic waste of manpower during the Indian wars, and MacArthur thought such a strategy should not be repeated in the Philippines. Otis repeated his orders, and MacArthur reluctantly complied.[3]

Initially, his division occupied 33 towns, but in the next few months, the division was spread even thinner to garrison over 117 small barrios along the railroad line. Buildings were rented to house the men, and canteens were opened so the troops could let off steam. All regular and systematic military operations ceased as the division's prime responsibilities became the repair, maintenance, and policing of the railroad.

Garrison duty sapped the morale of MacArthur's division. Days merged into weeks of inactivity. November passed. "Another stupid day is gone," declared one soldier after another in letters overflowing with homesickness. Military discipline became lax. Short tempers erupted into fistfights; many of the men drank too much and got into brawls or into altercations with local merchants, and others neglected their duties. The officers discovered some of the men were even sneaking off for a nap when assigned to guard duty.[4]

As the court-martial records reveal, the U.S. garrison soldier was not always well behaved, but if he misbehaved and if his misbehavior was reported to headquarters, he was punished. MacArthur's men quickly learned they could expect no leniency for misconduct. Rowdy behavior by intoxicated soldiers threatened discipline, and the general reminded his officers that the U.S. Army, theoretically at least, was responsible for the safety of the residents of the towns. Any man guilty of abusive acts against the townspeople ran a serious risk of punishment.[5]

In the first week of December, MacArthur's station commanders reported an increase in guerrilla activity. The fighting took on a pattern of punch and counterpunch. MacArthur sent out patrols that penetrated deep into the mountains, and they occasionally stumbled on small bands of guerrillas, who immediately fled. They would hide until the patrols withdrew, then sneak down into the plain to harass U.S. outposts. The telegraph lines buzzed with reports of hostile contact with small bands who attacked U.S. detachments repairing the railroad and the communication lines. Signal parties, railroad work parties, and supply wagons were favorite targets in well-planned hit-and-run attacks. As fast as telegraph lines were repaired, the guerrillas recut the wires. Railroad tracks and bridges were also destroyed. When chased, the guerrillas fled to the mountains or merged with the local village population that clearly supported them. By discarding their uniforms, the revolutionaries could appear and disappear almost at their convenience. Operating in scattered bands of 15 to 200 men, the guerrillas came down from the mountains to raid and to obtain food and supplies from the towns. "These men," historian Leon Wolff wrote, "could live and fight on very little; a sip of water, a few mouthfuls of rice and fruit and sometimes fish, and they were ready for another day's work. They had lost some of their confidence, they feared the burly U.S. sharpshooters, but they were as loyal as ever to Emilio Aguinaldo."[6]

The mountain camps of the guerrillas were difficult to locate, and the trails were ideal places for ambushes. If a U.S. patrol became the least bit careless, it fell into ingenious traps that allowed the guerrillas to attack at close range. Captured

U.S. soldiers were hacked to death with bolos instead of being killed by Mauser bullets.

The Republicans could not protect territory, nor could they afford to engage in any more set-piece battles. As a rule, the Filipinos allowed U.S. troops to take any town they wished. Whenever the troops captured a town, they set up a Filipino municipal government, but the underground government of the revolutionaries was the real authority. Often the U.S.-selected mayor and police chief were local leaders of the revolution. In addition, secret committees were formed in all the barrios and towns to obtain contributions and to maintain the loyalty of the masses. The towns also gathered information and supplies for the roving bands. Captain John Leland Jordan, 38th Volunteer Infantry, reported that in village after village, his men were greeted "with kindly expressions, while the same ones slip away, go out into the bushes, get their guns, and waylay you further down the road. You rout them & scatter them; they hide their guns and take to their houses & claim to be amigos." Frederick Presher, a young farm boy from New Jersey, who was a private in the 1st Cavalry, observed that the Filipinos were "quick change" artists. The U.S. troops no longer fought a recognizable, uniformed army but, instead, determined groups of men who tilled their fields by day and stalked the U.S. outposts by night.[7]

The U.S. Army occupied barrios but then abandoned many of them. When the Republicans reoccupied a village, they punished any Filipino who had assisted or collaborated with the U.S. forces. There was no room for neutrals. Every Filipino owed absolute loyalty to the revolution, and the penalty for assisting the U.S. soldiers was death. Harsh punishments were also meted out to any Filipino who swore allegiance to the United States or surrendered a weapon.

The new guerrilla tactics achieved a dramatic success on December 18, 1899. After the failure of the November mountain campaign, General Lawton had returned with his 1st Division to Manila, and Otis assigned him to garrison the small barrios south and east of Manila. Lawton, who constantly bickered with Otis over military strategy, protested. Like MacArthur, Lawton advocated concentrated military action to suppress the remnant bands of the Republican Army. Otis's plodding style, his political orientation, and his decision to spread the troops into small garrison towns throughout the Philippines disgusted Lawton, who complained loudly to U.S. correspondents in Manila. But the opposition of his two division commanders did not alter Otis's strategy; rather, it irritated him. Consequently, he refused to transmit the opinions of MacArthur and Lawton to Washington and censored all news dispatches leaving Manila.

Lawton waited impatiently for President McKinley to honor his promise to recall Otis and place Lawton himself in command of the 8th Army Corps. MacArthur also hoped Otis would soon be recalled and replaced by Lawton, for he was an aggressive officer, and nearly everyone believed that under his command, the U.S. Army could quickly pacify the islands.[8]

Lawton's popularity and public opposition to Otis naturally caused tension between the two men. Meanwhile, McKinley delayed recalling Otis, and Lawton became increasingly frustrated. Ultimately, he decided to lead a few small U.S. patrols against the guerrilla bands operating in southeastern Luzon. Reporters accompanied Lawton on his excursions and observed that he was able to instill his own tremendous energy into his officers and enlisted men whose privations and dangers he shared. If there was fighting, Lawton was utterly careless with his personal safety.[9]

On December 18, Lawton led a small patrol to San Mateo, a village 18 miles east of Manila. Conspicuous in his white pith helmet, he charged a band of guerrillas, and in the minor skirmish that followed, a Mauser bullet struck Lawton in the chest. He died shortly thereafter.

A nation mourned Lawton's death, and he became a national hero. In the next few months, reporters, politicians, bureaucrats, and many army officers praised his victories against the Republican Army in the 1899 offensive. When Major General John C. Bates replaced Lawton as commander of the 1st Division, Otis ordered him to sweep the area south and east of Manila with 8,000 men.[10]

The military situation in the Philippines continued to deteriorate. From December 1899 to April 1900, hundreds of light skirmishes occurred between U.S. units and the guerrillas. In the last two months of 1899, U.S. casualties in 229 engagements totaled 69 killed and 302 wounded. From January to April 1900, there were 442 encounters, and 130 U.S. soldiers were killed, with 325 wounded. Filipino losses were estimated at 3,227 killed, 694 wounded, and 2,864 captured.[11]

The nature of the war had changed dramatically. During the 1899 campaigns, the U.S. soldier respected the bravery and tenacity of the Filipino rebels. Soldiers seldom felt the animosity toward the enemy that was displayed by the wartime press or citizens at home. War was their business, and they sympathized with the plight of the Filipino soldiers who were in the same trade, albeit on the opposite side. Guerrilla warfare, however, destroyed that mutual admiration. Regular soldiers felt only animosity toward the guerrillas, who engaged in "uncivilized" warfare. Widespread stories of the mutilation of American captives raised the soldiers' blood lust. Captain Jordan of the 38th Volunteer Infantry reported that one of his men had carelessly wandered a quarter mile from town unarmed; when he was later found, his body had been terribly mutilated. The Filipinos had cut off his head and carried it away as a trophy. One soldier wrote home that the Filipino guerrillas mutilated dead soldiers by cutting "their pricks off [and putting] them in their mouths, that is the kind of people they have here." He angrily proclaimed that his company would "[take] no more prisoners. They take none, and they torture our men, so we will kill wounded and all of them."[12]

The Spanish word for friend became a bitter mockery. Unarmed Filipinos shouted out "Amigo!" to the soldiers in hopes they would not be shot, but later, these same Filipinos aided the Republican Army in killing Americans. Who was a noncombatant? The dilemma was solved by a simple sinister slogan: "There are no more amigos." To many U.S. soldiers, all "niggers" or "gugus" were indistinguishable anyway. "Our fighting blood was up," one soldier wrote home, "and we all wanted to kill niggers. When we find one that is not dead, we have our bayonets." William Eggenberger, an army cook, reported that when his company captured a "suspicious nigger, we generally lose him in the swamps. That is, he is lost and he isn't lost, but he never shows up any more."[13]

Some U.S. soldiers became specialists in the "water cure," usually administered to elicit information. "A blend of Castilian cruelty and American ingenuity," Leon Wolff observed, "the water cure consisted in forcing four or five gallons of water down the throat of the captive, whose body became an object too frightful to contemplate, and then squeezing it out by kneeling on his stomach." MacArthur abhorred such tactics, and he issued strict orders to his troops against torturing or harming captives. There was never the slightest hint that he condoned or participated in any torture or murder of a prisoner of war.[14]

Although many U.S. soldiers feared, distrusted, and loathed the Filipinos, many others had ambivalent feelings. On the one hand, soldiers in the field witnessed the torture and mutilation of their wounded and dead, causing many to view the Filipinos as savage beasts. On the other hand, living in garrison towns throughout the Philippines, U.S. soldiers became familiar with the people as they interacted in stores, at the local markets, and at concerts and fiestas. Relations were normally friendly during these encounters, and many U.S. soldiers came to admire and like the Filipino people.[15]

On January 2, 1900, MacArthur received good news from the War Department—Congress had approved his promotion to brigadier general in the Regular Army. On the same day, Samuel Young and Adna R. Chaffee were also promoted to brigadier general. MacArthur's promotion was only a prelude to even greater honor and power. In early April, he received official word from the War Department that he had been selected to replace General Otis and would become the new military commander and governor of the Philippines, effective May 5, 1900.

MacArthur had hoped to be appointed the new military commander, but he had assumed Otis's replacement would be either Bates, Wheaton, or Young, all of whom outranked him in the Regular Army. Instead (perhaps with the advice of MacArthur's old mentor, Adjutant General Henry Corbin), the new secretary of war, Elihu Root, had chosen MacArthur because of his seniority in field experience in the Philippines. Most of the officers and men of the new Division of the Philippines approved, and many celebrated when they heard the news. They appreciated the fact that, because of his extensive field service, MacArthur entertained no military illusions about the war. In addition, he was an excellent field commander and an able administrator. The guerrillas were also aware of MacArthur's ability. One revolutionary wrote that MacArthur was "the most able American General," whose astuteness was to be greatly feared.[16]

MacArthur's return to Manila was a high point in his military career. The city was the center of power and culture in the Philippines. And after eighteen months

*General Arthur MacArthur, c. 1900. (MacArthur
Memorial Library, Ph-1553)*

in the field, MacArthur returned to the busy city with great military fanfare. On
May 5, 1900, Otis relinquished command in a ceremony in front of the
Ayuntamiento, the government administration building located in old Manila.
Speeches were made, artillery salutes were fired, and Otis was escorted to the dock
to take a transport home to receive a hero's welcome.[17]

MacArthur moved into *Malacañan,* a massive, two-story Moorish edifice that
had served as Otis's residence and was the residence of the Spanish governor-gen-
erals. *Malacañan's* main floor had over twenty rooms, and the upper floor contained exquisite apartments for the governor and his staff. Situated on the Pasig
River, *Malacañan* had a white-tiled veranda on the river side, where MacArthur
could sit and enjoy the cool evening breezes while watching the boats on the water. The veranda was the most delightful spot in Manila on a clear, tropical summer evening when the moon and stars shone down on the river, the ricefields, and
the nipa huts beyond.

The *Malacañan* estate included 20 acres of grounds that were shaded by wide-
leafed palm trees, interspersed with beautiful lawns and exquisite flower beds.

The outer grounds contained five or six houses for the governor's staff, a large stable for the horses, and, out of view of the main structures, a colony of nipa huts for the servants. Except on the river side, a high granite wall surrounded the estate. Sentries were posted at the entrance gate, and guards patrolled the grounds.[18]

MacArthur longed for his wife to share in his glory. With the war contained, many officers sent for their wives, and arriving businessmen and politicians were usually accompanied by their spouses as well. All wanted invitations from the governor, but MacArthur was not a social man; he needed Pinky to manage the servants and his social life. But she refused to come to Manila. Douglas was entering his second year at West Point, and Pinky decided to stay with her son. Her failure to come to Manila may have haunted their marriage.

As governor, MacArthur needed to be, in the words of William Manchester, "an economist, a political scientist, an engineer, a manufacturing executive, [and] a teacher." Although he would devote most of his time to military affairs, his job now encompassed a myriad of other tasks, including education, customs, mining, forestry, and health and sanitation, throughout the archipelago. With Manila still under martial law, he appointed General Bell as provost marshal to maintain the peace. Other departments worked to transform the city's finances, social services, and judicial system.[19]

MacArthur's command, the Division of the Philippines, included 71,727 enlisted men and 2,367 officers scattered in 502 garrisons throughout the archipelago and organized into 4 departments: Northern Luzon, commanded by General Young; Southern Luzon, under General Bates; the Visayas, headed by General Hughes; and the Mindanaos, commanded by General Kobbé.[20]

When MacArthur took over as governor, he discovered that Otis, because of his insistence on examining every minor piece of paperwork, had left a cluttered desk. MacArthur's adjutant, Colonel Crowder, and three other officers quickly went through the piles of paper, disposed of most on their own initiative, and brought only the most important items to MacArthur's attention. The new governor appointed boards of officers to look into various problems involving tariffs, immigration, land reform, and municipal charters. They then turned their recommendations over to MacArthur, who took immediate action. As his son Douglas noted, his firmest rule was to postpone nothing until tomorrow, and he answered every letter or memorandum on his desk before the day was over. MacArthur was not the swashbuckling, hard-riding cavalry type, but he *was* a good administrator. His orders for each level of operation were strict and explicit, and the channels of authority and communications were clear.[21]

It is easy to visualize the hustle and bustle of military headquarters in the *Ayuntamiento.* Supply, staff, and communications officers and district and department commanders constantly demanded MacArthur's attention. His day's work carried on into the evenings, and he often had working dinners at *Malacañan.* He permitted himself only three diversions: reading, horseback rid-

MacArthur and staff, c. 1900. (National Archives, 111-SC-93884)

ing, and cards. Over dinner, MacArthur talked with his officers about military strategies, educational policies, sanitation problems, economic development, and many other topics of colonial administration. These meetings were not open to civilians, and MacArthur expected his officers to go through channels with any suggestions. Learning from his forty years of experience in the army, he wanted everything in writing. Informal discussions revealed the proper policies, but all plans had to be carefully developed to conform with army regulations. MacArthur also studied the history of the Far East and the colonial administrations of the European powers. In the following months, through books from Hong Kong and particularly through extensive interviews, he developed his own assessment of the problems facing his administration. Under his leadership, new health and sanitation laws were implemented, legal codes were revised, schools and hospitals were built, and a tariff system was developed.

Although MacArthur wanted to actively pursue the guerrilla bands, he found his hands were tied by the policies of his predecessor, who had spread the U.S. Army into small garrisons throughout the islands. As a result, there were precious few troops available for active pursuit of the enemy. Although he believed that Otis should have concentrated on pacifying Luzon before garrisoning the less im-

portant outer islands, concerns about U.S. prestige prevented MacArthur from abandoning the garrisons established by Otis.[22]

On June 3, 1900, the day after his fifty-fifth birthday, MacArthur's euphoria over assuming this high command was dampened. On that blistering summer Sunday, William Howard Taft arrived aboard the USS *Hancock* with the second Philippine Commission.

The first Philippine Commission, headed by Jacob G. Schurman, president of Cornell University, had failed dismally in its attempts to work with Otis. President McKinley had appointed Schurman, Dean C. Worcester (a zoologist from the University of Michigan), and Charles Denby (a former U.S. minister to China) to investigate the situation in the Philippines and make recommendations for the implementation of a civilian government. The commissioners had arrived in Manila on March 4, 1899, during the spring military offensive to capture Malolos. But despite the fact that he and Admiral Dewey were also members of the commission, Otis refused to cooperate with the Schurman commission. Otis felt the president had exceeded his powers when he appointed a civilian body to advise a military commander in a war zone. Schurman did not help matters—he took an extremely liberal stance, asserting that military control should be terminated

President William McKinley (far left) and his cabinet. (Library of Congress, LC-USZ62-4251)

quickly and power transferred to civilian authority. He recommended that a cease-fire be arranged with the Republican government so that the two sides could negotiate a settlement. Because of Otis's opposition, Schurman became disillusioned and left the Philippines in July 1899. The other civilian commissioners remained until September.

In Washington in November 1899, Schurman, Denby, and Worcester worked for two months preparing a four-volume report. The report concluded that the rebellion in the Philippines would be short and that a second commission should be appointed to develop a plan to transfer the government in Manila from military to civilian authority. McKinley accepted the advice, and on February 6, 1900, he appointed Taft to head a second commission to Manila with more detailed powers than the Schurman commission had had. Several authorities believed that Otis requested to be relieved in protest.[23]

Although Worcester had been reappointed, none of the other members of the second commission had ever been in the Philippines. Besides Taft and Worcester, the members were Luke E. Wright (usually called General Wright), a Democrat and former attorney general of Tennessee; Henry Clay Ide of Vermont, former chief justice of the U.S. Court in Samoa; and Bernard Moses, a professor of his-

William Howard Taft (center), with Luke E. Wright and Henry Clay Ide. (I. Pringle, p. 212a; probably Taft Papers, Library of Congress)

tory at the University of California and a noted writer on the Spanish colonies in the Americas.[24]

The commissioners left San Francisco on April 17, 1900, and traveled via Honolulu, Yokohama, and Hong Kong to arrive in Manila Bay on June 3. They expected MacArthur to come out to the ship to greet them, but that idea did not occur to the general any more than it would have occurred to Admiral Dewey or General Otis. For MacArthur to leave his headquarters to meet the commissioners would have been comparable to the president leaving the White House to greet his own cabinet. MacArthur was the governor, and in his mind, the commissioners were merely civilian advisers who represented political interests at home.[25]

The governor followed proper protocol. He acknowledged the importance of the commissioners without acknowledging that they held any real power. He sent his personal launch out to the *Hancock,* accompanied by Colonel Crowder, his secretary, legal adviser and, for all practical purposes, his second in command. The commissioners remained on board the *Hancock* in Manila harbor for one day while MacArthur arranged for them to be properly greeted. With great pomp and circumstance, they entered the city the next morning. A cavalry detachment acted as an honor guard, while infantry- and artillerymen lined the streets from the docks all the way through the old city to the *Ayuntamiento,* where MacArthur had his headquarters.[26]

Over lunch at *Malacañan* Palace, MacArthur welcomed the commissioners to the Philippines. Although the thermometer was in the nineties, a certain frigidness pervaded the atmosphere. The commissioners did not impress the general with their knowledge of the islands nor with their physical appearance. Nicknamed "the fat men" because their average weight was 227 pounds, the commissioners were politicians, not military men. Taft was the fattest of them all. Massively overweight, he traveled with his own bathtub because hotels did not have tubs large enough to accommodate him.[27]

Taft's credentials did not impress MacArthur either. Born on September 15, 1857, in Cincinnati, Taft was a mere boy of six when Lieutenant MacArthur charged up Missionary Ridge and won the congressional Medal of Honor. Taft's father, Alphonso Taft (1810–1891), a Vermonter of Scottish descent, moved to Cincinnati and practiced law before and after the Civil War. In 1876, Alphonso Taft became President Grant's secretary of war and later served as Grant's last attorney general. In the 1880s, the elder Taft became the U.S. minister to Austria-Hungary (1882–1884) and Russia (1884–1885). Meanwhile, his son attended Yale and graduated second in his class in June 1878. He returned to Cincinnati to study law and was admitted to the Ohio bar in 1880. In March 1887, he became a judge of the Superior Court of Cincinnati. Three years later, President Harrison appointed him solicitor general. In 1892, Taft accepted an appointment to the Sixth Circuit Court of Appeals.

Taft's appointment as president of the second Philippine Commission on February 6, 1900, came as a surprise and was based not on displayed ability but on his friendship with Elihu Root, the new secretary of war. A highly successful New York corporation lawyer, Root had become secretary of war in July 1899. Young and energetic, he was known for his incisive mind and his coolly deliberate manner.

MacArthur treated Taft with the same courtesy he would have extended any political appointee who knew absolutely nothing about the Philippines. He did not dislike Taft—few men did—but he did resent the commission. As a constitutional lawyer and a former member of the Adjutant General's Office, MacArthur assumed that the new commission was primarily an advisory body and that he, as military commander and governor of the Philippines, retained veto power over all the commission's actions. Like Otis before him, MacArthur did not believe that the president could, under the Constitution, appoint a civilian commission to command the military in a war zone.

MacArthur quickly learned that Taft disagreed. As the highest civil authority in the islands, Taft assumed that his commission's powers were greater than that of the military governor, and he expected MacArthur to do the bidding of the commission. In Taft's view, although MacArthur was the military commander and chief executive officer in the islands, the Philippine Commission was comparable to the United States Congress. Taft's directives from Secretary Root stated clearly that the commissioners would assume legislative and budget powers on September 1, 1900; at that time, MacArthur's civilian authority would be restricted to implementing laws passed by the commission. As president of the commission, Taft would therefore become the ranking authority.

Since the powers of the commission were drawn up by Taft in consultation with Root, he claimed his interpretation was correct. He refused to accept MacArthur's authority and wrote his brother that although the army was a necessary evil, it was not "adapted to administration of civil government and ... the sooner it be made auxiliary the better. We shall not be in control for sixty to ninety days, but we shall be in control when the time comes."[28]

Taft's attempt to usurp power irritated MacArthur, but to his credit, he did not openly complain about the presence of the commissioners. He attempted to work with them and to deal with the difficulties caused by inadequate instructions from Washington. When invited to attend commission meetings, the general accepted, and in his dealings with the commission, he was formal and reserved but not obstructive. He agreed to assist the commissioners in their endeavors and advised them to seek his aid when it was needed.

In the following days, MacArthur helped the commissioners find houses and provided them with a small, temporary office in the *Ayuntamiento*. When Taft complained that the homes were in disrepair and the office was too small for five men plus the innumerable clerks the commission would eventually need to hire, MacArthur informed Taft the best houses in Manila were already occupied; he assigned an officer to supervise the repairs of the commissioners' residences to make them more comfortable. As for the commission's office, MacArthur acknowledged the problem but informed Taft that there was no other space available in the *Ayuntamiento*. Because MacArthur used the building as his military headquarters, various military departments had long since occupied the best offices, and he refused to eject his officers simply to provide the commissioners with more space. As a compromise, he offered the commissioners plush offices in another public building in the *Intramuros*. Taft rejected the offer, feeling, perhaps correctly, that the commission's office should be in the most important government building in Manila.[29]

MacArthur devoted the majority of his time to military matters and disliked dealing with civilians, but he did try to cooperate with the commissioners. He listened to their complaints and resolved many of their problems. In their letters home, the commissioners praised the general for his obvious organizational skills. Taft observed that MacArthur was kept busy solving the tremendous problems associated with furnishing supplies for 500 different posts in a "country infested with guerrilla bands and in a country practically without roads [where escorts] were necessary, and combine with that the duty of chasing the guerrilla bands from point to point in the most impassable mountains, you can see what a tremendous task the army had."[30]

In letters to his brother, his wife, and to Secretary Root, Taft wrote that MacArthur was polite and considerate to the commissioners. He characterized the general as a pleasant, self-contained man with a genial but candid manner. MacArthur's abilities impressed Taft, and that impression was reinforced after Taft talked to several general officers in Manila who described MacArthur as an excellent military commander. MacArthur was not dashing like Lawton, but he was a clearheaded, efficient leader.[31]

Despite the praise, however, it was soon apparent that Taft and MacArthur disagreed on nearly every aspect of rule in the Philippines. Within days of his arrival, Taft was absolutely certain he knew more about the Philippines than MacArthur, who had been serving there for almost two years. While MacArthur insisted that the Filipinos still desired independence, Taft touted the Republican party line on the Philippines, and in letters home, he maintained that the rebellion was almost over. In reality, Taft was merely being a good politician. The elections of 1900 loomed on the horizon, and the upheaval in the Philippines haunted the McKinley administration. The Republican party wanted to convince the U.S. public that Otis had already won the war and that most Filipinos were overjoyed to be under U.S. control. A monumental effort was mounted to convert these fictions into reality for the electorate.

When Otis arrived back in the United States on June 3, 1900, Republican politicians greeted him with praise for his tremendous military victories and the triumph of his forces over barbarism in the Philippines. Otis loved the attention and played the role to the hilt. He pompously strutted down the gangplank in San Francisco to the tune of "See the Conquering Hero Comes," then exchanged salutes and inspected the troops with General William Shafter, who had assembled an honor guard for him. Otis would make his way slowly across the nation as guest of honor and conquering hero at increasingly elaborate ceremonies. The gala celebrations outstripped the honors rendered to Admiral Dewey on his triumphant return. It was as if the country desperately wanted to share in Otis's self-deception as he repeatedly declared in one city after another that the war in the Philippines was over. When he reached Washington, any doubts were washed away in a sea of toasts to his victory and in the thunderous applause a jointly convened Congress gave him during a standing ovation. President McKinley invited Otis to the White House and congratulated him on his splendid military achievements.[32]

MacArthur's reports, of course, contradicted Otis's rosy depiction of the situation in the Philippines. Even Stuart Miller, who seldom praised the military, admitted that MacArthur had the virtue of being a "realist who unlike his predecessor, refused to delude himself about the course of the war." The truth was that rebel attacks had not slackened during the rainy season, and MacArthur recounted hundreds of incidents in his official reports. Fortunately, most of the contacts were merely light skirmishes in military terms. Filipino guerrillas fired on garrison towns, set booby traps, and attacked U.S. patrols. Although American casualties were small in each rebel attack, the number of U.S. dead and wounded mounted: By June 1900, U.S. casualties in the guerrilla war had reached 524 men wounded and 150 killed. As Otis assured the American people the rebellion was over, guerrilla attacks actually escalated. During the summer, U.S. garrisons suffered 344 casualties, 118 killed and 226 wounded, and MacArthur estimated that from December 1899 to September 1900, 3,227 rebels had been killed, 694 wounded, and 2,864 captured. In one year, the U.S. Army had more hostile contacts with the Filipino guerrillas and suffered as many casualties as it had during the Indian wars from 1865 to 1890.[33]

MacArthur did not gloss over the rebellion in his official reports, nor did he support the myth that Filipinos were delighted with U.S. rule. He believed that although the majority of Filipinos publicly supported the U.S. occupation, they were, in reality, loyal to the revolution. This loyalty was almost universal. "That such unity exists," he wrote in his official reports, "is an undeniable fact."[34]

MacArthur supported his country's emerging international goals, but, as Carol Petillo observed, "he ... refused to deny the true nature of the undertaking. He knew that his Philippine adversaries had both the reasons and the ability to make America's quest for President McKinley's 'benevolent assimilation' a long and bloody struggle ... politically as well as militarily. In these assessments, MacArthur proved more farsighted than most of the American policy makers involved."[35]

The primary disadvantage facing the revolutionaries was disharmony, not lack of popular support. If the various Filipino factions had coalesced, they might have achieved independence. Unfortunately, their leaders disagreed on every issue, ranging from military strategy to religion, politics, economics, and morality. They fought among themselves as much as they challenged the policies of the United States.[36]

Taft disagreed with MacArthur's assessment and wrote Secretary Root that the general was too pessimistic in his view of the situation. "He regards all the people as opposed to the U.S. forces and looks at his task as one of conquering eight million recalcitrant, treacherous, and cruel people." But according to historian Henry A. Fant, "Nothing could be further from the truth. ... MacArthur felt no desire to crush the natives under a military heel and rule them in terror. He was a firm believer in democracy."[37]

Taft "drove his team at top speed." As president of the commission, he assigned other commissioners to spend the summer amassing information. As Stanley Karnow reported:

> They labored ten or twelve hours a day in the torrid heat, interviewing Filipinos, Americans, and other witnesses. Dean Worcester covered agriculture, mining and health. Luke Wright, an attorney, focused on the militia, the police and criminal codes while Henry Ide, the former Samoa judge, studied courts, banking and currency, and Bernard Moses, the historian, surveyed education. Taft reserved for him-

self the touchiest topics: the civil service, the disposition of public lands and the status of the remaining Spanish friars.[38]

The majority of Filipino witnesses were from the educated, wealthy *ilustrado* class, but the commissioners were qualified men, and as Lewis E. Gleeck points out, "There was nothing in the least naive about either their selection or their interrogation of those who appeared before them, as a prolonged reading of the minutes of the commission will reveal." The *ilustrado* constituted the upper stratum of Filipino society and most supported the independence movement, but they also wanted stability to protect their wealth. If the Americans fulfilled their promises of sharing authority and establishing an enlightened civil government, many of the *ilustrados* would become reluctant revolutionaries.[39]

Though they were among many bigoted Americans in Manila, MacArthur and Taft shared one trait—they displayed no racial prejudice. Taft entertained many wealthy Filipinos, and they responded by inviting him to social gatherings, where he was at his best. Accompanied by his wife, Helen, he gathered friends in the Filipino community as the local aristocracy welcomed a fellow aristocrat to their homes. The Filipinos enjoyed this big, friendly man, perhaps more than they liked the stiff governor who shunned social functions.[40]

MacArthur often ignored the commissioners. Without asking for their advice, he issued his first major proclamation on June 21, 1900, offering amnesty to any Filipino insurgent who surrendered to U.S. forces within ninety days and swore allegiance to the government of the United States. He offered 30 Mexican dollars for surrendered rifles, and as a further enticement, guaranteed to transport any Filipino revolutionaries who surrendered anywhere in the archipelago. MacArthur also recognized the need to treat the officers of the defeated Republican Army with dignity. The Filipinos were a proud people, and their officers would be accorded the respect due their rank. Any high-ranking officer or member of the Republican government who wished to confer with the military governor or with the U.S. Philippine Commission was to be permitted to visit Manila and was, as far as possible, to be provided with transportation for that purpose. After the amnesty period expired, any Filipino captured with arms would be classified as a bandit, or *ladrone,* not a Republican soldier. All bandits would be tried in U.S. military courts as murderers or common criminals.[41]

Taft criticized MacArthur's amnesty proclamation as too conciliatory and advocated a hard-line military policy to speed up pacification. A number of MacArthur's officers also urged a harsher military strategy. General Young, commander of the Department of Northern Luzon, proposed a policy of severe retaliations for the "constant sniping, small ambushes, and clever booby traps" claiming the lives of U.S. soldiers. General Wheaton agreed and proposed "swift methods of destruction"; he sneered at MacArthur's policy of "going with a sword in one hand [and] a pacifist pamphlet" in the other, adding that "you can't put down a rebellion by throwing confetti and sprinkling perfume." He urged that "bandits, spies, assassins, and murderers" be executed. Even J. Franklin Bell, the provost marshal of Manila and one of MacArthur's favorite officers, agreed with Young and Wheaton. He requested permission to arrest any Filipino in Manila suspected of supporting the rebellion. In the outer areas, Bell suggested that MacArthur establish free-fire zones by moving noncombatants into concentration camps in areas of military operations, and he wanted to destroy all foodstuffs that might support the guerrillas in the field.[42]

Taft wrote Root that he believed it was "time to put our foot down on leniency." If MacArthur did not want to execute captured Filipino bandits, he should hold them in concentration camps while he deported the leaders to Guam. Taft advised MacArthur to confiscate the property of Republican leaders like Aguinaldo and make them suffer economically for their participation in the rebellion.[43]

MacArthur listened to his officers and Commissioner Taft, but he was reluctant to implement the policies they recommended, partially because he did not wish to be remembered as "the butcher" of the Philippines and partially because he did not believe military actions alone would end the rebellion. The islands could be ruled by force, he believed, but there would be unending discord, conspiracy, and strife. The only way to achieve U.S. hopes and aspirations was through conciliation. "We have to govern them," MacArthur declared, and "government by force alone cannot be satisfactory to Americans." Benevolent and humanitarian action was needed to win the enduring friendship of the great mass of Filipinos. MacArthur believed the Filipinos should be in charge of building their country, and he did not want to interfere with their culture or customs, an attitude his son Douglas would later share in regard to the Japanese. He hoped that they would regard the United States as a protector rather than as a conqueror.[44]

MacArthur admitted there were many bandits in the Philippines that deserved execution if captured: In times of war, bands of thieves, murderers, and bullies always take advantage of the accompanying chaos. Aguinaldo and other high Republican officers issued constant orders prohibiting rape, brigandage, and robbery, but these proclamations were no more effective than orders emanating from MacArthur's headquarters. Thus, bandits continued to pillage for fun and profit. While portraying themselves as revolutionaries, the criminal element took advantage of the situation and robbed the people blind. MacArthur made a clear distinction between bandits and true Republican soldiers. He believed bandits should be executed for murder and extortion, but he refused to execute true Filipino patriots. He also refused to confiscate rebel property or deport captured leaders to Guam. He wanted to treat captured Republican leaders with respect and to hold out the hand of peace.[45]

In early July, MacArthur met secretly with General Jose Alejandrino, a top Republican leader, to discuss convening a peace conference. Unfortunately, Alejandrino demanded that the governor accept Philippine sovereignty before such a conference was held. MacArthur replied that U.S. sovereignty could not be questioned, but if the Republican leaders would surrender under the amnesty program, he personally promised to help establish a civilian government that would guarantee Filipinos the personal liberties guaranteed in the U.S. Constitution. "Not enough," was Alejandrino's reply. The Republican leaders needed concessions, not promises—they had heard enough promises from the Spaniards. MacArthur reluctantly terminated the discussions.[46]

The governor's problem was how to reconcile U.S. supremacy with the national aspirations of the people. After interviewing a number of Filipino leaders in Manila, MacArthur concluded that there were many areas of possible compromise. He became convinced that if he granted the Filipinos their personal liberties and treated them in a benevolent and humanitarian fashion, the rebellion would end. The Filipino intelligentsia impressed him as equal to any group of educated men in the world, and he consequently held them in high esteem. "American institutions are on trial," MacArthur told his staff, "not the Filipino people."[47]

As the first step in a good-faith contract with the Filipinos, MacArthur rejected the implementation of any draconian measures of martial law in Manila. Under orders from the War Department, press censorship continued, but MacArthur refused to curtail freedom of speech, except to prohibit any speech advocating the violent overthrow of the U.S. government in the Philippines. He allowed Filipino civic and fraternal groups (and even secret societies) to continue their meetings as long as they pledged not to use the meetings to support the rebellion. He also encouraged Filipino leaders to speak out publicly. When Provost Marshal Bell objected, seeing trouble ahead, the general responded by saying the Filipinos could have "a mass meeting on every corner in Manila where they could utter any sentiments they wished," except, of course, the violent overthrow of the government. The Filipinos were not to be treated as slaves nor exploited; rather, they would be treated as all citizens of the United States were treated. MacArthur ordered his staff to greet all Filipino visitors to *Malacañan* with respect, and he encouraged all his officers to form friendships with the local aristocracy. In sum, the Filipinos were not enemies but potential friends to be converted to MacArthur's brand of republicanism. In time, a festive mood settled over Manila as the people began to enjoy their unrestricted liberties.[48]

MacArthur worked on expanding a new educational program staffed by volunteer officers, which he considered the backbone for developing republican institutions in the Philippines. The Filipino people were hungry for schools, and MacArthur fed that hunger. In all matters touching schools, there was a fortunate coincidence of U.S. interest and Filipino aspirations, and education programs received cooperation even in areas of major guerrilla activity. MacArthur personally edited a condensed history of the United States, beginning with the discovery of America. Published in Spanish and English, the book explained the U.S. Constitution and government structure. The English edition proved more popular than the Spanish, for many Filipinos recognized the need to learn the English language as quickly as possible. Schools were expanded as soldiers, some still on active duty, volunteered to teach English to any Filipino who wished to learn.[49]

Taft scoffed at MacArthur's belief that the Filipinos could quickly absorb the principles of democracy and begin to rule themselves under a republican form of government. He felt that the vast majority of Filipinos were "nothing but grown up children who would need training for fifty or a hundred years." In a letter to Secretary Root, Taft observed:

> The population of the Islands is made up of a vast mass of ignorant, superstitious people, well intentioned, light-hearted, temperate, somewhat cruel, domestic and fond of their families, and deeply wedded to the Catholic Church. They are easily influenced by speeches from a small class of educated mestizos, who have acquired a good deal of superficial knowledge of the general principles of free government, who are able to mouth sentences supposed to embody constitutional law. ... They are generally lacking in moral character, are ... prone to yield to any pecuniary consideration, and are difficult persons out of whom to make an honest government.[50]

Taft mocked MacArthur for his condescending attitude that only he could understand the Filipino mind. The general agreed that his conclusions were tentative ones, but he believed he knew more about the Filipinos than Taft. Taft, in turn, resented MacArthur's patronizing lectures and thought the general was "haughty, arrogant, and conceited."[51]

The controversy between Taft and MacArthur retreated into the background when a rebellion erupted in China. In early June 1900, the Society of the Right Harmonious Fists, more commonly referred to as the Boxers, threatened foreigners in northern China. The Boxers took over the city of Peking and entrapped all the foreign diplomatic legations in the city. Supported by a conservative Chinese government controlled by the Empress Dowager Tzu Hsi, the Boxers visualized the death or expulsion of all foreigners in China. For the next three months, the prime topic on President McKinley's table was not the Philippines but U.S. participation in the China Relief Expedition.[52]

Secretary Root considered dispatching troops to China from the Philippines, but the possible consequences worried him. He telegraphed MacArthur for his opinion. The general wired back that he could immediately dispatch troops and offered to lead the expedition to China. A new war was on the horizon, and MacArthur wanted to go, but he advised Root that a permanent decrease in troops in the Philippines could have a disastrous effect on the suppression of the rebellion. "In sentiment, the natives are united against us," MacArthur again warned. If his forces were depleted for the China Expedition, security in the smaller towns in the Philippines would be threatened, and some of the U.S. garrisons were certain to be attacked. The Philippine Commission telegraphed Root substantiating MacArthur's position. In contradiction to their public stance, in which they proclaimed the backbone of the revolt had been broken, the commissioners reported that the rebels were "discouraged, but a favorable outcome would be hindered by further reducing the army and relaxing the military grasp."[53]

Root dispatched only the 9th Infantry from the Philippines, indicated to MacArthur he was too important in his post in Manila, and appointed Brigadier General Chaffee to command the China Relief Expedition. In the next couple of months, MacArthur provided intelligence, transport ships, and supplies for the U.S. men fighting in China. One of his staff officers, Lieutenant Colonel John S. Mallory, was in Hong Kong investigating the "Filipino junta" when the Boxer Rebellion erupted in north China. MacArthur sent Mallory to Tientsin. With support from U.S. Navy Captain Bowman McCalla, Mallory provided MacArthur with detailed reports on the situation in China, and MacArthur forwarded these reports to the Adjutant General's Office. An international rescue force of 18,000 men (2,100 Americans, 8,000 Japanese, 4,800 Russians, 3,000 British, 800 French, 58 Austrians, and 53 Italians) left Tientsin on August 4 and marched toward Peking, arriving on August 14 to relieve the besieged international legations.[54]

Soldiers in Manila celebrated the news of victory in China, which temporarily silenced the anti-imperialist critics in the United States. The Boxer Rebellion reinforced the imperialist argument that the United States needed a military base in the Philippines to protect U.S. interests in Asia.

For General MacArthur, one delightful outcome of the Boxer Rebellion was a visit to Manila by his older son, Navy Ensign Arthur MacArthur. Twenty-four years old, Arthur had graduated from the Naval Academy in 1896. In July 1898, he was onboard the gunboat USS *Vixen* during the battle of Santiago, when the Spanish fleet had been annihilated in Cuban waters. On his way to China, Ensign MacArthur stopped briefly in Manila to see his father.[55]

The general must have been thrilled to see his son, for the evidence indicates he loved Arthur deeply and that the affection was reciprocal. MacArthur probably displayed his son with great pride at staff dinners and at the Army and Navy Club in Manila, and the handsome young ensign likely was equally proud to be the governor's son. The evidence also suggests Ensign MacArthur was much like his father—a serious, proud, capable officer who would rise to high rank in the navy. Ensign MacArthur's Manila visit was brief, and his ship soon left for China.[56]

While General MacArthur was busy supporting the U.S. effort in China, Taft concentrated on completing the commission's study on the situation in the Philippines. Late in August, at the cost of $40,000, the commissioners cabled their findings to Root. The report proclaimed the rebellion was over, with only a few bandits remaining in the field, and it recommended the establishment of civilian government as soon as possible. The commission was instructed to begin the process on September 1, 1900, by assuming legislative powers.[57]

Although he did not wish to interfere with the Taft Commission, MacArthur had no intention of surrendering any executive or military power. His instructions from Washington were that on September 1, he was to relinquish control of the civilian budget to the commission, which would function as a legislative body with the authority to fix taxes, appropriate funds for civil projects, and assume control of civil government in pacified areas. On August 30, MacArthur met with the commissioners and informed them that, as governor and military commander, he retained all executive and military authority. No law could be implemented without his approval, and all military and civilian personnel came under his direct authority.[58]

Taft protested and declared that the commission had the power to enact any legislation pertaining to civil affairs and that, as the governor, MacArthur was required to implement any law passed by the commission. Taft informed MacArthur that he had drawn up the commission's instructions, in consultation with Secretary Root, and that these instructions placed the commission in charge of all civil matters. He expressed the idea that while it was MacArthur's job as military governor to curtail the Filipino rebels, it was Taft's job as president of the commission to implement civilian rule. MacArthur would retain control over the military while Taft became the de facto civil governor. MacArthur, he said, could not veto laws passed by the commission—only Taft had that power.[59]

MacArthur diasgreed. While the Philippines remained under martial law, "military authority was paramount and exclusive." As the military governor, he felt he held absolute power over all civilian and military personnel. The commission could advise him, but it could not act without his approval. MacArthur said he would obey any direct order from the president or the secretary of war, but he doubted that they intended to circumvent his military authority. Interpreting the Constitution very narrowly, he asserted that neither the president nor the secretary of war had the power to appoint a civilian authority in a military district. The creation of a civilian government required an act of Congress, not an order from the president of the United States acting as commander in chief.[60]

Taft fumed over MacArthur's interpretation of the Constitution and poked fun at his legal arguments. An expert on constitutional law, Taft expected to be appointed to the Supreme Court on his return to the United States. According to him, the military authority of the president could be exercised either through civil agents or military officers unless Congress passed legislation restricting the president. Thus, because President McKinley had delegated all civil authority in the Philippines to the Taft Commission, MacArthur was obligated to accept the commission's authority.

MacArthur requested clarification from Washington, and Taft wrote Root that it was "a curious phase of political human nature to me to observe that men who have not the slightest knowledge of legal principles feel entirely at home in the construction of the constitution and in using its limitations to support their views and to nullify action, the wisdom of which they dispute."[61]

Although Taft thought MacArthur was an amateur where the law was concerned, he was not. MacArthur, was licensed to practice law in Wisconsin and had served in the Adjutant General's Office for nine years. Equally significant was his upbringing and association with Judge Arthur MacArthur, who had been an associate justice of the Supreme Court of the District of Columbia for seventeen years, 1870 to 1887. His father had been the greatest intellectual influence in General

MacArthur's life, and the general had often consulted him on legal questions until the judge's death in 1896. But, silent as usual about his background, MacArthur never felt obligated to list his credentials for Taft.

MacArthur's objections to the Taft Commission echoed the feeling of many military men and some members of Congress. Prior to the appointment of the commission, Senator John C. Spooner of Wisconsin introduced a bill in the Senate to grant the president the power to establish a civil government in the Philippines, but the bill had met strong resistance because some senators, such as George F. Hoar of Massachusetts, opposed any law that implied the United States intended to remain in the islands. Since MacArthur maintained contacts in Wisconsin, Spooner's home state, he was fully aware of the progress of the Spooner Bill in Congress. And while Congress debated, President McKinley ruled the islands in his role as commander in chief rather than as the civilian leader of the United States.[62]

Taft and MacArthur never agreed on who had final authority, and despite efforts to clarify the issue, instructions from Washington remained vague. Taft wanted the commission to legislate and implement all programs in the civilian area. He refused to acknowledge that a war was still in progress and that the islands were subject to martial law rather than civilian rule. Meanwhile, MacArthur jealously guarded the prerogatives of his office, declaring that the commission could legislate but that the governor's office had exclusive executive powers.[63]

Despite the disagreements, MacArthur assisted the commission in establishing civil government in pacified areas. In most of the towns and villages of central Luzon, municipal governments were established with elected local officials. A town *presidente* and council controlled public schools, sanitation, police, and other civil functions under the close supervision of the local U.S. military commander, who retained the power to veto any action by the local Filipino officials. The franchise was restricted to wealthy property owners, and only about 5 percent of the population could vote. MacArthur did not, however, trust the local Filipino councils and correctly believed that many were controlled by Aguinaldo's Republican Army, which established shadow governments often composed of the same officials.[64]

Generals Young and Wheaton opposed the introduction of civil government in their areas and suggested that military government be maintained for some time to come. If the military commander of an area was forced to negotiate tactics with civilians, then the war effort was doomed—democracy in a war area was a non sequitur, and the establishment of civil government in areas under rebel attack would be a mere facade for public consumption back in the United States. MacArthur agreed and refused to initiate civil government in areas where the Republican Army was active, but in all pacified areas, he ordered his department commanders to work closely with Taft's civil appointees and avoid friction unless the public safety was threatened.[65]

Soldiers in the field feared that civilian authority might be implemented too quickly, for they were concerned about renewed guerrilla attacks. They also resented Taft's assertion that the war was over, with nothing but a few bandits remaining. They ridiculed Taft for referring to the Filipinos as "little brown brothers." The phrase drew sneers from the soldiers because these alleged kinfolk were killing and mutilating U.S. troops. To the tune of "Son of a Gamboleer," the men in uniform sang:

> *I am only a common soldier in the blasted Philippines.*
> *They say I've got brown brothers here, but I dunno know what it means.*
> *I like the word fraternity, but still I draw the line.*
> *He may be a brother of Big Bill Taft,*
> *But he ain't no brother of mine.*[66]

One soldier wrote home that Taft should have been forced to join the army for six months as a private to personally see if the Filipinos were little brown brothers. MacArthur's sympathies were with his men. Taft's constant assertion that the war was over except for a few bandits irritated MacArthur, who read the daily casualty lists.[67]

The power dispute between Taft and MacArthur disrupted the government for months. A typical example involved the powers of appointment. Taft asked MacArthur to detach a number of skilled military officers to fill civilian positions since there were few civilians in Manila with comparable abilities and experience. The general graciously agreed to do so if the officers could be released from military duties. But Taft then proceeded to appoint an officer to a civilian position without obtaining prior approval from military headquarters. MacArthur exploded and canceled the appointment: Only the military commander could detach military officers to civilian duty.

Taft protested. He claimed that, as president of the commission, he could detach any military officer to special duty in a civilian capacity without obtaining MacArthur's approval. He informed the general that "the power and duty of the Commission under its instructions to appoint all officers in the civil service are express, and no limitations are made upon its power when appointments are to be made of military officers to that service."[68]

MacArthur sent Taft a blistering reply. All army personnel, even officers temporarily working as civilian administrators, remained members of the U.S. Army and on active duty under the orders of the commanding general. Further, MacArthur stated, any officer accepting a civilian appointment without the approval of military headquarters would be removed from the active list and asked to resign his commission.[69]

Taft stewed but backed off. Later, the issue resurfaced when the commission appointed H. Phelps Whitmarsh to be the civilian governor in the province of Benguet in northern Luzon. Colonel Robert Duvall, the military commander of Benguet, became bitter enemies with Whitmarsh. Duvall blocked municipal governments in many of the villages because of guerrilla activities, but Whitmarsh claimed the areas were pacified. Duvall received MacArthur's support, and the general threatened to remove Whitmarsh from office if he continued to interfere with the military commander of the area.[70]

Taft objected. Although he had reluctantly admitted that MacArthur controlled all military personnel in the Philippines, he was certain that only the commission had the authority to appoint or remove civilian personnel. The general disagreed. As governor, he had the power to remove any civilian who refused to obey his orders. Taft and MacArthur referred the issue to the secretary of war, and to Taft's surprise, Root supported MacArthur and telegraphed Manila that the general had veto powers over all civilian appointments.[71]

Despite Root's telegram, Taft continued to grasp for power, and MacArthur continued to block his moves. Publicly, relations between Taft and MacArthur remained friendly, but privately, their exchanges grew colder through September and October. Taft continued to attack MacArthur in devastating letters to Secretary Root, his pipeline in Washington. Root, in turn, showed Taft's letters to President McKinley; although neither man had met MacArthur, they sympathized with Taft's problems—MacArthur appeared to be a difficult man to deal with and could be petty when he thought his powers were being threatened.

Critics of MacArthur seem to assume that he should have known Taft was destined to become secretary of war and eventually president of the United States. In that context, the general appears as an obstinate, patronizing, condescending military martinet. "His efforts now seem to have been barren of hope," William Manchester observed later, "but that is because there is a law of inertia in history: whatever happened usually seems to have been inevitable." But in 1900, "Taft was a placid star," Ralph E. Minger stated, "not a comet against the judicial and political sky." Even Taft was surprised when President McKinley appointed him as president of the commission based on Root's recommendation.[72]

Taft maintained his contact with Root through weekly letters that described conditions in the islands and his problems with MacArthur. He also wrote lengthy letters to his wife, his brother, and his friends. He packed his letters with interesting details and gossip about the people he met. The details were fascinating, and his character studies were delightfully entertaining. Taft loved to analyze people, and his style was witty and cutting. Not wishing anyone to proclaim him unfair, he invariably listed the good traits of the people with whom he associated before lowering the hammer with devastating results. This technique made Taft appear fair and objective in his analysis, but his criticisms were always more pronounced than his praise. MacArthur was one of Taft's constant targets, and he accurately described both the general's weaknesses and his strengths. Taft told Root that MacArthur had many good traits, but (and there was always a "but" in Taft's letters) he believed the general lacked "vigorous initiative" and was "naturally timid" and "set in his opinions." Although MacArthur was a courtly, kind man without racial prejudices, he also lacked a sense of humor and had "the weakness of thinking himself a profound and philosophical thinker [who] assumes the position of lecturing us everytime he gets an opportunity." According to Taft, MacArthur also lacked any great consideration for the views of others and was firmly convinced of the need to maintain military etiquette. Taft complained that it was trying "not to feel that we can consult freely and make suggestions concerning our common purpose without arousing a small but intense feeling our suggestions may transgress the line between civil and military operations."[73]

Scholars who have analyzed the Taft-MacArthur controversy, such as Rowland T. Berthoff and Ralph Minger, have usually relied heavily on Taft's letters in their evaluations. Although they treat MacArthur more gently than Taft did, their characterizations of him largely reflect Taft's impressions. Even William Manchester, who was favorably impressed with MacArthur, accepted Taft's view of the general's character and described him as "extremely jealous of his prerogatives" and "ready to take offense" at the slightest question to his authority.[74]

Scholars are also fond of quoting MacArthur's adjutant, Colonel Crowder, as saying that "Arthur MacArthur was the most flamboyantly egotistic man I had ever seen—until I met his son." But as pointed out by Clark Lee and Richard Henschel, "This is one of those pat and easily quotable descriptions that is repeated again and again, regardless of its accuracy."[75]

Taft's letters are persuasive but unfair. As Henry Fant, supported by Carol Petillo, observed, "Taft's remarks about the general have been magnified to such a degree as to make MacArthur appear as a military redneck." This portrait of the general as a "stuffy, proper martinet harassing the big, bluff negotiator [Taft] is overdrawn, the product of stereotypical assessments rather than a close examination of the facts of the case."[76]

Taft's catty style is very quotable, but he often exaggerated personality characteristics to entertain his audiences, and he was a good hater. He once denounced his brother Horace as a "theoretical pedant," and his cheerful manner was deceptive. "Like many fat men who outwardly appear to be jolly," Stanley Karnow observed, Taft "had a simmering and sometimes uncontrollable temper." He expected to persuade people to agree with him, and when he failed, he became privately angry while remaining jovial on social occasions. He also refused to read any news articles that commented negatively on his actions, and privately, he was an unyielding man. Years later, Theodore Roosevelt called Taft "one of the best haters" he knew.[77]

That said, there were at least elements of truth in Taft's description of MacArthur's personality. The general could be pompous, he did not like civilian interference, and he had an annoying habit of spouting grandiose generalizations couched in magniloquent, tedious prose. The same criticisms were later leveled at Douglas MacArthur during World War II and even later when he was Supreme Commander of Allied Powers (SCAP) in Japan. Franklin Roosevelt's secretary of the interior, Harold L. Ickes, echoed Taft's words when he described Douglas as "the type of man who thinks that when he gets to heaven, God will step down from the great white throne and bow him into His vacated seat." Certainly, the general, like his son, was "a bit of a peacock to begin with, and he deliberately played the part of an emperor in the belief that it would impress the 'Oriental mentality,' and to Taft's chagrin, he got away with his presumptions."[78]

MacArthur's extraordinary abilities as an officer were not matched with equal brilliance in his dealings with civilians. He preferred working with other military officers and usually remained very formal with people outside of the exclusive military club. The general also preferred the company of men and seldom gave social functions to which women were invited. William Manchester's description of Douglas MacArthur holds true of the general: He was almost "painfully shy in intimate social situations, wretched in the easy give-and-take of idle conversation, jollity, and good-fellowship." Even with other officers, MacArthur was seldom totally open. He believed, as had George Washington, that superior officers should not fraternize with subordinates: Fraternization could lead to slackness and discipline problems. Later, while serving in Japan, Douglas followed his father's example and expected his subordinates to keep a "respectful distance."[79]

MacArthur did not regard fraternization with civilians as part of his job. Though several of the commissioners invited him to dinner, he entertained only what Taft called a "select military circle" at *Malacañan*. This was an error on MacArthur's part but one that most other military men of the era would also have committed. The U.S. Army and Navy were, as Edmund Morris noted, "proud, hierarchical institutions, traditionally resistant to change and contemptuous of civilian authority." If Pinky had come to the Philippines, she could have acted as the governor's official hostess and practiced all the social skills she had learned in her Virginia girlhood. Because she recognized the advantages of networking with political as well as military contacts, she would have insisted that the general entertain Taft and the other commissioners. She would have charmed them and formed relationships with their wives. And she would have loved it. But Pinky felt Douglas needed her more. Besides, she never quite realized until it was too late how important her husband had become.[80]

Manchester, in his biography of Douglas MacArthur, observed that "as a commander he was a model officer"—an attribute equally true of Arthur MacArthur. And Manchester's description of Douglas's relations with the native population could also have been written about the elder MacArthur, who lacked Taft's open, democratic approach. The general "was less popular with the American community, but the Filipinos loved him. His very aloofness and inscrutability inspired respect in them. He talked to them, not in military jargon, but in spiritual terms, equating patriotism with morality, freedom, and Christianity. Above all he was to them a cherished, enigmatic father figure."[81]

When meeting with the commissioners, MacArthur often delivered discourses on Filipino society, the U.S. Constitution, and a myriad of other topics. He considered himself an intellectual and a profound thinker. Douglas was much like his father, and Dwight D. Eisenhower accurately described both MacArthurs when he observed that Douglas regarded "reading (and talking) in all subjects the most delightful form of occupation; he was a self-educated man [and] he could talk with informed interest on almost any subject." Actually, "discuss is hardly the correct word," Eisenhower complained. "Discussion suggests dialogue and the General's conversations were usually monologues. ... Unquestionably, the General's fluency and wealth of information came from his phenomenal memory, without parallel in my knowledge. Reading through a draft of ... a paper once, he could immediately repeat whole chunks of it verbatim."[82]

Other observers also noted the similarities between father and son. William L. Shirer described Douglas as "forceful, articulate, thoughtful, even a bit philosophical, and well read." He added, "Only his arrogance bothered me." John Gunther echoed the sentiment when he wrote, "MacArthur's qualities are so indisputably great in his own field that it comes as something of a shock to explore the record and find that in others he can be narrow, gullible, and curiously naive. He treads on unsure ground when he steps off the path of what he really knows [and in Gunther's opinion, MacArthur knew very little about] politics and the realm of news." C. L. Sulzberger reported in his diaries that what Douglas said "was a curious cocktail of earnest, decent, hopeful philosophy; a certain amount of rather long-range thinking and a good deal of highly impractical poppycock."[83]

The elder MacArthur's reports and his vocabulary, written and oral, illustrated both his delight in expounding on grand philosophical questions and the joy he had in using words that displayed his erudition. Shortly after meeting Taft, MacArthur noted that he objected to the commission as "mediatizing" his position as military governor. Although a Yale man, Taft had to fetch a dictionary, and even then, he did not correctly interpret the general's meaning. Taft read that *mediatize* meant to reduce someone to a vassal, and he interpreted MacArthur's use of the word to mean that the general felt he had been "deeply and personally humiliated" by the president's appointment of the commission. Perhaps Taft did not have an unabridged dictionary, which defines the word more as intervening agent. The word source is German and refers to the time of the Holy Roman Empire when a state or prince was reduced from status of an immediate vassal of the empire to that of a mediate vassal. Later, *mediatize* came to mean the annexation of a smaller state to a larger one, leaving the ruler his title but only some of his authority. Since the commission came under the authority of the War Department, MacArthur interpreted it as an intervening authority between the military governor and the secretary of war. But Taft missed MacArthur's point—that the appointment of the civilian commission insulted the military and that, as the military representative in Manila, MacArthur felt obligated to represent the military position.[84]

Interpreting MacArthur's use of *mediatize* as personal humiliation, Taft inferred that MacArthur was considering resigning. Such a suggestion was ridiculous. MacArthur liked being military governor and was smart enough to know he had been lucky to get the appointment: A half dozen other generals could have been selected. The arrival of the Taft Commission irritated him as an infringe-ment on his powers, but he still enjoyed his role immensely. As the governor of the Philippines, he commanded more U.S. soldiers in the field than any general since the Civil War. He had fulfilled a lifetime's dream.

Taft was on stronger ground when he complained of MacArthur's propensity to use esoteric words. MacArthur was proud of his eloquence, and he spent much of his time writing reports and letters. Like his father before him and his son later, the general thought of himself as a great writer, but his style was derived from the hundreds of academic and scholarly books that he had read. Many of these tomes were full of polysyllabic words known to force even the most educated reader to the dictionary and thesaurus. Concluding that a huge vocabulary was a prerequi-site to being admired as a scholar, MacArthur imitated their style. It is easy to vi-sualize him hovering over the dictionary as he read the works of Herbert Spencer, William James, or Thorstein Veblen; then, in the words of William Manchester, the vocabulary "built up during all those years of study ... burst forth like a pur-ple skyrocket." MacArthur's written reports were an "incredible" combination of compound sentences laced with pretentious words that confused readers rather than enlightening them.[85]

Scholars have delighted in quoting some of MacArthur's most ponderous and flowery prose. As an example, he described his arrival in the Philippines in the following manner: "When the command entered Manila Bay everybody was in a totally ignorant but especially sensitive and receptive state of mind. It was appar-ent, however, that we had entered in a new world ... teeming with a dense popula-tion that was in a paroxysmal state of excitement."[86]

Such language irritated Taft, who was not impressed. But the general loved words like "epigram, permeate, persuance, ethnological, academical, laudable, pursuance, propagate, psychological, and mitigate."[87]

Inevitably, Taft judged MacArthur's reports and observations much as Presi-dent Harry S. Truman would judge the reports written by Douglas while he was supreme commander in Japan. In his gritty, down-home style, Truman pro-claimed that Douglas MacArthur's reports were "nothing but a bunch of damn bullshit."[88]

Taft grumbled that he had to conduct what business he had with MacArthur "through the medium of formal correspondence," but the general realized that the portly Ohio politician was an adversary, not a friend, and he insisted that all communications between the governor's office and the commission be part of the official record. MacArthur was also acutely aware of the content of Taft's letters. Taft dictated his correspondence to Arthur Ferguson, executive secretary of the commission and its chief translator, who had a wide circle of acquaintances in the Filipino, Spanish, and U.S. communities. A massive man who loved eating as much as Taft did, Ferguson also loved to socialize. Gossip about the MacArthur-Taft feud raged through Manila as the contents of Taft's letters became public knowledge.[89]

Adjutant General Corbin, MacArthur's mentor and the most powerful staff officer in Washington, failed to warn MacArthur of the political developments brewing at home. Root had selected Taft as president of the commission and naturally accepted his interpretation of events in the Philippines and of his relationship with the general. If MacArthur had known how thoroughly Taft had Root's ear, he might have acted more cautiously.

Conflicts between military leaders and civilian politicians echo through history, and it is unlikely that Taft would have gotten along with any U.S. general. He basically disliked the military and was critical of nearly every general he met (and some he did not even know). Thus, for example, he described Otis, who had left the Philippines before he arrived, as a man who loved power and who minimized "the importance of people by implying he alone knew all the facts." Taft thought General Young was bullheaded and totally unfit to make the "transition from a state of war to a state of peace." And he described Bell as a poorly trained administrator of civil affairs, General Bates as a reactionary of a dangerous type, and General Hall as absolutely unfit for command.[90]

Despite his faults, Taft reluctantly admitted, MacArthur was the best military man in the Philippines. "If I have occasionally made a remark or two referring to General MacArthur which could be misconstrued," Taft informed Root, "I did not mean to imply that he is not working as hard as possible to secure good results because he is a very hard worker and earnest. Ultimately I have no doubt he will succeed." But Taft's minor praise of MacArthur did not mean he liked working with the general, and he continued to seek methods to get around military controls.[91]

To circumvent the military, Taft suggested that the commission be allowed to form a native militia and police force, a Filipino "constabulary," completely divorced from the army and under the control of the commission. He visualized training and equipping several thousand Filipinos to serve in a national Philippine army. He believed that such a Filipino force could suppress the bandits (that is, the guerrillas) more effectively than the U.S. Army. "If judiciously selected and officered," Taft asserted, a native constabulary would be an "efficient force for maintenance of order and will permit early, material reduction of United States troops." He recommended that the Macabebes, a minority group used by the Spanish in their colonial army, be recruited for the constabulary.[92]

MacArthur was unalterably opposed to creating a Filipino constabulary that would be equal in size to several U.S. regiments and armed in comparable fashion and to placing that constabulary under the commission's control. The U.S. Army was engaged in a guerrilla war supported by the majority of the Filipino people, and MacArthur believed it would be unwise to give thousands of rifles to Filipinos who might immediately join the revolution. He had already formed a small Filipino force, mostly Macabebes, and he insisted that the force remain under direct army control. He used the Macabebes as scouts, but he claimed they needed to be closely supervised because they were notoriously cruel to prisoners and often robbed and abused the local citizens. MacArthur did not wish to see an escalation of atrocities, a problem that haunted both sides.[93]

MacArthur constantly issued orders to his department commanders (who, in turn, issued comparable orders to their regiments) to severely punish any U.S. soldier found guilty of torturing prisoners, stealing from the people, or raping women. Despite these orders, atrocities continued on both sides. The implementation of the general's orders always rested on the commanders of 500 different garrisons spread throughout the Philippines.

The letters and diaries of U.S. soldiers were often laced with incidents of cruel and inhumane behavior, and the anti-imperialists in the United States, who opposed U.S. annexation of the Philippines, pounced on these accounts. MacArthur knew there were isolated instances of atrocities committed under his command, and when he learned of the incidents, he ordered the officers and men responsible to be court-martialed. Because of his policy of punishing soldiers for misconduct, according to Glenn May, "most of their day-to-day contacts with Filipinos appeared to be friendly enough."[94]

Although MacArthur refused to organize a Philippine constabulary, he was not opposed to using Filipinos as army scouts or as local policemen. In many towns and villages, he armed local police forces with shotguns and Colt .45 revolvers and allowed them to enforce the law in minor criminal cases.[95]

By late October, MacArthur reluctantly concluded that harsher military measures were needed to curtail the guerrilla bands harassing the U.S. garrisons. His lenient, humanitarian policies had failed. From June to October, 5,022 Filipino soldiers had accepted amnesty, but they were only a small percentage of the total rebels in the field. Guerrilla warfare demanded more stringent measures than MacArthur wished to employ, but he realized that the war could only be won by terminating the support the towns and villages gave to the revolutionaries in the form of information, supplies, and sanctuary. MacArthur again warned Washington that the war was not winding down and that the end was not even in sight.[96]

The secretary of war and the president were not pleased with MacArthur's official reports on conditions in the Philippines. In the midst of a presidential campaign, McKinley was upset that those reports contradicted the official Republican position that the rebellion was over. Indeed, MacArthur's analysis appeared to support Democratic candidate William Jennings Bryan's position that U.S. annexation of the Philippines was an act of imperialism opposed by the majority of the Filipino people, who were fighting for liberty and freedom from oppression. The administration suggested that MacArthur delay any new military offensive until after the November elections.

McKinley's dynamic running mate, Theodore Roosevelt, crisscrossed the United States at a frantic pace, castigating Bryan and his supporters for their unpatriotic stand on the Spanish-American War and the U.S. annexation of the Philippines. Roosevelt lumped "war critics, silverites, and Populists together as 'irresponsible,' 'anarchistic,' and 'treasonable.'" Albert Beveridge, the freshman

Republican senator from Indiana, received thunderous applause from packed galleries when he branded Bryan and members of the Anti-Imperialist League as traitors. Beveridge had toured the Philippines in 1899, and his patriotic pronouncements struck a chord with the highly nationalistic mood of the people. His dream of an American empire captivated audience after audience across the nation.[97]

Roosevelt, Beveridge, and a host of other Republicans preached that to support Bryan was to support Aguinaldo, who was killing "our boys" in the Philippines. Republican newspapers crucified Bryan, and "political cartoons often placed Aguinaldo on Bryan's right, cheering Bryan on with bloody hands or standing on the bodies of slain American soldiers."[98]

Bryan was closely associated with the Anti-Imperialist League, and the public viewed the league as composed of weary old intellectuals, idealistic aristocrats, and business and labor leaders who had a vested interest in opposing annexation of the Philippines. The league's pamphlets attacked the McKinley administration for the Spanish-American War, the annexation of the Philippines, and even the annexation of Hawaii. The pamphlets, according to Stuart Miller, "tended to be intellectual, even pedantic, and put forth historical, constitutional, economic, and moral arguments" that did not have much mass appeal. For most moderate Americans, the pamphlets verged on sedition and were "utterly distasteful," and league members were, for the most part, "ignored or denounced as traitors or copperheads."[99]

Soldiers in the Philippines deeply resented the Anti-Imperialist League. Captured rebel documents indicated that the Filipino Republican leaders hoped that a Bryan victory would lead to independence for the islands. One officer wrote home:

> I would to God that the truth of this whole Philippine situation could be known to every one in America as I know it. If the real ... conditions of the insurrection ... could be understood at home, we would hear no more talk of unjust ... government, ... or of hauling down our flag in the Philippines. If the so called anti-imperialists would honestly ascertain the truth on the ground and not in distant America, they ... would be convinced of the error of their statements. ... The continuance of fighting is chiefly due to reports that are sent out from America.[100]

Nearly all U.S. officers and enlisted men were angered when they discovered anti-imperialist pamphlets among the guerrillas. As one exclaimed, the war "would have ended long ago were it not for Bryan. ... Every American soldier that is killed ... can be laid directly to his door."[101]

Secretary Root viewed MacArthur's negative reports as potential ammunition for the Democrats and suppressed them until after the November elections. Releasing Taft's more optimistic statements to the press, Root declared that the Filipinos had no "conception of what self-government means, or the first qualification for its exercise."[102]

U.S. soldiers in the Philippines greeted McKinley's landslide victory with elation, and the Republican victory delivered a crushing blow to the Philippine revolution. Within three weeks, 2,000 revolutionaries on Luzon surrendered.

Despite the setback, the rebel leaders refused to surrender, and the rebellion continued. Colonel William E. Birkhimer, commander of the Second District in the Department of Southern Luzon, wrote military headquarters:

> The trouble ... is not our lack of military power. ... The great problem is to meet and overcome a foe that will not, as a foe, face us. ... It is a very powerful foe in a military sense: that is, it wears out our troops chasing a phantom [and] even when parties of armed insurrectos are ... located, the facility with which they can perform the chameleon act, by throwing away their arms under the bushes or grass ... and blandly greeting us as good amigos, utterly defeats our best trained and most skillfully conducted operations."[103]

Village leaders kept local Filipino commanders informed of U.S. troop movements, and Filipino soldiers had little difficulty in avoiding U.S. patrols. With their advanced knowledge of the troop movements, guerrillas often set up elaborate ambushes.

MacArthur ordered his garrison commanders to maintain close surveillance and to arrest anyone even suspected of aiding the guerrillas. Townspeople were made responsible for any action that supported the guerrillas. Anyone who aided or assisted a person involved in active, violent opposition to U.S. rule was to be arrested. And any Filipino who refused to swear loyalty to the United States was to be considered a rebel who was aiding the enemy. Suspicion was sufficient reason for arrest, and those who were arrested were not to be released until the end of the war. In Manila, MacArthur ordered General Bell, his provost marshal, to crack down on the Filipinos; in the next two months, Bell arrested and detained over 600 suspects for refusing to swear allegiance to the United States.[104]

Taft supported the new policies. MacArthur's lenient programs had not worked, and it was time, Taft declared, for the U.S. authorities "to give the men in arms an opportunity to come in, and if they do not accept it, declare them outlaws and either hang or transport them as they are captured. ... The resistance to American authority is nothing but a conspiracy of murder and assassination."[105]

In early December, MacArthur initiated a military campaign to isolate the Filipino guerrillas from local village support. He sent out his 70,000 veteran troops from their garrisons with the goal of cutting the towns off from the guerrillas. Under new orders, the soldiers were authorized to burn villages where they encountered guerrilla resistance. MacArthur's forces struck hard everywhere in the Philippines.[106]

The general simultaneously altered the treatment of prisoners. Filipino rebels were divided into two categories: Soldiers in uniform would be treated as prisoners of war if captured; guerrillas captured out of uniform could be executed. In the next three months, 79 captured Filipino bandits were hanged.[107]

MacArthur also accepted Taft's recommendation to deport captured Republican leaders to the island of Guam. He had been reluctant to take such action, but his experiences with Apolinario Mabini convinced him that a number of the Republicans were irreconcilables. The paralyzed Mabini, president of the Republican cabinet, had been captured in December 1899 and thrown into prison. When MacArthur became governor, he released Mabini to his family in Manila. A true Republican and highly intelligent, Mabini immediately began to engage in revolutionary activity. MacArthur ordered him rearrested and finally decided to deport him to Guam in January 1901, along with 38 of the most prominent captured rebel leaders.[108]

The new military tactics proved effective. Popular support for the revolution began to collapse. In the small garrison towns, the U.S. Army had less difficulty in obtaining guides, agents, and informants. In December and January, about 2,000 Filipino soldiers, including a number of high-ranking officers, surrendered or were captured; the number of Filipinos surrendering jumped dramatically in December to over 650 and rose to 800 in January 1901. Those who surrendered guns could obtain the release of prisoners of war in numbers equal to the number of arms surrendered. And relatives or sweethearts who surrendered weapons could obtain the release of their loved ones. In December and January, the army captured or accepted the surrender of 23,000 weapons.[109]

Taft saw the military successes as proof that the rebellion would soon be over. He wrote Root urging Washington to recall MacArthur and replace him with a civilian governor. In early January 1901, the secretary of war recommended to President McKinley that MacArthur be relieved as soon as the Spooner Amendment passed Congress. Privately admitting that MacArthur's constitutional arguments were correct, Root observed that the president did not have the power to appoint a civilian governor until Congress passed the enabling legislation. He wrote Taft that if the Spooner Amendment passed, "we intend to discontinue the military government and to establish a civil government" with Taft, of course, as the new governor. MacArthur would be recalled, and a new military commander who would acknowledge civilian control even of the military would be appointed. The army would then have substantially the same relation "to the new government as the army has to the government in the United States," Root wrote.[110]

Despite the military successes, MacArthur still believed peace could be achieved only through benevolent U.S. rule. In pacified areas, he encouraged the establishment of municipal governments and promised Filipinos their personal liberties. A number of former Republican leaders accepted MacArthur's olive branch and swore allegiance to the United States. With the encouragement of both MacArthur and Taft, some of the *ilustrados* (wealthy landowners, rich attorneys, bankers, and physicians) formed the Federal party and accepted U.S. rule. On his travels, Taft often took along Federal party members for propaganda purposes.[111]

MacArthur lifted martial law in Manila, allowed the establishment of a civilian police force, and even recommended that the Taft Commission take over the supervision of the Manila government. A military committee drew up a city charter and turned it over to the Taft Commission for consideration. The charter called for the appointment of a three-man Manila commission to oversee the city's government departments. Taft, however, disagreed with many of the details and delayed implementing the plan.[112]

On February 5, 1901, Congress rewarded MacArthur for his service in the Philippines by promoting him from brigadier general to major general in the Regular Army. In three years, he had risen from an obscure lieutenant colonel in the Adjutant General's Office to become the youngest major general in the U.S. Army.

Two other Civil War veterans, General Chaffee and General Young, were also promoted. Chaffee had joined the Regular Army in 1867 as a captain. Twenty-one years later, he was promoted to major of the 9th Cavalry and in 1897 to lieutenant colonel. Chaffee had achieved the rank of brigadier general on the same day as MacArthur, January 2, 1900. His command of the China Relief Expedition in the summer of 1900 propelled him into the limelight. On February 4, 1901, just one day before MacArthur's promotion, Chaffee was appointed to the rank of major general. Meanwhile, Young, who had been recalled to the United States, was promoted to major general on February 2, 1901, and thus outranked Chaffee by two days and MacArthur by three. Young had served in the Civil War with the 12th Pennsylvania and had joined the Regular Army in 1866. By 1897, he was a colonel commanding the 3rd Cavalry. As chief of cavalry for Lawton's 1st Division and later as commander of northern Luzon, Young achieved a reputation as a fighter. The obvious intent of Congress and the Army General Staff was for Young to succeed Lieutenant General Nelson Miles, for Chaffee to succeed Young, and for MacArthur to succeed Chaffee. MacArthur, as the youngest, could wait his turn.[113]

Pinky and Douglas were delighted with the general's new promotion. Douglas was doing exceptionally well at the military academy, ranking first in his class and participating in sports. Using the famous MacArthur foot speed as his prime weapon, Douglas played left field for the baseball team. During the Army-Navy game, the midshipmen razzed him about his famous father as they sang out: "MacArthur! MacArthur! Are you the Governor General or a Hobo? Who is the boss of this show? Is it you or Emilio Aguinaldo?" Douglas took the hazing with pride.[114]

General MacArthur missed his wife, and he certainly could have used her abilities and charms for the major social event of the season in Manila. To celebrate his promotion to major general and to introduce the leaders of the new Federal party to the army command, MacArthur held a grand reception at *Malacañan* on the evening of February 19, 1901. He invited over 2,000 people, including army officers, Filipino aristocrats, and the civilian commissioners. Hundreds of the foremost Filipino families of Manila, Cavite, and the outer cities attended. "Three

Major General Arthur MacArthur, c. 1901. (National Archives, 111-SC-99275)

thousand vehicles of all kinds were corraled and cared for within the grounds, and the contiguous streets, giving some idea of the vast number of persons present," General Isaac C. Catlin recalled.

> Two thousand electrical lamps shed their brilliant light on the grounds, illuminating as by midday sun every nook and corner of the vast, verdant enclosure. Many more lighted up the spacious apartments of the mighty Moorish structure from top to bottom. The unique and picturesque feature of the fete was the presence of several hundred Filipinas, dressed in their loose, dainty native gowns, wearing pretty slippers, displaying rich and resplendent jewels. The American matrons and maidens made also a brilliant and memorable picture of human loveliness in their bright, beautiful, gauzy gowns.[115]

Decorated with U.S. flags, *Malacañan*'s marbled entrance hall opened to an imposing hardwood staircase that led to a reception hall on the second floor. There, Venetian glass chandeliers hung from the ceilings, and massive tables with hand-carved scenes of Filipino peasants and carabao were loaded with food for the guests. Artificial flowers made of silk, paper, and tissue decorated smaller tables. Wicker chairs with fancy cotton cushions were in most of the rooms, and Persian rugs covered the hardwood floors. For the tobacco-chewing Americans and the betel-chewing Filipinos, cuspidors were placed in convenient locations. The rooms smelled of kerosene, which was used to wash the floors and keep the myriad tropical insects, particularly ants, from destroying the wood. The polished floors were maintained by Filipino servants who tied bags on their bare feet and skated up and down.

The first floor was built of stone, but the upper floor was of native woods. Instead of glass, the grated windows were paned with thin, flat, oyster shells set in little three-inch squares that allowed the sun in but prevented anyone from seeing into the house. Relics of the old Spanish period were everywhere. Dozens of U.S. military bands and Filipino bands provided music. General Catlin remembered that "everywhere one strayed, upstairs or downstairs or out on the great court and on the grand lawns, the ravishing strains of music saluted the ear and thrilled the senses."[116]

Taft foolishly wore a frock coat and silk hat, and he suffered in the heat. He had complained for months about MacArthur's refusal to socialize with members of the commission, and he now complained about the governor's failure to solicit his advice on the big party. Taft accused MacArthur of being too liberal in his guest list, which he felt should have been presented to the commission for approval.[117]

The party was a momentous occasion for MacArthur as his fellow officers gathered to celebrate his promotion. Over the years, MacArthur had been generous in his praise of his subordinate officers, and many had been promoted on his strong recommendation. Bell and Funston were the most obvious cases, but many other military leaders rose in the army partially because of MacArthur's support, including John Pershing, Peyton March, Charles Summerall, William Mitchell, and

General Arthur MacArthur (center) and General Frederick Funston (second from left), Philippines, c. 1900. (MacArthur Memorial Library, Ph-147)

Enoch Crowder. Although Taft questioned MacArthur's ability, many of his fellow officers considered him to be the best general in the U.S. Army.[118]

Shortly after the *Malacañan* reception, a bit of good fortune fell to the U.S. Army. In early February, General Funston, commander of a brigade at San Isidro in central Luzon, captured Cecilio Segismundo, who was carrying Republican government documents. Because of the possibility of traitors, Aguinaldo had taken great care in selecting his own base camps and allowed only a few of his more important generals to know where he was. He conducted the war through correspondence, carried by messengers to his subordinates in various parts of the islands. Segismundo was one of those messengers. During interrogation, he revealed that Aguinaldo had his headquarters deep in the mountains on the northeastern edge of Luzon, in the small village of Palanan. His staff included 50 well-armed soldiers. In early January, Aguinaldo had decided he needed a larger escort; he therefore ordered Segismundo to contact several rebel generals and deliver a coded letter requesting they send an additional 400 men to Palanan. Funston's men had captured the messenger.

Funston reported to MacArthur at *Malacañan*. He had served in MacArthur's 2nd Division as commander of the 20th Kansas Volunteers and was one of the general's most trusted officers. The two had a special relationship: MacArthur treated Funston almost like a son, and Funston looked on the general as the ideal military commander. Years later, he named his first son Arthur after the general, and he would protect the general's own son, Douglas, when he was criticized for disobeying orders.

Working with the headquarters staff, MacArthur and Funston worked out an audacious plan to capture Aguinaldo. The general did not want Aguinaldo killed, for the Filipinos had created a legend of invincibility around him, and if he were killed, millions of Filipinos would not believe he was dead. Even those who did would surely make him a martyr of the revolution. MacArthur hoped to capture Aguinaldo alive, dispel the myth of his invincibility, and end the rebellion. A large force could not approach Palanan because Aguinaldo would simply flee deeper into the mountains. Funston suggested a subterfuge. With a small force of 80 Macabebe scouts, indistinguishable from other Filipinos, he and 4 other U.S. officers would take a gunboat from Manila to northeastern Luzon. The sea trip would take from six to ten days. After a clandestine landing, the Macabebes would pose as reinforcements for Aguinaldo's headquarters, and the 5 U.S. officers would pose as prisoners. Funston hoped to penetrate Aguinaldo's headquarters and take the Filipino president alive.[119]

The possibility of failure or even disaster was great. If Funston's deception failed, he and the other officers would be captured or killed. Nonetheless, MacArthur proved as bold as Funston and gave the mission his backing. He accepted the possibility of failure, as well as full responsibility for the mission, because he believed that risks were necessary to end the rebellion.[120]

On March 6, Funston, 4 other army officers, and the 80 Macabebes boarded the gunboat *Vicksburg* and steamed out of Manila. General MacArthur waited anxiously as three weeks passed without a word from them. He began to fear that the mission had failed.

Around 6:30 on the morning of March 28, MacArthur was awakened by a member of his staff. Funston had returned and was waiting downstairs. The normally formal MacArthur dashed down in his pajamas. Funston later wrote that the general shook his hand, then looked at him in a quizzical way but did not ask the obvious question. He waited for Funston to report. Funston smiled and said, "Well, I have brought you Don Emilio." MacArthur could scarcely believe it and asked, "Where is he?" Funston replied, "Right in this house." The plan had worked perfectly. Funston had captured Aguinaldo and most of his headquarters staff.[121]

Ordering Funston to remain, MacArthur dashed to his quarters to dress while his staff prepared breakfast for the generals and their prisoner. During breakfast, MacArthur was jubilant. Aguinaldo, by contrast, was depressed and silent. A serious young man in his early thirties who did not smoke, drink, or gamble, he was about five feet tall and had a high forehead and coarse black hair that he brushed up in what was called the pompadour style. From a fairly wealthy Chinese Tagalog family in Cavite, Aguinaldo had features that were more Chinese than Filipino. MacArthur treated his prisoner as an honored guest and reiterated his earlier promises to guarantee all personal liberties to the Filipino people once the rebellion ended. He ordered quarters prepared for Aguinaldo and directed officers to notify his family that they could visit him.[122]

In high spirits, MacArthur telegraphed Washington and publicly announced Aguinaldo's capture. He lavished praise on Funston for his accomplishment and allowed him to receive most of the glory. He also recommended that Funston, who was a Volunteer officer, be rewarded with a commission in the Regular Army up to his Volunteer rank of brigadier general.[123]

The news of Aguinaldo's capture made Funston a hero in the United States. Vice President Roosevelt wired Funston to congratulate him for the crowning exploit of a career filled with "cool courage and iron endurance." Congress rewarded him with the Medal of Honor and a commission in the Regular Army as a brigadier general, the youngest in the U.S. Army at the time.[124]

U.S. soldiers throughout the Philippines were wild with excitement when the news of Aguinaldo's capture was released, hoping the long rebellion was finally over. In the interim, politicians, journalists, and military men offered suggestions for Aguinaldo's future. "Deport him to Guam," was Taft's advice; Admiral Dewey suggested that he be shot, and many supported this idea.

MacArthur had an even better idea. He hoped to persuade Aguinaldo to issue a proclamation declaring an end to the revolution, with a request that all his followers lay down their arms. To achieve his goal, MacArthur treated Aguinaldo with extreme consideration. He quartered Aguinaldo in a spacious villa near *Malacañan* and allowed his family and friends to visit. The ever-present U.S. guards were as unobtrusive as possible.

Despite this, Aguinaldo remained depressed and sullen. MacArthur visited him daily and explained "the U.S. point of view, the glories and prosperity which would follow as soon as the fighting ended, and the hopelessness of allowing the struggle to continue."[125]

Taft attempted to intervene in the negotiations, but MacArthur rejected his proposals and refused his request to attend the meetings. Taft appealed to Washington. In his opinion, MacArthur was treating Aguinaldo with too much respect. The man deserved to be executed or deported, said Taft, who considered Aguinaldo a man of little ability who had become the leader of the Philippine revolution largely as an accident of history. Taft telegraphed Root that Washington should carefully monitor the MacArthur-Aguinaldo negotiations because the general was likely to make some inappropriate concessions.[126]

Accepting Taft's recommendation, Root wired MacArthur to forward all proposals to Washington for approval. The general therefore telegraphed an outline of his plan to Adjutant General Corbin. MacArthur saw Aguinaldo's capture as a tremendous opportunity to end the war, and in the negotiations, he was actually more liberal than Taft or Washington. If Aguinaldo would swear allegiance to the United States and issue a proclamation that his followers should surrender, MacArthur proposed that the United States reissue the amnesty proclamation of June 1900 and release thousands of Filipino prisoners as a show of good faith. He also suggested that Aguinaldo travel to the United States with Funston and Bell as a demonstration that the United States intended to honor its promises. In that way, the army's victory would achieve maximum publicity, and the people of both the United States and the Philippines would have heroes to honor. Such a trip would also stimulate popular support in the Philippines for the civil government that MacArthur assumed would soon be established.[127]

MacArthur's proposals horrified Root and McKinley. In their view, the general was either very naive or very stupid. The anti-imperialist movement remained powerful in the U.S. Senate and the intellectual communities, particularly in Boston and New York. If Aguinaldo visited Washington, the controversy would only escalate. Root could visualize Aguinaldo being interviewed by the liberal press, talking about liberty, freedom, and equality for all, and becoming more of a hero than Funston. It would have been political stupidity to allow such a visit. Consequently, Root rejected any visit by Aguinaldo and also refused to allow MacArthur to reissue his amnesty proclamation. MacArthur disagreed with Washington but followed orders and forwarded all proposals to Root for approval.[128]

After twenty-three days of negotiations, during which Aguinaldo listened to vigorous lobbying by his wife, mother, sisters, and numerous prominent Federal party members, he agreed to terms on April 19. In return for Aguinaldo's swearing allegiance to the United States and issuing a proclamation requesting his followers to surrender, MacArthur released 1,000 captured rebels from prison and promised to release another 1,000 in early May and an additional 1,000 in June.[129]

Some rebels branded Aguinaldo a traitor, but many others responded to his call to surrender. From all over the Philippines, reports of surrenders poured into MacArthur's headquarters. Within weeks, over 20,000 rebels had turned themselves in and sworn allegiance to the United States. Rebel activity dropped dramatically, and by early May, MacArthur considered the rebellion over except for a few isolated hot spots like Batangas province south of Manila and a region on the island of Samar, where rebel General Vicente Lukban remained active.[130]

With rebel activity declining, MacArthur moved rapidly to turn over vast areas to civilian control. By June, over half the towns and villages on Luzon were administered by municipal governments appointed by the Taft Commission. Although Taft took all the credit, the civilian authorities were often army officers temporarily detached from military duty. U.S. troops were slowly withdrawn, and by June, the Division of the Philippines numbered only 42,000 men.

MacArthur realized that the war was over and that he would soon be replaced by a civilian governor. The Spooner Bill had finally passed Congress, enabling the president to govern the islands by authority of Congress rather than in his capacity as commander in chief. In meetings with Taft, MacArthur offered to assist in a smooth transition of power, but Taft, already informed he would be the new governor, was not in a compromising mood.[131]

In early April, the War Department notified MacArthur that Taft would replace him as governor and that Adna Chaffee would replace him as military com-

General Arthur MacArthur, military governor of the Philippines, and staff, 1901. MacArthur is seated in the front row, fourth from the left. (MacArthur Memorial Library, Ph-A83/p. 16; identification sheet available from the library)

mander of the Military Division of the Philippines. President McKinley made it official on June 20, 1901, by issuing a proclamation ending military government in the islands on July 4, 1901.

Chaffee arrived from China in late June. A dour Ohioan of sixty with narrow eyes, a lantern jaw, and the bowlegged gait of a cavalryman, he was described by one historian as "a soldier's soldier ... who felt more comfortable on a horse than at a desk." Joining the Union army during the Civil War, Chaffee fought at Gettysburg, served on the frontier after the war, saw combat in Cuba, and commanded the China Relief Expedition. He was "a throwback to the robust, mudsplattered leader of an earlier era [and he] had little use for civilians ... and ... pronounced that despised word with an exaggerated initial sibilant."[132]

In a series of meeting with MacArthur, Chaffee learned of the general's problems with Taft, and MacArthur learned that Root had actually notified Chaffee of his new assignment in late February. Although Root had also informed Taft of the intended change in military commanders, he had withheld the information from

MacArthur for over two months. The general felt betrayed by the secretary of war: Root should have been representing the military interest in the Philippines, not the interest of the politicians. Relations between MacArthur and Taft reached a low point.[133]

Although Taft ignored MacArthur during this period, military officers at the Manila Club honored him with a banquet on July 1, attended by over 400 English and U.S. officers. The officers toasted MacArthur's accomplishments as military commander of the Division of the Philippines. During his thirteen months in that post, he had successfully curtailed the guerrilla bands on most of Luzon while capturing and dealing honorably with Aguinaldo.

MacArthur's forces suffered 245 killed, 490 wounded, and 138 captured or missing in 1,026 encounters with Filipino forces from May 1900 to July 1, 1901. In the official reports, a list of the brief encounters consumed over 734 typewritten pages. In addition, for every man who died in battle, three others died of tropical diseases. Total Filipino casualties from the war (including battles, famine, pestilence, and other causes) were approximately 200,000. The United States had purchased the islands from Spain for $20 million and then spent $200 million suppressing the Filipino revolutionaries.[134]

MacArthur formally surrendered power on July 4, 1901, in a grand military ceremony in the Cathedral Plaza facing the *Ayuntamiento*. From a raised platform covered with canvas to block the tropical sun, he addressed an audience composed of hundreds of soldiers, thousands of Filipinos, and a few U.S. civilian dignitaries. He praised his officers and enlisted men for their hard work and proclaimed that the Filipinos would now obtain the full benefits of American civilization under civilian control. MacArthur admired the Filipino people and believed their future was to become a model of republican government in Asia.[135]

Taft followed MacArthur to the platform. In his address, he talked of the past accomplishments of the Philippine Commission and the future he visualized for the islands under civilian rule. Not once in his speech did Taft mention MacArthur's accomplishment nor grant him the normal accolades given to a departing leader. The insult did not go unnoticed by the general.[136]

The officers and soldiers of the Division of the Philippines showed their respect for MacArthur in the traditional military fashion. An artillery battery stationed in the *Intramuros* fired a military salute to their departing commander as he was escorted by an honor guard down streets lined with soldiers to the pier. Each regiment saluted as he passed. At the bay, the general boarded a launch to take him to the transport that would return him to the United States.[137]

The transport did not depart until the next day. That night, MacArthur and his staff returned to *Malacañan* for a final reception. Over 1,000 people, including Filipino aristocrats, army officers, and civilian dignitaries, gathered to honor MacArthur before he departed the islands the next morning. Although he would never return, his son Douglas would eventually become as closely associated with the Philippines as he himself had been.[138]

PART FOUR

Final Days

14

A Soldier's Odyssey

EARLY IN THE MORNING of July 5, 1901, accompanied by Colonel Enoch Crowder and two aides, General MacArthur left the Philippines aboard a transport bound for Japan. The ship reached Yokohama on July 9, and for three weeks, MacArthur waited before sailing to San Francisco on the transport USS *Sheridan*. Treating MacArthur as an honored guest, Japan's military leaders showed him the sights of Nagasaki, Kyoto, and Yokohama. The Japanese respected and admired MacArthur, and for the rest of his life, he maintained close ties with Japan. During this visit, he shopped for gifts for his wife and sons. Handcrafted Japanese goods were in great demand in the United States at that time; the most popular purchases were ivory tea boxes, porcelain vases, incense burners, kimonos, and lacquered boxes. On August 3, MacArthur and his colleagues departed for the States.

The general assumed his return to the United States would be greeted with great fanfare. When Dewey returned from the Philippines in October 1899, the nation had erupted in wild celebrations. Cities erected statues and renamed parks, streets, and schools after him. In Washington, D.C., President McKinley toasted the admiral, and a grateful nation even contributed to a fund to purchase Dewey a new home. Congress awarded Dewey a Tiffany sword of gold and jewels and minted a Dewey coin. In New York City, schoolchildren collected 7,000 dimes that were melted down and made into a silver cup for Dewey. A fireworks display capped his victory parade in New York City as colored rockets outlined a 1,000-square-foot portrait of Dewey in the night sky. Eight months later when Otis returned to the United States, the gala celebrations almost equaled the honors rendered Dewey. In Washington, a jointly convened Congress gave him a standing ovation, and during ceremonies at the White House, McKinley congratulated Otis on his splendid military achievements.[1]

MacArthur expected to receive comparable honors when he reached the United States. He was the first man down the gangplank when the *Sheridan* arrived in San Francisco on August 18, 1901. To his surprise, the ceremonies welcoming him back after three years in the Philippines were decidedly low key. General Samuel Young, an old comrade from the Philippines, was the commander of the Department of the Pacific with headquarters in San Francisco, yet he sent a mere captain to greet MacArthur. No representative from the U.S. government, no representative from the state of California, and no representative from the city of San Francisco were at the docks to greet the general. Although MacArthur made no comment, he felt the slight keenly. The lack of any welcoming ceremonies became a subject of general conversation among the members of MacArthur's staff and other army and naval officers in San Francisco.[2]

President McKinley and Secretary Root ignored MacArthur's return on the advice of William Howard Taft. On August 2, Governor Taft telegraphed Washington and advised the president not to award any great honors to MacArthur on his return. According to Taft, the general could not be trusted to follow the administration's official line on the Philippines. He even proclaimed that MacArthur's "head has been swelled to such an extent that he may make a fool of himself when he reaches the United States." Given Taft's advice, McKinley therefore decided it would be best if MacArthur's return was not accompanied by any fanfare—he might say something that would embarrass the administration.[3]

Even the general's family was absent. Although MacArthur had briefly seen his older son while in the Philippines, he had not seen Pinky or Douglas for three years. Pinky had remained in the hotel close to West Point to be near her son, and apparently, she planned to stay there for the next two years as well, despite her husband's return. Carol Petillo observed that Pinky became "even more strong-willed and overpowering as she grew older." She focused "her considerable energies entirely on Douglas's life at school, his social activities, and his unparalleled efforts to achieve success." Meanwhile, the general, "distanced by professional responsibilities, his own austerity, and often by temporary assignments away from home, provided scant buffer for her efforts. Indeed, there is every reason to believe that both of his parents were in essential agreement concerning Douglas's upbringing." During his years at West Point, Pinky even directed his social life. She could not control her husband or older son, but she had better luck with Douglas.[4]

Although Pinky had not seen her husband since June 1898, she decided not to travel to San Francisco but rather to await his return to Chicago. The general probably agreed with her practicality since his orders were to report to Washington, D.C., and Chicago was on the way. Still, he must have been disappointed by his family's absence in San Francisco after his long tour of duty in the Philippines.

Only Milwaukee honored MacArthur on his return. The city of his youth sent a special delegation to San Francisco to invite him to a gala celebration in his honor scheduled for September 11. Nearly every major Wisconsin politician and businessman had accepted invitations. MacArthur felt a renewal of faith in his beloved city and accepted the invitation. He wanted to go home, and Milwaukee was home.[5]

A reporter from the *Milwaukee Sentinel* interviewed MacArthur, and just as Taft feared, the general refused to claim a complete victory in the Philippines. He pointed out that pacification efforts were still needed in two major areas: southern Luzon (particularly in Batangas, where General Miguel Malvar still remained active) and on the island of Samar (where General Vicente Lukban remained in the field). Malvar had assumed the position of supreme commander of the remaining Filipino forces, and Filipino villages in Samar and Batangas continued to support the revolutionaries. MacArthur did not mention the Moro, or Moslem, problem on Jolo and Mindanao but concentrated his attention on Luzon and the central islands of the Philippines.[6]

The general did not waste time in San Francisco. Accompanied by his staff, he boarded a train for Chicago on August 20. The four-day trip was the most trying of the entire journey home because of his impatience to see his family. Due to arrive in Chicago in the morning of August 24, the train was twelve hours late and did not pull in until 9:30 P.M. Much to the general's delight, however, Pinky and Douglas were at the station to greet him. The general and his family stayed at the Auditorium Hotel in Chicago to await an invitation from Secretary Root and President McKinley to visit Washington.[7]

The family got reacquainted in the next few days. Pinky was proud of her husband's accomplishments, and she was genuinely pleased with his new distinguished rank. Douglas was doing well at West Point, ranking first in his class for two years, playing baseball and tennis, and socializing well with the other cadets. The general's older son, Arthur, who had been promoted to lieutenant, junior grade, in May 1901, was not in Chicago to greet his father; he had been assigned to the naval station at Newport, Rhode Island, to attend classes on torpedo training and could not get a leave.

The summer heat in Washington, D.C., drove President McKinley out of the White House to his home in Canton, Ohio, in late August. MacArthur was therefore ordered to Canton to meet with the president around September 1. A friendly, gregarious man, McKinley had never met MacArthur and had expected him to be rigid and unlikeable. Indeed, his only knowledge of the general came from Governor Taft via Secretary Root. And for two years, Taft had written devastating letters describing MacArthur as an egoistical military martinet who had the "weakness of thinking himself a profound and philosophical thinker."[8]

But on meeting MacArthur, McKinley quickly decided that Taft's characterization was brutally inaccurate. MacArthur was a quiet, almost shy, man, and after spending an entire evening together, he and McKinley discovered they had much in common. Both men had been Civil War officers, and the president loved to discuss his earlier military exploits. McKinley had joined the 23rd Ohio Volunteers in 1861, and during the war, he achieved the rank of major. Although MacArthur's 24th Wisconsin had served on the western front and the 23rd Ohio had served on the eastern front, the men could reminisce about common war experiences; Civil War veterans held a special place in both men's hearts. As old comrades in arms, McKinley and MacArthur respected each other. They were also members of the Grand Army of the Republic and the Loyal Legion. The Grand Army was an association formed after the war by veterans of the Union army. The organization significantly influenced local and national politics for fifty years. In 1900, the Grand Army's local posts remained powerful in local communities, and their annual reunions and parades were stirring events. The Military Order of the Loyal Legion, formed in Philadelphia in April 1865, was opened only to Union officers who served in the Civil War. The order was structured around twenty state commanderies with 7,500 members.[9]

A firm friendship blossomed between MacArthur and McKinley. During dinner, the president suggested that the general tour the country as Otis and Dewey had done. MacArthur rejected the idea—the thought of giving a hundred public speeches frightened him more than the prospect of going into battle. The president smiled but insisted. "General," he said, "speech-making is an established custom of the country, and you have got to get used to it. I am an old stager at this business, but I never get up before an audience to make a speech that I am not seasick for at least five minutes."[10]

When MacArthur left Canton the next day to return to Chicago, his spirits were high, and his visions of the future were rosy. With his own pipeline to the president, his position could no longer be undercut by Root and Taft. Fame and promotion seemed imminent. Milwaukee would honor him as its most famous military hero on September 11, and he seemed destined to receive national acclaim and recognition.

But forces of history intervened and again twisted MacArthur's life and career. Shortly after the general's audience with the president, McKinley left Canton to visit Buffalo, New York, and attend the Pan-American Exposition, a lavish international fair designed to dramatize the Western Hemisphere. McKinley arrived in Buffalo early in the evening of Wednesday, September 4, 1901. After a brief visit to the fair the next morning, he went to the Temple of Music in downtown Buffalo, where long lines had formed to meet him.

McKinley liked to mix with the people and often shook hands with thousands at public ceremonies: Anybody could walk right up and greet him. Guards at the temple were amazed that the president could shake hands at the rate of forty-five a minute.

Waiting in line on this day was Leon Czolgosz, a twenty-eight-year-old Polish American. Czolgosz was one among thousands. His right hand was wrapped in a white handkerchief, as though injured, and held against his side. When his turn came, Czolgosz extended his left hand, but though "the President reached for it ... the two never clasped. Instead, Czolgosz brushed McKinley's arm aside, raised his 'bandaged' right hand, and virtually pressed it against the President's vest. Two muffled shots came in quick succession." A swarm of soldiers and Secret Service men hurled themselves on the young Pole, but the damage was done. One of the bullets penetrated the president's stomach, and he was rushed to the hospital.[11]

In the first few days, reports were optimistic as the doctors predicted McKinley's recovery. But as MacArthur warned in an interview, any abdominal wound was extremely dangerous and might prove fatal. The general was correct. McKinley's wound became infected, and gangrene riddled his stomach, pancreas, and kidney. Eight days after the shooting, he died. Theodore Roosevelt assumed control of the government as the nation mourned their dead president.[12]

McKinley was buried in Canton on September 19. MacArthur attended the funeral as a member of a special honor guard of military leaders that included Admiral Dewey and General Otis. He returned to Chicago after the funeral to await a summons to Washington to meet the new president, but that summons never came. Roosevelt was busy, it is true, but it is also true that MacArthur's archenemies, Secretary Root and Governor Taft, were close friends of the new president.[13]

Postponed because of the assassination of President McKinley, Milwaukee's celebration to honor its favorite son was rescheduled for October 2. The chamber of commerce sent a committee to Chicago to escort MacArthur back home by special train. At the Milwaukee railroad station, Wisconsin's most famous and powerful men waited to greet the general. The dignitaries included former governors, senators, congressmen, mayors, business leaders, retired generals, and many old friends. MacArthur led a grand parade through the streets of downtown Milwaukee, and thousands cheered their returning hero. The MacArthur name meant something to the citizens of the city, and many were honoring not only General MacArthur but also his late father, Judge Arthur MacArthur. The judge had been one of the best-loved men in Milwaukee from the early 1850s until his death in 1896. Many of his old friends were still alive and active in Milwaukee politics.[14]

The honors touched MacArthur, who always had a special place in his heart for Milwaukee. His memories of the city were positive ones. He had played in the streets as a youth, and many of his boyhood friends, such as John Mitchell and Charlie King, still lived there. His most honored comrades in arms also lived in the city. Friends from his Civil War days, such as Captain Edwin Parsons of the 24th Wisconsin, were at the railroad station to greet the returning hero.

The Milwaukee chapter of the Loyal Legion gave a banquet that evening to climax the day's festivities.

> The hall was handsomely decorated for the occasion. Across the North end ... was the headquarters flag of General MacArthur, a large expanse of yellow bunting, bearing in its center a large figure "8" in white bordered in blue, and with red centers surmounted by a red scroll with the words "Division of the Philippines." Clusters of silk flags hid the chandeliers whose electric lights shone down upon long tables decorated with flowers and sparkling burnished silver and glassware. After dinner, Charles King gave the keynote address in praise of the guest of honor. Others rose to honor MacArthur including his old comrade Captain Parsons. Between speeches, they sang patriotic songs.[15]

After the celebrations, MacArthur returned to Chicago and waited another month before departing for Washington, D.C. When General Corbin, a widower, decided to remarry, he invited MacArthur to the wedding. Secretary Root and President Roosevelt also attended the wedding on November 6. Although Roosevelt was polite, he did not invite MacArthur to the White House: Secretary Root had advised against having the general remain in Washington because he might embarrass the administration. Roosevelt agreed, and Root assigned MacArthur to take command of the Department of the Colorado, with headquarters in Denver. As it turned out, however, his residency in Denver would be brief.[16]

A Senate committee was conducting detailed hearings on the Philippine Islands during this time. The U.S. Army there had implemented harsher tactics after MacArthur's departure, and quoting letters from the soldiers in the field, newspapers uncovered dozens of accounts of atrocities committed by U.S. soldiers in campaigns in southern Luzon under General Bell and on the island of Samar under General Jacob H. Smith.

On the day that MacArthur left the Philippines, Taft had asserted his new power. He moved the military personnel out of the *Ayuntamiento* and replaced them with his civilian administrators, most of whom were detached military officers. Taft informed General Chaffee that all members of the military in the Philippines were now subject to the orders of the civilian administrators.

Chaffee proved as stubborn as MacArthur in protecting military prerogatives. Over half the islands were still under martial law. In Batangas province south of Manila, on Leyte, and on Samar, the rebellion dragged on and required the continued presence of a large contingent of U.S. troops. In areas still under martial law, Chaffee believed he, not Taft, was in control, and he presented the same constitutional arguments that MacArthur had used back in September 1900. Taft exploded and wrote a thirteen-page legal rebuttal, but his arguments did not convince Chaffee. Once again, Taft complained to Washington, and Corbin was dispatched to Manila to deliver verbal orders to the general.[17]

To circumvent Chaffee, Taft created the Philippine Constabulary, composed of nine companies of armed Filipinos with U.S. officers. He still believed a Filipino constabulary would be more effective in countering the guerrillas than the U.S. Army. Taft's position was undercut when a company of U.S. troops at the village of Balangiga on Samar were massacred on September 29, 1901. Samar was the third-largest island in the Philippines, located about 350 miles southeast of Manila. Early in the morning of September 27, a Filipino force under the command of General Lukban had launched a surprise attack on Company C of the 9th Infantry, stationed at the small barrio of Balangiga. Lukban achieved a dramatic victory. Forty-seven men of Company C were killed in the assault, 10 were severely wounded, 12 slightly wounded, and only 5 uninjured. The survivors of the attack barely managed to escape to Basey, 30 miles north. Captain Edwin V. Bookmiller, commander of Company G of the 9th Infantry at Basey, boarded a gunboat with his company and steamed to the site of the massacre. There, he found that the dead of Company C had been stripped, and many were horribly mutilated. Some were covered with flour, others had their stomachs split open and stuffed with codfish. One officer had his face half severed off by a bolo, his eyes gouged out, and jam smeared in the sockets.[18]

The massacre at Balangiga shocked the U.S. public, and many newspaper editors noted that it was the worst disaster suffered by the U.S. Army since Custer's last stand at the Little Big Horn. Some editors criticized MacArthur for hoodwinking the public into believing the war was over, but MacArthur pointed out that he had never made that claim: In fact, he had warned Chaffee that trouble was brewing in Samar. Balangiga infuriated Chaffee, who assured the press that "the situation calls for shot, shells and bayonets as the natives are not to be trusted." Chaffee informed his officers that it was his intention "to give the Filipinos 'bayonet rule' for years to come."[19]

President Roosevelt set the tone. He ordered Chaffee to adopt, "in no unmistakable terms," the "most stern measures to pacify Samar." A special unit, the 6th Separate Brigade under Brigadier General Jacob Smith, was formed to punish the people of Samar. At Balangiga on October 23, 1901, Smith ordered a battalion of 300 U.S. Marines, under the command of Major Littleton W. Waller, to make Samar a "howling wilderness." "I want no prisoners," Smith declared. "I wish you to kill and burn, the more you kill and burn the better you will please me. I want all persons killed who are capable of bearing arms in actual hostilities against the United States." Smith set the minimum age limit at ten.[20]

For the next five months, the 6th Separate Brigade killed and burned. Waller's marine battalion was particularly active, fighting several major skirmishes with Lukban's guerrilla bands but also systematically burning villages in the interior, destroying food, slaughtering work animals, and killing many civilian inhabitants. The population of Samar dropped from 312,192 to 257,715. Major Waller concluded his campaign with the unwarranted execution of 11 Filipinos, whom he accused of treachery.[21]

Chaffee also instituted harsher policies in the other remaining guerrilla stronghold, located in Batangas province in southern Luzon. On November 30, 1901, he sent his best field commander, Brigadier General Bell, to take command of the area. Chaffee directed Bell to use whatever means necessary to end the rebellion in the area. According to Glenn May, between January 1 and April 30, 1902, Bell kept approximately half of his 8,000-man brigade in the field. The soldiers destroyed over 1,400 tons of rice and palay, hundreds of bushels of corn, and hundreds of hogs and chickens; they also burned more than 6,000 houses and killed 200 carabaos, 800 head of cattle, and 680 horses. Large sections of Batangas province were turned into a wilderness, "totally lacking in food supplies, domesticated animals, and human shelter."[22]

The army burned villages and herded the population of Batangas into the major cities or into concentration camps. Noncombatants were forced into designated zones, where they were ordered to remain as long as fighting continued. All areas outside the camps were labeled "dead zones," and the U.S. Army operated under minimal restraint and pursued the enemy relentlessly. "Freed from most of the prohibitions under which they had earlier operated and pressed by Bell to get quick results," May observed in his study, "many officers and enlisted men appeared to feel that, so long as they were successful, their actions were likely to be condoned." The water cure was used extensively on captured Filipinos, but Bell's men were also charged with "committing other types of torture (the tying up of prisoners by their elbows and knees for long periods, the administering of severe beating, the exposure of prisoners to the sun for seven days)." Deathrates soared in the province as many civilians perished in the concentration camps. From January to April 1902, May estimated that 8,344 people died in Batangas, or about 28 people out of every 1,000 in a population of 298,000.[23]

The anti-imperialist forces in the U.S. Senate, primarily members of the minority Democratic party, demanded an investigation. The Republicans grudgingly agreed and selected Senator Henry Cabot Lodge to chair a committee to conduct hearings on the Philippines. Lodge reluctantly convened the committee on January 28, 1902. Witnesses were called, including Dewey, Otis, MacArthur, and many other military officers. Senators William B. Allison and Albert Beveridge led the Republican majority in feeding the witnesses leading questions to elicit responses that justified both the acquisition of the Philippines and U.S. military actions. The anti-imperialist senators, such as Thomas M. Patterson, Edward W. Carmack, and Charles A. Culberson (all Democrats), feared a whitewash and searched for evidence to clearly prove that U.S. actions in the Philippines were morally wrong. The senators squabbled constantly among themselves and often interrupted testimony to express their own opinions. As historian Stuart Miller noted, the senators "jockeyed rather clumsily to introduce leading and loaded questions in order to enhance or to mitigate" their own positions. "Sometimes the hearing degenerated into shouting matches between the committee members. The proceedings might have been more laughable had not the subject been so grim."[24]

Lodge usually stood above the fray, although his presence could never be ignored—he was not the type of man anyone ignored. Another historian, Edmund Morris, described Lodge as

tall, haughty, quiet and dry. His beard was sharp, his coat tightly buttoned, his handshake quickly withdrawn. His eyes, forever screwed up and blinking, surveyed the world with aristocratic disdain. A heavy mustache clamped his mouth aggressively shut. On the rare occasions when the thin lips parted, they emitted a series of metallic noises which, according to Lodge's whim, might be a quotation from *Prosper Mérimée,* or a joke comprehensible only to those of the bluest blood and most impeccable tailoring, or a personal insult so stinging as to paralyze all powers of repartee. Only in conditions of extreme privacy would Henry Cabot Lodge unbend an inch or so, and allow the privileged few to call him "Pinky." Among his own kind, Lodge was said to be a man of considerable wit and charm, but the large mass of humanity, including most of the political establishment, found him repellently cold. By no amount of persuasion could he be made to see any other man's view if it differed from his own.[25]

Lodge occasionally interjected his wit in the committee hearings, but generally he left it up to other fire-breathing imperialists to carry the ball. Beveridge, the young freshman Republican senator from Indiana, seemed to enjoy the confrontation and often led the Republican defense of the administration.[26]

The Senate hearings were closed to the public, and the newspapers did not print any sensational headlines on the testimony of witnesses before the committee. Roosevelt considered the hearings so important that he recalled Governor Taft from the Philippines to testify. Arriving in Washington in early February 1902, Taft huddled with the president and Root to develop the party line. They met constantly at the White House, and soon the town was referring to them as the "Three Musketeers."[27]

In his testimony before the Senate, Taft denied that U.S. rule in the Philippines was harsh and cruel. He acknowledged

> that cruelties have been inflicted; that people have been shot when they ought not to have been; that there have been … individual instances … of torture … all these things are true." [By way of explanation, Taft observed,] a man's bunkie … comes alone and finds [him] mutilated in an outrageous way; a man whom he had seen alive an hour before. You must understand that a soldier has human nature, and that things are done which a commanding officer would not approve and yet can not be prevented because of the outrage of feelings.[28]

But despite these occasional outrages, Taft asserted that the military and civilian officials did everything in their power to prevent atrocities. "I desire to say," he continued, "that it is my deliberate judgment that there never was a war conducted, whether against inferior races or not, in which there were more compassion and more restraint and more generosity." Taft praised Bell's operations in Batangas, declaring that only harsher penalties could control the roving *ladrones*. He even wrote to a friend, "I am sorry that Bell did not include Cavite in his campaign. Bell has made a great success in Batangas."[29]

Taft also claimed that the majority of the Filipino people welcomed U.S. rule. The Filipinos, he asserted, simply were not ready for self-government, and if the United States withdrew, anarchy and massive slaughter would occur. The United States was therefore obligated to remain in the Philippines until the Filipinos could be trained in self-rule. Although Taft did not put a time limit on the appropriate period of political tutelage, he implied it might take 100 years. He also recommended that Congress pass laws to allow U.S. citizens to purchase large tracts of land so that sugar and coconut plantations could be developed. Cheap Filipino labor would make such ventures extremely profitable.[30]

Other witnesses echoed Taft's testimony as they paraded before the Senate committee. Otis denied that the U.S. military committed any atrocities in the

Philippines and proclaimed that, if granted independence, the islands would soon be in a state of "anarchy and military despotism." General Robert Hughes concurred and declared the Filipinos incapable of self-government.[31]

In early April, MacArthur arrived from Denver to begin his testimony before the Senate committee. When questioned about U.S. military atrocities, MacArthur defended the army. In this area, he agreed with Taft and Root that the reports of atrocities were "grossly exaggerated." Considering the "barbarous cruelty" of the Filipinos who had "tortured to death American prisoners, ... buried alive ... Americans ... and horribly mutilated the bodies of the American dead, it was understandable that American soldiers occasionally retaliated." Root philosophically added, "Such things happen in every war."[32]

When Senators Patterson and Carmack noted that over 350 U.S. soliders had been court-martialed for crimes ranging from thievery, rape, and torture to murder, MacArthur responded with copies of his official reports from August 1898 to July 1901 that supported his positions. The reports were acknowledged as "illuminating," and in them, both sides discovered material to support their positions. As a brigade and division commander and later as military governor, MacArthur asserted he did everything in his power to prevent atrocities from occurring. With over 125,000 U.S. soldiers in the Philippines during the war, only a few officers and enlisted men had violated the rules of war. As to the ferocity in human nature that is brought to the surface in wartime, MacArthur observed,

> To say that the Army committed excesses or that excesses were encouraged ... is to say that the character of Americans in the Philippines is immediately transformed by the question of latitude and longitude which is not the fact. Individual men have committed individual outrages; but when we compare the conditions that exist in the Philippines today in that respect with what have existed in all modern wars between civilized states the comparison is absolutely in favor of the self-restraint and high discipline of the American soldier. ... I doubt if any war—either international or civil, any war on earth—has been conducted with as much humanity, with as much careful consideration, with as much self-restraint ... as have been the American operations in the Philippine archipelago.[33]

MacArthur deftly responded to criticism with facts and philosophical evaluations. The senators soon discovered that he enjoyed talking on topics such as political theory and the principles of democracy. When asked whether the United States should have annexed the Philippines, MacArthur lectured the senators and presented the political, economic, and military reasons why the United States needed the islands as a place to sell its surplus manufactured goods, as a strategic base in the Far East to expand trade with China and to protect Hawaii, and as a political base from which to spread American ideas about republican government. "The archipelago affords an ideal strategic position," MacArthur informed the senators. "It is the stepping stone to commanding influence—political, commercial and military supremacy in the East."[34]

The general "operated almost like a one-man filibuster," according to Stuart Miller, and often ignored questions "to embark on endless and tangential soliloquies on just about any subject that entered his head." Miller, who attacked MacArthur for his language and style, saw the purpose of the Senate hearings as investigative, designed to explore the charges of atrocities; on the other hand, MacArthur saw them as a means of researching what had happened and deciding what should be done in the Philippines.[35]

MacArthur wanted to display "a global strategic vision," in the words of William Manchester, "and in places the yellowing transcript foreshadows 1951 testimony after his son's relief." Often grandiose in vision, MacArthur (like Douglas later) insisted on analyzing topics in the broadest possible terms. When Douglas testified before the Senate in May 1951, he displayed a trait he had in common with his father when a single question "would touch off a ten or fifteen minute performance in free association, during which he might cite the Caesars, medieval customs, the Magna Carta, the French Revolution, England's nineteenth-century corn laws, Ireland's potato famines, and the average daily caloric consumption of Japanese farmers."[36]

In essence, MacArthur viewed the Senate hearings as a forum on U.S. policies in the Philippines. In this, he infuriated the administration. When asked whether the Filipinos liked Americans, for example, the general responded,

> They like our institutions. They have some mistrust of us individually, because our deportment is so entirely different from anything they have been familiar with. The Filipino is naturally an exceedingly polite person. The poorest laborer is imbued with that idea. ... The American idea of deportment is not exactly the same thing. So that the first intercourse between the Filipino and the American is apt to lead to misunderstanding.[37]

MacArthur refused to depict the Filipinos as naked savages. The popular image of Filipinos as a corrupt, cruel, stupid, and miserable people appalled him. The opposite was true, he proclaimed. "I have a good deal of faith in them," he said. "They are smart, generous and intelligent people." MacArthur advised the committee that the Filipinos should be granted self-government as soon as possible. "The principal end to be attained by the retention of the Philippine Islands is the initiation of and promulgation of republican principles," he stated. "I do not think there is a question about the power of the Filipino to reach any standard of excellence in almost any direction."[38]

MacArthur also disagreed with Taft on the appropriate economic development of the islands. Despite a growing clamor in Washington, he opposed the sale of large tracts of land to U.S. speculators to build sugar, tea, coffee, and coconut plantations. In 1902, of the 35 million acres of land in the Philippines, only about 5 million were under cultivation, the rest being underdeveloped public lands. The general advised Congress to avoid granting any land, franchises, or licenses to U.S. speculators who visualized obtaining cheap land and employing cheap labor in sweatshops or on plantations. He also opposed Taft's recommendation that Congress allow the importation of even cheaper Chinese labor into the islands because he believed it would undercut the wages being paid to the Filipino people. An unlimited flood of Chinese would simply continue the situation that had prevailed in the islands for centuries and would display an utter lack of interest in the well-being of the laboring class. If, on the other hand, Filipino laborers were paid an adequate wage, they would provide a good, conscientious, and stable workforce. In other words, MacArthur felt that the United States needed to improve the lot of the laboring class in the Philippines rather than depress it through exploitive wages. Such exploitation would change the nature of the Filipino people—they would become doleful, sober, human machines. If permeated with U.S. ideals, exploitation would be a disaster and lead to continued rebellion. MacArthur contended the Filipinos should not be regarded as inferior and abused, but rather, they should be treated as all citizens of the United States were treated.[39]

MacArthur's testimony infuriated the "Three Musketeers," and Root publicly disagreed with MacArthur. In speeches around the nation, he declared that the Filipinos did not have the first conception of what self-government meant, nor did they have the first qualification for its exercise.[40]

As soon as his testimony was completed, MacArthur was shuttled out of Washington to command the Military Department of the Lakes. Then, in the fall of 1902, he was sent to San Francisco to assume command of the Department of the Pacific. Pinky stayed with Douglas in his last year at West Point.

From his headquarters in San Francisco, MacArthur continued to frustrate the administration. Army reorganization was the major topic in military circles at the time. Many believed the military organization needed to be revamped and streamlined. For over forty years, the military structure was based on the senior general, usually with the rank of lieutenant general, commanding the army through bureaus and regional departmental commands. Technically, the commanding general was in charge, but staff bureaus usurped much of his power. Staff was divided into ten corps or departments, each with a bureau chief and a number of subordinate officers. The most powerful was the adjutant general, who made personnel assignments. Next was the Quartermaster's Department, which performed a variety of duties, including providing transportation, furnishing animals, purchasing supplies and equipment for troops, and constructing and maintaining enlisted men's barracks, officers quarters, and all other garrison buildings.[41]

The army command structure proved to be fragmented and inefficient during the Spanish-American War. Although the president was commander in chief, he could not give orders directly to staff officers or field forces, nor could his representative, the secretary of war. Instead, they both depended on the commanding general of the army to translate the president's desires into action. In turn, the commanding general depended on his bureau chiefs and department commanders to render his orders into action. When a planned action actually occurred, it was more a triumph of luck than a triumph of the system.[42]

When Root became secretary of war, he decided to correct the problem by reorganizing the army into a new general staff system patterned after that of Prussia. On December 13, 1902, he submitted a bill to the House Committee on Military Affairs on the creation of a general staff. It would consist of a chief of staff with the rank, pay, and allowances of a lieutenant general, one major general, one brigadier general, four colonels, six lieutenant colonels, twelve majors, and twenty captains. Unlike the staff system in which appointments were permanent, appointments under the new system were to be for a period of four years. The president could bypass the senior generals in the army and appoint any officer as chief of staff.

From his headquarters in San Francisco, MacArthur joined with Lieutenant General Nelson Miles, the commanding general of the army, in opposition to Root's bill on army reorganization. MacArthur believed the plan was politically motivated and not in the best interest of the service. Under the existing structure, Miles, long an irritant in Root's side, could not be removed as the commanding general until he reached the mandatory retirement age of sixty-four, still two years away. By creating a chief of staff, Root could effectively eliminate Miles's position and replace him with a chief of staff who would serve only as long as he maintained the confidence of the secretary of war and the president. Root's plan, then, would create a chief of staff under his direct control.[43]

MacArthur wrote a paper in opposition to Root's bill before Congress. He asserted that the plan was inappropriate for the United States and would lead to chaos in the U.S. Army. The Prussian general staff on which it was based had evolved under the patronage of one man, Frederick William Louis of Hohenzollern, who patronized, encouraged, and maintained its efficiency during the nearly seventy-five years he was prince, king, and emperor. The general staff system worked in Prussia, MacArthur admitted, but it would not work in a republican form of government. The kaiser, as the executive head of the system, was the foundation for the Prussian general staff, but in the United States, the chief of the executive branch of government was transitory. Presidents came and went every four to eight years. Because each new president would select a new chief of staff, there would be no continuity of leadership in the army. Moreover, every time the president changed or a chief of staff irritated a politician, the leadership of the army would change. Thus, the general staff would be subjected to a series of violent shocks absolutely unknown in Prussia as each new chief brought in a new general staff. There would be none of the continuity of organization, of direction, or of leadership that was essential for good staff work. "The proposed plan," according to MacArthur, was an attempt "to adopt and foster, in a Republican form of Government a system peculiarly adapted to monarchies."[44]

MacArthur also opposed the new general staff concept because it ignored the principle of rank. Since the president could appoint any officer, regardless of military rank, to be chief of staff, the appointee might be a junior officer, perhaps a recently promoted major general; as chief of staff, he could then order a lieutenant general, the ranking general in the army, to obey his commands. Such a situation violated the basic principle of military organizations: An officer's rank determined to whom he gave orders and from whom he received them. Command by rank had absolutely no exception in the military, and MacArthur strongly believed in the concept. The idea that the chief of staff might not be the ranking officer in the army seemed ludicrous to him—a violation of military logic.[45]

Root branded MacArthur and Miles uncooperative for their opposition to his reorganization plan. With the support of Roosevelt, he attacked Miles and publicly censored him several times for minor violations. When Miles complained to news reporters, Root and Roosevelt developed a scheme to get the touchy commanding general away from Washington, D.C. He was soon ordered on a world tour to evaluate foreign military establishments.[46]

Root then turned to the other recalcitrant general, MacArthur. In a series of speeches in early 1903, he subtly insulted MacArthur. For example, in reevaluating the heroic actions of the U.S. Army in the Philippines, Root ignored MacArthur and instead praised the "swift, resistless marches of General Young and General Lawton through the island of Luzon" during the campaigns of 1899 and 1900. He never mentioned the military victories achieved by MacArthur's 2nd Division, and nearly every officer in the army and most foreign military observers noted the insult. Root's failure to acknowledge MacArthur's military triumphs with appropriate honors was a slap in the face that the general would never forget or forgive.[47]

Root skillfully maneuvered his army reforms through Congress. And in February 1903, Congress authorized the creation of a general staff commanded by a chief of staff under the direct control of the president and the secretary of war. The authorized strength of the U.S. Army was set by Congress at a record peacetime ceiling of 100,000 men, four times its size a decade earlier. Service schools were reorganized, and new ones were created, such as the Army War College. In March, Root appointed a board to recommend the forty-two officers who would fill the first general staff complement. Not surprisingly, Miles and MacArthur were ignored. Root selected Major General Samuel Young as board president, with Major Generals Adna Chaffee and John Bates, and Brigadier Generals William Carter, Tasker Bliss, and Wallace Randolph. When Miles retired on August 8, 1903, Young was promoted to lieutenant general and selected by President Roosevelt to be the army's first chief of staff.[48]

MacArthur obtained a leave from his duties in San Francisco to attend Douglas's graduation at West Point on June 11, 1903. To the general's chagrin, Secretary Root was the keynote speaker at the graduation exercises. By this point, MacArthur knew he was a marked man with the Roosevelt administration: Root disliked him, Taft hated him, and the president sided with his political cronies. Insulted by Root's earlier speeches, General MacArthur refused to sit on the same rostrum with the secretary of war. Instead, he and Pinky sat with the other parents and relatives of the graduating class.[49]

The general, it can be assumed, beamed with pride. Douglas was first captain of the corps of cadets during his final year, the highest military honor a cadet could receive. D. Clayton James notes that Douglas "ranked first in his class for three of his four years, dropping from the top to fourth only in his third or second-class year. He earned 2424.12 merits of a possible 2470.00, or 98.14 per cent, for the four-year program. In the standing on the general merit roll for the ninety-four man class which graduated in 1903, [Douglas was first]."[50]

Biographer Frazier Hunt related Douglas's memory of the graduation ceremony. As first captain, he "[led the line of] graduates from their seats in the front rows. After he saluted and accepted his diploma, there was an outburst of applause. He turned quickly from the rostrum and instead of returning to his seat he walked straight on to the rear. He handed the diploma to his father and smiled down at his mother."[51]

Douglas returned to San Francisco with his father and mother for a two-month furlough, and for the first time in years, the family was reunited. Douglas's brother, Arthur, had been promoted to lieutenant and transferred from Newport, Rhode Island, to Mar Island near San Francisco in March 1903, where his father-in-law, Captain Bowman McCalla, was in command. Arthur's wife, Mary, was expecting; Pinky, Douglas, and the general had barely reached San Francisco when Mary gave birth to her first son (named Arthur after his father, grandfather, and great-grandfather) on June 29, 1903.[52]

The general spent many an evening with his two sons talking of his experiences in the Philippines, where Douglas was assigned to report in October. As his father described the islands, according to Carol Petillo, Douglas visualized the

> tropical beauty, so different from the gray skies and windy plain of the academy. [The general's descriptions of the] fiery and romantic temperament of the Filipinos appealed to the young cadet's already well-developed propensities in that direction. General MacArthur's recollections undoubtedly provided a valuable balance for the views which Douglas may have formed from the often distorted press accounts. ... Recounting his views of Aguinaldo and other Philippine leaders, the General would have persuaded Douglas that the Filipinos were both skilled militarily and loyal to a vision of national destiny.[53]

In early October, Douglas sailed on the transport *Sherman* with a list of his father's friends in Manila in his pocket; when he arrived in Manila on October 28, they made him feel welcome. His next six months were filled with high adventure. Assigned to the Department of the Visayas, he saw duty on Panay, Samar, Cebu, and Leyte, the four major Visayan islands just south of Luzon. Assigned as an engineer, MacArthur commanded work parties that cleared roads and built bridges and piers in the area. He probably wrote home about a narrow escape when two Filipino bandits attacked a work detail he was commanding. As Douglas recounted in his memoirs: "While attempting to construct piers and docks at Guimairs Island, located at the mouth of Iloilo Harbor [on Panay Island], I had to procure my own piling, and took a small detachment to cut timber in the jungle forests. The place was dangerous, being infested with brigands and guerrillas." On a narrow jungle trail, Douglas's party was waylaid "by two of these desperadoes. ... Like all frontiersmen, I was expert with a pistol," Douglas bragged. "I dropped them both dead in their tracks, but not before one had blazed away at me with his antiquated rifle. The slug tore through the top of my campaign hat and almost cut the sapling tree immediately behind me."[54]

Lieutenant MacArthur's exposure to guerrilla activity on Samar, Panay, and Leyte reinforced his opinion that his father had been mistreated by Washington. Civil control was a sham in the area, and local commanders believed that military control would remain necessary for years to come.[55]

During his one-year tour of duty in the Philippines, Douglas spent much of his time in Manila, associating with his father's old contacts. According to D. Clayton James, he was "charmed" and "enjoyed the social life and amusements." The Filipinos began calling him "MacArthur the Younger" to distinguish him from his father, whom they referred to as "MacArthur the Elder." In April 1904, less than a year after his graduation from West Point, Douglas was promoted to first lieutenant.[56]

Meanwhile, back in San Francisco, General MacArthur was again in trouble with the politicians. He had accidentally become involved in a public controversy over the rising power of Kaiser Wilhelm's Germany. As commander of the newly renamed Division of the Pacific, Hawaii came under MacArthur's jurisdiction, and in November 1903, he went to Honolulu to inspect U.S. military facilities on the islands. On November 27, he had dinner with Colonel J. W. Jones, commander of the Hawaiian National Guard. The National Guard was attempting to persuade the War Department to cede some land near Honolulu as a training camp for their recruits. Jones asked MacArthur what reasons might impress the secretary of war and the president.[57]

MacArthur suggested that he stress the military importance of Hawaii. Colonel Jones looked puzzled, so the general explained the significance of the islands in any future war in the Pacific. A master of military strategy and well read in politics and international relations, MacArthur was candid in his evaluation of Hawaii's military importance. If the United States became involved in a war with either Germany or Japan, he believed that Hawaii would be attacked before the Pacific Coast states. No enemy force in the Pacific could afford to attack California without capturing Hawaii; otherwise, they would leave their lines of communication open to attack and subject themselves to the serious consequences of having their supply vessels captured or destroyed. Therefore, MacArthur believed a strong National Guard in Hawaii was essential for the defense of the islands. In time of war, it would form the nucleus of any defensive force.

Lieutenant Douglas MacArthur, c. 1904. (MacArthur Memorial Library, Ph-215)

When Colonel Jones asked if MacArthur thought a war was likely to erupt between the United States and Germany or Japan, the general replied, "Possible but not in the immediate future." A decade or two in the future, he said, such a war not only seemed likely, it seemed almost inevitable because of the rising nationalism in Japan and Germany. Germany, according to MacArthur, was a more immediate threat than Japan because it was expanding its markets into Latin America, where hundreds of thousands of Germans resided. It was inevitable that the Monroe Doctrine would be tested and strained. And if these tensions erupted into war between the United States and Germany, German-born Americans would have a conflict of loyalty. The pan-Germanic doctrine, fostered by Kaiser Wilhelm and the imperial government, was strong and getting stronger wherever German people settled, even among the Germans who were citizens of the United States.

MacArthur's fears of a rising Germany were not unique. For years, journals, magazines, and newspapers had speculated on the possibility of war between the United States and Germany, and many other military men, such as Admiral Dewey, expressed the same views as MacArthur had. In his conversations with Jones, MacArthur was candid in his evaluation primarily because he was discussing a military situation with another military officer in the line of duty as commander of the Military Division of the Pacific.[58]

A few days later, Colonel Jones had a conference with Governor George R. Carter. When questioned about the National Guard, he mentioned MacArthur's cogent arguments on the need for a strong Hawaiian guard. Carter was impressed and suggested that Jones type up a summary of his conversation with MacArthur: The arguments would be useful in Hawaii's negotiations with the War Department to obtain land for a new training facility for the National Guard.

On Wednesday, December 9, Jones turned in his report to Governor Carter. That afternoon, around 4:30, Daniel Logan, a reporter for the Honolulu *Pacific Commercial Advocate,* visited Carter and noticed Jones's report sitting on the desk. Logan asked to read the report, and Carter handed it over to the newsman. Carter was a politician, and public relations were important to him.

Logan saw a news story. Without asking permission or checking with MacArthur on the accuracy of Jones's report, which had been composed from memory six days after the conversation took place, Logan wrote his story. The next day's headlines in the *Commercial Advocate* read: "GENERAL MACARTHUR WARNS HAWAII OF A COMING WAR WITH GERMANY." The Associated Press picked up the story, and it was reprinted in a number of mainland newspapers, including the *New York Herald.*[59]

German American groups from New York to San Francisco protested. They declared that MacArthur was questioning their loyalty, and they demanded an apology and retraction. Although President Roosevelt and Secretary Root agreed with MacArthur on the danger of Kaiser Wilhelm's Germany, they were appalled by the news story: Political commentary was the province of politicians, not generals.

Root ordered the new chief of staff, Lieutenant General Young, to send a cablegram to MacArthur demanding an explanation for his actions.[60]

MacArthur was caught in a trap. The news story embarrassed him, and he was apologetic, although he did not believe the current flap was his fault. He had made no public speeches, had expressed his opinion in private, and had been badly misinterpreted. The story was an unauthorized version of a private conversation and should never have been published. MacArthur contacted Governor Carter and Colonel Jones and requested they explain the situation to the War Department.

A red-faced Carter responded immediately with a cablegram to the president. He wired:

> I feel, and feel very strongly, that no disciplinary action can justly be taken towards General MacArthur. He has been extremely diligent in the acquisition of knowledge for the War Department. In his conversation with Colonel Jones, he was impressing upon him the value of this group of Islands in case of any foreign war, emphasizing their importance to the War Department so as to stimulate the National Guard of Hawaii to increased activity.[61]

Carter explained that the news story was his fault, not MacArthur's; the general had never authorized nor even considered the possibility that his ideas would be made public.

Roosevelt was not impressed. How MacArthur's statements were leaked was irrelevant. The fact he had embarrassed the administration was more important. Dismissing Carter's explanation, he ordered Root to send MacArthur a letter of reprimand. Root responded with a critical letter to the general that began:

> By direction of the President, you are informed that the President feels obliged to express his grave regret that even in a private conversation you should have said the things stated in the Associated Press dispatch. Unjustifiable and unexpected as was the publication of your remarks, it shows how unwise it is for an officer of high rank to express opinions upon such subjects. The responsibilities of high military office include the obligation to carefully refrain, under all circumstances, from expressions which, if reported, may tend to disturb the good will and friendly feeling between our own and all other nations. The President especially regrets your reflection upon the patriotism of a large body of our fellow citizens who happen to be of a certain birth and origin. It is most unfortunate that any high official should use language tending to divide Americans one from another by exciting prejudices.[62]

Root's letter angered MacArthur. To demand that a military officer not express his military opinions in private conversations with other military officers was asinine and clearly an impossible order. Beyond that, his comments had nothing to do with racial or national prejudices—his old Milwaukee regiment had been full of German Americans during the Civil War. Rather, a military officer had privately asked him if he believed Hawaii might need to defend itself from an attack by a foreign power, and he had given his military opinion to inspire the officer to diligently train the Hawaiian National Guard. Ultimately, MacArthur believed it was unfair to reprimand him for doing his job. If a reprimand were issued, it should be directed at Governor Carter. MacArthur felt that Roosevelt and Root had sacrificed his reputation for political expediency and perhaps as a rebuke for his earlier positions on the Philippines and army reorganization. He now realized that he had little chance of being appointed chief of staff during the Roosevelt administration.

His troubles, however, were not over. MacArthur's standing with the War Department suffered a disastrous blow in January 1904 when his archenemy, William Howard Taft, was recalled from the Philippines and appointed secretary of war after Root resigned. Taft, a better propagandist than MacArthur, had convinced many that he was the instrumental force in civilizing the Filipinos. He presented himself as the humanitarian while depicting the military as a group of cruel men who believed in pacification by the sword. Taft continued to portray MacArthur as a pompous, overly proud military man with limited ability. Roosevelt sided with Taft.

MacArthur had expected more from Roosevelt, who had often said that those "who have dared greatly in war, or the work which is akin to war" deserved the best from their country. But Roosevelt did not particularly like career army officers. During his experiences with the Rough Riders in Cuba, he developed a disdain for high-ranking army officers, such as William Shafter. As Roosevelt had written to Henry Cabot Lodge: "I am more fit to command a Brigade or a Division or attend to this whole matter of embarking and sending the army than many of those whose business it is." During Taft's tenure at the War Department, he would favor the hard-line officers, such as Bell and Chaffee, over those who had preached a softer line in the Philippines.[63]

Fortunately, international events took MacArthur's mind off his deteriorating career. On February 8, 1904, the Japanese navy attacked the Russian Pacific fleet at Ports Arthur and Dairen (Dalny) in Manchuria. The attack surprised the world. President Roosevelt proclaimed the Japanese had illustrated bold initiative.

For the next few months, MacArthur watched the events in Korea and Manchuria with fascination. For thirty years, he had read nearly every book published on East Asia, and his deep interest in China and Japan had been reinforced by his experiences in the Philippines. Although the world assumed the Japanese would be defeated in the war with Russia, MacArthur knew better. The Russian population, the Russian army, and the Russian navy greatly outnumbered the Japanese, but Japan had carefully trained its troops and had a much shorter supply line. In battle after battle in Korea and southern Manchuria in the spring, summer, and fall of 1904, the Japanese army was victorious, although their losses were high.

Douglas's tour of duty in the Philippines was cut short when he contracted malaria, and he returned to San Francisco in November. With Lieutenant Arthur MacArthur, his wife, and his young son also living in the area, family get-togethers were frequent. Captain McCalla, Arthur's father-in-law, had recently been promoted to admiral. The men often discussed the Russo-Japanese War. It was shoptalk for them.[64]

As the war dragged on, MacArthur desperately wanted to visit the front. It was not simply because it was a war but because the war was in an area that he had been interested in for most of his adult life. East Asia called to him. In December 1904, he petitioned the War Department for an assignment to Japan as a military observer. "My purpose," he wrote, "would be to witness some general engagement. I don't know that I could present a report of very much practical value, as the only special qualification I can claim for the work is exceptional appreciation of the importance of the subject."[65]

MacArthur's request delighted Taft. The general was a potential thorn in the side of Taft's career, and if MacArthur wanted to leave the country for a year or two, Taft supported the idea. He believed that MacArthur simply wanted a trip to Tokyo, where he would socialize with the Japanese military and play bridge with the members of the U.S. legation. The only difficulty was that the War Department had already appointed five military observers to Japan, including Colonel Crowder, MacArthur's secretary in Manila; Major Peyton March, another former MacArthur aide; and Captain John J. "Black Jack" Pershing, a rising star in the army.[66]

Taft solicited the advice of Secretary of State John Hay, who queried Tokyo on whether the Japanese would accept General MacArthur as a military observer in Manchuria. Tokyo responded with enthusiasm. MacArthur's appointment displayed respect toward Japan, and most Japanese military men wanted to meet the famous general of the Philippine campaigns.[67]

On January 18, 1905, MacArthur received official notification of his appointment as a military observer in the Russo-Japanese War. To his surprise, Pinky opted to accompany him. He began immediate preparations for his trip, looking up shipping schedules and purchasing two tickets on the liner SS *Korea*. It was to leave San Francisco for Yokohama on February 15.

Through the military grapevine, MacArthur learned that Washington would extend his mandate if he requested it. He was, after all, a potential embarrassment to the administration since he was the logical candidate to succeed Lieutenant General Chaffee as chief of staff. General Young had retired in the summer of 1904, and the sixty-two-year-old Chaffee would retire within two years. Major General Arthur MacArthur was now the second ranking general in the army, and he would not reach the mandatory retirement age of sixty-four until 1909. But the prospect of MacArthur becoming the next chief of staff appalled Secretary of War Taft. The traditional method of getting rid of an irritating general who could not be fired was to send him on a world tour, as Root had done with Miles back in 1902. Consequently, since MacArthur was going to be in Japan, Taft suggested that he might like to tour military bases in Asia from Tokyo to New Delhi. He hoped such a tour would keep MacArthur out of the country until after Chaffee retired and a new chief of staff was appointed.[68]

To Taft's delight, MacArthur responded with enthusiasm. He had dreamed of visiting China for thirty years. Back in 1882, he had even tried, without success, to obtain an appointment as the military attaché to Peking. He knew the Philippines, but he wanted to see the great cultures of the East and to study their economic and military potential.

On February 14, 1905, Pinky and General MacArthur, accompanied by his aide, Captain Parker W. West of the 11th Cavalry, boarded the SS *Korea* in San Francisco harbor for the first stage of an adventure that would last eighteen months. Also aboard was Captain Pershing and his new wife, Frances, the daughter of Senator Francis E. Warren of Wyoming. Roosevelt selected Pershing as one of the military observers in Manchuria primarily as a wedding gift to the newly married couple with excellent political connections. While en route, the military group became friends; in later years, Pinky often reminded Pershing of their trip together.[69]

For the first five days, the sea was turbulent, but it became calmer as the ship approached Honolulu. MacArthur had described the beauty of the islands to his wife, and when they arrived in Honolulu on February 21, she was not disappointed. However, there was no time to see the city because the *Korea* sailed the next day for Yokohama. The ship reached Yokohama on March 5. The U.S. minister to Japan, Lloyd C. Griscom, met the party and traveled with the MacArthurs to Tokyo. The bustle of the city fascinated Pinky. Tokyo was home to over 1 million people, and, according to historian Frank E. Vandiver, "an odd mixture of old and new touched the city with tangled mystique. ... Commerce throbbed in the Ginza's circled avenues, and prosperous businessmen gave the Marinouchi district a kind of Western hurry." The MacArthurs took rooms at the Old Imperial Hotel, the only hotel in the city that catered to foreigners.[70]

The next day, General MacArthur met with the Japanese minister of war, General Terauchi Masatake, and the assistant chief of staff, General Murato. The Japanese considered most foreign military attachés and foreign reporters to be nuisances. The war had stimulated tremendous interest in Japan, and correspondents and observers inundated the Japanese Foreign Office with requests to visit the battle zone. Nearly 100 war correspondents and military observers languished in Tokyo and constantly badgered the Foreign Office for permission to travel to Manchuria. Although courteous to the foreign visitors, the government offered special consideration to only a few. Representatives of wire services and distinguished Western newspaper and magazine correspondents were often frustrated with the extensive paperwork and long delays required before being granted permission to visit the front. But General MacArthur was an exception—the Japanese military treated him as an honored guest. While Roosevelt and Taft ignored MacArthur's military accomplishments, the Japanese high command considered the general a great military tactician, and they had carefully studied his tactics in the Philippines and applied them in Manchuria.[71]

On Wednesday evening, March 8, General Terauchi honored MacArthur with a banquet. During the day, a hush of hope hung over the city as news from the front

Lieutenant General Arthur MacArthur in Japan, 1905. (MacArthur Memorial Library, Ph-A83/p. 17)

arrived. A major battle raged at Mukden, the capital of Manchuria, where the Japanese army was attacking the Russian forces. As more than 100 Japanese and foreign guests assembled to honor MacArthur, a buzzing excitement charged the air. Throughout the evening, dispatches kept arriving from Mukden, and Terauchi would stand and read them aloud. The Japanese were winning, and the quiet Tokyo streets changed as crowds assembled to cheer each news dispatch. Finally, riotous cheers of "banzai" erupted when news reached the city that Mukden had been captured. At the banquet, the highest Japanese military leaders grasped the full dimensions of the victory, and men who were normally formal and restrained shouted and cheered. "Banzai" rang out time and again as the guests toasted the Japanese army, the emperor, President Roosevelt, and General MacArthur.[72]

MacArthur realized the war would soon be over, and he wanted to visit the front immediately. Although most foreign observers experienced frustrating delays, the Japanese moved with alacrity in MacArthur's case. Minister Griscom wrote Secretary Hay that for once, the Japanese provided maximum help. The general got special attention and quickly received permission to travel to Manchuria.[73]

Accompanied by Captain West and Captain Pershing, MacArthur departed from Tokyo on March 9 for Kobe. The Japanese general staff arranged every detail and assigned a Japanese army lieutenant as an interpreter to accompany the party, which included two British officers, Colonel W. H. Birkbeck and Captain B. Vincent. At Kobe, the party transferred to a special railroad car and proceeded to Shimonoseki. They arrived at 5:30 A.M. on March 11 and were scheduled to depart Shimonoseki for Manchuria on the transport *Tamba Mara* that afternoon. Rather than waste the day waiting, MacArthur visited the Russian prisoner of war camp at Moji near Shimonoseki. The camp was crude, but the prisoners were well fed and comfortable. After a whirlwind tour, MacArthur returned to board the *Tamba Mara* for the voyage to Port Dairen (Dalny), the main Japanese supply base in Manchuria. Although not a large ship, the *Tamba Mara* was packed with troops and supplies for the front. The Japanese honored MacArthur and his party with the best staterooms on the vessel, and the group was served Western food by excellent attendants.[74]

After a two-day voyage, the *Tamba Mara* dropped anchor in Dairen harbor. Captured from the Russians early in the war, Dairen was on the Kwantung Peninsula about 40 miles east of Port Arthur. The harbor was alive with activity. Japanese war vessels and transports, international merchant ships, Chinese junks, small sampans, and naval launches crowded the bay. Ashore, overpacked warehouses were loaded with army supplies that spilled out in enormous stacks surrounding the buildings. All was in perfect order and covered with canvas tarpaulins lining the waterfront. Behind the docks and warehouses, a railroad line ran toward the city proper, 5 miles to the west. MacArthur remained aboard the *Tamba Mara* for two days as supplies were unloaded. A flotilla of junks then took the men and horses ashore. Pershing remembered that "the debarkation was a novel sight, the men, fifteen at each hoist, being lifted over the side and lowered into the junks in great nets of rope, and the horses going over in a sling one at a time."[75]

On March 15, the MacArthur party went ashore and took the train to Dairen. The city showed few signs of war damage. Built by the Russians, it looked more European than Asian. Massive brick structures served as government headquarters, and there were other large brick structures to house the Russian garrison. Everything looked new and modern, for the Russians had expected to remain. Still, Dairen had a depressing drabness. "It is very substantial in appearance," observed Pershing in his report to the War Department, "but the brick is poorly laid and the buildings are gradually crumbling away. The streets are narrow and the houses are surrounded by low brick walls on stone foundations."[76]

Japanese troops and supplies packed the city, and the streets were crowded with thousands of Chinese. Although there was much commotion, there was little confusion: The Japanese capacity for organization maintained order in what would otherwise have been chaos. Japanese staff officers quickly found MacArthur and his companions comfortable quarters heated by coal stoves to combat the cold Manchurian spring.

That evening, MacArthur dined with the Japanese commander of Dairen. The next day, he visited the docks, warehouses, and barracks and interviewed other Americans in Dairen, including C. H. Little, a correspondent for the *Chicago Tribune* who had been captured while with the Russian army. Little described his experiences and informed MacArthur that the Japanese had caught the Russians completely unprepared.[77]

On March 16, a very cold day in Dairen, MacArthur's party boarded a special railroad car attached to a supply train going to Liaoyang, 200 miles north. After running along the coast for a number of miles, the track veered northeast. From the train, they saw old battle sites, such as Nanshan Hill, where the Russian trenches had been overrun on May 26, 1904. The countryside appeared poor, with only occasional farming areas and stray squalid huts in poor villages. During the day, they passed trainloads of Russian prisoners being brought southward in open cars despite the bitterly cold weather. Among the prisoners were two U.S. officers, Colonel Valery Havard, Medical Corps, and Major William V. Judson, Engineer Corps, who had been military attachés with the Russian army at Mukden. They would be released in Japan and deported back to the United States—an ignoble fate that could befall MacArthur if he, too, were captured by the Russian army.[78]

The train continued through the night. The next morning, they arrived at Liaoyang on a bitterly cold St. Patrick's Day. Liaoyang was a typical Chinese city, with narrow, congested streets desperately in need of repair. The city reeked of garbage, but here and there were spots of striking beauty. MacArthur had complete freedom of movement, and he roamed the old city for the next three days. During his stay, he met America's most famous war correspondent, Frederick Palmer, a squat, bandy-legged little man. Palmer looked like a scholar and had a nose for other people's business. He had an aura of reckless bravado, donned a bandolier and pistol in tense situations, and walked the battlefields with pad and pencil in hand. The adventurous Palmer had covered more wars and achieved greater fame than any other U.S. correspondent of his generation.[79]

Palmer was bogged down in Liaoyang because of Japanese regulations. The Japanese censored all dispatches leaving Manchuria, and correspondents were under strict orders not to mention troop movements, unit strengths, names of regiments, morale of troops, or place-names. They were not even allowed to speculate on future military operations. If the censors decided any item in a correspondent's dispatch was militarily sensitive, the whole dispatch was deleted. Palmer also complained about the Japanese refusal to allow him to continue on to Mukden. He asked permission to join MacArthur's party, whose path was being smoothed by the general's high rank and prestige. After consultation with Colonel Yoda, the Japanese commander at Liaoyang, MacArthur allowed Palmer to join his group, which still included Captain West, Captain Pershing, and the two British officers.[80]

Considering MacArthur an honored guest, Colonel Yoda accompanied the party the next day when they boarded the train for the two-hour trip to Mukden. Yoda acted as the tour guide for the party. As the train moved north through the countryside, he described the many battles fought over the terrain in the previous year. As they approached Mukden, the gruesome reminders of war became increasingly evident. Villages were in ruins, and the fields were strewn with discarded military equipment, shattered artillery pieces, broken-down transports, and the unburied bodies of hundreds of dead Russian soldiers. The battle for Mukden had been ferocious; the Russians lost 89,000 men—20,000 killed, 49,000 wounded, and 20,000 captured. Japanese casualties had also been high, with 16,000 dead and 60,000 wounded.

Mukden was the capital and most important city in Manchuria. Under Japanese control, the city became the new headquarters of Field Marshal Oyama Iwao, the commander of Japanese armies in Manchuria. Supplies poured into the city from Japan, and the roads in and out of the city were packed with transports. The Chinese were at work reconstructing burned houses and salvaging every little article from among the ruins.[81]

MacArthur was allotted quarters in one of the better-constructed Russian buildings near Japanese headquarters. In the evening, he dined with Marshal Oyama and his staff. MacArthur wanted to proceed to the front immediately, but Oyama was reluctant to grant permission until he was sure his guest would be absolutely safe. MacArthur remained in Mukden for six weeks observing Japanese military organization. He reported to Washington that the military environment afforded a fine scope for professional study and military reflection.[82]

MacArthur also exchanged information with military observers from Germany, Austria, France, and Italy. The foreign observers took horseback rides together to the battlefields in the surrounding countryside. The roads out of Mukden were crowded with Japanese field transport trains; long columns of Japanese army carts, each drawn by one small horse and led by a soldier, stretched north for miles. The Japanese had also commandeered Chinese carts and conscripted coolies to assist them. Some of the Chinese carts were large, some small; some were drawn by ponies, some by bullocks, and some by coolies panting and grunting as they strained at the ropes as desperately as the animals under the lash. Pershing reported that "the Japanese engineers had not had time to put the roads in good condition or reconstruct the bridges the retreating enemy had destroyed." Men and animals paid the price in sweat and muscle. North of Mukden, the streaming lines of supply vehicles seemed endless. "In places there was hardly space on the roads for those that were laden going north and those that were empty coming south."[83]

MacArthur admired the organizational skills of the Japanese and the almost fanatical devotion of the Japanese soldiers to their officers and government. He formed a close friendship with General Kuroki Tametomo, the sixty-year-old commander of the Japanese 1st Army, that would be maintained for years. Kuroki never failed to appear when MacArthur visited army headquarters, and the two generals spent hours discussing military tactics and world history. On May 10, accompanied by Kuroki, MacArthur was allowed to visit the front at Tieling, 40 miles north of Mukden. For the next three months, he remained in the area observing minor skirmishes between the Japanese and the Russians.

War activity shifted from the land battles in Manchuria to the sea. At the beginning of the war, the Japanese navy crippled the Russian Pacific fleet at Port Arthur and later captured or destroyed most of the ships. Other Russian vessels in the Pacific were blockaded in Vladivostok harbor. The Japanese controlled the seas, but Tsar Nicholas had a solution. Russia had another fleet in European waters that was as large as the entire Japanese navy, and in October 1904, the tsar sent his European fleet (composed of 12 battleships plus about 25 destroyers and cruisers and dozens of smaller support vessels) to the Pacific to destroy the Japanese navy. The Russian fleet suffered innumerable catastrophes during the 18,000-mile journey that lasted eight months. Sailing up the China coast in mid-May 1905, the Russian commander decided to pass through the Straits of Tsushima that separate southern Korea from Japan. His goal was Vladivostok, where he hoped to break the Japanese blockade and to reoutfit his fleet before engaging the Japanese in a decisive naval battle. Vice Admiral Togo Heihachiro, in command of the Japanese navy, had other plans. On May 27, he engaged the Russian navy in the Straits of Tsushima and achieved one of the greatest naval victories in history. The Japanese navy sank or captured 32 of the 35 Russian vessels, killed 4,800 Russian sailors, and captured another 7,000. The Japanese losses were 110 dead.[84]

Russia sued for peace. When the tsar contacted President Roosevelt and asked him to act as mediator, Roosevelt agreed. Under the keen eye of the president, Russian and Japanese diplomats met in Portsmouth, New Hampshire, in August 1905. Meanwhile, in Manchuria, both sides waited for the treaty that would officially end the war. MacArthur decided it was time to return to Japan. On August 10, he returned to Mukden; from there, he traveled back to Dairen, then 30 miles north to Port Arthur, where he remained for a few days observing the Japanese military machine and administration of the area. To continue his observations, he traveled back to Dairen and took a steamship to Pusan, Korea, where he disembarked to travel to Seoul. He then took a train down the peninsula to Ping-yang, 153 miles south, arriving on September 3. After a brief rest, he reboarded a steamship for the final stage of his journey and arrived in Tokyo on September 10, 1905. He proceeded immediately to Yokohama, where his wife was waiting at the Oriental Palace Hotel. While the general had been in Manchuria and Korea, Pinky had spent the six months socializing with various Americans in Japan, including railroad magnate Edward H. Harriman, the controlling owner of the Union Pacific and Southern Pacific railroads.[85]

MacArthur was back in Japan only one day when anti-American demonstrations erupted in the major cities. The Japanese people were upset with the terms of the Treaty of Portsmouth, signed on September 5. Although Russia had ceded

Secretary of War William Howard Taft and party enroute to Manila, c. 1905. (MacArthur Memorial Library, Ph-1719)

its interests in Manchuria and northern Korea to Japan, the tsar had refused to pay an indemnity to Tokyo. The Japanese had accumulated a tremendous war debt, and the government had promised the nation that the Russians would be forced to pay that debt. When Russia refused and President Theodore Roosevelt sided with St. Petersburg, many Japanese blamed the United States. Millions demonstrated in the streets of Japanese cities, and hundreds committed suicide to protest the national disgrace.

MacArthur also learned that his archenemy, Secretary of War Taft, was in Yokohama. Taft's presence was not accidental—it was directly related to MacArthur. The general had indicated a desire to revisit the Philippines while he was in Asia, and the idea frightened Taft, whose reputation and political future were based on his days as governor of the islands. The Republican press depicted Taft as the savior of the islands, rescuing them from cruel military rule; nearly a century later, scholars were still portraying Taft as the defender of the Filipino people and condemning MacArthur for believing in rule by the bayonet—despite the fact that he had supported civil liberties in the Philippines and opposed harsh military tactics, such as those employed by J. Franklin Bell in Batangas.[86]

Since MacArthur was already in Japan, this was a perfect opportunity for him to visit the Philippines. The Manila aristocracy and the U.S. military would give him a grand reception. Also, Pinky would get to see the islands where he had achieved his greatest accomplishments.

Taft developed a plan to prevent MacArthur from returning to Manila and to preserve his own image as the benevolent governor of the islands. In May, Taft organized a grand political junket to tour Japan, China, and the Philippines. He invited eighty guests, including Alice Roosevelt (the president's daughter), seven senators, twenty-four congressmen, and Major General Henry Corbin, who had been appointed commander of the Military Division of the Philippines. The Taft party left San Francisco on the SS *Manchuria* in mid-July 1905 to arrive in Yokohama around July 27. At a grand reception, Taft met Pinky and Frances Pershing and invited them to accompany the party to Manila.

Pinky rejected the invitation, knowing the general's attitude toward Taft, but Mrs. Pershing accepted the offer. The Taft junket left Yokohama and arrived in Manila on August 13 for a two-week visit. The U.S. colonial government, the U.S. military, and the Filipino aristocracy organized banquets and tours for the politicians. Grandiose speeches lauded Taft at every stop, and the praise was picked up by the U.S. press.[87]

A week before MacArthur returned from Manchuria, Taft and his party arrived back in Japan, and on September 17, MacArthur met with Taft and Corbin. When he outlined his plans to visit the Philippines, they discouraged him: The situation in Manila, they proclaimed, was too delicate.

Taft, a master at political compromise, offered the general something in return. He would assign Lieutenant Douglas MacArthur as the general's new aide for the grand Asian tour. To Pinky's delight, the general accepted the offer.[88]

Shortly thereafter, Taft and his group left for Peking, while the general and Pinky waited for the arrival of their son from San Francisco. MacArthur's extended stay pleased the Japanese. Japan's military leaders normally had a policy of secrecy and silence, but in MacArthur's case, they opened up their establishments for his inspection. He visited the Tokyo Arsenal, the Military Cadet School, military hospitals, infantry and cavalry barracks, and military museums. With his aide, Captain West, he also finished a report on the Hotchkiss machine gun used by the Japanese army in Manchuria. The report was so detailed on the technical aspects of the machine gun that the chief of military intelligence distributed it to all department heads and recommended it be published in the *Infantry Journal*. In Tokyo, MacArthur had conferences with Field Marshal Yamagata Aritomo and General Terauchi Masatake, the minister of war, and on October 11, he met the Emperor Meiji at an official reception at Shibu Palace.

Douglas MacArthur finally arrived in Japan on Sunday, October 29, 1905, and joined his father and mother at Yokohama's Oriental Palace Hotel. Three days later, they departed on a trip that would greatly influence Douglas's life (see Map 14.1). The trip began with visits to Japanese military bases at Kyoto, Kobe, and Nagasaki, where the general introduced his son to the famous Japanese military leaders of the day, including Generals Oyama and Kuroki and Admiral Togo. Douglas was impressed with these "grim, taciturn, aloof men of iron character and unshakable purpose," but he was even more impressed with the respect these

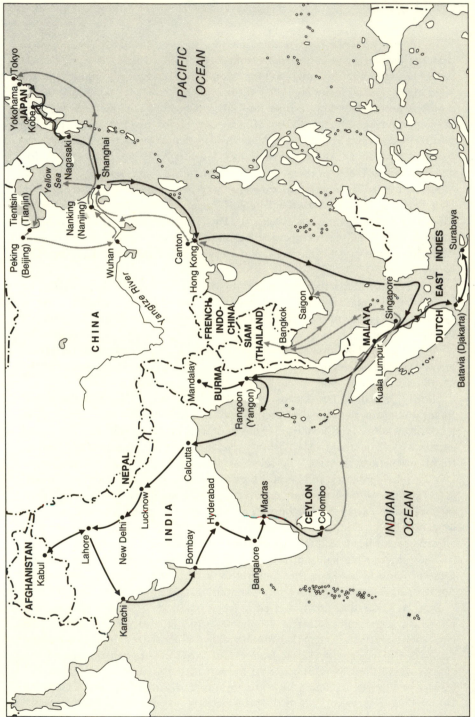

MAP 14.1 The Asian tour, November 1905–June 1906

hardened military men showed his father. During the eight-month, 19,949-mile Asian tour, Douglas would learn that professional soldiers throughout Asia appreciated his father's military and administrative talents. He later considered this trip "without doubt the most important factor of preparation for my entire life." He learned, according to his memoirs, "the strength and weakness of the colonial system, how it brought law and order, but failed to develop the masses along the essential lines of education and political economy." He also learned about poverty as he "rubbed elbows with millions of the underprivileged who knew nothing of the different [political and economic systems and peasants] interested only in getting a little more food in their stomachs, a little better coat on their backs, a little stronger roof over their heads." He took hundreds of photographs to record the experience.[89]

For the first time in his adult life, Douglas was continually in the presence of his father, the man he idolized more than any other. During the long journey, the son began to emulate his father and dreamed of making the general proud of him. In the words of William Manchester, "The flame of zeal burned ever brighter" in Douglas; "he awaited only an opportunity to prove himself the equal of the hero of Missionary Ridge." When Douglas received the congressional Medal of Honor after Corregidor, he indicated his regret that his father was not there to share his honor. When an acquaintance once remarked that Douglas was much like his father, Douglas responded by saying, "Thank you, sir. There is no tribute you could pay me that I would appreciate quite that much."[90]

The first rule of the MacArthur clan was to be prepared. The general ordered his son to purchase every book he could find on the countries they visited, and in the evenings, they read, talked, and analyzed their experiences. The general insisted that Douglas keep meticulous records, and each day his reading list grew. By the end of their trip, the MacArthurs had read dozens of books on the countries they visited. Teddy Roosevelt once told a friend, "Reading with me is a disease," and MacArthur was like Roosevelt in this and in many ways. Both had voracious appetites for books on almost any topic from Greek and Roman history to the culture of China. Before he retired, the general accumulated a library of over 4,000 books.[91]

General MacArthur's second rule for his son regarded appearance and decorum. A superior man, he believed, always appeared dignified, always dressed appropriately, and always communicated with others in the most intellectual language. The MacArthurs were traveling out of uniform at the time, although at social functions, they appeared in their dress whites. Manchester pictures Douglas in a "white linen suit, a Charles Dana Gibbons poster of what a young officer in mufti should look like, gazing at stirring Asia with the eyes of an impressionable American patrician." As his father's aide, Douglas kept the party's travel vouchers and acted as the general's secretary. He was soon emulating his father's academic tone in his speech and his writing. As Manchester notes, all his life Douglas employed "artifices he had learned from his father. ... He acted in the belief that he was a courageous and gifted officer, that he was entitled to more responsibility, and that bestowing it upon him would be a service to the country." In laters years, Douglas's Victorian style and turgid language, much like that of his father's, irritated many of his colleagues and most of the politicians who were forced to deal with him.[92]

Of all the things the general taught his son on this trip, the most important was a moral code that emphasized the inalienable rights of man. Carol Petillo observed that the general and his son

> clearly believed in the importance of long-term Western control of certain Asian countries, [but] on the other hand, the philosophy of democratic opportunity was also a factor in the background, experience, and education of both men. They had been influenced enough by the progressive milieu then current in the United States and by their Philippine experiences to believe that something must be done to alleviate the impoverished condition of the Asian poor. Even though they enjoyed the luxuries and tribute offered them [on the trip], at the same time they deplored the economic base [of colonialism]. It was a quandary which would provide Arthur MacArthur a subject for the philosophical and theoretical examinations of which he was so fond. For his son, these parallel, equally attractive and yet opposing concerns would be cause for a much more serious and concrete response in later life.[93]

General MacArthur often talked about the Philippines and his hope for the development of a republican form of government in the islands. Petillo, in her study of Douglas, asserts that the general's "unusual appreciation of the Filipinos and their national interest encouraged a parallel sympathy and understanding in his son" who would be closely associated with the Philippines for much of his military career. Years later, in a speech before Congress describing the aspiration of the Asian peoples, Douglas echoed the words of his father.[94]

As Frazier Hunt would note about Douglas, the general's philosophy of government was based on the ideals of democracy, and he "sought footholds on the bedrock of principles." Hunt wrote that for Douglas, as for his father, "issues automatically became moral issues, his decisions resting on the simple test of what is right and what is wrong. ... The ancient verities still remained the basis of the great decisions that MacArthur made."[95]

When Douglas was Supreme Commander of Allied Powers in Japan, he attempted to fulfill his father's mission. He remembered the general's lectures on the value of using conciliation rather than punishment when dealing with a defeated enemy, his hatred of racial bigotry, and, particularly, his strong belief in republicanism. In Tokyo, Douglas treated the Emperor Hirohito much as his father had treated President Aguinaldo. And like his father before him, Douglas refused to give an order against fraternization: "Soldiers will be soldiers," he said. His father had told him he should "never give an order unless I was certain it would be carried out. I wouldn't issue a no fraternization order for all the tea in China." Douglas's prime goal in Japan, like his father's main objective in the Philippines, was to stimulate the development of democratic principles and to guarantee to the Japanese people the personal liberties outlined in the U.S. Constitution.[96]

On November 6, the MacArthurs left Nagasaki for Singapore, where they arrived on November 23. Arthur MacArthur called on the British governor and reviewed British troops on the island. From Singapore, they traveled to several military bases on the Malay Peninsula, then returned to Singapore to sail for Batavia (Djarkarta) on November 28. They remained in the Dutch East Indies (Indonesia) for twenty days, traveling about 1,200 miles by train from Batavia to Surabaya and stopping at twelve military bases. On December 23, they returned to Singapore for Christmas. They then sailed for Rangoon, Burma, where they remained for about two weeks before traveling by boat up the Irrawaddy River to Mandalay and on to Bhamo. Returning to Rangoon, they caught a steamer for Calcutta, arriving there on January 14, 1906.

In Calcutta, the MacArthurs were warmly received by Lord Kitchener, who was in the midst of a power struggle with the civil governor-general of India, Viceroy George N. Curzon; as commander in chief of the British forces in India, Kitchener objected to Curzon's constant interference in military affairs. Kitchener was a grand entertainer, and the MacArthur party was probably treated like royalty. After dinner, the generals and their aides retired to the billiard room for a smoke and a glass of brandy or scotch. The two old heroes recounted their experiences with difficult civilians. MacArthur probably described the problems he had had with Taft, and Kitchener likely talked of his problems with Viceroy Curzon. Years later, Douglas would remember his father's problems and Kitchener's dilemmas. While chief of staff in India, Kitchener's power had been "mediatized" by a military officer who sat on the viceroy's council. Although Kitchener had triumphed in the dispute, both generals realized that victories over the politicians were generally temporary.[97]

Listening to his father and Lord Kitchener, Douglas developed "a disdain and contempt," notes biographer D. Clayton James, "for civilian officials who interfered in what he considered to be his domain, and, a corollary, his own outspokenness on matters beyond his jurisdiction." Critics would later castigate Douglas, as Taft had castigated his father, for his interpretation of the line between civilian and military authority. Like his father, Douglas studied his orders "like a scholar deciphering a palimpsest" and, as William Manchester observed, interpreted them "according to his own established theories." In later years, when Douglas was SCAP in Japan, historians would note that "the General assumed that he needed little or no advice from Washington" and that "he regarded his task as an exalted historical mission." It is interesting to note that in his memoirs recounting his father's exploits in the Philippines, not once does Douglas mention Taft.[98]

The MacArthurs remained in India for eight weeks, traveling from Calcutta to Allahabad, Lucknow, Agra, and Delhi and then journeyed up into the Himalayas to visit a frontier post at Darjeeling. Crossing the Indo-Gangetic Plain by rail, the party stopped at nine British military installations. By mid-February, they were in the mountains of northwestern India inspecting the posts around Peshawar and the fabled Khyber Pass. They returned south to Lahore, southwest to Karachi, north to Quetta, and back to Karachi to catch a steamship to Bombay. From there, they traveled by train east to Secunderabad, Hyderabad, south to Bangalore, east to Madras, then south to Tuticorin on the tip of the Indian continent.[99]

Leaving India in early March, the party stopped briefly at Colombo, Ceylon, before returning by ship to Singapore. After two weeks there, they set off for Bangkok, Siam (Thailand), arriving on Tuesday, March 27, 1906. General MacArthur's reception in Bangkok was representative of the entire trip. King Chulalongkorn gave a formal dinner at the Royal Palace to honor the famous general. Hamilton King, the U.S. minister in Bangkok, reported that "outside the reception given His Royal Highness Prince Heinrich of Prussia and Prince Waldemar of Denmark on their visit to Siam some years ago, no man has been accorded such a royal and generous welcome as was the General since I have been in this country."[100]

Cora Lee King, the wife of the U.S. minister, kept a diary recently discovered by historian Carol Petillo. Mrs. King's record indicates that the MacArthurs stayed in a comfortable guest house in the U.S. legation compound and that she herself "spent many hours each day in the company of the MacArthurs" and, on one excursion, took them to a Buddhist temple in Dusit Park. She also entertained Pinky while the general and Douglas inspected nearby military facilities, schools, and prisons and visited with government officials and military leaders.[101]

After spending the first two days in Bangkok, the general and his son, accompanied by a young Siamese army officer, took a private rail car to Rat Buri to visit several Protestant missionaries serving in the area. The general returned to Bangkok for a quiet weekend, then early on Monday, the group left Bangkok for a two-day trip to Ayuthia, the old capital of Siam, where there were some significant historical monuments. At Ayuthia, the MacArthurs were guests of the Siamese high commissioner, and Cora King reported that the "royal bungalows where they were quartered for the night were surprisingly comfortable." The next day, the high commissioner took the party on a tour of an old wat that contained the largest sitting Buddha in the world.[102]

The MacArthurs returned to Bangkok the next day and rested during the afternoon as the temperature hovered around 102 degrees. That evening, King Chulalongkorn honored General MacArthur with a state dinner at the palace. In her diary, Cora King described the "delicious dinner with all the 'delicacies of the season' most beautifully served on a table decorated with the King's wonderful red gold vases and urns full of tropical fruits and flowers."[103]

Douglas later remembered the dinner because "the lights suddenly went out and there was much confusion. I had noticed a fuse box near where I was seated and promptly replaced the burned-out fuse. The King (his father, King Mongkut, the subject of Margaret Landon's book *Anna and the King of Siam,* had ninety-two wives and seventy-seven children) was so delighted he proposed to decorate me there and then. Happily, I had the common sense to decline."[104]

After dinner, the king gave the MacArthurs a guided tour of the palace. "In such a setting," Petillo observed,

> the aging southern belle from Norfolk, Virginia, directed all her substantial charms toward the usually dignified and highly respected King of Siam. Mrs. King, appalled at the effrontery of the General's wife, described the scene which followed: "Passing through the throne room Mrs. MacArthur ... said to him [the King], 'Oh! I should like to see you on your throne!' He, entering into the joke of the thing, seated himself on the Royal throne! & when we entered the room there He was, smiling at Mrs. MacA. who in turn was making long bows to him! ... Mrs. MacA. seemed utterly unconscious of having done anything out of the ordinary and [later] took the King's arm as though it were the only thing to do, where no one ever does it!" Later, when the King requested the visitors to write their names and birth dates in his autograph book, once again Mrs. MacArthur responded informally. "Mrs. MacA. beseeched him to exempt her from this, which he graciously did. She grasped his hand and said, 'Oh! Your Majesty, you're a darling!' at which he laughed heartily but it nearly took our breaths away."[105]

Siam was a status-conscious society, and there was no one higher than the king—to touch his body or to treat him with familiarity, as Pinky MacArthur did, might have meant instant death for a Thai offender. But Chulalongkorn was knowledgeable in Western ways and perhaps found Pinky a delight.

On April 7, the MacArthurs left Bangkok for Saigon and from there went to Canton. From Canton, they took a train through the interior of south China to the Yangtze River, then traveled by boat up the river to Shanghai. From Shanghai, they went to Tsingtao on the Shantung peninsula where the general visited a number of German military bases. The tour continued with visits to Tientsin and Peking and from there by rail southward to Hankow and Wuhan, and then back up the Yangtze to Shanghai.

While in China, the MacArthurs learned of a terrifying tragedy in San Francisco. On April 18, 1906, a massive earthquake had struck the city; as buildings collapsed, fires erupted, burning for three days and destroying much of the city. General MacArthur probably wired his temporary replacement in San Francisco, Brigadier General Frederick Funston (the general's old protégé from the Philippines) to inquire about conditions in the city; he likely wired Admiral McCalla for news about the family. Naval Lieutenant Arthur MacArthur was at sea when the earthquake struck, and Mary and grandson Arthur IV were safe.[106]

Impatient to return home, MacArthur arranged passage from Shanghai to Japan. The party arrived back in Yokohama on June 22, 1906, but had to wait nearly a month for a ship leaving for San Francisco. The Japanese military leaders once again entertained the general, and Douglas remembered that a second audience with the emperor was arranged. The extra month gave father and son time to reflect on their long trip. Douglas later said, "It was crystal clear to me that the future and, indeed, the very existence of America, were irrevocably entwined with Asia. ... It was to be sixteen years before I returned to the Far East, but always was its mystic hold upon me."[107]

General MacArthur enjoyed the Asian trip immensely. In the words of historian John Marszalek, he "felt at ease among the monarchs, soldiers, and political leaders he met. He showed he was one of them—an important person of great accomplishment."[108]

The MacArthurs left Yokohama on the steamship SS *Manchuria* on July 17, 1906, and arrived in San Francisco on August 2. Within days, General MacArthur resumed command of the Pacific Division, with headquarters at Fort Mason just outside San Francisco. He spent the first few weeks solving problems and socializing with his family and friends.

The pressing question on General MacArthur's mind was whether he would be promoted to lieutenant general and appointed the new chief of staff. In the army reorganization bill passed in 1903, the role of the lieutenant general had been superseded by a general staff headed by a chief of staff with the permanent rank of major general (two stars). While chief, however, this officer temporarily held the rank of lieutenant general (three stars) in pay and power. The bill created some confusion because the rank of lieutenant general still existed, but Congress delayed abolishing the rank until October 1906 to reward the heroes of the Spanish-American War with a final promotion before they reached the mandatory retirement age of sixty-four. Congress had five major generals in mind: Young, Chaffee, Bates, Corbin, and MacArthur.[109]

In the summer of 1903, Young, the oldest of the five generals, was promoted to lieutenant general and appointed the first chief of staff. When he retired in early 1904, Chaffee became lieutenant general and was made chief of staff. Late the next year, when Chaffee retired, Bates had his turn as lieutenant general and new chief of staff. Within five months, however, Bates reached the mandatory retirement age of sixty-four. Next in line was Corbin, MacArthur's old boss in the Adjutant General's Office. On May 1, 1906, with only four months to retirement and very ill, Corbin was promoted to lieutenant general, but the position of chief of staff remained temporarily vacant.[110]

When Corbin retired on September 18, 1906, Congress immediately promoted MacArthur to lieutenant general. Thus, after forty-four years of military service, he had obtained the highest rank in the U.S. Army. The promotion meant a considerable increase in pay, from $7,500 to $11,000 per annum, but MacArthur was more interested in leading the army in the tradition of Grant, Sherman, and Sheridan. With two and a half years to go before he reached the mandatory retirement age, MacArthur assumed his career would be crowned with an appointment as the new chief of staff. Although the law did not require the president to appoint the ranking general of the army to this post, Roosevelt had selected every lieutenant general except Corbin to hold that position, and Corbin had declined the honor because of illness. MacArthur knew he did not have the support of Secretary of War Taft, but he did have the support of the general staff.[111]

The general underestimated Taft's influence. Back in Manila, MacArthur had thought Taft was an obscure Ohio politician; as it turned out, the general had alienated the one man who stood between him and the successful culmination of his military career. Taft was not about to allow the appointment of his old adversary as chief of staff.[112]

MacArthur's dream crashed in early January 1907, when President Roosevelt selected J. Franklin Bell as the new chief of staff. Only fifty years old, Bell was the youngest major general in the U.S. Army. He had been one of MacArthur's favorite officers in the Philippines, and it was through MacArthur's influence that Bell had won fame and promotion. In 1899, he had been a mere major when MacArthur selected him to be the intelligence officer of the 2nd Division. He performed extremely well, and MacArthur promoted him to colonel during the fall 1899 offensive. When the general became military governor of the Philippines in May 1900, he selected Bell to be provost marshal of Manila and later appointed him to command a department. With MacArthur's support, Bell ultimately rose to the rank of brigadier general in the Regular Army; he had been promoted to major general only days before being appointed chief of staff. Roosevelt proclaimed the office needed a man who could complete the four-year term of duty, not another lieutenant general who would shortly retire.

MacArthur would never forgive the politicians for this slap in the face, although Roosevelt tried to soothe his feathers with rewards to his sons. Lieutenant Arthur MacArthur was assigned to the Naval Academy in Annapolis as an aide to the superintendent, and Douglas received a plush assignment to the Engineer School at Fort MacNair outside Washington, D.C. Only eleven officers were selected that fall, and with this appointment, Douglas was a year ahead of any other member of his class at West Point. Then, on December 4, 1906, Roosevelt selected him as a military aide, and for the next year, he attended social functions at the White House and had many conversations with the president on the situation in the Far East. The talks did not improve his father's relations with the White House.[113]

Bell's selection as chief of staff placed MacArthur in a delicate position, for as a ranking general, he was taking orders from a subordinate officer. Moreover, his lofty rank of lieutenant general simply did not fit his command of the Division of the Pacific. When the War Department informed him that the division designation would change back to department, MacArthur requested a transfer to some job more suited to his advanced rank. He felt like an admiral commanding a cruiser instead of a battleship.[114]

Taft responded by offering MacArthur command of the Department of the East, headquarted on Governor's Island in New York harbor. MacArthur should have accepted. In New York City, the ranking general of the U.S. Army and his wife would have been invited to prestigious social gatherings, and the general

Lieutenant General Arthur MacArthur, c. 1906. (MacArthur Memorial Library, Ph-96)

would have met the rich and powerful men of the financial world—men who would have admired his meticulous, organized style much more than the flamboyant Roosevelt or the jolly Taft ever did.

But MacArthur angrily rejected the post, feeling that Taft simply refused to understand the underlying problem. The ranking lieutenant general of the army should not be assigned a position that a mere brigadier general could fill. Taft replied that there was no higher position available.

MacArthur's attitude probably seemed childish to Taft. After all, couldn't someone be temporarily appointed to command an organization without any regard for seniority? Business did it all the time. MacArthur did not disagree with the right of the War Department, with congressional approval, to promote an officer to a higher grade, but in each grade, every officer was ranked by seniority of appointment. Since lieutenant general was the highest grade possible, no other active officer could outrank MacArthur. In his opinion, that violated military logic and insulted the entire officers corps. Further, if politicians could abolish rank in grade for the lieutenant general, then the same could be done in all other grades. Since most officers were more than qualified for their jobs, MacArthur contended, seniority in grade was extremely important, not only for morale but also for military discipline. In battle, orders were delivered according to rank; as officers fell, in a well-trained unit, everyone knew instantaneously who was next in command.

Thus, MacArthur felt he could not ignore the War Department's basic violation of the principle of seniority in grade. One of his strongest traits was that he was a principled man, who always tried to live up to his own high expectations in military bearing, in scholarly interest, and in battle. He wanted to personify what he considered the perfect general, and his ideal was a composite of all the great military men he had served under, from General Rosecrans to General Corbin. And as his sons had learned, MacArthur's personal code of ethics was inflexible.

Taft (and many scholars in later years) interpreted MacArthur's emphasis on conforming to a code of conduct as the action of a pompous, self-important martinet. *Was* MacArthur pompous? The answer depends on how one defines the word. Although liberal in his thinking in many respects, MacArthur was a strict disciplinarian professionally and extremely conscious of rank. The Civil War had taught him that in the age of modern weapons, individual valor on the field was less important than organizational unity. He believed that unity was maintained by absolute obedience to orders, provided those orders were delivered by qualified officers. In his opinion, every military officer should strive to serve as an example for his men: One led by leading, and on the battlefield, generals and officers belonged with their men. As he was trained, so he believed. To maintain discipline, officers should not become chums with the enlisted men or even the noncommissioned officers. Moreover, men of all ranks were to be constantly aware of the grade of every officer and every enlisted man. MacArthur seldom, if ever, formed close personal friendships with junior officers; he was one of those officers who never let his guard down except around close personal friends, such as his old Civil War comrades.

MacArthur lived his life in an organization that emphasized rank, and ultimately, he decided that his position as a department commander was an insult to the army ranking system. On March 13, 1907, he wrote Taft and offered a compromise. He requested that he be detached from command and assigned to Milwaukee for his remaining two years of service. While on detached duty, he would serve as a consultant and senior statesman, whose advice on military maneuvers, training programs, and weapons systems would be sought by the chief of staff. He also assumed the president would request his attendance at social functions where the presence of the highest-ranking officer in the army was desirable. The assignment would also give him time to work on his report on the Russo-Japanese War and review his Asian tour. Taft quickly accepted MacArthur's request for detached duty since it resolved a sticky situation and placed MacArthur, for all practical purposes, into early retirement.[115]

Thus, on April 26, 1907, MacArthur was relieved of command of the Department of the Pacific. He was ordered to proceed to Seattle, Washington, to accompany a Japanese military delegation led by General Kuroki to the Jamestown Exposition, where the United States was celebrating the three-hundredth anniversary of the first European settlement in North America. The assignment delighted MacArthur. When he was in Manchuria in the spring of 1905, he had become friendly with Kuroki, a quiet, dignified gentleman of few words but iron determination. MacArthur and Kuroki renewed their friendship as they traveled across the country. After reaching Jamestown, the general left the Japanese delegation to proceed to Milwaukee, arriving there on May 20.[116]

By New York or Boston standards, Milwaukee was a small town, but MacArthur loved the city more than any other place in the world. To a news reporter, he admitted that he was "glad to be back home. I shall stay in Milwaukee for the rest of my days and renew old friendships just as fast as I can. In all the experiences of a long life spent moving about the world, no city has appealed to me as much as does Milwaukee."[117]

He rented a house at 575 Marshall Street in a nice suburban neighborhood and entered into the social life of the city. Many of his father's powerful friends were still alive, and their sons, his own boyhood friends, were now some of the wealthiest and most powerful men in Wisconsin. The influential citizens of Milwaukee were delighted with the return of the city's greatest military hero. They respected him as they had respected his father (and soon would respect one of his sons). Six weeks after his return to the city, fifty of his friends gave him a dinner party in the Colonial Room of the Plankinton Hotel. The guest list included senators, congressmen, mayors, former governors, business leaders, lawyers, and some of MacArthur's oldest friends. Charlie King was there, and so were John Mitchell, Paul Carpenter, Jerome Watrous, James G. Flanders, Edwin Parsons, Hugh Ryan, Ross Hunter, William E. Cramer, and retired Admiral James K. Cogswell.[118]

The MacArthur family, c. 1907. Back row, from left: Arthur III, his wife Mary, Douglas. Front row: Pinky, grandson Arthur IV, and General MacArthur. (MacArthur Memorial Library, Ph-1741)

Pinky was not as content living in Milwaukee as the general was—she was lonely and wanted her sons nearby, and only when they were in town was she truly happy. Lieutenant Arthur MacArthur visited with his wife, Mary, and four-year-old son, Arthur IV. Mary was pregnant and that August gave birth to another son, named Bowman McCalla after his maternal grandfather. The couple's visit to Milwaukee was brief, for Lieutenant MacArthur had to return to his post at the Naval Academy. Soon, Pinky was complaining again. Above all, she missed Douglas; in the previous ten years, she had spent more time with him than with her husband, and she was used to seeing her son every day.[119]

Pinky asked the general to use his influence to get Douglas transferred from Washington to Milwaukee. The general reluctantly complied and contacted his sources in the War Department. As a result, on August 10, 1907, the department assigned Douglas to river and harbor duties at the engineering office in Milwaukee. He soon moved into his parents' home on Marshall Street—a large, two-story, wooden frame house with a gracious porch and a lovely veranda that faced Lake Michigan on the east side. With her beloved son at her side, Pinky began to enjoy the Milwaukee social life and often invited the general's friends over on Sunday afternoons for long philosophical discussions.

Douglas enjoyed staying up late in the evenings with his father discussing politics, history, literature, and, most of all, Asia. They spent many hours reviewing their Asian trip and discussed the subtleties of Filipino politics, the mysteries of the Orient, and the rising power of Japan.[120]

The War Department remained a sour note in the general's life. MacArthur never made any serious effort to call public attention to his accomplishments, but among his fellow officers, he was much more aggressive. He expected to be rewarded for his accomplishments during his forty-five years of service with honor and respect. Instead, most active military officers realized that MacArthur was now out of the power loop and virtually in retirement. From the moment MacArthur arrived in Milwaukee on detached duty, Taft and Bell ignored him and acted as if he had already retired.

Meanwhile, expecting to be treated as the ranking general in the army, MacArthur opened offices in the Federal Building on Milwaukee Street and requested that the War Department assign him a staff appropriate to his rank. Bell acquiesced but allowed MacArthur only one aide and two clerks, a mere pittance of the staffs allowed all previous lieutenant generals. Weeks and then months passed, and still MacArthur received no assignment, no requests for research in any military area, no solicitation of his opinion on military affairs, and no invitations to military functions. These insults to his rank and illustrious career infuriated MacArthur. He never forgave either Taft or Bell.[121]

All his life, Douglas remembered how poorly Taft and the army's general staff treated his father in the final years before his retirement. As Stuart Miller notes, the other major actors in the Philippine war, except for Otis, "went on to reap richer rewards. Taft became president, and Root went on to represent New York in the U.S. Senate. General[s] Young, Chaffee, and Bell all reached the army's top post."[122]

Douglas developed an animosity toward civilian politicians and deskbound warriors of the general staff. In later years, according to William Manchester, he was "sensitive to slights [and] came to believe people in the army were out to get him—deskbound men who envied and resented a fighting officer." Douglas's paranoia, "which was to bring so much anguish to him and to others in the years ahead," actually began with the army's treatment of his father in his final years.[123]

In Milwaukee during his father's last years in the army, Douglas neglected his duties as an engineering officer, and for the first time in his career, he received a bad efficiency report from his commanding officer, Major Judson. He simply did not have enough time to listen to his father, take care of his mother, and perform his military duties. Pinky wanted him at home, and if she did not receive his constant attention, she became "ill." Carol Petillo suggests that Douglas was also distracted by a local young lady named Fanniebelle Stuart.[124]

When the general learned of Douglas's poor efficiency report, he intervened, realizing that his wife's demands were threatening his son's career. Using his army contacts, MacArthur arranged for his son to be transferred to Fort Leavenworth in Kansas. In April 1908, Douglas departed to assume his new job as commander of Company K and as instructor at the Mounted Service School at Fort Riley. Major Peyton March, one of the general's aides in the Philippines, looked out for the young lieutenant.[125]

Pinky was lonely again and assumed, incorrectly, that her son was upset with his assignment to Leavenworth. She wanted him to resign his commission and accept a job offer from Edward Harriman, owner of the Union Pacific, that she had secured in her son's behalf. He rejected the offer, and as Carol Petillo observes, "it is possible that Douglas believed that his decision ... reaffirmed the value of [his father's] life."[126]

With no assignment from Washington, General MacArthur concentrated on writing his reports on the Russo-Japanese War and his Asian tour. Although he admired the Japanese, he recommended that the United States recognize the eventual threat that Japan posed to the Philippines. Secretary Taft and General Bell, however, were not interested in MacArthur's observations on Asia. His reports were never circulated, and eventually they disappeared in the mass of material in the military archives.[127]

The general continued to feel overlooked and even insulted by the treatment he received from the War Department. A typical example of an incident almost designed to infuriate the ranking general in the army was a dispute with the War Department over one of his travel vouchers. When he left the Philippines in 1901, he had shipped some Filipino arts and crafts back to the United States, charging the government. The War Department ruled that such items were personal, not travel related, and demanded payment for the shipping cost. MacArthur paid but included an indignant letter challenging the decision.[128]

On June 2, 1909, General MacArthur reached the mandatory retirement age of sixty-four. The War Department did not honor his passage with any special ceremonies, and the national press took no notice of his retirement. His forty-seven years of service seemed insignificant to politicians who were simply glad to see another old military horse placed out to pasture. The insult turned MacArthur bitter, and on the day of his retirement, he proclaimed that he would never wear his uniform again. And he never did. Shortly after his retirement, the War Department added to his bitterness when it refused to allow him to accept a special decoration from the emperor of Japan.[129]

In spite of his disappointment in the War Department, General MacArthur's final years were happy ones. Although he would always resent the Washington politicians and berate the concept of a general staff, he had wisely retired to his old hometown of Milwaukee, where friends of his youth still lived. There, he was respected, honored, and treated like a famous son. He was Milwaukee's "boy colonel" of the Civil War, who had risen to the highest rank in the U.S. Army. The general was content with Milwaukee's praise. He was also content in the knowledge that his accomplishments in the military equaled, if not exceeded, the accomplishments of his father in the legal profession. And he expected his sons to continue the MacArthur tradition.

But his productive days were not over. The general was an active man, and he began to utilize his talents in new areas. For most of his life, he had been a reluctant public speaker, but now he began to emulate his father, the judge, whose speaking talents were renowned. Within a month of his retirement, the general was the keynote speaker at a Scottish celebration in Milwaukee to honor Robert Burns. The St. Andrews Society had commissioned William Grant Stevenson, a Scottish sculptor, to carve a statue of Robert Burns that was an exact replica of the eleven-foot-high, twenty-six-ton Burns statue in Edinburgh, Scotland. The general addressed the crowd at the dedication of the statue at Knapp and Prospect Streets on June 26, 1909. MacArthur was proud of his Scottish heritage and reminded the audience that his father had founded the Robert Burns Society in Milwaukee on January 24, 1851. The judge had also served as president of the St. Andrews Society, and the general himself had attended the society's annual meetings as a young man.[130]

Over time, the general became a good public speaker—not as great as his father nor as vibrant and Olympian as his son Douglas but competent and sought after nonetheless. No longer under War Department censorship, he accepted invitations to speak on topics ranging from the Civil War to the Philippines. Public speaking provided him with an opportunity to utilize his broad scholarly interests and his eloquent vocabulary, which was famous in military circles. It was widely acknowledged that MacArthur was the best-read man in his profession. He was looked on, far and wide, as perhaps the most intellectual of U.S. generals. "It may be said," Brigadier General Isaac Catlin observed, "that there were few, if any, of his contemporaries so scholarly."[131]

General MacArthur also became deeply involved in the activities of veterans' associations. He was elected the Milwaukee commandant of the Military Order of the Loyal Legion in 1909. Organized around state chapters, the Loyal Legion was open to officers of the army, navy, and marine corps, and MacArthur had been a member since 1873 when the Milwaukee chapter was organized. In 1909, the Milwaukee chapter had 212 members, including Charlie King, Edward Parsons, Billy Bishop, Jerome Watrous, and John Mitchell. MacArthur was punctilious in his legion post and each year attended all eight meetings of the Wisconsin chapter. When Rear Admiral George W. Melville, the national commander, died in early 1912, General MacArthur was selected as the Loyal Legion's new commander in chief. With over twenty state commanderies, the legion had around 7,500 members.[132]

Some of his friends wanted MacArthur to run for governor in 1910. One Wisconsin newspaper, proclaiming its support for the general, noted that since MacArthur had never been "identified with party politics, he would neither be a democratic governor nor a republican governor, but he would make a most excellent governor." MacArthur discouraged all such efforts on his behalf. Much like General Sherman in his retirement, MacArthur "had no political ambitions, nor did he want to translate his fame into some civilian profession. He saw himself as a soldier who had given his nation loyal service and wanted only to rest. He entered these years looking forward to no new challenges but rather hoping to enjoy the fruits of his past labor."[133]

He spent most of his time in his beloved library at his home on Marshall Street. His love for reading and study increased, and he lived among his books, surrounded by the memorabilia of forty-seven years of military service. On the walls were paintings of Grant, Sherman, Sheridan, Logan, Thomas, Kearny, and other soldier heroes in full dress uniforms. MacArthur's battle flags from the Civil War to the Philippines were there, too, and a number of small statues of Lincoln, Grant, and Burns stood on display stands. All about were the thousands of books that MacArthur had collected over the years—poetry, literature, and erudite books on every conceivable topic. His military collection was extensive and included scores of volumes on the Civil War, the Spanish-American War, and wars from Greek and Roman times to those of contemporary Europe and Asia.[134]

Admitting that he now belonged to the past—to the old days and the old memories—he began work on his memoirs. If he finished any portion of the manuscript, it was consumed by the flames of war or still lies forgotten in the basement of some family member. But even if his memoirs are discovered someday, it is unikely they will reveal much about the personal life of the general. Probably, MacArthur, much like Admiral McCalla and General Pershing in their unpublished memoirs, devoted most of his space to his military career rather than to descriptions of his feelings toward his father, mother, wife, and children. His accounts of the battles he fought in the Civil War likely would have emphasized strategy and tactics rather than a personalized account of his own experiences. He had been courageous in the war, as had all his comrades in the 24th Wisconsin, and he accepted that attribute as the norm among good officers. His main interest was infantry tactics, and he would probably have illustrated how each battle affected the development of such tactics. Modern weapons, he often said, meant that a force had to use all available cover when attacking, to be disciplined enough to obey orders in battle, and to always build fortifications when protecting a position. He opposed frontal assaults and likely would have illustrated how he used flanking movements in the Philippines.

The general would probably have concentrated on his experiences in the Philippines, where he had achieved his greatest successes. Despite the fact that the president, the secretary of war, the general staff, and many other senior officers had ignored MacArthur's accomplishments in the Philippines, there were a sizable number of officers who respected him and his achievements. That group of officers would have read of the battles of Calacoon and Angeles City with interest, enjoyed MacArthur's discussion of guerrilla tactics, and sympathized with his problems with Taft while he was military governor.

The general's trials with the Adjutant General's Office over brevets, with the War Department over promotions, and with the secretary of war over the general staff would probably have received considerable space in his memoirs. Ranking generals in the U.S. Army from Scott to Grant to Sherman to Miles to MacArthur grew to dislike the politicians in Washington, and each lieutenant general believed his status and power did not equal his high rank.[135]

In the summer of 1912, MacArthur's health, formerly so robust, began to decline. Sedentary habits, long hours in his library, and little exercise in the open air caused his health to deteriorate. His condition worsened in late August and aroused the anxiety of his wife and several of his close friends. He suffered from acute indigestion caused by hyperacidity of the stomach, from high blood pressure, and from kidney problems. Despite the advice of physicians, the general refused to give up his cigars and Scotch whiskey. The doctors and Pinky argued with him, but their arguments were useless, for a pronounced characteristic of the general was that he knew his own mind.[136]

Despite his illness, MacArthur insisted on attending the fiftieth reunion of the 24th Wisconsin Volunteers on Thursday, September 5, 1912. The Milwaukee Chamber of Commerce planned an all-day celebration to honor the survivors of the regiment with parades and a banquet at Wolcott Hall. Of the 1,150 members of the 24th Wisconsin, 750 had died in battle, of diseases, or in prison camps. By 1912, only 64 of the original group of the 400 survivors were still alive. These men were MacArthur's oldest comrades in arms. As the 24th's Civil War commander, he was invited to be the guest of honor and the keynote speaker at the elaborate banquet scheduled to end the celebration. He had accepted the invitation before becoming seriously ill, and he insisted he would attend the reunion even if it meant leaving his sickbed.[137]

Fearing the result, Pinky begged him not to go, but the general refused her request. Because of his illness, he reluctantly agreed to skip the public ceremonies, the business meetings, and even the dinner at Wolcott Hall. But he *would* give his speech, returning home as soon as possible.[138]

MacArthur's decision to restrict his schedule was a wise one. September 5, the day of the celebration, proved to be the hottest day of the year in Milwaukee. People lay prostrate in the streets during the day, and the evening brought little relief. But despite the heat, MacArthur was determined not to disappoint his old comrades. Over the opposition of his wife and in spite of the weakness that made dressing a slow and difficult process, he persisted. Shortly before 9:00 P.M., he smilingly told Pinky not to worry and bade her good-bye. Pinky wanted to accompany the general, but the reunion was an all-male affair. "I'll be back in three-quarters of an hour," he said as he went out the door to a waiting automobile.[139]

Driven to the University Building at Broadway and Mason Streets, MacArthur entered Wolcott Hall around 9:00 P.M. He tried to enter quietly, but the guests rose and gave him a tumultuous welcome, cheering wildly for over five minutes. Their former boy colonel was now the grand old commander. The crowd was looking forward to MacArthur's address, billed as the feature event of the day's celebration. The hall was filled with over 100 guests, including the survivors of the 24th Wisconsin, important members of the chamber of commerce, and many of MacArthur's closest friends—Charlie King, Jimmy Flanders, and Billy Bishop, among others. The crowded banquet room was like a furnace, and the general looked weak but dignified.[140]

Escorted to the dais, MacArthur was introduced by his old friend Captain Edwin Parsons, the toastmaster at the reunion. As MacArthur rose to give his speech, the audience erupted again and applauded him for six to seven minutes before they would let him begin.

"Comrades," MacArthur said, motioning the crowd to be seated, and the hall slowly quieted.

"Comrades," MacArthur began again, "little did we imagine fifty years ago, that [we would ever] gather in this way. Little did we think that on that march to Atlanta so many of us would be spared to see Wisconsin again."

For ten minutes, MacArthur spoke of the battles the 24th had fought during the Civil War, to the periodic applause of his highly patriotic audience. As he reached the battle of Peach Tree Creek, he stumbled over his words, then paused. The heat in the room was overpowering, and for a moment, he looked as if he might pass out. The toastmaster began to fan him, but MacArthur's pallor worsened as beads of sweat covered his face.

Everyone in the silent audience seemed to hold his breath as the general continued, choosing each word carefully. Then, after a long pause, he wavered and leaned heavily on the podium. A noticeable paleness spread across his cheeks. The silence dragged on for five seconds, then MacArthur said slowly, "Comrades ... I am ... too weak ... to proceed." He sank down in his chair, and his head fell forward onto the table.

Dr. William J. Cronyn rushed to the dais as the general's old friends crowded around him. Tenderly, MacArthur was moved to an improvised couch, where Cronyn examined him. The room was silent as the men stared in shock and disbelief; not a sound was heard but the beating of their hearts. After only a minute or two, Cronyn rose and shook his head. "Comrades," he said, "our commander has gone to his last rest." A blood vessel, weakened by sixty-seven years of life, had burst at the base of MacArthur's brain, and death was almost instantaneous.

A soft cry escaped somewhere in the crowd, and then all was still. One of the old soldiers, in a voice broken with sobs, began to say the Lord's Prayer. As the words left his lips, every man present knelt and joined in. At the conclusion of the prayer, the soldiers rose. One of Mac's old comrades removed a flag from the wall and draped it over his body.

MacArthur's death was a severe shock to his old friend Captain Parsons, who collapsed. He suffered a paralytic stroke on his right side, and an ambulance was called to transport him to the hospital; he would die within two weeks. Another ambulance was summoned to transport MacArthur's body to the George H. Thomas Undertaking Parlor at 467 Milwaukee Street.

Meanwhile, Dr. Cronyn telephoned Pinky but discovered he simply could not tell her over the phone that her husband was dead. Instead, he told her that her husband had been taken seriously ill. Charlie King, James Flanders, and William Bishop volunteered to go to 575 Marshall Street to give Pinky the sad news. Before departing Wolcott Hall, King called his wife and Dr. Robert Brown, Pinky's physician, and asked them to go to MacArthur's home as well. When King and the others arrived at MacArthur's house, Pinky hurried down the front steps to meet them. "Is the General dead?" she asked. The telephone call had prepared her for the worst. "Yes," they answered. She bowed her head, then quietly walked to her room, where she was joined by her pastor, Dr. Brown, and Mrs. King. Pinky insisted on writing telegrams to her sons, Lieutenant Commander Arthur MacArthur, stationed at Newport, and Captain Douglas MacArthur, stationed at Fort Leavenworth. Charlie King took the messages to the telegraph office within hours of the general's death.

Friday morning, newspapers across the nation ran feature stories on the death of General MacArthur. The nation did not engage in deep mourning, but in the next few days, many military and civilian leaders praised the general for his great accomplishments. Eulogies flowed from the mouths of the rich and famous, few of whom had known the general intimately.[141]

Only in Milwaukee was the mourning genuine. MacArthur was the city's favorite son and most famous military man. Flags flew at half-mast in the city for the next four days.[142]

At Pinky's request, Charlie King took over all the funeral arrangements. On Friday morning, MacArthur's body was brought from the funeral parlor to 575

Marshall Street. For a day, the general's body rested in a second-floor bedroom. Arthur and Douglas arrived in Milwaukee on Saturday. The closed coffin, draped in a U.S. flag, was moved to the general's library on the first floor and was surrounded with flowers and his beloved books.[143]

Browsing among the books, the family perhaps rediscovered Judge Mac-Arthur's essay on death. When Senator Matthew Carpenter, his closest friend, died in 1881, the judge wrote: "The death of a great man is nearly always sudden, unexpected, and appalling. When his death occurs, it comes upon us like a tropical sunset—sudden, instantaneous, involving us in darkness and despair." The judge reminded his family to remember the dying expressions of Gabriel Victor Mirabeau, a great leader of the French Revolution, who on his deathbed declared to his wife, "Throw aside the curtains and let the sunshine fill the apartment and bathe me in its beams, and let the incense of the garden reach my senses, for I would die amidst the perfume of its flowers. ... The great Frenchman ... feared not death [for he] believed it to be an eternal sleep."[144]

As Pinky and her sons sat by the coffin through Saturday night, the scene was a sad and touching tableau. "My whole world changed that night," Douglas wrote fifty years later; "never have I been able to heal the wound in my heart." And as historian Carol Petillo concludes, "There is no reason to doubt his judgment. The loss of his father ... almost immediately resulted in an unprecedented attack of insomnia serious enough to require medical attention."[145]

Long before he died, the general gave his wife very specific instructions on his funeral. Having become extremely embittered against the Taft administration and the army general staff for ignoring him in his final days, MacArthur directed that his body be laid to rest in Milwaukee's Forest Lawn Cemetery without any military ceremonies. "I want to be laid away here in our own lot, among my old friends and by my old friends without the pomp of a military funeral," he said. He wanted a funeral of the "utmost simplicity and utterly devoid of military display." The general did not even wish to be buried in his military uniform.[146]

Pinky wanted the funeral to occur on Sunday, but complications arose because Forest Lawn prohibited Sunday burials; Monday was the only alternative. Therefore, the general's closest friends in Milwaukee attended private services at the family residence at 10:30 Monday morning. A good number of friends and neighbors filled the spacious library. *Harper's Weekly* reported that

> the casket, hidden in the beautiful folds of the flag he loved and served, had been closed before ... the ceremony, but companions of the Loyal Legion and comrades of the Grand Army passed between the encircling banks of flowers and paid their final visit. The pallbearers, active and honorary, were grouped in the hall. Other soldier associates thronged the dining room. Not a uniform was to be seen.[147]

Colonel John L. Glenn, chief quartermaster of the Central Division and representing the commanding general, was the only active-duty officer present, except for

MacArthur's sons. Abiding by the general's wishes, all three dressed in civilian clothes.

As MacArthur had directed, the services were simple. At the family's request, the Reverend Paul B. Jenkins, pastor of the Immanuel Church, did not deliver a sermon but simply read brief selections from the Scriptures followed by William Wordsworth's poem "The Happy Warrior." An eloquent prayer completed the service at the house.

After the brief ceremony, sixteen honorary pallbearers, all residents of Milwaukee, formed in front of the casket to lead the procession to the waiting hearse. The actual pallbearers were young members of the Loyal Legion, but the honorary pallbearers represented the cream of Milwaukee society. As the procession moved down the sidewalk to the street, the general's old comrades from the 24th Wisconsin and about fifty members of the Loyal Legion lined the way. They bared their heads and raised their hands in mute salutes as MacArthur's casket passed. Then, with tears streaming from their eyes, they turned silently away. Beyond the ranks of the general's comrades, a crowd gathered to watch as the casket was carried to the waiting motored hearse. There was no music, no insignia of rank or station, no ceremonial rite, none of the trappings of the military funeral.

The family, the bearers, and the immediate friends accompanied the general's body to Forest Lawn. At the cemetery, Reverend Jenkins read Psalms 19 and 23 and the twenty-second chapter of Revelation. A lone bugler from the Loyal Legion softly played taps as the flag-draped casket was lowered in the ground.[148]

After the funeral, Douglas and his brother remained in Milwaukee for a few days to comfort Pinky, who exhibited symptoms of extreme grief and became desperately ill. Arthur's wife was already caring for three small children while he was at sea, and thus, the responsibility of taking care of Pinky fell on Douglas. He telegraphed the War Department to request a temporary transfer from Leavenworth to Milwaukee so that he could help his mother, whose condition was "alarming."[149]

Although General MacArthur had been ignored by Roosevelt and Taft, he had been a highly respected member of the military establishment. The Adjutant General's Office noted the passage of one of the last great Civil War heroes, and General Charlie King provided the other officers with a detailed report on the general's funeral, which generated a great deal of sympathy among MacArthur's many friends in the officers corps. General Leonard Wood, the chief of staff, contacted Henry L. Stimson, the secretary of war, and informed him of Douglas's situation and the plight of MacArthur's widow. Wood had known, liked, and respected MacArthur; the two had first met back in 1886 when both had been struggling young captains. At Wood's request, Stimson ordered the adjutant general to assign Douglas to Wood's staff as a special assistant. Pinky was pleased with this news, and Washington certainly suited her better than cold Milwaukee. Before Christmas, she and Douglas were settled into an apartment at Sixteen and U Streets.[150]

As Pinky recovered, she clung to Douglas. In her mind, her late husband assumed a godlike image, and she encouraged her son to equal his accomplishments. Douglas took up the mission with a passion. The death of his father seemed to propel him as he dreamed of achieving his father's greatness and tried to emulate him in all ways. "Now," Carol Petillo observed, Douglas "redoubled his attempts to succeed in his chosen field. In this way, he could incorporate into his personality the characteristics most obvious in his dead father, thereby relieving his immediate sense of loss." Douglas's manner, his speech, and his philosophical beliefs were all patterned after the general. And like his father, Douglas would be criticized in his later years for being a pompous martinet and praised for his heroic and scholarly ways. Philosophical words came as easily to his lips as to those of his father.[151]

Clark Lee and Richard Henschel noted that Douglas's career paralleled that of his father in many ways.

> His father was an officer for 46 1/2 years, Douglas for 47 1/2 years. ... In their respective careers, both men set many records of "youngest" and "firsts." Together they held the highest ranks ever attained in the American Army by members of the same family, and they are the only father-son combination to win our highest military award, the Congressional Medal of Honor. They served as a team in the Orient in the early part of the twentieth century; and each in his time was recognized as America's outstanding expert on Far Eastern affairs. Each man was military governor of an Asiatic nation. Each became involved in a dispute with his superiors. ... Each had a famous feud, Arthur with William Howard Taft and [Douglas with Harry Truman].[152]

Douglas's success in the army can be partially attributed to his father's influence. D. Clayton James suggests that Arthur MacArthur's "most significant legacy to his son was the talented gathering of young officers who served under him in the Philippines. ... These officers did not forget ... when General MacArthur's son served under them in future years. Talented as he was, Douglas would enjoy a meteoric rise due in no small measure to the special interest of officers who were beholden to his father." The name MacArthur meant something to them, and when Douglas's name appeared on the promotion lists, he always had a number of sponsors to aid and abet his career because they felt an obligation to his father.[153]

Frederick Funston would never forget the general, and as a brigadier general in charge of U.S. forces in Vera Cruz, Mexico, in 1914, Funston forgave Douglas for a major blunder. When Douglas, still a captain, was sent to Vera Cruz on a special assignment by General Wood, he ignored Funston's standing orders and engaged in a long-range reconnaissance mission behind Mexican lines. Although cited for bravery and recommended for a Medal of Honor, his actions had clearly violated Funston's orders. Ultimately, MacArthur did not receive the medal, but it was not Funston's fault. Douglas's actions angered him, to be sure, but he remembered his obligation to the boy's father and worded his report in the most gentle terms pos-

sible. General MacArthur, if he had still been alive, would have privately castigated his son while simultaneously admiring his heroics. And the general would
have thanked Funston for protecting his son's career. For his part, Douglas did
not believe his father would have disapproved: The general had disobeyed orders
when he charged up Missionary Ridge, and Douglas noted that "it's the orders
you disobey that make you famous."[154]

During World War I, Douglas commanded the Rainbow Division in France
under General Charles P. Summerall, who had served in the Philippines as a
young lieutenant under Douglas's father. Like his father, Douglas was heroic in
war, earning twelve decorations from his own government—including seven Silver Stars, a Distinguished Service Medal, and two Purple Hearts—and nineteen
honors from the Allied nations. The Medal of Honor, to his chagrin, eluded him
until World War II.[155]

After World War I, Douglas retained his rank as brigadier general primarily because of the support of General Peyton March, the new chief of staff. March had
served under and greatly respected Douglas's father, who had sponsored his career. March did not forget his obligation to the father and became the son's mentor. He assigned Douglas to be the new superintendent of the U.S. Military Academy at West Point.[156]

On November 21, 1930, after two tours of duty in the Philippines, General
Douglas MacArthur was selected by President Herbert Hoover to be the army's
chief of staff. After the swearing-in ceremonies, Pinky touched Douglas's four
stars and whispered, "If only your father could see you now! Douglas, you're
everything he wanted to be."[157]

Postscript

Mɪʟᴡᴀᴜᴋᴇᴇ ʟᴇᴀᴅᴇʀs talked about building a monument to honor General MacArthur, but no monument was ever built. During World War I, the U.S. Army belatedly honored the general by naming two minor forts after him—Camp MacArthur in Waco, Texas, and Fort MacArthur in San Pedro, California. When General Douglas MacArthur achieved great fame during and after World War II, the citizens of Chicopee, Massachusetts, suddenly remembered that Douglas's father had been born in their town and erected a monument to honor Lieutenant General Arthur MacArthur.[1]

Mary Pinckney Hardy MacArthur, his widow, lived another twenty-three years before dying in the Manila Hotel on December 3, 1935. Pinky had received an annual pension of only $1,200, although all other widows of lieutenant generals received more than twice that amount. After Milwaukee attorney James G. Flanders took the government to court, her pension was raised to $2,500.[2]

Arthur MacArthur III rose to high rank in the U.S. Navy during World War I. He commanded the *South Dakota* with the Pacific Fleet and later the cruiser *Chattanooga* in the Atlantic Fleet in 1917. In 1918, he was promoted to captain and awarded the Navy Cross and the Distinguished Service Medal. After the war, he served as commander of the San Diego Naval Training Station. On December 2, 1923, while in Washington, D.C., Captain MacArthur died of appendicitis at the age of forty-seven. He was buried in Arlington National Cemetery. He had fathered five children: Arthur IV, born June 29, 1903, who died in 1912; Bowman McCalla, born August 17, 1907; Douglas II, born May 7, 1909; Mary Elizabeth, born February 20, 1913; and Malcolm, born December 12, 1914.[3]

In 1926, General Douglas MacArthur had the body of his father moved from Milwaukee's Forest Lawn Cemetery to Arlington National Cemetery. Pinky would be laid to rest beside him in 1937.[4]

On February 21, 1938, Douglas's wife, Jean Faircloth, bore him a son, whom they named Arthur after his uncle, grandfather, and great-grandfather. Arthur V was christened on his grandfather's birthday, June 2, at an Episcopalian church in Manila. Manuel Quezon, then the president of the Philippine Commonwealth, was his godfather.[5]

Notes

Chapter 1: The Judge

1. Carol Morris Petillo, *Douglas MacArthur: The Philippine Years*, p. 1, quoting Douglas MacArthur, Tokyo, late 1940s.

2. When Judge MacArthur migrated to the United States from Scotland in 1828, he spelled his name McArthur rather than MacArthur and continued to do so for years. During the Civil War, for some unknown reason, both the judge and his son began to spell the name MacArthur. The change occurred gradually over a three-year period. Major MacArthur signed his name to his official report on the Atlanta campaign MacArthur, *Official Records*, Vol. 38, p. 330. But in letters of the same period, he signed his name McArthur. See RG20, MML, 24th Wisconsin, Field and Staff Muster Rolls, where name is consistently spelled McArthur: letter, May 15, 1864, from McArthur to Buck; letter, Sept. 9, 1864, from McArthur to Whipple. By the end of the war, both MacArthurs were using the Mac spelling (see MacArthur file, Milwaukee County Historical Society, document of Nov. 8, 1869). By the 1880s, the judge insisted people spell his name MacArthur, as illustrated in a letter, June 10, 1887, to Ben W. Austire (RG20, MML), in which the judge wrote: "Please note my middle name is Mac not Mc." See also *Springfield Scrapbook* and Harry H. Anderson, ed., *The MacArthurs of Milwaukee*, p. 49. In any case, whether spelled with Mac or with Mc, the name means "Arthur son of Arthur."

3. RG10, MML, letter, Oct. 28, 1843, Arthur McArthur of Springfield, MA, to Arthur McArthur of Limington, ME. See also Ellis B. Usher, *Wisconsin: Its Story and Biography, 1848–1913*, pp. 1837–1839; Howard Louis Conard, ed., *History of Milwaukee County from Its First Settlement to the Year 1895*, p. 192; Parker M. Reed, *The Bench and Bar of Wisconsin*, p. 130; Conklin Mann, "Some Ancestral Lines of General Douglas MacArthur," p. 171.

4. RG10, MML, letter, McArthur to McArthur, Oct. 28, 1843.

5. The judge is quoted in Robert S. Neenah, "A Worthy Scotsman"; see also Robert G. Carroon, "The Judge and the General," pp. 2ff, and Conard, *History of Milwaukee County*, p. 191.

6. *Springfield Scrapbook*; Neenah, "Worthy Scotsman"; Anderson, *The MacArthurs*, p. 49.

7. Neenah, "Worthy Scotsman"; William A. Mowry, *The Uxbridge Academy*, pp. 38–39, 74–75.

8. RG10, MML, letter, McArthur to Smith, Aug. 22, 1837, and letter, McArthur to McArthur, Oct. 28, 1843.

9. The claim in the MacArthur family is that through Aurelia Belcher, Douglas and Winston Churchill were related as eighth cousins and that MacArthur, like Churchill, was also a distant relative—sixth cousin, once removed—of Franklin D. Roosevelt. See Clark Lee and Richard Henschel, *Douglas MacArthur*, p. 11, and the photo section, which is sizable and includes photos of Sarah and Aurelia Belcher as well as the judge, his wife, Pinky, and Arthur Jr. at various ages.

10. RG10, MML, letter, McArthur to McArthur, Oct. 28, 1843, implies 1840 although others put the marriage date some time in 1844.

11. *Springfield Scrapbook*.

12. RG20, MML, letter, Thaddeus M. Szetela of Chicopee Falls, MA, to Dandridge P. West, Curator of the MacArthur Memorial Library, Jan. 29, 1965, 9 pages.

13. *Springfield Scrapbook*; RG10, MML, letter, McArthur to McArthur, Oct. 28, 1843.

14. RG10, MML, letter, McArthur to McArthur, Oct. 28, 1843.

15. Judge Arthur MacArthur, *Essays and Papers on Miscellaneous Topics,* pp. 19–20.

16. Don Russell, *Campaigning with King,* pp. 2–17.

17. Richard N. Current, *The History of Wisconsin,* pp. 5, 71–72, 76; Frank A. Flower, *Life of Matthew Hale Carpenter,* p. 59.

18. Robert G. Carroon, "Scotsmen in Old Milwaukee: 1810–1860," p. 31; Current, *The History of Wisconsin,* pp. 5, 71–72, 76; Flower, *Life of Matthew Hale Carpenter,* p. 59.

19. *Milwaukee Sentinel,* Oct. 17, 1850, Jan. 18, 21, 27, and 31, 1851, Jan. 12, 1852, March 20, 1858; Neenah, "Worthy Scotsman"; Carroon, "Scotsmen in Old Milwaukee," pp. 29–31; Arthur MacArthur, "Address of Arthur McArthur, Esq., on the Fourth Anniversary of the R. W. Grand Lodge of Wisconsin."

20. *Milwaukee Sentinel,* March 1, 3, April 6, 1852; *Daily Wisconsin,* March 3, 1852; RG20, MML, Genealogy Chart. MacArthur received 2,102 votes to 1,740 for his opponent, Charles K. Watkins, a plurality of 362 votes.

21. James M. McPherson, *Battle Cry of Freedom,* pp. 57, 70–77, 121.

22. Current, *The History of Wisconsin,* pp. 222–225.

23. Ibid.

24. *Argus,* Sept. 7–8, 1855.

25. *Argus,* Sept. 3–4, 8, 1855; *Daily Wisconsin,* Sept. 1, 1855; Moses M. Strong Papers, WHS, letter, Arthur McArthur to Strong, Sept. 4, 1855. There were two other prime contenders for the nomination: F. W. Horn and H. M. Billings. On the first ballot, MacArthur received 33 votes, well short of the 75 needed for a majority. But none of the other candidates came close to receiving 75 votes either. The convention was adjourned, and the delegates reconvened the following day to take up the issue again. Only 144 delegates were present, which meant that the nominee for lieutenant governor needed a minimum of 73 votes. On the first ballot, MacArthur received 68, Billings 44, and Horn 27, with eleven voters selecting other candidates or abstaining. A second ballot was called. MacArthur received 76 votes to Billings's 51 and Horn's 15. MacArthur was the candidate.

26. *Argus,* Sept. 4, 1855; Jerome A. Watrous, "An Old Time Routing of Grafters"; Edward M. Hunter, "Civil Life, Services and Character of William A. Barstow"; Current, *The History of Wisconsin,* p. 226.

27. *Argus,* Sept. 4, 1855; *Milwaukee Sentinel,* Sept. 1, Oct. 10 and 24, 1855.

28. *Milwaukee Sentinel,* Dec. 19, 1855; James R. Donoghue, *How Wisconsin Voted, 1848–1972,* p. 64.

29. Current, *The History of Wisconsin,* p. 228; Flower, *Life of Matthew Hale Carpenter,* p. 97.

30. For details on the Bashford–Barstow court case, see *Evening Argus and Democrat,* March 1–5, 8, 12, and 25–27, 1856; Current, *The History of Wisconsin,* p. 226.

31. *Milwaukee Sentinel,* March 24, 26, 29, and 31, 1856; *Argus,* March 28, 1856; *New York Times,* March 29, 1856; *Springfield Republican,* April 1, 1856; *New York Herald,* March 29, 1856. See also *Evening Wisconsin,* Aug. 27, 1896; Hunter, "William A. Barstow"; Watrous, "An Old Time Routing of Grafters"; Jerome A. Watrous, *Memoirs of Milwaukee County.*

32. Charles King, "Boys of the Loyal Legion"; Current, *The History of Wisconsin,* p. 5; Russell, *Campaigning with King,* pp. 2–17.

33. Chicopee, MA, City Hall, Death Records, 1864.

34. As a historian, trained to research and interpret factual events, I find hypothesizing on the effects of an event on the psychological development of an individual a challenge. With limited evidence, any conclusions are mere conjectures, and thus the reader is encouraged to draw alternate but equally appropriate conclusions. See Robert Coles, *Erik H. Erikson: The Growth of His Work;* Erik H. Erikson, *Life History and the Historical Moment;* Gail Sheehy, *Passages: Predictable Crises of Adult Life.*

35. *Milwaukee Sentinel,* March 26, 28, and 31, April 8, Oct. 14, 1857.

36. Ibid., Oct. 17, 1850, Jan. 21, 1851, Jan. 20 and 26, 1859, July 8, 1879; E. Bruce Thompson, *Matthew Hale Carpenter: Webster of the West,* p. 72; Carroon, "Scotsmen in Old Milwaukee," pp. 29–31; Usher, *Wisconsin,* p. 1839; Neenah, "Worthy Scotsman."

37. Sheehy, *Passages*, p. 78.

38. Coles, *Erikson*, p. 142, quoting Erikson.

39. Twain, quoted in Gerald F. Linderman, *Embattled Courage: The Experience of Combat in the American Civil War*, pp. 15–16.

40. Sheehy, *Passages*, p. 58; Petillo, *MacArthur*, p. 20, analyzing aspects of young Douglas's personality.

41. Anderson, *The MacArthurs*, quoting speech by Charlie King to the St. Andrews Society, Jan. 25(?), 1903, and speech by General MacArthur to the Old Schoolmates Association, 1907, pp. 18–22; Watrous Papers, WHS. Although Watrous knew the MacArthurs, he tended to elaborate on stories and must always be read with care.

42. Sheehy, *Passages*, pp. 35, 37, 56, 91.

43. McPherson, *Battle Cry*, pp. 205–206.

44. Anderson, *The MacArthurs*, quoting speech by Charlie King to the St. Andrews Society, Jan. 25(?), 1903, and speech by General MacArthur to the Old Schoolmates Association, 1907, pp. 18–22; Russell, *Campaigning with King*, p. 5; Watrous Papers, WHS. Although it is clear that Arthur went to a military school, which one is never mentioned.

45. Quoted in McPherson, *Battle Cry*, pp. 238, 316–317. This quote is a problem: I am quoting both McPherson and the people he quoted. The order of secession was: South Carolina, Dec. 20, 1860; Mississippi, Jan. 9, 1861; Florida, Jan. 10, 1861; Alabama, Jan. 11, 1861; Georgia, Jan. 19, 1861; Louisiana, Jan. 26, 1861; Texas, Feb. 1, 1861. The eight remaining states were Virginia, Arkansas, Missouri, North Carolina, Tennessee, Maryland, Delaware, and Kentucky. See McPherson, *Battle Cry*, pp. 234–235.

46. Ibid., p. 278. Missouri and Kentucky retained Union governments, although the loyalty in these two border states was split.

47. Quoted in and quoting McPherson, *Battle Cry*, p. 274.

48. *Milwaukee Sentinel*, April 22 and 28, 1861.

49. Oliver Knight, *Life and Manners in the Frontier Army As Depicted in the Novels of Charles King*, p. 11; Russell, *Campaigning with King*, pp. 10–14.

50. Jerome A. Watrous, "How the Boy Won: General McArthur's First Victory"; RG20, MML, newspaper clipping; also Watrous Papers (WHS).

51. McPherson, *Battle Cry*, p. 347.

52. Ibid., p. 349; Linderman, *Embattled Courage*, pp. 201–204.

53. *Milwaukee Sentinel*, May 29, June 7, 1861. RG94, NA, Document file, McArthur to Lincoln, May 13, 1862. RG94, NA, Document file consulted is on microfilm at MacArthur Memorial Library. The extensive file documents are organized chronologically.

54. Thompson, *Matthew Hale Carpenter*, pp. 68ff; Flower, *Life of Matthew Hale Carpenter*, p. 194.

55. RG94, NA, Document file, Doolittle to Lincoln, June 3, 1862; "Proceedings Attending the Reception and Banquet to Major General Arthur MacArthur," p. 501; Knight, *Life and Manners*, p. 11; Russell, *Campaigning with King*, pp. 10–14.

Chapter 2: Into the War

1. *Milwaukee Sentinel*, April 28, 1862; Current, *The History of Wisconsin*, p. 310.

2. Watrous, "How the Boy Won"; RG94, NA, Document file, letter, Edward Salomon, governor of Wisconsin, to President Lincoln, May 10, 1862, on official stationery of the Executive Department of the state of Wisconsin. Watrous's account is exaggerated but interesting.

3. RG94, NA, Document file, letter, Captain MacArthur to Adjutant General (AG), July 8, 1882, subject, birth records; *Milwaukee Sentinel*, Aug. 8, 1862; Robert G. Carroon, "Arms and the Clans: Milwaukee Scots in the Civil War," pp. 113–114.

4. See photos.

5. RG20, MML, newspaper clippings, *Milwaukee Telegraph*, April 1898, interview of Lieutenant Colonel MacArthur, and 24th Wisconsin, Field and Staff Muster Rolls.

6. Watrous, "How the Boy Won."

7. Major Howard Greene, "With the 24th Wisconsin Volunteers," in Howard Greene Papers, WHS.

8. Edwin B. Quiner, *Correspondence of Wisconsin Volunteers, 1861–1865*, Vol. 6, pp. 247ff; Bell I. Wiley, *The Common Soldier of the Civil War*, pp. 35–36.

9. Patricia L. Faust, ed., *Historical Times Illustrated Encyclopedia of the Civil War*, pp. 687–688.

10. Watrous, "How the Boy Won."

11. Ibid.; RG20, MML, newspaper clippings, *Milwaukee Telegraph*, April 1898, interview of Lieutenant Colonel MacArthur; RG20, MML, typed copy of a newspaper clipping, Jan. 1899, on a speech by a member of the 24th Wisconsin, probably from the *Milwaukee Sentinel*, describing "Wisconsin's boy soldier" of the Civil War; RG20, MML, newspaper clipping, source unknown, possibly the *Milwaukee Sentinel*, 1897, Watrous interview of Dunn.

12. Watrous, "How the Boy Won."

13. Faust, *Encyclopedia of the Civil War*, pp. 92–95; McPherson, *Battle Cry*, p. 528.

14. Watrous, "How the Boy Won."

15. Quiner, *Correspondence*, Vol. 6, pp. 248–249, letters, Sept. 8 and 22, 1862.

16. "Civil War Letters of Henry T. Drake," WHS; Mitchell Family Papers, "Civil War Letters of John Mitchell," WHS; Mitchell Family Papers, "Civil War Letters of Robert Chivas," WHS; Major Howard Greene, "With the 24th Wisconsin Volunteers," in Greene Papers, WHS.

17. Camp routine is described in "Civil War Letters of Henry T. Drake," WHS, Sept. 8 and 22, 1862; Wiley, *Common Soldier*, p. 42.

18. Wiley, *Common Soldier*, p. 23, passim.

19. Letters, Sept. 1862, in Howard Greene, Henry T. Drake, and Mitchell Family Papers, WHS; Quiner, *Correspondence*, Vol. 6, pp. 248ff, letter Sept. 8, 1862.

20. Wiley, *Common Soldier*, p. 42, passim; letters, Sept. 1862, in Howard Greene, Henry T. Drake Papers, WHS; Henry S. Commanger, ed., *The Blue and the Gray: The Story of the Civil War Told by Participants*, Vol. 1, pp. 417ff.

21. "Civil War Letters of Henry T. Drake," WHS, Sept. 7, 1862.

22. Quiner, *Correspondence*, Vol. 6, pp. 249ff; Howard Greene and Henry T. Drake Papers, WHS, Sept. 1862.

23. McPherson, *Battle Cry*, p. 544, observed: "The casualties at Antietam numbered four times the total suffered by American soldiers at the Normandy beaches on June 6, 1944. More than twice as many Americans lost their lives in one day at Sharpsburg as fell in combat in the War of 1812, the Mexican War, and the Spanish-American war—*combined*."

24. J. Montgomery Wright, "Notes of a Staff Officer," pp. 60–61. I used extensively the eyewitness accounts collected in Ned Bradford, ed., *Battles and Leaders of the Civil War*, Vols. 3 and 4.

25. McPherson, *Battle Cry*, p. 326 and note on p. 330. Four or five infantry regiments (later five or six) formed a brigade, three or four brigades comprised a division, and two or three divisions formed an army corps. At the start of the war, an infantry regiment numbered 1,000 men, a brigade 4,000, a division 12,000, and a corps 24,000. In practice, the size of each unit was about one-half or one-third of these numbers.

26. Wright, "Notes of a Staff Officer," pp. 60–61.

27. Commanger, *The Blue and the Gray*, Vol. 1, p. 423.

28. "Civil War Letters of Howard Greene," WHS, Nov. 4, 1862.

29. Letters, Oct. 1862, in Howard Greene, Henry T. Drake, and Mitchell Family Papers, WHS, "Civil War Letters of Robert Chivas."

30. Charles C. Gilbert, "On the Field at Perryville"; United States War Department, *The War of the Rebellion: A Compilation of the Official Records of the Union and Confederate Armies* [hereafter cited as *Official Records*], Vol. 16.

31. "Civil War Letters of Henry T. Drake," WHS, Oct. 13, 1862; Mitchell Family Papers, WHS, letter, Oct. 16, 1862; Wiley, *Common Soldier,* pp. 25, 55–56.

32. "Civil War Letters of Henry T. Drake," WHS, Oct. 13, 1862.

33. Sheehy, *Passages,* p. 3.

34. Linderman, *Embattled Courage.*

35. Watrous, "How the Boy Won."

36. Thomas J. Ford, *With the Rank and File,* pp. 6–8.

37. Mitchell Family Papers, WHS, letter, Oct. 10, 1862.

38. *Official Records,* Vol. 16; James Lee McDonough, *Stones River: Bloody Winter in Tennessee,* pp. 30ff.

39. "Civil War Letters of Howard Greene," WHS, Oct. 9, 1862.

40. First two quotes are from McPherson, *Battle Cry,* pp. 477, 574; Mitchell Family Papers, WHS, letters, Oct. 10 and 16, 1862; "Civil War Letters of Howard Greene," WHS, Oct. 21, 1862; see also Linderman, *Embattled Courage,* pp. 124–128.

41. "Civil War Letters of Henry T. Drake," WHS, letter, Oct. 11, 1862.

42. Ibid., letter, Oct. 16, 1862.

43. "Civil War Letters of Howard Greene," WHS, Oct. 24, 1862.

44. "Civil War Letters of Henry T. Drake," WHS, Oct. 16, 1862.

45. "Civil War Letters of Howard Greene," WHS, Oct. 24, 1862.

46. McDonough, *Stones River,* p. 38; Don Carlos Buell, "East Tennessee and the Campaign of Perryville," p. 31.

Chapter 3: The Battle of Murfreesboro

1. McDonough, *Stones River,* pp. 38–41.

2. The name is spelled both *Stone's* and *Stones*—each author seemed to make his or her own selection; I selected Stones.

3. "Civil War Letters of Howard Greene," WHS, Jan. 11, 1863.

4. Mitchell Family Papers, WHS, letter, Greusel to Alexander Mitchell, Jan. 9, 1863, letters, Larrabee to Mitchell, Dec. 8, 1862, and Jan. 1, 1863.

5. McPherson, *Battle Cry,* pp. 325, 340, 579.

6. "Civil War Letters of Howard Greene," WHS, Jan. 11, 1863.

7. Ibid., McDonough, *Stones River,* p. 75.

8. McDonough, *Stones River,* p. 75; G. C. Kniffin, "The Battle of Stone's River," pp. 613–632 and map on p. 616.

9. "Civil War Letters of Henry T. Drake," WHS, Jan. 8, 1863; "Civil War Letters of Howard Greene," WHS, Jan. 11, 1863.

10. "Civil War Letters of Howard Greene," WHS, Jan. 11, 1863; Mitchell Family Papers, WHS, "Civil War Letters of Robert Chivas," Jan. 5, 1863; Ford, *Rank and File,* pp. 9–10; *Official Records,* Vol. 29, pp. 354–357, 363–365; the name is spelled *MacArthur* for first time in these official reports—the army used both spellings.

11. McDonough, *Stones River,* p. 78.

12. Ford, *Rank and File,* pp. 9–10.

13. "Civil War Letters of Howard Greene," WHS, to Webb, Jan. 13, 1863.

14. "Civil War Letters of Henry T. Drake," WHS, letter, Jan. 8, 1863.

15. Ibid.; McDonough, *Stones River,* p. 87.

16. "Civil War Letters of Howard Greene," WHS, to Webb, Jan. 13, 1863; McDonough, *Stones River,* p. 111.

17. "Civil War Letters of Henry T. Drake," WHS, Jan. 8, 1863; Mitchell Family Papers, WHS, "Civil War Letters of Robert Chivas," to Aunty, Jan. 5, 1863, "Civil War Letters of John Mitchell," to mother, Jan. 8, 1863, and letter, Greusel to Alexander Mitchell, Jan. 9, 1863; Kniffin, "Stone's River," p. 625.

18. Adams quote is from Lloyd Lewis, *Sherman: Fighting Prophet,* p. 213. See also McPherson, *Battle Cry,* pp. 408, 473–477; Linderman, *Embattled Courage,* p. 135.

19. "Civil War Letters of Howard Greene," WHS, to Webb, Jan. 13, 1863; McDonough, *Stones River,* p. 125, quoting J. H. Haynie of the 19th Illinois, Negley's division.

20. "Civil War Letters of Howard Greene," WHS, Jan. 17 and 31, 1863.

21. Quoted in McDonough, *Stones River,* p. 104; Kniffin, "Stone's River," p. 625.

22. Ford, *Rank and File,* pp. 9–10.

23. McPherson, *Battle Cry,* pp. 409, 540.

24. "Civil War Letters of Henry T. Drake," WHS, Jan. 8, 1863; "Civil War Letters of Howard Greene," WHS, to Webb, Jan. 13, 1863; *Official Records,* Vol. 29, pp. 363–365.

25. Quiner, *Correspondence,* Vol. 10, citing letter, Jan. 2, 1863; Ford, *Rank and File;* Mitchell Family Papers, WHS, "Civil War Letters of Robert Chivas," to Aunty, Jan. 5, 1863; "Civil War Letters of Howard Greene," WHS, to Webb, Jan. 8, 1865; "Civil War Letters of Henry T. Drake," WHS, Jan. 8, 1863.

26. "Civil War Letters of Howard Greene," WHS, to Webb, Jan. 13, 1863.

27. Mitchell Family Papers, WHS, "Civil War Letters of John Mitchell," to mother, Jan. 8, 1863; McPherson, *Battle Cry,* p. 330; Linderman, *Embattled Courage,* passim.

28. RG20, MML, "Wisconsin's Boy Soldier."

29. Ford, *Rank and File,* pp. 9–10; McPherson, *Battle Cry,* pp. 581–582.

30. "Civil War Letters of Howard Greene," WHS, to Webb, Jan. 13, 1863.

31. McDonough, *Stones River,* p. 129.

32. Ibid., p. 117.

33. "Civil War Letters of Howard Greene," WHS, to Webb, Jan. 13, 1863; Mitchell Family Papers, WHS, "Civil War Letters of Robert Chivas," to Aunty, Jan. 5, 1863, and "Civil War Letters of John Mitchell," to mother, Jan. 8 and 19, 1863; *Official Records,* Vol. 29, pp. 356–357, 363–365.

34. "Civil War Letters of Howard Greene," WHS, to Webb, Jan. 13, 1863; Ford, *Rank and File,* pp. 9–10.

35. McDonough, *Stones River,* pp. 152, 157.

36. "Civil War Letters of Howard Greene," WHS, to Webb, Jan. 13, 1863; *Official Records,* Vol. 29, pp. 363–365.

37. Mitchell Family Papers, WHS, "Civil War Letters of Robert Chivas," Jan. 27, 1863.

38. McDonough, *Stones River,* p. 209, quoting John Beatty; Linderman, *Embattled Courage,* pp. 124–128.

39. Quoted in McDonough, *Stones River,* p. 205; "Civil War Letters of Henry T. Drake," WHS, Jan. 8, 1863.

40. RG20, MML, "Wisconsin's Boy Soldier."

41. Mitchell Family Papers, WHS, letter, Greusel to Alexander Mitchell, Jan. 9, 1863; *Official Records,* Vol. 29, pp. 356–357, 363–365.

42. Douglas MacArthur, *Reminiscences,* pp. 8–9.

Chapter 4: Interlude

1. Mitchell Family Papers, WHS, "Civil War Letters of Robert Chivas," to Aunty, Jan. 27, 1863.

2. Mitchell Family Papers, WHS, "Civil War Letters of Robert Chivas," to Aunty, Jan. 5 and 16, 1863, "Civil War Letters of John Mitchell," to mother, Jan. 8, 1863.

3. Mitchell Family Papers, WHS, "Civil War Letters of Robert Chivas," to Aunty, Jan. 5 and 16, 1863, "Civil War Letters of John Mitchell," to mother, Jan. 8, 1863, and Greusel to Alexander Mitchell, Jan. 9, 1863.

4. Edwin B. Parsons, "Sheridan."

5. Mitchell Family Papers, WHS, "Civil War Letters of Robert Chivas," Jan. 27, 1863.

6. Wiley, *Common Soldier,* pp. 53ff. Battlefield deaths totaled 204,000; death by diseases, 414,152.

7. Mitchell Family Papers, WHS, "Civil War Letters of Robert Chivas," to Aunty, Jan. 27, 1863, and "Civil War Letters of John Mitchell," to mother, Jan. 3, 1863; "Civil War Letters of Henry T. Drake," WHS, to brother, Jan. 24, 1863.

8. *Milwaukee Sentinel*, Feb. 7, 1863; "Civil War Letters of Howard Greene," WHS, Jan. 17 and 31, 1863.

9. Lewis, *Sherman*, pp. 239ff; "Civil War Letters of Henry T. Drake," WHS, letter, May 1, 1863.

10. *Legislative Manual of the State of Wisconsin*, WHS, p. 202. Other promotions included: Lieutenant David T. Horning to captain of Company E; Lieutenant William Kennedy to captain of Company G; Lieutenant Edwin B. Parsons to captain of Company K; Lieutenant Howard Greene to captain of Company B; and Sergeant Henry Drake to second lieutenant of Company A.

11. Mitchell Family Papers, WHS, "Civil War Letters of John Mitchell," Jan. 19, 1863, and "Civil War Letters of Robert Chivas," March 17, April 13, 1863.

12. "Civil War Letters of Howard Greene," WHS, to brother, March 28, 1863; "Civil War Letters of Henry T. Drake," WHS, to brother, March 4, 1863.

13. Mitchell Family Papers, WHS, "Civil War Letters of Robert Chivas," to Aunty, April 13, 1863.

14. Commanger, *Blue and Grey*, citing George Ward Nichols, pp. 417ff; Lewis, *Sherman*, p. 239.

15. "Civil War Letters of Henry T. Drake," WHS, Sept. 25, 1862; Wiley, *Common Soldier*, p. 42.

16. Quoted in Linderman, *Embattled Courage*, pp. 118–119.

17. Lewis, *Sherman*, p. 239; Linderman, *Embattled Courage*, pp. 37, 118–119.

18. Wiley, *Common Soldier*, p. 45. Other popular Civil War songs included: "Just Before the Battle Mother," "Annie Laurie," "Auld Lang Syne," "Juanita," "Lilly Dale," "Sweet Evalina," "Listen to the Mocking Bird," "The Captain and His Whiskers," "Gay and Happy Still," "All Hail the Power of Jesus," "How Firm a Foundation," and "Jesus Lover of My Soul."

19. Wiley, *Common Soldier*, p. 39.

20. Lewis, *Sherman*, p. 240.

21. "Civil War Letters of Henry T. Drake," WHS, April 24 and May 1, 1863.

22. Parsons, "Sheridan"; "Civil War Letters of Henry T. Drake," WHS, May 22, 1863; Mitchell Family Papers, WHS, "Civil War Letters of Robert Chivas," to Aunty, Oct. 7, 1862, and March 17, 1863; "Civil War Letters of Howard Greene," WHS, Nov. 4, 1862.

23. "Civil War Letters of Henry T. Drake," WHS, to brother, April 24 and May 1, 1863.

24. Linderman, *Embattled Courage*, p. 72.

25. "Civil War Letters of Howard Greene," WHS, to father, July 24, 1863.

26. McPherson, *Battle Cry*, p. 664.

27. Ibid., pp. 637–638.

28. *Milwaukee Sentinel*, July 14 and 18, Sept. 29, 1863; RG20, MML, Field and Staff Muster Rolls.

29. Faust, *Encyclopedia of the Civil War*, p. 307.

30. Thompson, *Matthew Hale Carpenter*, pp. 72ff.

31. Carpenter Family Papers, WHS, letter, Charles Robinson to Carpenter and MacArthur, Aug. 12, 1863, letters to Robinson, Aug. 24, 1863, and Sept. 10, 1863; *Green Bay Advocate*, Sept. 24, 1863; *Milwaukee Sentinel*, Sept. 25, 1863; Donoghue, *How Wisconsin Voted*, p. 65; Thompson, *Matthew Hale Carpenter*, pp. 72–79.

32. Linderman, *Embattled Courage*, pp. 216–217.

Chapter 5: Hero of Missionary Ridge

1. "Civil War Letters of Howard Greene," WHS, to mother, Sept. 30, 1863.

2. Parsons, "Sheridan," p. 278; *Official Records*, Vol. 30, pp. 586–588.

3. *Milwaukee Sentinel*, Sept. 29, 1863.

4. Linderman, *Embattled Courage*, p. 235.

5. James Lee McDonough, *Chattanooga: A Death Grip on the Confederacy*, pp. 42ff and map on p. 46; Ulysses S. Grant, "Chattanooga," p. 684.

6. Joseph S. Fullerton, "The Army of the Cumberland at Chattanooga," pp. 719–727.

7. Ibid., pp. 719ff; McDonough, *Chattanooga*, p. 58; Glenn Tucker, "The Battle for Chattanooga," pamphlet, *Historical Times* (1971), p. 8.

8. Linderman, *Embattled Courage*, p. 235.

9. Fullerton, "Chattanooga," p. 719; Tucker, "Chattanooga," p. 8; Grant, "Chattanooga," p. 684; Ford, *Rank and File*, pp. 25ff.

10. Lewis, *Sherman*, pp. 316–325; John F. Marszalek, *Sherman: A Soldier's Passion for Order*.

11. Lewis, *Sherman*, p. 315.

12. Fullerton, "Chattanooga," p. 721.

13. Ibid.

14. Ibid.

15. Quiner, *Correspondence*, Vol. 10, p. 297, letter, McArthur to father, Nov. 26, 1863.

16. Tucker, "Chattanooga," p. 30.

17. Fullerton, "Chattanooga," p. 723.

18. Quiner, *Correspondence*, Vol. 10, p. 297, letter, McArthur to father, Nov. 26, 1863.

19. Fullerton, "Chattanooga," p. 725; Tucker, "Chattanooga," p. 40; McDonough, *Chattanooga*, pp. 171–176; Edwin Parsons, "The True Story of the Assault on Missionary Ridge," p. 197.

20. Parsons, "Missionary Ridge," pp. 195ff.

21. Quoted in McDonough, *Chattanooga*, pp. 179–180; Parsons, "Missionary Ridge," pp. 195ff.

22. Fullerton, "Chattanooga," p. 725.

23. Ibid.

24. Quiner, *Correspondence*, Vol. 10, p. 297, letter, McArthur to father, Nov. 26, 1863.

25. McDonough, *Chattanooga*, pp. 188–189; Tucker, "Chattanooga," p. 40.

26. RG20, MML, "Wisconsin's Boy Soldier."

27. Quiner, *Correspondence*, Vol. 10, p. 297, letter, McArthur to father, Nov. 26, 1863.

28. Edmund Morris, *The Rise of Theodore Roosevelt*, p. 654, see also pp. 639ff.

29. Ford, *Rank and File*, pp. 28ff.

30. McPherson, *Battle Cry*, p. 680.

31. Ford, *Rank and File*, p. 28.

32. Ibid., pp. 28ff.

33. Parsons, "Missionary Ridge," pp. 198ff; *Official Records*, Vol. 55, pp. 207–208; Howard Greene Papers, WHS, letter, Lieutenant Rogers to mother, Nov. 26, 1863.

34. Fullerton, "Chattanooga," p. 726; Parsons, "Missionary Ridge," p. 193.

35. Carroon, "The Judge and the General," p. 6, quoting Parsons.

36. "Summary of Service Record of Lieutenant General Arthur MacArthur," Estabrook Papers, WHS, letter, June 7, 1890, Baumbach to secretary of war, supported by statements of Captain Edwin Parsons, Second Lieutenant George Allanson, and Lieutenant J. E. Armitage; *Official Records*, Vol. 55, pp. 207–208; Quiner, *Correspondence*, Vol. 10, p. 297, letter, McArthur to father, Nov. 26, 1863.

37. MacArthur, *Reminiscences*, p. 9.

Chapter 6: The Atlanta Campaign

1. Parsons, "Sheridan," pp. 279–280.

2. Diary of George A. Cooley, WHS. There are surprisingly few personal observations here, but Cooley kept a daily record of the weather, marches, skirmishes, etc.

3. Parsons, "Sheridan," pp. 279–280.

4. *Wisconsin State Journal*, Jan. 9, 1864; *Milwaukee Daily News*, Jan. 7, 1864; *Milwaukee Sentinel*, March 24, 1864; RG20, MML, Field and Staff Muster Rolls; Jerome Watrous, "About High Ranking Officers"; "Summary of Service Record of Lieutenant General Arthur MacArthur," Estabrook Papers, WHS; Carroon, "The Judge and the General," quoting Parsons, p. 6.

5. See Chapter 9.

6. Diary of George A. Cooley, WHS, March 26, 1864; Parsons, "Sheridan," pp. 283–284.

7. Diary of George A. Cooley, WHS, April 10–21, 1864.

8. Lewis, *Sherman*, p. 357; William T. Sherman, "The Grand Strategy of the Last Year of the War," pp. 247–259; Joseph E. Johnston, "Opposing Sherman's Advance to Atlanta," pp. 260–277; Oliver O. Howard, "The Struggle for Atlanta," pp. 293–325; *Official Records*, Vol. 38, pp. 309–312, 327–330.

9. Diary of George A. Cooley, WHS, April–May 1864.

10. See McPherson, *Battle Cry*, pp. 473–474, or Linderman, *Embattled Courage*, p. 135, for a discussion of muzzle-loading muskets.

11. Sherman, "The Grand Strategy," p. 255.

12. *Official Records*, Vol. 38, pp. 327–330; Diary of George A. Cooley, WHS, May 14, 1864.

13. Carlton McCarthy of the Richmond Howitzers, quoted in Linderman, *Embattled Courage*, p. 142; see also Lewis, *Sherman*, p. 371.

14. "Proceedings Attending the Reception and Banquet to Major General Arthur MacArthur," comments by Parsons, pp. 510–511.

15. Diary of George A. Cooley, WHS, May 15–16, 1864.

16. Ibid., May 17–19, 1864; letters, Major McArthur to father, May 16 and 18, 1864, quoted in *Milwaukee Sentinel*, May 28, 1864; *Official Records*, Vol. 38, pp. 327–330.

17. "Summary of Service Record of Lieutenant General Arthur MacArthur," Estabrook Papers, WHS, quoting Arthur L. Wagner.

18. *Official Records*, Vol. 38, pp. 327–330.

19. For a vivid description of rain in the summer in Tennessee, see "Civil War Letters of Howard Greene," WHS, to father, July 24, 1863.

20. *Official Records*, Vol. 38, pp. 327–330.

21. Diary of George A. Cooley, WHS, June 3, 1864.

22. McPherson, *Battle Cry*, pp. 732–734, 742–743.

23. A good summary of the battle of Kennesaw Mountain is in Charles Royster, *The Destructive War*, pp. 296–320.

24. *Official Records*, Vol. 38, pp. 327–330; Henry F. Graff, *American Imperialism and the Philippine Insurrection*, p. 128.

25. *Official Records*, Vol. 38, pp. 327–330; Diary of George A. Cooley, WHS, June 24, 1864; RG94, NA, Document file, letter, MacArthur to General Sidney Burbank, Oct. 20, 1866.

26. This seems like an apocryphal story, but the episode was recounted by a number of people, including eyewitness Private George A. Cooley (Diary), WHS, June 22, 1864. See also RG20, MML, newspaper clippings, *Oregonian*, Aug. 29, 1866, newspaper clippings (probably *Milwaukee Sentinel*, 1897 and Jan. 1899; Watrous, "How the Boy Won," and Watrous, "About High Ranking Officers."

27. *Official Records*, Vol. 38, pp. 327–330.

28. Diary of George A. Cooley, WHS, June 28–July 1, 1864.

29. Lewis, *Sherman*, pp. 401–402.

30. McPherson, *Battle Cry*, p. 751.

31. Sherman, "The Grand Strategy," p. 253.

32. Lewis, *Sherman*, pp. 383ff.

33. "Summary of Service Record of Lieutenant General Arthur MacArthur," Estabrook Papers, WHS, extract of letter from Captain T. E. Balding, describing reconnaissance made by the 24th Wisconsin, vicinity of Atlanta, GA, July 19–20, 1864. See also D. Clayton James, *The Years of MacArthur*, p. 15.

34. Linderman, *Embattled Courage*, pp. 213–214.

35. *Official Records*, Vol. 38, pp. 309–312, 327–330.

36. Diary of George A. Cooley, WHS, Sept. 8, 1864.

37. *Official Records*, Vol. 38, pp. 327–330.

Chapter 7: The Battle for Franklin

1. RG20, MML, letter, Major McArthur to General Whipple, Sept. 9, 1864; Chicopee, MA, City Hall, Death Records, 1864; *Milwaukee Sentinel*, Oct. 4, 1864.
2. Carroon, "The Judge and the General," pp. 2ff; Conard, *History of Milwaukee County*, p. 191; Usher, *Wisconsin*, p. 1838; Mann, "Ancestral Lines," p. 171; Reed, *Bench and Bar*, p. 130.
3. RG20, MML, letter, Major McArthur to General Whipple, Sept. 9, 1864.
4. Linderman, *Embattled Courage*, p. 134.
5. *Milwaukee Sentinel*, Oct. 4, 1864.
6. Diary of George A. Cooley, WHS, Oct. 1864.
7. Sherman, quoted in Marszalek, *Sherman*, p. 358.
8. First quote is from Alexander Hunter of the 17th Virginia, in Linderman, *Embattled Courage*, p. 235; second quote appears on p. 234.
9. Diary of George A. Cooley, WHS, Oct.–Dec. 1864.
10. Sherman, quoted from McPherson, *Battle Cry*, p. 808; see also pp. 807–809.
11. The prime sources used for the battle of Franklin were *Official Records*, Vol. 45, pp. 114–118, 239–241, 252–254; Fred W. Byers, "Battle of Franklin"; Sims Crownover, "The Battle of Franklin"; J. B. Hood, "The Invasion of Tennessee"; Henry Stone, "Repelling Hood's Invasion of Tennessee"; Dan M. Robison, "The Carter House"; James Lee McDonough and Thomas L. Connelly, *Five Tragic Hours: The Battle of Franklin*; and Wiley Sword, *Embrace an Angry Wind*.
12. Chicopee, MA, City Hall, Death Records, 1864. The records do not indicate the type of mental illness—"insanity" is the word used.
13. The seven regiments were the 24th Wisconsin, the 125th Ohio, and five Illinois regiments (the 36th, 44th, 73rd, 74th, and 88th).
14. *Official Records*, Vol. 45, pp. 239–240.
15. Sword, *Embrace an Angry Wind*, pp. 173–174.
16. Ford, *Rank and File*, p. 16; *Official Records*, Vol. 45, p. 253; RG20, MML, "Wisconsin's Boy Soldier"; Byers, "The Battle of Franklin," pp. 233ff.
17. Ford, *Rank and File*, p. 16.
18. Watrous, "About High Ranking Officers."
19. *Official Records*, Vol. 45, p. 116.
20. Sword, *Embrace an Angry Wind*, p. 201.
21. RG20, MML, "Wisconsin's Boy Soldier," implies the words, and thus, the liberty.
22. Sword, *Embrace an Angry Wind*, p. 203.
23. RG20, MML, medical certificate, Jan. 23, 1865. For a more heroic version, see MacArthur, *Reminiscences*, p. 10.
24. RG20, MML, "Wisconsin's Boy Soldier."
25. *Official Records*, Vol. 45, pp. 239–240, 252–254; Byers, "The Battle of Franklin," pp. 237–238. The battle for Franklin was one of the bloodiest of the Civil War. In comparison, in the long Seven Days' campaign of 1862 in Virginia, General George McClellan's federal army of 105,000 men fought Robert E. Lee for seven days and suffered a loss of only 1,734 men. At Chancellorsville in 1863, the Army of the Potomac, 97,000 strong, suffered fewer casualties than Hood's army at Franklin. At Chickamauga, the 60,000-man Army of the Cumberland lost only 1,657 men killed.
26. RG94, NA, Document file, letters, Stanley to Stanton, June 5, 1865, and Opdycke, April 11, 1865.

Chapter 8: A Hero's Return

1. *Milwaukee Sentinel*, Dec. 6, 8, 19, 24, and 29, 1864.
2. RG94, NA, Document file, letters to Stanton from General Kimball, April 13, 1865, from General Opdycke, April 11, 1865, from General Stanley, June 5, 1865, from General Thomas, Aug. 13, 1865.

3. Ibid., letter, no date (April 1865?), from Wisconsin senators and congressmen to secretary of war.

4. RG20, MML; Wiley, *Common Soldier*, p. 15; Frazier Hunt, *The Untold Story of Douglas MacArthur*, p. 6.

5. These figures are estimates from official records and diaries. Hunt, *The Untold Story*, p. 6, lists the survivors in June 1865 as 25 officers and 334 enlisted men.

6. Major Howard Greene, "With 24th Wisconsin," in Greene Papers, WHS; Watrous Papers, WHS.

7. Linderman, *Embattled Courage*, pp. 267–268.

Chapter 9: Into the Wilderness

1. *Milwaukee Sentinel*, Aug. 22, 1866; William D. Love Papers, WHS, letters, Judge MacArthur to Reverend Love, Aug. 22, 1866, and Feb. 22, 1867.

2. I owe a debt to a number of scholars for their work on the U.S. Army after the Civil War, including: Robert M. Utley, *Frontier Regulars: The United States Army and the Indian, 1866–1890*; Jack D. Foner, *The United States Soldier Between Two Wars: Army Life and Reforms, 1865–1898*; Don Rickey, *Forty Miles on Beans and Hay: The Enlisted Soldier Fighting the Indian Wars*; William A. Ganoe, *History of the U.S. Army*; Oliver Knight, *Life and Manners in the Frontier Army as Depicted in the Novels of Charles King*; Edward M. Coffman, *The Old Army: A Portrait of the American Army in Peacetime, 1784–1898*; Frances C. Carrington, *My Army Life and the Fort Phil Kearney Massacre*; and George A. Forsyth, *The Story of the Soldier*.

3. Petillo, *MacArthur*, p. 6.

4. RG94, NA, Document file, memo, AG to Captain MacArthur, July 18 and 26, 1882, MacArthur to AG, Aug. 5, 1882.

5. Ibid., letters, Aug. 6, 8, 12 and Sept. 20, 1866.

6. Ibid., letter, Oct. 20, 1866.

7. See RG94, NA, Document file.

8. *Milwaukee Sentinel*, June 21, 1867, Jan. 30, 1868; *Evening Wisconsin*, Aug. 27, 1896; John R. Berryman, *History of the Bench and Bar of Wisconsin*, pp. 386–388.

9. RG94, NA, Document file, Officer's Individual Report filed by MacArthur to AGO, May 1, 1890; *Report of the Proceedings of the Meetings of the State Bar Association of Wisconsin*, Vol. 10 (1912–1914), pp. 38–39.

10. *Milwaukee Sentinel*, Sept. 15, 1869, quoting the *Boston Transcript*; also *Milwaukee Sentinel*, Sept. 30 and Oct. 11, 12, and 14, 1869.

11. Ibid., March 12, May 14, Nov. 9 and 26, and Dec. 14 and 17, 1869.

12. Ibid., July 15–16, 1870.

13. RG94, NA, Document file, letters, Captain MacArthur to Sheridan, July 27, 1870, Sheridan to lieutenant general of the army, July 27, 1870, MacArthur to AG, July 30, 1870.

14. Philippe de Trobriand, *Military Life in Dakota: The Journal of Philippe Regis de Trobriand*; Ulysses G. Alexander, *History of the Thirteenth Regiment, United States Infantry*.

15. Petillo, *MacArthur*, p. 13

16. RG94, NA, Document file, Officer's Individual Report filed by MacArthur to AGO, May 1, 1890; RG165, NA, "Chinese Memorandum," Jan. 15, 1883.

17. *Milwaukee Sentinel*, Jan. 14, 1871.

18. Ibid., April 9, 1874, and July 8, 1879; Carpenter Family Papers, WHS, diary of Lilian Carpenter, March 20, 1877.

19. *Milwaukee Sentinel*, Feb. 10, 1872.

20. RG165, NA, "Chinese Memorandum," Jan. 15, 1883.

21. RG94, NA, Document file, letters, Carpenter to Grant, July 20, 1872, Twambly to Grant, May 31, 1872.

22. Ibid., letter, secretary of war to Carpenter, Aug. 21, 1872.

23. Quoted in Richard Hofstadter, William Miller, and Daniel Aaron, *The American Republic*, Vol. 2, p. 28.

24. MacArthur, *Reminiscences*, p. 13.

25. Ibid., p. 14; William Manchester, *American Caesar: Douglas MacArthur, 1880–1964*, p. 24; Hunt, *The Untold Story*, p. 8.

26. See *Milwaukee Sentinel*, Dec. 4, 1866, for an example of the judge's pride in his Scottish heritage.

27. Hunt, *The Untold Story*, p. 8.

28. RG20(?), MML, Marriage certificate, note attached.

29. Quoted in Hofstadter, *The American Republic*, Vol. 2, p. 98.

30. Petillo, *MacArthur*, pp. 9–10, quoting RG165, MML, letter, mother to Mary, April 30, 1877; Frank MacArthur, *Reports of Cases: Cases Arising upon Applications for Letters-Patent for Inventions Determined in the Circuit and Supreme Courts of the District of Columbia*.

31. See Duane Merritt Greene, *Ladies and Officers of the United States Army*; Petillo, *MacArthur*, p. 12.

32. Knight, *Life and Manners*, pp. 6–7.

33. First quote is from Foner, *United States Soldier*, p. 74; Sherman quote is from Knight, *Life and Manners*, p. 6.

34. Ralph E. Minger, "Taft, MacArthur, and the Establishment of Civil Government in the Philippines," p. 310.

35. All quotes are from Linderman, *Embattled Courage*, p. 273.

36. Rickey, *Forty Miles*, p. 105. The army required every enlisted man to fire ninety rounds of ammunition at the rifle range. Riflemen participated in sight drills to perfect their knowledge of the effects of wind on the bullets. By 1878, rifle and carbine practice was done at ranges progressing from 100 to 1,000 yards. The target had a bull's-eye of 3 to 36 inches in diameter. At 500 yards, a 50 percent hit ratio was required to pass. In addition to shooting at conventional targets, experienced men fired at silhouette figures of mock enemies. Cutouts were placed at various distances in all conceivable positions. The number and placement of hits in the figure targets determined the shooter's score.

37. Petillo, *MacArthur*, p. 12.

38. Quote from Coffman, *Old Army*, p. 263.

39. James, *MacArthur*, pp. 49–50; MacArthur, *Reminiscences*, pp. 15–16; Frank E. Vandiver, *Black Jack: The Life and Times of John J. Pershing*, p. 74.

40. Knight, *Life and Manners*, pp. 4, 5, 110.

41. Manchester, *American Caesar*, p. 42.

42. Marszalek, *Sherman*, quoting Sherman, pp. 49–50.

43. Linderman, *Embattled Courage*, p. 285.

44. Coffman, *Old Army*, p. 265.

45. Hofstadter, *The American Republic*, Vol. 2, pp. 197–198, 204, 230.

46. Petillo, *MacArthur*, p. 253, note 20, citing Brown to Douglas MacArthur, Oct. 16, 1937.

47. Ibid., pp. 13–14.

48. Ibid., pp. 9–10, quoting letter, April 30, 1877, mother to Missy, see also p. 253, note 16; Hunt, *Untold Story*, p. 112. Pinky's mother's name was Elizabeth Pierce Hardy.

49. *Evening Wisconsin*, Aug. 27, 1896; Usher, *Wisconsin*, p. 1839.

50. RG94, NA, Document file, letter, Knight to Spooner, March 20, 1889; RG165, NA, letter, Grant to Judge, June 10, 1882; RG165, NA, Box 128, "Russo-Japanese War and the Asian Tour," MacArthur, commanding the Pacific Division, San Francisco, to Secretary of War Taft, Feb. 4, 1905.

51. RG94, NA, Document file, memos, AG to Captain MacArthur, July 18 and 26, 1882, MacArthur to AG, Aug. 5, 1882, AG to MacArthur, Sept. 15, 1882, and Oct. 2, 1882.

52. RG165, NA, "Chinese Memorandum," sent to Grant on Jan. 15, 1883.

53. RG94, NA, Document file, memo, Bradley, Sept. 15, 1882.

54. RG165, NA, "Chinese Memorandum," Jan. 15, 1883; Petillo, *MacArthur*, pp. 45ff.

55. MacArthur's ideas reflected the opinions General Sherman presented in his 1880 annual report as commanding general (Nov. 10, 1880) to the secretary of war. See Marszalek, *Sherman*, p. 393.

56. Petillo, *MacArthur,* p. 19.
57. Ibid., p. 253, note 21, p. 254, note 32.
58. Sheehy, *Passages,* pp. 6, 11–13.
59. MacArthur, *Reminiscences,* p. 14; Petillo, *MacArthur,* pp. 16–19; James, *MacArthur,* p. 51.
60. MacArthur, *Reminiscences,* p. 15; RG94, NA, Post Returns, March 14, 1884.
61. RG94, NA, Post Returns, March 14, 1884.
62. Ibid.
63. Herbert M. Hart, *Old Forts of the Southwest,* pp. 132–134, photo of Fort Selden, p. 133.
64. Ibid., p. 132.
65. RG94, NA, Post Returns, March–April 1884.
66. Quoted in Petillo, *MacArthur,* citing a letter, May 11, 1884, "Pink" to "My Precious Sister," also p. 254, note 27.
67. RG165, NA, "Chinese Memorandum," Jan. 15, 1883.
68. RG20, MML, newspaper clipping, *Leavenworth Times,* Sept. 10, 1912.
69. RG94, NA, Post Returns, Selden, 1884–1886.
70. Manchester, *American Caesar,* pp. 42, 135; Hunt, *Untold Story,* pp. 4, 7, 11; Coffman, *Old Army,* p. 322; James, *MacArthur,* p. 11; Petillo, *MacArthur,* p. 1.
71. Manchester, *American Caesar,* p. 119, quoting William A. Ganoe, *MacArthur Close-up.*
72. First quote is from Manchester, *American Caesar,* p. 41; second quote is from Hunt, *Untold Story,* p. 11; see also Coffman, *Old Army,* p. 316, and Petillo, *MacArthur,* p. 20.
73. MacArthur, *Reminiscences,* pp. 12–13.
74. RG94, NA, Post Returns, Selden, 1884–1886; James, *MacArthur,* pp. 53–54. For an exciting account of Lawton and the Geronimo campaign, see Hermann Hagedorn, *Leonard Wood,* pp. 48–103.
75. RG94, NA, Document file, Extract from report of inspection of Fort Selden, Major G. H. Burton, Sept. 15, 1885.
76. *Milwaukee Sentinel,* Nov. 20, 1879; Judge Arthur MacArthur, "Welcome Address," to the 11th Reunion of the Society of the Army of the Cumberland, Nov. 1879.

Chapter 10: On Staff

1. Coffman, *Old Army,* pp. 274, 290.
2. Hunt, *Untold Story,* p. 12.
3. "Summary of Service Record of Lieutenant General Arthur MacArthur," Estabrook Papers, WHS, quoting Arthur L. Wagner. See Timothy K. Nenninger, *The Leavenworth Schools and the Old Army,* for a description of the course of instruction at Leavenworth in September 1887, p. 29.
4. "Summary of Service Record of Lieutenant General Arthur MacArthur," Estabrook Papers, WHS; Coffman, *Old Army,* pp. 275–276. Wagner's textbook was *Organization and Tactics* (1895); see Nenninger, *The Leavenworth Schools,* pp. 36–44, and Graff, *American Imperialism,* pp. 128–132, for further comments on Wagner.
5. Sheehy, *Passages,* pp. 5, 8, 16.
6. The other staff departments were the Judge Advocate General's Department, the Subsistence Department, the Medical Department, the Ordnance Department, the Pay Department, the Engineer Corps, and the Signal Corps.
7. McCook quote is from Estabrook Papers, WHS, letter, McCook to AG, July 16, 1888; see also RG94, NA, Document file, various letters, 1887–1889, particularly Knight to Vilas, Dec. 15, 1887, and Knight to Spooner, March 29, 1889.
8. *Army Register,* 1887–1890.
9. RG94, NA, Document file, "Memorandum" written by Judge MacArthur, print date May 28, 1889, pp. 13–14.

10. RG94, NA, Document file, MacArthur letters on brevet issue, Nov. 9, 1868, April 24, 1869, Jan. 10 and 28, 1873, Sept. 11, 15, and 20, Oct. 8, 24, and 28, Nov. 6, 1879, May 10 and 20, June 2 and 4, 1881, Oct. 13 and Nov. 1, 1883.

11. James B. Fry, *The History and Legal Effect of Brevets in the Armies of Great Britain and the United States,* passim.

12. Utley, *Frontier Regulars,* pp. 13, 22, and 38.

13. See brevet letters, cited in Note 10.

14. RG94, NA, Document file, July 1 and 2, 1889.

15. James, *MacArthur,* p. 57; MacArthur, *Reminiscences,* p. 16; Manchester, *American Caesar,* p. 44.

16. Quoted in Morris, *Roosevelt,* p. 414.

17. Quoted in James, *MacArthur,* pp. 44–45; Manchester, *American Caesar,* p. 28.

18. Manchester, *American Caesar,* p. 124; "Summary of Service Record of Lieutenant General Arthur MacArthur," Estabrook Papers, WHS.

19. Coffman, *Old Army,* pp. 233, 273, 281.

20. "Summary of Service Record of Lieutenant General Arthur MacArthur," Estabrook Papers, WHS, quoting letter, Kelton to MacArthur, n.d.; see also RG94, NA, Document file, Baumbach to secretary of war, June 7 and 30, 1890.

21. "Summary of Service Record of Lieutenant General Arthur MacArthur," Estabrook Papers, WHS.

22. 54th Congress, 2nd Session, House Report 2585; *Army Register,* passim.

23. "Summary of Service Record of Lieutenant General Arthur MacArthur," Estabrook Papers, WHS, extract from letter by Lieutenant E. K. Holton, n.d. (1890?), with reference to the battle of Stones River.

24. Ibid., extract from letter by Baumbach on Missionary Ridge, June 7, 1890.

25. *Army Register,* 1891–1896.

26. MacArthur, *Reminiscences,* p. 5.

27. MacArthur, *Essays,* pp. 18, 33, 83.

28. Hunt, *Untold Story,* p. 156; see also Petillo, *MacArthur,* p. 3, and Manchester, *American Caesar,* pp. 79, 135.

29. MacArthur, *Reminiscences,* pp. 8–9.

30. Nimitz Library, U.S. Naval Academy, Archives, MacArthur File.

31. Hofstadter, *The American Republic,* Vol. 2, p. 39, see also p. 291.

32. Ibid., p. 309, quoting Twain, p. 364, quoting Lloyd.

33. Ibid., pp. 245, 292–293, 297, 310, 355–356.

34. Petillo, *MacArthur,* p. 26.

35. Halstead-Maus Papers, *Memoirs,* U.S. Army Military History Research Collection at Carlisle Barracks, PA, hereafter cited as Carlisle; see also Hunt, *Untold Story,* p. 14.

36. MacArthur, *Reminiscences,* pp. 17–18; Hunt, *Untold Story,* p. 14; Petillo, *MacArthur,* p. 30; Manchester, *American Caesar,* pp. 44–45; James, *MacArthur,* p. 60.

37. RG94, NA, Document file, letters, April 9 and 18, 1895.

38. *Annual Registers,* 1892–1896, and *The Lucky Bag,* yearbook for class of 1896, pp. 93–94, Nimitz Library, U.S. Naval Academy.

39. MacArthur, *Essays;* Mann, "Ancestral Lines," p. 171; Neenah, "Worthy Scotsman."

40. Morris, *Roosevelt,* pp. 415–416.

41. William F. Vilas Papers, WHS, letters, Mrs. MacArthur to Vilas, Jan. 2 and 10, 1897. Mary lived three more years before dying on April 30, 1899, at the age of seventy-five. She was interred in Rock Creek Cemetery, next to her husband, in section 1 Lot. 91, site 6.

42. RG94, NA, Document file, will of Arthur MacArthur.

43. MacArthur, *Reminiscences,* p. 17; Hunt, *Untold Story,* p. 15.

44. Petillo, *MacArthur,* p. 31; James, *MacArthur,* p. 63.

45. James, *MacArthur,* p. 65; Manchester, *American Caesar,* pp. 44–45; MacArthur, *Reminiscences,* p. 17; Hunt, *Untold Story,* p. 18.

46. See Knight, *Life and Manners,* and Russell, *Campaigning with King;* see also Morris, *Roosevelt,* pp. 462–463.

Chapter 11: The Spanish-American War and the Philippines

1. Charles H. Brown, *The Correspondents' War: Journalists in the Spanish-American War,* passim; Morris, *Roosevelt,* pp. 569–607; Stuart Creighton Miller, *Benevolent Assimilation: The American Conquest of the Philippines, 1899–1903,* p. 9; Stanley Karnow, *In Our Image: America's Empire in the Philippines,* p. 88.

2. Hofstadter, *The American Republic,* Vol. 2, pp. 280, 333; Miller, *Benevolent Assimilation,* pp. 8–9.

3. Quoted in Karnow, *In Our Image,* p. 89.

4. Linderman, *Embattled Courage,* pp. 271 and 275.

5. Quoted in Hofstadter, *The American Republic,* Vol. 2, p. 337.

6. Morris, *Roosevelt,* pp. 596–597; Miller, *Benevolent Assimilation,* p. 10; Hofstadter, *The American Republic,* Vol. 2, p. 333.

7. Karnow, *In Our Image,* p. 95; Morris, *Roosevelt,* pp. 593, 599; Miller, *Benevolent Assimilation,* pp. 10–11; Hofstadter, *The American Republic,* Vol. 2, pp. 333–335.

8. Morris, *Roosevelt,* p. 607; Karnow, *In Our Image,* p. 99.

9. Karnow, *In Our Image,* p. 171.

10. Charles King, *Memories of a Busy Life;* RG20, MML, newspaper clippings, *Milwaukee Sentinel* and *Milwaukee Telegraph,* May–April 1898.

11. Jesse George, *Our Army and Navy in the Orient,* p. 19.

12. Quoted in Morris, *Roosevelt,* p. 627.

13. Hofstadter, *The American Republic,* Vol. 2, p. 335; Morris, *Roosevelt,* pp. 586–587, 611; Karnow, *In Our Image,* pp. 102–105, 160–163.

14. Petillo, *MacArthur,* p. 47.

15. RG94, NA, Document file.

16. James, *MacArthur,* p. 66; Manchester, *American Caesar,* p. 47.

17. MacArthur, *Reminiscences,* p. 19.

18. Petillo, *MacArthur,* p. 257, note 11.

19. Charles King Papers, WHS, "Diary of Brigadier General Charles King, U.S. Volunteers, June 11, 1898, to Feb. 5, 1899"; King, *Memories,* pp. 52–54; Knight, *Life and Manners,* pp. 7–8, 16–18.

20. 55th Congress, 3rd Session (1899), House Document 2, *Annual Report of the War Department;* William T. Sexton, *Soldiers in the Sun,* pp. 22ff.

21. King, *Memories,* pp. 52–54; Russell, *Campaigning with King,* pp. 115–116.

22. George, *Our Army,* pp. 25–28; Frank Merrill Papers, Memoirs, Carlisle.

23. Sexton, *Soldiers in the Sun,* pp. 22–24; George, *Our Army,* pp. 29–31. MacArthur's brigade included: the 98 men of the Astor Battery under First Lieutenant Peyton C. March; the 1st North Dakota Volunteers commanded by Lieutenant Colonel W. C. Trenman with 645 men and 30 officers; the 1st Idaho Volunteers with 631 men and 22 officers under Lieutenant Colonel John W. Jones; the 13th Minnesota Volunteers under Colonel C. Mc. Reeve with 914 men and 43 officers; the 1st Wyoming Volunteers with 297 men and 13 officers under Major F. M. Foote; elements of the 18th and 23rd Infantry under Colonel Samuel Ovenshine, about 1,200 men; plus hospital staff, elements of the Signal Corps, engineers, and the 3rd Artillery.

24. Peyton C. March Papers, Library of Congress; Private Frederick J. Podas Diary, Carlisle; George, *Our Army,* pp. 31–33.

25. George, *Our Army,* pp. 33–34.

26. Ibid., pp. 32–34; Frank Merrill Memoirs, Carlisle.

27. George, *Our Army*, pp. 34–36.

28. Frank Merrill Memoirs, Carlisle; Henry C. Corbin Papers, Library of Congress, letter, Kennon to Corbin, Oct. 25, 1899.

29. George, *Our Army*, pp. 38–39; George R. Fisher Diary, Carlisle.

30. Frank Merrill Memoirs, Carlisle; George, *Our Army*, pp. 40–44.

31. Frank Merrill Memoirs, Carlisle.

32. George, *Our Army*, p. 44.

33. Peyton C. March Papers, Library of Congress; Enoch H. Crowder Papers, University of Missouri, journal, July 8 and 9, 1898.

34. Fred Arnold, letters of Mrs. Arnold, Carlisle; Enoch H. Crowder Papers, University of Missouri, July 10 forward.

35. George, *Our Army*, pp. 45–51; Forest A. Haight Papers, Carlisle; Frank Merrill Memoirs, Carlisle; George R. Fisher Diary, Carlisle.

36. George, *Our Army*, p. 51; Frank Merrill Memoirs, Carlisle; 55th Congress, 3rd Session (1899), HD2, *Annual Report of the War Department*, Vol 1, pp. 1–165, "Annual Report of Major General Otis," Aug. 29, 1898, to Aug. 31, 1899, hereafter cited as HD2-O-1899.

37. Roosevelt quote from Morris, *Roosevelt*, p. 634.

38. Forest A. Haight Papers, Carlisle; George, *Our Army*, pp. 51–54.

39. George, *Our Army*, p. 54.

40. Frank Merrill Memoirs, Carlisle.

41. Henry C. Corbin Papers, Library of Congress; George, *Our Army*, p. 54.

42. Enoch H. Crowder Papers, University of Missouri; Morris, *Roosevelt*, pp. 638ff.

43. Quote from Morris, *Roosevelt*, p. 578; see also Karnow, *In Our Image*, p. 90.

44. In the next three chapters, a number of secondary sources were used extensively; although they varied in interpretation, each provided insight and should be examined for further study. The list includes: Miller, *Benevolent Assimilation*; Karnow, *In Our Image*; Sexton, *Soldiers in the Sun*; John M. Gates, *Schoolbooks and Krags: The United States Army in the Philippines, 1898–1902*; Leon Wolff, *Little Brown Brothers*; Virginia F. Mulrooney, "No Victor, No Vanquished: American Military Government in the Philippine Islands, 1899–1901."

45. Gates, in *Schoolbooks and Krags*, Sexton, in *Soldiers in the Sun*, and many other military historians explain the military position; Miller, *Benevolent Assimilation*, Mulrooney, "No Victor," and a number of other historians analyze the political commitments and usually support the Filipino side.

46. Enoch H. Crowder Papers, University of Missouri.

47. George R. Fisher Diary, Carlisle; George, *Our Army*, p. 55.

48. George, *Our Army*, pp. 79–80; Sexton, *Soldiers in the Sun*, pp. 33–34.

49. Ernest Hewson quoted from Mulrooney, "No Victor," p. 28; see also Spencer Kuhn Letters, Carlisle.

50. Sexton, *Soldiers in the Sun*, p. 34. Frank Merrill Memoirs, Carlisle.

51. Henry F. Pringle, *The Life and Times of William Howard Taft*, Vol. 1, pp. 167–168.

52. George, *Our Army*, pp. 81–85; Sexton, *Soldiers in the Sun*, p. 34.

53. MacArthur quote from 57th Congress, 1st Session (1902), *Hearings on Affairs in the Philippines*, Senate Document 331 (hereafter cited as SD331), pp. 1406–1407; Anderson quoted in Mulrooney, "No Victor," p. 41.

54. Wolff, *Little Brown Brothers*, pp. 126–131; George, *Our Army*, p. 85.

55. George, *Our Army*, pp. 87–88.

56. A. B. Feuer, *Combat Diary: Episodes from the History of the Twenty-Second Regiment, 1866–1905*, pp. 68, 76.

57. RG20, MML, letter, William Compton, Company C, 13th Minnesota, to brother, Dec. 14, 1898; Frank Merrill Memoirs, Carlisle; Samuel Lyon Diary, Carlisle.

58. Feuer, *Combat Diary*, pp. 70–71, quoting Private Watterson. Peyton March rose to be chief of staff during World War I. Douglas owed a part of his success in the army to March, who admired General MacArthur. See Manchester, *American Caesar*, pp. 116–117, 159.

59. George, *Our Army*, pp. 88, 94–96; Sexton, *Soldiers in the Sun*, pp. 40–43; Wolff, *Little Brown Brothers*, pp. 134–135; 55th Congress, 3rd Session (1899), House Document 2, "MacArthur's Brigade Command Report," Aug. 22, 1898, Vol. 3, pp. 111–115.

60. Enoch H. Crowder Papers, University of Missouri, letter, Aug. 15, 1898; George, *Our Army*, p. 125, passim.

61. Petillo, *MacArthur*, p. 50.

62. SD331, pp. 874–875, 1384–1385, and 1899.

63. Mrs. William Howard Taft, *Recollection of Full Years*, pp. 95–98.

64. David H Bain, *Sitting in Darkness: Americans in the Philippines*, pp. 199–201; Frank Merrill Memoirs, Carlisle.

65. Taft, *Recollection of Full Years*, pp. 95–98.

66. Feuer, *Combat Diary*, pp. 82–83; King, *Memories*, pp. 54, 55–58.

67. George, *Our Army*, p. 123; James Blount, *The American Occupation of the Philippines, 1898–1912*, p. 292.

68. Samuel J. Ovenshine Papers, Carlisle, telegram to MacArthur, Sept. 10, 1898; RG94, NA, Document file, letter, MacArthur to Corbin, Sept. 1898.

69. Peyton C. March Papers, Library of Congress; Frank Merrill Memoirs, Carlisle; Louis W. Hubbard, letters, Carlisle.

70. Bain, *Sitting in Darkness*, p. 80; Frederick Funston, *Memories of Two Wars*, p. 175.

71. Louis W. Hubbard, letters, Carlisle; Frank Merrill Memoirs, Carlisle; Charles Soules letters, Sept. 24, 1898, Carlisle; Wolff, *Little Brown Brothers*, pp. 176–183.

72. Charles Soules letters, Carlisle; William B. Landon letters, Carlisle.

73. George, *Our Army*, pp. 119, 209; Peyton C. March Papers, Library of Congress; Henry T. Allen Papers, Library of Congress.

74. Lenihan Papers, Carlisle; George R. Fisher Diary, Carlisle; Frank Merrill Memoirs, Carlisle; George, *Our Army*, pp. 131–133.

75. Frank Merrill Memoirs, Carlisle.

76. George, *Our Army*, p. 124; George R. Fisher Diary, Carlisle.

77. Spencer Kuhn letters, Carlisle; Frank Merrill Memoirs, Carlisle.

78. George, *Our Army*, p. 131; Charles Soules letters, Carlisle; Frank Merrill Memoirs, Carlisle.

79. Quoted in Graff, *American Imperialism*, p. XIII.

80. Mulrooney, "No Victor," pp. 102–104, 117.

81. Bain, *Sitting in Darkness*, p. 182, paraphrasing Miller, *Benevolent Assimilation*, pp. 113–114.

82. McKinley, quoted in a dozen books: For example, see Miller, *Benevolent Assimilation*, p. 23, and Margaret Leech, *In the Days of McKinley*, p. 345. See also Miller, *Benevolent Assimilation*, p. 16; Graff, *American Imperialism*, pp. VII–VIII; Karnow, *In Our Image*, p. 129; Mulrooney, "No Victor," pp. 96–124; Glenn Anthony May, *Battle for Batangas*, p. 74.

83. Leech, *In the Days of McKinley*, p. 345.

Chapter 12: The Philippine Revolution

1. Miller, *Benevolent Assimilation*, pp. 31, 195, see also pp. 42–43, 46, 55, 66, and passim; Mulrooney, "No Victor," pp. 117–118. In the new national era, Filipinos are very sensitive about the use of the term *insurgent* and prefer the use of the term *Republican soldiers*. Although I tried to keep the use of *insurgent* to the minimum, this book primarily presents the U.S. side of the war, and the Americans did call the Republican soldiers *insurgents*.

2. Anderson to AGO, July 21, 1898, quoted in Mulrooney, "No Victor," p. 29; see also p. 119.

3. McKinley quote is from Mulrooney, "No Victor," p. 110.

4. Wolff, *Little Brown Brothers*, map, endpiece; Sexton, *Soldiers in the Sun*, pp. 90–91; 55th Congress, 3rd Session (1899), House Document 2, *Annual Report of the War Department*, Vol. 5, "MacArthur's 2nd Division Report," Feb. 4, 1899, to Feb. 28, 1899, p. 422, hereafter cited as HD2-1st-M-1899.

5. Samuel J. Ovenshine Papers, Carlisle.

6. Utley, *Frontier Regulars*, pp. 74–79; Feuer, *Combat Diary*, p. 69; May, *Battle for Batangas*, p. 96.

7. Frederick J. Podas Diary, Carlisle; Daniel Doyle Diary, Carlisle; George, *Our Army*, pp. 131–134; Wolff, *Little Brown Brothers*, pp. 141–143.

8. King, *Memories*, pp. 58–62; George, *Our Army*, pp. 175–179; Wolff, *Little Brown Brothers*, pp. 202–203.

9. SD331, pp. 898–899; Samuel J. Ovenshine Papers, Carlisle, telegram, MacArthur to Ovenshine, Sept. 10, 1898.

10. King, *Memories*, p. 62; HD2-1st-M-1899, p. 424.

11. Karnow, *In Our Image*, pp. 139–140.

12. Ibid.; SD331, pp. 898–899, 1389–1393.

13. SD331, pp. 1393–1394, 1397–1398; Funston, *Memories of Two Wars*, pp. 177–180.

14. George Deshon Papers, Carlisle; Wolff, *Little Brown Brothers*, p. 225.

15. George, *Our Army*, pp. 178–179; Charles Soules letters, Carlisle.

16. Sexton, *Soldiers in the Sun*, pp. 91–92.

17. Ibid., pp. 92–94.

18. Charles Soules letters, Carlisle; Sexton, *Soldiers in the Sun*, pp. 94–95.

19. May, *Battle for Batangas*, p. 96.

20. Peyton C. March Papers, Library of Congress; George, *Our Army*, p. 180.

21. Peyton C. March Papers, Library of Congress; Miller, *Benevolent Assimilation*, pp. 67–68.

22. Bass, quoted in Karnow, *In Our Image*, p. 145; see also Mulrooney, "No Victor," p. 125, Miller, *Benevolent Assimilation*, p. 68, and Gates, *Schoolbooks and Krags*, p. 77. As Glenn May, *Battle for Batangas*, p. 152, noted, it is likely the Filipino casualties were a "bit inflated," for "ambitious" American officers occasionally padded the counts to improve their chances of promotion.

23. SD331, p. 1397; Funston, *Memories of Two Wars*, pp. 183–187.

24. SD331, pp. 1394–1398.

25. Ibid., pp. 894–896, 1393–1398; Graff, *American Imperialism*, pp. 114–115.

26. Quoted in Bain, *Sitting in Darkness*, p. 185.

27. Ibid.

28. HD2-1st-M-1899, p. 425; Sexton, *Soldiers in the Sun*, p. 97.

29. Lodge, quoted in Karnow, *In Our Image*, p. 138.

30. Hofstadter, *The American Republic*, Vol. 2, p. 340.

31. Reed, quoted in Karnow, *In Our Image*, p. 138. Various sources cited the population of the Philippines in 1898 from 7 to 13 million; 10 million seems as good a guess as any other figure in that range.

32. Funston, *Memories of Two Wars*, p. 193.

33. War Departament, *Annual Report* (1899), "Report of Major General Arthur MacArthur," commanding 2nd Division, 8th Army Corps, March–May 1899, Vol. 1, Part 5, pp. 378–379, hereafter cited as AR-M-1899; Taft, *Recollection of Full Years*, pp. 91–92.

34. HD2-1st-M-1899, pp. 425–428.

35. Bass, quoted in Karnow, *In Our Image*, pp. 145–146; George, *Our Army*, p. 201; Peyton C. March Papers, Library of Congress.

36. Funston, *Memories of Two Wars*, pp. 160ff and passim.

37. Sexton, *Soldiers in the Sun*, pp. 97–98.

38. George, *Our Army*, pp. 215–217.

39. Quote from ibid., p. 218.

40. 56th Congress, 2nd Session, *Annual Reports of the War Department*, "Report of General MacArthur," Commander of 2nd Division, 8th Army Corps, June 1899 to April 6, 1900, Vol. 9, p. 19,

hereafter cited as HD2-M-1900; Sexton, *Soldiers in the Sun,* pp. 119, 148; William A. Kobbé Diary of Field Service, 1898 to 1901, typed copy, 378 pages, Carlisle.

41. AR-M-1899, p. 377.

42. Funston, *Memories of Two Wars,* pp. 220–221.

43. HD2-M-1900, pp. 44, 66.

44. AR-M-1899, pp. 378–381.

45. Miller, *Benevolent Assimilation,* p. 70; see Lawton photograph.

46. George Deshon Papers, Carlisle. Deshon was with Lawton during the voyage from the United States to the Philippines. See also Dean C. Worcester, *The Philippines: Past and Present,* Vol. 1, pp. 320–321; Sexton, *Soldiers in the Sun,* pp. 122–124.

47. Henry C. Corbin Papers, Library of Congress.

48. RG94, NA, Document file, letters, Otjen to secretary of war, Nov. 29, 1898, Flanders to Congressman Otjen, Nov. 30, 1899, letters from all the members of the Wisconsin congressional delegation to the president, Dec. 1898; Mary MacArthur to Corbin, circa Dec. 1898; see Manchester, *American Caesar,* p. 80.

49. AR-M-1899, pp. 378–379, 385–389; William A. Kobbé Diary, Carlisle.

50. Charles Soules letters, Carlisle; AR-M-1899, p. 379.

51. Sexton, *Soldiers in the Sun,* p. 119; Frederick J. Podas Diary, Carlisle; HD2-M-1900, p. 21.

52. Feuer, *Combat Diary,* p. 100; Sexton, *Soldiers in the Sun,* p. 119.

53. William A. Kobbé Diary, Carlisle.

54. Feuer, *Combat Diary,* p. 92; May, *Battle for Batangas,* p. 120; George R. Fisher Diary, Carlisle.

55. William A. Kobbé Diary, Carlisle; Sexton, *Soldiers in the Sun,* p. 150; SD331, pp. 906–908; May, *Battle for Batangas,* note on p. 101.

56. William B. Landon, Carlisle; AR-M-1899, p. 401.

57. Sexton, *Soldiers in the Sun,* pp. 111–112; AR-M-1899, pp. 389–396; HD2-M-1900, p. 20.

58. HD2-M-1900, pp. 28–30.

59. May, *Battle for Batangas,* p. 100.

60. Kreps, quoted in Feuer, *Combat Diary,* p. 104; AR-M-1899, pp. 391–392.

61. AR-M-1899, pp. 391–392.

62. HD2-M-1900, p. 17.

63. Sexton, *Soldiers in the Sun,* pp. 141–149; AR-M-1899, pp. 395–397; SD331, pp. 894–895, 1888, and 1932.

64. Sexton, *Soldiers in the Sun,* pp. 141–145.

65. 56th Congress, 2nd Session, HD2, "Report of Major General E. S. Otis," Sept. 1, 1899, to May 5, 1900, Vol. 5, p. 209, hereafter cited as HD2-O-1900; see also AR-M-1899, pp. 395–397, 401.

66. AR-M-1899, pp. 410–411.

67. Ibid., pp. 401, 406.

68. Sexton, *Soldiers in the Sun,* pp. 194–196; AR-M-1899, pp. 407–411.

69. AR-M-1899, pp. 395–401; HD2-M-1900, p. 31; Vandiver, *Black Jack,* p. 245.

70. Henry C. Corbin Papers, Library of Congress, letter, Schwan to Corbin, Oct. 6, 1899; Vandiver, *Black Jack,* p. 243.

71. Vandiver, *Black Jack,* p. 243; Miller, *Benevolent Assimilation,* pp. 46, 79–80; James, *MacArthur,* p. 35.

72. Sexton, *Soldiers in the Sun,* pp. 148–149; May, *Battle for Batangas,* pp. 26–27.

73. George, *Our Army,* p. 127; William B. Landon letters, Carlisle; 20th Kansas Volunteers files, Carlisle.

74. AR-M-1899, p. 401, Field Orders, April 2, 1899; SD331, pp. 985–986, also pp. 862–869, 873.

75. AR-M-1899, p. 411; SD331, p. 1942, and throughout MacArthur's testimony.

76. Funston, *Memories of Two Wars,* p. 307.

77. HD2-M-1900, p. 18.

78. Sexton, *Soldiers in the Sun,* pp. 162–165.

79. Quoted from Miller, *Benevolent Assimilation,* p. 97, see also pp. 73, 181; May, *Battle for Batangas,* p. 80.

80. Sexton, *Soldiers in the Sun*, p. 163.

81. Miller, *Benevolent Assimilation*, p. 73.

82. Ibid., pp. 83–84; Karnow, *In Our Image*, pp. 121, 155.

83. Miller, *Benevolent Assimilation*, p. 102; Karnow, *In Our Image*, pp. 121, 155.

84. Miller, *Benevolent Assimilation*, pp. 87–88.

85. Manchester, *American Caesar*, pp. 48, 53–54; James, *MacArthur*, p. 68.

86. Quote from James, *MacArthur*, pp. 69–70; Manchester, *American Caesar*, p. 50.

87. Quoted in Manchester, *American Caesar*, p. 53; James, *MacArthur*, p. 72.

88. 13th Minnesota pamphlet, Carlisle, says the promised $500 bonus money was not paid until 1944; William A. Kobbé Diary, Carlisle; Sexton, *Soldiers in the Sun*, pp. 161–162.

89. HD2-M-1900, p. 19; Lewis S. Sorley, Some Recollections, Carlisle; William A. Kobbé Diary, Carlisle.

90. HD2-M-1900, p. 20.

91. Morris, *Roosevelt*, pp. 639–645.

92. Sexton, *Soldiers in the Sun*, pp. 192–195.

93. Ibid., p. 195.

94. HD2-M-1900, pp. 28–29.

95. Ibid., pp. 36–37, 40.

96. Ibid., pp. 37–40.

97. Ibid., pp. 31, 40; HD2-O-1900, pp. 209ff; Sexton, *Soldiers in the Sun*, p. 168.

98. HD2-M-1900, pp. 30, 55; Sexton, *Soldiers in the Sun*, pp. 192, 196–197.

99. HD2-M-1900, pp. 57, 59; 57th Congress, 1st Session, *Annual Report of the War Department*, HD2, Vol. 5, "Report of General MacArthur," Oct. 1, 1900, to July 4, 1901, pp. 89–90, hereafter cited as HD2-M-1901.

100. HD2-M-1900, pp. 54–56.

101. Ibid., pp. 36–37, 40.

102. Ibid., p. 57.

103. Sexton, *Soldiers in the Sun*, pp. 196–197.

104. HD2-M-1900, pp. 56–57.

105. Ibid., pp. 60, 68.

Chapter 13: Military Governor

1. Brian M. Linn, "Provincial Pacification in the Philippines, 1900–1901," p. 63; May, *Battle for Batangas*, pp. 131–133.

2. HD2-M-1900, pp. 58–63; James, *MacArthur*, pp. 33–34.

3. Ibid., p. 61.

4. May, *Battle for Batangas*, pp. 153–154.

5. Ibid., p. 155.

6. Wolff, *Little Brown Brothers*, p. 253; May, *Battle for Batangas*, pp. 82, 132, 151; HD2-M-1900, pp. 59–68.

7. Quotes from May, *Battle for Batangas*, pp. 132, 142; see also SD331, pp. 1942ff, HD2-M-1900, pp. 60–63, and Gates, *Schoolbooks and Krags*, pp. 156ff; Wolff, *Little Brown Brothers*, pp. 277–299.

8. Worcester, *The Philippines*, Vol. 1, p. 320.

9. Ibid.

10. May, *Battle for Batangas*, p. 95.

11. War Department, *Annual Report*, 1900, Part 3, pp. 62–63, hereafter cited as WDAR, Part 3; SD331, pp. 894–896; William McKinley Papers, Library of Congress, letter, MacArthur to Corbin, June 4, 1900; Sexton, *Soldiers in the Sun*, p. 237; May, *Battle for Batangas*, p. 191.

12. Quotes from May, *Battle for Batangas*, p. 150; Miller, *Benevolent Assimilation*, p. 188; Wolff, *Little Brown Brothers*, pp. 253–254.

13. Quotes from Miller, *Benevolent Assimilation,* p. 188; Wolff, *Little Brown Brothers,* pp. 252–253; Mulrooney, "No Victor," p. 194.

14. Wolff, *Little Brown Brothers,* pp. 252–253; Mulrooney, "No Victor," p. 194; Henry A. Fant, "Arthur MacArthur and the Philippine Insurrection," p. 35.

15. May, *Battle for Batangas,* p. 154.

16. Quoted in Gates, *Schoolbooks and Krags,* p. 198.

17. RG20, NA, Headquarters, Division of the Philippines, General Orders #14, May 5, 1900.

18. *Army and Navy Journal,* Sept. 21, 1912, quoting Brigadier General Isaac S. Catlin, who visited Manila around 1901; Taft, *Recollection of Full Years,* pp. 212–214.

19. Manchester, *American Caesar,* p. 119; Mulrooney, "No Victor," pp. 53–95.

20. HD2-M-1900, p. 68.

21. Mulrooney, "No Victor," p. 151; Manchester, *American Caesar,* pp. 118–119, 479; Fant, "Arthur MacArthur," p. 56; Miller, *Benevolent Assimilation,* p. 46.

22. Quote from HD2-M-1901, p. 104; William Howard Taft Papers, Library of Congress, Aug. 18, 1900; William McKinley Papers, cablegram, MacArthur to Corbin, June 16, 1900.

23. Fant, "Arthur MacArthur," p. 53; Mulrooney, "No Victor," pp. 1–2, 129, 137–141, 146, 202; Miller, *Benevolent Assimilation,* pp. 76–77, 131, 133; Worcester, *The Philippines,* Vol. 1, passim.

24. Ralph E. Minger, "Taft, MacArthur and the Establishment of Civil Government," p. 308; see also Ralph E. Minger, *William Howard Taft and United States Foreign Policy: The Apprenticeship Years, 1900–1908.*

25. Worcester, *Philippines,* Vol. 1, pp. 325ff.

26. Taft, *Recollection of Full Years,* pp. 80–82.

27. Worcester, *Philippines,* Vol. 1, p. 331. Being obese seemed to be the fad of the times. Many businessmen (such as J. P. Morgan), presidents (such as Grover Cleveland), and other politicians of the era were massively overweight. A prime example was Thomas B. Reed, speaker of the House of Representatives, who was a gigantic man weighing 300 pounds. Morris, *Roosevelt,* p. 414, described Reed as "a vast, blubbery whale of a man, poised on two flipper-like feet."

28. William Howard Taft, Library of Congress, letter, Taft to brother, June 12, 1900; Taft, *Recollection of Full Years;* Rowland T. Berthoff, "Taft and MacArthur: A Study in Civilian-Military Relations," pp. 207–208.

29. Worcester, *Philippines,* Vol. 1, pp. 330–335; Berthoff, "Taft and MacArthur," p. 206; Gates, *Schoolbooks and Krags,* p. 177.

30. Taft Senate testimony, quoted in Graff, *American Imperialism,* p. 127.

31. William McKinley Papers, Library of Congress, and William Howard Taft, Library of Congress, June–Aug. 1900; Mulrooney, "No Victor," pp. 221–222; Graff, *American Imperialism,* p. 139.

32. Miller, *Benevolent Assimilation,* pp. 66, 100–101.

33. Quote from Miller, *Benevolent Assimilation,* p. 150; HD2-M-1901, p. 98; WDAR, 1900, Part 3, pp. 62–63; William McKinley Papers, Library of Congress, cablegram, June 4, 1900, MacArthur to Corbin. See Coffman, *Old Army,* p. 254, on Indian wars casualty figures.

34. WDAR, 1900, Part 3, pp. 63–64.

35. Petillo, *MacArthur,* pp. 48 and 50.

36. WDAR, 1900, Part 3, pp. 63–64; Gates, *Schoolbooks and Krags,* pp. 196–197; Wolff, *Little Brown Brothers,* p. 310; May, *Battle for Batangas,* pp. 85ff; Petillo, *MacArthur,* pp. 48–50.

37. William Howard Taft, Library of Congress, letters, Taft to Root, July 26, Aug. 18, and Oct. 1, 1900; quote from Fant, "Arthur MacArthur," p. 65.

38. Karnow, *In Our Image,* pp. 172–173.

39. Lewis E. Gleeck, Jr., *The American Governors-General and High Commissioners in the Philippines,* p. 19.

40. Mulrooney, "No Victor," p. 10.

41. WDAR, 1900, Part 3, pp. 59–71.

42. Young quote is from Miller, *Benevolent Assimilation,* p. 162, see also pp. 153–154; Wheaton quote from Karnow, *In Our Image,* p. 179, and from Mulrooney, "No Victor," p. 229; Bell position from May, *Battle for Batangas,* p. 247; see also Sexton, *Soldiers in the Sun,* p. 252.

43. William Howard Taft, Library of Congress, letters, Taft to Root, Sept. 21, Oct. 1, 1900, Root to Taft, Oct. 10 and Nov. 14, 1900; Gates, *Schoolbooks and Krags,* p. 193.

44. SD331, MacArthur's testimony, pp. 1940ff; WDAR, 1900, Part 3, pp. 64–65; Gates, *Schoolbooks and Krags,* p. 199; Manchester, *American Caesar,* p. 472.

45. WDAR, 1900, Part 3, pp. 65–66; William Howard Taft, Library of Congress, letter, Nov. 30, 1900; May, *Battle for Batangas,* p. 181; Peter W. Stanley, *A Nation in the Making,* p. 78.

46. William McKinley Papers, Library of Congress, letter, MacArthur to Alejandrino, July 16, 1900, and memorandums, MacArthur to Corbin, July 28 and 30, 1900.

47. Arthur MacArthur, "Address to Wisconsin Banker's Association"; WDAR, 1900, Part 3, pp. 70–71; HD2-M-1901, p. 111; SD331, p. 1921.

48. WDAR, 1900, Part 3, p. 70; HD2-M-1901, pp. 111ff; SD331, pp. 874–875, 1384–1385, and 1954; Graff, *American Imperialism,* p. 59.

49. Mulrooney, "No Victor," p. 70; WDAR, 1900, Part 3, p. 64; RG20, MML, newspaper clipping, *Boston Transcript,* Sept. 6, 1912.

50. William Howard Taft, Library of Congress, letters, Taft to Root, July 14, Dec. 14, 1900; see also Aug. 18, 1900, in which Taft's negative criticism of the Filipino people runs on for five typed pages.

51. William Howard Taft, Library of Congress, letters, Taft to Root, July 26, Aug. 18, Oct. 1, 1900; Miller, *Benevolent Assimilation,* p. 210.

52. William McKinley Papers, Library of Congress, June–Sept. 1900. To remain consistent with documents, Peking spelling is used instead of current Beijing.

53. Papers of Elihu Root, Library of Congress, cablegram, MacArthur to Root, June 24, 1900; William McKinley Papers, Library of Congress, cablegram, Commission to Root, June 25, 1900.

54. William McKinley Papers, Library of Congress, cablegram, MacArthur to Corbin, July 18, 20, 1900, topic, China Relief; on Mallory reports, see Enoch H. Crowder Papers, University of Missouri, July 1900 onward; Miller, *Benevolent Assimilation,* pp. 135–136.

55. Nimitz Library, U.S. Naval Academy, Arthur MacArthur Archives File.

56. Ibid. See also Petillo, *MacArthur.*

57. Karnow, *In Our Image,* pp. 172–173.

58. Worcester, *Philippines,* Vol. 1, pp. 335–338; RG20, MML, General MacArthur, *Governor's Letterbook for 1900,* letter, Taft to MacArthur, Oct. 8, 1900.

59. Pringle, *William Howard Taft,* Vol. 1, p. 192; Graff, *American Imperialism,* pp. 95, 192; RG20, MML, General MacArthur, *Letterbook for 1900,* letter, MacArthur to Taft, Oct. 8, 1900.

60. Elihu Root Papers, Library of Congress, letter, MacArthur to Taft, Jan. 10, 1901; Graff, *American Imperialism,* p. 123; Petillo, *MacArthur,* p. 54. After the Civil War, comparable constitutional arguments arose. Historian James McPherson, in *Battle Cry,* p. 700, notes that "if the Southern states reverted to the status of territories, Congress had the right to frame the terms of their readmission under its constitutional authority to govern territories and admit new states."

61. William Howard Taft, Library of Congress, letter, Taft to Root, March 17, 1901; Berthoff, "Taft and MacArthur," p. 208.

62. Minger, "Taft, MacArthur and the Establishment of Civil Government," p. 317. In his annual report to Congress in 1901, Root acknowledged that "the sole power which the President was exercising in the Philippines was a military power derived from his authority under the Constitution as Commander in Chief." Elihu Root, *The Military and Colonial Policy of the United States: Addresses and Reports,* pp. 252–255.

63. Elihu Root Papers, Library of Congress, letter, MacArthur to Taft, Dec. 7, 1900; RG20, MML, General MacArthur, *Letterbook for 1900,* letter, Oct. 6, 1900; Manchester, *American Caesar,* p. 34; Mulrooney, "No Victor," pp. 210–212.

64. Mulrooney, "No Victor," pp. 149, 167–185, 229; Linn, "Provincial Pacification," p. 63.

65. Mulrooney, "No Victor," pp. 171, 229; Elihu Root Papers, Library of Congress, telegram, MacArthur to division commanders, Jan. 19, 1901.

66. Wolff, *Little Brown Brothers*, p. 313.

67. James Blount, *The American Occupation of the Philippines, 1898–1912*, pp. 275ff; Manchester, *American Caesar*, pp. 32–33.

68. RG20, MML, General MacArthur, *Letterbook for 1900*, letter, Oct. 9, 1900.

69. Ibid.

70. Mulrooney, "No Victor," pp. 212–221.

71. RG20, MML, General MacArthur, *Letterbook for 1900*, letter, Oct. 9, 1900; William Howard Taft, Library of Congress, cablegram, Root to Taft, Aug. 8, 1900; Henry C. Corbin Papers, Library of Congress, cablegram, Corbin to MacArthur, Aug. 7, 1900.

72. Minger's quote is from his "Taft, MacArthur and the Establishment of Civil Government," p. 309; Manchester quote is from his *American Caesar*, p. 637; Gleeck, *The American Governors-General*, pp. 8–9.

73. William Howard Taft, Library of Congress, letters, Taft to Root, Aug. 18 and Nov. 14, 1900. Taft provided many details on the Philippines, and researchers have used his letters extensively. For an excellent example of Taft's style as a letter writer, see Taft to Root, July 30, 1900.

74. Berthoff, "Taft and MacArthur," pp. 196–213; Minger, "Taft, MacArthur and the Establishment of Civil Government," pp. 308–331; Minger, *Taft*, pp. 26–54; Manchester, *American Caesar*, p. 33; see also Miller, *Benevolent Assimilation*, pp. 133–135.

75. Lee and Henschel, *MacArthur*, p. 26. I could not find the quote in the Enoch H. Crowder Papers, University of Missouri. For a typical view of MacArthur, see Miller, *Benevolent Assimilation*, pp. 160–167.

76. Fant, "Arthur MacArthur," p. 65; Petillo, *MacArthur*, p. 54.

77. Taft quote is from Gleeck, *The American Governors-General*, p. 10; Karnow and Roosevelt quotes are from Karnow, *In Our Image*, p. 167.

78. Manchester, *American Caesar*, p. 153, quoting Ickes; second quote is from Miller, *Benevolent Assimilation*, p. 167.

79. Manchester, *American Caesar*, pp. 119, 519. In a comment on the manuscript of this book, Carol Petillo wrote: "It is interesting that intimacy is a quality Erik Erikson describes as developing in adolescence just when AMA's mother was having her breakdown and leaving him."

80. Quote from Morris, *Roosevelt*, p. 580; Manchester, *American Caesar*, p. 33; Peyton C. March Papers, Library of Congress; William Howard Taft, Library of Congress, letter, Taft to Root, Sept. 21, 1900; William Carey Brown Diaries, Carlisle.

81. Manchester, *American Caesar*, p. 166.

82. Ibid., p. 148, quoting Eisenhower; second quote is from Lee and Henschel, *MacArthur*, p. 9.

83. Manchester, *American Caesar*, p. 140, quoting Shirer, and pp. 482–483, quoting Gunther and Sulzberger.

84. Manchester, *American Caesar*, p. 33; Minger, "Taft, MacArthur and the Establishment of Civil Government," p. 323. *Mediatize* had a number of other meanings, and it is possible that MacArthur used the word to mean that the commission's arrival altered his position from executive in charge of the Philippines to mediator between the American civilian authority and the Filipino people.

85. Manchester, *American Caesar*, p. 32.

86. Quoted in Graff, *American Imperialism*, p. 135.

87. See SD331, MacArthur testimony, Graff, *American Imperialism*, quoting MacArthur, pp. 135–136, RG20, MML, General MacArthur, *Letterbook for 1900* or any of his official reports.

88. Quoted in Manchester, *American Caesar*, p. 657, see also pp. 633 and 662; Hunt, *Untold Story*, pp. 405–406; William Howard Taft, Library of Congress, letter, Taft to Root, Sept. 18, 1900; Taft, *Recollection of Full Years*, p. 218. For a more flattering view of MacArthur's language and style, see *Army and Navy Journal*, Sept. 21, 1912, quoting Brigadier General Isaac C. Catlin, who visited Manila around January 1901.

89. Gleeck, *The American Governors-General*, p. 13; Blount, *The American Occupation*, p. 280; Man-chester, *American Caesar*, p. 33; William Howard Taft, Library of Congress, letter, Taft to Root, Aug. 18, 1900; RG20, MML, General MacArthur, *Letterbook for 1900*, which is over 500 typed pages, illus-trates the volume of paperwork.

90. William Howard Taft, Library of Congress, letter, Taft to Root, Aug. 18, 1900, Feb. 28 and March 17, 1901.

91. First quote is from Elihu Root Papers, Library of Congress, letter, Taft to Root, Oct. 3, 1900; second quote, William Howard Taft, Library of Congress, letter, Taft to Root, Aug. 18, 1900.

92. William McKinley Papers, Library of Congress, letter, Taft to Root, Aug. 21, 1900; William Howard Taft, Library of Congress, letters, Taft to Root, July 26, Aug. 11, 23, and 31, Dec. 14, 1900; RG20, MML, General MacArthur, *Letterbook for 1900*.

93. HD2-M-1901, p. 102; William Howard Taft, Library of Congress, letter, Taft to Root, Nov. 14, 1900; Gates, *Schoolbooks and Krags*, p. 214; Henry T. Allen Papers, Library of Congress.

94. May, *Battle for Batangas*, p. 158, see also pp. 150, 193, 237; Brian McAllister Linn, *The U.S. Army and the Counterinsurgency in the Philippine War, 1899–1902*, p. xi; Mulrooney, "No Victor," pp. 192–193; Miller, *Benevolent Assimilation*, pp. 182, 188, 189. After reading May, Miller, Gates, Linn, and others, the resounding conclusion is that if a writer (see Miller, *Benevolent Assimilation*, pp. 88–89, 182, 188, passim), opposed the U.S. acquisition of the Philippines, they invariably described U.S. military pol-icy as harsh. If a writer was primarily a military historian, not an area historian (such as Gates), they viewed U.S. military policy as extremely liberal. During the Otis and MacArthur periods, Gates's interpretation appears correct; after July 1901, under Taft and Chaffee, Miller's view seems valid.

95. WDAR, 1900, Part 3, p. 65; William McKinley Papers, Library of Congress, cablegram, MacArthur to Corbin, May 12, June 16, 1900. After MacArthur left the Philippines, a native constabulary, the "Brownies," was formed—see Henry T. Allen Papers, Library of Congress, box 7, for details.

96. WDAR, 1900, Part 3, pp. 61–62; SD331, pp. 862–869; William Howard Taft, Library of Congress, let-ter, Taft to Root, Dec. 14, 1900; Blount, *American Occupation*, p. 290.

97. Miller, *Benevolent Assimilation*, pp. 2, 130–131, 137, 144.

98. Ibid., pp. 102, 142, 145.

99. Ibid., pp. 105–106, 108–109, 111–114, 131.

100. Root, *The Military and Colonial Policy*, p. 52, speech, Oct. 24, 1900, quoting General Lawton.

101. Gates, *Schoolbooks and Krags*, p. 173.

102. Root, *Military and Colonial Policy*, speech, Oct. 24, 1900, pp. 52ff; Miller, *Benevolent Assimilation*, p. 143; Mulrooney, "No Victor," pp. 206–207.

103. Birkhimer, quoted in May, *Battle for Batangas*, p. 161, see also p. 173.

104. Gates, *Schoolbooks and Krags*, pp. 196–197; May, *Battle for Batangas*, pp. 250ff; Linn, "Provincial Pacification," pp. 62–65. During 1900–1901, the military and native police of Manila arrested 24,934 people, including 729 for political reasons: see Mulrooney, "No Victor," p. 79.

105. Taft to H. C. Hollister, Oct. 15, 1900, quoted in Mulrooney, "No Victor," p. 228.

106. William Howard Taft, Library of Congress, letter, Taft to Root, Dec. 14, 1900; May, *Battle for Batangas*, p. 149.

107. War Department, *Army Regulations*, General Order 100, 1863, on Army rules on guerrilla warfare. See also Graff, *American Imperialism*, comments by Wagner, pp. 129–131; SD331, pp. 949ff; HD2-M-1901, pp. 90–94; Sexton, *Soldiers in the Sun*, p. 252; Gates, *Schoolbooks and Krags*, pp. 204–220.

108. William McKinley Papers, Library of Congress, cablegram, MacArthur to Corbin, Feb. 8, 1901; HD2-M-1901, pp. 90–94; SD331, pp. 909–911, 991; Sexton, *Soldiers in the Sun*, p. 252. The deported Filipinos included Artemio Ricarte, Pio del Pilar, Maximo Hizon, Mariano Lianera, Francisco de los Santos, Pablo Ocamp, Maximiono Trias, Simon Tecson, Pio Variacan, Anastasio Carmona, Mariano Sevilla, and Manuel E. Roxas. Filipino names generally do not have accent marks.

109. Gates, *Schoolbooks and Krags*, pp. 229–230. Among the prisoners were General Martin Delgado of Panay, General Simon Tecson of northern Luzon, General Mariano Trias of southern Luzon, and General Ananais Diocno of Panay.

110. William Howard Taft, Library of Congress, letters, Taft to Root, Dec. 14, 1900, and Root to Taft, Jan. 21, Feb. 28, 1901; cablegram, Commission Report, Jan. 2, 1901; memo Root to McKinley, Jan. 24, 1901; Henry C. Corbin Papers, Library of Congress, memo, Root to Corbin, Feb. 26, 1901.

111. Mulrooney, "No Victor," pp. 238–239; May, *Battle for Batangas,* p. 183; Miller, *Benevolent Assimilation,* p. 39. Federal party members included Felipe Buencamino, Pardo de Tavera, Cayetano Arrellano, Florentino Flores, Pedro Paterno, Felipe Calderon, Don Benito Legarda, and Ambrosio Flores.

112. Mulrooney, "No Victor," pp. 88–94.

113. RG20, MML, newspaper clipping, *New York Herald,* Sunday, April 15, 1901.

114. MacArthur, *Reminiscences,* p. 26, remembers this as May 1901, but the date was likely earlier, i.e., before Aguinaldo was captured.

115. *Army and Navy Journal,* Sept. 21, 1912, quoting Catlin, who was at the party; Forest A. Haight Papers, Carlisle.

116. Ibid.

117. Taft, *Recollection of Full Years,* pp. 147–149; William Howard Taft, Library of Congress, letter, Taft to Root, Jan. 9, 1901.

118. *Army and Navy Journal,* Sept. 21, 1912; Funston, *Memories of Two Wars,* passim.

119. Bain, *Sitting in Darkness,* pp. 344–374; Funston, *Memories of Two Wars,* pp. 425ff; Sexton, *Soldiers in the Sun,* pp. 259–260; William Carey Brown Diaries, Carlisle; Mark Twain, "On American Imperialism," pp. 49–65.

120. SD331, pp. 1890, 1901, 1932; HD2-M-1901, pp. 99–100; Bain, *Sitting in Darkness,* pp. 344–374.

121. Funston, *Memories of Two Wars,* pp. 425ff; William Carey Brown Diaries, Carlisle. Although aboard the *Vicksburg,* Brown did not go on the land expedition. Funston told his story to Brown, who wrote the official report as well as a magazine article on the incident.

122. HD2-M-1901, pp. 99ff; Peyton C. March Papers, Library of Congress, newspaper clipping, *New York World;* Funston, *Memories of Two Wars,* pp. 425ff; Bain, *Sitting in Darkness,* pp. 384–385.

123. HD2-M-1901, p. 100.

124. Miller, *Benevolent Assimilation,* p. 168.

125. Wolff, *Little Brown Brothers,,* p. 345; Funston, *Memories of Two Wars,* pp. 425ff; Sexton, *Soldiers in the Sun,* pp. 264–265.

126. William Howard Taft, Library of Congress, letter, Taft to Root, April 3, 1901.

127. Elihu Root Papers, Library of Congress; William McKinley Papers, Library of Congress, cablegram, MacArthur to AG, April 1, 1901.

128. Elihu Root Papers, Library of Congress, cablegram, Root to MacArthur, April 3, 1901.

129. HD2-M-1901, p. 100; Sexton, *Soldiers in the Sun,* p. 265; Gates, *Schoolbooks and Krags,* pp. 233–236; Bain, *Sitting in Darkness,* p. 385. Aguinaldo remained under house arrest until July 4, 1902, when he was allowed to return to Kawit province: He lived the rest of his life there. Occasionally, but not often, he engaged in politics. He died on Feb. 6, 1964, just short of his ninety-fifth birthday.

130. Gates, *Schoolbooks and Krags,* pp. 235–236; Sexton, *Soldiers in the Sun,* pp. 265–266.

131. HD2-M-1901, p. 106; Minger, "Taft, MacArthur and the Establishment of Civil Government," p. 317.

132. Miller, *Benevolent Assimilation,* p. 196.

133. Henry C. Corbin Papers, Library of Congress, memo, Root to Corbin, cablegram, Corbin to Chaffee, Feb. 26, 1901; William Howard Taft, Library of Congress, letter, Taft to Root, March 17, 1901.

134. *Army and Navy Journal,* Aug. 10, 1901, p. 1206; Sexton, *Soldiers in the Sun,* pp. 266–267; Root, *Military and Colonial Policy,* p. 248.

135. Frederick Brown, *History of the Ninth U.S. Infantry, 1799 to 1909,* p. 557.

136. Pringle, *William Howard Taft,* Vol. 1, pp. 200–201; Taft, *Recollection of Full Years,* pp. 206–210.

137. Brown, *Ninth Infantry,* p. 557; Lewis S. Sorley, *History of the Fourteenth U.S. Infantry.*

138. *Army and Navy Journal,* Aug. 10, 1901, p. 1206.

Chapter 14: A Soldier's Odyssey

1. Miller, *Benevolent Assimilation,* pp. 100–101.
2. RG20, MML, newspaper clipping, probably the *Milwaukee Sentinel,* Aug. 23, 1901.
3. Elihu Root Papers, Library of Congress, letter, Taft to Root, Aug. 2, 1901; Miller, *Benevolent Assimilation,* p. 174.
4. Petillo, *MacArthur,* p. 30.
5. *Milwaukee Sentinel,* Aug. 21, 1901.
6. Ibid.; May, *Battle for Batangas,* pp. 212–214; Miller, *Benevolent Assimilation,* p. 198.
7. See Enoch H. Crowder Papers, University of Missouri, July 5 to Sept. 1901.
8. William Howard Taft, Library of Congress, letters, Taft to Root, Sept. 18, Oct. 10, 1900; Jan. 9, 1901.
9. A. Ross Houston, "The Loyal Legion," pp. 81–86.
10. Anderson, *The MacArthurs,* pp. 20–22, quoting a speech by General MacArthur, probably given to the Old Schoolmates Association in 1907.
11. Walter Lord, *The Good Years: From 1900 to the First World War,* pp. 50–51.
12. RG20, MML, newspaper clipping, Sept. 1901, interview of General MacArthur on McKinley's assassination.
13. RG20, MML, newspaper clipping, *Chicago Record Herald,* Sept. 17, 1901. Besides MacArthur, the honor guard included Lieutenant General Nelson A. Miles, Major Generals James R. Brooke and Elwell S. Otis, Brigadier Generals George L. Gillespie and Leonard Wood, Admiral George Dewey, Rear Admirals A. S. Crowinshield and Charles O'Neil, Paymaster General A. S. Kenny, and U.S. Marine Corps General Charles S. Heywood.
14. "Proceedings Attending the Reception and Banquet to Major General Arthur MacArthur."
15. Ibid., pp. 510–511; RG20, MML, newspaper clipping, *Milwaukee Sentinel,* Oct. 3, 1901.
16. Henry C. Corbin Papers, Library of Congress, Oct.–Nov. 1901; RG94, NA, Document File.
17. Henry C. Corbin Papers, Library of Congress, Chaffee to Corbin, cablegram, Sept. 2, 1901; Elihu Root Papers, Library of Congress, letter, Taft to Root, Aug. 21, 1901; William McKinley Papers, Library of Congress, Chaffee memorandum, Oct. 11, 1901; Taft, *Recollection of Full Years,* pp. 218–221; William H. Carter, *The Life of Lieutenant General Chaffee,* pp. 238–258.
18. Kenneth R. Young, "Guerrilla Warfare: Balangiga Revisted," *Leyte-Samar Studies,* p. 26.
19. Quoted in Miller, *Benevolent Assimilation,* pp. 196 and 205, see also p. 204.
20. Roosevelt, quoted in Miller, *Benevolent Assimilation,* p. 206; Smith, quoted in Young, "Guerrilla Warfare," p. 27.
21. Young, "Guerrilla Warfare," p. 27; Kenneth R. Young, "Atrocities and War Crimes: The Case of Major Waller and General Smith."
22. May, *Battle for Batangas,* pp. 255–256, 239; Linn, "Provincial Pacification," p. 65.
23. Quotes from May, *Battle for Batangas,* pp. 242–243, 254, 257, 259, 264; see also Miller, *Benevolent Assimilation,* p. 208; Graff, *American Imperialism,* pp. 74–75, 80–81, 85, 87, 97–113; SD331, on Balangiga, pp. 1591–1602, on Batangas, pp. 1629ff.
24. Miller, *Benevolent Assimilation,* p. 213; SD331, General MacArthur's testimony, pp. 862–907, 1377–1410, 1885–1968; Graff, *American Imperialism,* pp. xvi, xx, 55, 62–63.
25. Morris, *Roosevelt,* p. 259.
26. Graff, *American Imperialism,* pp. xvi, xx.
27. Taft, *Recollection of Full Years,* pp. 234–235; Graff, *American Imperialism,* p. 171.
28. Quoted in Graff, *American Imperialism,* pp. 92–93, 94.
29. First quote, ibid., p. 95; second quote, letter, Taft to Colonel Crowder, Sept. 19, 1902, Enoch H. Crowder Papers, University of Missouri.
30. Graff, *American Imperialism,* p. 41.
31. Ibid., pp. 50, 60.
32. SD206, I, pp. 1–4, covering statement by Root, quoted in Young, "Atrocities and War Crimes," p. 72. See also MacArthur's testimony before the Senate, SD331, pp. 849–1968.

33. SD331, p. 870, and also pp. 949ff; Graff, *American Imperialism*, pp. 57, 141–144, 155; Miller, *Benevolent Assimilation*, p. 151.

34. SD331, pp. 866–869.

35. Quote from Miller, *Benevolent Assimilation*, p. 239.

36. Manchester, *American Caesar*, pp. 35, 467, 666.

37. SD331, p. 873, also quoted in Graff, *American Imperialism*, p. 139.

38. SD331, pp. 867, 876, 885, 894, 1572, and 1942.

39. SD331, pp. 906–907; HD2-M-1901, p. 111; MacArthur, "Address to Wisconsin Banker's Association."

40. Root, *Military and Colonial Policy*, speech, Oct. 24, 1900.

41. The other departments were Inspector General, Judge Advocate General, Subsistence, Medical, Ordnance, Payroll, and the Engineer and Signal Corps.

42. Vandiver, *Black Jack*, pp. 329–330.

43. Root, *Military and Colonial Policy*, pp. 417–439; Nelson Miles Papers, Carlisle, Folder F.

44. RG20, MML, letter, MacArthur to AG, July 18, 1902; Nelson Miles Papers, Carlisle, Folder F.

45. James, *MacArthur*, pp. 87, 111.

46. Nelson Miles Papers, Carlisle, Root to Miles, Dec. 21, 1901.

47. Root, *Military and Colonial Policy*, speech Jan. 27, 1903, pp. 22–25, passim.

48. Vandiver, *Black Jack*, pp. 329–330.

49. RG20, MML, newspaper clipping, source and date unknown; James, *MacArthur*, p. 78.

50. James, *MacArthur*, p. 78.

51. Hunt, *Untold Story*, p. 33.

52. RG20(?), MML, Genealogy Chart; Nimitz Library, U.S. Naval Academy, Arthur MacArthur III Archive file, letter, McCalla to Lieutenant MacArthur, July 4, 1903. Sometime in the fall of 1901 or spring of 1902, Lieutenant Arthur MacArthur married the daughter of Navy Captain Bowman H. McCalla. A check of city hall records from Newport News, Virginia, to Newport, Rhode Island (where the clerk refused to allow me to examine the marriage records), and a check of newspapers and the records of the MacArthur Memorial Library did not reveal the exact date of the marriage nor did material in the MacArthur or McCalla files at the Nimitz Library. McCalla had met General MacArthur in the Philippines, and yet in his memoirs, he never mentions the marriage of his daughter and the general's son. Records at the MacArthur Memorial Library state that the marriage occurred on August 21, 1901, in Newport, Rhode Island. If true, the groom's father would have missed the wedding, yet Douglas remembered the day as the first time the family had been together in years. Hunt, *Untold Story*, p. 33, stated that Douglas was granted a special leave in 1902 to attend his older brother's wedding at Newport News, Virginia. According to Hunt, Douglas acted as best man and was in his cadet's full dress uniform with the shining gold chevrons of a first captain. It was the first time that the MacArthurs had been together in several years. The fact that Lieutenant MacArthur married Mary McCalla sometime in this period is obvious, but I was never able to confirm the exact date of August 21, 1901.

53. Petillo, *MacArthur*, pp. 56–57.

54. MacArthur, *Reminiscences*, p. 29; Petillo, *MacArthur*, pp. 68–69.

55. Petillo, *MacArthur*, p. 70.

56. James, *MacArthur*, p. 89.

57. RG94, NA, Document file. In this period, command designations kept changing from departments to divisions and made it difficult to always get the correct official title.

58. Miller, *Benevolent Assimilation*, p. 19.

59. RG94, NA, Document file, *Hawaii Commercial Advocate*, Dec. 10, 1903.

60. RG94, NA, Document file, memo, Lieutenant General Young to White House, Dec. 11, 1903; cablegram, Young to MacArthur, Dec. 11, 1903.

61. RG94, NA, Document file, cablegram, Carter to President, Dec. 15, 1903.

62. RG94, NA, Document file, cablegram, Root to MacArthur, Dec. 22, 1903. See also Manchester, *American Caesar*, p. 37.

63. Quotes from Morris, *Roosevelt,* pp. 570, 630; Miller, *Benevolent Assimilation,* p. 260.

64. James, *MacArthur,* p. 90; Nimitz Library, U.S. Naval Academy, Bowman Henry McCalla Papers.

65. RG165, NA, Box 128, "Russo-Japanese War and the Asian Tour," letter, MacArthur to Chaffee, Dec. 24, 1904.

66. John J. Pershing Papers, Library of Congress, *Memoirs,* Vol. 2, Chapter 15, "Diary," Box 21, and "Report of Military Attaché," Box 324.

67. The Japanese sent their approval on Jan. 11, 1905, RG165, NA, Box 128, "Russo-Japanese War and the Asian Tour."

68. The *Army Register,* 1905, lists the ranking as Chaffee, MacArthur, and John C. Bates. Adjutant General Corbin's major general's commission dated from June 6, 1900, and thus he technically ranked MacArthur (Feb. 5, 1901) and Bates (July 19, 1902).

69. Vandiver, *Black Jack,* pp. 352–355; John J. Pershing Papers, Library of Congress, Box 371; David A. Lockmiller, *Enoch H. Crowder: Soldier, Lawyer, Statesman.*

70. RG165, NA, Box 128, "Russo-Japanese War and the Asian Tour," dispatch, U.S. Minister Lloyd Griscom to secretary of state, March 15, 1905; Vandiver, *Black Jack,* p. 355; John J. Pershing Papers, Library of Congress, *Memoirs,* Chapter 11.

71. Vandiver, *Black Jack,* pp. 363; John J. Pershing Papers, Library of Congress, "Military Attaché," Box 324.

72. Vandiver, *Black Jack,* pp. 356ff; John J. Pershing Papers, Library of Congress, "Military Attaché," Box 324.

73. RG84, NA, dispatch, Griscom to Hay, March 15, 1905.

74. John J. Pershing Papers, Library of Congress,, "Military Attaché," Box 324.

75. Ibid.

76. Ibid.; Vandiver, *Black Jack,* pp. 359–360.

77. John J. Pershing Papers, Library of Congress, "Military Attaché," Box 324.

78. Ibid.; Vandiver, *Black Jack,* p. 362.

79. Vandiver, p. 364.

80. Ibid., p. 363.

81. John J. Pershing Papers, Library of Congress, "Military Attaché," Box 324, and *Memoirs,* Chapter 15.

82. RG165, NA, Box 128, "Russo-Japanese War and the Asian Tour," letter, MacArthur to Chaffee, March 24, 1905.

83. John J. Pershing Papers, Library of Congress, "Military Attaché," Box 324.

84. Denis and Peggy Warner, *The Tide at Sunrise: A History of the Russo-Japanese War,* pp. 514–556.

85. RG10, MML, Pinky to Harriman, April 17, 1907.

86. Enoch H. Crowder Papers, University of Missouri, letter, Taft to Crowder, Sept. 19, 1902; see also H. W. Brand, *Bound to Empire: The United States and the Philippines,* pp. 39–79.

87. Henry C. Corbin Papers, Library of Congress, "Autobiography"; Minger, *Taft,* pp. 153–162.

88. RG165, NA, Box 128, "Russo-Japanese War and the Asian Tour," letter, West to Beach, Sept. 19, 1905, and letters, MacArthur to Major William Beach, General Staff, Intelligence, Oct. 29, Dec. 3, 1905, Jan. 15, 1906.

89. MacArthur, *Reminiscences,* pp. 31–32; see also Hunt, *Untold Story,* p. 38.

90. First quote is from Manchester, *American Caesar,* p. 73, see also pp. 38 and 44, as well as Petillo, *MacArthur,* pp. 87–92; second quote is from Lee and Henschel, *MacArthur,* p. 13; third quote is from Manchester, *American Caesar,* p. 44.

91. Morris, *Roosevelt,* p. 28; Manchester, *American Caesar,* pp. 164, 177, 217, 519. The list of books (from RG165, NA, Box 128, "Russo-Japanese War and the Asian Tour") included: Brooke, *An Eyewitness in Manchuria;* Burley, *On the Japanese Russian War;* Hall, *The Soul of the People;* Barring, *With the Russians in Manchuria;* Smith, *The Siege and Fall of Port Arthur;* Hamilton, *A Staff Officer's Scrapbook;* Weale, *The Reshaping of the Far East;* Scidmore, *Winter India;* Murray, *India;* Doumer, *L'Indo-China-Francaise;* Curtis, *Modern India;* Griffis, *The Kikado's Empire;* Wood, *From Yalu to Port Ar-*

thur; Curzon, *Problems of the Far East*; Astor, *Japanese Literature*; Smith, *Chinese Characteristics*; Day, *The Dutch in Java*; and Hitobo, *Soul of Japan*.

92. Quotes from Manchester, *American Caesar*, pp. 66 and 96, see also p. 499; Lee and Henschel, *MacArthur*, pp. 11, 14.

93. Petillo, *MacArthur*, p. 89.

94. Ibid., p. xvi; Douglas quoted in Manchester, *American Caesar*, p. 658.

95. Hunt, quoted in Manchester, *American Caesar*, 479.

96. Douglas, quoted in ibid., pp. 468–469, see also pp. 492–494.

97. Philip Magnus, *Kitchener*, pp. 205, 214; Petillo, *MacArthur*, p. 87.

98. Quoting James, *MacArthur*, p. 44; second quote is from Manchester, *American Caesar*, p. 633, quoting Robert Payne; third quote is from idem, p. 467; fourth quote is from MacArthur, *Reminiscences*, pp. 19–25.

99. Singapore Consulate Reports, m464, Roll 16; RG165, NA, Box 128, "Russo-Japanese War and the Asian Tour."

100. RG165, NA, Box 128, "Russo-Japanese War and the Asian Tour," dispatch, King to Secretary of State, April 10, 1906; MacArthur, *Reminiscences*, p. 32.

101. Petillo, *MacArthur*, pp. 90–91, citing Cora King Diary. Petillo, p. 262, note 11, thanks Colonel William F. Strobridge of the Center for Military History, Washington, D.C., for bringing the King Diary to her attention.

102. Ibid.

103. Ibid., p. 91, citing Cora King Diary.

104. MacArthur, *Reminiscences*, pp. 31–32.

105. Petillo, *MacArthur*, p. 92, citing Cora King Diary.

106. Nimitz Library, U.S. Naval Academy, Arthur MacArthur III Archive file.

107. Douglas, quoted in Manchester, *American Caesar*, p. 67; MacArthur, *Reminiscences*, p. 31.

108. See Marszalek, *Sherman*, p. 363, describing Sherman's feeling during a trip to Europe.

109. Henry C. Corbin Papers, Library of Congress, letter, John McCook to Corbin, June 30, 1905.

110. Henry C. Corbin Papers, Library of Congress, letter, Beach to West, May 17, 1905; Watrous, "About High Ranking Officers"; *Army Register*, 1902–1907.

111. RG165, NA, Box 128, "Russo-Japanese War and the Asian Tour," letter, Beach to MacArthur, Jan. 13, 1906. *Army Register*, 1907, listed the official date MacArthur became lieutenant general as Sept. 15, 1906.

112. Miller, *Benevolent Assimilation*, p. 265; Manchester, *American Caesar*, p. 36.

113. Petillo, *MacArthur*, p. 100; James, *MacArthur*, p. 95; Manchester, *American Caesar*, p. 69.

114. Petillo, *MacArthur*, pp. 93–94.

115. RG94, NA, Document file, letter, MacArthur to Taft, March 13, 1907; letter, Bell to MacArthur, March 25, 1907. See also James, *MacArthur*, p. 2, Hunt, *Untold Story*, p. 39; Edward M. Coffman, *The Hilt and the Sword: The Career of Peyton C. March*, p. 232. Petillo, *MacArthur*, p. 93.

116. RG94, NA, Document file; RG165, NA, Box 128, "Russo-Japanese War and the Asian Tour," letter, MacArthur to Chaffee, March 24, 1905, from Mukden.

117. RG20, MML, newspaper clipping, *Milwaukee Free Press*, Sept. 6, 1912.

118. *Milwaukee Sentinel*, June 25, 1907; Anderson, *The MacArthurs*, pp. 18–20, quoting King speech to the Old Schoolmates Association, 1907.

119. James, *MacArthur*, p. 105.

120. Manchester, *American Caesar*, p. 69.

121. Anderson, *The MacArthurs*, p. 24, quoting King speech to the Old Schoolmates Association, 1907.

122. Miller, *Benevolent Assimilation*, p. 265.

123. Manchester, *American Caesar*, p. 84.

124. Petillo, *MacArthur*, pp. 101–106; James, *MacArthur*, pp. 97, 105; Manchester, *American Caesar*, p. 69.

125. James, *MacArthur*, pp. 101, 105; Petillo, *MacArthur*, pp. 107, 109; Manchester, *American Caesar*, p. 72.

126. Petillo, *MacArthur*, p. 109.

127. RG20, MML, Folder #1; Arthur MacArthur, "Our American Shipping: Address to Old Settlers Club," Milwaukee, Feb. 22, 1908, WHS.

128. Petillo, *MacArthur*, p. 78.

129. RG20, MML, *Harper's Weekly*, Sept. 14, 1912. For an excellent photo of MacArthur in civilian clothes, see RG20, MML, *Milwaukee Free Press*, Sept. 6, 1912. In October 1905, Count Katsuro Taru, the Japanese minister of foreign affairs, requested permission from the United States to present decorations to the eleven U.S. officers who had served as military observers in Korea and Manchuria during the Russo-Japanese War (RG94, NA, Document file, letters, U.S. Minister in Japan to Taft, the secretary of war, and to Root, the secretary of state, Dec. 16, 1905, Jan. 4, 1906). The Japanese wanted to award the highest decoration, Second Class of the Imperial Order of the Rising Sun, to MacArthur. Colonel Crowder was to receive the Third Class award of the same decoration, and Captain Pershing and Major March would receive the Fourth Class of the Imperial Order of the Sacred Treasure. See Enoch H. Crowder Papers, University of Missouri, letter March 19, 1906, from U.S. minister in Japan to Taft. Taft rejected the proposal to give medals to U.S. officers based on a law that U.S. military personnel could receive no decorations from foreign countries.

130. *Milwaukee Sentinel*, June 27, 1909.

131. RG20, MML, *Milwaukee Free Press*, Sept. 6, 1912, quoting General King; *Army and Navy Journal*, Sept. 21, 1912; MacArthur, "American Shipping"; *Report of the Proceedings of the Meetings of the State Bar Association of Wisconsin*, Vol. 10, 1912–1914.

132. Jerome A. Watrous, *Memoirs of Milwaukee County*; A. Ross Houston, "The Loyal Legion."

133. Marszalek, *Sherman*, p. 364; RG20, MML, newspaper clipping, *Wausau Pilot*, April 19, 1910; Carroon, "The Judge and the General," p. 12.

134. RG20, MML, *Harper's Weekly*, Sept. 14, 1912. Manchester, *American Caesar*, p. 217, estimated the library at 4,000 volumes.

135. See Marszalek, *Sherman*, pp. 383–389.

136. RG94, NA, Document file, "Medical Records, General MacArthur, 1909"; RG20, MML, newspaper clippings, *Milwaukee Free Press*, Sept. 12, 1912, and *Harper's Weekly*, Sept. 14, 1912.

137. Theabold Otjen Papers, WHS, letter, MacArthur to Otjen, Nov. 16, 1909; RG20, MML, newspaper clippings, *Evening Wisconsin*, Sept. 6, 1912, and *Army and Navy Journal*, Sept. 21, 1912.

138. RG94, NA, Document file, letter, King to AG, Sept. 7, 1912.

139. RG20, MML, *Harper's Weekly*, Sept. 14, 1912.

140. RG20, MML, newspaper clippings, *Harper's Weekly*, Sept. 14, 1912; *Milwaukee Sentinel*, Sept. 6, 1912; *Milwaukee Journal*, Sept. 6, 1912; *Evening Wisconsin*, Sept. 6, 1912; *Milwaukee Free Press*, Sept. 6, 1912; *Army and Navy Journal*, Sept. 21, 1912; RG94, NA, Document file, letter, King to AG, Sept. 7, 1912.

141. RG20, MML, newspaper clippings, *Boston Post, Providence Daily Journal, Boston Daily Globe*, Sept. 6, 1912.

142. RG20, MML, *Milwaukee Free Press*, Sept. 6, 1912; *Army and Navy Journal*, Sept. 21, 1912.

143. RG94, NA, Document file, letter, King to AG, Sept. 7, 1912.

144. Quoted in Flower, *Life of Matthew Hale Carpenter*, pp. 573–574.

145. Douglas quote, Petillo, *MacArthur*, p. 111; see also James, *MacArthur*, p. 43.

146. RG94, NA, Document file, letter, King to AG, Sept. 7, 1912; RG20, MML, *Evening Wisconsin*, Sept. 6, 1912.

147. RG94, NA, Document file, letter, King to AG, Sept. 7, 1912; RG20, MML, *Harper's Weekly*, Sept. 14, 1912.

148. RG20, MML, *Milwaukee Free Press*, Sept. 10, 1912; photos of funeral, front page, RG20, MML, *Evening Wisconsin*, Sept. 9, 1912; RG94, NA, Document file, letter, King to AG, Sept. 7, 1912. The honorary pallbearers were: Governor Francis E. McGovern, Governor George W. Peck, George F.C.

Winkler, General Charles King, Judge Paul D. Carpenter, Judge James G. Flanders, Professor G. W. Peckham, E. G. Wall, George Ogden, Major James Sawyer, and Major P. E. Balchvin.

149. Manchester, *American Caesar,* p. 77.

150. RG94, NA, Document file, letter, King to AG, Sept. 7, 1912; Manchester, *American Caesar,* p. 73; James, *MacArthur,* p. 208. Manchester and James say that MacArthur met Wood at Fort Wingate, but Wood's service record seems to deny that possibility. Douglas says he first met Wood when he traveled through Fort Selden with Captain Henry Lawton's troop of cavalry in pursuit of Geronimo; see MacArthur, *Reminiscences,* p. 39.

151. Petillo, *MacArthur,* p. 111; Manchester, *American Caesar,* p. 38.

152. Lee and Henschel, *MacArthur,* pp. 13–14.

153. James, *MacArthur,* p. 44; Manchester, *American Caesar,* p. 30; Hunt, *Untold Story,* pp. 17–18.

154. Quoted in Manchester, *American Caesar,* pp. 74–76; Hunt, *Untold Story,* pp. 55–58.

155. Manchester, *American Caesar,* pp. 88, 110.

156. Hunt, *Untold Story,* pp. 98, 106; MacArthur, *Reminiscences,* p. 46.

157. Manchester, *American Caesar,* p. 144.

Postscript

1. RG20, MML, newspaper clipping, Oct. 3, 1912; RG20, MML, letter, Colonel Hicks to General Douglas MacArthur, Sept. 12, 1941.

2. James, *MacArthur,* p. 43.

3. Nimitz Library, U.S. Naval Academy, Arthur MacArthur III Archive file.

4. James, *MacArthur,* p. 495.

5. Manchester, *American Caesar,* p. 178.

Bibliography

The bibliography has been arranged in the following parts:

Part One: Primary Resource Libraries
MacArthur Memorial Library (MML)
U.S. National Archives (NA)
Wisconsin Historical Society (WHS)
Milwaukee County Historical Society
U.S. Library of Congress
U.S. Army Military History Research Collection (Carlisle)
Nimitz Library, U.S. Naval Academy
Miscellaneous

Part Two: U.S. Government Documents

Part Three: Newspapers

Part Four: Books and Articles
A. Family Background: Judge Arthur MacArthur
B. The Civil War Period
C. Frontier Days
D. The Spanish-American War and the Philippines
E. Final Days

Part One: Primary Resource Libraries

MACARTHUR MEMORIAL LIBRARY (MML), BUREAU OF ARCHIVES, NORFOLK, VIRGINIA

Record Group 10 (RG10, MML).
Record Group 12 (RG12, MML), Collection of photographs.
Record Group 20 (RG20, MML), Newspaper and magazine clippings.
Record Group 20 (RG20, MML), Material from National Archives, microfilm, Records of General Arthur MacArthur, 1880–1912.

U.S. NATIONAL ARCHIVES (NA)

Record Group 84 (RG84, NA), State Department, Consular, Embassy Reports.
Record Group 94 (RG94, NA), Records of the Adjutant General's Office. Adjutant General's Office (AGO), Old Record Files.
 *RG94, NA, Document File of Lieutenant General Arthur MacArthur.
RG94, NA, Miscellaneous 201 File of Lieutenant General Arthur MacArthur (AM-201 Misc.).
RG94, NA, Post Returns, Microfilm Roll 1147.

Record Group 108 (RG108, NA), Records of the Headquarters of the Army, Letters Sent and Letters Received by the Commanding General, 1895 to 1903.

*Record Group 165(RG 165, NA), Records of the War Department, General and Special Staff, Entry 310, Historical Section, War Department Correspondence.

*RG165, NA, Arthur MacArthur, "Chinese Memorandum," Jan. 15, 1883.

*RG165, NA, Major General MacArthur, Military Observer, Russo-Japanese War, Box 128, G-2, Box 128—"Asian Tour—MacArthur's Correspondence."

*RG165, NA, War College Division of the General Staff, File 1322, NA, "Chief WCD to MacArthur, Dec. 28, 1907." "Death of General MacArthur," *Milwaukee Journal*, Sept. 6, 1912; ANR, Sept. 7, 14, and 28, 1912; ANJ, Sept. 7, 14, 21, 1912.

*Asterisk indicates this material was examined on microfilm from MacArthur Memorial Library.

WISCONSIN HISTORICAL SOCIETY (WHS), UNIVERSITY OF WISCONSIN, MADISON

Carpenter Family Papers.

Cooley, George, Diary. Company A, 24th Wisconsin, June 23, 1863, to Dec. 11, 1864.

Drake, Henry T., Papers. "Civil War Letters."

Estabrook, Charles E., Papers. "Summary of Service Record of Lt. General Arthur MacArthur, born June 2, 1845, died Sept. 5, 1912." Box 1. See also James G. Flanders Papers, WHS, and Francis G. Newland Papers, Yale University Library, Summary of Record, Extracts from 201 file of Lt. General Arthur MacArthur (AM Extract 201).

Ford, Thomas J. *With the Rank and File*. Sergeant of Company H, 24th Wisconsin Infantry. Addresses delivered at E. R. Wolcott Post, Milwaukee, Nov. 19, 1897, March 11, 1898.

Greene, Howard, Papers. "Civil War Letters."

Greene, Major Howard, "With the 24th Wisconsin Volunteers." Paper read Nov. 1, 1920, Loyal Legion, Milwaukee, in Howard Greene Papers.

Jenkins, James, Papers.

Love, William D., Papers.

———. McArthur, Arthur. "History of the 24th Wisconsin." Speech by judge at Anniversary Banquet of Company B, Aug. 20, 1866, Love Papers, Misc. box.

King, Charles, Manuscript Collection.

Mitchell Family Papers.

———. "Civil War Letters of Robert Chivas."

———. "Civil War Letters of John Mitchell."

Otjen, Theabold, Papers.

Quiner, Edwin B. *Correspondence of Wisconsin Volunteers, 1861–1865*. Ten scrapbooks of newspaper clippings.

Robinson, Charles D., Papers.

Strong, Moses M., Papers.

Vilas, William F., Papers.

Watrous, Jerome A., Papers.

———. "About High Ranking Officers," Box 3.

———. "An Old Time Routing of Grafters." 1905(?).

Whyte, William F., Papers.

Wisconsin Blue Books: Election results, 1849–1858.

MILWAUKEE COUNTY HISTORICAL SOCIETY

Bureau of the Census: Milwaukee County, 1850, 1860, 1870, 1910.

King, Charles, Biographical File.

MacArthur File.

U.S. LIBRARY OF CONGRESS, MANUSCRIPT DIVISION

Allen, Henry T., Papers.
Corbin, Henry C., Papers.
McKinley, William, Papers.
March, Peyton C., Papers.
Pershing, John J., Papers.
Root, Elihu, Papers.
Taft, William Howard, Papers.

U.S. ARMY MILITARY HISTORY RESEARCH COLLECTION, CARLISLE BARRACKS, CARLISLE, PA (CITED AS CARLISLE)

A. Reference

Special Bibliographic Series, Number 6, *The U.S. Army and the Spanish-American War, 1895–1910.* Manuscript Holdings.
Special Bibliographic Series, Number 9, *The U.S. Army and the Spanish-American War, 1895–1910.* Part 1–2.

B. Manuscripts

Arnold, Fred, Adjutant, 4th U.S. Cavalry, Letters of Mrs. Arnold, 62 pages.
Bender Family Papers, Jacob Bender, Company K, 24th Wisconsin.
Bradley, Luther P., Papers.
Brown, William Carey, Brigadier General, Diaries of service from 1874 to 1902.
Deshon, George, Papers.
Doyle, Daniel, 13th Minnesota, Diary.
Fisher, George R., Musician, Utah Light Artillery, Diary, June 14, 1898, to May 16, 1899.
Haight, Forest A., 6th U.S. Artillery, Letters.
Halstead-Maus Papers. *Memoirs.*
Hubbard, Louis W., 1st South Dakota Volunteers, Letters.
20th Kansas Volunteers, 1 Box, Letters and Survey Forms.
Kobbé, William A., Major General, Diary and Papers on the Philippines.
Kuhn, Spencer, 17th U.S. Infantry, Letters.
Landon, William B. 35th Volunteers, Letters.
Lenihan Papers.
Line, Claude F., 20th U.S. Infantry, Diary, 1900–1902.
Lyon, Samuel, Diary.
Merrill, Frank, 13th Minnesota, Memoirs.
Miles, Nelson, Papers, Folder F.
13th Minnesota, 1 Box, including pamphlet.
Ovenshine, Samuel J., Papers.
Podas, Frederick J., 13th Minnesota, Diary.
Sorley, Lewis S., Some Recollections.
Soules, Charles, 3rd Artillery, seven letters, Sept. 1898 to Feb. 1899.
Vaughn, John B., 21st U.S. Infantry, "My Memoirs."
Young, Samuel Baldwin, General, Papers.

NIMITZ LIBRARY, U.S. NAVAL ACADEMY, ANNAPOLIS, MARYLAND

MacArthur, Arthur III, Archives File.
McCalla, Bowman Hendry, Papers, Manuscript, No. 215, *Memoirs,* c. 1909.

Annual Registers, 1892–1896.
The Lucky Bag, Yearbook for Class of 1896.

MISCELLANEOUS

Crowder, Enoch H., Papers. University of Missouri, Microfilm Roll 2, Folders 31–71.
Chicopee, MA, City Hall, Death Records, 1864.

Part Two: U.S. Government Documents

A. CIVIL WAR PERIOD

United States. War Department. *The War of the Rebellion: A Compilation of the Official Records of the Union and Confederate Armies.* Series 1, 128 Vols. Washington, D.C., 1880–1901. Cited as *Official Records.*
 Vol. 16: Perryville or Chaplin Hills, Oct. 28, 1862.
 Vol. 23: Tullahoma Campaign, Middle Tennessee Campaign, June 29–30, July 1, 1863.
 Vol. 29: Battle of Stones River or Murfreesborough, Tenn., Dec. 26 to Jan. 5, 1863.
 ———. "Report of Captain Asahel K. Bush," 4th Indiana Battery, pp. 354–356.
 ———. "Report of Colonel Nicholas Greusel," 36th Illinois, commanding 1st Brigade, pp. 356–357.
 ———. "Report of Major Elisha C. Hibbard," 24th Wisconsin, pp. 363–365.
 Vol. 30: Chickamauga, Ga., Sept. 19–20, 1863.
 ———. "Report of Major Carl von Baumbach," 24th Wisconsin, pp. 586–588.
 Vol. 31: Missionary Ridge, Chattanooga, Orchard Knob, Lookout Mountain, Tenn.: Nov. 23–27, 1863; Knoxville Expedition, Tenn.: Nov. 6–Dec. 4, 1863.
 Vol. 32: Dalton Tunnel Hill, Buzzard Roost, Rocky Face Ridge, Ga.: Feb. 22–27, 1864.
 Vol. 38: The Atlanta Campaign, May 13 to Sept. 5, 1864.
 ———. "Report of Colonel Emerson Opdycke," Sept. 10, 1864, 1st Brigade, 2nd Division, 4th Army Corps, pp. 309–312.
 ———. "Report of Major Arthur MacArthur, Jr.," Sept. 12, 1864, 24th Wisconsin, pp. 327–330.
 Vol. 45: Franklin, Tenn.: Nov. 30, 1864; Nashville, Tenn., Dec. 15–16, 1864.
 ———. "Report of Major General David S. Stanley," Dec. 1, 1864, 4th Army Corps , pp. 114–118.
 ———. "Report of Colonel Emerson Opdycke," Nov. 29–30, 1864, 1st Brigade, 2nd Division, 4th Army Corps, pp. 239–241.
 ———. "Report of Captain Edwin B. Parsons," Dec. 1, 1864, 24th Wisconsin, pp. 252–254.
 Vol. 55: Missionary Ridge, Battle of Chattanooga, Ringgold Campaign.
 ———. "Report of Major Carl von Baumbach," 24th Wisconsin, pp. 207–208.

B. FRONTIER DAYS

Army and Navy Journal, Sept. 7, 14, 21, 1912.
Army Register, 1867 to 1909.
U.S. Congress, House of Representatives, Committee of Military Affairs, Reorganization of the Army. House Miscellaneous, No. 354, 44th Congress, 1st session. Documents No. 56, 45th Congress, 2nd session.
———. 45th Congress, 2nd Session, House Miscellaneous Document 56.
U.S. War Department. *Annual Report*, 1877, 1888, 1889.
———. Historical Records, G-2, Box 128, Grant to Judge MacArthur, June 10, 1882.

C. THE SPANISH-AMERICAN WAR AND THE PHILIPPINES

United States Congress, Senate Documents (SD).

56th Congress, 1st Session, Senate Document 148, cited as SD148.

57th Congress, 1st Session, *Hearings on Affairs in the Philippines*, Senate Document 331, Vol. 2, pp. 849–879, 890–912, 1377–1420, 1885–1902. "Hearing Before the Committee on the Philippines," General MacArthur's testimony, April 7, 1902, to May 2, 1902, pp. 849–1968. Cited as SD331.

57th Congress, 1st Session, Senate Documents 205, 259, 323, 331, 347, 422.

United States Congress, House Document 2 (HD2), *Annual Report of the War Department*, 1898 to 1902. See also War Department, *Annual Reports.*

55th Congress, 3rd Session, HD2, *Annual Report.*

Vol. 1: "Report of Major General E. S. Otis," Commander of the 8th Army Corps, Aug. 29, 1898, to Aug. 31, 1899, pp. 1–165, cited as HD2-O-1899.

Vol. 3: "Report of Brigadier General Arthur MacArthur," 2nd Brigade, 8th Army Corps, Aug. 22, 1898, pp. 111–115.

Vol. 4: "Report of Major General Arthur MacArthur, 2nd Division, 8th Army Corps, March–May 1899, pp. 372–414.

56th Congress, 1st Session, HD2, *Annual Report.*

Vol. 5: "Report of Major General Arthur MacArthur," 2nd Division, 8th Army Corps, Feb. 4, 1899, to Feb. 28, 1899, pp. 422–428, cited as HD2-1st-M-1899.

56th Congress, 2nd Session, HD2, *Annual Report.*

Vol. 5: "Report of Major General E. S. Otis," Commander of 8th Army Corps, Sept. 1, 1899, to May 5, 1900, pp. 199–561, cited as HD2-O-1900.

Vol. 9: "Report of General MacArthur," 2nd Division, 8th Army Corps, June 1899 to April 6, 1900, pp. 14–76, cited as HD2-M-1900.

57th Congress, 1st Session, HD2, *Annual Report.*

Vol. 5: "Report of General MacArthur," Commander of the Division of the Philippines, Oct. 1, 1900, to July 4, 1901, pp. 88–135, cited as HD2-M-1901.

United States War Department, *Annual Report*, 1899, "Report of Major General Arthur MacArthur," 2nd Division, 8th Army Corps, March–May 1899, Vol. 1, Part 5, pp. 372–414, cited as AR-M-1899.

_____. *Annual Report*, 1900, "Report of Major General Arthur MacArthur," Commanding Division of the Philippines, May 1900 to October 1900, Vol. 1, Part 3, pp. 59–71, cited as WDAR.

_____. *Philippine Insurgent: Records of the U.S., 1896–1906.* 4 microfilm reels.

_____. *Regulations and Decisions Pertaining to the Uniform of the Army of the United States.* Annual, 1899–1902.

_____. *Report of the Philippine Commission:* 1902–1915. Special Hearings.

_____. Adjutant General's Office, *Military Notes on the Philippines.*

_____. Adjutant General's Office. *Correspondence Relating to the War with Spain Including the Insurrection in the Philippine Islands and the China Relief Expedition: April 15, 1898 to July 30, 1902.*

Other United States Government Documents

Executive Minutes of the United States Philippine Commission (ms): Sept. 19, Oct. 4, 6, 8, 16, 17, and 22, Nov. 7, 10, and 14, Dec. 7, 1900, Jan. 16, Feb. 20, 1901.

Philippine Commission, 1900–1916. "A Compilation of the Acts of the Philippine Commission." Manila: Bureau of Printing.

Philippine Commission, Executive Minutes of the United States Philippine Commission (ms): Sept. 19, Oct. 4, 6, 8, 16, 17, and 22, Nov. 7, 10, and 14, Dec. 7, 1900, Jan. 16–Feb. 20, 1901.

Philippine Islands, Military Governor: General Orders and Circulars. 1900–1901.

Taylor, John R.M., ed. *The Philippine Insurrection Against the United States: A Compilation of Documents with Notes and Introduction.* U.S. War Department, 5 Vols.

D. FINAL DAYS

U.S. State Department, Singapore Consulate Reports, m464, roll 16.

U.S. War Department, General Staff, 2nd Division, Reports of Military Observers in Russo-Japanese War, 5 Vols.

Part Three: Newspapers

Atlantic City Daily Press, Aug. 27, 1896.

Atlantic City Daily Union, Aug. 27, 1896.

Daily Argus and Democrat (Madison). Name changed: First was *Argus,* later the *Evening Argus and Democrat,* then simply *Argus and Democrat.*

Daily Wisconsin.

Evening Wisconsin.

Green Bay Advocate, Sept. 24, 1863.

Milwaukee Daily News, Jan. 7, 1864.

Milwaukee Sentinel.

New York Herald, March 29, 1856.

New York Times, Feb. 16, 1905, Dec. 4, 1906, and Sept. 6–8, 1912.

North Adams (MA) Hoosac Valley News, Feb. 12, 1868.

Springfield Republican, April 1, 1856.

Springfield Scrapbook, Vol. 26, p. 47, newspaper clipping dated July 24, 1951.

Part Four: Books and Articles

A. FAMILY BACKGROUND: JUDGE ARTHUR MACARTHUR

Anderson, Harry H., ed. *The MacArthurs of Milwaukee.* Milwaukee: Milwaukee County Historical Society, 1979.

Berryman, John R. *History of the Bench and Bar of Wisconsin.* Chicago, 1898, pp. 386–388.

Carroon, Robert G. "The Judge and the General," in Anderson, *The MacArthurs of Milwaukee,* pp. 2–14.

————. "Scotsmen in Old Milwaukee: 1810–1860," *Historical Messenger of the Milwaukee County Historical Society,* Vol. 25 (March 1969), pp. 20–33.

Celebration of the Hundredth Anniversary of the Birth of Robert Burns by the Boston Burns Club, pamphlet. Boston: Dulton, 1859.

Coles, Robert. *Erik H. Erikson: The Growth of His Work.* Boston: Little, Brown, 1970.

Conard, Howard Louis, ed. *History of Milwaukee County from Its First Settlement to the Year 1895.* Vol. 3. Chicago: American Biographical Publications, 1896(?).

Current, Richard N. *The History of Wisconsin.* Vol. 2, *The Civil War Era, 1848–1873.* Madison: State Historical Society of Wisconsin, 1976.

Dictionary of National Biography, Vol. 12, pp. 400–404.

Dictionary of Wisconsin Biography.

Donoghue, James R. *How Wisconsin Voted, 1848–1972.* Madison: University of Wisconsin, 1974.

Erikson, Erik H. *Life History and the Historical Moment.* New York: Norton, 1975.

Featherstonaugh, George W. *Centennial Anniversary.* Milwaukee: St. Andrews Society, 1859.

Flower, Frank A. *Life of Matthew Hale Carpenter.* Madison: Atwood, 1883.

History of Milwaukee. 1890(?).

Hofstadter, Richard, William Miller, and Daniel Aaron. *The American Republic.* Vol. 1: *to 1865*; Vol. 2: *Since 1865.* New York: Prentice-Hall, 1959.

Hunt, Frazier. *The Untold Story of Douglas MacArthur.* New York: Devin-Adair, 1954.

Hunter, Edward M. "Civil Life, Services and Character of William A. Barstow," in Lyman C. Draper, ed., *Collections of the State Historical Society of Wisconsin,* Vol. 6 (1872), pp. 93–109.

James, D. Clayton. *The Years of MacArthur.* Vol. 1: *1880–1941.* Boston: Houghton Mifflin, 1970.

Lee, Clark, and Richard Henschel. *Douglas MacArthur.* New York: Holt, 1952.

MacArthur, Judge Arthur. "Address of Arthur McArthur, Esq., on the Fourth Anniversary of the R. W. Grand Lodge of Wisconsin," Milwaukee, July 1850, Milwaukee County Historical Society. 21-page pamphlet.

———. *A Biography of the English Language.* Washington, D.C.: W. H. Lowdermilk, 1893.

———. *Education in Its Relation to Manual Industry.* New York: Appleton, 1884.

———. *Essays and Papers on Miscellaneous Topics.* Washington, D.C.: author, 1891.

———. *Historical Study of Mary Stuart,* 1889.

———. *History of Lady Jane Grey,* 1891.

———. *In Memoriam of Matthew H. Carpenter.* Published in pamphlet form, titled "Proceedings of the Bench and Bar of the Supreme Court of the United States." 1881. In Carpenter Papers, WHS.

———. *Law as Applied in a Business Education,* 1892.

———. "Opening Address by Judge Arthur MacArthur at the Graduating Exercises of the Law School, National University," June 8, 1882 (Washington, D.C.: 1882), 11 pages.

———, ed. *Reports of Cases.* The Supreme Court of the District of Columbia. Vols. 8 to 11, 1879–1882. Baltimore: M. Curlander, 1884.

———. "Welcome Address by Justice MacArthur," *Society of the Army of the Cumberland,* 11th Reunion, Nov. 1879, pp. 62–64.

MacArthur, Douglas. *Reminiscences.* New York: Time, 1964.

MacArthur, Frank. *Reports of Cases: Cases Arising upon Applications for Letters-Patent for Inventions Determined in the Circuit and Supreme Courts of the District of Columbia.* Washington, D.C.: Morrison, 1885.

Mackey, Franklin H., ed. *Reports of Cases.* The Supreme Court of the District of Columbia. Vol. 12 (1882), pp. 498–562. Washington, D.C.: Ginck, 1883(?).

Manchester, William. *American Caesar: Douglas MacArthur, 1880–1964.* Boston: Little, Brown, 1978.

Mann, Conklin, "Some Ancestral Lines of General Douglas MacArthur," *New York Genealogical and Biographical Record,* Vol. 73 (July 1942), pp. 170–172.

Mitchell, Alexander. *Reception and Banquet.* Milwaukee, 1884.

Mowry, William A. *The Uxbridge Academy.* Boston: Everett Press, 1897.

Muggah, Mary Gates, and Paul H. Raihle. *The MacArthur Story.* Featured in the *Chicago Tribune,* May 28, 1944. Chippewa Fall, WI: Chippewa Falls Book Agency, 1944(?).

Neenah, Robert S. "A Worthy Scotsman," *New York Scottish American,* Oct. 7, 1896.

Petillo, Carol Morris. *Douglas MacArthur: The Philippine Years.* Bloomington: Indiana University Press, 1981.

Reed, Parker M. *The Bench and Bar of Wisconsin.* Milwaukee: author, 1882.

Sheehy, Gail. *Passages: Predictable Crises of Adult Life.* New York: Bantam Books, 1976.

Shelton, Mary (MacArthur). *The Origins of Clan MacArthur,* edited by Robert C. MacArthur, privately printed, 1983.

Thompson, E. Bruce. *Matthew Hale Carpenter: Webster of the West.* Madison: State Historical Society of Wisconsin, 1954.

Thomson, Alexander M. *A Political History of Wisconsin to 1895.* Milwaukee: Caspar, 1902. Also in the *Milwaukee Sentinel,* Jan. 1898 to 1900.

Usher, Ellis Baker. *Wisconsin: Its Story and Biography, 1848–1913.* Chicago: Lewis Publishing. The judge, pp. 1837–1839; the general, pp. 1839–1847.

Watrous, Jerome A. *Memoirs of Milwaukee County,* Vol. 1. Madison: Western Historical Association, 1909.

B. CIVIL WAR PERIOD

Boatner, Mark M. *The Civil War Dictionary.* New York: Vintage, 1991.

Bradford, Ned, ed. *Battles and Leaders of the Civil War.* Vols. 3 and 4. Secaucus, NJ: Castle (reprint), 1982.

Buell, Don Carlos. "East Tennessee and the Campaign of Perryville," in *Battles and Leaders of the Civil War,* edited by Ned Bradford, Vol. 3, pp. 31–51.

Byers, Fred W., "The Battle of Franklin," address Oct. 7, 1885, Loyal Legion (Wisconsin), *War Papers,* Vol. 1 (1891), pp. 228–240.

Carroon, Robert G. "Arms and the Clans: Milwaukee Scots in the Civil War," *Historical Messenger of the Milwaukee County Historical Society,* Vol. 25 (Sept. 1969), pp. 109–119 (Dec. 1969), pp. 140–152.

Commanger, Henry S., ed. *The Blue and the Grey: The Story of the Civil War Told by Participants.* 2 Vols. New York: Bobbs-Merrill, 1950.

Crownover, Sims. "The Battle of Franklin," *Tennessee Historical Quarterly,* Vol. 14, Dec. 1955, reprint, 31 pages.

Estabrook, Charles E., ed. *Records and Sketches of Military Organization Related to Wisconsin in the Civil War.* Madison: State of Wisconsin, 1914.

Faust, Patricia L., ed. *Historical Times Illustrated Encyclopedia of the Civil War.* New York: Harper Perennial, 1991.

Fullerton, Joseph S. "The Army of the Cumberland at Chattanooga," in *Battles and Leaders of the Civil War,* edited by Ned Bradford, Vol. 3, pp. 719–727.

Gilbert, Charles C. "On the Field at Perryville," in *Battles and Leaders of the Civil War,* edited by Ned Bradford, Vol. 3, pp. 52–59.

Grant, Ulysses S. "Chattanooga," in *Battles and Leaders of the Civil War,* edited by Ned Bradford, Vol. 3, pp. 679–711.

Hill, Daniel H. "Chickamauga—the Great Battle of the West," in *Battles and Leaders of the Civil War,* edited by Ned Bradford, Vol. 3, pp. 638–662.

Hood, J. B. "The Invasion of Tennessee," in *Battles and Leaders of the Civil War,* edited by Ned Bradford, Vol. 4, pp. 425–439.

Howard, Oliver O. "The Struggle for Atlanta," in *Battles and Leaders of the Civil War,* edited by Ned Bradford, Vol. 4, pp. 293–325.

Johnston, Joseph E. "Opposing Sherman's Advance to Atlanta," in *Battles and Leaders of the Civil War,* edited by Ned Bradford, Vol. 4, pp. 260–277.

King, Charles. "Boys of the Loyal Legion," address, Dec. 7, 1892, Loyal Legion (Wisconsin), *War Papers,* Vol. 2 (1896), pp. 201–206.

Kniffin, G. C. "The Battle of Stone's River," in *Battles and Leaders of the Civil War,* edited by Ned Bradford, Vol. 3, pp. 613–632.

Legislative Manual of the State of Wisconsin. Bluebook 1863, p. 202, list of officers of 24th Wisconsin as of Aug. 1862.

Lewis, Lloyd. *Sherman: Fighting Prophet.* New York: Harcourt, 1932.

Linderman, Gerald F. *Embattled Courage: The Experience of Combat in the American Civil War.* New York: Free Press, 1987.

Love, William D. *Wisconsin in the War of the Rebellion: A History of All Regiments.* 1866.

McDonough, James Lee. *Chattanooga: A Death Grip on the Confederacy.* Knoxville: University of Tennessee Press, 1984.

————. *Stones River: Bloody Winter in Tennessee.* Knoxville: University of Tennessee Press, 1980.

McDonough, James Lee, and Thomas L. Connelly. *Five Tragic Hours: The Battle of Franklin.* Knoxville: University of Tennessee Press, 1983.

McPherson, James M. *Battle Cry of Freedom*. New York: Ballantine Books, 1988.

Marszalek, John F. *Sherman: A Soldier's Passion for Order*. New York: Free Press, 1993.

Parsons, Edwin B. "Sheridan," address, Oct. 3, 1888, Loyal Legion (Wisconsin), *War Papers*, Vol. 1 (1891), pp. 275–284.

———. "The True Story of the Assault on Missionary Ridge," address, March 7, 1888, Loyal Legion (Wisconsin), *War Papers*, Vol. 1 (1891), pp. 189–200.

Quiner, Edwin B. *The Military History of Wisconsin*. Chicago: Clarke, 1866.

Robison, Dan M. "The Carter House," reprint of article from *Tennessee Historical Quarterly*, Vol. 22, March 1963.

Royster, Charles. *The Destructive War*. New York: Vintage, 1991.

Sherman, William T. "The Grand Strategy of the Last Year of the War," in *Battles and Leaders of the Civil War*, edited by Ned Bradford, Vol. 4, pp. 247–259.

Stone, Henry. "Repelling Hood's Invasion of Tennessee," in *Battles and Leaders of the Civil War*, edited by Ned Bradford, Vol. 4, pp. 440–464.

Sword, Wiley. *Embrace an Angry Wind*. New York: HarperCollins, 1992.

Tucker, Glenn. "The Battle for Chattanooga," pamphlet, *Historical Times*, 1971.

Watrous, Jerome A. "How the Boy Won: General McArthur's First Victory," *Saturday Evening Post*, Philadelphia, Feb. 24, 1899.

Wheeler, Joseph. "Bragg's Invasion of Kentucky," in *Battles and Leaders of the Civil War*, edited by Ned Bradford, Vol. 3, pp. 1–25.

Wiley, Bell I. *The Common Soldier of the Civil War*. National Park and Monumental Association, 1984.

Wisconsin Historical Society, Vol. 6, pp. 101–106.

Wisconsin State Journal, January 9, 1864.

Wright, J. Montgomery. "Notes of a Staff Officer at Perryville," in *Battles and Leaders of the Civil War*, edited by Ned Bradford, Vol. 3, pp. 60–61.

C. FRONTIER DAYS

Alexander, Ulysses Grant. *History of the Thirteenth Regiment, United States Infantry*. Fort McDowell, AZ: Regimental Press, 1905.

Carrington, Frances C. *My Army Life and the Fort Phil Kearney Massacre*. Philadelphia: Lippincott, 1910.

Carrington, Colonel Henry B. (Mrs. Margaret I.) *Ab-sa-ra-ka, Land of Massacre: Being the Experience of an Officer's Wife on the Plains*. 4th ed. Philadelphia: Western Americana, 1878.

Coffman, Edward M. *The Old Army: A Portrait of the American Army in Peacetime, 1784–1898*. New York: Oxford University Press, 1986.

Foner, Jack D. *The United States Soldier Between Two Wars: Army Life and Reforms, 1865–1898*. 1970.

Forsyth, George A. *The Story of the Soldier*. New York: Appleton, 1900.

Fry, James B. *The History and Legal Effect of Brevets in the Armies of Great Britain and the United States*. New York: Van Nostrand, 1877.

Ganoe, William A. *History of the U.S. Army*. 1924.

Greene, Duane Merritt. *Ladies and Officers of the United States Army*. Chicago: Central Publishing, 1880.

Hart, Herbert M. *Old Forts of the Southwest*. Seattle: Superior Publishing, 1961.

King, Charles. *Memories of a Busy Life*. Madison. Reprinted from *Wisconsin Magazine of History*, Vols. 5–6, pp. 52–54, 66–82. WHS.

Knight, Oliver. *Life and Manners in the Frontier Army as Depicted in the Novels of Charles King*. Norman: University of Oklahoma Press, 1978.

Nenninger, Timothy K. *The Leavenworth Schools and the Old Army*. Westport, CT: Greenwood Press, 1978.

Rickey, Don. *Forty Miles a Day on Beans and Hay: The Enlisted Soldier Fighting the Indian Wars.* Norman: University of Oklahoma Press, 1963.

Russell, Don. *Campaigning with King.* Lincoln: University of Nebraska Press, 1991.

de Trobriand, Philippe Regis. *Military Life in Dakota: The Journal of Philippe Regis de Trobriand,* translated and edited by Lucile M. Kane. St. Paul: Minnesota Historical Society, 1951.

Utley, Robert M. *Frontier Regulars: The United States Army and the Indian, 1866–1890.* New York: Macmillan, 1973.

Vandiver, Frank E. *Black Jack: The Life and Times of John J. Pershing.* Vol. 1. College Station: Texas A & M University, 1977.

D. THE SPANISH-AMERICAN WAR AND THE PHILIPPINES

Alexander, Ulysses G. *History of the Thirteenth Regiment.* 1905.

American Monthly Review, "Arthur MacArthur," May 1900.

American Monthly Review of Reviews, "Arthur MacArthur," Sept. 1902.

Army and Navy Journal, Aug. 10, 1901, p. 1206.

Bain, David H. *Sitting in Darkness: Americans in the Philippines.* Boston: Houghton, 1984.

Berthoff, Rowland T. "Taft and MacArthur, 1900: A Study in Civilian-Military Relations," *World Politics,* Vol. 5 (Jan. 1953), pp. 196–213.

Blount, James. *The American Occupation of the Philippines, 1898–1912.* New York: Putnam and Sons, 1913.

Brand, H. W. *Bound to Empire: The United States and the Philippines.* New York: Oxford University Press, 1992.

Brown, Charles H. *The Correspondents' War: Journalists in the Spanish-American War.* New York: Scribner's, 1967.

Brown, Fred. *History of the Ninth U.S. Infantry, 1799 to 1909.* Chicago, 1909.

_____. *The Life of Lieutenant General Chaffee.* Chicago: University of Chicago, 1917.

Coffman, Edward M. *The Hilt and the Sword: The Career of Peyton C. March.* Madison: University of Wisconsin Press, 1966.

Fant, Henry A. "Arthur MacArthur and the Philippine Insurrection," Master's thesis, Mississippi State University, 1963, 72 pages.

Feuer, A. B. *Combat Diary: Episodes from the History of the Twenty-Second Regiment, 1866–1905.* New York: Praeger, 1991.

Funston, Frederick. *Memories of Two Wars.* New York: Scribner's, 1911.

Gates, John M. *Schoolbooks and Krags: The United States Army in the Philippines, 1898–1902.* Westport, CT: Greenwood, 1973.

George, Jesse. *Our Army and Navy in the Orient.* Privately published, 1899.

Graff, Henry F. *American Imperialism and the Philippine Insurrection: Selected Testimony from Senate Document SD331.* Boston: Little-Brown, 1969.

Gleeck, Lewis E. *The American Governors-General and High Commissioners in the Philippines.* Quezon City: New Day, 1986.

_____. *The Manila Americans, 1901–1964.* Manila: 1977.

Greene, Francis V. "The Capture of Manila," *The Century Magazine,* Vol. 52, March 1899, pp. 785–791, and April 1899, pp. 915–937.

Hagedorn, Hermann. *Leonard Wood.* Vol. 1. New York: Harper, 1931.

Karnow, Stanley. *In Our Image: America's Empire in the Philippines.* New York: Ballantine, 1989.

Leech, Margaret. *In the Days of McKinley.* New York: Harper, 1959.

Linn, Brian M. "Provincial Pacification in the Philippines, 1900–1901," *Military Affairs,* Vol. 51 (April 1987), pp. 62–66.

_____. *The U.S. Army and the Counterinsurgency in the Philippine War, 1899–1902.* Chapel Hill: University of North Carolina Press, 1989.

Lockmiller, David A. *Enoch H. Crowder: Soldier, Lawyer, Statesman.* Columbia: University of Missouri Studies, 1955.

MacArthur, Arthur. *Governor's Letterbook for 1900.* RG20, MacArthur Memorial Library.

McDonnell, Percy G. "The Battle of the Blockhouses," *Harper's Weekly,* Vol. 25 (1899), pp. 657–668.

Magnus, Philip. *Kitchener.* London: Murray, 1958.

May, Glenn Anthony. *Battle for Batangas.* New Haven: Yale University Press, 1991.

Miller, Stuart Creighton. *Benevolent Assimilation: The American Conquest of the Philippines, 1899–1903.* New Haven: Yale University Press, 1982.

Minger, Ralph E. "Taft, MacArthur, and the Establishment of Civil Government in the Philippines," *Ohio Historical Quarterly,* Vol. 70 (Dec. 1961), pp. 308–331.

————. *William Howard Taft and United States Foreign Policy: The Apprenticeship Years, 1900–1908.* Chicago: University of Illinois Press, 1975.

Morris, Edmund. *The Rise of Theodore Roosevelt.* New York: Coward, McCann and Geoghegan, 1979.

Mulrooney, Virginia F. "No Victor, No Vanquished: American Military Government in the Philippine Islands, 1899–1901." Ph.D. dissertation, University of California, 1975.

Pringle, Henry F. *The Life and Times of William Howard Taft.* 2 Vols. New York: Farrar and Rinehart, 1939.

Root, Elihu. *The Military and Colonial Policy of the United States: Addresses and Reports,* edited by Robert Bacon and James B. Scott. Cambridge, MA: Harvard University Press, 1916.

Sexton, William T. *Soldiers in the Sun.* Harrisburg, PA: Military Service Publishing, 1939.

Sorley, Lewis S. *History of the Fourteenth U.S. Infantry.* Chicago: author, 1909.

Stanley, Peter W. *A Nation in the Making.* Cambridge, MA: Harvard University Press, 1974.

Taft, William Howard, Mrs. *Recollection of Full Years.* New York: Dodd, Mead, 1914.

Twain, Mark. "On American Imperialism," *Atlantic,* Vol. 269 (April 1992), pp. 49–65.

Wolff, Leon. *Little Brown Brothers.* Manila: Erehwon Press, 1961.

Worcester, Dean C. *The Philippines: Past and Present.* 2 Vols. New York: Macmillan, 1914.

Young, Kenneth R. "Guerrilla Warfare: Balangiga Revisted," *Leyte-Samar Studies,* Vol. 11 (1977), pp. 21–31.

————. "Atrocities and War Crimes: The Case of Major Waller and General Smith," *Leyte-Samar Studies,* Vol. 12 (1978), pp. 64–77.

E. FINAL DAYS

Army and Navy Journal, Sept. 21, 1912.

Carter, William H. *Creation of the American General Staff: Personal Narrative of the General Staff System of the American Army.* U.S., 68th Congress, 1st Session (1919), Senate Document 119.

————. "A General Staff for the Army," *North American Review,* Vol. 175 (Oct. 1902), pp. 558–565.

Harper's Weekly, May 27, 1909.

Houston, A. Ross. "The Loyal Legion," address, Dec. 3, 1891, Loyal Legion (Wisconsin), *War Papers,* Vol. 2 (1896), pp. 81–86.

In Memoriam, Arthur MacArthur. Military Order of the Loyal Legion, Headquarters Commander of New York, 1912.

Literary Digest, "Up From the Ranks," Sept. 21, 1912.

Lord, Walter. *The Good Years: From 1900 to the First World War.* New York: Harper, 1960.

MacArthur, Arthur. "Address to Wisconsin Banker's Association by Lt. General Arthur MacArthur, retired," some time after 1909—in microfilm file from MML.

————. "Our American Shipping: Address to Old Settlers Club, Milwaukee, Feb. 22, 1908," WHS.

Outlook, "Arthur MacArthur," Sept. 21, 1912.

"Proceedings Attending the Reception and Banquet to Major General Arthur MacArthur, U.S. Army," Milwaukee, Oct. 3, 1901, Loyal Legion (Wisconsin), *War Papers,* Vol. 3 (1903), pp. 492–524.

Report of the Proceedings of the Meetings of the State Bar Association of Wisconsin. Vol. 10 (1912–1914), Milwaukee, 1915, pp. 38–39.

Sullivan, Mark. *Our Times:* Vol. 1: *The Turn of the Century.* New York: Scribner's, 1926.

Warner, Denis, and Peggy Warner. *The Tide at Sunrise: A History of the Russo-Japanese War.* New York: Charterhouse, 1974.

Vandiver, Frank E. *Black Jack: The Life and Times of John J. Pershing.* Vol. 1. College Station: Texas A & M University, 1977.

About the Book and Author

GENERAL ARTHUR MACARTHUR's extraordinary life spans the history of the United States from the Civil War through the Indian Wars to the Spanish-American War and the heyday of American imperialism in the Philippines. And in a sense, as the father of Douglas MacArthur, his influence extends well into our own century. *The General's General* is the first biography of Arthur MacArthur, and it clearly establishes his importance in American history.

Arthur MacArthur's military career began as a scrawny seventeen-year-old lieutenant, his commission owed not to any evidence of his ability but to family connections. His squeaky voice, barely audible on the parade field, combined with an adolescent conception of proper military bearing to make the young officer an object of ridicule. But MacArthur overcame this bad start and went on to become a bona fide Civil War hero. The youngest regimental commander of the war, he led his troops with distinction in battle and became one of the very first officers to be awarded the congressional Medal of Honor.

In the 1870s MacArthur served in forts in the West during the Indian Wars, married "Pinky" Hardy, and started a family. He next commanded a division in the Philippines during the Spanish-American War. MacArthur went on to become the governor-general of the Philippines—the most imperial post in that blatantly imperialistic period of American history. His blunt opposition to aspects of Washington's colonial policy in the Philippines led to a series of conflicts with Taft, McKinley, and other civilian authorities. After his return to the United States in 1907, these same leaders blocked MacArthur's appointment as chief of staff of the army. Instead, an embittered MacArthur was forced to retire. The MacArthur family, including Douglas, never forgave the powerful men who had thwarted Arthur in his greatest ambition and denied him his place in history.

After one of the most distinguished careers in the history of the U.S. Army, Arthur MacArthur died in relative obscurity while delivering a speech at the fiftieth reunion of his original Civil War regiment. A man whose whole life had been soldiering left instructions forbidding a military funeral and asking to be buried in civilian clothes rather than in the uniform he had worn so proudly from the age of seventeen.

MacArthur died too soon to witness the military exploits of his famous son. But there can be no doubt that Arthur made a profound impression on Douglas, who regarded the general with awe and spent much of his own life following in his father's footsteps. Arthur MacArthur had spent his life striving to be a soldier's soldier; in the end it can be truly said that he was the general's general.

Kenneth Ray Young, a Fulbright scholar to the Philippines in 1979, is professor of history at Western Connecticut State University, where he specializes in U.S. military actions in Asia.

Index